THE JPS LIBRARY OF JEWISH CLASSICS

HEBREW ETHICAL WILLS

Selected and Edited
and with an Introduction by

ISRAEL ABRAHAMS

two volumes in one

Facsimile of original 1926 edition

New Foreword by JUDAH GOLDIN

The Jewish Publication Society of America
PHILADELPHIA

Library of Congress catalog card number 76-2898
ISBN 0-8276-0081-X hardcover
ISBN 0-8276-0082-8 paperback
Manufactured in the United States of America

FOREWORD

JUDAH GOLDIN

There's no lineage like right conduct,
no legacy like trustworthiness.

1

THE introduction of a beautiful Hebrew book, *Mesillat Yesharim* (The Highway of the Upright), opens with the following words by the author, Moshe Hayyim Luzzatto (1707–47): "Author to reader: I have not composed this work to teach people what they do not already know, but to remind them . . . of what is well known to them indeed. For most of what I say is nothing more than what most people do know and have absolutely no doubts about. But what is said in the following pages is constantly ignored, most often forgotten, *because* it is common knowledge and obvious. That is why no profit will be derived from a single reading of this book, for quite likely after such reading the intelligent reader will find little that is new. Only constant reading and rereading will prove beneficial. Then the reader will recall those things that naturally tend to be forgotten and take to heart the obligations he tends to ignore."

The frustration felt by Luzzatto accompanies or haunts every moralist: what he wishes to say has been said, he knows, hundreds of times before and is therefore hardly audible any longer. Virtue is praised in literature of remote antiquity, as far back as the third millennium before our era, and even then is probably repetition. There is no lack of later parallels for Babylonian-Assyrian counsels of wisdom like

> Unto your opponent do no evil;
> Your evildoer recompense with good. . . .
> Do not slander, speak what is fine.
> Speak no evil, tell what is good.

Similarly at a later date in China:

> To the good I act with goodness;
> To the bad I also act with goodness:
> Thus goodness is attained.

Such counsel is hard to pay attention to even when it is delivered orally, when the words can be related to the emphasis created by the speaker's gestures and facial expression and voice-pitch. Read in printed text or written document, the response almost inevitably is, *déjà entendu.*

All moralistic discourse is at a disadvantage, however, not only because it says nothing new. Novelty or lack of novelty as such is not ultimately the determining factor. We are capable of revisiting certain paintings, granted not endlessly but at least many times, or rereading certain poems or listening again to some musical compositions, with considerable (though not necessarily the same kind of) enjoyment. On the other hand, moral treatises fail to affect us this way because what they say is not only not new, but even when we listen with only half an ear we know that they are an invasion into the most private interiors of our nervous system. They not only impinge on our esthetic or intellectual receptiveness. They attack us in the secret regions where the total personality has already settled down in the habits and tastes and excuses it prefers, and does not want to be disturbed. To change these is more than addition or variation of understanding. It is mutation, possibly forced reclamation, of human character. Since ethical warnings aim to upset what has become customary and comfortable, it takes more than one telling to get the painful message across. The necessary repetition, even if tolerated out of politeness, doesn't make listening easier.

And there is this too about repetition. Everyone repeats. Painters look at a landscape with eyes that have looked and look at earlier pictures ("looking alone [at nature] has never sufficed to teach an artist his trade"—E. H. Gombrich), and even as they compose, composers study earlier compositions and, wittingly or unwittingly, borrow—here the position of a tree or a hill, there a chord or motif. But principally the effect the artist is after is originality, or at least novelty; and that can emerge from the successful transformation of the loan-image or musical bar into individual statement: by free association, by subduing or salience, by disguising. The artist strives to become a creator.

Moralists likewise repeat. They likewise read earlier moralists and take over from them: vocabulary, illustrations, rhetoric of persuasion, the subject headings that require more than a single review. The moralist too seeks to convert what he has borrowed into personal declaration; but theoretically his principal ambition is not originality. Nor is it to increase our capacity for (spiritual) pleasure or the extension of our enlightenment. The moralist wants to rehabilitate the inner as well as the outer man.

He wishes to be a *re*former. With little self-consciousness, therefore, he repeats—sometimes verbatim—what has been said before, for he feels that until man is remade, the inherited appeals are not outdated. (How often has one been advised to reread Psalms or *Pirqe Abot*?) His aim is almost exclusively didactic, practive, as they would have said in the sixteenth and seventeenth centuries. In his own name the moralist will say again what has been said, because to him that still sounds urgent. Maybe someone else will finally hear. How many times have you been told . . . , he likes to say, as though that helps. Sometimes he may not even trouble to transpose what he took over. It might almost take him by surprise to find out that he has said something not said before.

One word more about moralists: While in their formal treatises they exhibit different approaches to their theme—some content simply to appropriate terms of the classical midrashic-talmudic homilies and anecdotes, others a combination of the midrashic-talmudic teachings and philosophical argument, and still others kabbalistic demonstrations and reinforcement—the tone of voice they adopt is, if not uniform, then predictable and seldom dispassionate. It is paternal, experienced (no one is better informed of the subtle devastations of sin than the saints: Isaiah seems to have known the names of every dangle and bangle of Jerusalem flirts), threatening, and beseeching. The very literature they create encourages those who take it seriously to address their own children similarly in both private and semiprivate communications.

Of course fathers have "always" exhorted their sons to choose the right course of life. The biblical historian (1 Kings 2:1–4) reports that when David was close to death, he instructed his son and successor, Solomon, not only to settle some old scores but to mind the following: "I am going the way of all the earth; be strong and show yourself a man. Keep the charge of the LORD your God, walking in His ways and following His laws, His commandments, His rules, and His admonitions as recorded in the Teaching of Moses, in order that you may succeed in whatever you undertake and wherever you turn. Then the LORD will fulfill the promise that He made concerning me: 'If your descendants are scrupulous in their conduct, and walk before Me faithfully, with all their heart and soul, your line on the throne of Israel shall never end' " (JPS new translation, with permission).

Back in the third–second century before our era there appeared a Jewish work that Byzantine scribes called "The Testaments of the Twelve Patriarchs" (E. J. Bickerman). In it each of the sons of Jacob (the Fathers of the twelve tribes of Israel) is represented as repenting of some transgression (when that is relevant) and proceeding at once to admonish his children to avoid sin, to beware of the spirit of deceit and envy, to keep the law of God, to fear the Lord and love their neighbor: "For he that feareth God and loveth his neighbor, cannot be smitten by the spirit of Beliar, being shielded by the fear of God." And much more along these lines.

The Talmud too preserves several brief obituary accounts of sages who in their last hours teach their students a lesson to remember all their lives. For example, "May you fear Heaven as much as you fear flesh and blood." "Only that much?" "Would it were that! Whenever a man commits a transgression, what does he say? I hope nobody sees me!" (Babylonian Talmud, Berakot 28b).

In other words, it may well be that those who were reflective and articulate, and had responsibilities to hand on, always and everywhere spoke to their descendants and successors in hortatory words which they hoped would be heeded in the future. But it is a fair guess (not certainty) that the *writing down* of ethical testaments by individuals for the reading on the part of their immediate family and kin (though they might sometimes wish for a wider circle too) became something of a "general" practice, a kind of adopted, personal ritual, only after moralistic *treatises* began to circulate. ("In the Geniza there are no ethical wills, a document so frequent in later centuries"—S. D. Goitein.) The formal, written treatises would have provided a model of themes that should be uppermost in a person's mind as he thinks about guiding principles for a righteous life. Not that multitudes of virtuous admonitions were unavailable in the classical sources, nor are quotations from these lacking in the written informal testaments. But the written testaments suggest the development of a genre, a more or less distinctive form of composition, beyond the ad hoc address. Once moralistic treatises began to be read, a focus was provided and even, one might say, a table of contents, a concentrated assembly of directives that a human being required and could consult if he was not to disgrace his life in this world now and had hopes of the world to come.

Here finally were systematic works for inculcation of moral conduct: memorandums for immediate and future performances. The author of moralistic treatises gave to the writer of private testaments a rhetorical example to imitate, to adapt to his particular condition, to invent variations on. The testaments gathered together by Israel Abrahams in this volume are thus a refraction of the whole tradition of Jewish moralistic expression, and at the same time completely personal admonitions to intimates. One may be a scholar but now he speaks chiefly as parent. One may be a simple man but he is not an illiterate parent; he has obviously read, if not a lot then a little.

2

ISRAEL ABRAHAMS called these testaments *Hebrew Ethical Wills* (he may actually have invented the expression "ethical wills"). In Hebrew, testaments that are drawn up in contemplation of death are called simply *ṣawwaot* (in the singular, *ṣawwaah*), "commands," "injunctions" (to the survivors), and of course may refer to material inventories as well as ethical instructions. The *Oxford English Dictionary,* relating the term to law, defines testament as "a formal declaration, usually in writing, of a person's wishes as to the disposal of his property after his death; a will." *Hebrew Ethical Wills* is not an unattractive title for the collection of writings in the following pages. For here too is a declaration of wishes, if not as regards the disposal of property, then as regards the attempt to transfer magnanimity. To avoid possible misunderstanding, however, it's not so much the word "testament" or "will" that must detain us, as the word "ethical."

For us, perhaps not altogether justifiably, the

ethical is taken as the rubric for rules governing only the relations of human beings to one another. Regardless of philological or philosophical explorations of the terms "ethics" and "morality," for the post-Enlightenment man the ethical can be autonomously prescriptive of human conduct—as though, so to speak, the second half (or three-fifths or more) of the Ten Commandments would be acceptable and compelling without the first. There is the human domain, and it can be ordered without reference to any authority beyond human sanction. What relates to God is another, independent province of speculation and actions, although interhuman relationships interest Him too. At all events, according to this view, ethics and ritual piety draw on separate sources of imperatives.

The recognition that there are indeed different provinces of conduct is far from new in historic Judaism. Long ago the biblical prophets underscored the fact that ceremonial fasting, for example, could never serve as a substitute for feeding the hungry and letting the oppressed go free; and to this day Jews recite the passage, from which this example is taken, in their *ritual*! Prophetical illustrations are too familiar to need review. More immediately plainspoken is the talmudic formulation of the categories "man vis-à-vis God" and "man vis-à-vis his fellowman": *ben adam la-maqom, ben adam la-ḥavero;* thus it is said toward the end of the Mishnah treatise Yoma: "Sins of a man against God—that's what the Day of Atonement atones for; sins of a man against his fellowman—that the Day of Atonement does not atone for unless the guilty one has first made his peace with his fellow." The consciousness of the presence of this twofoldness never disappears.

Nevertheless, the ethical in Judaism, at least until modern times (and even then not always), is not an independent field of values. It is not a secular exercise with its own momentum and accomplishments. *Ben adam la-maqom* and *ben adam la-ḥavero* are a description or classification, if you wish, of the contents of the whole Law, but both are regarded as equally the statement of one divine will. Both serve each other. Both are of religious origin and concern. There is one overarching expectation to which the obligations to God and to man belong. It follows then that the moralist sees nothing incongruous about including in one and the same treatise, or testament, exhortations about prayer at the proper hour, a married woman's monthly religious duties, the halakhic regulations of animal slaughter for meats, the appointment of a beadle to announce the hour for the beginning of the Sabbath, as well as self-evidently moral warnings: be sure to visit the sick; honor your wife; set aside a tithe of your income for charity; abandon anger and do not lose your temper; remember that truth and righteousness (= honest dealing) are the ornaments of the soul, that controversy is an abomination, that whiskey will undo you, that when in a rage, husband and wife should not make love, that from the poor the physician is not to demand a fee. And more of the same. The mood may be summed up in the words of one father: My son, remember, "He brought you into this world, not you Him; for He has no need of you, but you need Him!" (See *Midrash Debarim Rabbah,* ed. Lieberman, 70.)

It is true that all the examples brought together above, ritualistic along with the moralistic, do not come from the same testament but are lifted ad lib from many selections in the volumes. But the choosing and the choice are not unfair to them. Not one of the testators whom the reader will meet would have denied that both the ritual fastidiousness demanded by the Law and what we call moral conduct derive from One Sovereign. For them, the human is never separated from the divine inspection, even at its most human. A philosophical moralist (in a well-known passage in Baḥya ibn Pakuda, *Ḥovot ha-Levavot,* of the eleventh century) may be upset by intellectuals who take pains with recherché and complicated religiolegalistic problems but neglect to explore fervently the duties that are the piety of heart and soul: "You ask about something where ignorance won't kill you; do you know what you have to know about those commands where ignorance is fatal?" This is natural impatience with those for whom only complex intellectual concerns are respectable. Is a milk spoon in a meat pot a weightier matter, protests a father who is trying to persuade his son to study philosophy, than questions about the existence or unity of God? He is not minimizing the seriousness of milk spoons in meat pots; he is pleading for what he considers a proper balance. No one within the framework of the classical Jewish tradition is tempted to propose a dualism of ritual obligations and ethical doctrine or of the strictly legal and the unlimited humane. All the statutes of God bear His imprint. Of course the unity is a biblical inheritance. And the writers of the testaments accept the legacy.

3

THEY may be at one in the fundamental assumptions and in some modes of rhetoric, and I think it would not be unjust to say that taken all in all and scrambled together—particularly if they are (unwisely) all read in one sitting—an astonishing consensus could be achieved, to the point of monotony. Fear God, obey His commandments, live honestly and forgivingly, avoid the disgraceful and demoralizing, and remember what I taught you all my life. This may summarize a characteristic last will of a Jew to his children. Except that we may add one more detail that deserves notice: biblical verses are on the tips of their tongues and at their fingertips. And it is not as a literary "showing off," some flourish to add elegance to their own sentiments and speech, though it is invoked as confirmation. They talk Bible. For when they express themselves in Hebrew, it is virtually their deepest reflex and at the same time their most precise, indispensable, natural vocabulary: they have made it their own voice, all of them. We have here a consequence of pedagogy from midrashic centuries on. If you have something to say, get the Scriptures to help you out. "My son, cast your burden on the Lord (Ps. 55:23) and what you regard as very far off from you, may be ready at hand. Know that your mouth is not yours nor is your hand within your own reach. For everything that will be done is in *God's* hand. Always take this to heart, Unless the Lord builds the house, its builders labor on it in vain (Ps. 127:1); but if the Lord builds it, those who would wreck it labor in vain. Unless the Lord watches over the city, the watchman keeps vigil in vain (ibid.); but if the Lord watches over a city, the watchman goes to unnecessary troubles."

So one father, now a second: "And now, behold, I am going the way of all the earth (1 Kings 2:2). Take care not to be lured away and turn (Deut. 11:16) from the course in which I directed you, and the Lord be wrathful with me [!] on your account (cf. Deut. 3:26). But, if you will obey me faithfully and keep my covenant (Exod. 19:5), know that reverence for the Lord will be your treasure (cf. Isa. 33:6) and in the grave my lips will always whisper (Babylonian Talmud, Yebamot 97a) in your behalf. My prayer will be set out in order before the Lord for your sake at all times. He will slake your thirst in drought and you shall be like a watered garden, like a spring whose waters do not fail (cf. Isa. 58:11)."

There is an artfulness, a self-consciousness in the second selection that is almost entirely absent from the first, in which one doesn't hop from one biblical book to the next and figures of speech are minimal. But it would be a mistake to treat the latter selection as only contrived and belabored prose. (The talmudic phrase is no departure from the norm.) The testator is not posturing. These men reach up for biblical speech (and talmudic expression) because it is within easy reach of their own manners of speaking as a result of a lifetime of prayer. Even when they are not scholars, by constant synagogue attendance they have become thoroughly familiar with psalms that are recited daily, with the Scriptures that are read in recurring cycles, as well as with the interpretations of the most popular commentators. The writers of the testaments are hardly "quoting," or if they are, there's nothing unexpected or dramatic about it; they are using the sacred dialect they were raised in from childhood on. This, plus the constancy of the universal themes of moral instruction, gives to these testaments a quality of sameness.

But they are not the same. I do not mean (what is true enough) that sometimes we find touches of superstition in one, or more than one, that we do not find in others—"It was my practice Friday afternoons to recite the afternoon prayer *(minḥah)* with a congregational quorum and after that, as an unbroken rule, to do my fingernails . . . , and in honor of the sabbath, another unbroken rule, to go to the bathhouse. How fortunate is he who in the ritual bath can concentrate on some mystical meditations and confessions of what he did the past week." Or again: "Don't spend the night alone in any house. For then Lilith is disposed to attack." Or: "My father, of blessed memory, wrote in his book: When the time comes for a man to die, Satan stands by his side and tempts him with, 'Deny (forsake) the God of Israel.' At that moment, God spare us, a man is not in control of his mind. Therefore, as of now, I stand up to declare before the Great and Blessed Name and His Shekinah and the court on high and the court below, and I solemnly proclaim that if at that moment I say anything improper, Heaven forbid, what I then say is null and void. . . . Only what I am now saying is binding."

Superstition is revealing but not singular, and every age, rationalistic ones no less, has its favorite fears and hocus pocus, springing from the terrors of life and death. Especially from the terrors of death. What is noteworthy indeed is that, although we are dealing with last testaments in this volume, there is not more of superstitious conceit in them than we find. And some may have advanced beyond superstition regardless of what they were in origin. They have by now become a hand held out tremblingly for supererogative assistance: "With a rope drag my coffin to the grave, and after each four ells stop and wait a bit. Do this seven times up to the grave and may this be atonement for my sins." To break the habit of slander and taking the Lord's name in vain it helps to put up a tablet over the doors of rooms, with the inscription (Exod. 20:7), "Thou shalt not take the name of the Lord thy God in vain." In the movie "The Garden of the Finzi-Continis," over the entrance to the dining room of Giorgio's family, there was a plaque with the verse, "The Lord our God be with us" (1 Kings 8:57), in Hebrew.

But individuality breaks through notwithstanding a unanimity of assent to traditional values. Partly this is because of differences of personality and social background; partly, no doubt, because some forms of conduct appeal especially to one's temperament; partly too because one has been offended by particular exhibitions of misconduct. One father can't stop reminding his son that it is very important to write Arabic beautifully if he is to succeed in life (this was true enough in his time and place). His testament, which as a matter of fact he worked on for many years with an author's eye and polish, is a mirror of life in a well-to-do ménage where almost no tension is visible between piety and the graces (but appearances may be deceptive). The author is even something of a bore as he quotes endlessly from the poetry of Samuel ha-Nagid—lines that were doubtless fresh and sparkling once upon a time and now read like wilted middle-class practical advice. Needless to say, someday we too will sound like that: nothing goes out of date faster than the up-to-date.

Then there is the testament of a grandfather with almost no pretensions to outstanding accomplishments. He is not without learning, for what pious Jew would be without it unless he was the victim of some outrageous misfortunes or heartbreaking retardation. But there is nothing in what this man writes to hint at extraordinary scholarly attainments. An average Jew, Abrahams calls him, but the average is high. He urges his sons and daughters (note well!) to behave as befits a decent person, to be careful with Sabbath observances, not to overindulge in games of chance (would that my children gave it up altogether!), to be humble and forgiving but to resist false accusations against themselves, not to be extravagant in expenditures for food but to dress well (though eschewing gentile styles and buckles!), to engage in study, to keep away from slander and falsehood and envy. From all this it is difficult to distinguish the individual features of a person. But as he closes, something happens. For a moment the instructions still sound as though they might have come from any number of men like himself; suddenly a vibrato: "Bury me to the right side of my saintly father, of blessed memory. And even if it's a bit crowded there, I can depend on my father's love that he will draw himself in to make room for me to be beside him. And if under no circumstance will it be possible to lie at the right side of my father, try his left side, or near my grandmother Mistress Yuta. And if that's impossible, bury me by the side of my daughter."

His immediate family apart, and even they not certainly, who without that last sentence in this last will would have guessed the grief our gentle man carried with him to the grave? Or the love of his own father *he* still feels?

Another man wants his children always to keep in their homes a bench on which is to lie a volume of the Talmud or a talmudic composition, so that the first thing met with on entering the house will be a summons to study. So frequent is the reminder to study Torah in these testaments, by the way, that its occasional chance absence goes unnoticed at first. The Gaon of Vilna advises his womenfolk to keep away from the synagogue (and other public places obviously), because whenever women get together they gossip, and besides, envy is stirred up by the sight of other women in their elegant and modish dress. He pleads with his mother (whom he loves and who, he knows, is saintly) and his wife to live peacefully with each other. One man is grateful that he had a private room to himself for prayer and meditation and thanks God when his snuffbox falls out of his hands yet doesn't break. And still another, on the night before his execution, composes a long poem (it is not a testament strictly speaking) to remind the zodiac of all he had studied in a very short lifetime.

All the moral testaments are a reaffirmation of what all moral writers and preachers have emphasized and defended in their treatises. But since in his "last" will a person chooses to talk about those moral injunctions that best correspond with his own fears and past experiences and ideas of right and wrong (what else is there to talk about at the irreversible transition?), his testament becomes a unique statement. He may even knowingly say what others have said, but because *he* says it and wants to say it, and may say it with an accentuation of his own, his message is genuinely his.

4

Even today a person frequently draws up his last will long before his last days and then in the course of time changes his original text in various ways. The same is true of course among authors of Hebrew ethical wills. A quarter of a century may sometimes elapse between a man's composition of his will and the day of his death. It seems fair to say therefore that the testament he finally leaves represents those ideals of his that he wants made explicit and memorable. His most cherished commitments are now on display and to be put on record: This is what I want of you, this is what I stand for, this is the counsel I transfer to you. "Reread this book at least once a week, and all the chapter-headings at the beginning," the anonymous author of "The Ways of the Righteous" *(Orḥot Ṣaddiqim)* recommends ("end of the 15th–early 16th century . . . either in the Italian or mideast region"—H. Z. Dimitrovsky). In the same spirit fathers are prompted to ask their sons and other members of the family to "read this communication once a day" or once a week, "along with two other testaments which I reproduce below"! One man hoped that his testament might be printed as a preface to the prayer book, for all to contemplate. "My son," one father will say—and in a sense this is implied by all of them—"remember me at all times. Let the image of me be before your eyes and may it never be withdrawn from before your eyes. Don't develop a taste for doing what you know I abhor. Be with me at all times. Keep my commandments and you will live. May the following verse of Scripture be on your lips, 'I am only a sojourner in the land; do not hide Your commandments from me' (Ps. 119:19). Then the good and gracious God will increase your tranquillity and prolong your life in pleasantness. Then will your honor and good repute thrive as you wish and as is the wish of your father who begot you."

From the monitions and pleas to the son emerges the outline of the father's self-portrait, including a measure of self-approval, even when he does not spare himself in self-criticism. A last will and testament thus attempts to preserve for descendants and disciples the image one wishes to leave of himself. The ways of the fathers are urged in part because they are the fathers' ways, and because the fathers want to be remembered as having always practiced what they now preach. In dreams our vices catch up with us; in fantasy our virtues grow to more than life-size. In exhorting or reprimanding others, there is a little of both. By definition sons fall short: "Why don't you walk in the way of your fathers, and why isn't fear of the Lord before your eyes always? Why don't you study His Torah day and night? Why don't you get to the synagogue early morning and evening?" Another father has still other complaints: "Thank God that you are God-fearing in all your ways, as I know, except in the matter of honoring your father!" He continues peevishly: "When you wrote your letters or composed poems to send to another country, you never showed me a thing. . . . And when I used to say to you, 'Show me,' you used to say to me, 'Why do you want to see it?' . . . Why, R. Zerahiah of blessed memory, who was sui generis in his day, and was more gifted than I, from the time he knew me never wrote a letter or composed a poem to send to anyone without showing it to me first."

Typical parental talk that sons will later adopt with their sons, spontaneously too, and it will not be confined to the contents of testaments. But this forward projection of self, natural enough at any time and well-nigh inescapable in closest relationships ("Let the boy discover the truth for himself" is either humbug or callousness), is especially likely to take place as thoughts of death come to mind.

For although there may be varieties of terror crowding in as one tries to imagine extinction, it is intolerable (so long as there is life) to acquiesce to being silenced—not to being silent, but to being silenced. There is still something left unsaid, still something to tell to one's flesh of his own flesh or mind of his mind. And within those to whom right attitude and action and loyalty to the faith of the fathers are the supreme government of life, there is a compulsive wish to speak from beyond the grave. They know how close lies chaos to the disorders of the living, and they want the volume of their warning not to be reduced. They want to be heard across the deadening silence. Read me once a week or once a month, the fathers plead. Maybe this will save the descendants, and maybe this will protect the one who leaves the world from becoming zero.

The Hebrew ethical will is not mere valediction but an audacious attempt at continuing speech from fathers in the grave to children in a reckless world. The teacher's absence is not the end of instruction. It was said a long time ago, When the dead are quoted, their lips move.

ADVERTISEMENT

The present Series of JEWISH CLASSICS was projected in continuation of the previous publication of the English Translation of the HOLY SCRIPTURES—the greatest classic of Hebrew literature and of all times.

When the New Translation of the Scriptures was approaching completion, the late Jacob H. Schiff, through whose munificence the publication of that translation was rendered possible, further proposed to the Jewish Publication Society of America that they should issue a representative selection of the various classes of literature produced by Jewish writers after the close of the Biblical Canon, and for that purpose placed a fund at the disposal of the Society.

In the deed of gift of Mr. Schiff, which was intended to make the present Series possible, a Committee was named by him consisting of the following:

Dr. Solomon Schechter, Chairman
Dr. Cyrus Adler, Vice-Chairman
Rev. Dr. H. G. Enelow
Prof. Israel Friedlaender
Rev. Dr. Kaufmann Kohler
Prof. Alexander Marx
Rev. Dr. F. de Sola Mendes

Rev. Dr. David Philipson
Rev. Dr. Samuel Schulman
The Hon. Mayer Sulzberger

Later the Committee was increased by the addition of Prof. Louis Ginzberg, Prof. Jacob Z. Lauterbach, and Prof. Henry Malter. Upon the death of Dr. Schechter, on November 19, 1915, Dr. Cyrus Adler was elected Chairman. After the tragic death of Professor Israel Friedlaender in 1920, Professor Israel Davidson was named as his successor. The Committee has since been deprived of the aid of Judge Sulzberger, who passed away on April 20, 1923; of Professor Malter, who died on April 4, 1925; and of the Rev. Dr. Kaufmann Kohler, who died on January 28, 1926. Dr. Solomon Solis Cohen was appointed to succeed Judge Sulzberger.

The plan of the Series was outlined during the Chairmanship of our distinguished colleague, the eminent scholar, Dr. Solomon Schechter.

The first principle adopted was that in all cases in which a Hebrew text was extant, it was to be printed along with the English translation, and that an endeavor should be made to present a critical text based not only upon previous editions, but also upon the available manuscripts. For this purpose manuscripts in America have been employed, and those in the libraries of England, Italy, Germany, Austria and Hungary—wherever important manuscripts bearing upon the Series were to be found—have been photographed. The Committee feel that in offering this Series they are not only making accessible to English readers some of the treasures of Jewish literature, but are adding to Jewish scholarship by presenting carefully edited texts, which they hope will become the standard texts of the Jewish Classics.

In giving the original Hebrew text the Committee have been able to add a feature which was absent in the publication of the translation of the Scriptures, the English text of which was published without the original Hebrew. This was not due to any desire on the part of the Board in charge to substitute the English text for the original; but the demand for an English version on the part of English-speaking Jews was so urgent, and the facilities in the United States for printing Hebrew at the time so meager, that the Board felt any further delay of a work that had been anxiously expected for twenty years would be inadvisable. It is the hope of the Jewish Publication Society to publish, when its opportunities permit, the Hebrew text of the Bible, side by side with the translation.

The Committee were limited in the preparation of the Series by the amount of the fund, which, though most generous, could not provide for a complete presentation of the Jewish Classics, which might well cover hundreds of volumes.

They therefore decided, in the first instance, to omit, by reason of their availability in the English language, certain works which would otherwise naturally be expected to appear in such a Series. This is notably the case in regard to two great philosophical works—the *Kuzari* of Jehudah Halevi, which has been translated into English by Doctor Hartwig Hirschfeld, and the *Guide of the Perplexed* of Moses Maimonides, which has an English version at the hands of the late Doctor Michael Friedländer. Similarly two great names like those of Flavius Josephus and Philo of Alexandria, although rightfully belonging to a series of Jewish Classics, were not included because we were given to understand that they had already been selected for publication in the Loeb Classical Library.

The Committee deemed it necessary to limit the Series to about 25 volumes, and they will endeavor to include in this number representative works of the various classes of Jewish literature under the headings of Apocrypha and Pseudepigrapha, Mishnah, Talmud, Midrash, Codes, Hebrew Poetry, Philosophy, Ethics, Mysticism, History, Epistles, Travels, Homiletics, and Folklore.

The Series was inaugurated with a selection from the religious poems of Solomon Ibn Gabirol, edited by Professor Israel Davidson, and put into English verse by Mr. Israel Zangwill; followed by a selection of the poems of Jehudah Halevi, translated into English by Mrs. Nina Salaman, based chiefly on the critical text of Doctor Heinrich Brody.

The present volume, being a selection from the Ethical Wills of Jewish worthies, is the first collection of its kind brought together. Such Wills, whose beginnings are found in the Bible, have a continuous history throughout Jewish literature and were also known in Christian and Mohammedan circles. The text and translation are from the pen of Doctor Israel Abrahams, Reader of Rabbinics at the University of Cambridge. The work of Doctor Abrahams was carried on under many difficulties and exacting labors in other directions and the proofs were read during the summer of 1925, shortly before his lamented death. Doctor Abrahams read the first proof and while the pages did not have the advantage of his revisions, no material additions or alterations have been made by the Committee.

It is a source of great sorrow to the members of the Committee that this gifted man did not live to see the issuance of a volume which contains the fruition of studies begun by him more than thirty-five years ago. May not this work be considered as his last Testament to two generations of students and readers whom he instructed and delighted?

It is expected that the next volume to appear in this Series will be a critical edition with translation of the Tractate Taanit of the Babylonian Talmud, edited and translated by the late Professor Henry Malter. Following this the Committee expect to publish a critical edition of the Mekilta, edited and translated by Professor Jacob Z. Lauterbach, and a translation of the Maase Book, by Doctor Moses Gaster.

The Committee trust that this Series will awaken the interest and command the support of those who feel the obligation to see to it that the Jewish Classics, which, with few exceptions, have been unknown to English readers, shall come into their own, and take their rightful place among the classic literatures of all peoples.

June, 1926.

HEBREW ETHICAL WILLS

SELECTED AND EDITED

BY

ISRAEL ABRAHAMS

Reader in Talmudic in the University of Cambridge,
formerly Senior Tutor at Jews' College, London.

PART ONE

PHILADELPHIA
THE JEWISH PUBLICATION SOCIETY OF AMERICA
1926

צואות גאוני ישראל

לקטו נערכו הוגהו ונעתקו

על ידי

ישראל בן ברוך בר אברהם

חלק א

פילאדלפיא
החברה היהודית להוצאת ספרים אשר באמיריקא
תרפ"ז

THE JEWISH PUBLICATION SOCIETY PRESS
PHILADELPHIA, PENNA.

מנחת אהבה

לזכרון

מוהר"ר שניאור זלמן שעכטער זצ"ל

כִּי יְדַעְתִּיו לְמַעַן אֲשֶׁר יְצַוֶּה אֶת־בָּנָיו וְאֶת־בֵּיתוֹ
אַחֲרָיו וְשָׁמְרוּ דֶּרֶךְ ה׳ לַעֲשׂוֹת צְדָקָה וּמִשְׁפָּט
לְמַעַן הָבִיא ה׳ עַל אַבְרָהָם אֵת אֲשֶׁר־דִּבֶּר עָלָיו׃

(בראשית יח, יט)

For I have known him, to the end that he may command his children and his household after him, that they may keep the way of the Lord, to do righteousness and justice; to the end that the Lord may bring upon Abraham that which He hath spoken of him.

(Genesis 18.19)

CONTENTS

INTRODUCTION

THE present volume includes specimens which, either as complete texts or as extracts, are representative of the type of literature known as Ethical Wills.

The practice of *writing* testamentary directions for the religious and secular guidance of children cannot be traced with certainty earlier than the twelfth century. The oldest, however, is usually dated as belonging to about the year 1050. But the habit of addressing *verbal* counsels is, of course, very much more ancient.

What shall he murmur with his latest breath,
When his proud eye looks through the film of death?

asks Keats when, towards the close of his brief life, he allowed his despondency to doubt the value of the poet's service. The moralist has usually been of more robust faith. Through the ages he has felt the longing to convey to his offspring at the end the ideals which he himself has striven after from the beginning. The Bible records several such instances. Prominently among these may be mentioned the blessing of Jacob, the dying requests of Joseph to his brethren, the addresses of Moses and Joshua to the people of Israel, the advice of David to his son Solomon, the ascetic restriction imposed against the use of wine or settled abodes by Jonadab son of Rechab, and such injunctions as that of the prophet of Bethel to his sons (I Kings 13.31). The injunctions contained in the Wisdom Literature, and especially in the first nine chapters of Proverbs, are cast in the form of admonitions by the sage, in the guise of father, to the disciple, in the aspect of son. Very interesting is it to note that in the Book of Proverbs, the mother also appears in the guise of counsellor.

Hear, my son, the instruction of thy father,
And forsake not the teaching of thy mother (1.8).

There is, further, the remarkable 'burden wherewith his mother corrected' king Lemuel, in the last chapter of Proverbs. To this must be added the ever-memorable instance of the mother of the Maccabean martyrs (2 Macc. 7), whose brave encouragement of her sons in the moment of death justifies the historian's description of her (verse 20): 'but above all was the mother marvelous.' And though the Jewish Ethical Wills are predominantly paternal, the maternal genre has survived into recent time, as in the *Zeker 'Olam* of Rebekah Luria (Jerusalem, 1891).

The Apocrypha still further develops the ethical testament. The address of the dying Mattathias to his five sons is matched in pathos and excelled in beauty by the counsels of Tobit when he sent his son on a mission from which he scarce expected to live to see him return. The fourth chapter of Tobit can, indeed, no longer be described as the oldest specimen of the Jewish ethical will. Much earlier, at least as soon as 400 B. C., comes the story of Aḥiḳar, a long section of which consists of that very species of exhortation, directly spoken to a son, which is characteristic of the type of literature which we are considering. So ingrained was the habit that the Maccabean period gives us several pseudepigraphic specimens. Thus the Book of Jubilees contains some, so does Enoch XCI, the Apocalypse of Moses, and above all the Testaments of the Twelve Patriarchs. And the death scenes in the Talmud continue the record of the fondness of the Jewish parent for this method of offering counsels of perfection from one generation to the next.

The importance of the Testaments of the Twelve Patriarchs, as a pre-Christian Jewish document, has only become realized of recent years. These apocryphal last words and admonitions of the twelve sons of Jacob were long regarded as of Christian origin; they are now generally considered to be Jewish with some later interpolations. The reader will find these points discussed by Dr. K. Kohler in the *Jewish Encyclopedia* (vol. xii, p. 113). The date usually assigned to parts at least of the Testaments is the reign of John Hyrkanus. Dr. Charles very definitely assigns the year 109–107 B. C. for the original Jewish work. The Testaments have close parallels to passages in the New Testament. Their ethical worth is high. Dr. Kohler ably characterizes the moral of the Testaments, in which "each of the twelve sons of Jacob delivers a farewell address, giving an account of such of his experiences as offer some lesson, either warning against sins that he had committed or exhorting to virtues that he had practised." Thus: Reuben's theme is Unchastity; Simeon's, Envy; Levi's, the Priesthood and Pride;

Judah's, Courage, etc; Issachar's, Simplicity; Zebulun's, Compassion; Dan's, Anger; Napthali's, Natural Goodness; Gad's, Hatred; Asher's, the Two Characters of Vice and Virtue; Joseph's, Chastity; Benjamin's, Purity of Heart. Another ancient document, the *Didachê*, is similarly of Jewish provenance with Christian changes, but the least characteristically Jewish factor in the *Didachê* is the compiler's mode of addressing the proselyte as 'my son'.

Thus the ethical testament has a long and continuous history in Jewish literature. That literature did not monopolize the genre. The Arabs held the ethical will (included under the general title "Wasaya") in such high esteem that they would ascribe documents of the kind to revered sages like Lokman. In Christian circles, too, we find similar phenomena. In 717 Bishop Egwin spent several days before his death in exhorting his monks and other disciples. Similarly with Abbot Gildas and Joachim de Flore. In the preambles of many Christian wills may be found declarations of faith, directions as to burial which belong to the same category. The letter of Sir Henry Sidney to his son Philip (written in 1566) may be also cited as an illustrative parallel. The age of the Renaissanse was rich in such products.

Despite these, and other parallels, the ethical will is in a sense a distinctive Jewish genre. The word used (צַוָּאָה from צָוָה, piel צִוָּה, *to command*) is the same as describes the ordinary will. But it derives from texts which give the ethical key-note of the special type. Isaiah bids Hezekiah, who was sick unto death, "Set thy house in order" (literally "command thy house," Isa. 38.1). The same word is used in the charge of Moses (Deut. 32.46). But most operative of all texts in this connection has been Gen. 18.19, where God says of Abraham: "I have known him (Abraham) to the end that he may *command* his children and his household after him, that they may keep the way of the Lord." This text (which is printed in Hebrew and English as the motto of the present book) has inspired many a Jewish parent in after centuries, and it has been made the basis of an actual rubric in modern Jewish codes. It has been held to enjoin on every father the bounden duty to leave moral exhortations for his children's guidance. This feeling is well brought out in the following Midrash. "Jacob felt that his end was near, and besought the divine mercy: Ruler of the World, he cried, Take not my soul until I have exhorted my children. And his wish was granted." A similar gracious impulse led many a Rabbi to offer dying instructions to his disciples and community. In imitation of Moses it was held obligatory for a teacher, before his demise, to impart abundantly of his wisdom, a duty which Moses Recanati beautifully quotes at the end of his commentary on Deuteronomy.

These wills have been spoken of as continuous. Seeing, however, that most of them were *verbal*, it is not surprising that there are gaps in the literary records. Amid all the wealth of past lore which the Cairo Geniza brought to light, not a single instance of an ethical will has been discovered. This merely implies that they were not written down or preserved, not that they were unspoken.

Both the occasion and the motive of these testaments differ. Sometimes they were written when the father was near death, at other times when he was separated from his family by the exigencies of travel. Especially when about to go to Palestine, or when arrived there, letters of admonition might be despatched. Sometimes the parent would write his testament at a comparatively early age, and modify and expand it as years passed by. Occasionally the testament would take the form of an elaborate treatise on ritual and ethics. Here and there a father would content himself with directions for his burial; mostly such directions would be incorporated in a longer testament. Sometimes the testament would be intended for the son, sometimes for a whole family, sometimes for the public.

The testaments give an intimate insight into the personal religion of Jews in various ages. The wills convey much information as to social life, the position of women, habits of dress and domestic economy, schemes of education, and indeed as to the many interests of business and culture.

All these topics can be studied with effect in the testaments, and the present writer may refer to an essay of his own in the third volume of the first series of the *Jewish Quarterly Review*. He hopes also to print, on a subsequent occasion, a complete bibliography and running synopsis of the large number of wills now known to him from actual perusal. The present volume contains a small fraction of the whole, nineteenth century wills being excluded by the scheme of the series. But even so, the testaments show, in a striking manner, the popularity of just those elements of the rabbinic literature which, in a special sense, may be termed ethical. The favorite quotations are beyond question the finest passages. It is necessary to call attention to this, because the wills naturally differ very considerably in point of view. In some the outstanding influence is scholasticism, in others mysticism, in others the modernism of the Mendelssohn type. Very interesting is it to witness the gradual and constant growth of affection for Maimonides. It is superfluous, however, to enter into fuller details, seeing that the texts speak for themselves. A bibliographical descriptive note is prefixed to each. The selection is mainly the editor's own, but he received valuable suggestions from the Committee, and to them as to Prof. Reuben Levy he is indebted for assistance in correcting the proofs.

The texts themselves reflect the phases of Jewish experience and the literary and moral reactions to it through many centuries. But whatever the passing indications of contemporary manners and thought, the Jewish code of morality remains essentially the same throughout. There is never a sordid thought or hateful sentiment, though there may be occasional narrowness of horizon. Intellectually some may be comparatively low, morally all are high. Indeed if one were writing apologetically, one could find in the confidential pronouncements which constitute the testaments a most effective vindication of the Jewish character.

לקוטים מתלמוד ומדרש

SELECTIONS FROM THE EARLY RABBINIC LITERATURE

I

SELECTIONS FROM THE EARLY RABBINIC LITERATURE

The early rabbinic literature records the passing of many heroic figures—heroic whether the scene be a restful deathbed or the martyr's stake. Both served as future models. Thus in the present volume, Nathaniel Trabotti, in his last quiet hours, follows the model of the Nasi Judah the first (cf. p. 19 with p. 264 below). On the other hand, Moses Rimos, in face of his more violent taking off, finds encouragement in Akiba's precedent (cf. p. 15f. with p. 247 below). Heroism has its message alike for times of tranquillity and agitation.

Some of the passages which follow are direct quotations of the words of dying teachers. These last words are rarely the best words their authors uttered. Some seem to show a touch of rather smug self-satisfaction, but this appearance is not always accurate. Judah the first, for instance, holds his ten fingers up and claims that he has done no wrong with them, a rather arrogant assumption of virtue. Yet the last Mishnah in Soṭah declares that with Judah the First there ceased "humility and the fear of God", so little was his nature given to self-pride. In some of the sayings we have illustrations of the Jewish view that laws of hygiene are laws of religion. Again some belong in the category of the curious and superstitious rather than to the ethical or literary. But there is more than literary worth to be considered. The ruling passion is strong still in death, and the veteran teacher, surrounded by his disciples, sometimes men more famous than himself, seeks to impart to the last both his worldly wisdom and his exposition of Torah. To impart and to receive. It is the latter consideration that has justified

א

לקוטים מתלמוד ומדרש

בספרות התלמוד והמדרש נמצאים ספורים ע״ד פטירת גבורים רבים–בין שמתו בשלוה והשקט על ערש דוי בין שנהרגו על קדוש השם. אלה ואלה שמשו בתור אנשי מופת לדורות הבאים. כמו שנראה בכרך שלפנינו, נתנאל טרבוט בשלות רגעיו האחרונים הולך בעקבות רבי יהודה הנשיא (השוה דף 19 לדף 264 למטה); ולהפך, משה רימוס, שמת מיתה חטופה ואכזרית, תולה את עצמו באילן הגדול רבי עקיבא (השוה דף 15 וכו׳ לדף 247 למטה). מעשי גבורה רישומם נכר גם בימי שלום וגם בימי מהומה.

יש דבורים בין אלה הבאים להלן שיצאו מפי מורים גוססים, ובכ״ז רק מעטים מהם הם מן המעולה והמובחר שיצא מפיהם. יש מהם המגלים קורטוב של ספוק עצמי מוצנע, אבל לפעמים כל זה הוא רק למראית עין. יהודה הנשיא, למשל, זוקף את עשר אצבעותיו כלפי מעלה ואומר שלא נהנה אפילו באצבע קטנה–הלא זו תפיסת יושר שיש בה משום יהירות. ובכ״ז המשנה האחרונה בסוטה סבורה כי „משמת רבי בטלה ענוה ויראת חטא", כל כך היה טבעו רחוק מן הגאוה והיהירות. יש מימרות המבליטות את השקפת היהודים שתורת הבריאות הוא תורת הדת; ויש עוד כאלה השייכות לממלכת הדברים הזרים והאמונות הטפלות יותר מאשר לדברי מוסר ועניני ספרות. אכן לא די להבחין רק את הערך הספרותי של הדברים האלה. התאוה השליטה ה״א עזה גם בשעת המות, והרבי המנוסה המיסב בחברת תלמידיו, אשר לפעמים הם יותר מפורסמים ממנו, משתדל לתת עד רגעו האחרון מחכמתו הכללית ומפירושיו על התורה. ולא רק לתת כי גם לקבל. מפני הטעם האחרון

the inclusion of one or two scenes, not necessarily final scenes, in which the Rabbi on a bed of sickness is visited by pupils and colleagues and asks for their report of the doings in the Academy. This act of receiving belongs to the testamentary category almost as fully as does the act of giving counsel.

Another series of extracts contains the explanations given by Rabbis of their longevity. Juniors inquire and the seniors answer. The answers easily fall within the scope of this volume, for they are in essence advice in the science of life by those whose tenure of life is near its end. Some of the answers are strange enough, but they have a value of their own on the moral side and as elements in contemporary folk-lore. The editor himself did not plan the inclusion of these early rabbinic passages, for they need ampler discussion than is here possible. But he acquiesced in the Committee's desire so as to make the selection more representative.

It has not seemed necessary to enter into biographical details regarding the Rabbis cited. Articles on most of them will be found in the Jewish Encyclopedia, while their teaching is displayed and expounded in Bacher's works on the Hagada. In the notes to the Hebrew text, V. refers to variant readings in the editions, and M. to the readings of the Munich MS.

1

Eleazar b. Hyrkanos and Johanan b. Zakkai.

Our Rabbis have taught: When R. Eleazar was ill, his disciples went in to visit him.[1] They said unto him: Our Master, teach us the Ways

[1] For the version given in Sanhedrin 68a, see p. 7 below.

נכללו פה ספור אחד או שנים שאין להם יחס כלל לקץ החיים, כי בהם הרבי שוכב על ערש דוי ותלמידיו וחבריו באים לבקרו והוא שואל אותם מהנעשה בבית המדרש. המעשה הזה של קבלת עצה הוא חלק מסוג הצואה לא פחות מן המעשה של נתינת עצה.

סדר אחר של לקוטים מכיל סברות רבנן לאריכות ימיהם. הצעירים שואלים והזקנים משיבים. התשובות האלה יש להן יחס ישר אל הכרך שלפנינו, יען כי בעקרן הן עצות להבנת החיים ע"י אנשים אשר חייהם קרבים אל קצם. אחדות מן התשובות זרות הן למדי, אבל יש להן ערך מיוחד מן הצד המוסרי ובתור יסודות בפולקלור של הימים ההם. העורך עצמו לא היה בדעתו להוסיף את הלקוטים האלה של חכמי התלמוד והמדרש, יען כי דורשים הם חקירה יותר עמוקה מאשר אפשר לתת פה, אבל הוא נכנע לחפץ הועד בכדי לעשות את הלקוט יותר כולל ומקיף.

לא חשבתי לנחוץ לתת פרטים מתולדות תלמידי החכמים הבאים להלן. רובם מפורטים באנציקלופדיה היהודית האנגלית, והוראותיהם נדרשות בספריו של באכער על האגדה. בהערותי לנוסח העברי V משמש לשנוים במהדורות, M למקראות של כת"י מינכען.

א

רבי אליעזר בן הורקנוס ור' יוחנן בן זכאי

תנו רבנן כשחלה ר' אליעזר נכנסו תלמידיו לבקרו. אמרו לו. רבינו. למדנו אורחות חיים

of Life, whereby we may be worthy of the life of the world to come. He answered unto them: Take heed to the honor of your colleagues; withhold your children from recitation,[2] and cause them to sit between the knees of the disciples of the wise; and when you pray, know before whom you stand. Thereby will you be worthy of the life of the world to come.

And when Rabban Joḥanan b. Zakkai was ill, his disciples went in to visit him. When he saw them he began to weep. His disciples said unto him, O Lamp of Israel,[3] right-hand pillar,[4] mighty hammer! Why dost thou weep? He answered unto them: If I were being led before a king of flesh and blood, who is today here and tomorrow in the grave, who if he were angry with me, his anger need not be everlasting,[5] who if he imprison me his imprisonment need not be everlasting, who if he put me to death the death would not be for ever, whom I could appease with words and bribe with money—even then I would weep; but now,

[2] So Jastrow, *Dictionary*, p. 331, renders; interpreting "Restrain your children from parading a superficial knowledge of the Bible by verbal memorizing." Others hold that the reference is to some debatable literature, apocryphal or metaphysical (Cf. Bacher, *Agada der Tannaiten* i. ch. vi. Comp. I. Z. Lauterbach, *Midrash and Mishnah*, New York 1916, pp. 89–90).

[3] According to another reading, "Lamp of the World."

[4] I Kings 7.13.

[5] According to another reading: "would only be in this world;" similarly in other clauses.

ונזכה[1] בהם לחיי העולם הבא. אמר להם. הזהרו בכבוד חבריכם. [ומנעו בניכם מן ההגיון, והושיבום בין ברכי תלמידי חכמים].[2] וכשאתם מתפללים דעו לפני מי אתם עומדים. ובשביל כך תזכו לחיי העולם הבא:

וכשחלה רבן יוחנן בן זכאי נכנסו תלמידיו לבקרו. כיון שראה אותם התחיל לבכות. אמרו לו תלמידיו. נר ישראל[3] עמוד הימיני פטיש החזק[4] מפני מה אתה בוכה? אמר להם. אילו לפני מלך בשר ודם היו מוליכין אותי. שהיום כאן ומחר בקבר. שאם כועס עלי אין כעסו כעס עולם.[5] ואם אוסרני אין איסורו איסור עולם. ואם ממיתני אין מיתתו מיתת עולם. ואני יכול לפייסו בדברים ולשחדו בממון. אף על פי כן הייתי בוכה.[6] ועכשיו שמוליכין

[1] M. כדי שנזכה.

[2] Aboth de R. Nathan I, 19 omits the whole bracketed passage. M. omits the second clause. At the end of the paragraph M. has a considerable addition.

[3] In some texts of the Aboth de R. Nathan the reading is נר עולם (see ed. Schechter p. 159).

[4] M. omits these two words.

[5] A. de R. N. (loc.cit.) אלא בעה"ז.

[6] M. מתיירא ממנו.

when I am being led before the King of Kings, the Holy One, blessed be He, Who lives and endures to all eternity, Who if He be angry with me, His anger is eternal,[6] Who if He imprison me, His imprisonment would be everlasting, Who if He sentenced me to death, the death would be for ever, and Whom I cannot appease with words nor bribe with money—nay more, when before me stretch two ways, one to the Garden of Eden and the other to Gehinnom, and I know not in which I am to be led—shall I then not weep? They said unto him: Our Master, bless us! He answered unto them: "May it be His will that the fear of Heaven be upon you as great as the fear of flesh and blood." His disciples exclaimed: Only as great? He answered unto them: Would that it be as great! for know ye, that when a man designs to commit a transgression, he says: I hope that no man will see me. In the hour of his death Joḥanan said unto them: Remove the utensils because of defilement,[7] and prepare a seat for Hezekiah King of Judah, who is coming.[8] (Berakot 28b).

R. Eleazar fell ill and R. Tarphon, R. Joshua, R. Eleazar b.'Azaria, and R. 'Akiba went to visit him. R. Tarphon spake, saying: 'Rabbi, thou art dearer to Israel than the Sun, for the Sun shines in

[6] Acc. to another reading: "in the world to come;" sim. in other clauses.

[7] Caused by the presence of a dead body.

[8] To accompany him (Rashi). On the whole of this passage see *Studies in Pharisaism*, II, 46.

אותי לפני מלך מלכי המלכים הקדוש ברוך הוא שהוא חי וקיים לעולם ולעולמי עולמים. שאם כועס עלי כעסו כעס עולם.[7] ואם אוסרני איסורו איסור עולם. ואם ממיתני מיתתו[8] מיתת עולם. ואיני יכול לפייסו[9] בדברים ולא לשחדו בממון. ולא עוד אלא שיש לפני שני דרכים אחת של[10] גן עדן ואחת של גיהנם[11] ואיני יודע באיזו מוליכים אותי. ולא אבכה?[12] אמרו לו. רבינו ברכנו! אמר להם. יהי רצון[13] שתהא מורא שמים עליכם כמורא בשר ודם. אמרו לו תלמידיו. עד כאן? אמר להם ולואי! דעו[14] כשאדם עובר עבירה אומר שלא יראני אדם: בשעת פטירתו אמר להם פנו כלים מפני הטומאה. והכינו כסא לחזקיהו מלך יהודה שבא:[15] (ברכות כ״ח ב׳)

וכבר היה ר׳ אליעזר חולה ונכנסו רבי טרפון ורבי יהושע ור׳ אלעזר בן עזריה ור׳ עקיבא לבקרו: נענה ר׳ טרפון ואמר רבי! חביב אתה לישראל יותר מגלגל חמה. שגלגל חמה מאיר בעולם הזה

7 A. de R. N. לעה״ב. 8 M. מיתתי. 9 A. de R. N. לגונבו. 10 M. לנן. So A. de R. N. p. 79. 11 M. לגיהנם.
12 Instead of this clause A. de. R. N. quotes Psalm 22.30.
13 M. 30., יהי מורא וכו׳ 14 Var. תדעו. M. עובד עבודה (עובר עבירה?) בסתר ואמר לא יראני האדם אעפ״י שיודע שהכל גלוי לפניו אינו מתיירא ואינו מונע מלעשות. 15 M. omits.

this world only, but thou dost illumine this world and the next.' R. Joshua spake, saying: 'Rabbi, thou art dearer to Israel than the gift of rain; for the rain giveth life in this world only, and thou hast given life in this world and the next.' R. Eleazar b. 'Azariah addressed him in these words: 'Rabbi, thou art dearer to Israel than father and mother, for a man's parents bring him into this world, while thou bringest us into this world and the next.' R. 'Akiba shook his head, and said 'Rabbi, dear is affliction.' R. Eleazar said to his disciples: 'Support me!' He sat up and said: 'speak on, 'Akiba!' 'Akiba replied: The Scripture[9] says, Manasseh was twelve years old when he began to reign and he reigned five and fifty years in Jerusalem, and he did that which was evil in the sight of the Lord. Another text tells us:[10] These also are proverbs of Solomon, which the men of Hezekiah king of Judah copied out. Is it conceivable that Hezekiah taught all Israel law, yet neglected to teach his own son, Manasseh? But all his instructions, all his efforts failed, and the only effective teacher was affliction. For it is written further how the Lord spake to Manasseh and to his people, but they gave no heed, wherefore the Lord brought upon them the captains of the host of the king of Assyria, who took Manasseh with hooks and bound him with fetters and carried him to Babylonia. And when he was in distress he besought the Lord his God, and humbled himself greatly before

[9] II Chron. 33.1.

[10] Prov. 25.1.

ואתה מאיר לעולם הזה ולעולם הבא: נענה רבי יהושע ואמר רבי! חביב אתה לישראל ממתן גשמים. שהגשמים נותנים חיים בעולם הזה ואתה נתת להם חיים בעולם הזה ובעולם הבא: א"ל ר' אלעזר בן עזריה רבי! חביב אתה לישראל מאב ואם. שאב ואם מביאים את האדם לעולם הזה ואתה מביא אותנו לעולם הזה ולעולם הבא: נענה רבי עקיבא ואמר רבי! חביבים יסורים: ואמר להם רבי אליעזר לתלמידיו סמכוני! ישב לו ר' אליעזר אמר לו אמור עקיבא! אמר לו הרי הוא אומר בן י"ב שנה מנשה במלכו ונ"ה שנה מלך בירושלים ויעש הרע בעיני ה'. ואומר גם אלה משלי שלמה אשר העתיקו אנשי חזקיה מלך יהודה. וכי עלתה על דעתך שחזקיהו לימד תורה לישראל ולמנשה בנו לא לימד תורה? אלא כל תלמוד שלימדו וכל עמל שעמל בו לא הועיל לו אלא ייסורים. שנאמר וידבר ה' אל מנשה ואל עמו ולא הקשיבו ויבא ה' עליהם את שרי הצבא אשר למלך אשור וילכדו את מנשה בחוחים ויאסרוהו בנחושתים ויוליכוהו בבלה וכהצר לו חלה את פני ה' אלהיו ויכנע מאד מלפני

the God of his fathers. And he prayed unto Him, and He was entreated of him, and heard his supplication, and brought him back to Jerusalem into his kingdom. So, said 'Akiba, thou mayest learn that precious is affliction! (Sifre on Deut. 32).

The record is that it was on a friday, when R. Eleazar lay sick, that R. 'Akiba and his colleagues visited the dying sage. [They asked him several questions]; he answered 'unclean' concerning the unclean, and concerning the clean he answered 'clean', and his soul departed in purity at the word. (Abot de R. Nathan, ch. 25; Sanhedrin, 68a).

2

'Akabya son of Mahalalel.

'Aḳabya son of Mahalalel testified to four teachings. The Sages said to him: "Aḳabya! Withdraw the four teachings which thou hast declared, and we will appoint thee a President of the Court[11] for Israel." He answered them: "Rather would I be called a fool all my life, than become for a single hour a sinner before God." (Also,) he did not wish people to say that he recanted to gain office.

In the hour of his death he said to his son: "My son! Give up those four things which I used to declare." His son asked: "Why didst thou not thyself abandon them?" 'Aḳabya an-

[11] According to the Mishnah Ḥagigah 2.2, the Ab Beth-din was vice-president of the Sanhedrin.

אלהי אבותיו ויפן אליו ויעתר לו וישיבהו לירושלים למלכותו. הא למדת שחביבים ייסורים[16]: (ספרי דברים פ׳ ל״ב).

כשחלה רבי אליעזר אמרו אותו היום ערב שבת היה ונכנס רבי עקיבא וחביריו[17] לבקרו... והיה משיב על טמא טמא ועל טהור טהור עד שיצתה נשמתו בטהרה[18]: (אבות דר׳ נתן כ״ה. סנהדרין ס״ח א׳).

ב

עקביא בן מהללאל

עקביא בן מהללאל העיד ארבעה דברים. אמרו לו. עקביא חזור בך בארבעה דברים שהיית אומר ונעשך אב בית דין לישראל. אמר להן מוטב לי להקרא שוטה כל ימי. ולא ליעשות שעה אחת רשע לפני המקום. שלא יהיו אומרים בשביל שררה חזר בו:

...בשעת מיתתו אמר לבנו. בני! חזור בך בארבעה דברים שהייתי אומר. אמר לו, ואתה למה לא חזרת בך? אמר לו אני שמעתי מפי

16 For notes on this text see Friedmann, *Sifre*, p. 73b.

17 M. נכנסו חכמים אצלו.

18 In Sanh. 68a the passage ends: מנעל שעל גבי האמוס.

swered: "I heard these decisions from a majority, so did the others hear their decisions from a majority.[12] I stood by my tradition, and they by theirs. But thou hast heard (opposite views) from (me) an individual, and from (them) a majority. 'Twere better for thee to reject the words of the individual and hold to those of the majority." He said to him: "Father, commend me to thy colleagues." 'Aḳabya answered: "I will not commend thee." The son asked: "Hast thou detected some fault[13] in me?" "No," said 'Aḳabya, "but thine own deeds will bring thee near (to the Sages), or thine own deeds will thrust thee far (from them)." (Mishnah 'Eduyot V, 6–7).

3

Jose son of Ḳisma and Ḥanina son of Teradyon

Said Rabbi Jose, the son of Ḳisma: Once I was walking by the way, when a man met me, and gave me "Peace," and I returned him "Peace".[14] He said to me, "Rabbi, from what place art thou?" I said to him, "From a great city of Sages and Scribes[15] am I." He said to me, "Rabbi, should it be thy pleasure to dwell with us in our place, I will give thee a thousand thousand[16] golden dinars[17], and precious stones and

[12] Either the majority decided differently on different occasions or there were divergent traditions as to what *was* the majority decision.

[13] Or, according to the other reading, "cause" for complaint.

המרובים. והם שמעו מפי המרובים. אני עמדתי בשמועתי. והם עמדו בשמועתן. אבל אתה שמעת מפי היחיד ומפי המרובין. מוטב להניח דברי היחיד ולאחוז בדברי המרובין: אמר לו פקוד עלי לחבריך. אמר לו איני מפקיד. אמר לו שמא עולה[19] מצאת בי? אמר ליה לאו! מעשיך יקרבוך ומעשיך ירחקוך: (עדיות פרק ה')

ג

יוסי בן קיסמא וחנניה בן תרדיון

אמר רבי יוסי בן קיסמא. פעם אחת הייתי מהלך בדרך ופגע בי אדם[20] אחד ונתן לי שלום והחזרתי לו שלום. אמר לי רבי מאיזה מקום אתה? אמרתי לו מעיר גדולה של חכמים ושל סופרים[21] אני. אמר לי רבי רצונך שתדור עמנו במקומנו ואני אתן לך אלף אלפים דינרי זהב ואבנים טובות ומרגליות.

מהו? אמר להם הוא טהור] ויצתה נשמתו בטהרה: The bracketed words, however, are missing in M.

[19] V עילה. [20] V זקן. [21] V omits these two words.

---

[14] The usual form of salutation.

[15] See *J.E.*, xi, 123. Jose's city was Caesarea Philippi, but he may be referring to Usha, the seat of learning in his age.

[16] *i. e.* a million. [17] Lat. denarius.

pearls." I said to him, "Wert thou to give me all the silver, and gold, and precious stones, and pearls in the world, I would not dwell except in the home of the Torah. And thus is it written in the Book of Psalms,[18] by the hands of David King of Israel: The Law of Thy mouth is better unto me than thousands of gold and silver."

Moreover, in the hour of a man's decease, not silver nor gold nor precious stones and pearls accompany him, but Torah and good works alone,[19] as it is said,[20] When thou walkest, it shall lead thee, when thou liest down, it shall watch over thee; and when thou awakest, it shall talk with thee. "When thou walkest, it shall lead thee"—in this world; "when thou liest down, it shall watch over thee"—in the grave; "and when thou awakest, it shall talk with thee"—in the world to come[21]. (Chapter of R. Meir, so-called ch. 6 of Abot).

The Rabbis taught: When Rabbi Jose son of Ḳisma lay sick, R. Ḥanina son of Teradyon went to visit him. Jose said to him: Ḥanina, my brother, knowest thou not that this nation[22] has received its domination from Heaven? It has wasted God's House, burned His Temple, slain His saints, destroyed His excellent ones, yet it still endures. And I have heard of thee, that thou (despite the Roman prohibition) sittest and art occupied with teaching the Torah, summoning public assemblies, and bear-

[18] Ps. 119.72.

[19] This idea is widely spread in literature. Cf. J.

אמרתי לו אם אתה נותן לי כל כסף וזהב ואבנים טובות ומרגליות שבעולם איני דר אלא במקום תורה: וכן כתוב בספר תהלים על ידי דוד מלך ישראל טוב לי תורת פיך מאלפי זהב וכסף:

ולא עוד[22] שבשעת פטירתו של אדם אין מלוים לו לאדם לא כסף ולא זהב ולא אבנים טובות ומרגליות אלא תורה ומעשים טובים בלבד. שנאמר בהתהלכך תנחה אותך בשכבך תשמור עליך והקיצות היא תשיחך: בהתהלכך תנחה אותך בעולם הזה. בשכבך תשמור עליך בקבר. והקיצות היא תשיחך לעולם הבא: (פרק ר׳ מאיר או פרק קנין תורה)

תנו רבנן כשחלה רבי יוסי בן קיסמא הלך רבי חנינא בן תרדיון לבקרו. אמר לו חנינא אחי אי אתה יודע שאומה זו מן השמים המליכוה. שהחריבה את ביתו ושרפה את היכלו והרגה את חסידיו ואבדה את טוביו ועדיין היא קיימת. ואני שמעתי עליך שאתה יושב ועוסק בתורה ומקהיל קהלות ברבים.[23]

[22] V לפי שבשעת פטירתו (cf. ed. Taylor, text, p. 49). [23] V omits this phrase.

Jacobs, *Barlaam and Josaphat*, pp. lxxvii ff.

[20] Prov. 6.22.

[21] Follows a quotation of Haggai 2.8.

[22] Rome.

ing a Scroll of the Torah at the breast. Ḥanina answered: Mercy will be shown from on high! Jose rejoined: I address reasonable words to thee, and thou answerest, Mercy will be shown from on High! I shall be surprised if they do not burn thee and the Scroll in fire. Ḥanina said: Master, what will be my lot in the life of the world to come? He answered, Has any occurrence happened to thee?[23] Ḥanina replied, Purim money was once mixed with[24] alms-money, and I distributed it to the poor.[25] Jose exclaimed: This being so, may thy portion be my portion, and thy lot my lot! It was said that very soon afterwards R. Jose son of Ḳisma died, and all the magnates of Rome attended his funeral, and mourned over him with a great mourning.

On their return they found R. Ḥanina son of Teradyon, sitting occupied with the Torah, gathering public assemblies, carrying a Scroll of the Torah at his breast. They took him, wrapped the Scroll about him, and encompassed him with faggots of vine branches, to which they set fire. They brought woolen tufts, soaked them with water, and laid them on his heart, so that his soul should not depart quickly.[26]

[23] Any incident from which I may judge your conduct.

[24] Or interchanged with, mistaken for.

[25] Money set aside (either for his own use or for meals for the poor on Purim) was mistaken by Ḥanina for general alms money and so he distributed the deficiency out of his own pocket.

[26] To make his death lingering.

וספר תורה[24] מונח לך בחיקך: אמר לו מן השמים ירחמו: אמר לו אני אומר לך דברים של טעם ואתה אומר לי מן השמים ירחמו! תמה אני אם לא ישרפו אותך ואת ספר תורה באש: אמר לו רבי! מה אני לחיי העולם הבא? אמר לו כלום מעשה בא לידך? אמר לו מעות של פורים נתחלפו לי במעות של צדקה וחלקתים לעניים. אמר לו אם כן מחלקך יהי חלקי ומגורלך יהי גורלי! אמרו לא היו ימים מועטים עד שנפטר רבי יוסי בן קיסמא. והלכו כל גדולי[25] רומי לקברו. והספידוהו הספד גדול:

ובחזירתן מצאוהו לרבי חנינא בן תרדיון שהיה יושב ועוסק בתורה. ומקהיל קהלות ברבים. וספר תורה מונח לו בחיקו. הביאוהו וכרכוהו בספר תורה. והקיפוהו בחבילי זמורות. והציתו בהן את האור. והביאו ספוגין של צמר ושראום במים והניחום על לבו כדי שלא תצא נשמתו מהרה:[26]

[24] V omits.

[25] V בני רומי והספידוהו.

[26] V שלא ימות מהרה.

His daughter said to him: Father, must I see thee in this plight? He answered: Were I being burned alone, the matter would be hard for me; but seeing that I am now being burned together with the Scroll, He who will resent the insult to the Torah will take account also of my wrong. His disciples asked of him: Rabbi, what seest thou? He answered, the Scroll burns but the letters soar (on high). They said to him: Open thy mouth that the fire may penetrate.[27] He replied: Better is it that He who gave the soul should take it, and that a man should do himself no injury. Then the executioner said to him: Master! If I increase the flame and remove the woolen tufts from off thy heart, wilt thou bring me to the life of the world to come?—Yes, said Ḥanina.—Swear it (demanded the executioner). Ḥanina took the oath. Forthwith the officer increased the flame and removed the woolen tufts from over Ḥanina's heart, and his soul departed quickly. The executioner thereupon leaped up and plunged into the fire. Then a Daughter of the Voice[28] went forth and cried: Rabbi Ḥanina son of Teradyon and the executioner are both appointed for eternal life! Rabbi (Judah) wept and said: One acquires his world in a single hour, and another acquires it in many years! ('Abodah Zarah 18).[29]

[27] Thus hastening the end of his sufferings.

[28] See *J.E.*, ii, 588, on this "heavenly voice."

[29] Cf. 'Abodah Zarah 10b. A very human comment on life's inequalities. It may be suggested that a negative has dropped out of this oft-quoted saying, which should

אמרה לו בתו אבא אראך בכך? אמר לה אילמלא אני נשרפתי לבדי היה הדבר קשה לי. עכשיו שאני נשרף וספר תורה עמי[27] מי שמבקש עלבונה[28] של ספר תורה יבקש עלבוני: אמרו לו תלמידיו רבי מה אתה רואה? אמר להן גליון[29] נשרפין ואותיות פורחות. אמרו לו[30] אף אתה פתח פיך ותכנס האש.[31] אמר להם מוטב שיטלנה מי שנתנה ואל יחבל הוא בעצמו: אמר לו קליסטנרי[32] רבי! אם אני מרבה בשלהבת ונוטל ספוגין של צמר מעל לבך אתה מביאני לחיי העולם הבא? אמר לו הן. השבע לי! נשבע לו. מיד הרבה בשלהבת. ונטל ספוגין של צמר מעל לבו. ויצאה נשמתו במהרה: אף הוא קפץ ונפל לתוך האור:[33] יצאה בת קול ואמרה רבי חנינא בן תרדיון וקליסטנרי מזומנין הן לחיי העולם הבא: בכה רבי ואמר יש קונה עולמו בשעה אחת ויש קונה עולמו בכמה שנים! (עבודה זרה י"ח)

27 V This whole clause in third person.
28 V עלבונו.
29 V גוילין.
30 M adds these two words.
31 V add בך. M שלהבת.
32 V קלצטונירי.
33 M האש.

4

Joshua son of Ḥananya

In the old age of R. Joshua b. Ḥananya his disciples visited him, and he said to them: 'My children, what new ideas did you acquire at the college today?' They answered: 'We are thy disciples and drink of thy waters!'[30] He replied: 'God forbid that there should be a generation orphaned of men of wisdom.[31] Whose Sabbath was it?'—'The Sabbath of R. Eleazar b. 'Azariah'—'On what topic was the lecture to-day?'—'On the section (Deut. 31. 12): Assemble the people, the men and the women and the little ones'—'What did R. Eleazar expound on this text?'—'Thus he expounded: the men came to learn[32], the women to listen, but the children, why did they come? To give a reward to those who brought them'—'A precious pearl ye had in your hands and ye sought to deprive me of it! Had ye not come but to tell me[33] this single thing, 'twere enough'—'He further discoursed on Ecclesiastes 12. 11: The words of the wise are as goads. Just as the goad directs the heifer in her furrow, so the words of the Torah direct mankind to the paths of life.' (Abot de R. Nathan, ch. 18).

run: "One attains eternity in an hour, another fails in many years."

[30] We have come to learn, not to teach.

[31] There were others besides himself and to replace himself, as teacher.

[32] To take part in the discussion.

[33] Lit. 'to hear'; but the meaning is 'to tell me'.

ד

ר׳ יהושע בן חנניה

לעת זקנותו של רבי יהושע נכנסו תלמידיו לבקרו. אמר להם בני מה חידוש היה לכם בבית המדרש? אמרו תלמידיך אנו ומימיך אנו שותים. אמר להם ח״ו שאין דור יתום של חכמים. שבת של מי היתה? אמרו לו שבת של רבי אלעזר בן עזריה היתה. אמר להם ובמה היתה ההגדה היום? אמרו בפרשת הקהל את העם האנשים והנשים והטף (דברים ל״א י״ב). אמר להם ומה דרש בה? אמרו לו כך דרש בה אנשים באים ללמוד ונשים לשמוע טף למה הם באים? כדי לתת שכר טוב למביאיהם. אמר להם מרגלית טובה היתה בידכם וביקשתם לאבדה ממני! אלמלא לא באתם אלא לשמוע דבר זה די. אמרו לו ועוד דרש בה דברי חכמים כדרבונות... (קהלת י״ב י״א) מה דרבן זה מכוון את הפרה לתלמיה כך דברי תורה מכוונים את האדם לדרכי חיים:[34] (אבות דר׳ נתן י״ח)

34 For notes on the Hebrew text see Schechter's ed.

When the soul of R. Joshua ben Ḥananya was departing, the Rabbis said unto him: What will become of us at the hands of the Minim?[34] He answered them with the text, Jeremiah 49.7: 'If counsel is departed from the sons, then is their wisdom vanished'—if the sons[35] lose their skill in argument, so does the heathen's wisdom also perish. Or, if you will, he added: take comfort from the experience of Jacob who said to Esau:[36] 'Let us take our journey, and let us go, and I will go with thee'[37] (Genesis 33.12). (Ḥagigah, v, 1).

5

Samuel the Younger

Once they were assembled in the upper chamber of the house of Gorya in Jericho, when a Daughter of the Voice manifested itself, saying: There is among you one who is fit that the Shekinah should rest upon him, but his generation is unfit for it. They turned their eyes toward Hillel the Elder. When he died, they said of him in their elegiac lament: O thou saint! O thou gentle-man! O thou disciple of Ezra! On another occasion they were gathered in an upper chamber in Jabneh. Again a Daughter of the Voice manifested itself, saying: There is here one fit that the Shekinah should rest upon him, but his

[34] Heathen and Judeo-Christian disputants. Cf. Bacher, *Agada der Tanaiten* I 161 (ed. 2 p. 156). Some editions read 'Epicureans'. Joshua was famed for his controversial ability, see *J. E.* vii 291.

כי קא ניחא נפשיה דרבי יהושע בן חנניה אמרו ליה רבנן מאי תיהוי עלן ממיני[35]? אמר להם אבדה עצה מבנים נסרחה חכמתם. כיון שאבדה עצה מבנים נסרחה חכמתן של אומות העולם: ואי בעית אימא מהכא נסעה ונלכה ואלכה לנגדך (חגיגה ה׳ א).

ה

שמואל הקטן

פעם אחת היו מסובין בעליית בית גוריא ביריחו. נתנה עליהן בת קול מן השמים ואמרה יש בכם אדם אחד שראוי שתשרה שכינה עליו אלא שאין דורו ראוי[36] לכך. נתנו עיניהם בהלל הזקן. וכשמת הספידוהו הי חסיד הי עניו תלמידו של עזרא! ושוב פעם אחרת היו מסובין בעלייה ביבנה. נתנה להן בת קול מן השמים ואמרה להן יש בכם אדם אחד שראוי שתשרה שכינה עליו אלא שאין דורו זכאין

35 Censored editions read מאפיקורוסין.

36 The readings זכאי and ראוי vary in the Mss. and editions.

---

35 i. e. of God—Israel being meant.

36 Typifying Rome.

37 Jacob and Esau keep pace together.

generation is unworthy of it. They turned their eyes to Samuel the Younger, and when he died they keened for him in the terms: O thou modest one! O thou saint! O thou disciple of Hillel. On his death-bed he prophesied: 'Simeon and Ishmael are destined to the sword, their comrades to death, the rest of the people will be a spoil, and many sorrows will befall Israel.' Also of Judah b. Baba they would have wished to use a similar lamentation: 'O saint, O gentle-man', but it was an unsettled time and it was impossible to make public elegy over those executed by the Roman government.[38] (Soṭah, 48b).

6

'Akiba

Our Rabbis have taught: Seven injunctions did Rabbi 'Aḳiba lay upon Joshua his son. My son! Dwell not on the height of the town while studying;[39] live not in a city whose heads are scholars;[40] enter not thy house suddenly,[41] still less thy neighbor's house; withhold not shoes from thy feet;[42] rise up early and eat, in Summer because of the heat, in Winter because of the cold;[43] make thy Sabbath a week-

[38] See J. E. xi, 21. Both Hillel and Samuel ha-Ḳaṭon were celebrated for their meek and gentle disposition.

[39] To avoid the disturbance of the traffic.

[40] They would be devoted more to their books than to public affairs.

לכך. נתנו עיניהם בשמואל הקטן וכשמת הספידוהו הי עניו הי חסיד תלמידו של הלל! ואף הוא אמר בשעת מיתתו שמעון וישמעאל לחרבא וחברוהי לקטלא ושאר עמא לביזא ועקן סגיאין עתידין למיתי על עמא. ואף על ר׳ יהודה בן בבא בקשו לומר הי חסיד הי עניו אלא שנטרפה שעה שאין מספידין על הרוגי מלכות (סוטה מ״ח ב׳)

ו

ר׳ עקיבא

תנו רבנן, שבעה דברים צוה ר׳ עקיבא את ר׳ יהושע[37] בנו. בני! אל תשב בגובהה של עיר ותשנה[38]. ואל תדור בעיר שראשיה תלמידי חכמים. ואל תכנס לביתך פתאום כל שכן לבית חבירך. ואל תמנע מנעלים מרגליך. השכם ואכול בקיץ מפני החמה ובחורף מפני הצינה. ועשה שבתך חול ואל

37 M omits the name. 38 M omits.

---

41 Give warning of your approach: cf. Leviticus Rabba ch. xxi.

42 To go unshod was disgraceful: cf. T. B. Shabbat, 129a.

43 Derived in T. B. Baba Ḳama 92b from the text Isaiah 49. 10.

day,[44] so as to avoid needing help from thy fellow-creatures; and be on good terms with one on whom the hour smiles.[45] (Pesaḥim 112a).

Five things did Rabbi 'Aḳiba command R. Simeon b. Yoḥai, when he was confined in prison. Simeon said to him: Master, teach me Torah! 'Aḳiba replied, I will not teach thee. Simeon said to him: If thou teach me not, I will inform my father Yoḥai, and he will give thee up to the government. 'Aḳiba answered: My son! more than the calf desires to suck, the cow desires to suckle. Who is in danger, asked Simeon, is it not the calf? 'Aḳiba then said unto him: If thou wishest to be strangled, hang thyself on a big tree,[46] and when thou teachest thy son, teach him out of a correct book. Cook not in a pot in which thy comrade has cooked.[47] His is an act of charity and also a good investment who helps to produce fruits, while he has a reward.[48] His is a religious act which also keeps his body pure, who marries a wife though he already has children (Pesaḥim 112 a-b).

"And thou shalt love the Lord thy God with all thy heart, and with all thy soul, and with all thy substance."[49] It has been taught: R. Eleazar said, If it is written "with all thy soul",[50] why

[44] Do without luxurious meals.

[45] The Talmud cites in illustration association with Job, of whom it is said: "Thou hast blest the work of his hands."

[46] Go for instruction to a high authority.

[47] Explained in the Talmud as referring either to marriage with a divorced woman in her first husband's life-

תצטרך לבריות. והוי משתדל עם אדם שהשעה משחקת לו: (פסחים קי"ב א')

חמשה דברים צוה רבי עקיבא את ר' שמעון בן יוחי כשהיה חבוש בבית האסורין. אמר לו רבי למדני תורה! אמר לו איני מלמדך. אמר לו אם אין אתה מלמדני אני אומר ליוחי אבא ומוסרך למלכות. אמר לו בני! יותר ממה שהעגל רוצה לינק פרה רוצה להניק. אמר לו ומי בסכנה? והלא עגל בסכנה! אמר לו אם בקשת ליחנק היתלה באילן גדול. וכשאתה מלמד את בנך[38a] למדהו בספר מוגה ...ולא תבשל בקדירה שבישל בה חבירך. מצוה וגוף גדול אוכל פירות ולו[39] שכר. מצוה וגוף טהור נושא אשה ולו בנים: (שם)

ואהבת את ה' אלהיך בכל לבבך ובכל נפשך ובכל מאדך. תניא ר' אליעזר אומר אם נאמר בכל

[38a] M adds תורה. [39] Following Jastrow's reading of לו for לא (see Dictionary, p. 225).

---

time, or to marriage with a widow.

[48] So Jastrow, *Dictionary*, p. 225; he explains: "e. g. one who loans money to a husbandman on security, allowing payment in small instalments." Rashi explains somewhat differently (Cf. Baba Mezi'a 67b).

[49] Deut. 6.5. [50] Life or self.

is it written "with all thy substance"?[51] and if it is written "with all thy substance", why is it written "with all thy soul"? The reason is: should there be a man who holds his life dearer than his wealth, it is written "with all thy soul;" and should there be a man whose money is dearer to him than his life, it is written "with all thy substance." R. 'Aḳiba said: "With all thy soul," even if He take thy soul.

Our Rabbis have taught: Once the wicked government[52] decreed that the Israelites should not occupy themselves with the Torah. Pappos b. Judah came and found R. 'Aḳiba gathering public assemblies and teaching the Torah. He said: 'Akiba dost thou not fear the government? 'Akiba answered: "I will tell thee a parable. To what is the matter like? To a fox who was walking along the river and saw some fishes gathering and fleeing from place to place. He said to them: from what are you fleeing? They answered: From nets which men are casting against us. The fox said: Let it be your pleasure to come up to the dry land, and I and you will dwell together, as my fathers once dwelt with your fathers. They answered: Art thou indeed he whom they declare the shrewdest of animals? Thou art not shrewd, but a dullard! For if we are afraid in the place which is life to us, how much more must we fear in the place which means to us death? So we,

[51] Usually rendered "with all thy might", but see commentaries on the text.

[52] Rome.

נפשך למה נאמר בכל מאדך? ואם נאמר בכל מאדך למה נאמר בכל נפשך? אלא אם יש לך אדם שגופו חביב עליו מממונו לכך נאמר בכל נפשך. ואם יש לך אדם שממונו חביב עליו מגופו לכך נאמר בכל מאדך: רבי עקיבא אומר בכל נפשך, אפילו נוטל את נפשך:

תנו רבנן. פעם אחת גזרה מלכות הרשעה[40] שלא יעסקו ישראל בתורה. בא פפוס בן יהודה ומצאו לרבי עקיבא שהיה מקהיל קהלות ברבים ועוסק בתורה. אמר לו עקיבא אי אתה מתירא מפני מלכות? אמר לו אמשול לך משל. למה הדבר דומה? לשועל שהיה מהלך על גב הנהר[41] וראה דגים שהיו מתקבצים ורצים ממקום למקום. אמר להם מפני מה אתם בורחים? אמרו לו מפני רשתות שמביאין עלינו בני אדם. אמר להם רצונכם שתעלו ליבשה ונדור אני ואתם כשם שדרו אבותי עם אבותיכם? אמרו לו אתה הוא שאומרים עליך פקח שבחיות? לא פקח אתה אלא טפש אתה! ומה במקום חיותנו אנו מתיראין במקום מיתתנו על אחת כמה

40 V מלכות יון.

41 M. שפת הים, but M's readings vary throughout too

if we are now in such a case while we sit and engage in the Torah of which it is written: 'for that is thy life and thy length of days',[53] how much worse would be our case were we to go and neglect it!"

It is reported that shortly afterwards they arrested R. 'Aḳiba and bound him in prison, and they arrested Pappos b. Judah and bound him at his side. 'Aḳiba asked: Pappos, for what reason are thou brought hither? He answered: Happy art thou Rabbi 'Aḳiba, inasmuch as thou hast been imprisoned on account of the Torah; alas for Pappos, who has been arrested for a trivial cause!

In the hour when they took forth R. 'Aḳiba to execution, it was the time for reading the Shema';[54] they combed his flesh with iron combs, but he went on receiving upon himself the yoke of the Kingship of Heaven.[55] His disciples said unto him: Our Master, thus far?[56] He answered: All my days I was concerned about this text: "(And thou shalt love the Lord thy God) with all thy soul", which means, even if He take thy soul. I said: When shall it be in my power to fulfil it? And now that I have the opportunity, shall I not fulfil it? He dwelt long over the word One, until his soul went forth with the word One

[53] Deut. 30.20.

[54] Which includes Deut. 6.4 and 5, *seq.*

[55] This idea was associated with the recital of the passage referred to.

[56] Do you still recite the Shema' despite these tortures?

וכמה! אף אנחנו עכשיו שאנו יושבים ועוסקים בתורה שכתוב בה כי היא חייך ואורך ימיך כך אם אנו הולכים ומבטלים ממנה על אחת כמה וכמה!

אמרו לא היו ימים מועטים עד שתפסוהו לרבי עקיבא וחבשוהו בבית האסורים. ותפסו לפפוס בן יהודה, וחבשוהו אצלו. אמר לו פפוס! על מה הביאך לכאן? אמר ליה, אשריך רבי עקיבא שנתפסת על דברי תורה! אוי לו לפפוס, שנתפס על דברים בטלים!

בשעה שהוציאו את ר' עקיבא להריגה זמן קריאת שמע היה. והיו סורקים את בשרו במסרקות של ברזל והיה מקבל עליו עול מלכות שמים. אמרו לו תלמידיו רבינו! עד כאן? אמר להם, כל ימי הייתי מצטער על פסוק זה בכל נפשך אפילו נוטל את נשמתך. אמרתי מתי יבא לידי ואקיימנו? ועכשיו שבא לידי לא אקיימנו? היה מאריך באחד

considerably for collation here. The passage may be also found in B. Halper's *Post Biblical Hebrew Literature*.

on his lips[57]. There issued a Daughter of the Voice[58] which proclaimed: Happy art thou Rabbi 'Aḳiba, that thy soul went forth with the word One. The Ministering Angels spake before the Holy One, blessed be He, Is this the Torah and this its reward? Is Thy hand governed by men, O Lord, by men of the world?[59] He replied to them: "Their portion is in the (future) life."[60] A Daughter of the Voice went forth and proclaimed: Happy art thou Rabbi 'Aḳiba, inasmuch as thou art ready for the life of the world to come. (Berakot 61b).

7

Judah ha-Nasi[61]

Our Rabbis have taught: In the hour of the demise of Rabbi (Judah), he said: I require the presence of my sons. His sons came to his side. He said to them: Take heed to honor your mother; let the lamp be lit, the table prepared and the couch spread in their wonted places. Joseph of Haifa and Simeon Ephratha ministered to me in my life-time, and they shall attend to me in my death... He then said unto them: I desire to see the Sages of Israel. They came in unto him. He said unto them: Make no mourning for me in the cities,[62] but hold an

[57] "The Lord is One", Deut. 6.4.

[58] Comp. p. 11, note 28.

[59] Ps. 17.14. Should such a man have died at the hand of torturers, and not at God's hand?

[60] These words are the continuation of Ps. 17.14; they are interpreted to refer to the future life.

עד שיצתה נשמתו באחד. יצתה בת קול ואמרה אשריך רבי עקיבא שיצתה נשמתך באחד! אמרו מלאכי השרת לפני הקב"ה זו תורה וזו שכרה? ממתים ידך ה' ממתים מחלד. אמר להם חלקם בחיים. יצתה בת קול ואמרה אשריך רבי עקיבא שאתה מזומן לחיי העולם הבא: (ברכות ס"א ב')

ז

רבי יהודה הנשיא

ת"ר בשעת פטירתו של רבי אמ:ר. לבני אני צריך! נכנסו בניו אצלו. אמר להם הזהרו בכבוד אמכם.[42] נר יהא דלוק במקומו. שולחן יהא ערוך במקומו. מטה תהא מוצעת במקומה. יוסף חפני שמעון אפרתי הם שמשוני בחיי והם ישמשוני במותי:[43] ...אמר להן לחכמי ישראל אני צריך! נכנסו אצלו חכמי ישראל. אמר להן אל תספדוני בעיירות.[44]

42 T. J. Ketubot ix, 3 reads אל תזח אלמנתי מביתי.

43 In T. J. the direction is more general.

44 T. J. adds מפני המחלוקת. See T. B. Sanhedrin 47a.

---

61 Compiler of the Misnah: usually cited as "Rabbi" (simply).

62 T. J. interprets: because of dissension there would be too much emulation among those desirous of delivering orations. Another view was that Rabbi wished to spare his colleagues from trouble.

assembly (for study) after thirty days. Simeon my son is a Sage, Gamaliel my son shall be the Nasi, Ḥanina bar Ḥama shall sit at the head (of the assembly)...He then said unto them: I wish to see my younger son. R. Simeon came into his presence, and he delivered unto him the orders of wisdom. He then said unto them: I require the presence of my eldest son, and Rabban Gamaliel entered. He said unto him: Conduct thy office with the exalted, and act with aloofness toward the disciples...[63]

He stretched his ten fingers on high and said: Master of the World! It is revealed and known before Thee that I have toiled with my ten fingers in the Torah, and have never derived personal advantage even with the little finger. May it be Thy will that peace may abide in my resting-place. A Daughter of the Voice went forth and said: He shall come in peace, they shall rest in their bed. (Ketubot 103 a-b).

Rabbi Hezekiah adds (that Rabbi Judah also directed): Place not many shrouds on me, and let my coffin be set open to the earth (T. J. Ketubot XII, 3).[64]

Four things did our sainted Master[65] command his sons: Dwell not in Shekanzib;[66] sit not on

[63] Lit. 'cast bile amongst'. So Jastrow, *Dictionary*, p. 838. The meaning would be: "avoid over familiarity with them." On the Patriarch's severity, cf. Graetz, *History of the Jews*, E. T., ii, ch. 17.

[64] Not to delay decomposition.

[65] R. Judah ha-Nasi.

[66] A town in Babylonia (Persia), where (according to the Talmud) the people were mockers. (Cf. *J. E.* xi, 257).

והושיבו ישיבה לאחר שלשים יום. שמעון בני חכם גמליאל בני נשיא חנינא בר חמא ישב בראש: ...אמר להן לבני הקטן אני צריך! נכנס ר׳ שמעון אצלו. מסר לו סדרי חכמה: אמר להן לבני הגדול אני צריך! נכנס רבן גמליאל אצלו. ומסר לו סדרי נשיאות: אמר לו בני! נהוג נשיאתך ברמים. זרוק מרה בתלמידים!...

זקף עשר אצבעותיו כלפי מעלה. אמר רבונו של עולם! גלוי וידוע לפניך שיגעתי בעשר אצבעותי בתורה. ולא נהניתי אפילו באצבע קטנה. יהי רצון מלפניך שיהא שלום במנוחתי. יצתה בת קול ואמרה. יבא שלום ינוחו על משכבותם! (כתובות ק״ג)

רבי חזקיה מוסיף. אל תרבו עלי תכריכין ותהא ארוני נקובה לארץ. (ת״י כתובות י״ב ג׳)

ארבעה דברים צוה רבינו הקדוש את בניו.[45] אל תדור בשכנציב... ואל תשב על מטת[46] ארמית...

[45] M בנו.
[46] V. מטה.

the couch of an Aramaean woman;[67] do not seek to escape the payment of taxes; and stand not before an ox when it goes up from the meadow.[68] (Pesaḥim 112b).

8

Rab

And Rab said unto Rab Asi: Dwell not in a place where no horse neighs and no dog barks; dwell not in a place whose headman is a physician;[69] do not marry two wives, but if thou hast done so, marry a third.[70]

Rab said unto R. Kahana: Deal in carcasses but not in words;[71] strip the skin off a carcass in the market and take the profit, but say not I am a priest, I am a great man, and the thing is detestable to me. If thou hast ascended to the roof, take provision with thee. Though a hundred gourds may be bought in the city for a zuz, nevertheless take them under thy wings.[72] (Pesaḥ. 113a).

Rab said unto Ḥiyya his son: Drink no drugs, leap not over a ditch, have no tooth extracted, anger neither a snake nor an Aramaean.[73] (Ibid.)

[67] Comp. note 95 below.

[68] The Talmud adds: "because Satan dances (or leaps) between its horns," i. e. the animal is dangerous.

[69] He would be too occupied with professional duties.

[70] A humorous reminder that three would hardly combine against the husband.

[71] "Gossip, sophistry," etc. (Jastrow, *Dictionary*, p. 361).

[72] However short the journey, or however cheap food may be, never travel without provisions.

[73] Comp. note 95.

ואל תבריח עצמך מן המכס... ואל תעמוד בפני השור בשעה שעולה מן האגם: (פסחים קי״ב ב׳)

ח

רב

ואמר ליה רב לרב אסי[47] לא תדור במתא דלא צניף בה סוסיא ולא נבח בה כלבא, ואל תדור בעיר דריש מתא אסיא,ולא תנסיב תרתי, אי נסבת תרתי נסיב תלת:

אמר ליה רב לרב כהנא[48], הפוך בנבילתא ולא תיפוך במילי. פשוט נבילתא בשוקא ושקיל אגרא ולא תימא כהנא[49] אנא וגברא רבא אנא וסניא בי מילתא. סלקת לאיגרא, שירותך[50] בהדך. מאה קרי במתא בזוזא, תותי כנפיך ניהוו: (פסחים קי״ג א׳)

אמר ליה רב לחייא בריה, לא תשתי סמא. ולא תשוור ניגרא. ולא תעקר ככא. ולא תקנא בחיויא. ולא תקנא בארמאה: (שם)

47 M. אמר רב אסי. 48 M רבא לרב הונא.
49 M adds רבה. 50 M בכנפיך מאה קרי במעה תותי
כנפיך א׳ל רב לרב חייא.

Rab said to his son Aibo: I have labored to teach thee law, without success; come, I will instruct thee in worldly affairs. While the dust is still on thy feet,[74] sell thy wares; you may regret a (premature) sale of anything except wine; untie thy purse, then open thy sack;[75] better a kab from the ground than a kor from the roof;[76] if thou hast dates in thy cask, run to the brewer.[77] (Ibid.).

9

Joshua b. Levi

It was reported to Rabbi Joḥanan that aged men were to be found in Babylonia. He was surprised and said: "It is written: 'That your days may be multiplied, and the days of your children *on the land,*' but outside the land not so." When, however, they told him that (these old Babylonians) are early and late in the Synagogues, he exclaimed: "This is what helps them." This agrees with what Rabbi Joshua son of Levi said to his sons: "Rise up early and stay up late and go to the Synagogue, so that you may prolong your life." R. Aḥa son of R. Ḥanina asked: "What Scriptural text is authority for this?" (The answer was:)

[74] Immediately on reaching the market.

[75] First receive the money.

[76] Do business with what is near, and trust less to distant ventures.

[77] Do not delay lest the dates be consumed.

אמר ליה רב לאיבו בריה, טרחי בך בשמעתא ולא מסתייע מילתא תא אגמרך מילי דעלמא. אדחלא אכרעיך זבינך זבין. כל מילי זבין ותחרט בר מחמרא דזבין ולא תחרט. שרי כיסיך פתח שקיך.[51] קבא מארעא ולא כורא מאיגרא. תמרא בחלוזך לבית סודנא רהוט: (שם)

ט

ר׳ יהושע בן לוי

אמרו ליה לרבי יוחנן איכא סבי בבבל. תמה. אמר למען ירבו ימיכם וימי בניכם על האדמה כתיב אבל בחוצה לארץ לא. כיון דאמרי ליה מקדמי ומחשכי לבי כנישתא אמר היינו דאהני להו. כדאמר רבי יהושע בן לוי לבניה קדימו וחשיכו ועיילו לבי כנישתא כי היכי דתורכו חיי.[52] אמר ר׳ אחא ברבי חנינא מאי קראה? אשרי אדם

[51] M שרי שקך ופתח כיסך.

[52] M ויתקיים תלמודייכו בידיכו א״ר אחא בר אדא.

"Happy is the man that hearkeneth to Me,[78] watching daily at My gates, waiting at the posts of My doors," after which it is written: "For who findeth Me findeth life". (Berakot 8a).

10

A GROUP OF SAYINGS

i

King Jannaeus (on his death-bed) said to his wife (Queen Alexandra): Fear neither the Pharisees nor their opponents, but fear the hypocrites who pretend to be Pharisees, whose deeds are the deeds of Zimri, and who claim a reward like that of Phinehas[79]. (Sota 22b).

ii

Onias the circle-drawer begged mercy and died. Raba said, this illustrates the popular saying: Either friendship or death.[80] (Ta'anit 23a).

iii

Rabbi Yannai said unto his sons: My sons:

[78] Prov. 8.34; applied here to God.

[79] Numbers 25.14. See Schürer, *Geschichte des jüdischen Volkes im Zeitalter Jesu Christi*, beginning of § 11.

[80] On Onias, see J.E. ix, 404; I. Abrahams, *Studies in Pharisaism*, Second Series, p. 81. He was the Rip Van Winkle of the Talmud; awaking after seventy years he found himself without comrades, and preferred death to isolation.

שומע לי לשקוד על דלתותי יום יום לשמור מזוזת פתחי. וכתיב בתריה כי מצאי מצא חיים:[53]

(ברכות ח' א')

י

מאמרים שונים

א

אמר לה ינאי מלכא לדביתהו אל תתיראי מן הפרושין ולא ממי שאינן פרושין אלא מן הצבועין שדומין לפרושין שמעשיהן כמעשה זמרי ומבקשין שכר כפנחס:[54] (סוטה כ"ב ב")

ב

בעי (חוני המעגל) רחמי ומית. אמר רבא היינו דאמרי אינשי או חברותא או מיתותא (תענית כ"ג א").

ג

והאמר להו רבי ינאי לבניו, בני! אל תקברוני

53 M omits this text.

54 On this passage see Derenbourg, *Essai sur l'Histoire et la Géographie de la Palestine*, p. 101.

Bury me neither in white nor in black shrouds;[81] not in white, lest I be not found worthy and I shall be as a bridegroom among mourners; not in black, lest I be found worthy, and I shall be as a mourner among bridegrooms. But bury me in court garments[82] that come from overseas. (Niddah 20a).

iv

In earlier times, the funeral was a more serious matter to a man's relatives than his death[83], so that they would leave him and flee. Then came Rabban Gamaliel who directed simpler obsequies for himself, and (in obedience to his instructions)[84] they carried him out in a linen shroud. This custom thereafter became the general habit. R. Papa said: Nowadays it is the general rule to spend but a zuz[85] on the shroud. (Ketubot, 8b).

v

'Ulla had gone down from Palestine (to Babylonia). When his end was approaching, he started to weep. 'Why weep?' his associates

[81] Similar orders are recorded of other Rabbis; cf. Joḥanan (Bereshit Rabba 96.5). See also T. J. Kil. ix,3, Ketubot ix,3. Thus the Palestinian Amora Jeremiah asked to be so clothed and equipped as to be ready to rise and follow the Messiah.

[82] Of mixed colors. See S. Krauss, *Talmudische Archaeologie*, I, 145, 549.

[83] Owing to the costly funeral rites.

[84] His instructions are found in T. B. Mo'ed Ḳaṭan, 27b.

[85] A very small coin.

לא בכלים לבנים ולא בכלים שחורים. לבנים, שמא לא אזכה ואהיה כחתן בין אבילים. שחורים, שמא אזכה ואהיה כאבל בין חתנים. אלא בכלים האוליירין הבאין ממדינת הים: (נדה כ' א')

ד

בראשונה היתה הוצאת המת קשה לקרוביו יותר ממיתתו. עד שהיו מניחים אותו ובורחים. עד שבא רבן גמליאל ונהג קלות[55] בעצמו. והוציאוהו[56] בכלי פשתן ונהגו כל העם אחריו להוציא בכלי פשתן. אמר רב פפא והאידנא נהוג עלמא אפילו בצרדא[57] בר זוזא (כתובות ח' ב').

ה

עולא נחותא הוה אידמך תמן שרי בכי. אמרין ליה מה לך בכי? אנן מסקין לך לארעא דישראל.

[55] M. adds ראש.
[56] In Mo'ed Ḳaṭan 27b ויצא.
[57] For variants see Jastrow, *Dictionary*, p. 1299, s. v.

asked, 'we will carry thee to the land of Israel for burial.' He rejoined, 'What will that profit me, if I lose my jewel[86] in an unclean land; to place it in a strange woman's bosom is far different from placing it in the bosom of one's mother.' R. Meir was dying in Asia and he said: Say ye to the sons of the land of Israel, behold your Messiah![87] (Though he knew that he would be buried in Palestine), he nevertheless said to them: 'Place my coffin by the sea-shore,[88] for it is written: He hath founded it upon the seas and established it upon the floods'[89]. (J. T. Kilaim IX, 4).

vi

Three things did Rabbi Ishmael son of R. Jose command his son: Cause no blemish to thyself;[90] do not negotiate a purchase when thou hast no money;[91] and when thy wife has taken a ritual bath, do not approach her on the first night. (Pesaḥim 112b).

vii

Three things did Rabbi Jose son of R. Judah

[86] i. e. soul.

[87] An impassioned claim for burial in Palestinian soil.

[88] Thus the sea which washes the land of Israel might touch his bones. The text quoted is Psalm 24.2.

[89] On the desirability of interment in the Holy Land, see Genesis Rabbah, ch. 96 and parallels.

[90] The Talmud explains this of bringing a lawsuit against three people, as each defendant would have cor-

אמר לון ומה הנייה לי? אנא מובד מרגליתי גו ארעא מסאבתא. לא דומה הפולטה בחיק אמו לפולטה בחיק נכריה: רבי מאיר הוה אידמך ליה באסייא. אמר אימורין לבני ארעא דישראל הא משיחכון דידכון. אפילו כן אמר לון יהבי ערסי על גיף ימא דכתיב כי הוא על ימים יסדה ועל נהרות יכוננה (ירושלמי כלאים פרק ט' ד')

ו

שלשה דברים צוה ר' ישמעאל ברבי יוסי את בנו.[58] אל תעש מום בעצמך. ואל תעמוד על המקח בשעה שאין לך דמים. אשתך טבלה אל תזקק לה[59] לילה הראשונה: (פסחים קי"ב ב')

ז

שלשה דברים צוה רבי יוסי ברבי[60] יהודה את

58 V רבי.
59 M עמה.
60 M omits יוסי ברבי.

---

roborative support. The sentence can be interpreted more generally.

[91] Thereby preventing the vendor from finding a firmer customer.

command Rab:[92] Go not out alone by night; stand not naked in front of a lamp; and enter not a new bath.[93] (Ibid.).

viii

Raba said to his sons: When you cut meat, do not cut it on your hand;[94] do not sit on the couch of an Aramaean[95] woman; and do not pass a Synagogue[96] at the time when the congregation is at prayer.[97] (Berakot 8b).

ix

Rabbi Joḥanan said:[98] The Holy One, blessed be He, daily proclaims the virtues of three: a bachelor who lives in a great city and maintains his chastity; a poor man who restores a lost object to its owners; and a rich man who gives a tithe of his profits in secret. (Pesaḥim 113a).

Three doth the Holy One, blessed be He, love: him who does not yield to anger; him that never becomes intoxicated; and him who does not stand on his rights. Three doth the Holy One, blessed be He, hate: him who says one thing with his mouth and (thinks) another thing in his heart;

[92] These acts would be dangerous or immodest. The Talmudic glosses explain these precautions in terms of demonology.

[93] The bath may need inspection as to its safety.

[94] The Talmud explains that this was either to avoid danger or spoiling the food.

[95] Aramaean is used of Gentile in general; here Roman may be meant. The Talmud gives various explanations of Raba's rule: among them that the meaning was not to

רב.[61] אל תצא יחידי בלילה, ואל תעמוד בפני הנר ערום, ואל תכנס למרחץ חדש[62]: (שם)

ח

אמר להו רבא לבניה כשאתם חותכין בשר אל תחתכו על גב היד...[63] ואל תשבו על מטת ארמית. ואל תעברו אחורי בית הכנסת בשעה שהצבור מתפללין. (ברכות ח׳ ב׳)

ט

אמר ר׳ יוחנן. שלשה מכריז עליהם הקדוש ברוך הוא בכל יום על רווק הדר בכרך ואינו חוטא. ועל עני המחזיר אבידה לבעליה. ועל עשיר המעשר פירותיו בצינעה: (פסחים קי״ג א׳)

שלשה הקב״ה אוהבן. מי שאינו כועס. ומי שאינו משתכר ומי שאינו מעמיד על מדותיו: שלשה הקב״ה שונאן. המדבר אחד בפה ואחד בלב. והיודע עדות

61 V רבי. 62 The following words שמא תפחת seem an addition. 63 M adds א״ד על פיסת היד.

---

lie down to rest before reciting the Shema' (Deut. 6.4, *etc.*), for this would be to play the heathen.

96 Lit., behind a Synagogue.

97 This would be an irreverent action.

98 The following, with several other passages in the context, is often cited by the authors of Ethical Wills.

him who can give testimony in a fellowman's favor but does not testify; him who sees a disgraceful thing in his neighbor and charges him singly.[99] (Pesaḥim 113b).

X

A certain Elder said to him[100]: We have learned that one should neither anticipate nor postpone[101] (the readings); as R. Joshua son of Levi said to his sons: Finish your Parashot with the congregation, twice the Hebrew text and once the Targum; also take care with the jugular vein in accordance with R. Judah's opinion.[102] Take heed moreover (to show respect) to an old man who has forgotten his learning under compulsion,[103] for we say: The whole tablets (of stone) and the fragments of the broken tablets were both placed in the Ark.[104] (Berakot 8b).

[99] A single witness could not cause a conviction, but could merely bring the defendant into ill-repute.

[100] R. Bebai b. Abbai.

[101] The discussion concerns the home readings of the weekly lesson (parashah). This lesson (besides being read in Synagogue) was read at home, twice in the Hebrew and once in the Aramaic Version (Targum). The home reading was to be the same portion as the Synagogue lesson. It thus linked together each home with all homes, and all with the communal service.

[102] The reference is to the slaughter of birds. Cf. Mishnah Ḥullin ii, 1.

[103] Of age, sorrow or illness.

[104] Cf. Baba Batra 14b. "Similarly one must respect the old though they be broken by years of trouble" (Cohen).

לחבירו[64] ואינו מעיד. הרואה דבר ערוה בחבירו ומעיד בו יחידי: (שם ב׳)

י

אמר ליה ההוא סבא תנינא ובלבד שלא יקדים ושלא יאחר.[65] כדאמר להו רבי יהושע בן לוי לבניה אשלימו פרשיותייכו עם הצבור שנים מקרא ואחד תרגום והזהרו בורידין כרבי יהודה... והזהרו בזקן ששכח תלמודו מחמת אונסו.[66] דאמרינן לוחות ושברי לוחות מונחות בארון:[67] (ברכות ח׳ ב׳)

64 V בחבירו.

65 M adds: וכך א״ל אביי לבניה אשלימו פר׳ בהדי צבורא תרי קרא וחד תרגום ואפילו עטרות ודיבון כ״ה דתורכו יומי.

66 M שאין נוהגים בו מנהג בזיון דאמר מר לוחות.

67 M adds: מכאן לזקן ששכח תלמודו מחמת אונס שאין נוהגים בו מנהג בזיון.

11
CAUSES OF LONGEVITY

His disciples inquired of R. Joḥanan b. Zakkai: How didst thou prolong thy days? He answered unto them: I never passed water within four cubits of the place of prayer; I never called my fellow-man by a nickname;[105] nor did I ever omit the Sanctification of the Day.[106] My aged mother once sold the cap off her head and brought to me (wine for) the Sanctification of the Day...

His disciples inquired of R. Eleazar son of Shammu'a: How didst thou prolong thy days? He answered unto them: I never made use of the Synagogue as a short cut; I never stepped on the heads of the holy people;[107] nor did I ever raise my hands[108] without a (previous) benediction.

The disciples inquired of R. Perida: How didst thou prolong thy days? He answered unto them Never in my life did another arrive at the Bet Hamidrash[109] before me; I never said the Grace before a priest;[110] nor did I ever eat of an animal from which the priestly dues had not been separated.[111]

His disciples inquired of R. Neḥunya ben Haḳana: How didst thou prolong thy days? He answered unto them: I never won honor at the

[105] Cf. Baba Mezi'a 58b.

[106] The sanctification over the wine-cup on Sabbaths and feasts.

[107] In the assembly, the disciples sat on the ground; Eleazar did not push them aside to reach his place.

[108] In the priestly blessing.

[109] House of Study.

יא

במה הארכת ימים?

שאלו תלמידיו את רבי זכאי. במה הארכת ימים? אמר להם. מימי לא השתנתי מים בתוך ארבע אמות של תפלה. ולא כניתי שם לחבירי. ולא ביטלתי קידוש היום. אמא זקינה היתה לי. פעם אחת מכרה כפה שבראשה והביאה לי קידוש היום:

שאלו תלמידיו את ר' אלעזר בן שמוע. במה הארכת ימים? אמר להם. מימי לא עשיתי קפנדריא לבית הכנסת.[68] ולא פסעתי על ראשי עם קדוש. ולא נשאתי כפי בלא ברכה:

שאלו תלמידיו את רבי פרידא. במה הארכת ימים? אמר להם. מימי לא קדמני אדם לבית המדרש. ולא ברכתי לפני כהן. ולא אכלתי מבהמה שלא הורמו מתנותיה:

שאלו תלמידיו את רבי נחוניא בן הקנה. במה הארכת ימים? אמר להם. מימי לא נתכבדתי בקלון

68 M לא עשיתי בהכ"נ קפנדריא.

---

[110] If a Cohen were present, he took precedence in saying Grace after meals.

[111] Such scrupulosity was not general after the destruction of the Temple.

cost of a colleague's[112] disgrace; never did the curse of my fellow-man come up on my couch—just as Mar-Zuṭra, when he went to bed, was wont to say: Let every one be forgiven who has done me annoy. Further, I was generous with my money.

R. 'Aḳiba inquired of R. Neḥunya the Great, saying: How didst thou prolong thy days? He answered unto him: I never in my life accepted presents; I never exacted retaliation;[113] and I was generous with my money.

So was R. Eleazar wont to refuse gifts sent from the house of the Patriarch. Nor would he accept invitations there, saying, Is it unpleasant to you that I should live? for it is written (Prov. 15. 27): He who hates gifts shall live. R. Zera refused gifts and accepted invitations under similar circumstances, regarding it as a compliment to his host. Nor did I bear resentment for offences against me. For Raba said: He who pardons others is himself pardoned of his own transgressions. As it is written (Micah 7.18): He forgives iniquity and he passes over transgression. To whom does He forgive iniquity? The one who passes over transgression.

His disciples inquired of R. Zera: How didst thou prolong thy days? He answered unto them: Never did I lose my temper in my home; never

[112] Or fellow-man's.

[113] More generally: "I never insisted on my just rights." Rashi's note is: "I never repaid an evil requital to one who had troubled me."

חבירי. ולא עלתה על מטתי קללת חבירי.[69] כי הא דמר זוטרא כי הוה סליק לפורייה אמר שרי ליה[70] לכל מאן דצערן. וותרן בממוני הייתי.

שאל ר׳ עקיבא את ר׳ נחוניא הגדול. אמר לו במה הארכת ימים? אמר לו. מימי לא קבלתי מתנות. ולא עמדתי על מדותי. וותרן בממוני הייתי:

לא קבלתי מתנות כי הא דרבי אלעזר. כי הוו משדרי ליה מתנות מבי נשיאה לא הוה שקיל. כי הוה מזמני ליה לא הוה אזיל. אמר להו לא ניחא לכו דאחיה? דכתיב ושונא מתנות יחיה. רבי זירא כי הוה משדרי ליה מבי נשיאה לא הוה שקיל. כי הוה מזמני ליה אזיל. אמר אתייקורי דמתייקרי בי. ולא עמדתי על מדותי. דאמר רבא כל המעביר על מדותיו מעבירין[71] ממנו כל פשעיו. שנאמר נשא עון ועבר על פשע. למי נשא עון? למי שעבר על פשע:

שאלו תלמידיו את רבי זירא. במה הארכת ימים? אמר להם. מימי לא הקפדתי בתוך ביתי.

69 M קללת חברי על מטתי לא עלתה עמי.
70 M שרי להו מחיל לכל מאן דצערן.
71 M. לו על כל.

did I step in front of one greater than myself; I never even meditated in foul alleys; I never walked four cubits without Torah and Tephillin; I never slept or dozed in the Bet Hamidrash; I never rejoiced at a colleague's disgrace; I never called a fellow-man by a nickname[114] (Megillah 27b–28a.)

It was said of R. Ḥanina B. Ḥama that when eighty years of age he was still able to stand on one foot while removing or putting on his shoe. He said: 'The warm baths, and the oil with which my mother anointed me in my youth have stood me in good stead in my age'.[115] (When the Patriarch Judah appointed him head of the college on his death-bed) Ḥanina refused any higher than third place, and he survived many years. His longevity in office was attributed by himself alternatively to that act of self denial or to his making a detour on his journey from Tiberias to Sepphoris in order to pay his respects to R. Simeon b. Ḥalafta. (Ḥullin, 24b; J. T. Ta'anit, 68a; Kohelet Rabbah, vii, 6).

[114] "An opprobrious surname" or "a by-name." (Jastrow, *Dictionary*, p. 482). The use of such names would be both frivolous and offensive.

[115] Ḥanina was a physician, cf. Bacher, *Die Agadah der Palästinensischen Amoräer*, I. 3.

ולא צעדתי בפני מי שגדול ממני. ולא הרהרתי במבואות המטונפות. ולא הלכתי ארבע אמות בלא תורה ובלא תפלין.[72] ולא ישנתי בבית המדרש לא שינת קבע ולא שינת ארעי. ולא ששתי בתקלת חבירי. ולא קראתי לחבירי בחניכתו[73] (מגלה כ"ז כ"ח)

אמרו עליו על רבי חנינא (ב' חמא) שהיה בן שמונים שנה והיה עומד על רגלו אחת וחולץ מנעלו ונועל מנעלו. אמר ר' חנינא חמין ושמן שסכתני אמי בילדותי הן עמדו לי בעת זקנותי... קביל עלוי ר' חנינא למתמני תליתוי וזכה למארכה שנין סגין. אמר לית אנא ידע מן בגין מה זכיתי מארכה שנין סגין. מן בגין הדא מילתא. ואם מן בגין דהוינא סליק מן טבריה לציפורין והוינא עקים איסטרטיא שאיל בשלמיה דרבי שמעון בן חלפתא: (חולין כ"ד ב', ירושלמי תענית ס"ח א, קהלת רבה ז' ו).

72 M תפלה. 73 M בהכינתו.

ספר ארחות חיים להרב ר׳ אליעזר הגדול

THE "PATHS OF LIFE", BY R. ELEAZAR THE GREAT.

II

THE "PATHS OF LIFE"

BY R. ELEAZAR THE GREAT.

In 1544 there appeared at Venice an octavo volume containing various items, fourth among them (pp. 79b-84a) the "Paths of Life by Rabbi Eleazar the Great" (ספר ארחות חיים לרבי אליעזר הגדול ז"ל). It is generally held that this Testament is the earliest extant specimen of the type of ethical literature dealt with in the present volume; and its author was Eleazar ben Isaac of Worms; and that its date is the middle of the eleventh century. This Eleazar, known as the Great, was a highly reputed authority (see *J. E.*, v, 115).

This identification of the author is due to Lonzano (*Shete Yadot* 122a) and is accepted by Zunz (*Zur Geschichte und Literatur*, Berlin, 1845, p. 124). Jellinek was inclined to place the work a century or more earlier, or at all events to associate it with the same period as another work attributed to Eleazar the Great, viz. the *Chapters of Rabbi Eleazar*, which is probably a ninth century product. The present writer is inclined to place the *Paths of Life* later, not earlier, than the date assigned by Lonzano. The similarity between the Testament and the Zohar, a similarity well brought out by the title-page of the Salonica edition of 1568 and by the notes in Leiner's Lublin edition of 1903, seems to point to a period when the mystical school had made its influence felt.

Popularly and in the editions, the author is described as a much earlier Eleazar than Lonzano's. This would be

ב

ספר ארחות חיים להרב ר׳ אליעזר הגדול:

בשנת ש״ד יצא לאור בויניציה כרך אקטאווא המכיל ענינים שונים, ומהם הרביעי (דף ע״ט:-פ״ד.) ספר „ארחות חיים" לרבי אליעזר הגדול ז״ל. הכל מסכימים שהצואה הזאת היא הדוגמא היותר מוקדמת שנשארה לנו מספרות המוסר ממין זה אשר אנחנו עוסקים בו בכרך שלפנינו, שמחברה היה רבי אליעזר בן יצחק מוורמיזה, ושזמנה הוא אמצע המאה האחת עשרה. אליעזר זה, המכונה „הגדול", היה בר אורין משובח ובר סמכא מפורסם (עיין באנציקלופדיה היהודית האנגלית, כרך חמישי, דף קט״ו).

מנחם לונזאנו (שתי ידות, דף קכ״ב.) המציא את שם המחבר הנעלם, וצונץ (צור געשיכטע אונד ליטעראטור, ברלין תר״ה, דף קכ״ד) הסכים לו. יעללינעק נטה להאמין שספר זה נכתב כמאה שנים או יותר קודם לזמן הנזכר לעיל, ובכל אופן השתדל ליחסו לתקופתו של חבור אחר המיוחס לרבי אליעזר הגדול, הלא הוא „פרקי רבי אליעזר" אשר מוצאו הוא בלי ספק מן המאה התשיעית. כותב הטורים האלה נוטה לקבוע לספר „ארחות חיים" זמן יותר מאוחר, ולא מוקדם, מזה שקבע לו לונזאנו. הדמיון שבין הצואה והזהר, דמיון הבולט היטב ע״י שער הספר של מהדורת סלוניקא שכ״ח וההערות במהדורת לובלין תרס״ג של ליינער, מורה על תקופה שבה השפעת האסכולה המיסתית היתה כבר נכרת ומורגשת.

במסורת העם ובמהדורות הספר מתואר המחבר אליעזר כמו איש שחי שנים הרבה לפני אליעזר של לונזאנו. אפשר

Eleazar ben Hyrḳanos (on whom see *J.E.*, v,113), who lived in the first and second centuries of the current era, and is also the reputed author of the *Chapters* already alluded to. The text opens with the talmudic account of the last illness of this older Eleazar (T. B. Sanhedrin 68a). Elsewhere (Ber. 28b) we are told how R. Eleazar on his deathbed taught his disciples the "*Paths of Life*", and this fact would easily suggest the compilation of just such a work as we are now considering.

Recently a distinguished scholar, G. Klein of Stockholm, has urged that the Testament is a genuine work of the earlier Eleazar son of Hyrḳanos. His arguments are interesting but quite unconvincing (See his work *Der älteste christliche Katechismus und die jüdische Propaganda-Literatur*, Berlin, 1909, pp. 101 seq.).

According to the popular view now reinforced by the opinion of Klein, the son addressed is Hyrḳanos. If Lonzano's theory be true, the son referred to is the famous medieval writer, Tobiah son of Eleazar, a contemporary of Rashi. (On Tobiah and his writings, see Zunz, *G. V.*, ed. 1892, p. 307; S. Buber's Preface to Tobiah's *Leḳaḥ Tob*, Wilna, 1844; and the article in *J. E.*, xii, 169). Thus this son, so frequently admonished in the Testament, was a worthy offspring of a worthy father. It may be suggested that, in the injunction to seek the knowledge of God, the citation of Prov. 19. 2 (בלא דעת נפש לא טוב) is a play on the son's name.

שחשבוהו לאליעזר בן הורקנוס (ראה אודותיו באנציקלופדיה היהודית האנגלית, כרך חמישי, דף קי"ג) שחי במשך המאות הראשונה והשניה של התאריך הנוכחי ואשר אליו מיחסים את „פרקי רבי אליעזר" הנזכרים לעיל. הצואה פותחת בספור התלמוד ע"ד מחלתו האחרונה של אליעזר זה הקדום (תלמוד בבלי, סנהדרין ס"ח.). במקום אחר (ברכות כ"ח:) אנחנו קוראים שעל ערש מיתתו הורה רבי אליעזר לתלמידיו „אורחות חיים", ואין כל ספק שעובדא זו היא אחראית בעד חבור ספר כזה אשר אנחנו עוסקים בו כעת.

בימים האחרונים השתדל תלמיד חכם מובהק, ג. קליין משטוקהולם, להוכיח שהצואה הזאת היא באמת מעשה ידי אליעזר בן הורקנוס. סברותיו יש בהן טעם, אבל אינן מוכיחות כלום (עיין בחבורו „דער אלטעסטע כריסטליכע קאטעכיזמוס אונד דיע יודישע פראפאגאנדא-ליטעראטור", ברלין תרס"ט, דף ק"א וכו').

לפי השקפת העם, המסתייעה כעת ע"י דעתו של קליין, הבן אשר אליו שלוחה הצואה הוא הורקנוס. אכן אם סברתו של לונזאנו היא נכונה, הבן הוא המחבר המפורסם של ימי הבינים, טוביה בן אליעזר, בן דורו של רש"י (ע"ד טוביה וספריו ראה צונץ, גאטטעסדיענסטליכע פארטרעגע, הוצאת תרנ"ב, דף ש"ז; הקדמת שלמה בובער ל„לקח טוב" של טוביה, ווילנא תר"ב; וגם המאמר עליו באנציקלופדיה היהודית האנגלית, כרך שנים עשר, דף קס"ט). ובכן הבן הזה, אשר אביו מיסרהו כל כך בצואתו, היה זרע הגון של אב הגון. נחוץ להעיר שבאזהרתו להשתדל לדעת את הבורא יתברך אפשר שהכתוב ממשלי י"ט ב' (בלא דעת נפש לא טוב) הוא רמז לשמו של הבן.

The Testament, besides its ethical value, has also folklore interest. Some parallels between the Testament and the German *Winsbeke* of 1210 are drawn by M. Güdemann in his *Geschichte des Erziehungswesens*, etc. Vienna, 1880, p. 121.

For editions of the text see Benjacob, p. 50. The present text is based on the Venice editions of 1544 (A) and 1623 (C). The British Museum MS. Add. 27100 (B) has also been collated, and so has the Lublin edition apparently of the year 1572 (L). The MS. referred to agrees closely with the edition of 1544, from which it was possibly copied. Yet it offers some useful variants.

The esteem in which the Testament was held is shown by the not infrequent citations of it as authoritative by important writers on Jewish law and custom.

[They told[1] how, when Rabbi Eleazar the Great lay sick, the Sages paid him a visit. When he saw them he said to them: "I doubt whether the wise men of this generation have enough regard for their lives".[2] They asked: "Rabbi, why speakest thou so?" He answered, "In that ye have not waited upon me." Later, R. 'Aḳiba entered, excusing his previous neglect on the ground of lack of leisure. 'Aḳiba's heart melted within him at R. Eleazar's rebuke. "My Master," cried 'Aḳiba, "instruct me!" In that hour Eleazar taught him three hundred definite decisions concerning the "spot sparkling as snow".[3]

[1] See the Variants in T. B. Sanh. 68a; Abot de R. Nathan, ch. 25; and parallels.

[2] A threat is implied to the effect that the offence may have fatal consequences.

[3] With reference to the plague. Cf. Nega'im i, 1, etc.

מלבד ערכה המוסרי יש לצואה זו גם ערך פולקלורי. מ. גידעמאן, בספרו „געשיכטע דעס ערציעהונגסוועזענס אונד דער קולטור דער אבענדלענדישען יודען וועהרענד דעס מיטטעלאלטערס", וויען תר"ם, דף קכ"א, מצא איזו נקודות מקבילות בין הצואה הזאת ושיר המוסר שכתב המשורר האשכנזי ווינסבעקע בערך שנת 1210.

בנוגע להוצאות הצואה עיין ב„אוצר הספרים" של בן־יעקב, דף ן'. הנוסח הנוכחי נוסד על מהדורות וויניציאה של ש"ד (A) ושפ"ג (C). השויתי גם כ"י Add. 27100 אשר במוזיום הבריטי (B) ומהדורת לובלין אשר כפי הנראה מוצאה משנת של"ב (L). כ"י הנ"ל מתאים עפ"י רוב למהדורת ש"ד, ואפשר שהוא העתק ממנה; ובכ"ז נמצאים בו איזה שינוים מועילים.

חשיבות הצואה נראית מן העובדא שלפעמים קרובות נסתייעו בה מחברים גדולים ופוסקים מפורסמים ויביאו את דבריה בתור סעד וסמך לחוקים ומנהגים ידועים.

[1]ואמרו שכשחלה רבי אליעזר הגדול נכנסו חכמים אצלו: כשראה אותם, אמר להם, תמה אני על חכמי הדור אם ימותון מיתת עצמן: אמרו לו, רבי למה? אמר להם, מפני שלא שמשתם אותי: לאחר כך נכנס רבי עקיבא ברבי יוסף: אמר לו, מפני מה לא באת לשמש אותי? אמר לו, לא היה לי פנאי: אמר לו, עקיבא תמה אני אם תמות מיתת עצמך: באותה שעה נתחלחלו[2] איבריו של רבי עקיבא ונמס לבו[3] בקרבו: אמר לו, רבי למדני!

[1] This introduction appears in all versions of the text.
[2] B נתח לו. [3] A דמו.

Then he called for his son Hyrḳanos, and placed him at his right hand. R. Eleazar wept and said: "My son! Up to this day I have treated thee severely, and have shown little affability. My object was to subdue thee to the fear of thy Maker. But now, my son, behold I go into the pleasance of the Lord and His beauty. Come, I will teach thee the Paths of Life." Then R. Eleazar opened his discourse with the text[4]: "Lord I have heard the report of thee and am afraid."]

My son! Give glory to God and offer unto Him thanks. Remember that He created thee out of clay, and brought thee into the world, fashioning thy body and its parts without help from thee. For thou hast need of Him, He has no need of thee.

My son! Trust not in thyself until the day of thy death[5]; a decision according to the Rabbis is law (i. e. overrides individual opinion). Have no confidence in thy physical well-being in this world. Many have lain down on their couch never to rise again. Many have gone to their beds in good cheer and in robust health to awake in trouble and pain.

My son! Take heed to hold constant intercourse with the wise. Rely not on thine own

[4] Hab. 3.2.

[5] Hillel's saying, Abot ii, 5. It has not been thought necessary to give the reference to the many quotations from Abot, in the course of this and other Testaments.

באותה שעה שנה לו שלש מאות הלכות פסוקות על בהרת עזה כשלג: קרא להורקנוס בנו. וישימהו על יד ימינו: בכה רבי אליעזר ואמר, בנִי! עד היום הייתי מתנהג עמך ברוגז. ולא הסברתי לך פנים כדי לכוף אותך ביראת קונך. ועתה בני! הנני הולך לנועם ה׳ והדרו. בא ואלמדך אורחת חיים: פתח רבי אליעזר ואמר, ה׳ שמעתי שמעך יראתי:

בני! שים נא כבוד לה׳ ותן לו תודה, וזכור כי מחומר עשאך והוא הוציאך לאויר העולם. וכוננך בעצמות עצם אל עצמו. והכניסך בעולם הזה ואתה לא הכנסתו[4] בו. כי הוא אינו צריך לך ואתה צריך לו:

בני! אל תאמין בעצמך עד יום מותך. הלכתא כרבנן הלכתא. אבל לא תאמין עצמך בשלות גופך בעולם הזה: כמה שכבו על מטתם ולא קמו.[5] כמה שכבו על מטתם שמחים וטובי לב וקמו בחלאים רעים. כמה שכבו על מטתם בריאים והקיצו במכאובים רבים:[6]

בני! הוי זהיר להתאבק תמיד באבק עפר רגלי

[4] So L. The usual reading is הכנסת.

[5] C omits this clause. [6] So C. A רעים.

opinion, nor art thou permitted to say to others: "Accept my view!"

My son! Fear the God of thy father and serve Him[6]. Be diligent in reciting the evening Shema' and the morning prayer[7]. Thus David, of blessed memory, said[8]: "Evening and morning and at noonday will I complain and moan,—and He hath heard my voice." These prayers were the ordinance of the first Fathers[9]. Attach chief importance to the evening prayer, for Jacob our Father instituted it. Indeed, the Scripture has made him first of the Patriarchs, as it is said[10]: "And behold the Lord stood beside him and said, I am the Lord, the God of Abraham thy father, and the God of Isaac." Thus, in the first instance God mentioned His holy name over Jacob, and afterwards spoke of Himself as God of Abraham and of Isaac.

My son! Be thou fleet as a hart, in thine eagerness to read the Shema' at the proper hour. Postpone it not to the latest moment allowed by prescription. For the enthusiastic and the scrupulous perform their duties at the earliest instant.[11] Whoever reads the Shema' in its due time glorifies his Creator. Take care, on retiring to rest, to recite this same declaration of Unity and Love, sanctifying thyself and ador-

[6] The context shows that the author is referring to the fine rabbinic idea that "Prayer is the service of the heart" (T. B. Ta'anit 24).

[7] The text seems corrupt here.

[8] Psalms 55.18.

[9] T. B. Ber. 26b.

החכמים. ואל תסמוך על דעתך. ואינך רשאי לומר קבלו דעתי!

בני! ירא את ה׳ אלהי אביך ועבדהו. והוי[7] זהיר בקריאת שמע של ערבית ובתפלה של שחרית. כמו שאמר דוד ע״ה, ערב ובקר וצהרים אשיחה ואהמה וישמע קולי. כמו שתקנו אבות הראשונים: ותפלת ערבית שים ראשונה לכל התפלות. כי יעקב אבינו תקן אותה. והכתוב עשהו[7] ראש לכל האבות. שנאמר, והנה ה׳ נצב עליו ויאמר אני ה׳ אלהי אברהם אביך ואלהי יצחק. בתחלה הזכיר שמו הקדוש עליו ואחר כך אלהי אברהם ואלהי יצחק:

בני! הוי קל כצבי ואל תהי עצל לקרוא ק״ש בעונתה. ואל תעכב אותה לשיעור דרבנן. כי הזריזים והזהירים מקדימים למצות. וכל הקורא ק״ש בעונתה נותן כבוד לבוראו: הוי זהיר בק״ש על מטתך ולקדש עצמך ולברך לבוראך. ושכבת וערבה שנתך: ולאחר שתקדש עצמך בזה[8] אל תספר

[7] A and C עשאו. Such variants are not here collated.
[8] So L., A, etc. read ואל.

---

[10] Gen. 28.13. Cf. Tanḥuma and Zohar on this text.
[11] T. B. Yoma 28b.

ing the Lord, then shalt thou lie down and thy sleep will be pleasant. After thou hast sanctified thyself by these means, speak no idle phrase, do no carnal act, for thou art hallowed with the holiness of thy Maker. Thy soul ascends, and thou knowest not whether it deserve admission before Him. "When thou awakest it shall talk with thee".[12] The sons of the priests enter to partake of their appointed meal and thy soul ascends at that hour; if thou art worthy, thou shalt go in with them; if unworthy, they will thrust thee outside.[13]

My son, when thou wakest from thy sleep at midnight, converse with thy wife in chaste terms, using no indecent expression, even in jest, for this too wilt thou be called to account! If thou wakest at other hours, let not thine heart indulge in impure fancies, for evil thought leads to evil deed.[14] How goodly and how sweet that thou be ever prepared to form one of the righteous company which enters with God, thus drawing o'er thyself the thread of His Love, and finding thy pleasant lot with the righteous in Paradise! Shouldst thou be worthy of this, happy art thou, well will it be with thee![15]

My son! Keep a vessel of water always near thy couch. On rising at morn do not begin to dress before washing thy hands, nor receive thy garments from another in the same condition, for

[12] Prov. 6.22.

[13] Cf. Midrash to Psalm 25; Rabbah on Eccles. 10.4.

[14] Kallah Rabbete ch. 2; Derek Erez Zuṭṭa ch. 6.

[15] Psalm 128.2.

בדברים בטלים. ואל תעסוק עם אשתך בדבר אחר הואיל וכבר קדשת עצמך בקדושת קונך. כי נשמתך תעלה ואינך יודע היאך יקבלוה לעמוד לפניו. והקיצות היא תשיחך. בני! הכהנים נכנסין לאכול בתרומתן ונשמתך עולה באותה שעה. אם תזכה תכנס ביניהן ואם לאו ידחו אותך בחוץ:

בני! כשתעור משנתך בחצות הלילה, אז תספר עם אשתך בקדושה. ואל תנבל את פיך, ואפילו דרך שחוק. כי אתה עתיד ליתן דין וחשבון על שיחה שבינך ובין אשתך: וכשתקיץ[9] משנתך אל יפנה לבך בהרהורים רעים. כי ההרהור מביא לידי מעשה: הנה מה טוב ומה נעים כשהקב"ה נכנס עם הצדיקים, שתהיה מצוי בתוכן. למשוך חוט של חסד עליך, להיות גורלך[10] עם הצדיקים בגן עדן. ואם תזכה ותהיה עמהם אשריך וטוב לך!

בני! הוי זהיר בכלי של מים סמוך למטתך. וכשתקום בבקר, אל תטול חלוקך ללבוש בלא

[9] B וכשתקוע A. וכשתקוץ.
[10] L גור לך.

the spirit of uncleanness rests on the hands. Pass not thine unwashed hands over thine eyes, intending harm to an enemy, lest thy plot fail and thy gaze prove baneful to thy friends, though harmless to thy foes.[16]

My son! Keep thy body pure, cleanse the abode of thy soul! Beware lest thou make it detestable, thyself the cause of thine own rejection!

My son! Be not impatient when I thus insist on this subject. Laving the hands is one of the sublime things which stand on the height of the world. Beware, lest by neglect in this regard, thou become as one excommunicated, and forfeit future bliss. For when thou washest thy hands thou art bound to stretch them on high in adoration of thy Maker[17]; it were unseemly to do so with foul fingers.

My son! Never attire thyself without benediction. Even as men should offer thanks for the enjoyment of food, so must they do for the gift of raiment. He who dresses without blessing shall wear worm and clod in the grave, and the worms cause as much pain to the dead as a needle in raw flesh.[17a]

[16] T. B. Shabb. 62b, 108b; Ber. 19a, 60b; Maimonides Hilk. Tephilah, ch. 4. See *J. E.*, v, 280. The combination of mysticism with popular folk-lore is exemplified in parts of the Zohar, which has many parallels to this Testament (See the Notes of Leiner, in the edition Lublin, 1903).

[17] T. B. Soṭah 4b.

[17a] Ber. 18b.

נטילת ידים. לא מידך, ולא מיד אחר שלא נטל ידיו. כי רוח הטומאה שורה בידים: ואל תעביר אותם על גבי עיניך, פן יכשלו רבים במראית עיניך. כי אין ברכה שורה במראה עין שקבל טומאה. ואי עביד להסתכל בשונאו, שונא נמלט ואוהבו נכשל:

בני! הוי זהיר לנקות גופך ולפנות דירת נפשך שלא תשקצנה. ואל תהי גורם להיות נמאס:

בני! הוי זהיר בנטילת ידים. כי נטילת ידים בכלל הדברים העומדים ברומו של עולם. וכל המזלזל בנטילת ידים מנודה לשמים. וכל שכן דאין לו חלק לעולם הבא: וכשתרחץ ידיך, זקוף אצבעותיך למעלה, וברך ליוצרך: ואל תברך עד שיהיו הידים רחוצות. כי אסור להזכיר קדושת שמו בלכלוך הידים כשהן מזוהמות. ואל תטול ידיך ממי שלא נטל ידיו:

בני! אל תלבש בגדיך בלא ברכה. כי כשם שנהנה האדם לתת אוכל לנפשו, וצריך לברך על הנאת האוכל, כך צריך לברך על הנאת המלבוש בכל עת שילבש. וכל מי שלא בירך על מלבושיו ילבש ברמה וגוש עפר בקבר. וקשה אותה רמה כמחט בבשר החי:

My son! Wrap thyself in the wrapping of duty[18], that on the body of the righteous may rest the robe of the commandment. If one is not so enwrapped, his attire is called the garment of the treacherous; he beareth false witness against himself.[19]

My son! Prepare to meet thy God,[20] with a diadem of honor on thy brow,[21] precious oil on thy head.[22] These are the phylacteries, bearing thy Creator's Name, a chaplet of grace for thine adornment. "And all the peoples of the earth shall see that the Name of the Lord is called upon thee, and they shall stand in awe of thee"[23]. Bind them also on thine arm, the seal[24] of His image, the likeness of the Glory of God. Day by day goeth forth a Heavenly Voice, which proclaims:[25] "Be ye clean, ye that bear the vessels of the Lord." Before a man, in that hour, there walk three Angels,[26] who cry: "Give glory to the Icon (image) of the King," and they apply to such a one the Scripture: "Thou art My servant, Israel, in whom I will be glorified."[27]

[18] The fringed garment—a phrase used also in the Zohar. For the whole paragraph, cf. the Zohar on Beshallaḥ (163, 175, etc.)

[19] Applying Isaiah 24. 16. Cf. T. B. Ber. 14b.

[20] Amos 4.12. Applied in this sense T. B. Shabb. 10a.

[21] T. B. Ber. 11a, Ta'anit 16a. Ṭur O. Ḥ. 25.3.

[22] Ps. 133.2. So interpreted T. B. Shabbat 153a.

[23] Deut. 28.10. On this point see my *Studies in Pharisaism and the Gospels*, 2nd series p. 203.

בני! הוי זהיר להתעטף בעטיפת מצוה, כסוי מצוה על גוף צדיק ינוח. וכל מי שאין כסוי מצוה בגופו נקרא לבושו בגד בוגדים בגדו, כי מעיד עדות שקר בעצמו:

בני! הכון לקראת אלהיך. ושים עטרת תפארת בראשך. השמן הטוב על הראש. והם התפלין. שם יוצרך ולוית חן הם לראשך. וראו כל עמי הארץ כי שם ה' נקרא עליך ויראו ממך. וקשור על זרועך חותם תבניתו הוא דמות כבוד ה': בת קול יוצאת בכל יום ואומרת, הברו,[11] נושאי כלי ה'! שלשה מלאכים הולכים לפני האדם באותה שעה ומכריזים ואומרים[12] תנו כבוד לדיוקנו של מלך ששכינת אל על ראשו ואומר לך עבדי אתה ישראל אשר בך אתפאר:

[11] Several versions give the quotation inaccurately; thus A reads הבריות.

[12] A. ואומר.

---

[24] Cant. 8.6 is so applied in the Midrash.

[25] Cf. Rashi's note on Isaiah 52.11.

[26] On guardian angels see *J. E.*, i, 587.

[27] Is. 49.3.

My son! Go not early to thy comrade's abode, greeting him before thou hast greeted God.[28] It is written: "For three things the earth doth quake," and one of the three is, "for a handmaid that is heir to her mistress."[29] Do not thou let thy fellow-man usurp the dignity due to his Master!

My son! Be among the first ten in Synagogue, that thou mayest enjoy the reward of all the ten[30]. Each of the other nine being in like case with thee, thy reward is increased a hundred-fold. Thus does public worship increase the worth of each man's prayer.[31] Happy he who is numbered!

My son! Enter the presence of thy Creator with the deepest reverence; and when thou prayest, know before Whom thou standest![32]

My son! Exert all thy bodily powers to attain to holiness, to subdue thy will unto God! "All my bones shall say: Lord who is like unto Thee, Who deliverest the poor from him who is too strong for him." And again: "Ascribe ye strength unto God," "God the Lord is my strength."[33]

[28] T. B. Ber. 14a, Nedarim 32b.

[29] Prov. 30.21

[30] T. B. Ber. 47b.

[31] Based on a verbal play on the text Prov. 8.17. The double נ in the word ימצאנני would amount numerically to 100 by *Gematriah*.

[32] T. B. Ber. 28b, in the name of Eleazar the Great.

[33] Ps. 35.10, 48.35; Ḥab. 3 (end). Cf. Yalḳuṭ on first passage.

בני! אל תשכים לבית חבירך[13] להזכיר עליו שם שמים לברכו. כתיב תחת שלש רגזה ארץ. ואחת מהם שפחה כי תירש גבירתה. וכל המברך נשמת חבירו קודם ברכת השם מוריש לשפחה הגברת:[14]

בני! הוי זהיר שתהיה מעשרה הראשונים בבית הכנסת. להיותך נוטל שכר כנגד כולם. כנגד כל העשרה, או כנגד כל הבאים? הלכתא כרבנן הלכתא. אלא נוטל שכר כנגד כל העשרה. וכל אחד מן העשרה הראשונים שכרו כנגד כלם והם כלל מאה. וזהו ומשחרי ימצאנני[15] בשני נונין. אשרי הנמנה!

בני! כשתכנס לפני יוצרך תכנס באימה וביראה. וכשאתה מתפלל דע לפני מי אתה עומד: בני! כל עצמותך תרגיש לקדש[16] בקדושה בכח גדול, לכוף יצרך אצלו. משום, כל עצמותי תאמרנה ה׳ מי כמוך. מציל עני מחזק ממנו. ומשום, תנו עוז לאלהים, למנצח בנגינותי:

13 A. חבריך.
14 C ירושת הגברת.
15 A ימצאונני.
16 A לקדיש.

My son! In the house of learning, speak no idle words; but incline thine ear to the discourse of the wise. Consider nothing negligible; despise no man. For many pearls are found in the poor man's tunic. Nor may any man invade his neighbor's bounds,[34] nor expect to discover doctrine which his fellow is appointed to reveal, seeing that all was ordained before the Lord from the day on which the Law was created.

My son! Be zealous in visiting the sick, for sympathy lightens pain. Urge the patient to return, a penitent, to his Maker. Pray for him, and depart! Do not fatigue him by staying too long, for his malady is heavy enough already. Enter cheerfully, for his heart and eyes are on those who come in.[35]

My son! Bear thy part regularly in the burial of the dead, delivering them into the hand of their Maker, for great is this duty. Unto one who does a kindness which the receiver cannot requite, God renders unmerited favors.[36]

My son! Comfort the mourners, and speak to their heart.[37] The companions of Job were held punishable merely because they reproached when they should have consoled him.[38] Thus it is written[39]: "Ye have not spoken of Me the thing that is right, as My servant Job hath."

[34] Cf. Yoma 38b. Mid. on Prov. 2.7.

[35] Cf. Midrash on Ps. 41, T. B. Shabbat 32a, Ned. 40a.

[36] T. B. Ber. 18a, Sukkah 49a; Rabbah on Gen. 47.29.

[37] Gen. 50.21. Cf. Abot de R. Nathan 14.

[38] Pesiḳta (Buber) p. 117b.

[39] Job 42.7.

בני! אל תשיח שום שיחה בבית המדרש. והט אזנך ושמע[17] דברי חכמים. ואל תהי בז לכל דבר ואל תהי בז לכל אדם. כי כמה מרגליות ימצאו באפקריסתו של עני: אין אדם נכנס לתחומו של חבירו. ואין אדם יכול לחדש דבר בתורה שחבירו מזומן לחדשו. כי הכל מוכן לפניו, מיום שהתורה נבראת:

בני! הוי זהיר לבקר את החולה. כי המבקרו מקל חליו. והשתדל עמו לשוב לקונו. והתפלל עליו וצא! אל תכביד עליו ישיבתך, כי די לו מכובד חליו[18]: כשתכנס לחולה תכנס אצלו בשמחה. כי לבו ועיניו על הנכנסים עליו:

בני! הוי זהיר להוצאת המת לקוברו. ולהכניסו ביד קונך. כי מצוה גדולה היא עליך: כל העושה חסד חנם הקב"ה עושה עמו חסד חנם:

בני! הוי זהיר לנחם אבלים ולדבר על לבם. כי לא היו ראויים להענש חביריו של איוב אלא על שאמרו לו דברי קנטורין ולא דברי ניחומים. דכתיב, כי לא דברתם אלי נכונה כעבדי איוב:

17 לשמע.

18 A חוליו.

My son! "Better is it to go to the house of mourning than to the house of feasting,"[40] to discipline thy soul and pour out tears from thine eyes. He who sheds tears for a worthy man will not weep over his own children in their youth.[41]

My son! Join in bringing the bride to the canopy, help to gladden the bridegroom, for he who thus acts is as though he participated in the nuptial ceremony of the giving of the Law at Sinai.[42]

My son! Show honor to the poor, and draw out thy soul unto him[43]. Be punctilious to offer thy gift in secret, not in the public gaze. Give him food and drink in thy house, but do not watch him while he eats. His soul famishes, and perchance he swoops on the viands.[44]

My son! Crush not the poor with harsh words, for the Lord will plead his cause. Such conduct rouses on high many accusers, to whom there is no defence. But he who treats the poor with good-will and generosity acquires intercessors to plead his cause.[45]

My son! Prepare a viaticum for thy soul[46] and kindle a lamp to give light before thee. Leave it

[40] Eccles. 7.2. Cf. T. J. Ketub. 7.5.

[41] T. B. Shabb. 105b.

[42] Cf. Midrash on Numbers 7.1. There is a play on the words כלתו and כלה (bride).

[43] Isaiah 58.10.

[44] Job 9.26. Cf. Maim. Hilk. Berakot 7.6.

[45] Cf. Abot 4.11 for these terms.

[46] Cf. Tana Debe Eliyyahu 8, and parallels.

בני! טוב ללכת אל בית אבל מלכת אל בית משתה. לתת מוסר לנפשך, ולשפוך דמעות מעיניך. כי כל השופך דמעות על אדם כשר לא ישפוך דמעות על בניו כשהם קטנים.

בני! הוי זהיר בהכנסת כלה לחופה ולשמח חתן. שכל המשמחו כאלו קבל תורה מהר סיני. שנאמר, ויתן אל משה ככלותו. ככלתו כתיב. ודאי יום שנתנה תורה כיום שנכנסה כלה לחופה:

בני! הוי זהיר לכבד לעני ולהפק לו נפשך. ולתת לו מתנה בסתר ולא בפרהסיא. והאכילהו והשקהו בביתך. והעלים עינך מלהסתכל בו כשהוא אוכל. כי נפשו רעבה ותטוש עלי אוכל[19]:

בני! אל תדכא לעני בדבריך. כי ה׳ יריב ריבם. ועון זה גורם לכמה קנטורין[20] למעלה, לגלות חטאתיו לרעה. ומליץ לא נמצא עליו. וכל העושה לו רצונו ודברים טובים, קונה לו כמה פרקליטין למעלה. וכולם מליצים עליו לטובה:

בני! תקן צדה לנפשך. והדליק נר להאיר לפניך. ואל תניחהו להאיר אחריך שמא לא יוכלו

[19] So A. Some texts corrupt the quotation to ותטוב עליו אוכל. [20] Read קטיגורין.

not to those who come after thee, lest they be unable to kindle it, and it be left forever unlit. And thou wilt remain "in the twilight, in the evening of the day, in the blackness of night and the darkness."[47]

My son! Stop not thine ears at the cry of the poor, that the Lord may hearken to thy voice when thou criest. For he who is deaf to the appeal of others, when he crieth shall himself obtain no answer.[48]

My son! Whenever thou prayest, hold thyself as destitute in the presence of thy Maker. For there are many accusers against thee[48a]. Thus, Jacob realized this truth, for observe that he made himself like one poor and needy, for it is written: "I have an ox and an ass," like a poor and needy man.[49] So, too, King David describes himself in the same lowly terms, saying: "Incline thine ear, O Lord, and answer me; for I am poor and needy,"[50] though after a day of prayer[50a] he ascribes to himself a divine quality, and says in the sequel: "Keep my soul, for I am godly." Strive thou to fulfil the text: "Glorify not thyself in the presence of the King."[51]

[47] Prov. 7.9. Cf. Midrash on Ps. 119.105. The metaphor is applied to the darkness of a future consequent on a wasted life.

[48] Prov. 21.13.

[48a] A reference to Satan and his demons.

[49] Gen. 32.6. The Bible has the singular "ox" and "ass," used as collectives. But the author infers from this that Jacob intended to indicate poverty.

אחריך להאירו[21]. ואפילו שהוא לאחור לא ידליקוהו לעולם. ותשאר אתה בנשף בערב יום באישון לילה ואפלה:

בני! אל תאטם אזניך מזעקת דל, למען ישמע ה׳ את קולך בזעקתך. וכל האוטם אזנו מזעקת דל גם הוא יזעק ולא יענה:

בני! בכל תפלתך שים עצמך עני ואביון בפני בוראך. כי כמה הם מקטרגים עליך. כאשר ידע יעקב הענין. וראה שעשה דוגמתו כעני ואביון דכתיב[22] ויהי לי שור וחמור כעני ואביון. ודוד המלך ע״ה אמר הטה ה׳ אזנך ענני כי עני ואביון אני. כיון שעבר היום והמקום הכניס עצמו בחסד בוראו שנאמר לאחריו שמרה נפשי כי חסיד אני. וקיים בך אל תתהדר לפני מלך:

21 B. reads להאריך and omits next six words.

22 The reading of B is here adopted as against עשו for עשה of other texts.

---

50 Ps. 86.1.

50a The author plays upon the expression, "For unto Thee do I cry all the day," Ps. 86.3.

51 Prov. 25.6, applied to humility in prayer (Cf. Numbers Rabbah 4).

My son! Make full provision for the Sabbath joy, honoring it with all thy resources, nay beyond, in preparing repasts for day and night. Omit not the third meal. And order thy conversation aright on the Sabbath day.[52]

My son! Enter not thy house suddenly, still less enter thy neighbor's house without announcement.[53] Make not thyself too much feared in thine home, for this is the cause of many evils.[54]

My son! Drive anger out of thine heart, "for anger resteth in the bosom of fools[55], and a strange god rests on their head."[56]

My son! Love the wise, and attach thyself to them. Seek to know thy Maker, for "that the soul be without knowledge is not good."[57] Salute all men and speak the truth.

My son! Be chaste, and self-restrained in all thine actions. When thou sittest at thy table to eat, remember that thou art in the presence of the King. Be not a snatcher or a glutton. Wash thy hands before and after the meal, for both actions are essential.[58] If thou drinkest while

52 T. B. Shabbat 113b, 117, etc.

53 T. B. Pesaḥ. 112a.

54 T. B. Giṭṭin 6b and often.

55 Eccles. 7.8.

56 Anger is compared to idolatry. See T. B. Shabb. 105b, Maim. Hilk. De'ot 2.3.

57 Prov. 19.2.

58 T. B. Ber. 53b.

בני! הוי זהיר בעונג שבת לכבדו כפי כחך ולעננו במאכל ובמשתה ובסעודת הלילה[23]. אל תשים עצמך כעני כי אם תכבדהו[24] יותר מיכלתך והזהר בסעודה השלישית. והוי זהיר בדבורך ביום השבת. כי על הכל אתה עתיד ליתן דין וחשבון:

בני! אל תכנס ·לביתך פתאום. וכל שכן לבית חבירך. ואל תטיל אימה יתירה בתוך ביתך כי כמה רעות גורמת האימה:

בני! הסר כעס מלבך. כי כעס בחיק[25] כסילים ינוח ואל זר שורה על ראשם:

בני! אהוב את החכמים, ורדוף אחריהם, השתדל לדעת בוראך. כי בלא דעת נפש לא טוב. והוי זהיר לתת שלום לכל אדם, ודבר אמת:

בני! הוי זהיר להיות צנוע בכל מעשיך[26]. והוי צנוע בדבר אחר: בני! כשתשב על שולחנך לאכול, דע שאתה עומד לפני המלך. אל תהי חצוף ובלען. הוי זהיר במים הראשונים ובמים אחרונים, כי שניהם לצורך. כשאוכלין בני השולחן, ואתה שותה, אל

[23] B omits these two words, substituting חלילה after כעני. [24] So B adds. [25] A inaccurately בלב.

[26] So B. But A, L read במקום מגולה. C, D בבית הכסא ואל תפרע עצמך במקום מגולה.

the rest are eating, do not obtrusively recite the benediction over the wine. Speak not during the meal,[59] not even words of Torah.

My son! Nevertheless never omit to discourse of the Torah at the table,[60] for a table whereat there is no discourse of Torah is full of filthy vomit, in that the All-present is not in their thoughts.[61]

My son! When thou visitest a sick man who is without means, go not to him with empty hands. When he awakes, be quick to offer refreshment to him, and he will esteem it as though thou didst uphold and restore his soul[62]. The Lord will requite thee!

My son! Reveal not thy secret to thy wife.[63] Be of faithful spirit to all,[64] betray not another's confidence even when thou art at strife with him.[65]

My son! Eat herbs rather than beg from others, and if thou beggest, ask only for thine absolute need.[66] Prefer death to making thyself a burden on thy fellow-creatures![67]

My son! It is incumbent on thee to beget children, and to rear them for the study of the Torah.[68] For their sake thou wilt be worthy of eternal life.[69]

59 T. B. Ta'anit 5b.

60 After the meal.

61 For this application of Isaiah 28.8, see Abot 3.4.

62 T. B. Nedarim 40a.

63 Micah 7.5. Genesis Rabbah 54.

64 Prov. 11.13.

65 Prov. 25.9. Cf. T. B. Ḥullin 89a.

תרים קולך בברכת היין. ואל תשיח בתוך הסעודה, ואפילו בדברי תורה:

בני! הוי זהיר בדברי תורה לאמר על השולחן. וכל שולחן שאין עליו דברי תורה נקרא קיא צואה בלי מקום:

בני! הוי זהיר כשתכנס לחולה, ואין לו, אל תכנס בידים ריקניות. כשיקום, הוי מקדים לו המאכל. ויהשב עליך כאלו אתה מקימו ומשיב נפשו. וגמולך ישלם לך בוראך:

בני! אל תגלה סודך לאשתך. הוי נאמן רוח אצל כל אדם. ואל תגלה סוד חבירך[27] בריבך עמו. כל שכן בהיותו בשקט עמך:

בני! הוי זהיר לאכול את העשבים ואל תשאל מבני אדם. וכשתשאל שאל לצורך: תבחר מחנק לנפשך ואל תצטרך לבריות:

בני! הוי זהיר להיות לך בנים, ולגדלם לתלמוד תורה. כי בשבילם תזכה לחיי העולם הבא: בני!

[27] So B; while A reads סודך and C סודו.

---

[66] T. B. Pes. 114a; Sanh. 108b.

[67] Job 7.15. Cf. Rabbah on Exod. 31.12 and often.

[68] T. B. Yeb. 63b.

[69] T. B. Shabb. 127a; Sanh. 104a.

My son! Beware lest thy wife be over generous to her first son-in-law. Appoint not the latter as administrator over thy household.[70] My son! Approach not thy wife near her menstrual period. Avoid all grossness. Hold aloof from what is foul and from what has the appearance of foulness.[71] Pass not behind a woman in the street nor between two women.

My son! Be on thy guard lest thou provoke any of the wise, for his anger is as a viper's venom, the poison of a basilisk which will not be charmed.[72] But if there be death in such a one's wrath, there is life in his good-will.[73]

My son! Walk not alone, judge not alone, testify not alone, nor be witness and judge at the same time. None may judge alone save One.[74]

My son! Be no cause of plaint to orphan or widow, for God is the father of the fatherless and judge of the widows. Rob them not, seeing that He hath already deprived them of all their happiness.[75] Hence "He will despoil of life those that despoil them."

70 T. B. Pes. 113; Ber. 63a. 71 T. B. Ḥullin 44b.

72 Ps. 140.4, Jer. 8.17. See the variant Abot ii, 6. Cf. *J. E.* v, 280. Contrast Hillel's proverbial graciousness (T. B. Shabb. 30). 73 T. B. Ketub. 103a.

74 Ȧbot 4.4, 8; T. B. Makk. 12a.

75 Klein renders: "Seeing that all the good that befalls them He has ordained." This is very forced, for קבע is taken in two senses: *to rob* and *to fix*. A possible alternative is: "Seeing that he (their oppressor) robs them of all good." The texts quoted are Ps. 68.6, Prov. 22.23.

הוי זהיר באשתך מחתנה הראשון. ואל תמנהו אפטרופוס בביתך: בני! אל תקרב לאשתך קרוב לוסתה. והתרחק מן הכיעור ומן הדומה לו. ואל תעבור אחרי אשה בשוק. ואל תעבור בין שתי נשים:

בני! הוי זהיר שלא תקפיד לחכם. כי חמתו חמת עכשוב. וחמתו צפעוני שאין לו לחש. חמתו מות ורצונו חיים:

בני! אל תלך יחידי ואל תדין יחידי ואל תעיד יחידי[28] ואל תהי עד ודיין כאחד[29]. כי אין יחידי ודיין זולתי אחד:

בני! הוי זהיר מזעקת יתום ואלמנה. כי הוא אבי יתומים ודיין אלמנות. אל תהי להם קובע, הואיל והוא קובע כל טוב שלהם. על כן הוא קובע את קובעיהם נפש:

28 This clause is omitted in several texts.

29 B יחידי.

My son! Set all thy sins in the scale, and thy repentance will make even the balance. Thereafter add confession and prayer, to make overweight in thy favor.

My son! Keep far from a wicked neighbor, and from him whose reputation is evil, for what they say of him below accords with what they say of him on high.[76]

My son! "Rejoice not when thine enemy falleth, and let not thy heart be glad when he stumbleth, lest the Lord see it and it displease Him, and He turn away His wrath from him [to thee]." But "if thine enemy be hungry give him bread to eat."[77]

My son! Pursue not after authority, for every thing is decreed from on high. God confers greatness where He wills, and daily He proclaims those whom He hath called by name. Thus is it written that Israel was called upon to recognize: "Behold the Lord hath called by name Bezalel."[78]

My son! Be not as a fly o'er thy fellow-man's sore, leaving the healthy parts and pouncing on the plague spot. Cover up thy neighbor's disease, and lay not his corruption bare to the world.[79]

My son! Haste to the performance of a duty, and let it not seem light in thine eyes. Say not, this is light, that is important, for thou knowest

[76] Cf. Abot 3.10.

[77] Prov. 24.17, 25.21.

[78] Exod. 31.2, 35.30. T. B. Ber. 55a. On Predestination see *J. E.* v, 351; x, 181.

[79] Cf. Mid. Tanḥuma on Deut. 25.17.

בני! כל חטאתיך שים במשקל, ותשובתך במאזנים ישאו יחד. ואחרי כן תן וידוי ותפלה להכריע המשקל:

בני! התרחק משכן רע, ומאדם ששמועתו רעה. כשם שאומרים עליו מלמטה, אומרים עליו מלמעלה:

בני! בנפול אויבך אל תשמח פן יראה ה׳ ורע בעיניו[30] והשיב מעליו אפו. אבל אם רעב שונאך האכילהו לחם:

בני! אל תרדוף אחר השררה. כי הכל גזור מלמעלה, ולאשר יחפוץ יתננה. בכל יום הקב״ה קורא על זה בעצמו, ראו קראתי בשם! ראו קרא ה׳ בשם בצלאל:

בני! אל תהי כזבוב[31] לחבירך על נגעו. שמניח מקום בריא ושורה על הנגע. כסה לחבירך על נגעו ואל תגלה קלקולו[32] לעולם:

בני! הוי רץ לדבר מצוה. ואל תהי המצוה קלה בעיניך. ואל תאמר זו קלה וזו חמורה. כי אינך

30 So A. Several texts have לו.

31 So C, D; but A, B, L have the curious reading כאוב.

32 L קלקול.

not the grant of reward for each. Let all thy deeds be done in the Name of Heaven![80]

My son! Be not righteous overmuch, neither be thou overmuch wicked.[81] Nor let thyself become over-yielding to the extent of drinking water left over from the lips of thy friend.[82] For the breath cometh out from within his throat, and thou art unaware who is suffering from disease. Be bashful in all matters, but efface not thyself at the cost of thy health. Yet in the house of study be thou modest. Behave there as one unlearned, even though thy comrades laugh at thee for it.[83]

My son! Sit not in the company of calumniators and slanderers, for all is noted on high, and is recorded in a book. And all who are present are inscribed in the list of offenders.

My son! Drink not borrowed waters[84], eat not from everyman's hand. Cook not in a pan which has already been used by another, still less if two have previously cooked in it and have departed from the world. For already the angel of destruction recognizes it[85].

[80] T. B. Ber. 6b; Abot 2.1, 4.2, etc.

[81] Eccles. 7.16,17.

[82] Cf. Comm. on Ṭur Oraḥ Ḥayyim Ch. 8.

[83] T. B. Ber. 43b.

[84] See *J.E.*, iv, 516.

[85] T. B. Pes. 111, 112; Yeb. 64b. These metaphors are often applied to cases of re-marriage.

יודע מתן שכרן של מצות. כל מעשיך יהיו לשם שמים:

בני! אל תהי צדיק הרבה ואל תרשע[33] הרבה. ואל תהי בישן הרבה, אפילו לשתות מים הנשארים מפיו של חבירך. כי ההבל יוצא מבית חללו ואינך יודע איזה חולה[34] בגופו: בכל דבר הוי בישן, ובמקום שההיזק שכיח[35] אל תהי בישן: לעולם הוי מנבל עצמך בבית המדרש. ואפילו ששחקו חביריך עליך:

בני! אל תשב בחבורת האומרים גנאי מחביריהם ובעלי לשון הרע. כי כל הדברים עולים, ובספר נכתבים. וכל העומדים שם נכתבים בחבורת[36] הרשע ובחבורת לשון הרע:

בני! אל תשתה מים שאולים. ואל תאכל מאכל מיד כל אדם. הוי משתין בפני מאה, ואל תשתה מים בפני אחד: בני! אל תבשל בקדרה שבשל בה חבירך. וכל שכן אם בשלו בה שנים ונסתלקו מן העולם. כי כבר מלאך משחית מכיר בה:

[33] B תרשיע. [34] A חולי. [35] A שכיב ההיזק.

[36] A B L חבורת, and so in next occurrence of word.

My son! Wed not an unworthy woman: woe to the tarnished who tarnishes his seed![86] Absalom and Adonijah, the offspring of such a union, wrought many evils to Israel. They were unchaste and stirred up rebellion. My son! Have no marital intercourse with thy wife while she is suckling her child. Do not leave an infant in his cradle alone in the house by day or night, nor pass thou the night alone in any abode. For under such circumstances, Lilith seizes man or child in her fatal embrace.[87]

My son! Zealously bring up thy children in the study of the Law. Withdraw them not from it! For he who so acts shortens his life; the Holy One weeps over such a one day by day.[88]

My son! Drink no water that has been left uncovered overnight. Many pitfalls exist in the world, and in them men are caught, as birds are trapped in a snare.

My son! Sit not in the sun's shadow in the summer months (Tammuz and Ab); still less mayest thou sleep in the light of the moon, especially when it is crescent. Concerning these things does the text speak[89]: "The sun shall not

[86] T. B. Ḳidd. 70a.
[87] On Lilith see *J.E*, viii, 87.
[88] T. B. Ḥagigah 5b.
[89] Ps. 121.6

בני! הוי זהיר מאשה שאינה הגונה לך. אוי לו לפסול[37] שפוסל את זרעו! אבשלום גרם כמה רעות לישראל. רדף אחר אביו להרגו ושכב את נשיו. אדוניהו אחיו הפליג על המלוכה ובקש לאשת אביו[38]: בני! הוי זהיר שלא תשמש מטתך בשעה שהיא מיניקת את בנה. ואל תניחהו[39] בעריסתו יחידי בבית, בין ביום ובין בלילה: ואל תהי ישן יחידי בלילה בשום בית. כי בדברים אלו לילית מזומנת להזיק. וכיון שאוחזת לאדם או לתינוק, היא מוציאתו מן העולם:

בני! הוי זהיר לגדל בניך לתלמוד תורה, ואל תסלקם ממנה. שכל המסלק בנו מן התורה יסתלקו ימיו מן העולם. מפני שהקב"ה בוכה עליו בכל יום ויום:

בני! הוי זהיר שלא תשתה מים מגולים בלילה. כי כמה מקטרגים משתכחים בעולם. ובהם נוקשים בני אדם כצפורים[40] הנאחזים בפח:

בני! אל תשב בצל חמה בימי תמוז ואב. וכל שכן שלא תישן בלילה לאור הלבנה. ועל זה נאמר

37 L למי. 38 A omits לאשת. The omission is explained by the reading of L ובקש אביו להרגו. 39 C תנוח בנך.
40 A, C, L ובהם יוקשים בני אדם חסרים כדגים.

smite thee by day nor the moon by night," by day because of Keteb Meriri, by night because of Igrath bath Mahalath.[90] But "the Lord shall keep thee from all evil, He shall keep thy soul. The Lord shall guard thy going out and thy coming in, from this time forth and for ever."[91]

My son! Snatch not at flesh while the steam is rising from it, whether the meat be roasted or boiled. Eat no food prepared in a pan in which no cooking had been done for thirty days.[92]

My son! Give unto thy Creator His share of all thy food. This, God's portion, belongs to the poor. Therefore select of the choicest viands on thy table and present them to thy Maker. "Thou shalt not curse the deaf, but thou shalt fear thy God."[93]

My son! Be it known unto thee that the hope of the righteous is the happiness which is reserved in the fairest region of the universe, a treasured place and secret, wherein none may abide but the clean and sanctified souls invited to enter. It is the Holy One's Plantation of Delight, 'twas formed ere earth came into being, and is not of this world![94]

[90] Names given to evil spirits, T. B. Pes. 112b, etc. See *J.E.*, iv, 516.

[91] Ps. 121.7.

[92] For the folklore elements see *J.E.*, art. Demonology, and list of articles pp. 425–6. The coincidence of certain folk-superstitions with modern hygienic rules is very arresting. As Sir J. Frazer has shown, magic is in a sense early empirical science.

[93] This quotation of Levit. 19.14 seems to mean that the benefactor must not impose on the recipient's ig-

יומם השמש לא יככה וירח בלילה. ביום מפני קטב מרירי, ובלילה מפני אגרת בת מחלת. וכל שכן כשלבנה[41] בחידושה. ה' ישמרך מכל רע ישמור את נפשך. ה' ישמור צאתך ובואך מעתה ועד עולם:

בני! אל תאכל בשר בעוד שמסלקת ההבל, בין צלי בין מבושל. ואל תאכל תבשיל מקדרה שלא בשלו בה שלושים יום:

בני! הוי זהיר מכל מאכל לתת חלקו לבוראך. והחלק שלו הוא של עניים. לפיכך טול מן היפה שבשולחנך לתת לקונך: אל תקלל חרש ויראת מאלהיך:

בני! דע כי בטחון הצדיקים הוא הטוב הגנוז מבחר תבל ארצו. והוא מקום גנוז וסתור ואין כל בריה יכולה לעמוד באותו מקום זולתי הרוחות הקדושות הטהורות המזומנות ליכנס לאותו מקום. והמקום ההוא מטע שעשועים של הקב"ה. ונברא קודם שנברא העולם. אינו מן העולם הזה:[42]

[41] Interesting, as showing how variants arise, is the reading of A which has וכשלבנה for these 3 words.

[42] B ואינו בעולם הזה רק בעולם הבא.

---

norance by bestowing the less dainty morsels. God is not deceived. [94] See *J.E.*, ix, 575, *seq.*

מוסר אב: צואת ר׳ יהודה אבן תבון

A FATHER'S ADMONITION BY JUDAH IBN TIBBON

III

A FATHER'S ADMONITION

BY JUDAH IBN TIBBON.

Born in Granada about 1120, Judah son of Saul Ibn Tibbon was forced to leave Spain in the middle of the twelfth century. The cause may be presumed to have been the same persecution by the Almohades which drove Maimonides from Cordova. Ibn Tibbon went to Provence and in 1160 Benjamin of Tudela found him practising as a physician at Lunel. His Testament is obviously the work of a medical man; equally it is the work of a cultured man of letters. Indeed he fills an important place in the history of Hebrew literature, for, to use his son Samuel's justly eulogistic phrase, Judah Ibn Tibbon was the "father of translators". He was the translator of works by Baḥya, Jehuda Halevi, Ibn Gabirol, and Ibn Janaḥ. It is very doubtful whether he translated also the *Choice of Pearls*. He quotes the work in the Testament, but scarcely in terms implying that he had himself rendered the maxims. He refers to two of his own works otherwise unknown. On his activity as translator see Steinschneider, *Heb. Ueber.* 4, 215; *J. E.* vi, 544.

In Lunel, Judah Ibn Tibbon enjoyed the friendship of a scholarly circle (cf. *J. E.* loc. cit.). He was an ardent collector of books, and it is no doubt his library that is referred to by his son in the latter's preface to the Hebrew translation of Maimonides' *Guide for the Perplexed.* The

ג

מוסר אב: צואת ר׳ יהודה אבן תבון

יהודה בן שאול אבן תבון נולד בעיר גראנאדא בערך שנת תת״ף לאלף החמישי, וכבן שלשים הוכרח לעזוב את ספרד. אפשר לשער שסבת גלותו מארץ מולדתו היתה רדיפת היהודים ע״י האלמוהדים אשר לרגלה נגרש גם הרמב״ם מקורדובה. אבן תבון הלך למדינת פרובינצא, ובשנת תתק״ך מצא אותו בנימין מטודילא מתפרנס בתור רופא בלוניל. נקל לראות שצואתו היא מעשה ידי רופא וגם סופר משכיל. אין כל ספק שאבן תבון ממלא מקום חשוב בתולדות הספרות העברית, ובצדק אומר עליו בנו שמואל שהיה „אבי המעתיקים״. הוא העתיק מערבית לעברית את ספריהם של בחיי, יהודה הלוי, אבן גבירול ואבן גנאח. ספק גדול הוא אם העתיק גם את „מבחר הפנינים״. הוא מביא בצואתו איזה פתגמים ומבטאים מן הספר הזה, אבל לא בסגנון שאפשר היה להסיק ממנו שהוא בעצמו העתיק אותם. בצואתו הוא מזכיר ג״כ שנים מחבוריו שאינם נודעים משום מקור אחר. בנוגע למלאכת ההעתקה שלו עיין בספרו של שטיינשניידר, העברעאישע איבערזעטצונגען, דף ד׳ ורט״ו; האנציקלופדיה היהודית האנגלית, כרך ששי, דף תקמ״ד.

בלוניל התרועע יהודה אבן תבון לחברת אנשים חכמים ומלומדים (עיין באנציקלופדיה היהודית האנגלית, במקום הנזכר לעיל). הוא אהב לאסוף ספרים הרבה, ואין כל ספק שבהקדמתו אל ההעתקה העברית של „מורה נבוכים״ להרמב״ם

J. E. states that Samuel was born c. 1150 and that the Testament was written in or after 1190. It seems difficult to reconcile some of the expressions in the Testament with a forty-year old recipient; on the other hand, some parts clearly require us to think of Samuel as no longer young. The puzzle is solved when we remember that parents often began such Testaments when their child was young, and completed them many years later, just as nowadays codicils are added to wills. The Testament of Judah Ibn Tibbon bears many marks of having been more than once supplemented and revised. As rendered below, the last lines of the metrical epilogue seem to confirm this. "Thrice these counsels have I written out." It must, however, be confessed that the word rendered "thrice" is employed by Judah in another poem of his to mean "excellent things" (see the lines printed by L. Dukes in *Path of Good Men*, p. xi).

The author's laments as to his sufferings refer to his earlier years. In Lunel he appears to have prospered well. But he was clearly a sensitive soul, and he was distressed when his daughters, on their marriage, left him for other cities. His tone of querulous affection for his son is also very human. He obviously believed in his son's abilities, and resolved to cultivate them to the utmost. His resolve bore fruit, for Samuel attained to fame, yet the father certainly diagnosed his son's disposition with accuracy, for Samuel was of a restless nature and does not appear to have settled for long in any one place after his father's death. Judah's advice as to the study of Arabic was taken to heart by Samuel, who was complimented on his Arabic proficiency by Maimonides. Judah's insistent declaration that the "style is the man" applied to handwriting as well as to the substance of what was written. So, later on, Joseph Ezobi in his Silver Bowl told his son:

בנו שמואל מרמז לאוצר הספרים שלו. לפי האנציקלופדיה היהודית האנגלית נולד שמואל בערך תתק"י והצוואה נכתבה בשנת תתק"ן או אח"כ. קשה להלום איזה מן המבטאים של הצוואה לזרע בן ארבעים; ולהפך, מבטאים אחרים מכריחים אותנו להניח ששמואל כבר לא היה צעיר. החידה הזאת נפתרת כשזוכרים אנחנו שלפעמים קרובות התחילו האבות לכתוב צוואות בשעה שבנם היה עוד צעיר ועול ימים ולא השלימון כי אם שנים רבות אח"כ, כמו שבימינו החדשים סמפונים נוספים אל צוואות מזמן לזמן. ובאמת צואת יהודה אבן תבון נושאת תוים רבים המעידים על מלואים והגהות שנצטרפו אליה לעתים תכופות. כפי שנעתקה להלן, החרוזים האחרונים בסופה כמו מחזקים את ההשערה הזאת: „ושלישים כתבתים לך". אבל נחוץ להודות שהמלה הנעתקת „שלש פעמים" משמשת בשיר אחר של יהודה במובן „דברים נעלים" (ראה את הטורים שהדפיס יהודה ליב דוקעס בספר „אורחות צדיקים", דף XI).

תרעומות המחבר על עינויו ויסוריו מוסבות על חייו הקדומים בספרד. בלוניל, כנראה, זרחה עליו שמש ההצלחה. אכן ברור הוא שהיה בעל מזג רך ונפש מתרגשת, ויצטער הרבה כשבנותיו נשאו לאנשים ויעזבוהו ללכת לערים אחרות. דבריו המוכיחים והמלטפים לבנו הם ג"כ כדרך הבריות. אין כל ספק שהאמין בכשרונות בנו ויחליט לפתחם ולשכללם בכל האפשר. עמלו זה נשא פרי ישוה לו, כי שמע שמואל יצא לשם ולתהלה; ובכ"ז הכיר האב היטב את תכונת בנו הסוערת שאינה יודעת מרגוע, כי כידוע נשאר שמואל נע ונד תמיד וכנראה לא התישב לעולם לזמן ארוך במקום קבוע אחרי מות אביו. שמואל שם לבו לעצת אביו בנוגע ללמוד שפת ערב, כי הרמב"ם הלל אותו על ידיעתו הרבה בשפה זו. המימרא השגורה של יהודה ש„הסגנון הוא האיש" מוסבה גם על הכתב גם על התוכן של הכתב. דומה לה מה שאמר יוסף אובי לבניו ב„קערת הכסף" שלו:

For in his penmanship man stands revealed,
Purest intent by chastest style is sealed.

Judah Ibn Tibbon's hero was Samuel the Nagid, who in Judah's youth attained to high place in Granada because of his skill as a writer of Arabic. The Nagid was indeed worthy of Judah's homage. For as statesman, scholar and philanthropist the Nagid stands out for the beauty of his character no less than for the splendor of his attainments. As to Judah Ibn Tibbon's own character, his fidelity to his friends and his generosity as to lending his books are notable, as is his desire that his son should emulate his example. His beautiful comparison of his library to a garden is worthy of Ruskin; he anticipates the charm of the sylvan vignettes on the Bewick ex libris of a much later date—*inter folia fructus*, or again *In tali nunquam lassat venatio sylva.*

The text of the Testament depends on a single MS. in the Bodleian Library (Cat. Neubauer, No. 2219, 3). It was printed from this MS. twice in one year, 1852, in Berlin and in London. The present edition has been derived directly from the MS. and several misreadings and misprints in the former editions have been corrected. The many quotations from Samuel the Nagid's poems have been checked with the readings in Harkavy's edition of the Nagid's verses, and Harkavy's text has often been preferred. It has not been possible to collate these quotations with the MS. in the possession of Mr. David Sassoon. (In the Notes S refers to Steinschneider's Berlin edition, O to the Oxford MS.). To the English edition of 1852 (*The Paths of Good Men*, ed. H. Edelman) a translation was added by M. H. Bresslau. This has been of much service, but has not been bodily adopted. The original

בספרו האנוש נכר וכתב
לשכל שולחו עדות ברורה.

גבורו של יהודה אבן תבון היה שמואל הנגיד אשר בימי בחרותו של יהודה התמחה בגראנאדא לסופר בקי ומהיר בשפת ערב. באמת היה שמואל הנגיד ראוי והגון לתהלתו של יהודה אבן תבון, כי בתור איש מדינה, תלמיד חכם ובעל צדקה היה עולה ובולט משום מזגו היפה באותה מדה שהיה נבדל ונפרד בכשרונותיו המצוינים. בנוגע לאפיו של יהודה אבן תבון, הנה יש להרים על נס את מסירת נפשו לרעיו ונדבת רוחו בהלואת ספריו, כמו שיש להלל את חפצו שבנו ילך בעקבותיו. הדמיון היפה שהוא מדמה את אוצר הספרים שלו לגן הוא ראוי והגון לאיש כרוסקין; והוא טועם מראש את קסם העולם הצומח הנמצא בציורי עקס-ליברים של בעוויק בתקופה יותר מאוחרת–inter folia fructus או שוב in tali nunquam lassat venatio sylva.

נוסח הצואה תלוי בכתב־יד יחיד ומיוחד הנמצא בבית עקד הספרים הבודליאני (רשימת נייבויער, נומר 3, 2219) ונדפס מן הכ"י הזה פעמים בשנה אחת, שנת תרי"ב, בברלין ובלונדון. המהדורה הנוכחית נוסדה על הכ"י, ועל ידו תקנתי איזה שגיאות קריאה ודפוס של ההוצאות הראשונות. השויתי גם את החרוזים הרבים שהוא מביא משירי שמואל הנגיד לנוסח המזוקק של שירי הנגיד בהוצאת הרכבי, ולפעמים קרובות בכרתי את האחרון על הראשון. לדאבוני אי אפשר היה לי להשוות את החרוזים האלה לכ"י הנמצא תחת ידו של דוד ששון. בהערותי קראתי S למהדורת ברלין של שטיינשניידר, O לכ"י אוקספורד. למהדורת לונדון של תרי"ב („אורחות צדיקים", הוצאת צבי הירש עדעלמאן) נוספה העתקה אנגלית ע"י מרדכי ברעסלוי, והעתקה זו היתה לי לעזר גדול, אבל לא

text is sometimes in rhyme, and both Prologue and Epilogue are in rhymed verse. These have been turned into rhythmical prose.

The generosity of the author with regard to the loan of his books is paralleled by the Testament of R. Eleazar bar Peraḥyah (apparently of the fourteenth century). This is to be seen in the Oxford MS. of Maimonides' *Code* (Cat. Neub. No. 577, cf. Edelman, *Treasures of Oxford*, 1851, p. xxi). This testator died young, and bequeathed the whole of this MS., which bears Maimonides' autographic declaration that the copy is accurate, to the Beth-Din. It was not to be sold or otherwise disposed of, nor was it to be used for study. But it was to remain for ever at the disposal of students for the correction of their copies. As a rather grim comment on the bequest, Edelman tells us that Prof. Huntingdon had no difficulty in acquiring the Codex at Cairo "at a comparatively cheap price."

In the Name of God,[1] whose Memorial be exalted and praised for ever!

[This Admonition was composed by the great philosopher, Rabbi Judah son of Saul Ibn Tibbon, for his son, the distinguished scholar Samuel, in his youth; be their memory for a blessing!]

Take a Father's Admonition, from a heart disturbed
At parting from thee, like a sea in storm;

[1] Heb. in the name of the Name.

הבאתיה כמות שהיא. יש אשר הנוסח העברי הוא בחרוזים, כמו הראש והסוף. חרוזים כאלה העתקתי לפרוזה שקולה אף כי לא חרוזה.

נדבת רוחו של המחבר ביחס להלואת ספריו מוצאת את משלה בצואת רבי אלעזר בר פרחיה (כמדומה במאה הארבע עשרה). זאת אפשר לראות בכ"י אוקספורד של ה„יד החזקה" להרמב"ם (רשימת נייבויער, נומר 577, ראה עדעלמאן, „גנזי אוקספורד", תרי"א, דף XXI). בעל הצואה הזאת מת בדמי ימיו וינחיל לבית דין את הכ"י כלו, הנושא מודעה מהרמב"ם בכתיבת יד עצמו ששטר הצואה הוא נכון ומדויק. הוא אסר למכור אותו או למסור אותו לאחרים באיזה אופן שיהיה, וגם התנגד לשמושו בלמוד; אבל התלמידים הורשו להשתמש בו בכדי לתקן את השגיאות הנמצאות בהעתקיהם. בתור באור מר על עזבון המנוח מודיענו עדעלמאן שעלה ביד הפרופיסור הונטינגדון לקנות את הכ"י היקר הזה בקהירה „במחיר נמוך בערך".

בשם השםי יתעלה וישתבח זכרו לנצח. זה מוסר חבר אותו החכם הגדול ר' יהודה בר' שאול בן תבון זצ"ל לבנו החכם הכולל שמואל בבחרותו זכרונם לברכה:

קח מוסר אב מלב נכאב
לפרידתך כים הומה.[2]

[1] The MS. always has השם with a horizontal line over the last two letters.

[2] The division of the lines into two halves follows the MS. The H. edition disregards it.

With boundless grief without all intermission,
His eye is poured out and ceaseth never![2]
God has tried him by migration of his children
As none among fathers has been tried before![3]
Against him, too, Destiny has conspired,
Beguiling him with its enticements;
It cast him into depths of loneliness,
And threw him into a sea of sorrows!
With exile and yearning it afflicted him,
And in their robes was he disguised;[4]
Yea, Time came with storm and raging,
To stir and overwhelm his heart![5]
On his platter it put wormwood,
And poison it mixed in his cup;[6]
Strained were his eyes with weeping; well-
Nigh was he sightless as the blind;
Had his tears dropped down on a desert,
They had made reeds and rushes flourish!
So he ate the bread of misery, and drank
Athirst, tears in flowing measure;[7]

[2] Lam. 3.49.

[3] For the personal history of the author, see above p. 51f.

[4] E. renders: "It afflicted him with wandering and shame. And by their pains he was struck dumb."

[5] Job 39.24.

[6] Ps. 69.22.

[7] Ps. 80.6.

וברוב תוגה מאין פוגה
עינו נגרה לא תדמה.
נסהו אל בנדוד בנים
עד אין לו באבות דומה.
וזמן הסית את לבו בו
ויפתה אותו וירמה.
השליכו במצולות פירוד
ובים תוגות אותו ירמה.
בנדוד ובכוסף יענהו
ובמדויהם יהיה נדמה.
וברעש ורוגז יבוא
לרגיז את לבו ויגמא.
ובברותו לענה ישים
לצמאו רוש אותו יגמא.
כלו עיניו בדמעיו כמ־
עט[3] לא יראה אור כסומא.
לו ירדו על ארץ ציה
הצמיחו קנה וגומא.
יאכל לחם דמעה ישתה
בדמעות שליש בצמא[4]

[3] The MS. divides כמעט [4] H. כצמא.

His soul abhorred all viands,[8]
In his eyes his meat was unclean!
My God, O wherefore hath befallen me
So grievous an ill, or for what sin?
Till when must I live on enduring
This separation, O Lord, how long?[9]

My son, list to my precepts, neglect none of my injunctions. Set my Admonition before thine eyes, thus shalt thou prosper and prolong thy days in pleasantness!

Thou knowest, my son, that the Creator did not specify a recompense for any of the Ten Commandments except for honoring parents. Length of days and happiness were the appointed meed of obedience. For the Pentateuch says:[10] "Honour thy father and thy mother....that thy days may be long, and that it may go well with thee;" and in the Prophecies, God asks of Israel: "If then I be a father, where is My honour?"[11] I need not recall to thee the recompense of the children of Jonadab, son of Rechab, who kept their father's ordinance; and how the Creator used their example for reproof of Israel, and granted to the Rechabites the appointed requital of happiness and longevity, as thou wilt find in the section referring to that subject.[12]

8 Ps. 107.18.

9 Several phrases in these verses are reminiscent of Samuel ha-Nagid, whom our author cites so often. Cf. e. g. No. iv in Harkavy's edition of ha-Nagid's poems.

10 Deut. 5.16.

11 Mal. 1.6.

12 Jer. 35.

ותתעב כל אוכל נפשו
ובעיניו כל לחמו טמא.
אלי אלי במה היתה
לי זאת הרעה או על מה?
או עד מתי אשא עלי
פירוד[5] הזה או עד כמה?

בני! למצותי הקשיבה. ואל תפל דבר מכל הדברים אשר אצוך. ושים מוסרי נגד עיניך ונוכח פניך. כי אז תצליח את דרכיך ואז תשכיל. והארכת ימים בטוב ובנעימים!

בני! כבר ידעת כי הבורא לא פירש גמול על אחת מעשרת הדברים כי אם על כבוד אבות. שייעד עליהם באורך חיים וימים טובים. כמו שאמר למען יאריכון ימיך ולמען ייטב לך. ואמר בתוכחות, אם אב אני איה כבודי? וכבר ידעת מה היה גמול בני יונדב בן רכב ששמרו מצות אביהם. והוכיח הבורא בהם את ישראל וייעד אותם במה שייעד מהגמול הטוב ואריכות ימים. כאשר תמצא בפרשת הענין ההוא:

[5] H. הפירוד.

Thou knowest, my son, how I swaddled thee and brought thee up, how I led thee in the paths of wisdom and virtue. I fed and clothed thee; I spent myself in educating and protecting thee. I sacrificed my sleep to make thee wise beyond thy fellows, and to raise thee to the highest degree of science and morals. These twelve years I have denied myself the usual pleasures and relaxations of men for thy sake, and I still toil for thine inheritance.

I have honored thee by providing an extensive library for thy use, and have thus relieved thee of the necessity to borrow books. Most students must bustle about to seek books, often without finding them. But thou, thanks be to God, lendest and borrowest not. Of many books, indeed, thou ownest two or three copies. I have besides made[13] for thee books on all sciences, hoping that thy hand might "find them all as a nest."[14] Seeing that thy Creator had graced thee with a wise and understanding heart, I journeyed to the ends of the earth, and fetched for thee a teacher in secular sciences. I minded neither the expense nor the danger of the ways. Untold evil might have befallen me and thee on those travels, had not the Lord been with us!

But thou, my son! didst deceive my hopes. Thou didst not choose to employ thine abilities, hiding thyself from all thy books, not caring to

[13] Apparently referring to compendia made for the son's use by the father.

[14] Isa. 10.14.

ואתה ידעת בני! כי טפחתיך וריביתיך. וגדלתיך ורוממתיך. ובדרך חכמה הוריתיך. במעגלי יושר הדרכתיך. ובמאכל ובמשתה ובמלבוש כבדתיך. וטרחתי בלימודך מכל פחד שמרתיך. ונודדתי שנתי לחכמך מכל חביריך. ולהעלותך אל המעלות הרמות בחכמה ובמוסר. מנעתי עצמי מכל טובה ותענוגות בני אדם בעבורך זה שתים עשרה שנה. ועוד יגעתי להנחילך:

כבדתיך בהרבות לך ספרים. ולא הצרכתיך לשאול ספר מאדם כאשר אתה רואה רוב התלמידים ישוטטו לבקש ספר ולא ימצאו. ואתה שבח לאל! משאיל ואינך שואל. וברוב הספרים יש לך שניים ושלישים. ויותר עשיתי לך ספרים מכל החכמות. הייתי מקוה שתמצא ידך כקן לכולם. כיון שחננך צורך לב חכם ונבון. טרחתי לקצות ארץ והבאתי לך מלמד חכמות חיצונות. ולא חסתי על הוצאה ועל סכנת דרכים. וכמעט הייתי בכל רע אני ואתה בהליכה ההיא, לולי השם שהיה לנו:

ואתה בני! הכזבת את תוחלתי ואת תקותי. ולא חפצת להשתמש בבינתך. והתעלמת מכל ספריך.

know them or even their titles. Hadst thou seen thine own books in the hand of others, thou wouldst not have recognized them; hadst thou needed one of them, thou wouldst not have known whether it was with thee or not, without asking me; thou didst not even consult the Catalogue of thy library. *Ben Mishle*[15] says:

He who has toiled and bought for himself books,
But his heart is empty of what they contain–
Is like a lame man, who engraved on a wall
The figure of a foot, and tried in vain to stand!

All this thou hast done. Thus far thou hast relied on me to rouse thee from the sleep of indolence, thinking that I would live with thee for ever! Thou didst not bear in mind that death must divide us, and that there are daily vicissitudes in life. But who will be as tender to thee as I have been, who will take my place—to teach thee out of love and good-will? Even if thou couldst find such a one, lo! thou seest how the greatest scholars, coming from the corners of the earth, seek to profit by my society and instruction, how eager they are to see me and my books. But thou, though all this was thine without silver and price, thou wert unwilling; and the Lord hath not given thee a heart to know, eyes to see, or ears to hearken unto this day. May thy God en-

[15] On the author's frequent quotations from the poems of Samuel ha-Nagid see above, p. 53. *Ben* (Son of) *Mishle* is a series of metrical aphorisms based on the Biblical *Mishle* or Proverbs. For editions see above p. 53.

אפילו לא היית רוצה לראות מה הם ומה שמותם. כי אם היית רואה אותם ביד אחרים לא היית מכירם. ואם היית צריך לאחד מהם, לא היית יודע אם ישנו אתך[6] אם אין, עד שהיית שואל אותי.[7] ואפילו המזכרת של ספריך לא היית מעיין אותה. ובן משלי אמר,

אשר יגע וקנה לו ספרים
ולבו מאשר בם ריק וריקם.
כפסח אשר חקק עלי[8] קיר
דמותי[9] רגל. ובא לקום ולא קם:

כל זה עשית, עד עתה היית סומך עלי להעיר אותך משנת העצלה. ודמית שאחיה לך לעולם. ולא נתת אל לבך ועינך. כי המות יפריד ביני ובינך. או ילדי יום מחיים: כי מי יחמול עליך בני כחמלתי? ומי יעמוד לך במקומי ללמד מאהבה ומחפץ? אפילו אם היית מוצא, הנה אתה רואה החכמים הגדולים שהם מבקשים ומשתדלים מכנף הארץ להועיל בחברתי ובישיבתי. ונכספים לראותי ולראות ספרי. ואתה כאשר מצאת בלא כסף ובלא מחיר לא רצית. ולא נתן לך השם לב לדעת ועינים לראות ואזנים לשמוע עד היום הזה. אלהיך יתן

6 MS. אותך. 7 E reads אותו. 8 H. אלי 9 O מאת

dow thee with a new heart and spirit, and instil into thee a desire to retrieve the past, and to follow the true path henceforward!

Seven years and more have passed since thou didst begin to learn Arabic writing but, despite my entreaties, thou hast refused to obey. Yet thou art well aware how our foremost men only attained to high distinction through their proficiency in Arabic writing.[16] Thou hast already seen what the Nagid (of blessed memory) has recorded as to his rise to power being solely due to this cause, when he sang: "O Pen, I tell of thy kindness!"[17] Similarly with his son. In this country, too, as well as in the kingdon of Ishmael[18] the Nasi, R. Shesheth, acquired wealth and honor through his Arabic. By means of it, he paid his debts, met all his expenditure, and made splendid gifts.

Nor hast thou acquired sufficient skill in Hebrew writing, though I paid, as thou must remember, thirty golden pieces annually to thy master, the clever R. Jacob son of the generous R. Obadiah. And when I persuaded him to teach thee to write the letters, he answered: "It will be enough for him to learn one letter a year." If

[16] For Samuel ha-Nagid's debt to his Arabic caligraphy see Graetz, *History*, E. T., iii, 255. The "Song of the Pen" is no longer extant. The Nagid's son Joseph collected his father's poems (Cf. Harkavy, Introduction, p. ix).

[17] E. "I am weary of relating thy mercy."

[18] Spain or Morocco; Shesheth was a noted physician in Barcelona. Cf. Dukes' note in Edelman's *Path of Good Men*, p. 57.

לך לב חדש ורוח חדשה וחפץ שתשיג בו מה שחלף. ותשיב כל מה שאבד. וישכילך ויורך בדרך זו תלך!

גם כתיבת הערבי שהחלות ללמוד אותו היום שבע שנים ועוד הייתי מפייס אותך עליה. ולא רצית לעולם שמוע אלי: ואתה יודע כי הגדולים שבעמינו לא הגיעו אל הגדולה והמעלות הרמות כי אם בכתיבת הערבי: כבר ראית[10] מה שספר הנגיד ז"ל מן הגדולה שהגיע אליה בעבורה באמרו, עט אני חסדך מספר וכו'. ומה שהגיע בנו אחריו גם כן מן הגדולה בה. גם בארץ הזאת אתה רואה כי הנשיא ר' ששת ז"ל הגיע בה אל העושר והכבוד גם במלכות ישמעאל. ובה יצא מכל חובותיו, ועשה כל הוצאותיו הגדולות ונדבותיו:

גם על כתב העברי לא השגחת כראוי. הלא תזכור שהייתי נותן למשכיל ר' יעקב בן הנדיב ר' עובדיה רבך שלשים דינר זהב בכל שנה. וכאשר פייסתי אותו ללמדך כתיבת האותיות אמר אלי, והלא יספיק לו אם ילמוד אות אחת לשנה. ואם

10 MS. ראיתי.

thou hadst paid attention to this remark of his, thou wouldst have striven to become a better scribe than he or his sons. Hast thou not seen R. Shesheth's son, a boy of twelve, whose writing so resembles that of his teacher, R. Patur, that the scripts are indistinguishable? Handwriting is but an art[19], and with attention, intelligence, and practice, anyone can imitate his model. "If anyone asserts, 'I have labored but did not find,' believe him not."[20] Now, if the reputation—for the most part false—which thou hadst acquired far and wide embarrassed thee, thou wouldst have exerted thyself to prove the report an underrating rather than an exaggeration, from fear of exposure, should people actuallv come to thy place. As *Ben Mishle* says:

When men commend thee with their lips,
  Unto their words apply thine heart;
And if they laud for parts not thine,
  Strive hard to justify their praise!

High qualities have been ascribed to thee by R. Shesheth, and what wilt thou do in the day of visitation? Woe for that indignity, alas for that disgrace! May God lead thee into wiser ways, and teach thee for thy profit[21]; may He make this separation the cause of thine amendment and awakening. O that thy lethargy prove but a passing slumber! As *Ben Mishle* says:

[19] Lit. "form".

[20] T. B. Megillah 5b.

[21] Isa. 48.17.

היה לך לב בעבור הדבר הזה שיצא מפיו, היית משתדל שתהיה סופר יותר ממנו ובניו: והלא ראית בנו של ר׳ ששת והוא בן י״ב שנים כתיבתו דומה לכתיבת רבו ר׳ פטור. וכאלו היא היא בעצמה. כי הכתיבה היא צורה מן הצורות ובעיון ובהתבוננות יוכל אדם לחקותה ובהרגל. ויגעתי ולא מצאתי אל תאמן. וכן אם היית בוש בעצמך בעבור השם אשר יצא לך למרחוק ורובו שקר. היית משתדל להוסיף על השמועה. והיית ירא מהבושת והכלמה כשיגיעו למקומך. בן משלי[11],

בעת יענו עמך שבחיך
בפיהם, תנה לבך למלתם.[12]
ואם יהללוך באשר אין בך,
שקוד עד תהי[13] צדק תהלתם.[14]

ואתה רואה המעלות הרמות אשר הנשיא קורא לך בהם. ומה תעשה ליום פקודה? אוי לאותה בושה אוי לאותה כלמה! אלהיך יישרך להשכיל. וילמדך להועיל. וישם הנדוד הזה סבה לטובתך. ולהקיץ מתנומתך. ולא תהיה תנומה כי אם תרדמה! ב׳. מ׳.

11 The MS. mostly omits ואמר, and merely introduces the quotation with בן משלי or the abbreviation ב'מ'.
12 O למלותם. 13 O שתהא. 14 O תהלותם.

Woe to the man who stands awake,
  Yet seeth not his path;
Happier he who lies asleep,
  And eyes within his heart!

Thou art still young, and improvement is possible, if Heaven but grant thee the helping gift of desire and resolution, for ability is of no avail without inclination. So King David said[22]: "His *delight* is in the law of the Lord." Thou knowest, too, what the Nagid has written (in *Ben Mishle*):

A brother of knowledge, if indeed he possess a heart,
  For his heart's sake his heart will strive with him!

And in another place:

A green tree while still moist thou canst straighten[23],
  But thou canst not straighten a dry log.

If the Lord please to bring me back to thee, I will take upon me all thy wants. For whom indeed do I toil but for thee and thy children? May the Lord let me see their faces again in joy!

Therefore, my son! Stay not thy hand when I have left thee, but devote thyself to the study of the Torah and to the science of medicine. But chiefly occupy thyself with the Torah, for thou hast a wise and understanding heart,[24] and all that is needful on thy part is ambition and

[22] Ps. 1.2. [23] E. "prune".

[24] Rather touching is the father's wavering between pride in his son's ability (afterwards justified by his son's literary fame), and discontent with the same son's indolence.

אבוי לאיש אשר נעור
ולא ראה נתיבתו!
ואשרי איש אשר יישן
ועינים בלבתו![15]

כי עדיין נער אתה. ואיפשר שתתיישר אם יעזרוך מן השמים לתת לך חפץ ורצון. כי תבונה בלי חפץ אינה מועילה: ודוד ע"ה אמר, כי אם בתורת ה'[16] חפצו. וכבר ראית מה שאמר הנגיד ז"ל, ב'. מ'.

אחי מדע אשר לבב יהי בו
לבבו בעבור לבו יריבו:

ואמר עוד,

ועץ רטוב בעודו לח תיישר.
ולא תיישר לך קורה יבשה:

ואם שוב ישיבני אליך השם אעמס כל מחסורך עלי. כי למִי אני עמל כי אם לך ולבניך?[17] אלהי יראני פניהם בשמחה!

על כן בני! אל תרף ידך אחרי מעסוק בתלמוד תורתך ובחכמת הרפואות. והוי מעט עסק ועסוק בתורה. כי יש לך לב חכם ונבון אם תחפוץ לקבוע

15 Kaempf reads ועינו היא. H. renders as though the text read ועיניו בלכתו.

16 The MS. (here and elsewhere) has ייי with a horizontal line over the three letters.

17 MS. reads ולבנך.

application. I know that thou wilt repent of the past, as many have repented before thee of their youthful indolence. As the Nagid (*Ben Mishle*) says:

Learning's robe the good disciple decks,
And youthful study sweet increase bestows;
But he who in his age would wisdom gain
Dies ere he wisdom's savor tastes:[25]

Therefore, my son! Exert thyself whilst still young, the more so as thou even now complainest of weak memory. What, then, wilt thou do in old age, the mother of forgetfulness? Awake, my son! from thy sleep; devote thyself to science and religion; habituate thyself to moral living, for "habit is master over all things."[26] As the Arabian philosopher[27] holds, there are two sciences, ethics and physics; strive to excel in both! The Sage of blessed memory said: "The wise shall inherit honour,"[28] while as for wisdom, "length of days is in her right hand, in her left riches and honour."[29] And further: "Better is a poor and wise child than an old and foolish king."[30] But I need not dwell longer on this subject, nor quote more on the same point from Proverbs and the Son of Proverbs.[31]

25 E: "Will depart life without wisdom and understanding."

26 Cf. *Choice of Pearls.*

27 Al-Ghazali.

28 Prov. 3.35.

29 Ibid. 3.16.

30 Eccles. 14.13.

31 Ha-Nagid's *Ben Mishle.*

וללמוד. ויודע אני שתתחרט על מה שעבר כאשר התחרטו רבים לפניך על התעצלם בימי הנערות והבחרות. והנגיד ז״ל אמר, ב׳. מ׳.

סדין חכמה לתלמיד טוב ילובש.
ותלמוד[18] נערות חוסן ונועם.
ומי ילמד בזקנה לא בנוער,
יאוסף מבלי חכמה וטעם:

על כן בני! השתדל בעוד ימי הבחרות והנערות. כל ׳כן אתה מתרעם עתה מן השכחה. ומה תעשה לימי הזקנה שהיא אם השכחה? הקיצה בני! משנתך. והתעסק בחכמה ובמוסר. והרגל עצמך במדות טובות. וההרגל על כל דבר שלטון. ואמר החכם הערבי, החכמות שתים. חכמת התורות וחכמת הגופות. השתדל בני! שתהיה נכבד מחביריך בכבוד החכמה. והחכם ע״ה אמר, כבוד חכמים ינחלו. ואמר עוד, אורך ימים בימינה. ואמר, טוב ילד מסכן וחכם ממלך זקן וכסיל. ואינני[19] צריך להאריך בענין הזה. ומה שנזכר בו במשלי ובבן משלי:

[18] O ובתלמוד. [19] MS. ואיניני.

Well art thou aware, my son! that the companionship of the ungodly is noxious, that their example cleaves like the plague. O "enter not into the path of the wicked!"[32] Loiter not in the streets, sit not in the highway, go not with him whose society is discreditable. As the Sage says:[33] "He that walketh with wise men shall be wise," and *Ben Mishle* writes:

Choose upright men for friends, with them
  Take counsel, but the fool despise!
With the wise thou canst a rock o'erturn,[34]
  And safety find 'gainst giants' rage!

My son! Make thy books thy companions, let thy cases and shelves be thy pleasure-grounds and gardens. Bask in their paradise, gather their fruit, pluck their roses, take their spices and their myrrh. If thy soul be satiate and weary, change from garden to garden, from furrow to furrow, from prospect to prospect. Then will thy desire renew itself, and thy soul be filled with delight! For, remember the lines of the poet:[35]

How shall I fear man, when a soul is mine
  Whose whelps can dismay lions?
Why fret about poverty, when in her[36] is wisdom

[32] Prov. 4.14.

[33] Ibid. 13.20.

[34] Cf. T. B. San. 24a.

[35] See note on Hebrew text.

[36] Her, i. e. the soul.

בני! כבר ידעת כי חברת הרעים מזיקה. וכצרעת דבקה. והחכם ע"ה אמר, בארח רשעים אל תבא. בני! אל תעמוד ברחובות. ואל תשב במסלות. ואל תלך עם מי שלא תתכבד בחברתו. והחכם ע"ה אמר, הולך את חכמים יחכם. ב'. מ'.

בחר את בעלי שכל[20] לחברה
ומועצה. וקוצה בכסילים!
במשכיל תעקור סלע. ותבוא
במו צרה. ותשך[21] אף נפילים![22]

בני! שים ספריך חביריך. וארגזיך ותיבותיך פרדסיך וגנותיך. רעה בגנותיהם ולקוט שושניהם. וארה מפריהם בשמיהם ומוריהם. ואם תקוץ נפשך ותלאה העתק מגן אל גן. ומערוגה אל ערוגה. וממראה אל מראה. כי אז יתחדש חפצך ותנאה נפשך!

וזכור מה שאמר המשורר בשירו,[23]
איך אפחדה מאיש ולי נפש,
חתו אריות מכפיריה?
איך אדאגה מריש[24] ובה חכמה[25]

20 O צדק. 21 H. וחשך. 22 O כסילים.

23 MS. has בן משלי. But the poet is Judah ha-Levi. See Dukes, *Treasures of Oxford*. p. 60.

24 O מאיש. Margin מריש. 25 D. ובחכמה.

From whose hills I may hew jewels?
If I hunger, lo! her dainty fruits;
If I thirst, I find [37] her streams!
Sit I desolate, when her harp
Charms me with her melodies?
Why seek a friend to hold converse,
And lose her cunning accents?
My harp, my lyre, are at her pen's[38] point,
Her scrolls are my garden and paradise!

So *Ben Mishle* says:

The wise of heart forsakes the ease of pleasure,
In reading books he finds tranquillity;
All men have faults, thine eyes can see them,
The wise-heart's failing is—forgetfulness!

Consult a man of sense and well-beloved,
Put not thy trust in thine own device;
For if thou turnest to thy heart's desire,
Desire will hide from thee the right;
Is it a yearned-for end? Thy heart
Doth make thy lust seem fair before thee!

[37] Note the clever play on words in the Hebrew.

[38] Perhaps render: "style", the instrument with which the harp is struck. Or cf. Ps. 45.2.

אחצוב פנינים מהרריה?
אם ארעבה הנה מגדיה.
או אצמאה אמצא[26] נהריה!
איך אשבה שומם, וכנורה
אותי ישעשע בשיריה?
איך אדרשה[27] ריע ישיחני,[28]
עת[29] אשמעה חכמת דבריה?
נבלי וכנורי בפי עטה,[30]
גני ופרדסי ספריה!
[וכן אמר] בן משלי,
חכם לב יעזוב נוח עדנים,
ובקרוא בספרים לו מנוחה.
ומומים יש באישים אם תחפש.
ומום חכמי לבבות השכחה:
היה נועץ באיש שכל ואהוב,[31]
ואל תבטח בנפשך אל עצתך.[32]
ואם תט אחרי אהבת לבבך,
תכסה על נכונה אהבתך.
למען כי לך אוה, ולבך
ייפה נגדך את תאותך!

26 O .הנה 27 O .אשאלה 28 H .שיחני 29 O .בל
30 D. .עטי 31 O .ואוהב 32 O .לנפשך את Margin .אל

In all thine acts, therefore, take counsel with him on whose affection and prudence thou canst rely. Desert not thy friend, thy father's friend. Lo! "Aaron and Hur" are with thee, the accomplished R. Aaron and R. Asher.[39]

Contend not with men, and meddle not "with strife not thine own".[40] Enter into no dispute with the obstinate, not even on matters of Torah. On thy side, too, refrain from subterfuges in argument, to maintain thy case even when thou art convinced that thou art in the right. Submit to the majority and do not reject their decision. Risk not thy life by taking the road and leaving thy city, in times of disquiet and danger. Even where large sums are involved, travel only on the advice of men of mature judgment who are well disposed to thee; trust not the counsel of the young in preference to that of the old. Let not the prospect of great gain blind thee, to make light of thy life; be not as a bird that sees the grains but not the net.[41] Remember what the Sage, of blessed memory, said: "A wise man feareth and departeth from evil, but the fool behaveth overbearingly and is confident".[42]

My son! Take upon thee to write one leaf daily and to meditate for an hour, in the *Ben Mishle*.

[39] Sons of Meshullam of Lunel. Aaron was a spirited Maimonist partisan in the famous controversy. Cf. Graetz, *History*, E. T., iii, 524.

[40] Prov. 26.17.

[41] Dukes compares a poem by Judah ha-Levi. Cf. Prov. 1.17.

[42] Prov. 14.16.

בני! התייעץ עם מי שתבטח באהבתו וחכמתו. ורעך ורע אביך אל תעזוב. והנה אהרן וחור עמך, החכם ר׳ אהרן והחכם ר׳ אשר:

בני! אל תרב עם אדם. ואל תתעבר לריב לא לך. ואל תחלק על העקשים אפילו בתלמוד תורה. ואל תתעקש אתה להחזיק בדעתך אפילו אם תדע שהאמת אתך. והודה לרבים ואל תחלק עליהם: בני! אל תסכן בנפשך ללכת בדרכים בעתות החרם[33] והסכנה. אפילו על ממון גדול. כי אם בעניין שיורו לך רבים וחכמים אוהביך. ויכירו כי הוא בטוח: ואל תסמוך על עצת הבחורים להניח עצת הזקנים. ואל יעוורך רוב השכר להקל בנפשך. ואל תהיה כעוף שרואה הגרגרים ואינו רואה הרשת: וכבר ידעת מה שאמר החכם ע״ה, חכם ירא וסר מרע וכסיל מתעבר ובוטח:

בני! קבל עליך לכתוב עלה אחת בכל יום ולעיין שעה אחת בבן משלי. ולקרוא בכל שבת

[33] MS. החרום.

Read every week the Pentateuchal section in Arabic. This will improve thine Arabic vocabulary, and will be of advantage in translating, if thou shouldst feel inclined to translate.[43]

Show honor to thyself, thy household, and thy children, by providing decent clothing, as far as thy means allow; for it is unbecoming for any one, when not at work, to go shabbily dressed. Spare from thy belly and put it on thy back!

Thou knowest, my son! the trouble and expense that I endured for the marriage of thy elder and younger sisters. Never in my life had I undergone such dangers, thrice crossing the sea at great cost though my means were scanty[44]. I pledged my books, I borrowed from my friends, though I was never wont to do so, and all this not to reduce thy share. Also, at thine own marriage, thou art aware that I did not sell thee for silver, as others richer than I have done with their sons. None of thy companions made a more honorable union. I took for thee the daughter [45] of a cultured and distinguished lineage, all of them the "seed of truth", learned and of high standing. The community showed its consideration by imposing on thee no tax or due. Thou wast honored

[43] On Samuel Ibn Tibbon's translations, see *J.E.*, vi, p. 549.

[44] This departure of his daughter on their marriage seems referred to in the metrical Prologue.

[45] She seems to have been a sister of the famous Jacob Anatoli. See *J.E.*, i, 562.

הסדר ערבי. כי יועיל לך במלות הספרים הערביים.[34] ובהעתקה אם תרצה להעתיק:

בני! כפי יכלתך כבד את עצמך ואת ביתך ואת בניך במלבושים הגונים. כי אין ראוי לאדם ממלאכתו להיות מלבושיו פחותים. וחסר מבטנך ותן על גבך!

בני! כבר ראית מה שסבלתי מן היגיעה ומן הטורח וההוצאה בנשואי אחותך הגדולה. ומה שסבלתי בנשואי אחותך הקטנה. הכנסתי עצמי בסכנה שלא נכנסתי בה מימי. בעבור הים שלשה פעמים. וההוצאה הרבה מבלי יכולת. משכנתי ספרי. לויתי על פני. שמתי לאוהבי יד עלי במלוה. מה שלא נהגתי בזה. כל זה עשיתי בעבור שלא תפחות אתה בהם: גם בנשואיך אתה ידעת שלא מכרתיך בכסף כאשר עשו אחרים שהיו עשירים ממני בבניהם. ושאין בחבריך נכבד ממך בנשואיו. לקחתי לך[35] בת גדולי הארץ בחכמה וביחס. כלו זרע אמת קרובים חכמים ואצילים ונשאים: היית מכובד בחופתך מכל חבריך. והיית מכובד מהקהל שלא הטילו עליך מס ולא מעמס. היית נכבד מן

[34] H. incorrectly העבריים.

[35] MS. adds (redundantly) בת חכמים ומיוחסים.

at thy wedding by princes and priests, men of the highest lay and clerical distinction, for my sake.

And now, my son! if the Creator has mightily displayed His love to thee and me, so that Jew and Gentile have thus far honored thee for my sake, endeavor henceforth to so add to thine honor that they may respect thee for thine own self. This thou canst effect by good morals and by courteous behavior; by steady devotion to thy studies and thy profession, as thou wast wont to do before thy marriage.[46]

As *Ben Mishle* says:

In outside books[47] oft meditate, thou'lt find
What brings repute to its doer in the gates;
Will make thy voice respected 'mid the great,
Thy name extolled o'er thine associates.

Let thy countenance shine upon the sons of men; tend their sick, and may thine advice cure them. Though thou takest fees from the rich, heal the poor gratuitously; the Lord will requite thee. Thereby shalt thou find favor and good understanding in the sight of God and man. Thus wilt thou win the respect of high and low among Jews and non-Jews, and thy good name will go forth far and wide. Thou wilt rejoice thy

[46] Obviously, the father's previous complaints of his son's indolence must not be taken too literally. See above p. 52.

[47] i. e. secular, scientific; lit. outside the biblical canon (cf. Mishnah, Sanh. 10.1).

השרים והפרשים וההגמונים והכומרים והגלחים והכפירים בעבורי:

ועתה בני! אם הגביר הבורא חסדו עלי ועליך וכבדוך לכבודי ישראל וגוים עד עתה. השתדל אתה מעתה להוסיף כבוד על כבודך ויכבדוך בעבור עצמך. וזה תשיג במדותיך הטובות ומנהגיך הנעימים עם בני אדם. ושתקבע ללמוד ולעסוק במלאכתך ביום ובלילה כאשר היית עושה[36] קודם נישואיך: ב׳. מ׳.

הגה הרבה בספרי חוץ ותמצא
אשר יכשר עשהו בשערים.
ויארך לשונך בין גדולים,
ויתגדל שמך על החברים:

בני! האר פניך לבני אדם. ובקר חוליהם. ויהיה לשונך להם למרפא. ואם תקבל מעשירים היה מרפא חנם לענייהם. והשם ישלם גמולך ויתן את שכרך. ובזה תמצא חן ושכל טוב בעיני אלהים ואדם. ותהיה מכובד מן הגדולים ומן הקטנים, מישראל וגוים. ויצא לך שם טוב בקרוב ורחוק,

[36] This word must be inserted.

friends and make thy foes envious. For remember what is written in the *Choice of Pearls*:[48] "How shall one take vengeance on an enemy? By increasing his own good qualities." Remember also what I have written in my essay on the last chapter of Proverbs.[49]

My son! Examine regularly, once a week, thy drugs and medicinal herbs, and do not employ an ingredient whose properties are unknown to thee. I have often impressed this on thee in vain when we were together.

My son! If thou writest aught, read it through a second time, for no man can avoid slips. Let not any consideration of hurry prevent thee from revising a short epistle. Be punctilious as to grammatical accuracy, in conjugations and genders, for the constant use of the vernacular sometimes leads to error in this regard. A man's mistakes in writing bring him into disrepute; they are remembered against him all his days. As our Sages say: "Who is it that uncovers his nakedness here and it is exposed everywhere? It is he who writes a document and makes mistakes therein." Be careful in the use of conjunctions and adverbs[50] (particles), and how thou appliest them and how they harmonize with the verbs. I have already begun to compose for thee a book on the subject, to be called "Principles of Style", may God permit me to complete it! And what-

[48] Ch. 53, ed. Ascher, 617.

[49] Nothing is known of this work by the author of the present text.

[50] E. "prepositions and copulative words."

ותשמח[37] אוהביך ותקניא שונאיך ואויביך. וכבר ידעת מה שנזכר במבחר הפנינים, מי שרוצה להנקם מאויביו יוסף מעלה יתירה בעצמו. וזכור מה שפרשתי לך במאמר אשת חיל מי ימצא:

בני! הרגל עצמך לראות הסמנים ועשב הרפואות יום אחד בשבוע. ואל תשמש בדבר שלא תכיר אותו. וכמה פעמים פייסתיך שתרגיל בזה בעודי עמך. ותשלך דברי אחריך:

בני! כאשר תכתוב כתב שוב אליו וקראהו. כי אין אדם נצל מן השכחה. ואל יבהלך החפזון לשוב על אגרת קטנה להגיהה: והזהר מהטעות בלשון ובבניינים ובדקדוק ובלשון זכר ונקבה. כי פעמים מטעה בזה שגרת לשון הלעז. והטעות שתצא מיד האדם הוא הנתפש עליה ונזכר בה כל ימיו: וחכמים אמרו, מי הוא המגלה ערותו בכאן ונראית בכל? הוי אומר זה הכותב כתב וטועה בו: והוי זהיר בקשרים ומלות הטעם איך תביאם. ואיך יתחברו[38] הפעלים אל השמוש בהם: וכבר החילותי לחבר לך בזה ספר אם יזכיני השם להשלימו והוא

[37] MS. ותשמוח.

[38] MS. in margin יתעברו.

ever thou art in doubt about and hast no book to refer to, abstain from expressing it! Endeavor to cultivate conciseness and elegance, do not attempt to write verse unless thou canst do it perfectly. Avoid heaviness, which spoils a composition, making it disagreeable alike to reader or audience.

The same rules apply to poetry. The lines must not drag, verbosity must be eschewed. The words must be harmonious to the ear and light on the tongue. Use no rare constructions or foreign idioms or terms, for though the latter may be justified by analogy, they are none the less unnatural. And remember what I said to thee when thou didst make a blunder over an infinitive![51] Avoid all such faults. But choose what is sweet to thy palate and pleasant to those who hear thee.

See to it that thy penmanship and handwriting is as beautiful as thy style.[52] Keep thy pen in fine working order, use ink of good color. Make thy script as perfect as possible, unless forced to write without proper materials, or in a pressing emergency. The beauty of a composition depends on the writing, and the beauty of the writing on pen, paper, and ink; and all

[51] Lit: "when thou didst write בישבי instead of בשבתי." E. has the impossible rendering: "When thou wrotest, 'When I sat in the place on my seat.'"

[52] On this subject see remarks on p. 52.

סוד צחות הלשון. ומה שתסתפק בו ולא יהיה לך ספר לעיין עליו רחק מעליו! והשתדל בכתבך שתהיה מליצתך קצרה וצחה. ואל תרדוף החרוז בכתבך אם לא יבואך לתמו. ואל תנהגהו בכבדות. כי אם תנהגהו בכבדות יפסיד כתבך. ולא יהיה ערב לקוראיו ולשומעיו:

וכן תעשה בשיר. רחק מהבא מליצותיו בכבדות ובמלות רבות. ויהיו המלות ערבות. וקלות[39] על הלשון. ובנייניו בניינים נמצאים. ואל תביא בניינים זרים ולא מלות זרות אפילו אם הם עוברות מדרך ההקשה. כי הדבר הנכרי אינו מקובל לטבע: וזכור מה שאמרתי לך כשכתבת בישבי במקום בשבתי. הרחק מעל כל כיוצא בזה דרכך. ובחר מה שיהיה מתוק לחכך וערב לשומעו!

ויפה כתבך וכתיבתך. והטיב מלאכת קולמוסך. והדיו אשר תהיה כותב בו יהיה טוב במראהו. ואגרתך תהיה טובה מאד כפי יכלתך. אלא אם תכתוב בעת שלא יזדמן לך אחת מאלה. ובשעה דחוקה ובדבר נחוץ: כי יפי הכתב בכתיבה. ויפי הכתיבה בקולמוס ובאגר ובדיו. ויופי כתב האגרת

[39] MS. נקלות.

these excellencies are an index to the author's worth. Do not get into the habit of contracting the characters or of running them together, but make each long, broad, straight. Do not swallow up the *yod* but draw it out precise and clear. Another mark of beautiful handwriting is that the *lamed* should be long at the top and the neck properly turned;[53] also that the *kuf*, and the final *caf* and *nun* should have long and even down strokes. A point on which great care is needed is that if there be in the same line several cases of the letters named, one should not be shorter or longer than the other. Thou hast seen books in my handwriting and my precision in these matters, and must remember how the son of thy master, R. Jacob, expressed his admiration in thy presence. For writing, as I said above, is an art among the arts,[54] and the more care one takes the better is the result. Be fastidious, too, in the alignment; the lines must be straight, and the spacing uniform, so that one does not go up and another down. And may thy God prosper thee, and make thee straight in all thy ways!

And now, my son! in many of these matters,

[53] Perhaps the author means that the *lamed* must have a straight neck, a translation of which the Hebrew is susceptible.

[54] Lit. "a form among the forms".

מורה עלי יקרת הכותב: והשתדל להיטיב כתיבתך כפי יכלתך. ואל תרגיל להיות[40] אותיותיך קצרות ומובלעות זו בזו. אך הרגל עצמך לעשותם ארוכות ומרווחות ועומדות. ואל תבליע היוד בין אות לאות כאשר אתה רגיל. אך עשה אותו בקו היושר: ומנואי הכתיבה והכתב שיהיו הלמדים ארוכות למעלה וצואריהם נטוי על קו היושר. וכן הקופין והכפין והנונין הארוכה שיהיו[41] שוקיהם למטה ארוכים ושוין. ומן הזריזות בכתיבה שאם יתקבצו למדין או נונין או קופין או כפין בשטה אחת שלא תהיה אחת קצרה מחברתה ולא ארוכה מחברתה. וכבר ראית ספרי בכתב ידי ושמירתי בעניין זה. עד שתמה על זה בנו של ר׳ יעקב רבך לפניך. כי הכתיבה כאשר אמרתי לך היא צורה מן הצורות וכל אשר יזהר אדם בתיקונה תראה נאה יותר: ועל שטותיך שים דעתך שיהיו ישרות. וערך כל אחת מהנה אל חברתה שוה. ושלא תהיה אחת עולה למעלה ואחת יורדת למטה. ואלהיך ישכילך ויישרך בכל דרכיך!

ועתה בני! מה שנהגת עמי עד עתה שלא שמעת

[40] MS. adds כתיבת. [41] MS. שיהיה.

wherein thou didst not obey me when I was with thee, obey me at this time, when I am far off.[55] In all thy business, thy buying and selling, thou didst not do me the honor to ask my advice, nor didst thou even keep me informed. Whenever I asked thee, thou wast impatient, and didst conceal the facts from me. If I gave thee advice thou didst reject it, though never didst thou succeed when thou didst act against my counsel. *Ben Mishle* says:

The father of a son who brought
 His child to the house of the wise,
And pointed out the way of life,
 But he chose the path of the proud;
Who breathed in him, to fire his mind,
 But he refused to tend the fire;
Leave him! and reliance place
 On time for his discipline![56]

Long ago thou didst see what happened to thee with Solomon, son of the learned R. Joseph, when thou refusedst my order and advice. I will not further narrate how thou didst show me disrespect in this matter. Even in Marseilles, when we were together in a strange land, and thou didst purchase many worthless wares,[57] my advice

[55] The author makes several pregnant allusions to the fact that at the time of writing this Testament father and son were separated.

[56] Harkavy explains the verse in another sense. The son who has been set on the right way may be trusted to continue on it.

[57] Perh. render: "wares of great and small value."

לי ברוב העניינים בהיותי עמך. שמע לי עתה בהיותי רחוק ממך! כי אתה יודע כי בכל עסקיך ומקחיך וממכריך לא חלקת לי כבוד לשאול ממני עצה בדבר ולא להודיעני: ואם הייתי שואל אותך, היית קץ בשאלתי ומעלים ממני. ואם הייתי נותן לך עצה היית עובר על עצתי. ואתה יודע כי מעולם לא עברת על עצתי בדבר והצלחת בו! בן משלי,

אבי הבן אשר הביא
בנו אל בית מחוכמים,
והורהו נתיב חיים,
ובחר הוא נתיב רמים,
ונפחו בו להשכילו,[42]
ולא נפחו בפחמים,[43]
עזוב אותו! והשען
במוסרו עלי ימים!

וכבר ראית מה שקרה לך עם שלמה בנו של החכם ר׳ יוסף כשעברת על דברי ועל עצתי. ומה אזכור או אספר מהקלותך[44] אותי בעניין הזה: אפילו במרשיליאה הייתי עמך ביחד בארץ נכריה. וקנית מסחרים רבים ופחותים ולא שאלת עצתי

[42] O להשכיל [43] ? כפחמים. [44] MS. מהקלותיך.

was not asked, nor was I told anything. I knew nothing of all thy doings and dealings until thou didst unload the goods from the ship in the city of Arles.[58] If a non-Jew from my city had happened to be there, he would have consulted or informed me as to his buying and selling. Worse still, when thou didst write thy letters or compose thine odes to send abroad, thou wast unwilling to show a word to me and didst prevent me from seeing. When I said to thee, "Show me!", thou wouldst answer: "Why dost thou want to see?" as if thinking that my help was unnecessary. And this was from thy folly, in that thou wast wise in thine own eyes.[59] *Ben Mishle* says:

Who is wise in his own sight,
  E'er thinks his errors just;
And oft the cloud to him doth seem
  The sun, the sun a cloud!

Even R. Zerahyah[60], of blessed memory, who stood alone in his generation, and was more learned than I, never, from the day he knew me, wrote a letter or a poem to send to anyone, without showing it to me before it left his hand. Even of his letters to his brother he showed many to me before he sent them off. On my part, when I wrote letters, I said to thee: "Look at them,

[58] The journey to Arles from Marseilles would be about 40–50 miles by water (partly by sea, partly up the Rhone), and then some 25 miles by land from Arles to Lunel.

[59] It is strange that our author should so misinterpret a youth's natural reluctance to show his verses at home.

[60] On this scholar and poet see *J. E.*, xii, 660.

גם לא הודעתני. ולא ידעתי מכל מעשיך ומסחריך דבר עד שהוצאת אותם מן הספינה בעיר ארלדי: ואלו היה גוי שרוי ומעירי היה שואל עצתי או מודיע אותי במקחו וממכרו: ולא עוד אלא כשהיית כותב כתביך או עושה שיריך[45] לשלוח לארץ אחרת לא היית רוצה להראות לי דבר. והיית מונע ממני לראות: וכאשר הייתי אומר לך, הראיני! היית אומר לי, מה אתה רוצה לראות? כאילו היית חושב בעצמך כי אינך צריך לי בדבר. וזה מסכלותך וממה שהיית חכם בעיניך: ב׳ מ׳

אשר יהיה חכם לבב[46] בעיניו,
תעיתו יהי[47] חושב נכונה.
ותתחלף[48] ענוה לו פעמים
באור שמש ושמש בעננה:

והרב ר׳ זרחיה ז״ל שהיה יחיד בדורו. והיה חכם ממני. מיום שידעני לא כתב ולא עשה שיר לשלוח לשום אדם שלא הראהו לי קודם שיצא מידו. ורבים מכתביו לאחיו היה מראה לי קודם שישלחם: ואתה יודע כי אני כשהייתי כותב כתבי הייתי אומר לך, ראה אותם אם יש בהם להשיג

[45] MS. שירך. [46] H omits. [47] O תהי. [48] H ונתחלף.

perhaps there is something in them to alter or correct!" This I did from the day that I discovered in thee a knowledge of style and grammar. As the Arab says: He who sits at the brink bends.[61] All these evil courses hast thou adopted towards me. I bore them though deeply grieved, whilst thou didst provoke me, treating my honor as a light thing, neglecting the duty imposed on thee by God to show me respect! May the Omnipresent grant thee perfect pardon here and hereafter, may He be gracious and teach thee to do His will, and cause thee to find favor and good understanding in His sight and in the sight of all mankind! If, my son, thou desirest to undo the past, the Creator will grant His pardon, and I shall forgive thee all without reserve or reluctance.[62] Reject not my word in all that I have written for thee in this, my Testament, and wherein thou hast not honored me heretofore, honor me for the rest of my days and after my death! All the honor I ask of thee is to attain a higher degree in the pursuit of wisdom, to excel in right conduct and beautiful character, to behave in friendly spirit to all and to gain a good name, that greatest of crowns! to deserve applause for thy dealings and association with thy fellows, to cleave to the fear of God and the performance of His commandments,—thus wilt thou honor me in life and in death!

[61] i. e. to drink.

[62] Perhaps render: If thou desirest pardon, God will grant it; and if thou desirest my forgiveness, reject not, etc.

או לתקן! כי מיום שהכרתי בך שאתה יודע מליצה ודקדוק[49] לא עשיתי כתב שלא אמרתי לך, ראה אם יש בו להשיג או לתקן! כי הערב אומר, היושב על השפה שוחה: כל אלה המנהגים הרעים נהגת בי וסבלתי והייתי דואג מאוד עליהם. והקצפתני והכעסתני והמריתני והקילות בכבודי. ובמה שחייבך הבורא ממני. ועברת על מצותו[50] בזה: המקום ימחול לך בעוה"ז ובעולם הבא מחילה שלימה. וירצך וילמדך לעשות רצונו. וימציאך חן ושכל טוב בעיניו ובעיני כל אדם! ואם תרצה בני להשיג כל מה שחלף לך מכל זה ויסלח לך הבורא. ואסלח לך אני גם בנפש חפיצה וברצון על כל מה שעבר: אל תמרה את פי בכל מה שכתבתי לך בצואתי זאת: ומה שלא כבדתני עד עתה, כבדני במה שנשאר מימי ואחרי מותי! וכל כבודי שתוסיף מעלה בבקשת החכמה ובמנהגים טובים והמדות החמודות. ושתהיה רצוי לכל ושיהיה לך שם טוב שהוא הכתר הגדול. ושתדבק ביראת האל ובשמור מצותיו. ושיהיו עסקיך וחברתך עם בני אדם בעניין שיודוך הכל. ובזה תכבדני בחיי ובמותי! ב׳ מ׳

49 MS. ובדקדוק. 50 MS. מצותי.

Ben Mishle says:

In the son of the wise are three virtues:
  His errors are few and his follies;
He bows, feeling humble, to his people;
  He is raised above them all by his wisdom.

Thanks to my Creator, I know of thee that thou fearest Heaven in all thy ways, except as regards honoring thy father. Thou hast transgressed my commands and refused me obedience. Great, however, is this thing in the sight of God and man. Acquire the virtue of obedience and prosper! I trust to God that this, my separation, will be for thy good, and that thou wilt take it to thy heart to receive instruction, for thou hast none beside me, except thine own soul, mind and understanding. The Nagid of blessed memory has said:

What good is there in life if my work
To-day remains as 'twas yesterday?

Therefore, my son! Strive to honor me and thee from this day onwards. All the honor I desire is to be remembered for good because of thee in life and death; that those who behold thee may exclaim: "Blessed be he who begat this one, blessed be he who reared him!"[63] For I have no son but thee by whom my name may be recalled, and all my memory and glory are centered in thee. Reward from God and renown from men shall accrue to thee, in that thou continuest my name for good!

[63] Reversing T. B. Sanh. 52a.

בבן חכם שלשה מעללים,
שגיאותיו מתי מספר וסכלו,
וישח בעבור קטנו לעמו,
ויתנשא לראש[51] כלם בשכלו:

ותהלה ליוצרי! יודע אני בך כי ירא שמים אתה בכל דרכיך. רק בדבר כבוד אב בלבד. שעברת על מצותי ולא שמעת לקולי. וגדולה היא בעיני הבורא ובעיני כל בני אדם. והשג תשיג והצל תציל! ואני יודע ובוטח ביוצרי שפרידתי זאת תהיה לך לטובה. כי תשיב אל לבך לקחת מוסר. כי אין לך בלעדי כי אם נפשך ודעתך ושכלך: והנגיד ז״ל אמר,

מה טוב בחיים אם פעולתי
היום כמו היתה ביום אתמול?

על כן בני! השתדל בכבודי וכבודך מעתה וכבודי כולו שאזכר[52] לטובה בעבורך בחיים ובמות. ויאמרו רואיך, ברוך שזה ילד! ברוך שזה גדל! כי אין לי בן להזכיר בו שמי זולתך. וכי כל זכרי ותפארתי אינם כי אם בך. על כן במה שתשים זכרי לטובה יהיה לך שכר טוב אצל הבורא ותפארת בני אדם:

[51] O בראש. [52] MS. שאזכור.

Thou knowest what I suffered in bringing thee up. Thou hast seen what the learned R. Moses, son of R. Judah, did. He had four sons, and he dispersed them here and there, and went and left them, to marry again. But I, from out of my compassion towards thee, did not wish to bring thee into the hand of another woman.[64] But I bore all the anxiety, and great it was, of rearing and caring for thee. Thou knowest this, and all men know it, for, but for my great devotion thou wouldst have died, or lived deformed. Remember these things, my son! and take it to thy heart to hear and perform my instructions. Very important is it that thou shouldst fulfil my commands regarding thy diet. Slay me not before my time! For thou knowest my distress, my soul's sorrow, my fear for thee in thy sickness. Better death to me than life, that I look not on my wretchedness.[65] Yearly, as thou knowest, thou art visited with sickness (for my sins!), and the chief cause of thy complaints is unwholesome food. *Ben Mishle* says:

Dost thou desire thy health to hold,
  O'er thy lust make long thy furrow;[66]
Wage war against thyself as though
  Opposed to archer or to spearman!

And now, O my son! by the God of heaven,

[64] E. has misunderstood the whole of this passage. The author clearly refers to his disinclination to provide a stepmother for his son. E. takes it to refer to Samuel's marriage.

[65] Cf. Jonah 4.3, Num. 11. 15. [66] Ps. 129.3.

וכבר ידעת מה שסבלתי בעבור גדולך. וראית מה שעשה החכם ר' משה בר' יהודה שהיו לו ארבעה בנים. ופזרם אצל כל פנה והלך והניחם לקחת אשה. ואני בחמלתי עליך לא רציתי להביאך ביד אשה אחרת. וסבלתי כל הצער אשר סבלתי מגדול ומשמירתך הגדולה. כי אתה יודע ההפלגה שהגעתי בשמירתך. ובני אדם יודעים זה כי לולא השמירה הגדולה ההיא היית מת או בעל מום קבוע או מחוסר: זכור אלה בני! והשב אל לבך לשמוע בקולי ולקחת מוסרי. ומן הדבר הגדול שתקיים בו מצותי ותשמר דברי שתשמר במאכליך. ואל תמיתני בלא עתי. כי אתה יודע צערי וצרת נפשי ופחדי עליך בחלייך ויראתי בעבורך. וטוב היה לי מותי מחיי ואל אראה ברעתי. ותדע כי אתה מנוסה בחליים בכל שנה בעוונותי. ורוב סבותם המאכלים הרעים: ב' מ'

אם תאהב הרבות שלומים לך,
על תאותך הארך מענית!
ולחם לך עם נפשך כאשר
תלחם באיש יורה בחץ וחנית!

ועתה בני! אני אשביעך באלהי השמים ובמה

by the obedience to me imposed by His law, by the gratitude due for my rearing and educating thee, I adjure thee to abstain, with all thy resolution, from noxious food! Experience has taught thee how much thou hast suffered from carelessness in this regard. Be content with little and good, and beware of hurtful sweets. "Eat no eating that prevents thee from eatings."[67] What is the use of all thy wisdom if "thou layest a snare for my life, to cause me to die?"[68] Art thou not ashamed before thyself and the world when all know that thou art periodically sick because of thy injurious diet? There is no more disgraceful object than a sick physician, who shall forsooth mend others when he cannot mend himself.[69] *Ben Mishle* says:

Turn from one who enjoins the doing
 Of right, but himself is a man of wrong!
How shall *he* heal the malady,
 Who himself suffers from its pain?

Take heed to thyself! Preserve thy life, be not thine own destroyer! And if thou hast no pity on me and on thyself, have compassion on the child of thy delight, the object of thy yearning! For I shall be but a little while with you. Give me ease for that short space, be not a transgressor because of me! As *Ben Mishle* says:

[67] Quoted, later, by Joshua Ibn Shuaib (Discourse 44) as a proverb.

[68] I Sam. 28.9.

[69] Gen. Rabbah 20; Luke 4.23.

שחייבך הבורא מכבודי. ובמה שיש לי עליך מן הגדול ולמוד תורה. שתשמר בכל יכולתך מן המאכלים הרעים. כי כבר ידעת ונסית כי כל חלייך הן מאשר הקלות במאכלים הרעים: והסתפק בני! במעט הטוב והרחק מן הערב המזיק. ואל תאכול אכילה שתמנע אכילות. ולמה חכמת אתה אז יותר ואתה מתנקש בנפשי להמיתני? ולמה לא תבוש מעצמך ומבני אדם שכולם יודעים כי בעבור מאכליך הרעים אתה חולה בכל שנה? כי אין גנות ובושה כמו רופא שיהיה חולה. ויקשט אחרים ואינו יכול לקשט עצמו: בן משלי.

סור ממצוה לעשות
צדק, והוא איש עולה!
איכה ירפא החלי
מי בו כחליו מחלה?

השמר לך בני! ושמור נפשך ואל תחבל בעצמך. ואם לא תחמול עלי ולא על נפשך חמול על ילד שעשועיך והמון מעיך. כי אני מעט יש לי לעמוד עמכם. הנח לי בני! במעט ההוא ואל תאשם בעבורי! בן משלי.

If one follow the counsel of the foolish,
His foes will see his fall;
Who scorns the word of his doctor,
Falls indeed—into disease![70]

Thanks, thanks, to God, thou hast good food to eat and good wine to drink; but even wert thou to live on bread and water if I so commanded, 'twould but be thy duty. Lo, the sons of Jonadab son of Rechab denied themselves most of the enjoyments of life, they, their wives, and their children. But I seek to restrain thee only from things injurious to thy health. *Ben Mishle* says:

Who eateth naught but wholesome food,
His food is *for* him;
But if he eat unwholesome food,
His food is against him.

Say not in thy heart: "I will venture as before and will escape."[71] For all the world knows that but for the mercy of God and for my nearness to thee, thou hadst been near to death.[72] (May the Lord preserve thee in happy life). But not at every hour does a miracle happen![73] "Lo, all these things doth God work, twice, yea thrice, with a man" [but not always].[74]

[70] E: "Will have no comfort in sickness."

[71] I have translated as though the Heb. text read ואנצל.

[72] The Heb. has euphemistically "life".

[73] T. B. Meg. 7b.

[74] Job 33.29.

מהלך בעצת סכל[53]
משנאיו בו יהיו[54] רואים.
והמיקל בניב רופא
יהי נופל בתחלוים:

ושבח לבורא! תוכל לאכול לחם טוב ולשתות יין טוב. ואפילו אם היית אוכל לחם ומים בעבור כבודי וכדי לעשות רצוני היה לך לעשות: והנה בני יונדב בן רכב כאשר אמרתי לך מנעו עצמם מרוב הנאות העולם הם ונשיהם ובניהם. ואני איני מונע אותך כי אם מן המזיקים: בן משלי,

אשר יאכל אכלים הראוים
לגופתו, יהי[55] לו מאכלו.
והאוכל אכלים לא ראוים,
תהי עליו אכילתו ולא לו:

ואל תאמר בני בלבך אצא כפעם בפעם ואנצר. כי כל העולם יודעים כי לולא חסד השם ורחמיו. ושהייתי קרוב אליך. קרוב היית לחיים. המקום יחייך חיים טובים! ולא כל שעתא ושעתא מתרחיש ניסא. והן כל אלה יפעל אל פעמים שלש עם גבר:

[53] O מיקל. [54] O יהי. [55] O תהי.

Bethink thyself that I shall not be far from thee a day or two, or ten or twenty days, [but for a very long time]. Take all this to thy heart and act accordingly. Gossip not overmuch in the public streets, and do not dine away from home all the days of my absence. If an esteemed friend or relative invite thee to a banquet, pay him thy respects by thy presence and courtesy only.[75]

My son! Acquire a knowledge of the Calendar;[76] take occasional lessons in the subject from R. Aaron. It is a most necessary science.

My son! I command thee to honor thy wife to thine utmost capacity. She is intelligent and modest, a daughter of a distinguished and educated family. She is a good housewife and mother, and no spendthrift. Her tastes are simple, whether in food or dress. Remember her assiduous tendance of thee in thine illness, though she had been brought up in elegance and luxury. Remember how she afterwards reared thy son[77] without man or woman to help her. Were she a hired nurse she would have earned thy esteem and forbearance; how much the more, since she is the wife of thy bosom, the

[75] i. e. attend, but do not partake of the feast.

[76] E.: "study chronology." On Aaron ben Meshullam see *J. E.*, i, 18.

[77] The variation of the use of "son" and "sons" (unless it be due to the carelessness of the scribe) points to the fact (confirmed by the statement at the end of the metrical epilogue) that the author more than once re-touched his Testament, which bears several signs of different dates.

ועתה בני! אינני[56] רחוק ממך יום אחד ולא יומיים ולא עשרה ימים ולא עשרים יום. השב אל לבך כל זה ועשה כפיהו: בני! אל תרבה לשוח במסלות ובדרכים. ואל תאכל בסעודה חוץ לביתך כל ימי נדודי ממך: ואם יקראך לסעודה מי שיקר בעיניך אוהב או קרוב כבדהו בעמידתך ושמושך בלבד:

בני! למוד לעתים לפני החכם ר' אהרן מן העבור. כי חכמה שהצורך אליה היא:

בני! גם אני מצוך שתכבד אשתך בכל יכלתך. כי אשה משכלת וצנועה ובת גדולים בחכמה וביחס. ושמשת טובה לך ולבנך. ואינה מפזרת. ולא מבקשת גדולות לא במאכל ובמשתה ולא בכסות. וזכור שמושה הטוב לך בחלייך והיא כבודה ויחידה. וגדולה את בנך[57] אחר כן בלא עוזרת ובלא עוזר. ואפילו אם היתה מְיניקת לבניך היה לך לכבדה ולפַייסה. כל שכן אשת חיקך ובת גדולים אל תנהג

[56] MS. אינני.

[57] Perh. read לבניך; see note to translation.

daughter of the great, art thou bound to treat her with consideration and respect. To act otherwise is the way of the contemptible. The Arab philosopher says of women: "None but the honorable honoreth them, none but the despicable despises them." *Ben Mishle* also says:

Pardon thy child and wife their failings,
And persevere in thine exhortations;
As an armorer sharpens the edge of a sword,
By oft drawing it to and fro on the stone.

If thou wouldst acquire my love, honor her with all thy might; do not exercise too severe an authority over her; our Sages have expressly warned men against this.[78] If thou givest orders or reprovest, let thy words be gentle. Enough is it if thy displeasure is visible in thy look, let it not be vented in actual rage. Let thy expenditure be well ordered. It is remarked in the *Choice of Pearls*:[79] "Expenditure properly managed makes half an income." And there is an olden proverb: "Go to bed without supper and rise without debt." Defile not the honor of thy countenance by borrowing; may thy Creator save thee from that habit! *Ben Mishle* says:

When thou art poor, ride on the back of a lion,[80]
To seek thy sustenance, and beg of none!
Nor covet other's wealth, for in such envy
Thine own heart thou painest more than another's!

[78] T. B. Gittin 7b.

[79] Ch. i (beginning).

[80] i. e. go through any danger rather than beg alms.

לקלות ולהבזות כי כן מנהג הפחותים. וחכם הערב אמר על הנשים לא יכבדם כי אם נכבד. ולא יבזם כי אם נבזה: בן משלי,

סלח לבן ולאשה מריהם
ושובה עוד וצוה בן ואשה.
כמו לוטש פני חרב אשר הוא[58]
ברוב הולך[59] ורוב הבא לטושה:

ואם רצונך לקנות אהבתי כבדנה בכל יכלתך. ואל תטיל עליה אימה יתירה. ורבותינו ז"ל הזהירו מזה: ואם תצוה ותוכיח יהיו דבריך בנחת. ותספיק שתראה הכעס בפניך במה שלא כרצונך ואל תוציאהו למעשה: ושתנהוג בהוצאתך בסדר[60] נאה. וכבר נאמר במבחר הפנינים, הסדר בהוצאה חצי הספוק. ומשל הקדמוני לין בלא סעודה והשכם בלא חוב: ולא תחלל בני הדר פניך בשאלה. ויוצרך יצילך ממדה זו! ב' מ'

בעת תדל רכב על גב ארי אל[61]
מזונך, ואל תשאל לאישים!
ואל תחמוד! למען כי בחמדך
לבבך תעציב טרם אנשים!

58 O היא. 59 O הביא, הוליך. 60 MS. בסתר. 61 O אריאל.

Thou knowest already what is said on this subject in the *Choice of Pearls*[81] and in *Ben Mishle*; how they denounced this failing, which indeed cleaves like leprosy and degrades all self-respect. *Ben Mishle* says:

Eat herbs in safety,[82]
  And not meat in danger;
Take one thing by commerce,
  And not a thousand by gifts!

My son! Devote thy mind to thy children[83] as I did to thee; be tender to them as I was tender; instruct them as I instructed; keep them as I kept thee! Try to teach them Torah as I have tried, and as I did unto thee do thou unto them! Be not indifferent to any slight ailment in them, or in thyself (may God deliver thee and them from all sickness and plague), but if thou dost notice any suspicion of disease in thee or in one of thy limbs, do forthwith what is necessary in the case. As Hippocrates has said: Time is short, and experiment dangerous. Therefore be prompt, but apply a sure remedy, avoiding doubtful treatment.

Examine thy Hebrew books at every new moon, the Arabic volumes once in two months, and the

[81] Ch. 48.

[82] Cf. Prov. 15.17. It seems (as Kahana has suggested) that the sentiments of the *Ben Mishle* are mostly, if not invariably, epigrammatic expansions of texts in Proverbs. So with the same poet's Ben Tehillim (Psalms) and Ben Koheleth (Ecclesiastes); they are modelled on texts in the books after which they are named.

[83] Here the *plural* is used several times in the Hebrew.

וכבר ראית מה שנאמר בזה במבחר הפנינים ובבן משלי. כי המדה הזאת דבקה כצרעת ומפחיתה כל מעלה: ב׳ מ׳

אכול ירק במבטחים,
ולא בשר בסכנה!
וקח אחת בחק מקח,
ולא אלף במתנה!

בני! הרגיש על בניך כאשר הרגשתי עליך. וחמול עליהם כחמלתי. ויסרם כמוסרי. ושמרם כשמירתי. והשתדל ללמדם תורה כשהשתדלתי. וכאשר עשיתי לך כן תעשה להם. ואל תקל במעט מיחוש שיקרה להם וכן בעצמך. והאלהים יצילך ויצילם מכל מחלה ומכל נגע! ואם תרגיש בשום מיחוש בעצמך או באחד מאבריך[62] מיד תשתדל לעשות כל הצריך לעניין. וכבר ידעת מה שאמר אבוקרט, כי העת צר והנסיון סכנה. על כן היה זריז ואל תאריך! והשתמש במובטח ורחק מן הספק:

ופקוד ספריך העבריים בכל ראש חודש. והערביים פעם בשני חדשים. והכרכים הקשורים

[62] Pesh. read מבניך.

bound codices once every quarter. Arrange thy library in fair order, so as to avoid wearying thyself in searching for the book thou needest. Always know the case[84] and chest where the book should be. A good plan would be to set in each compartment a written list of the books therein contained.[85] If, then, thou art looking for a book, thou canst see from the list the exact shelf it occupies without disarranging all the books in the search for one. Examine the loose leaves in the volumes and bundles, and preserve them. These fragments contain very important matters which I collected and copied out. Do not destroy any writing or letter of all that I have left. And cast thine eye frequently over the Catalogue so as to remember what books are in thy library.

Never intermit thy regular readings with thy teacher, study in the college of thy master on certain evenings before sitting down to read with the young. Whatever thou hast learned from me or from thy teachers, impart it again regularly to worthy pupils, so that thou mayest retain it, for by teaching it to others thou wilt know it by heart, and their questions will compel thee to precision, and remove any doubts from thine own mind.

Never refuse to lend books to anyone who has not the means to purchase books for himself, but

[84] See note to Hebrew text. The word is obviously the Sp. armario (Fr. armoire).

[85] This method was often adopted in old libraries, see the example in the fine book-cases in St. John's College, Cambridge.

פעם בשלושה חדשים: וסדר הכל סדר נאה כדי שלא תיגע לחפש ספר כשאתה צריך אליו. ושתדע מקומו מן הארמרים[63] והתיבות: ואם היית כותב ספרי כל בית מן הארמרים באגרת, ותשימנה בבית ההוא, כדי שאם תחפש ספר תראה באגרת באי זה בית הוא, קודם שתבלבל הספרים, היתה זריזות נאה! וכן תעשה בתיבות. ועיין בעלים אשר בכרכים ובאגורות ושמרם! ואל תבז להם. כי יש בהם חמודות גדולות ממה שקבצתי וכתבתי. ואל תאבד כתב ולא אגרת מכל מה שהנחתי. וכן עיין במזכרת ספריך תמיד כדי שתזכור מה שיש אתך מן הספרים:

ואל תניח לעסוק בתלמודך לפני רבך. ואל תקבע ללמוד עם הבחורים כי אם אחר שתקום מבית מדרש רבך בקצת הלילות. וכל מה שלמדת ממני ומרבותיך למד לתלמידים הגונים תמיד. כדי שיתקיים למודך בידך. ובלמודך להם תדע אותו על פה. ויחדדוך בשאלותם לצאת מן הספק שבלמודך:

ואל תמנע מלהשאיל ספריך למי שאין בידו

63 MS. here and below הארמדים.

only act thus to those who can be trusted to return the volumes. Thou knowest what our Sages said in the Talmud,[86] on the text: "Wealth and riches are in his house; and his merit endureth for ever."[87] But, "Withhold not good from him to whom it is due,"[88] and take particular care of thy books. Cover the book-cases with rugs[89] of fine quality; and preserve them from damp and mice, and from all manner of injury, for thy books are thy good treasure. If thou lendest a volume make a memorandum before it leaves thy house, and when it is returned, draw thy pen over the entry. Every Passover and Tabernacles call in all books out on loan.

Make it a fixed rule in thy home to read the Scriptures, and to peruse grammatical works on Sabbaths and festivals, also to read *Proverbs* and the *Son of Proverbs*. Also I beg of thee, look at the chapter concerning Jonadab son of Rechab every Sabbath, to instil in thee diligence to fulfil my commands.

My son! If thou hearest abuse of me from the lips of fools, be silent and make no reply. Take no notice of aught that they may say against me. Remember what *Ben Mishle* says:

The good will of others is the fruit of meekness,
And the fruit of contentment is tranquillity;

[86] T. B. Ketubot 50a.

[87] Ps. 122.3. The Talmud applies the verse to one who writes the Scriptures and lends his copies to others.

[88] Prov. 3.27.

[89] Sp. tapeta. Cf. Fr. tapis. Ger. Teppich. There is also the Rabbinic טפיטא, a loan word from the Greek *τάπης* (*ητος*).

יכולת לקנות ספר. ובלבד שהוא מובטח שיחזירם לך: וכבר ידעת מה שאמרו רבותינו בכתובות בפסוק הון ועושר בביתו וצדקתו עומדת לעד: ואל תמנע טוב מבעליו ושמור ספריך שמירה רבה. וכסה הארמרים בתביט כסוי יפה. ושמור אותם מן המים מלמעלה ומן העכברים ומכל נזק כי הם אוצרך הטוב: וכאשר תשאיל לאדם ספר כתבהו במזכרת קודם שיצא מן הבית. וכאשר ישיבהו העבר עליו קולמוס: ובכל פסח וסוכות השב לביתך כל מה שהשאלת מן הספרים לחוץ:

וקבע בביתך לקרוא המקרא ולעיין בספרי הדקדוק בשבתות ובימים טובים. ובמשלי ובבן משלי: בני! אני מפייס ממך גם כן שתעיין בכל שבת בפרשת בני יונדב בן רכב. כדי שתהיה זריז לשמור מצותי:

בני! אם תשמע הרפתי ונידופתי בפי הנבלים שתוק ואל תענם. ואם ידברו בי אל תרגיש להם: ב׳ מ׳

אהבת בני אדם פרי לענוה.
ופרי לשמח בחלקו מנוחה.

The fruit of hearing others in silence
  Is peace of mind, confidence, and joy!

Show eagerness in honoring thy teachers and do them service. Attach thyself to their friends, make their foes thine. Treat them with respect in all places and under all circumstances, even though thou hast no need of them[90] while they have need of thee, a thousand and a thousand times more if thou needest them. As *Ben Mishle* says:

The wise is beloved of all,
  And loveth all whom he meeteth;
The fool is hated of all,
  And hateth all who may see him;
Therefore keep watch and ward,
  To be a brother of wisdom,
And keep far thy name from the name
  Of all the brothers of folly!

But, my son, honor thy comrades, and seek opportunities to profit them by thy wisdom, in counsel and deed. And unto the son of R. Zerahyah, of blessed memory, thy master, remember his father's affection for me and for thee. Love him as a brother, esteem him as a fine scholar, for his father ever esteemed, loved and praised thee; he also left thee a praise and a blessing

[90] i. e. for further instruction.

ופרי לשומע ושותק היותו
שוקט ובוטח ונפשו שמחה:

בני! היה זריז בכבוד מוריך ומלמדיך. ועבוד אותם ואהוב אוהביהם ושנא שונאיהם. והדרם בכל מקום במעמד ומושב. ואע"פ שאינך צריך להם והם צריכים לך. כל שכן אלף אלפי כפלים אם אתה צריך להם: ב' מ'

חכם לב אהוב הכל.
ואוהב לכל בואיו:
וסכל שנוא הכל.
ושונא לכל רואיו:
ולכן שקוד ודרוש
היותך אחי חכמה.
ורחק שמך משם
אחי ריק וסכלות מה![64]

אבל בני! כבד חביריך. והרגיש עליהם להועיל להם בחכמתך בעצה ובמעשה. ולבן הר' ר' זרחיה ז"ל רבך תזכור אהבת אביו בי ובך. ותאהב אותו כאח ותכבדהו כחבר גדול. כי כן היה מכבדך[65] ואוהבך ומשבח אותך אביו זצ"ל. גם הניח לך ברכה

[64] O omits מה and writes the last four lines as prose.
[65] MS. מכבודך.

after his death. My son! It can never be in thy power to requite such kindnesses; for no man can, all his days, repay one who has been in advance of him in friendship. As the Scripture says:[91] "Who hath given me anything beforehand that I should repay him?" And O beware of the inimical and envious.

My son! Visit thy sisters constantly in thy letters,[92] and inquire after their welfare. Show honor to thy relatives, for they will appreciate thy courtesies.

I enjoin on thee my son to read this, my Testament, once daily, at morn or at eve. Apply thy heart to the fulfilment of its behests, and to the performance of all therein written. Then wilt thou make thy ways prosperous, then shalt thou have good success.[93] If my advice seem good in thine eyes, select from among thy Arabic books one whose script pleases thee. Strive to imitate it. For in the instance of R. Samuel the Nagid, no one taught him to write Arabic. But he took a manuscript written by a scribe of repute and strove to copy it. He persevered until he succeeded in equalling his model. And now, my son! emulate such wisdom, and endeavor to follow men of virtue! Let not thy heart be envious of sinners, but let it be zealous in the fear of God all day!

[91] Job 41.3.

[92] The daughters of the author removed from Lunel on their marriage. In one of his poems 14 (ed. Harkavy), ha-Nagid uses the phrases "to visit in a letter".

[93] Judg. 1.8.

תהלה אחרי מותו ז"ל: בני! אל יספיק לך במי שגמלך טוב במעשה או בכבוד או בדבור שתשלם לו כמעשהו בלבד. כי לא יוכל אדם לשלם למקדים כל ימיו. כמו שאמר הכתוב, מי הקדימני ואשלם. והזהר מהשונא והמקנא!

בני! פקוד אחיותיך תמיד בכתביך. ושאל בשלומן וחלוק כבוד לקרוביך. ויתכבדו בך:

ואני מצוה בני! וגוזר עליך לקרות צואתי זאת פעם אחת בכל יום או בלילה. ותן לבך לקיימה ולעשות ככל הכתוב בה. כי אז תצליח את דרכיך ואז תשכיל. ואם טובה עצתי בעיניך בחר לך מספריך הערביים ספר אחד שתהיה כתיבתו נאה בעיניך. והשתדל לדמותה ולחקותה. כי הנשיא ר' שמואל לא למדהו אדם כתיבת הערבי. אך לקח כתב אחד מכתבי הסופרים החשובים והשתדל לכתוב כדמותו. וטרח עד שעלה בידו: ועתה בני! קנא במשכילים ובאנשי מדות חמודות. ואל יקנא לבך בחטאים. כי אם ביראת ה' כל היום!

And now I place before thee in verse[94] all the preceding Letter, so that all my admonitions may be told to thee in song!

Obey my mandate, heed thou my advice,
And make, my son, the Law thy heart's desire!
Incline to wisdom an attentive ear,
Pursue the right, be faithful to the true!
Then Wisdom shall enthrone thee mid the great,
And fame become the meed of loyalty!
Serve but thy God with undivided love,
With dainties shall thy soul be satisfied!
To keep His Law hold ready hand and heart,
Heart to remember, hand as firm to do!
For lo, His word a lamp, His Law a light,
A refuge sure in storm and darkest wrath!

Honor thy parents, do them reverence,
Bind up thy soul in loving bond with theirs!
From evil turn, ne'er choose a rogue for friend,
And know thy God, act justly, and be saved!
Early and late attend at Learning's hall,
Make those thine intimates who seek her too!

[94] The rhymes of the original are not retained in the metrical paraphrase which follows. Nor have Scriptural references been appended; the snatches of quotation are numerous.

והנה לך בחרוז כל האגרת. אשר כל המוסר בשיר אוגרת ומספרת!

שמור מצוה בני ושמע לעצה.
בתורת אל תהי לבך חפצה!
והטה את לבבך לתבונה.
והצדק רדוף ורעה אמונה!
תשימך התבונה רק למעלה.
ותתנך אמונתך תהלה!
ועבדה את אלהיך בכל לב.
ואז תשבע בכל דשן וחלב!
ומצותיו ותורותיו לשמרה.
וחוקיו לעשות הכון וזכרה!
הכי מצוה ותורה נר ואורה.
ומגדל עוז ביום זעם ועברה!

וכבד אב ואם כבוד ומורה.
ושים נפשך בנפשותם קשורה!
וסור מרע ואל תתרע לרשע.
וצורך דע תהי צדיק ונושע!
והשכם אל נוה חכמה והערב.
וחברת דורשה תבחר ותקרב!

Whene'er thou speakest, let thy words be few,
Each phrase the best, and chosen every clause!
Rule o'er thy tongue in silence mid the throng,
Then o'er the silent throng thy tongue shall rule!
Fix not thine aim on frivolous jests and joys,
Nor waste in soft delights thy precious hours!
Let not thine heart to indolence incline,
The langor passes, but regret endures!
Engage in toil, yet all excess avoid,
Rely not on thy father's heritage:
Labor enough thine own wants to provide,
Happy the mortal whom his lot contents!
The fool, by trust in fortune, is destroyed,
While idleness the sluggard doth enslave!
If wealth be thine, let not thy heart be high,
Due honor show, and thy Creator laud!
Thy plenty share with all who are in need,
Load them, nay pamper, from thine ample store!
A tower of strength be thou, a present help,
Be humbly rich, if thou a Help wouldst find!

וקצר את דבריך בדברך.
וברר מאמריך באמרך!
בהחרישך תהי מושל בניבך.
והוא ימשול בדברך בניבך![66]
וחק אל תתנה לשחוק ושמחה.
ואל תבחר בתענוג והנחה!
ואל יטה לבבך למנוחות.
למען אחריתם לאנחות!
ויגע נפשך אך לא להרבות.
ואל תבטח עלי נחלה לאבות!
יגע אך עד מלאת די מחסורך.
ושמח בחלקו הוא יבורך!
הכי שלות כסילים תאבידם.
ועצלת העצלים תעבידם!
ואל ירום לבבך בעשרך.
ושים כבוד ותן תודה ליוצרך!
ותן מלחמך לדל והענק
לאביונך. ולרעב תפנק!
ומגדל עוז היה להם ומעוז.
ואל תגאה ברוב עשרך ותעוז!

[66] So the MS. Perhaps we should read בלבך in the first line of the couplet..

To prayer attend at all appointed hours,
And make the House of God thine earliest goal!
O'er sons of men protecting wing outspread,
With gracious speech, my son, their sickness heal!
In pleasant places cast for thee the lines,
And boast not in the vanities of fools!
Assist thy kin, respect thy friends' demand,
Preserve thy wealth by giving generously!
Use all thy means the falling to upraise,
And cast not o'er thy pelf a miser's eye!
Nor covet what in other hands is found,
Lest thus thy soul with bitterness be filled,
While all thy days in grief and rage are spent;
And how can anger help or profit thee?
Thy want supplied, thou needst no fuller store,
Scorn him who cries enough is not enough!
And covet not thy neighbor's wife, my son,
Great though her charm, though beautiful her form!

From men who utter falsehood keep aloof,
In slander's mischief see thou bear no hand!
From faction-mongers steadfastly withdraw,

והתפלל בעתות התפלה.
ואל בית הכנסת בא תחלה!
ולבני איש כנפיך תרפה.
בני. ולשונך יהיה למרפא!
והפל בנעימים לך חבלים.
ואל תהבל בהבלי הכסילים!
וקרב את קרוביך וכבד
חביריך. והונך אל תאבד!
בהכשלם עזור להם כיכלך.
ועינך אל תהי רעה בשלך!
ואל תחמוד אשר בידי אחרים
בני! פן נפשך תשבע מרורים.
וימיך במכאובים וכעס.
ומה יועילך כעסך ויעש?
ובמלאת ספקך תשבע בכל הון.
ותלעג לאשר לא אמרו הון!
ואל תחמוד בני! אשת עמיתך.
ורוב לקחה ויופיה אל יסיתך!

רחק מדוברי שקר וסורה
בני, מהולכי רכיל וגורה!
ומעל דוברי סרה והפכם

Lest they entice thee to their erring ways!
The Rock that formed thee hold thou still in awe,
And fear to use His Name for frivolous ends!
From faults of other men avert thine eyes,
On thine own blemish gaze and know thy state!
Show kindness unto all thy fellow men,
Tender thy substance as well as thy advice;
If to thy counsel they incline deaf ears,
Then cease to pester them with futile words!

Forgive thy friend the injury he does,
Join not his foes, nor share their wicked plan!
With all the world deal ever honestly,
Lest thine own soul thou draggest down in shame!
If thou hast borrowed, pay before 'tis asked,
Avoid disputes, and tremble at an oath;
If thou hast lent, forbear to press thy debt,
Rely on God for certain recompense!

What thy lips utter let thine hands confirm,
Ne'er break the law this maxim inculcates!

נטה. פן יחטיאוך בדרכם!
ואת צור בוראך תירא. ותפחד
להשבע בשם אל המיוחד!
והעלם עינך ממום חבירך.
ומומך דע. והבט אל חסרך![67]
וברר לחבירך אהבתך.
והועילו בהונך ועצתך!
ואם לא יאזין אל מאמרך
בני, אל תוסף שנייה על דברך!

ולאוהבים היה נושא פשעים.
ואל תבוא בסוד זרים ורעים!
ויהיה עסקך טוב עם בני איש
בני, פן נפשך תחפיר ותוביש!
ועת תלוה פרע קודם תביעה.
וסור מדין וגורה משבועה!
ואל תגוש בהלוותך חברך
ואל שדי ישלם את שכרך!

ושמרה ועשה את מוצא שפתך.
ושימה זאת בני חקך ודתך!

67 The MS. reads מעמדך. Perhaps correct to אשריך ("thine own mode of life"). The rhyme needs a ר for the ד.

Thy tongue deliver from the liar's snare,
E'en in thine anger moderate thy taunts!
Than liars none are held in greater scorn,
For on them rests the stigma of their lies!
How honored in all eyes are men of faith,
How fair the path of upright men and true!
Thy secret unto others ne'er reveal,
Lock it within the prison of thine heart!
As strangers treat thy friends who fain would pry,
An alien her who in thy bosom lies!
For sacred still another's secret hold,
Nor gad about a dangerous gossiper!

Sell not thy self-respect by asking boons,
Beg not, nor all thy dignity degrade;
Eat simple herbs, and feed on barley bread,
And do not veil thy countenance with shame!

Honor thy wife, and love and draw her nigh,
Speak to her heart with sweet and soft address;
Through thee let her be glorified, and thou
In her repute shalt find thyself renowned!

והצל מדבר שקר לשונך.
והארך אפך בגלות חרונך!
הכי כל דוברי שקר גרועים
בעיני כל. ובשקר ידועים!
ומה נכבד בעין כל איש אמונים.
ומה יקרו דרכיו הנכונים!
וסודך אל תגלה לאחרים.
ושים את לבך לו לבית אסורים!
ושים אוהבים בזה כנכרים.
ושוכבת בחיקך כזרים!
וסוד אחר לאדם לא תגלה.
ורכיל אל תהי הולך לכלה!

ואל תתן כבודך בשאלה.
הכי משאל מחלל כל גדולה!
והירק אכול עם פת שעורים.
ואל תפל הדר פנים יקרים!

ואשת חיקך כבד וקרב.
ויהיה לה דברך טוב וערב!
למען זאת תכובד בעבורך.
ובכבודה כבודך והדרך.

Because of her, hold thou her kindred dear,
Set them among thy brothers and thy friends!
And if thou must reprove, be gentle still,
Forbear from rough retort or violence;
Better she render service of her love,
Than that, compelled, she yield enforced consent!
Learn not to curse, for curses are enrolled
Among the grievous, not 'mong trivial sins!
Unto thine offspring be compassionate,
Direct them in the Law by day and night!
At freshest dawn the rule of life impart,
In earliest youth O teach them to be wise!
So save them from all pitfalls in the path,
And keep their souls from straying into ill!

Take care in writing to avoid mistakes,
Lest in the reading others laugh at thee;
Such error brings the scribe to shame, and adds
A blemish to his count, nay e'en a crime!
So still re-read thy scroll, with zeal revise,
Supply defective words or syllables;
For know, the style of tongue or pen full oft

וכבד בעבורה הקרובים.
ושיתמו לאחים ואהובים!
והוכיח וצוה אך ברכות.
ואל תלמוד ענות עזות והכות!
וטוב שתעבוד אותך באהבה.
ואל תעש בהכרח ואיבה!
ואל תלמד לקלל. כי קללה
גדולה היא ואיננה נקלה!
וחוסה על ילדיך וחמלה.
ותורה למדם יומם ולילה!
ומוסרם תשחר לבקרים.
והשכילם והורם מנעורים!
ושמרם מנתיב מכשול ותועה.
ואת נפשם שמור מבוא ברעה!
והזהר בכתבך משגיאה
לבל יבזו לך אם הקריאה.
ולבושת במקהלות מביאה
ותחשב לך מום וחטאה!
ושוב על ספרך אחר כתיבה.
לבלתי תחסר בו אות ותיבה!
ודע כי מדברי פי איש וספרו

Reveals the author's wit and inmost worth!
For style, they praise the writer from afar,
For style, behold him mocked and put to scorn!
By Wisdom man excels above the herd,
And prudence wins him favor from his peers!

O bind the testimony, seal the Law,
More precious they than gold or richest gem!
Thy masters serve, obey thy teacher's voice,
Rejoice my heart, let envy find good cause!
Let conduct be the end of all thou learnest,
By goodness joined to wisdom earn applause!
Restrain thyself beneath discretion's hand,
And, thus controlled, be thou from passion free!
Despise no critic, welcome chastisement;
Before thy comrades bow, and thereby rule!
Thyself abase, let others lift thee up,
And thus thy poverty will lose its lack!

Receive thy father's doctrine, keep my words,
Treasure my orders, guard them in thy soul!
For, thrice these counsels have I written out,

מעידים על צפון שכלו וסתרו!
ובכתבו יהולל איש לרחוק.
ובכתבו יהי לבוז ולשחוק:
ובחכמה יהי יתר שאתו.
ובתבונה יכובד בעדתו:

חתום תורה בני ונצור תעודה.
אשר מפז ומזהב חמודה!
ומוריך עבוד ומלמדיך.
תשמח אב ותקניא חומדיך!
ולשמור לעשות הכון ולמדה.
תהי נכבד בכל קהל ועדה!
היה נעצר ביד שכלך ונמסר.
ומכל תאוותיך תהי סר!
ואל תקוץ בתוכחת ומוסר.
והכנע לרעך תהי שר!
והתנשא בהתנבל כטפסר.
וימעט רישך בזה ויחסר!

ומוסר אב קחה ושמור אמרי.
ומצותי צפון ונצור דברי!
ושלישים כתבתים לך וחכמות

Esteem thou them as pearls and corals rare!
Practise these rules, and more to them I'll add
For thine instruction if my life endure!

Behold a small cloud rising from the sea of science and learning, carried by the breeze of wisdom and understanding! If the cloud empty itself on a fertile soil, causing righteousness and faith to spring up, making pleasant knowledge to flourish,—ripeness will come in due season, and the roots of wisdom will be made firm; the branches will bloom, its food will be for nourishment, its leaves for healing! The loving-kindness of the Lord will guard it, will water it every moment, and shield it from all mishap. May He who gives prudence to the simple and to young men knowledge and discretion, bestow on thee a willing heart and a listening ear! Then shall our soul be glad in the Lord and rejoice in His salvation!

שמח בהם כעל גביש וראמות![68]
עשה בהם ועוד אוסיף עליהם
לך אם אחיה כהם וכהם!

הנה עב קטנה עולה מים השכל והתבונה. ברוח חכמה ובינה. ואם תריק על ארץ שמינה. להצמיח מוצא הצדק והאמונה. ולהפריח כנת הדעת הנעמנה. תבכר לחדשיה. ותשרש שרשיה. ותהי פוריה וענפה. והיה פריה למאכל ועליה לתרופה. וחסד יוצרה יצרנה. ולרגעים ישקנה. ומכל רע ישמרנה. ונותן לפתאים ערמה. לנער דעת ומזמה. יתן לך לב שומע ואוזן שומעת. ונפשינו תגיל בה׳ תשיש בישועתך!

[68] MS. ורמות.

אגרת מוסר ששלח הרמב"ן ז"ל לבנו.

THE VIRTUE OF HUMILITY BY NAHMANIDES

IV

THE VIRTUE OF HUMILITY

BY NAHMANIDES

In 1267 Moses, son of Naḥman (Naḥmanides), left Europe for Palestine. His departure was involuntary. He had, in 1263, been compelled to champion the Jewish cause in the public controversy held in Barcelona before the King of Aragon. The result of Naḥmanides' outspokenness was his banishment.

Born c. 1195, he was thus seventy-two years of age at the moment of his migration. He survived the ordeal for three years. Naḥmanides "represented Judaism from the side of emotion and feeling, as Maimonides did from the side of reason and logic " (S. Schechter, *Studies in Judaism*, first series, pp. 120 seq.). The same tenderness which marks his formal writings is revealed in his letters from Palestine. He suffered the keenest distress at his separation from family and home. Nor was the then condition of Palestine, which he pathetically depicts in one of his letters, able to console him. But he set himself to the direction of those whom he had been compelled to forsake, and wrote several letters with that object. In one of these (printed in the *J.Q.R.*, first series, v, 115) he communicated to his son Solomon counsels on various subjects, among them the duty of leading a chaste life amid the allurements of the Castilian court, where the son seems to have held a post. Solomon was his second son, the grandfather of Gersonides (see table in *J.E.*, ix, 87).

ד

אגרת מוסר ששלח הרמב"ן ז"ל לבנו

בשנת כ"ז לאלף החמישי הוכרח רבי משה בן נחמן לעזוב את אירופא ולהשתקע בארץ ישראל. רק ארבע שנים עברו אז למן היום אשר הגין על כבוד ישראל בוכוח פומבי שהיה בברצלונה במעמד מלך אראגוניה, אבל הוא נתפש בדבורו החפשי ובעטים של מתנגדיו נדן לגלות.

שנת לידתו היתה תתקנ"ד לאלף הרביעי, ובכן היה בן שבעים ושתים בשעת גלותו. אחרי הנסיון המר הזה הוסיף לחיות עוד שלש שנים. הרמב"ן הוא „בא־כח היהדות מצד הלב והרגש כמו שהרמב"ם הוא בא־כח היהדות מצד השכל וההגיון" (שלמה שכטר, Studies in Judaism, כרך ראשון, דף ק"כ וכו'). אותה הרכות המצינת את ספריו וחבוריו נראית גם באגרותיו מארץ ישראל. הפרידה מביתו ומשפחתו הסבה לו עינוים רבים ויסורים קשים, ובשום אופן לא יכול למצוא נוחם וספוק בתנאי ארץ ישראל בימים ההם, תנאים שהוא מתאר בהשתפכות הנפש באחת מאגרותיו. אכן הוא התמכר בכל לבו ונפשו להדרכת צאצאיו הנעזבים לנפשם, ויכתוב אגרות אחדות למטרה זו. באחת מאלה (נדפסה ברבעון היהודי האנגלי, סדר ראשון, כרך חמישי, דף קט"ו) יעץ לבנו שלמה עצות שונות, ביניהן החובה לחיות חיים טהורים וצנועים בתוך הפריצות של חצר המלכות הקסטילית, אשר כנראה היתה לבנו איזו משרה שם. שלמה היה בנו השני, אבי אביו של רבי לוי בן גרשון או רלב"ג (ראה הטבלה באנציקלופדיה היהודית האנגלית, כרך תשיעי, דף פ"ז).

The most famous of his letters was addressed to his elder son Naḥman. This letter is included in many editions of the Prayer book. Straight from his triumph at Barcelona, when his fame was ringing from end to end of the Jewish world, Naḥmanides eulogizes Humility as the source of Reverence and as the condition of receiving the divine spirit.

The text is printed from the חפוחי זהב of Yeḥiel Milli, Mantua, 1623. Various other editions have been collated. In translating the biblical texts it was sometimes necessary to depart from the usual renderings, in order to bring out Naḥmanides' application of the passages quoted. Another text with interesting expansions, is printed in B. Halper's Anthology of *Post Biblical Hebrew Literature*, Philadelphia, 1921. See vol. i, p. 133 and p. 253; vol. ii, p. 175. These two volumes were issued under the auspices of the Jewish Publication Society of America.

Hear, my son, the instruction of thy father, and forsake not the teaching of thy mother![1] Accustom thyself to speak in gentleness to all men, at all times. Thus wilt thou be saved from anger, the fertile cause of sin. As our Sages say[2]: "Over the man of wrath rules every manner of Gehinnom, and it is written[3]: Remove anger from thy heart, and [thus] put away evil from thy flesh.

[1] Prov. 1.8. Some versions omit "the teaching of thy mother." But Naḥmanides' wife certainly was alive when the writer was compelled to leave Spain for Palestine.

[2] T. B. Nedarim 22a. See other quotations in support of this moralization of Gehinnom in *J. E.* v, 584.

[3] Eccles. 12.10.

האגרת היותר מפורסמת של הרמב"ן נכתבה לבנו בכורו נחמן, והיא נמצאת במהדורות רבות של סדר התפלה. נפלא הוא שמיד אחרי נצחונו בברצלונה, כששמו הלך מסוף העולם היהודי עד סופו, הלל ושבח הרמב"ן את הענוה בתור יסוד ליראת הרוממות ובתור תנאי להשראת רוח הקדש.

הנוסח הנדפס פה הוא מן הספר „תפוחי זהב" לר' יחיאל מילי, מנטובה שפ"ג, אף כי השויתי גם מהדורות שונות אחרות. בהעתקת הפסוקים מן התנ"ך יש אשר חשבתי לנחוץ לשנות מן התרגומים המצוים בכדי להטעים את שמוש הרמב"ן בפסוקים האלה. נוסח אחר עם הוספות חשובות נדפס ע"י בן־ציון הלפר ב„אנתולוגיה של הספרות העברית שאחרי התנ"ך", פילדלפיה תרפ"א, ראה כרך א' דף קל"ג ורנ"ג, גם כרך ב', דף קע"ה. שני הכרכים האלה יצאו לאור ע"י החברה היהודית להוצאת ספרים באמיריקה.

שמע בני מוסר אביך ואל תטוש תורת אמך[1]. והתנהג תמיד לדבר בנחת כל דבריך לכל אדם בכל עת! ובזה תנצל מן הכעס, שהיא המדה הרעה להחטיא את האדם: וכן אמרו חז"ל, כל הכועס כל מיני גיהנם שולטים בו. שנאמר, והסר כעס

1 Some versions complete the quotation. M., however, omits the last two words.

Evil here (in the passage of Ecclesiastes) is nothing else but Gehinnom, as when it is said (in Proverbs): 'And the wicked for the day of evil.'"[4]

Being delivered from anger, there will arise in thy heart the quality of humility, better than all things good! For "the reward of humility is the fear of the Lord."[5] Reverence is thus the fruit of humility. For humility it is that must impel thee to lay to thine heart always the memory of whence thou camest and whither thou goest;[6] it is humility that reminds thee that in life thou art but a worm, and the more so in death; it is humility that warns thee that the One before whom thou must be judged and called to account is the King of Glory. "Behold heaven and the heaven of heavens cannot contain Him"[7]—how much less the hearts of the children of men! "Do not I fill heaven and earth? saith the Lord."[8] Pondering over all these things, [the exaltation of God, the lowliness of man], thou wilt stand in awe of thy Creator, and be on thy guard against sin. Endowed with these qualities, thou canst but rejoice at whatever lot befall thee. If thou indeed takest humility for thy rule in life, holding thyself modestly before the world, a God-fearer and a sin-fearer,—then will there rest upon thee the spirit of the Shekinah[9] and the radiance of the divine Glory, and thou wilt live the life of the world to come![10]

[4] Prov. 16.4. On Naḥmanides' conception of the soul, see S. Schechter, *Studies in Judaism*, first series, p. 140.

[5] Prov. 22.4. [6] Mishnah Abot 3.1.

[7] I Kings 8.27. [8] Jer. 23.24.

מלבך והעבר רעה מבשרך. ואין רעה אלא גיהנם. שנאמר, וגם רשע ליום רעה:

וכאשר תנצל מן הכעס, תעלה על לבך מדת הענוה, הטובה מכל הטוב! שנאמר, עקב ענוה יראת ה׳. ובעבור הענוה תעלה על לבך מדת היראה, כי תתן אל לבך תמיד מאין באת ולאן אתה הולך. ושאתה רמה ותולעת בחייך, אף כי במותך. ולפני מי אתה עתיד ליתן דין וחשבון, לפני מלך הכבוד. שנאמר, הנה השמים ושמי השמים לא יכלכלוך אף כי לבות בני אדם. ואמר, הלא את השמים ואת הארץ אני מלא נאם ה׳: וכאשר תחשוב את כל אלה, תירא מבוראך, ותשמר מן החטא. ובמדות האלה תהיה שמח בחלקך המגיעך: וכאשר תתנהג במדת הענוה, להתבושש מכל אדם, ותתפחד[2] ממנו ומן החטא, אז תשרה עליך רוח השכינה וזיו כבודו[3] וחיית חיי העולם הבא!

[2] M. ומהתפחד. [3] So M. Another reading: כבודה. Also וחיי for the next two words.

---

[9] i. e. the "Divine Presence". See Abelson (op. cit. next note) ch. iv.

[10] For Naḥmanides' views on the future life see his *Gate of Requital* at the end of his treatise the *Law of Man*. As to the "radiance" (*ziv*), he conceived it almost as a

And now, my son! Understand clearly that he who prides himself in his heart over other men is a rebel against the Kingship of Heaven. Such a one presumes to adorn himself in the robe of the Omnipresent. For it is God, enthroned, who wears the mantle of majesty.[11] And wherefore shall the heart of man be puffed up? Is it because of wealth? It is God who maketh poor and maketh rich.[12] Or is it because of honor? But honor is of God.[13] And how shall a man boast in an honor which is his Maker's? Does he glorify himself because of his wisdom? Lo, God "removeth the speech of men of trust and taketh away the sense of the elders."[14] In a word, all are equal before the Lord. For in His anger He bringeth down the high and in His good pleasure He elevates the low. Therefore debase thyself and let the Omnipresent raise thee up![15]

Accordingly I will explain how thou must habituate thyself to the quality of humility in thy daily practice. Let thy voice be low, and thy head bowed; let thine eyes be turned earthwards and thy heart heavenwards. Gaze not in the face of him whom thou dost address. Every man should seem in thine eyes as one greater than thyself. If he be wise or wealthy, it is thy duty to show him respect. If he be poor and thou the richer, or if thou be wiser than he, bethink thee in thy heart, that thou art the more

mystical union of the soul of man with the soul of God. Cf. J. Abelson, *The Immanence of God in Rabbinic Literature*, p. 87. See also my *Glory of God*, p. 44f.

[11] Ps. 93.1. The word גאות means both pride and majesty.

ועתה בני! דע וראה כי המתגאה בלבו[4] על הבריות הוא מורד במלכות שמים. כי מתפאר הוא בלבוש המקום. שנאמר, ה׳ מלך גאות לבש. ולמה יתגאה לב האדם? אם בעושר, ה׳ מוריש ומעשיר. ואם בכבוד, הלא לאלהים הוא. שנאמר, והעושר והכבוד מלכניך. ואיך יתפאר בכבוד קונו? ואם יתפאר בחכמה, מסיר שפה לנאמנים וטעם זקנים יקח: נמצא הכל שוה לפני המקום. כי באפו משפיל גאים וברצונו מגביה שפלים. לכן השפל עצמך וינשאך המקום!

על כן אפרש איך תתנהג במדת הענוה, ללכת בה תמיד: כל דבריך יהיו בנחת. וראשך יהיה כפוף. ועיניך יביטו למטה לארץ, ולבך למעלה. ואל תבט בפני אדם בדברך עמו: וכל אדם יהיה גדול ממך בעיניך. אם הוא חכם אם הוא עשיר[5] עליך לכבדו. ואם הוא רש ואתה עשיר ממנו, או שאתה חכם ממנו, חשוב בלבבך כי אתה חייב

[4] M. לבו. [5] M. עשיר וחכם.

[12] I Sam. 2.7.
[13] I Chron. 29.12.
[14] Job 12.20.
[15] T. B. ‘Erubin 13b.

guilty, he is the more innocent. If he sin, it is from error; if thou sin, it is with design![16]

In all thy doings, words, and thoughts, and at all times, regard thyself as one standing before the Omnipresent[17], with His Shekinah upon thee, for the glory of the Lord filleth the universe. Let thy words be spoken in the deepest reverence as though a servant addressed his master. Hold thyself abashed before all men, and if one call thee do not answer noisily, but respond without agitation and in lowered tones, as an inferior would use to his superior.

Read in the Torah regularly, so that thou mayest be able to fulfil its precepts. When thou risest from the book, think closely over what thou hast learned, perchance there may be some thing in it for thee to translate into conduct. Examine thine actions at morn and at eve, and by this means all thy days will be passed in repentance.

And when thou prayest, remove all worldly considerations from thy heart. Set thy heart right before God, cleanse thine inmost thoughts and meditate before uttering thy devotions. Act thus all thy days, in all things, and thou wilt not sin. By this course thy deeds will all be upright, and thy prayer pure and clean, innocent and devout, and acceptable before the Lord. As it is written: "Thou, God, wilt direct their heart, Thou wilt cause Thine ear to attend."[18]

[16] For rabbinic parallels see Derek Erez *passim*.

[17] On the application to God of the term Maḳom (lit. Place, here rendered Omnipresent), see *J. E.*, iii, 460.

[18] The first clause of the verse (Ps. 10.17) runs: "Lord,

ממנו והוא זכאי ממך. שאם הוא חוטא הוא שוגג ואתה מזיד:

ובכל מעשיך ודבריך ומחשבותיך, ובכל עת, תחשוב כאלו אתה עומד לפני המקום ושכינתו עליך. כי כבודו מלא העולם: ודבריך יהיו באימה וביראה, כעבד לפני רבו: והתבייש מכל אדם ואדם. ואם יקראך איש לא תעננו בקול רם, רק בנחת ובקול נמוך, כעומד לפני גדול:[6]

והוי זהיר לקרות[7] בתורה תמיד אשר תוכל לקיימה. וכאשר תקום מן הספר חפש באשר למדת אם יש בו דבר שתוכל לקיימו: ופשפש במעשיך בבקר ובערב. ובזה יהיו כל ימיך בתשובה:

והסר כל דברי העולם[8] מלבבך בעת התפלה. והכן לבך לפני המקום. וטהר רעיונך[9]. וחשוב הדבר קודם שתוציאנו מפיך: וכן תעשה כל ימי חייך בכל דבר ודבר ולא תחטא. ובזה יהיו כל מעשיך ישרים. ותפלתך זכה וברה ונקייה ומכוונת ומקובלת לפני המקום. שנאמר, תכין לבם תקשיב אזנך:

[6] So corrected from usual reading רבו.

[7] M. omits, and transposes next two words.

[8] M. והסר כל דבר מלבך.

[9] M. omits this phrase.

Read this Letter once a week, and be as regular in carrying out[19] its injunctions, by its aid walking forever after the Lord, blessed be He; that thou mayest prosper in all thy ways, and be held worthy of all the good which is treasured up for the righteous!

Thou hast heard the desire of the humble." The verse is applied also by Samuel b. Naḥman (T. J. Berakot end) to enforce the moral that only the prayer of a devout heart avails.

[19] Or: "once a week at least; so as to carry out, etc."

תקרא האגרת הזאת פעם אחת בשבוע לא תפחות לקיימה וללכת בה תמיד אחרי השם יתברך למען תצליח בכל דרכיך. ותזכה לכל הטוב[10] הצפון לצדיקים![11]

10 Sometimes it would seem that לעולם הבא, the usual reading here, is an inaccurate expansion of the abbreviation ל״ה which might be לכל הטוב.

11 Another version (see היקב 1894, p. 39) adds: וביום שתקראנה יענוך מן השמים אשר יעלה על לבך לשאול עד העולם שנא׳ ויתן לך משאלות לבך ויתן מעדנים לנפשך.

שערי המוסר (המיוחס להרמב"ם)

THE GATE OF INSTRUCTION ATTRIBUTED TO MAIMONIDES

V.

THE GATE OF INSTRUCTION

Attributed to Maimonides

There are two Testaments attributed to Maimonides (1135–1204). One of them, that most usually described as Maimonides' Testament, occurs in many libraries in manuscript, and has often been printed, since the first edition appeared in Venice in 1544. It is of polemical rather than of ethical interest, for it culminates in an ungracious, not to say abusive, denunciation of the French school of Jewish scholars. It is true that in other letters ascribed to Maimonides a similar tone is sometimes heard. Here and there, too, there are touches worthy of Maimonides, as this: "The perfect rest of the Sabbath is the attuning of the heart to the comprehension of God." Then, again, there is a circumstantial statement in a Bodleian MS. (Cat. Neubauer No. 2386) to the following effect. The Testament was written in Arabic on two leaves by Maimonides; the said leaves were detached from the book containing them, soon after the philosopher's death; and the Testament was thereupon translated into Hebrew. There is no probability in the story. The most that can be urged for the document is that it may contain some authentic points (Steinschneider, *Hebr. Ueber.* p. 931). But on the whole it seemed best to omit the document from the present collection.

But what *has* been included has no better claim to authenticity. It is however a far finer work, and deserves inclusion on its own merits. It was printed by Steinschneider

ה

שערי המוסר (המיוחס להרמב"ם)

יש שתי צואות המיוחסות לרבי משה בן מיימון (תתצ"ה–תתקס"ד לאלף החמישי). האחת, הנודעת עפ"י רוב כצואת הרמב"ם, נמצאת בכתב יד בבתי־עקד־ספרים רבים ונדפסה פעמים רבות למיום הופעתה הראשונה בויניציה בשנת ש"ד. הצואה הזאת יש לה חשיבות פולמית יותר ממוסרית, יען כי כל עיקרה לא בא אלא להלשין באופן גס ומעליב על חכמי ישראל בצרפת. · אמנם הד קול כזה נשמע לפעמים גם באגרות אחרות המיוחסות להרמב"ם. בכלל נמצאים בה פה ושם קוים ושרטוטים הראוים להנשר הגדול הזה, כמו הרעיון שהמנוחה השלמה והאמתית ביום השבת מסייעה לתקן ולשכלל את הלב להשגת הבורא יתברך. מלבד זאת יש ידיעה מפורסמת בכ"י בודליאני (רשימת נייבויער, נומר 2386) שהצואה הזאת נכתבה ע"י הרמב"ם בערבית על שני עלים ותיכף אחרי מותו נפרדו העלים האלה מן הספר שבו היו נתונים ונעתקו לעברית. אבל אי אפשר לתת אמון בידיעה הזאת. לכל היותר אפשר להניח שהצואה הזאת יש לה איזה קוים מקוריים (שטיינשניידר, העברעאישע איבערזעטצונגען, דף תתקל"א), אבל בשלמותה חשבתי לטוב ונכון להשמיטה מן הכרך שלפנינו.

והנה צואת הרמב"ם שנתתי פה איננה בחזקת מקוריות יותר גדולה, אבל לכל הפחות היא חבור יותר יפה ומעולה מן הראשונה, וראויה היא למקום פה בשביל מעלותיה העצמיות. שטיינשניידר ועדעלמאן הדפיסו אותה בספריהם המכילים את

and Edelman in the same volumes which contain Ibn Tibbon's Testament (See p. 53). In the Bodleian MS. from which Steinschneider derived it, it is an introduction to the Testament mentioned above, and claims to be by Maimonides (מוסר נאה מאד מאד מהרמב"ם ז"ל להרב החכם ר' אברהם בנו ז"ל). In 1852 Steinschneider was rather inclined to accept this ascription, but he afterwards withdrew his opinion (*Hamazkir*, ii, 8, iv, 107). For it turned out that the same text had been published anonymously under the title ס' המוסר in Cracow, in 1586. Moreover L. Dukes discovered a MS. of the text in the British Museum, entitled שערי המוסר אל השלם השר איש רומי. This MS. is written on the margin of fol. 137b, seq. of Harleian MS. 5686. In the present writer's opinion, though the MS. is a fifteenth century copy, it points to an older original. In several places the copyist must have had an old and faded MS. before him, as he frequently was unable to read his original. It seems most probable that the text is a product of the early part of the thirteenth century. It was thus written soon after Maimonides' death, and is therefore placed in the position it occupies in the chronological sequence of this volume. In order, however, to indicate that the text is later than Maimonides, it is placed *after* the letter by Naḥmanides, which it would precede, if it were really by Maimonides himself. The writer adopts several of the most prominent Maimonist views: Free-will, the doctrine of the Mean, and so forth. That the text is not by Maimonides is indicated unmistakably by the fact that the writer addresses his *children* in the plural. We know of only one child, Abraham, who carried on the reputation of Maimonides into the next generation. It is clear that the writer of this text was, like Maimonides himself, a physician.

הצואה של אבן תבון (ראה דף 53). בכ"י הבודליאני אשר ממנו דלה שטיינשניידר את הצואות הרי היא כעין הקדמה אל הצואה הנזכרת לעיל והרמב"ם נזכר בפירוש בתור מחברה (מוסר נאה מאד מאד מהרמב"ם ז"ל להרב החכם ר' אברהם בנו ז"ל). בשנת תרי"ב נטה שטיינשניידר להאמין שהרמב"ם הוא מחברה, אבל אח"כ חזר על דעתו זו (המזכיר, כרך שני, דף ח'; כרך רביעי, דף ק"ז), יען כי נודע הדבר שאותו הנוסח עצמו נדפס בהעלם שם המחבר בקראקוי בשנת שמ"ו תחת השם „ס' המוסר". מלבד זאת גלה יהודה ליב דוקעס כ"י ממנו במוזיאום הבריטי בלונדון תחת השם „שערי המוסר אל השלם השר איש רומי". כתוב בשולי העמודים קל"ז: וכו' של כת"י הארלעס נומר 5686. לפי דעתי, אף כי הכ"י הוא מן המאה החמש עשרה בכ"ז נראה שמקורו הוא יותר עתיק. במקומות אחדים אפשר לראות שהמעתיק העתיק מכ"י בלוי מוזקן, כי לפעמים קרובות לא עלה בידו לקרוא את מקורו כראוי. אפשר מאד שהחבור הזה נכתב בתחלת המאה השלש עשרה, קרוב לפטירת הרמב"ם, וע"כ קבענו לו מקום פה בהתאם אל הסדר הכרונולוגי של הכרך הזה. אכן בכדי להראות שנוסח הצואה הוא מאוחר מן הרמב"ם הצגנו אותו אחר האגרת של הרמב"ן, כי להפך אם היה מעשה ידי הרמב"ם עצמו כי אז צריכים היינו להקדימו. כנראה קבל המחבר מן הרמב"ם איזה מדעותיו היותר חשובות: רצון חפשי, הכלל של שביל הזהב וכו'. הוכחה גמורה שהאגרת הזאת לא נכתבה ע"י הרמב"ם היא העובדא שהמחבר פונה אל בניו בלשון רבים. אנחנו יודעים רק ע"ד בן אחד של הרמב"ם, אברהם, אשר התעטר בשם אביו. אין כל ספק שמחבר האגרת הזאת, כמו הרמב"ם עצמו, היה רופא.

In the notes to the Hebrew text, S. indicates Steinschneider's readings, B. those of the British Museum MS. This MS. has, for the first time, been collated with the Oxford version.

I will bless the Lord, who hath given me counsel, and hath led me in the right way.[1] I will make mention of His mercies, according to all that He hath bestowed upon me.[2] He hath chastened me sore, but hath not given me over unto death.[3] He held me by my right hand, and in the shadow of His hand He hid me.[4] From the burdens of fortune's wheel He delivered me, and saved me from life's vicissitudes. In the melting pot of time He tried me, and from the blackness of youth He made me white.[5] From its perverseness He kept me aloof, and from the conflict of passion He hath given me rest. He rebuked the serpent which enticed me, and gave me to taste the sweet[6]. From the dust He raised me, and with princes He hath made me sit.[7] My days have taught me, experience hath made me wise, time hath been my reproof. Thus far hath the Lord blessed and preserved me,[8] granting unto me widsom beyond my fellows, and enabling me to distinguish between good and evil. My end is in His hand, and He hath made me conscious of it, though I know not how long, nor how short-lived am I![9] Therefore hath His love stirred me to admonish the children whom He hath graciously bestowed on me, that they may observe the way of the Lord. I would teach them what He hath taught me, bequeath

בהערותי לנוסח העברי S משמש למהדורת שטיינשניידר, B לכ״י הנמצא במוזיאום הבריטי. השויתי את הכ״י הזה בפעם הראשונה לכ״י אוקספורד.

אברך את ה׳ אשר יעצני. ובדרך אמת הנחני. חסדיו אזכיר כעל כל אשר גמלני. יסר יסרני. ולמות לא נתנני. בימיני[1] אחזני. ובצל ידו החביאני. מסבלות הגלגל הוציאני. ומתהפוכותיו הצילני. בכור הזמן צרפני. ומשחרות הילדות הלבינני. וממשובותיו הבדילני. וממלחמת[2] יצרי השקיטני. ויגער בנחש השיאני. ומתוק[3] הטעימני. ומעפר הקימני. ועם נדיבים הושיבני. הימים הורוני. והנסיון השכילני. והזמן הוכיחני. ועד כה ברכני. והחייני. מזולתי הבינני. ובין טוב לרע הבחינני. אשר בידו קצי הודיעני. ולא אדע מתי ומה חדל אני. ולכן אהבתו הערתני.[4] לצוות את הילדים אשר חנני.

[1] S בימינו. [2] S ממלחמות. [3] B מר ומתוק. [4] S תעירני.

---

[1] Ps. 16.7; Gen. 24.48.
[2] Is. 63.7.
[3] Ps. 118.18.
[4] Ps. 73.23; Is. 49.2.
[5] i. e. cleansed him from the faults of youth.
[6] Add "of contentment".
[7] I Sam. 2.8 [8] Jos. 17.4. [9] Ps. 39.5.

to them the heritage which He gave me, ere He call me away, and His Glory shall gather me in![10]

Hear me, my children! Blessed be ye of the Lord, who made heaven and earth,[11] with blessing of heaven above, blessings of the deep that coucheth under, blessings of the breasts and of the womb![12] Be strong and show yourselves men![13] Fear the Lord, the God of your father, the God of Abraham, Isaac, and Jacob; and serve Him with a perfect heart, from fear and from love. For fear restrains from sin, and love stimulates to virtue. Know that He will bring all to judgment, for what is open and for what is hidden, for good and for evil.[14] He who leads a good life finds good even in this world; for they that see him glorify him, and those who know him declare him blessed. And when the tale of his years is full, and he departs from the children of men, he will rejoice in the worthiness of his work and will find comfort. No fear of death will distress him, for he will not be anxious concerning punishment; he will await the good reward, to see the bliss treasured up for them that fear the Lord, and his house will be established for ever. But if a man corrupt his way and pursue

[10] To Himself, or as E. takes it "to my fathers". The text (Isa. 58.8) is applied to death in T. B. Soṭa 9b, (cf. also Kimḥi's comm. on Isaiah ad loc.). Besides the references given, there are in this introduction several other biblical reminiscences, which are not direct quotations, as the author sometimes paraphrases, sometimes alters for his rhymes, sometimes modifies by the introduction of

לשמור דרך ה׳. ולהורותם מאשר הורני. ולהורישם
אשר הורישני. בטרם יקראני. וכבודו יאספני:
שמעוני בני! ברוכים אתם לה׳ עושה שמים וארץ.
ברכות שמים מעל. ברכות תהום רובצת תחת.
ברכות שדים ורחם. חזקו והיו לאנשים![5] יראו את
ה׳ אלהי אביכם.[6] אלהי אברהם יצחק ויעקב.
ועבדוהו בלבב שלם מיראה ומאהבה.[7] כי היראה
מביאה הזהירות מן החטא. והאהבה מביאה
הזריזות[8] למצות: דעו כי הכל יביא במשפט. על
גלוי ועל נעלם. על טוב ועל רע: המטיב פעלו
יטיבו לו בעולם הזה. רואיו יפארוהו ויודעיו[9]
יאשרוהו. ובהמלא מספר ימיו בהפרדו מבני אדם
ישמח על כשרון פעלו ויתנחם ולא יכאב[10] מאד
למות כי לא ידאג לעונש. אבל יצפה לגמול טוב.
לראות בטוב הצפון ליראי ה׳. וביתו יהיה נכון
עד עולם: והמשחית דרכו וירדוף הרע. הרע

[5] B omits this clause. [6] B אבותיכם. [7] S omits מיראה.
[8] S reads in both cases זריזות; B in both cases זהירות.
[9] B omits this and previous word. [10] S ידאג.

---

post-biblical phraseology. But the result is a singularly fine specimen of the "mosaic" type of composition.

[11] Ps. 115. 15. [12] Gen. 49. 25.
[13] I Kings 2. 2. [14] Eccles. 12. 14.

evil, evil shall pursue and overtake him and in turn corrupt his conduct farther. They that see him will despise and condemn him in his life-time; and in his death "his flesh grieveth for him, and his soul mourneth over him."[15] For "he departeth in darkness and with darkness is his name covered;"[16] yea, "he shall lean upon his house, but it shall not stand!"[17]

I entreat you to recognize the excellency of light over darkness. Reject ye death and evil, choose ye life and good, for the free choice is given unto you![18] Accustom yourselves to habitual goodness, for habit and character are closely interwoven, habit becoming as it were second nature. Again, the perfection of the body is an antecedent to the perfection of the soul, for health is the key that unlocks the inner chamber. When I bid you to care for your bodily and moral welfare, my purpose is to open for you the gates of heaven! Conduct yourselves with gravity and decency; avoid association with the wanton; sit not in the streets, sport not with the young, for the fruit thereof is evil. Be found rather in the company of the great[19] and learned, but behave modestly in their presence, occupying the lower seats.[20] Incline your head, and open

[15] Job 14. 22.

[16] Eccles. 6. 4.

[17] Job 8. 15. In the previous verse, the house of the wicked is likened to a spider's web for frailty. There are throughout this part of the Testament reminiscences of the *Choice of Pearls*.

ירדפהו וישיגהו וישחית מעשיו. רואיו יעקשו עליו פיהם. וילזו[11] שפתותיהם. ובמותו בשרו עליו יכאב. ונפשו עליו תאבל. כי בחשך ילך[12] ובחושך שמו יכוסה. וישען על ביתו ולא יעמד:

אחלי לפניכם תכירו יתרון האור מן החושך. ומאסו במות וברע ובחרו בחיים ובטוב כי הרשות נתונה לכם.[13] הנהיגו עצמכם במדות הטובות. כי טבע האדם תלוי במנהג. והמנהג יוקבע בטבע: דעו כי שלמות הגוף קודם לשלמות הנפש. והוא כמפתח הפותח טרקלין. ולכן עיקר כוונת מוסרי על שלמות גופכם ותיקון מדותיכם לפתוח לפניכם דלתות השמים: התנהגו בכבדות ובכבודות. חדלו לכם מחברת הקלים. ומישיבת הרחובות. ומשחוק הבחורים. כי משם יצא פרי רע: המצאו תמיד בין כבירים וחכמים.[14] אך בענוה ובהכנעה ובשפל המקומות. והטו אזני[15] ראשיכם ופתחו אזני לבבכם

[11] B ויליזו. [12] B הולך. [13] B לפניכם.
[14] B בין נכבדים. [15] S omits.

---

[18] Eccles. 2. 13; Deut. 30. 19; Mishnah Abot iii, 15. Cf. *J. E.* v, 505.

[19] Job 15. 10.

[20] In olden times the disciple sat on the ground (cf. Abot i.4, T. B. Megillah 21a). Cf. also Matthew 23. 6.

the ears of your heart to listen and to understand their words, and what they praise and blame; weigh[21] their opinions and thus will ye be set in the right way. Guard your tongue from wearying them, measure your words with judgment, for the more your words the more your errors. Be not supercilious or conceited when with them; be not ashamed to ask explanations, but do so at the right moment and in fitting terms. Ponder well over every word before you utter it, for you cannot recall it afterwards.

Love wisdom, seek her as silver, search for her as for hidden treasures.[22] Be found on the threshhold of the wise, those that learn and those that teach. There obtain your recreation; there take delight in hearing discourse of science and morals, as well as the new thoughts and ingenious arguments of the students. Emulate those who seek knowledge, despise those who have no intellectual curiosity. Whether you ask a question or answer one, speak without haste or obscurity, softly and without stammering.[23] Use refined phrases, let your utterance be clear, tranquil, and apt to the point. Behave as one who wishes to learn and to discover the truth, not as one whose aim is to dispute and win a wordy victory. Attend there in a receptive frame of mind, determined to profit by your attendance; then will study be pleasant

[21] Or, following a different punctuation, "weigh what they praise and blame."

[22] Prov. 2.4.

[23] Is. 28.11.

לשמוע ולהבין[16] דבריהם ומה יגנו ומה ישבחו. ושקלו[17] הענינים קצתם על קצתם. ואז תשכילו: שמרו פיכם ולשונכם מהעתיר דברים לפניהם. כלכלו דבריכם במשפט. כי בהרבות דבריכם ירבו טעייותיכם[18]. ואל תתהדרו ותתגאו לפניהם. ואל תבושו לשאול הנעלם מכם. אך בעת ראוי[19] ובלשון ראוי. חשבו ושקלו הדבר טרם תוציאוהו מפיכם כי לא תוכלו להשיבו:

אהבו החכמה. בקשוה ככסף. וכמטמונים חפשוה.[20] הסתופפו בבתי החכמים. הלומדים[21] והמלמדים. שם יהיה טיולכם. והתענגו שם בשמוע החכמות והמוסרים והחדושים ופלפולי התלמידים. קנאו ליודעים[22] ובזו בלבבכם הגולמים: כאשר תשאלו או תענו דבר. אל תמהרו ואל תבהלו ואל תצעקו ואל תדברו בלעגי שפה. דברו במבחר הלשון. בצחות[23] השפה. בקול נחת.[24] בכיוון הענינים. כמבקש ללמוד ומחפש האמת. לא כמריב ומבקש לנצוח: עמדו שם ברצון[25]. והתבוננו להוציא משם תועלת ואז ינעם לכם ויקל עליכם. ואם

[16] S ולהאזין. [17] S שקלו, putting stop at דבריהם.
[18] S טענותיכם. [19] B adds ובחכמה. [20] S. תחפשוה.
[21] B omits. [22] B לתלמידים. [23] B בכבדות.
[24] B omits phrase. [25] S ברצונכם.

and facile. But if you allow your heart to wander hither and thither, you will fail in the main purpose of your attendance, for you will learn nothing, and the heavy confinement will wear out your body. When ye leave the college, realize what you are taking home; grave it on your brain, bind it to your heart! Learn in your youth, when ye eat what others provide; while your mind is still free, and unencumbered with cares; ere the memory lose its vigor. For the time will come when ye will wish to learn but will be unable. And, even if ye do not entirely fail, ye will labor much to little effect; for your mind will lag behind your lips, and when it does keep pace, the memory will not hold fast what the mind attains.

Behold, my counsel is committed into your hand, you may profit much from the study of it to confirm truth,[24] to settle the mind, and to remove doubt. When you find in the Law or the Prophets, or the books of the Sages, a deep text or an obscure saying, which you cannot understand nor can penetrate into its secret; which appears subversive of the corner-stones of the Torah or altogether absurd; do not budge from your faith, let not your mind be confounded. Stand fast in your stronghold, and attribute the fault to yourselves, for it is not a vain thing, and if it be vain, it is because of your lack of understanding.[25] Place

[24] According to another reading: "faith".

[25] Maimonides, *Guide*, iii, ch. 26, cites this use of the text, Deut, 32. 47. "The giving of these commandments [whose object is not clear] is not a vain thing and without

תשלהו לבכם אנה ואנה תפסידו מן[26] הקרן במעמדכם.[27] כי לא תלמדו ויכבד עליכם המסגר[28] המחלה הגוף: ובצאתכם דעו מה תוליכו לבתיכם. חקוהו במוחכם. וצוררוהו בלבבכם: למדו בבחרותכם באכלכם הכנת זולתכם. ובעוד לבכם פנוי טרם ימלא מחשבות וכח המזכיר יחלש. כי יבוא עת שתרצו ולא תוכלו. ואפילו מה שתוכלו תתיגעו עם מעט תועלת. כי לא ירדוף הלב את הפה. ואפילו במה שירדפהו לא יחזיקהו כי ישכחהו:

הנה מוסרי בידכם מסור.[29] יש בו תועלת רב בלמוד לחזקת האמונה.[30] ולישב בדעת ולהסיר המבוכה: כאשר תמצאו כתוב עמוק ומאמר נבוך בתורה או בנביאים או בספרי חכמים. אשר לא תבינוהו ולא תדעו מסתרו. ונראה כסותר פנות התורה או דברי הבאי. אל תזוזו מאמונתכם. ואל יתבלבל שכלכם. עמדו בחזקתכם. והפחיתות ההוא חשבוהו בכם. כי לא דבר רק הוא כי אם[31] מכם.

26 S omits.

27 S בעמדכם. 28 B כמסגר.

29 B הנני מוסר בידכם מסורת. 30 S לחזק האמת.

31 S omits כי אם.

it "in a corner"[26] and do not abominate the whole of your faith because you are incompetent to solve a single problem of philosophy. "God understandeth the way thereof, and knoweth its place."[27]

Love truth and righteousness, and cleave to them. Prosperity so obtained is built on a sure rock. Hate falsehood and injustice, lust not after their dainties, for such happiness is built on sand.[28] To one who so acts apply the Scriptural words: "Say unto them that daub a wall with whited plaster, that it shall fall."[29]

Therefore, let truth and righteousness, by which ye may seem to lose, be more lovely in your sight than falsehood and unrighteousness, by which ye may seem to gain. For thus said the Wise Man in his admonition: "Buy the truth, and sell it not."[30] Know that truth and righteousness are adornments of the soul and givers of strength and durability to the body. I have found no remedy for weakness of heart[31] comparable to an infusion of truth and righteousness. Nor could the company of friends, the deep shelter of Ashteroth Karnayim, javelin or coat of mail, give me the same sense of security as the helmet of truth and the shield of righteousness![32]

useful purpose, and if it appears so to you in any commandment, it is owing to the deficiency in your comprehension."

[26] A talmudic phrase, T. B. Kiddushin 66a. Here the sense is: "set it apart for further thought.'

[27] Job 28.23.

[28] Cf. Abot de R. Nathan I, xxiv. See particularly Matt. 7. 24–7. Cf. I. Abrahams, *Studies in Pharisaism*,

הניחוהו בקרן זוית. ואל תשקצו כל אמונתכם על חסרון הבנת דבר חכמה.[32] אלהים הבין דרכה והוא ידע את מקומה:

אהבו האמת והצדק ובהם תדבקון. כי תצליחו בהם ותקיים[33] ההצלחה ההיא כבונה על צור החלמיש: שנאו השקר והעול. ואל תתאוו למטעמידם. כי הוא כבונה[34] על החול. וקראו עליהם, אמור אל טחי תפל[35] ויפול!

לכן ינעם לכם האמת והצדק שנראה שתפסידו בהם יותר מן השקר והעול שנראה שתרויחו בהם.[36] וכן אמר החכם במוסרו. אמת קנה ואל תמכור: דעו כי האמת והצדק הם תכשיטי הנפש. ונותנים גבורה ובטח ונצח לגוף. ולא מצאתי רפואה לרכות הלבב כהרכבת האמת והצדק. ולא הבטיחוני אחוזת מרעים ועשתרות קרנים ושלח ושריון ככובע האמת ומגן הצדק:[37]

[32] B הדבר ההוא או חכמה אחת.
[33] S omits. [34] B נבונה. [35] S תחי טפל. [36] S in both cases בו. [37] B is here defective.

---

p. 92. [29] Ezek. 13.11. [30] Prov. 23.23.
[31] Prob. in the sense of "timidity"; cf. Deut. 20.8.
[32] Gen. 26.26 (as interpreted by the Targum). Ashteroth Karnayim, situated E. of the Jordan, in a deep

So shall it come to pass in the day when I bequeath unto you the possessions which the Creator has preciously bestowed on me, I will hand on to you the honesty of purpose by which God has enabled me to possess this store, for with my staff I crossed over to gain my daily bread and its drink offering, and lo! the Lord has blessed me thus far. Faithfulness has introduced me into places where my kinsmen could not admit me, and has dowered me with more than my fathers had to leave unto me. It has given me authority over men greater and better than I, and I have prospered myself and have been a source of profit to others. Therefore take heed therein, even toward one whose good the Law does not enjoin us to seek.[33] Stand by your words, let not a legal contract or witnessed deed be more binding than your verbal promise, whether publicly or privately given. Disdain reservations and subterfuges, tricks, sharp practices, and evasions. Woe to him that builds his house thereon! For if one getteth riches and not by right, "in the midst of his days he shall leave them and at his end he shall be a fool."[34] Live in sincerity, integrity, innocency! Touch not that which is not yours, be it a small matter or great. Taste not that which is not clearly and decisively your own. Flee from doubtful possessions, treat

dale between two hills, was a type of the completely sheltered spot (cf. T. B. Sukkah 2a).

[33] The Talmud has a beautiful term for those aspects of morality which are not susceptible of legal definition:

והיה ביום הנחילי אתכם את אשר חנני[38] הבורא. אנחילכם הנאמנות אשר בה הקנני הבורא את החיל הזה. כי במקלי עברתי להרויח לחם התמיד ונסכו. והנה ברכני ה׳ עד כה. והנאמנות הכניסני במקום שלא הכניסוני קרובי. וירשתי מה שלא הורישוני אבותי. והמשילני על גדולים וטובים ממני. והצלחתי והועלתי לי ולזולתי: לכן הזהרו בו אפילו במה שלא הזהירה התורה אשר תדרוש שלומו. עמדו[39] בדבוריכם. אל יכבד בעיניכם שטר ועדים וקנין על הבטחת הדבר גלוי ונסתר. בטלו ומאנו במודעי מרמות ומזמות ודקדוקים ועמוקים ועקשיות ותושיות ודתות תחתיות. הוי לבונה ביתו עליהם! כי בחצי ימיו יעזבנו ובאחריתו יהיה נבל: תחיו[40] בתמות ובתמימות ובנקיות. אל תגעו בשל זולתכם דבר קטן וגדול. ואל תטעמו מאומה ממה שאינה שלכם ברור ומוחזק. ברחו מן הספקות והעמידום בחזקת

[38] S הנחילני. [39] B adds קיים. [40] B תהיו.

---

they are described as "matters given over to man's heart" (Cf. e. g. T. B. Baba Mezi'a 58b.).

[34] Jer. 17.11. The terms used by the author in explanation refer literally to the commodities about which the duty of tithing is doubtful or certain.

them as the property of others. Remember that the tasting of the doubtful leads to indifference as to the certain; the little to the great, the inadvertent to the designed, till one becomes a hardened cheat, liar, thief and bandit, from whom men turn hastily away.[35] "The buyer from him will not rejoice, nor the seller mourn."[36] He shall be ashamed in his life and confounded in his death. All this have I seen and laid it to my heart. "He that conceives chaff shall bring forth stubble," but "he that sows according to righteousness shall reap according to mercy."[37] Let your moral life be your pride of lineage, and your loyalty to truth your sufficient wealth, for there is no pedigree noble[38] as virtue, no heritage equal to honor.

Bring near those who are far off, bow to the lowly, and show the light of your countenance to the downcast. Be pitiful to the poor and the sorrow-stricken. See to it that they share your joys! Help them in your feasts, according to the good hand of the Lord upon you. But beware lest they be put to the blush by reason of your gifts. Never cease to do good to all whom it is in your power to serve, and be on your guard against working ill to any man whatsoever.

Contemn idleness and loath ease, for these corrupt the body, and lead to all manner of penury

[35] Or "and bandit. Turn ye hastily away from such a one."

[36] Ezek. 7.12.

[37] Isa. 33.11; Hos. 10.12. The quotations are

זולתכם: דעו כי טעימת[41] הדמאי גורמת ליגע מן הודאי. והמעט להרבה והנסתר לנגלה. עד שיוחזק לעקש כפרן גנב וגזלן יברחו[42] מפניו. הקונה ממנו אל ישמח והמוכר אל יתאבל. יבוש בחייו ויכלם במותו. כל זה ראיתי ונתון אל לבי מי שיהר חשש ילד[43] קש והזורע לצדקה קוצר לפי חסד: התיחסו במוסרכם והסתפקו בנאמנותכם[44]. כי אין יחס כמוסר ואין ירושה כנאמנות:

קרבו הרחוקים. השחו[45] לקטנים. האירו פניכם לשפלים. רחמו על האביונים והעלובים. שמחום בשמחתכם והפקידום[46] בחגיכם כיד ה' הטובה עליכם. והזהרו שלא יבושו ויחורו פניהם בסבת מתנותיכם. ואל תחדלו להטיב לכל אשר תוכלו והזהרו מהרע[47] למי שיהיה:

מאסו הבטלה וגעלו השלוה. כי הם סבות להשחתת הגוף. ולמחסור ולשעמום. ולפטפוט.

41 B נגיעת. 42 S ברחו.
43 B תלד and תהר. 44 B באמונתכם. 45 B השחר.
46 B ותפקדום. 47 S omits מהרע.

---

slightly modified by the author to suit the structure of his sentence.

38 Cf. the quotations in Ben Jehuda's *Millon*, 2025 a.

and perversity, in pocket and in conversation. They are the ladder to Satan and his servitors.[39] Such is the fruit of pernicious sloth, whereas "in all labour there is profit".[40]

Make not your souls abominable by dissension, which wastes body and soul and substance. And what else remains? I have seen the white become black, the high of station brought low, families smitten sore, princes humiliated from their position, great cities ruined, assemblies dispersed, the pious destroyed, men of faith like to perish, and the honorable held in light esteem,—all because of contention. Prophets have prophesied, sages have spoken wise words, philosophers have probed, all have dilated on the evils of faction without exhausting the subject.[41] Therefore hate dissension and flee from it; keep aloof from its lovers, its supporters, its admirers. If your own flesh and blood be among the lovers of strife, make yourselves as strangers unto them—ignore your kinship, lest ye be consumed in all their sin.[42] Glory in forbearance, for that is real strength and true victory. If ye seek

[39] See *J.E.*, xi, 70b. [40] Prov. 14.23.

[41] The evils of contention and faction are a fertile theme of Jewish moralists of all epochs. Our author writes with a heat patently due to personal experience. If the author be indeed Maimonides, his denunciation is prophetic of what occurred after his death, and in connection with his philosophical writings. But the ascription of the Testament to Maimonides is highly improbable. See above p. 101.

[42] The allusion is to the story of Koraḥ, Num. 16.

ולעקשות פה. ולזות שפתים. וסולם לשטן ולעובדיו. והיא היא העצלה המנולה[48] ובכל עצב יהיה מותר:

אל תשקצו את נפשותיכם במחלוקת המכלה הגוף והנפש והממון. ומה נשאר עוד? ראיתי לבנים הושחרו[49]. ופחות נפחתו. ומשפחות נספחו. ושרים הוסרו מגדולתם. ועיירות גדולות נתערערו. וקיבוצים נפרדו. וחסידים נפסדו. ואנשי אמונה אבדו. ונכבדים נקלו ונתבזו. בסבת[50] המחלוקת: נביאים נבאו. וחכמים חכמו. ופילוסופים חיפשו. ויספו לספר רעת המחלוקת. ולא הגיעו לתכליתה: לכן שנאו אותה ונוסו מפניה! והתרחקו מכל אוהביה וגואליה ורעיה[51]: וגם אל כל שאר בשרכם אוהב מדנים התנכרו[52]. ורחקו קרבתם פן תספו בכל חטאתם[53]. התפארו בסבל כי הוא הגבורה הישרה והנצחון האמיתי. כי בבקשכם הנקמה שמא

48 B המגונה.

49 S השחירו.

50 B מחמת.

51 The MSS. have masc. terminations throughout this sentence.

52 B התנכרו ממנו.

53 B חטאתיך.

revenge, perchance ye will not attain it, and your heart will be sick with hope deferred;[43] and ye may add shame to your disgrace, like one who rolleth a stone which returns unto himself.[44] And if ye do attain the sought-for revenge, behold ye have sinned against the Lord! For, realize what the result must be to *yourselves*! Hatred, a vindictive heart, confusion of mind, sleeplessness, interruption of your work, the exposure of your faults and failings, degeneration in look and speech, destruction of the soul, a devouring jealousy, disturbance of family peace, and in the end remorse!

Therefore, recognize the worth of forbearance. Sanctify yourselves and be ye holy in the eyes of your enemies. They will relent of their animosity, and your soul will be great in their eyes. They will repent and will better their heart, if they be indeed men of heart. If they are hopelessly base, they will be pained that ye are not as despicable as themselves, in that ye do not as they do, and ye will reign over them with the crown of virtue. Behave, then, with humility, for it is the ladder to the topmost heights;[45] if ye possess that quality, forbearance itself will not be necessary. There is no ornament so comely as meekness. The Master of the Prophets Moses was not so distinguished in Scripture for any of his qualities as for his virtue of humility.[46] Keep

[43] Prov. 13.12.

[44] Prov. 26.27.

[45] Or: "to the highest virtues."

[46] Num. 12.3.

לא תשיגוה ותחלו לבבכם בתוחלת ממושכה. ושמא תוסיפו על בשתכם חרפה.[54] כי גולל[55] אבן אליו תשוב. ואם תשיגוה הנה חטאתם לה׳! ודעו את אשר תמצא אתכם. שנאה. לב נוקם. בלבול השכל. טרוד שינה. ביטול[56] פעולה. גילוי מומים. וג״כ[57] יולידוהו שינוי פנים והלחשים. אבדן הנפש. קנאה אוכלת. עכירות פמליא.[58] חרטה באחרית:

לכן תכירו מעלת הסבל.[59] והתקדשתם והייתם קדושים בעיני אויביכם. ויתחרטו מזיקיכם ותגדל נפשכם בעיניהם. וישובו ויטיבו לבם[60] אם הם אנשי לבב. ואם הם אנשי בליעל יכאבו ויצר להם על אשר לא תתבזו עמהם. לעשות כמוהם. ותמלכו עליהם בכתר המוסר: תתנהגו בענוה. כי הוא סולם לעלות המעלות[61] הרמות. ועמה לא תצטרכו לסבל: דעו כי אין עדי כענוה. הנה[62] רבן של נביאים לא נתיחס על כל טוב[63] מדותיו כמו על הענוה: שמרו מחסום

54 B omits. 55 B כגולל.
56 S בלבול. 57 B אם אין.
58 S adds לומר לאחרים חוטא ומחטיא.
59 B השכל.
60 B להם.
61 B במעלות.
62 B משה הנקרא.
63 S omits.

a curb on your mouth,[47] a bridle on your tongue. God bestowed the faculty of speech on man, because He loved man above all other creatures; a faculty desirable for understanding and lauding God and declaring His wonders; a gift fitted to help man meditate in His Law, learning and teaching, an instrument by which man might promote peace among human kind. It would be ungrateful to turn good into evil, to utter indecent or lying words and to slander—this is indeed an iniquity to be punished by the Judge![48]

But make matter subject to mind, the body to the soul, for this subjection is your freedom, here and hereafter! Therefore, as to the body, "further not its evil device,"[49] for to minister to its cravings is to increase its demands, until it[50] yearns for the unattainable, and in the end the divine element perishes with it. But if the spirit[51] rule, and the body is dominated and humbled, man will seek nothing beyond the necessary; he will be satisfied with the little and will disdain superfluities; he will be contented in life and comforted in death!

Eat, then, that ye may live, and lay a ban on excess. Do not imagine that abundance of food and drink strengthens the body and expands the mind as though you were dealing with a sack which is filled by what is put therein. The

[47] Ps. 39.1.

[48] Job 31.11.

[49] Ps. 140.9.

[50] Perhaps render "*he* yearns", and refer the pronouns to the man.

[51] Or: "mind".

לפיכם ורסן ללשונכם. דעו כי מעלת הדבר חנן האל באדם באהבתו אותו על כל הברואים. נחמד להשכיל. וטוב להודות לה׳[64] ולרוממו ולספר נפלאותיו. ולהגות בתורה וללמוד וללמד. ולהטיל שלום בין אדם לחבירו.[65] לכן לא יתכן להמיר טוב ברע. ולדבר נבלה ושקר ורכילות.[66] כי הוא עון פלילי:

ושעבדו החומר לשכל. כלומר הגוף לנפש. כי שעבודו הוא חירותכם בזה ובבא. לכן זממו אל תפיקו. כי בהפיק[67] מאוייו יוסיף לבקש[68] ולא ישבע עד שישתוקק למה שלא ישיג, ויאבד עמו חלק האלהי[69]: ואם ימשול השכל וישתעבד הגוף ויכנע. לא יבקש רק הצריך[70]. וישבע מן המעט ויקוץ המותר. וינעם בחיים ויתנחם במות:

אכלו כדי שתחיו והיותר תחרימו. ואל תאמינו שרוב המאכל והמשתה יגדיל הגוף וירבה השכל. כשק המתמלא מן המושם לתוכו. כי הוא ההפך.

64 S לו. 65 S omits the previous 8 words.
66 B adds ודברי הבאי. 67 S כהפיק.
68 S לבקשו.
69 S אלהי.
70 B יכנע מאוייו יבקש רק מה שצריך.

contrary is true. By taking the little food which is easily digested by the natural heat, a man's vigor and health increase, his mind becomes clear and calm. But if he eat more than enough, overtaxing his digestion, his food "is a vile thing, it shall not be accepted."[52] His body is emaciated, his intellect dulled, his purse emptied. Overeating is, in fact, the cause of many maladies. Work before ye eat, rest after ye have eaten. Feed not ravenously, like people afflicted with bulimy;[53] fill not your mouths gulp after gulp without breathing space.

Hate injurious viands as you would hate a foe who seeks to slay you. Eat not in the public ways, do not incessantly nibble like mice, take your meals at fixed hours in your homes.[54] Avoid frequent feastings with young men. The breeding of a man, whether for good or ill, is discerned by his manner at a public banquet. Many a time have I returned to my house hungry and thirsty, because I was aghast at the shame of some of the other guests. Beware of wine, which destroys the strong and degrades the honored. How excellent in my eyes is the ordinance of Jonadab unto his children,[55] yet will I not lay

[52] Lev. 19.7.

[53] A medical term (Yoma, viii, 6) derived from the Greek. It denotes excessive appetite.

[54] T. B. Ḳiddushin 40b. Against dining out see T. B. Pesaḥim 49a.

[55] Jer. 35.6. The sons of Jonadab were commanded by their father to abstain from wine. This sentiment of our author is opposed to that of Maimonides, see *Eight Chapters*.

באכול מעט יש כח באצטומכא לקבלו. ובחום הטבעי לעכלו.[71] אז יגדל ויבריא לסובלו ודעתו תתישב:[72] ואם יאכל יותר מדאי האצטומכא לא יקבלנו. והחום הטבעי לא יעכלנו. נכחו יצא. פגול הוא לא ירצה. גופו ירזה. ושכלו יתבזה. וכיסו יתרוקן: הזהרו שלא תאכלו עד אשר תעכלו. כי הוא הפסד הגוף והכיס. כי הוא סבת רוב התחלואים: ועמלו טרם שתאכלו. ותנוחו אחר שתאכלו.[73] אל תאכלו בבהלה כבעלי בולמוס. אל תמלאו פיכם, הלוגמא לא תשיג[74] חברתה:

שנאו המאכלים המזיקים. כאשר ישנא איש את שונאו המבקש[75] להמיתו: אל תאכלו בדרכים ואל תאכלו תמיד[76] כעכברים. כי אם לשעות הקבועות ובבתיכם. והמנעו מהתמיד סעודות עם הבחורים: דעו כי בסעודות הקבוצים יוודע תרבות האדם אם טוב ואם רע. והרבה פעמים חזרתי רעב וצמא בביתי מיראתי. בראותי חרפת זולתי: הזהרו מן היין המשחית עצומים. ומבזה הנכבדים. ומה טוב בעיני צוואת יהונדב לבניו. אמנם לא אצונו. כי

71 B לסובלו. 72 B תישב. 73 B omits clause.
74 S בלוגמא כי תשיג. 75 S רעהו השונאו ומבקש.
76 S omits.

the same command on you; for I have not accustomed you to complete abstinence from wine from your earliest years. But break the strength of the wine with water, and drink it as food not as a pastime.[56] Not without purpose was the shame of Noah written;[57] the record was preserved to point a moral.

Expenditure is divisible into four categories: Profit, Loss, Aversion, Honor. *Profit*, is the expenditure on the bestowal of loving-kindness, the interest of which ye enjoy while the capital remains.[58] *Loss*, is expenditure on gambling, by which a man loses his money, his dignity, his time. If he win he weaves a spider's web; it is a trespass, certainly he is guilty![59] *Aversion*, is the designation of expenditure on food. *Honor*, is the expenditure on wearing apparel, on which one should spend what he can afford.[60] But eat less than your means allow, enough to keep you alive; loathe gambling, keep aloof from gamblers. Stretch your means beyond their capacity to sow in charity, and reap according to mercy![61]

Enjoy life in the society of your friends and the wife of your young manhood.[62] Remember the warnings of Scripture against unchastity. "She hath cast down many wounded, yea a

[56] Lit: "luxury"; mere enjoyment.

[57] Gen. 9.21.

[58] Mishnah Peah 1.1.

[59] Isa. 59.5; Lev. 5.19.

[60] T. B. Ḥullin 84b.

[61] Hosea 10.12.

לא התנהגתי אתכם מתחלת בריאתכם. אך שברו כחו במים ושתוהו דרך מזון ולא דרך[77] תענוג: ראו[78] כי לא לחנם נכתב גנות נח הצדיק. כי אם ליקח מוסר:

דעו כי ההוצאה מתחלקת לארבעה חלקים, ריוח, הפסד. מאוס. כבוד: ריוח, הוא גמילות חסדים שתאכלו הריוח והקרן קיימת: הפסד, הוא השחוק שמפסיד בו אדם מעותיו וכבודו. ומבטל ימיו. ואם ירויח קורי עכביש יארוג. ואשם הוא. אשם אשם! מאוס, הוא מה שנאכל: כבוד, הוא שמלתו לעורו. לכן לבשו כפי השגתכם. אכלו פחות מהשגתכם רק כדי מחייתכם. מאסו השחוק והתרחקו מן השוחקים. זרעו לצדקה יותר מכדי השגתכם. וקצרו לפי חסד!

ראו חיים עם חברתכם ואשת נעוריכם. ואל תגעו בשל זולתכם. כי רבים חללים הפילה

[77] B על דרך.
[78] B דעו.

---

[62] This combination of the society of friends and the love of wife, as conditions of a happy life, is directly derived from Maimonides, *Guide*, iii, ch. 49.

mighty host are her slain."[63] Imagine that ye had been in Noah's ark, and be comforted. Never excite desire, and when in the course of nature it comes upon you, satisfy it in the manner ordained by moral rule, to raise up offspring, and perpetuate the human race. Though it is not meet that ye should be dominated by your wives or reveal to them secrets placed in your keeping,[64] you must honor your wives, for they are your honor. "All glorious is the King's daughter within the palace."[65] Serve those who love you, and those near unto you, with your person and your substance, according to the good hand of the Lord upon you. But take heed lest ye serve them with your soul, for that is the divine portion![66]

[63] Prov. 7.26.

[64] Lit.: "the mysteries of your heart". Cf. Micah 7.8.

[65] Ps. 45.14, often used by moralists to typify the home as woman's sphere.

[66] A fine caution, finely expressed. Ardent devotion to the cause of one's family and friends may tempt one to sacrifice ideals. Cf. the Sifra on Levit. 19. 3; T. B. Baba Mezi'a 32a. Closely parallel to some of the sentiments in the latter sections of this Testament, are the views of Maimonides as expressed in the *Guide*, chs. 8, 38, 48, of Part III, and in the passages cited there by Maim. in cross-reference to his other works.

ועצומים כל הרוגיה. חשבו כאשר הייתם בתבת נח ותתנחמו. ואף בשלכם בסדר ובמשפט.[79] להעמיד זרע ולהתמיד הבריאות: הנה האש היושב עליו יכוה. והמשכיל יתחמם נגדו ויגע בו לעת הצורך. ויקבל ממנו תועלת. הניחו לרצון שירדפכם ואתם לא תרדפוהו: כבדו את נשיכם כי הם כבודכם. אל תרפו מהם מוסר ולא תמשילון עליכם. כבודן פנימה. במעט ראותם ימעט הזיקם. אל תגלו להם מסתורי לבכם: עבדו אוהביכם וקרוביכם בגופכם ומאודכם. כיד ה׳ הטובה עליכם. רק השמרו מאד פן תעבדון בנפשכם כי הוא חלק אלהי!

[79] B כסדר ומשפט.

קצור ההנהגה אשר תקן הר׳ ר׳ אשר

EXTRACTS FROM THE "RULE" DRAWN UP BY R. ASHER

VI

EXTRACTS FROM THE "RULE"

Drawn up by R. Asher

Asher son of Yeḥiel (known as the "Rosh" from the initials of the words Rabbenu Asher) was born in Germany c. 1250; he migrated to Spain, where he died in 1327. The work on which his fame rests is his compendium of the halakic parts of the Talmud (see *J.E.*, ii, 182). But he was author of much else, including the "Rule" or "Rules", from which some extracts are printed in this volume. Sometimes the "Rule" is described as "*Paths of Life*" (cf. Zunz, *Zur Geschichte und Literatur*, Berlin, 1845, p. 128). It is also known as "Rule for Health of the Soul" (MS. Ha. cited below).

The Rule differs in extent in various texts. The fullest form consists of two parts with distinct numberings. Part I contains 23 short paragraphs, the first of which enjoins the payment of a tithe of all profits. See the full statement on this subject in Judah ben Asher's Testament (p. 192 below). Part II consists of 131 or 132 paragraphs, mostly short.

Apart from the question of the 23 paragraphs of Part I (which are sometimes omitted, sometimes transposed to the end of Part II), the Rule as contained in Part II is not a unity. Thus §§ 1 to 24 are in the third person; §§ 25 to 46 are in alphabetical sequence; §§ 47 to end (like the alphabetical section) are in the second person. The Aleppo edition of 1875 contains only 52 paragraphs. The interesting MS. now at Jew's College (Cat. Hirschfeld, No.

קצור ההנהגה אשר תקן הר' ר' אשר[1]

אשר בן יחיאל (הנודע בשם רא"ש-ראשי תיבות של רבינו אשר) נולד באשכנז בערך שנת ו' לאלף הששי; גלה לספרד ונפטר שם בשנת פ"ח. חבורו היותר מפורסם הוא קצור ההלכות על התלמוד הנודע בשם „פסקי הרא"ש" (עיין באנציקלופדיה היהודית האנגלית, כרך שני, דף קפ"ב). אבל הוא חבר גם ספרים אחרים, ביניהם ה„הנהגה" או ה„הנהגות" אשר קצור ממנה נדפס בכרך שלפנינו. יש אשר ה„הנהגה" נקראת „ארחות חיים" (ראה צונץ, צור געשיכטע אונד ליטע־ראטור, ברלין תר"ה, דף קכ"ח), ונודעת היא גם בשם „הנהגה לבריאות הנפש" (כ"י האלבערשטאם המובא להלן).

ההנהגה שונה במדתה בנוסחאות שונים. בתכנה המלא יש לה שני חלקים, וכל חלק מסתעף לסעיפים מיוחדים. החלק הראשון מכיל כ"ג סעיפים קצרים, והראשון מהם מזהיר על הפרשת מעשר מכל מיני רוח. הענין הזה נידן באריכות בצואת יהודה בן אשר (להלן דף 192). החלק השני הוא בן קל"א או קל"ב סעיפים, רובם קצרים.

מלבד השאלה ע"ד כ"ג הסעיפים של החלק הראשון (אשר יש שהם נשמטים לגמרי, ויש שהם נדחים לסוף החלק השני), ההנהגה כפי שהיא מופיעה בחלק השני איננה חטיבה שלמה בפני עצמה. כן הסעיפים א'-כ"ד הם בלשון נסתר; כ"ה-מ"ו ערוכים בסדר אלף בית; מ"ז עד גמירא (כמו החלק האלפביתי) הם בלשון נוכח. המהדורה של אחלב תרל"ה מכילה רק נ"ב סעיפים. כ"י חשוב הנמצא כעת בבית מדרש הרבנים בלונדון

[1] For title, and plan of citation see p. 119.

247, 5, here called Hb.) contains, with other matter, most of the negative precepts of the Rule. But they are arranged in an order which suggests that the copyist of one or the other version read a double-columned page vertically instead of horizontally.

It is not specifically stated that the Rule is a Testament. But it is so described by Zunz, Güdemann (*Quellenschriften*, Berlin 1891, p. 22), and Bäck (in Winter u. Wuensche, *Die Jüdische Litteratur*, Trier, 1896, iii, 636).

The variations in order indicated above, justify the action of Zunz, who extracted sentences and arranged them in his own order. The same plan has been adopted here. Zunz's selection has been followed, though not exactly.

The Hebrew editions represent two types of text: one is contained in the Venice edition of 1578 and the Mantua edition of 1623 (here named A and L); the other is contained in the Venice edition of 1616 and the Frankfort edition of 1717 (here named B and D). In the Metz edition of 1767 the work is arranged into seven parts for daily reading, the whole Rule would thus be read once a week. The basis of the text used in the present volume is A, but the other editions have been consulted, and use has been made of the MS. Hb. as well as of Ha., which is bound in the same codex (§ 10).

These are the things to which thou must give heed, if thou wouldst depart from the snares of death, and bask in the light of life!

Be not prone to enter into quarrels; beware of oppressing fellow-men whether in money or word. Never feel envy or hate. Keep far from

(רשימת הירשפעלד, נומר 5, 247, מכונה פה Hb) מכיל יחד עם כתבים אחרים רוב המצוות השליליות של ההנהגה, אבל הן מסודרות בסדר כזה הנותן לנו טעם להחליט שהמעתיק של הנוסח האחד או השני קרא עמוד בעל שתי צלעות לאורך ולא לרוחב.

לא נאמר בפירוש שההנהגה היא צואה, אבל צונץ, גידעמאן (קוועללענשריפטען, ברלין תרנ"א, דף כ"ב), ובעק (בספרם של ווינטער ווינשע, דיא אידישע ליטעראטור, טריער תרנ"ו, כרך שלישי, דף תרל"ו) מכנים אותה כך.

השינוים בסדר הנזכרים למעלה מצדיקים את מעשהו של צונץ אשר לקט פסוקים ויסדר אותם בסדר המיוחד לו. בדרך זה הלכתי גם אני: החזקתי בסדר הלקוט של צונץ, אף כי לא בדיוק גמור.

המהדורות העבריות מציגות שני מיני נוסח: האחד נמצא בהוצאת ויניציה של"ח ובהוצאת מנטובה שפ"ג (נקראות פה A, L), השני נמצא בהוצאת ויניציה שע"ו ובהוצאת פרנקפורט תע"ז (נקראות פה D, B). במהדורת מעץ תקכ"ז ההנהגה היא מסודרת בשבעה חלקים לקריאת יום יום, באופן שכל ההנהגה נקראת פעם אחת בשבוע. הנוסח בכרך שלפנינו נוסד על A, אבל חזרתי גם על המהדורות האחרות, והשתמשתי בכ"י Hb וגם בכ"י Ha הכרוך באותו קודקס (10 §).

ואלה הדברים שיזהר האדם בהם לסור ממוקשי מות ולאור באור החיים:

אל תצא לריב מהר. ותזהר מאונאת הבריות. הן בממון הן בדברים. ומקנאתם ומשנאתם:

oaths and the iniquity of vows[1], from laughter[2] and anger which confuse alike the spirit and the mind. Use not the name of God for vain purposes or in foul places. Rely not on the broken reed of human support, make not gold thy hope[3], for therein lies the first step to idolatry. Rather distribute thy money where the Lord so wills, He can make good thy deficit! 'Tis a fine and right course to think little of thy virtues and much of thy vices; to magnify the mercies of Him who made thee and provideth thy sustenance in due season. Act not aright from hope of reward, nor avoid the wrong from fear of punishment; but serve from love. Esteem the utterance of thy money as of less import than the utterance of thy words; issue no base coin from thy lips, weigh thy words in the balance of thy judgment. Hide behind the walls of thy heart what is said in thy presence, even though thou be not pledged to confidence. If thou hearest the same report from another, say not: "I have heard it already!"

Habituate thyself to wake at dawn, and to leave thy couch at the song of the birds[3a]. Rise not as a sluggard, but with eagerness to serve thy Maker! Be not a drunkard or a glutton, lest thou forget thy Creator and fall into sin. Look

[1] Cf. T. B. Nedarim 22a.

[2] So Zunz renders.The author means that lack of seriousness which reveals itself in frivolity and insincerity.

[3] Zunz: "*Lebenshoffnung.*" Cf. Job 31.24.

[3a] Eccles. 12.4.

ותתרחק מן השבועות ומעון[2] הנדרים. מן השחוק ומן הכעס. כי מבלבל רוחו ודעתו של אדם: ואל תוציא שם שמים לבטלה. ולא במקום מטונף: הסר ממך משענת הקנה הרצוץ משענת בני אדם. ואל תשים זהב כסלך. כי זאת תחלת עבודת אלילים. ופזר ממונך באשר הוא רצונו. כי בידו למלאות חסרונך: טוב וישר לך להמעיט בעיניך פעולותיך הטובות. ולהגד״ל פשעיך. ולהרבות חסדי בוראך ויוצרך מבטן ונותן אכלך בעתו. ואל תהיה משמש על מנת לקבל פרס בעשותך מצותיו. ואל תרחק מן העבירות מפני העונש. רק עבוד מאהבה: ותקל בעיניך הוצאת ממונך מהוצאת דבריך. ופיך אל ימהר להוציא דבר רע עד אשר תשקלהו במאזני שכלך: גם על הדברים אשר ידברו לפניך שלא על דרך סוד טומנם בקירות לבך. גם אם תשמענו מאחר אל תאמר כבר שמעתי זה:[3]

ותרגיל את עצמך להקיץ בהנץ החמה. ולקול הצפור קום ממטתך: אל תקום כאיש עצל. כי אם בזריזות כדי לעבוד ליוצרך: אל תהי בסובאי יין בזוללי בשר פן תשכח בוראך ותחטא:[4] אל תשים

[2] So A. Some other texts read רמן.

[3] §§ 8, 23, 24, 28, 29, 34, 52, 30, 41.

[4] So Hb. D omits with A and C. B reads ותחליא.

not at him who is above thee in riches but at him who is below; turn thine eyes to thy superior, not to thy inferior, in the service and fear of God. Rejoice when thou sufferest reproof, hear counsel and receive instruction[4]. Exalt not thyself over thy fellow creatures, but be humble of spirit, and like the dust on which all tread. Speak not insolence with a haughty neck[5], lifting high thy forehead, thereby rejecting the fear of Heaven. Never do in private what thou wouldst be ashamed to do in public, and say not: "Who will see me?"

Raise not thine hand against thy neighbor. Circulate no false reports; slander no man. When men address thee in unseemly fashion, be not too apt with insolent retort. Let no man hear thee in the street, bellow not like a beast, but let thy voice be soft. Put not thy fellow man to the blush in public. The first of all fences against wronging thy fellow man is the avoidance of covetousness. Never be weary of making friends, consider a single enemy as one too many. If thou hast a faithful friend, hold fast to him; let him not go, for he is a precious possession. But entice not friendship by adulation and hypocrisy,[6] and speak not with a double heart! Retain not thine anger against a fellow-man for a

[4] Prov. 19.20.

[5] Ps. 75.6.

[6] Zunz: "aber Schmeichelei und Falschheit halte fern von ihm."

עיניך למי שעלה לעושר יותר ממך. אלא למי שתחתך: אל תבט למי שהוא קטן ממך בעבודה וביראה אלא לגדול ממך: שמח בשמעך תוכחת. ושמע עצה וקבל מוסר: אל תתגאה על הבריות. ותהיה שפל רוח וכעפר שהכל דשים בו: אל תדבר בצוואר עתק. ואל תרים[5] מצח שלא לקבל עליך יראת שמים: אל תעשה בסתר מה שתתבייש בגלוי. ואל תאמר מי יראני?[6]

אל תרים ידך על חבירך. אל תוציא דבה ולשון הרע על שום בריה: אל תהי נבהל להשיב בעזות למי שאמר דברים אשר לא טובים: אל תשמיע בחוץ קולך. ואל תהי צווח כבהמה. ודבריך יהיו בנחת: אל תלבין פני חבירך ברבים: וראש כל הגדרים שישמור האדם את עיניו מכל דבר שאינו שלו: אל תרף ידך מלבקש ריעים ואוהבים.[7] ואל ימעט לפניך שונא אחד: אל תרף ידך לקנות לך חבר נאמן. ושמור אותו. ואל תאבדהו כי טוב: אל תפתה את חבירך בשפתי חלקות ובחניפות. ואל תדבר בלב ולב:[8] אל תחזיק כעסך נגד חבירך

[5] B. D תעיז.

[6] §§ 70, 48, 95, 59, 81, 45, 47, 66, 63, 109.

[7] Hb ואהובים. [8] D. בלא לב.

single day, but humble thyself and ask forgiveness. Let not thy heart be high, saying: "I am the injured party, let him make the first overtures." But, every night before thou retirest to rest, forgive whoever has offended thee. If men curse or revile thee, answer not a word, be of the insulted, (not of the insulters)![7]

Keep thy feet evenly in the track,[8] holding thyself firmly in the middle path in the satisfaction of thy appetites. So, be neither accessible to all nor a recluse from all. In all thy moral characteristics seek the mean, turning neither to right nor left.[9] Rejoice not overmuch, for remember that thy life is a breath; formed from the dust, thou wilt end with the worm! Be not offended at trifles, lest thou gather enemies without cause.[10] Pry not into other men's secrets. Be not overbearing towards the men of thy city; yield to the wishes of others. Will that which God wills; rejoice in thy portion, be it little or much; pray continually to God that He incline thine heart unto His testimonies. Never show ingratitude, but do honor to everyone who opens a door for thee to earn the necessaries of life.[11] Never utter a falsehood, but be faithful to all men, irrespective of creed. Be not slow to offer the greeting

[7] T. B. Shabbat 88b.

[8] Applying Prov. 4.26.

[9] On the "Mean" as ethical standard, see Maimonides, *Eight Chapters*, ch. 4; *De'ot* i, 4.

[10] Zunz: "du machst dir unnöthig Feinde."

[11] Zunz: "Bleibe dankbar jedem, der dir zu deinem Brote geholfen."

יום אחד. ותכנע לפניו לבקש ממנו מחילה. אל[9] יגבה לבך לאמר, יש לי עון ממנו. הוא יבא לבקש לי מחילה קודם: ותמחול בכל לילה קודם שתישן לכל מי שחטא לך בדברים: ואם יקללוך בני אדם או יחרפוך. אל תשיב להם מאומה. אלא תהי מן הנעלבים:[10]

פלס מעגל רגליך לישר עצמך בדרך בינוני במאכל ובמשתה. אל תהי הפקר ולא חדל אשים.[11] ובכל מדותיך אל תט ימין ושמאל: אל תרבה לשמוח. וזכור כי רוח חייך. ואתה נוצר[12] מעפר ואחריתך רמה: אל תהי קפדן לדבר מועט נגד שום אדם. פן תלקט שונאים על חנם: אל תהי להוט לדעת הסתרים שבין אדם לחבירו: אל תהי סרבן אל אנשי עירך. ובטל רצונך מפני רצון אחרים: רצה כאשר ירצה יוצרך. שמח בחלקך אם מעט ואם הרבה. והתחנן לפניו תמיד להטות לבבך אל עדותיו: אל תהי כפוי טובה. וכבד כל מי שפתח לך פתח לבקש די ספוקך: אל תוציא מפיך דבר שקר וכזב. ותהיה נאמן[13] לכל אדם. אל תתעצל

[9] From here till end of sentence is derived from Hb.
[10] §§ 82–86, 20, 90, 102, 103, 62, 11 (A), 22.
[11] Ha has been adopted.
[12] Hb נוצרת. [13] Hb אמיתי.

of peace to all, be they Jew or Gentile; and never give a fellow-man cause for resentment.

Show invariable hospitality to wayfarers; welcome them with a smiling face. When they take their leave, provide them with food for the journey, accompany them for a space[12], let them depart with a cheery farewell. Break not thy body by intemperance, thou mayest be betrayed into indecent speech and suffer thereafter remorse. Never be angry with thy wife; if thou put her off from thee with thy left hand, delay not to draw her to thee again with thy right hand![13]

Be ever responsive to the call of charity.[14] Never contribute less than a half shekel annually, and at one time. Give every month and every week the full amount that thou canst spare. On no day let there be lacking some small gift before prayer. Pay the "continual offering" every Friday. When thy means reach a tithable amount, set aside the tithe. Thus wilt thou possess an ever-ready store, at hand for all occasions of loving-kindness, whether to the living or the dead, whether to the poor or the rich.[15]

Enjoy nor food nor drink without benediction before and after, tendering thanks to Him who

[12] See e. g. Mishnah Soṭah 9.6.

[13] T. B. Soṭah 47a.

[14] Applying Deut. 16.20.

[15] The family of Asher ben Yeḥiel—the author of this Testament—was distinguished for the popularization of the tithing practice in the early part of the fourteenth century. See Abrahams, *Jewish Life in the Middle Ages*, p. 320. Cf. p. 192, in present volume. The last clauses

להקדים שלום לכל אדם ואפילו לעכו״ם. ואל תכעיס לשום אדם:[14]

אל יהיו פניך זעומים נגד עוברים ושבים. וקבל אותם בפנים מאירים: אל תשכח להעניק להם צידה לדרך ולעשות לויה להם. ותנחמם בדברים: אל תשבור גופך להשתכר מיין. פן תהיה מגונה ותנבל את פיך ותתחרט: אל תכעס באשתך. ואם רחקת אותה בשמאל, קרב אותה בימין בלא איחור:[15]

צדק צדק תרדוף. ואל תחסר ממחצית השקל בכל שנה בפעם אחת. ובכל חדש ובכל שבוע כפי מסת ידך. ובכל יום לא תחסר מתנה מועטת לכל הפחות קודם תפלה. ותפרע התמיד בכל יום הששי. ואם הגיע למעשר תתן. ויהיה טרף בביתך בכל אשר תמצא ידך לגמול. הן לחיים הן למתים. הן לעניים הן לעשירים:[16]

מכל מאכל אשר תאכל, ומכל משקה אשר תשתה, אל תהנה בלא ברכה תחלה וסוף. ותזהר

14 Another reading is לשום עכו״ם, §§ 43, 74, 107, 108, 120, 69, 129–131, 104.

15 §§ 57, 58, 122, 123.

16 §§ 68, 14 (A).

hath satisfied thy longing soul. Cover thy head when thou namest God.[16] Let thine innermost being be stirred when thou speakest of Him; be not among those of whom the Scripture says: "With their mouth and with their lips they honour Me, but they have removed their heart far from me."[17] Wash thy hands before prayer and meals. Sanctify thyself in all things; never behave with levity; let the fear of God be upon thee. Before meals, and before retiring to rest, regularly read the Torah, and derive from its pages topics for table-talk. Direct thy household in accordance with the Law, in all matters needing direction.

Pray not as a matter of rote, for prayer is the service of the heart.[18] If thy child address thee, and speak not from his heart, art thou not angry? How then shalt thou, insignificant wite, act in presence of the King of the universe? Be not as a servant to whom hath been committed for his own good an important work and he hath spoilt it! How shall such a one stand before the King? How excellent would it be to ask pardon for praying "Pardon us"[19] without sincerity! Relax not confession for thy sins mor-

in the paragraph may be differently rendered if we put a full stop at בביתך. The sense will then be that if a man gives a tithe, God provides sustenance for his household. The rest of the sentence will be an independent thought, calling for constant acts of charity and love.

[16] T. B. Shabbat 56b.

[17] Isa. 29.13.

[18] T. B. Ta'anit 2a.

לברך את בוראך שהשביע נפש שוקקה: וכסה ראשך כשתזכור את ה׳. ויהמו מעיך[17] מדי דברך בו. ואל תהיה כאמור, בפיו ובשפתיו כבדוני ולבו רחוק ממני: נטול ידיך לתפלה ולאכילה. וקדש עצמך בכל דבריך. ואל תנהג עצמך בקלות ראש. ויהי מורא שמים עליך: קבע עתים לתורה קודם אכילה ושכיבה. ודברת בם על שולחנך. והזהרת בם אנשי ביתך להדריכם על פי התורה בכל הדברים הצריכים אזהרה[18]:

כוון בתפלתך. כי התפלה היא עבודה שבלב. ואם בנך ידבר לך ולא מלבו הלא יחר לך. ומה תעשה טפה סרוחה לפני מלכו של עולם? ולא תהיה כעבד שמסרו לו מלאכה נכבדה לטובתו וחבלה.[19] ואיך יעמוד לפני המלך? ומה טוב לבקש סליחה על אמרך סלח לנו בלא כוונה: וידוי על

[17] This seems the true reading. Usually the text is ויזמו עיניך. Ha has מעיך.

[18] §§ 38, 22, 39, 40, 44.

[19] In place of this and the previous words, Ha reads לטובה ומסרה משובשת וחבולה.

---

[19] In the eighteen benedictions of the daily liturgy. Similarly with the rest of the sentences; they refer to passages in the prayers.

ning and evening, nor omit to remember Zion and Jerusalem with a broken heart and bitter tears. And when thou recitest the verse which bids thee love the Lord thy God,[20] speak as one ready to deliver up life and substance for His sanctification, thus fulfilling in thy person the words of the Singer: "For Thy sake are we killed every day."[21] Yet have a whole-hearted confidence in Him, and believe in His special providence, for the eyes of the Lord run to and fro throughout the whole earth, and He regards all the ways of a man.[22] Day and night let thy lips make mention of Him. When thou liest down luxuriate in His love, and in thy dream thou wilt find it. When thou awakest thou wilt delight in Him, and He will direct thy paths. So fulfil all thy virtuous acts in the spirit of humbly walking before Him. This is the service which He has chosen, this the service acceptable in His sight!

[20] Deut. 6.5. Cf. Sifre on the text.

[21] Ps. 44.23.

[22] II Chr. 16.9; Job 34.21

עונותיך ערב ובקר אל יחסר. וזכרון ציון וירושלם בשברון לב ובדאגה ובדמעה: והסכם באומרך את ה׳ אלהיך וגו׳ למסור גופך וממונך על קדושתו. ובזה תקיים בעצמך דברי המשורר. כי עליך הורגנו כל היום: ותבטח בה׳ בכל לבבך. ותאמין בהשגחתו פרטית. כי עיניו משוטטות בכל הארץ ועיניו על כל דרכי איש: יומם ולילה זכרו מפיך אל ימוש. בשכבך תשגה באהבתו ובחלומך[20] תמצאנה. והקיצות בו תשתעשע. והוא יישר אורחותיך: ותקיים בהצנע לכת[21] מעשיך הטובים כי היא עבודת ה׳ הנבחרת והרצויה לפניו:[22]

[20] So Ha. The usual reading is: ובקומך ובהלוכך.

[21] So Ha. Usual reading: בהצנע לכלכל.

[22] §§ 36, 31, 25, 26, 35, 23 (A).

ספר המוסר הנקרא יורה דעה
לר׳ יוסף אבן כספי

GUIDE TO KNOWLEDGE
BY JOSEPH IBN KASPI

VII

GUIDE TO KNOWLEDGE

By Joseph Ibn Kaspi

Kaspia (from kesef "silver") is the Hebrew equivalent of L'Argentière, a city of Languedoc, where Joseph (called also Bonafos) ibn Kaspi was born about the year 1280 (H. Gross, *Gallia Judaica*, Paris, 1897, pp. 67 seq.). He travelled much, and he and his children were separated. At the time when he wrote his Testament, in the autumn of 1332, he himself was in Valencia; he had a daughter in Perpignan; an elder son (Abba Mari to whom he dedicated his Commentary on Maimonides' *Guide*) at Barcelona; and a younger son (Solomon, to whom the Testament was addressed) at Tarascon. But though a wanderer; though at the age of fifty he describes himself as old; and though he is said to have suffered from the Pastoureaux persecution of 1320; Ibn Kaspi was not unhappy. He possessed adequate means, was everywhere respected, and, despite his lament as to the dearth of congenial friends, he wrote many works, of which a full list may be found in *J.E.*, iii, p. 600.

Most of his books had to wait long for publication. His Commentary on the *Guide* appeared in 1848, some others of his works followed, and then from 1903 onwards I. Last printed a long series of Ibn Kaspi's treatises, including his much discussed Metaphysics (Ha-Sod).

The Testament, called "*Book of Admonition*" (ספר המוסר) and also "*Guide to Knowledge*" (יורה דעה), was

ז

ספר המוסר הנקרא יורה דעה לר' יוסף אבן כספי

כספיא (ממלת „כסף") היא העתקה עברית של ארג'נטיער, עיר בחבל לאנגעדוק בצרפת, אשר שם ראה יוסף (הידוע גם בשם טוב עלם) אבן כספי אור חיים בערך שנת מ' לאלף הששי (ה' גראס, Gallia Judaica, פריז תרנ"ז, דף ס"ז וכו'). אבן כספי נסע הרבה ויהי רחוק מביתו ומבניו. בשעה שכתב את צואתו, בסתיו של שנת צ"ב, הוא בעצמו היה בבלנסיה, בתו היתה בפרפיניאן, בנו בכורו (אבא מרי, אשר אליו הקדיש את פירושו ל„מורה נבוכים" של הרמב"ם) היה בברצלונא, ובנו הצעיר (שלמה, אשר אליו נשלחה הצואה הזאת) היה בטרסקון. אבל אף כי היה נע ונד ובשנת החמשים לחייו כבר התאמר לזקן, ואף כי לפי השמועה סבל מרדיפות הרועים בשנת פ', בכ"ז לא היה מזלו של אבן כספי כ"כ רע. כפי הנראה היה איש בעל אמצעים נאותים וחביב על הבריות בכל מקום שהוא, ולמרות תלונתו כי רעים נאמנים הם יקרי המציאות עלה בידו לחבר חבורים הרבה (רשימה מלאה מהם נמצאת באנציקלופדיה היהודית האנגלית, כרך שלישי, דף ת"ר).

רוב ספריו עבר עליהם זמן רב ללא דפוס. פירושו אל ה„מורה" הופיע רק בשנת תר"ח, אחריו באו איזה מחבוריו האחרים, ומשנת תרס"ג ואילך הדפיס יצחק לאסט שורה ארוכה של מחברות אבן כספי, ביניהן „ס' הסוד" על מה שלמעלה מן הטבע, אשר עורר ויכוחים הרבה.

הצואה, המכונה „ספר המוסר" וגם „יורה דעה", נדפסה

printed in part by Benjacob in 1846, but the first full edition was that of E. Aschkenasi (in his טעם זקנים, Frankfurt a. M., 1854). A second edition appeared in Prag, 1857 (in E. Bondi's *Hebräische Chrestomathie*, ed. W. Pascheles). A third edition was that of I. Last (in עשרה כלי כסף vol. ii, p. 59, Pressburg, 1903).

For the present edition, the edds. of Aschkenasi (A) and Last (L) have been consulted, and the MS. of the London Beth Hamidrash (Cat. Neubauer No. 40 fol. 26b), and the Halberstam MS. now in the Jews' College, London (Cat. Hirschfeld, No. 279 fol. 23b) have been freshly collated. These MSS. are referred to in the critical notes as B. and H. respectively. Except that H. has no introduction and opens with Chapter i, it agrees generally with B., though it differs in detail.

The main theme of Ibn Kaspi's Testament, as of others of his works, is the vindication of philosophy. The well-known controversy as to the metaphysical writings of Maimonides was still keen, and later on Ibn Kaspi was assailed by advocates of the opposite view to his. In particular his Testament was attacked by J. Jabez, the fifteenth-century author of what Steinschneider rightly describes as an Apology of Theology against Philosophy (אור החיים, Ferrara 1554). In the ninth chapter of that work, Jabez uses strong terms, denouncing Ibn Kaspi as one who ridiculed the study of the Talmud. Jabez can hardly have had the full text of the Testament before him. For Ibn Kaspi was no bigot. He urges the claims of science, but he also eulogizes the Talmud. He agrees that the end of life is the performance of the Law, and the very incident which rouses the ire of Jabez shows Ibn Kaspi to have been himself a punctilious observer of rabbinic rules. What he really contended for was the

לקטועין ע"י בךיעקב בשנת תר"ו, אבל במלואה נדפסה ראשונה ע"י אליעזר אשכנזי (בספרו „טעם זקנים", פרנקפורט על נהר מאין תרי"ד). מהדורה שניה הופיעה בפראג בשנת תרי"ז (בספר „העברעאישע כריסתומטיה" של בונדי, הוצאת וואלף פאשעלעס). מהדורה שלישית היתה זו של יצחק לאסט (ב„עשרה כלי כסף", חלק שני, דף נ"ט, פרעסבורג תרס"ג).

למטרת ההוצאה שלפנינו השתמשתי במהדורות אשכנזי (A) ולאסט (L), ועברתי עוד הפעם על הכ"י של בית המדרש בלונדון (רשימת נייבויער, נומר 40, עמוד כ"ו:) וכת"י האל־ברשטאם הנמצא כעת בבית מדרש הרבנים בלונדון (רשימת הירשפעלד, נומר 279, עמוד כ"ג:). בהערותי בשולי הגליון נקרא הכ"י הראשון B והכ"י השני H. מלבד אשר H אין לו הקדמה והוא פותח בפרק א' הוא מתאים בכללו אל B, אף כי שונה הוא בפרטים.

הנושא הראשי של צואת אבן כספי, כמו של חבוריו האחרים, היא ההגנה על הפילוסופיה. המחלוקת הידועה ע"ד ספרי הרמב"ם העיוניים היתה עוד חדה ושנונה, וגם בזמן מאוחר התנפלו על אבן כספי כל אלה שהתנגדו לדעותיו. ביחוד נעשתה צואתו מטרה לחצי י. יעבץ שחי במאה החמש עשרה ויחבר מה ששטיינשניידר קורא בצדק התנצלות התיאולוגיה כנגד הפילוסופיה („אור החיים", פירארא ש"יד). בפרק התשיעי של הספר הזה מדבר יעבץ קשות כנגד אבן כספי וממיט עליו אשם שעשה את למוד התלמוד לשחוק ולקלס. אי אפשר שנוסח הצואה במלואו היה לפני עיניו, כי הלא הצביעות לא היתה ממדותיו של אבן כספי. אמנם דורש הוא עיון חכמה, אבל הוא מהלל ומשבח גם את התלמוד. מסכים הוא שקיום המצוות הוא תכלית החיים, ואותו המאורע עצמו המעלה קצפו של יעבץ מוכיח שאבן כספי היה מדקדק מאד בשמירת דיני התלמוד. מה שהתעצם להוכיח היתה החובה

duty to seek a philosophical justification of religion, which he based on certain fundamental principles, themselves precepts of the Law. Like Jewish writers of the pre-Christian age, Ibn Kaspi claimed that Aristotle derived his ideas from Jewish sources. He also credited the medieval legend that Aristotle at the end of his life recanted those views which ran counter to the Hebrew Scriptures (Cf. *Mind*, July, 1888; *Monatsschrift*, xlv, 453).

Another ground of attack on Ibn Kaspi was, curiously enough, his lucidity. Kalonymos, the famous Italian poet, while holding Ibn Kaspi in high esteem, blamed him for writing so as to disturb the "simple faith" of the masses (See *Kalonymos' Sendschreiben an Joseph Kaspi*, ed. Perles, Munich, 1879, pp. 3 and 6). Finally Ibn Kaspi was denounced as one who accepted the Aristotelian doctrine of the eternity (as against the creation) of the world. But he does not seem to have differed on this point from the object of his worship—Maimonides, the "holy", the "perfect", the "light of the world", as he delights to call him.

It is worth noting that Jabez quotes an otherwise unknown Testament by a disciple of Solomon ben Adereth: who applies to the philosophers the following biblical passages: "Shall a man go to the coals and his feet not be burnt? Shall children eat sour fruit and their teeth not be set on edge " (Prov. 6.28 and Ez. 18.2.)

Ibn Kaspi had his detractors (cf. *J. E.* loc. cit.), but he also won many admirers. In 1372 Isaac Lattes spoke favorably of his commentaries on the Bible (see Neubauer, *Mediaeval Jewish Chronicles*, ii, 239). Moses Rieti, in the early part of the fifteenth century, places him in Paradise in the good company of the Ibn Tibbons and the authors

לבקש הצטדקות פילוסופית בעד הדת, ואותה בסס על עקרים יסודיים ידועים שכשהם לעצמם הם הם מצוות התורה. כמו סופרים יהודיים שחיו לפני התקופה הנוצרית טען אבן כספי שאריסטו קבל את דעותיו ממקורות יהודיים, ויאמין גם בהאגדה של ימי הבינים שבקץ ימי חייו התחרט אריסטו על דעותיו המתנגדות לכתבי הקדש (ראה את העתון Mind לירח יולי 1888; מאנאטסשריפט, כרך ארבעים וחמשה, דף תנ"ג).

יש גם טעם אחר, טעם נפלא חזר, להתנפלות זו על אבן כספי, וזה הוא צחות לשונו ובהירות סגנונו. קלונימוס, המשורר האיטלקי המפורסם, אף כי הוקיר מאד את ערכו של אבן כספי, בכ"ז האשים אותו בעד נטיתו לכתוב בסגנון העלול לבטל את „האמונה הפשוטה" של ההמון (ראה קלונימוס, זענד־שרייבען אן יוסף כספי, הוצאת פרלס, מינכען תרל"ט, דף ג' וגם ו'). לאחרונה הלשינו עליו על אבן כספי שהאמין בעקר אריסטו של נצחיות העולם (כנגד בריאת העולם של היהודים); אבל, כנראה, לא שנה בזה ממורו אשר העריץ, הרמב"ם ה„קדוש", ה„מושלם", „אור העולם", כמו שהוא מכנהו בחבה. נחוץ להעיר עוד שיעבץ מביא צואה בלתי נודעת מתלמיד של שלמה בן אדרת, הקורא על הפילוסופים את הכתובים האלה של כתבי הקדש: „אם יהלך איש על הגחלים ורגליו לא תכוינה?" (משלי ו' כ"ח); „אבות יאכלו בסר ושני הבנים תקהינה (יחזקאל י"ח ב').

אבן כספי היו לו מגנים (ראה את האנציקלופדיה היהודית האנגלית, במקום הנזכר לעיל), אבל הוא רכש לו גם מכבדים ומעריצים רבים. בשנת קל"ב המליץ רבי יצחק לאטעס על פירושיו לספרי הקדש (ראה נייבויער, סדר החכמים וקורות הימים, כרך שני, דף רל"ט). בתחלת המאה החמש עשרה מיחד לו משה ריאטי מקום בגן עדן יחד עם יהודה ושמואל

of the Rokeaḥ and the Book of the Pious. Gross well sums up the truth about him when he says (*Gallia Judaica*, p. 68); "En effet, ses ouvrages ne contiennent pas que de l'argent pur, on y trouve aussi des scories, mais, dans tout se révèle un esprit net, pénétrant, épris de vérité."

Introduction

Saith Joseph ibn Kaspi: All my days I have toiled to live in the society of the wise, but I have found no rest. Twenty years ago, I became an exile to a place reputed for learning. I dwelt in the uttermost part of the sea, I crossed to Egypt, where I visited the College of that renowned and perfect sage, the Guide.[1] I found there the fourth and fifth generations of his holy seed, all of them righteous, but none of them devoted to science. In all the Orient there were no scholars, and I applied to myself the text,[2] "Woe to them that go down to Egypt for help."

I returned to my country disappointed, after having spent five months in going and coming. Then I passed a considerable interval at home, studying philosophy, and the commentaries on the Pentateuch and the whole of the Bible. A day came when the spirit of the Lord moved me to search among the capitals of the West; so I travelled through Catalonia and Aragon, and at

[1] i. e. Maimonides, so called from the title of his book, *Guide of the Perplexed*.

[2] Isa. 39.1.

אבן תבון ומחברי ה„רוקח" ו„ספר החסידים". גראס חדר לתוך האמת באמרו עליו (Gallia Judaica, דף ס"ח): „באמת חבוריו מלאים כסף טהור, אף כי נמצאת בהם גם פסולת; אבל בכלם מתגלה לב טהור, חוקר ודורש, ומשועבד אל האמת".

אמר יוסף אבן כספי:[1] כל ימי יגעתי להתגדל[2] בין החכמים ומנוחה לא מצאתי. זה לי עשרים שנה גליתי למקום תורה לפי הנשמע. שכנתי באחרית ים. ירדתי מצרים[2a] בית מדרשו של הרב הגדול החכם השלם המורה. ומצאתי שם זרעו זרע קודש דור רביעי ובניהם חמישי. כלם צדיקים אבל בחכמות לא היו מתעסקים. וגם בכל המזרח[3] לא היו שם חכמים. וקראתי על עצמי הוי היורדים מצרים לעזרה:

ואשוב אל ארצי בבשת פנים. וכל זמן עמידתי בהליכה ובחזרה היו חמשה חדשים: אחר כן שקדתי ימים רבים בארצי ובביתי[4] בחכמות ובפרושי התורה והמקרא כולה: ויהי היום רוח ה' העירני לחפש בבירות[5] ארץ המערב. ואסובי[6] קטלוניא

[1] H omits the introduction and begins with פרק א.

[2] L omits. [2a] B בארץ מצרים.

[3] So B. L reads המורה or התורה suggesting the correction to המדינה. [4] L ובניתי. [5] B Omits. [6] B ואשוב.

this moment[3] I am living in the great city of Valencia. If the Quickener of the dead grant me life, I will again traverse the whole of Aragon and Spain. I will cross to Fez, for I have heard that it is a seat of learning. Wherever I may go, wealth and honor are with me, thanks be to God! Perchance once in my life-time I may happen upon a teacher or companion in my studies. Or the Lord may work a miracle for me and I may find a disciple after my mind, to whom I may bequeath my inmost thoughts and opinions, —weak and poor though they be. Therefore I have resolved, before departing to distant shores, to write this Admonition, and to despatch it to my younger son Solomon, who is settled in Tarascon. I hope that it may be a memorial constantly between his eyes, so that he may order his ways aright. Peradventure the spirit of God may carry me to a far-off land, or death may cut me off, and I and my son be found sinners.[4] This Admonition may prove useful also for the instruction of many of the inhabitants of the land. Therefore I have called it: *A Guide to Knowledge*, and in the help of God may I find support (to accomplish my purpose).—

Chapter I

Solomon, my son! Know thou the God of thy father and serve Him. He will cause thee to ride in His "second chariot"[5] and thine own conduct

[3] Autumn of 1332.

[4] The father because he failed to admonish, the son because of the father's neglect.

[5] i. e. in the angelic rank.

וארגון והנני היום העיר הגדולה בלנציאה[7]. ואם יחייני מחיה המתים אסוב עוד כל ארגון וספרד ואעבור פאס. כי שמעתי שמה ישבו[8] כסאות לחכמים: ובכל מקום אשר אני הולך עושר וכבוד אתי תהלה לאל. אולי פעם אחת בימי אעשה לי רב או אקנה לי חבר או בריאה יברא ה׳ תלמיד הגון אנחילנו ירושת סודותי ודעותי החלושים והדלים: לכן טרם ארחיק ללכת אמרתי בלבבי לעשות זה המוסר ולשלחו לשלמה בני צעירי[9] היושב טרשקון[10]. יהיה לו לזכרון בין עיניו תמיד והוא יישר אורחותיו. פן רוח ה׳ ישאני בארץ[11] רחוקה או יפסקני המות. והייתי אני ושלמה בני חטאים: ואולי יועיל זה המוסר להבין ולהורות לרבים מיושבי הארץ. ולכן קראתיו יורה דעה[12] ובהשם אעזור:

פרק א

שלמה בני! דע את אלהי אביך ועבדהו. והוא ירכיבך במרכבת המשנה אשר לו וגם המעשה[13]

[7] L בלנסייא. [8] L omits.
[9] So B. Other readings: A בעירי, L בחורי, W. בכורי.
[10] B טרשקו, L טרסקון. [11] L omits, adding from A.
[12] B omits these four words. [13] B, H omit.

must raise thee in its chariot[6], drawing thee as near as thy faculty avails unto Him. Even so David said to his son Solomon, "If thou seek Him He will be found of thee."[7]

Now, the knowledge of God is the primary precept of all our 613 laws, as may be seen from the texts enforcing this knowledge.[8] It is the basis of the four precepts enumerated by Maimonides at the beginning of his Code. He specifically terms them the Foundations of the Torah. These four[9] precepts are (1) to know that there is a First Cause, (2) to recognize that He is One, (3) to love Him, and (4) to fear Him. They are designated the Foundations of the Torah, for they are at once the purpose and the root of all the commandments, the observance of which is the whole end of man.

Chapter II

Beware, however, lest thou draw from this a wrong inference, arguing: "Seeing that these four precepts are root and end, what concern have I with the rest of the precepts? Surely it is good for me to lighten myself of the other 609 laws." God forbid that thou shouldst act thus! As the Lord liveth, *all* the precepts are of great profit,

[6] Or, according to the other reading, "and He will raise thee in His chariot," etc.

[7] I Chron. 28.9.

[8] E. g. Exod. 20.2, Deut. 7 9; Ibn Kaspi (or the copyist) confuses two texts.

[9] Maimonides really includes 10 precepts as the "Foundations". But the four to which Ibn Kaspi reduces them are not unjustifiably selected.

יעלה אותך במרכבתו להתקרב אליו בכל אשר בכחך. אך כמו שאמר דוד ע"ה לשלמה בנו[14] אם תדרשנו ימצא לך:

ודע כי ידיעת ה' הנכבד שזכרתי לך היא המצוה הראשיית לכל תרי"ג מצות שלנו כמו שכתוב וידעת את[15] ה' אלהיך. וזה יסוד לארבע המצות שסדר המורה בראש ס' המדע. וקראם יסודי התורה. והם לדעת שיש מצוי ראשון. ושהוא אחד. ולאהבו[16] וליראה ממנו. ונקראו אלה יסודי התורה כי הם תכלית ועיקר לכל המצות. וזה סוף כל האדם:

פרק ב

השמר לך פן יהיה עם לבבך בליעל לאמר. אחר שאלה הד' מצות הם העיקר והתכלית מה לי וליתר המצות? הלא טוב לי שאקל מעלי תר"ט[17] מצות! חלילה לך מעשות כדבר הזה: חי ה' כי יתר המצות[18] כולם מועילות תועלות גדולות מצד

14 L לבנו.

15 So the MSS. read.

16 A, L ולאהבה.

17 L תרינ.

18 A omits these three words.

both in and for themselves and as reinforcements of the four basic rules. Thou canst not truly fulfil these four, unless thou fulfillest all the rest. If thou becomest proficient in philosophy, thou wilt understand that man is compounded of body and soul, and that the rational faculty, which belongs to the soul, is itself partly practical, partly speculative. Neither of these can exist without the other, just as the soul cannot exist without the body. For this reason the Commandments are divided first into those which effect the well-being of the body and those which effect the well-being of the soul, and secondly into the practical and speculative.

Maimonides has fully explained this in his Code and Guide.[10] Our honored Sages were the first to point this out in several passages, and Aristotle expounded their words with perfect lucidity in his *Ethics*. The Greek philosopher lived during the Second Temple, and he learned from the Jewish Sages all the true things that he wrote. Nor do I remember that Aristotle departed from the tenets of the Rabbis except with regard to the eternity of the world and the question whether the sphere or the stars move. In the second case, the Rabbis admitted[11] that the heathen Sages had the correct opinion, [in the first Aristotle retracted his opinion]. And, in general, if thou livest and acquirest a knowledge of these matters, it will become clear to thee

[10] In the Hilkot Madda' and in the *Guide for the Perplexed*, e. g. III, ch. 27.

[11] T. B. Pesaḥim 94; Shabb. 54.

עצמם ומצד הישרתם לאלה הארבע. ולא תוכל לקיים אלה הארבע קיום אמיתי אלא בקיום כל המצות: ואם תזכה לדעת החכמות על השלמות. אז תבין כי האדם מורכב מגוף ומנפש. ותדע כי הכח הדברי מן הנפש ממנו מעשי וממנו עיוני. ואין לאחד מאלו השנים קיום בלעדי חבירו. וכן אין קיום לנפש בלעדי הגוף: ולכן נחלקו המצות תחלה לתקון הגוף ותקון הנפש ואחר למעשיות ולעיוניות:

וכבר ביאר זה המורה באור שלם בס' המדע וכן בס' המורה: וזכרו זה תחלה רבותינו המכובדים במקומות מפוזרים. ובאר דבריהם אריסטו בס' המדות ביאור שלם: כי בזמן בית שני היה זה החכם[19] ומהם למד בכל[20] מה שאמר אמת. ואין אני זוכר שיצא מגדר דבריהם רק בענין הקדמות ובענין מזלות חוזרין וגלגל קבוע[21] שהודו הם בעצמם שבזה[22] נצחו חכמי אומות לחכמי ישראל: ובכלל אם תחיה[23] ותזכה להבין הדברים

[19] L הדבר.

[20] So H, B. L and A read וכל.

[21] L גלגל חוזר ומזלות קבועים. H as in text but reverses order.

[22] H ובזה.

[23] L תרצה.

that not "in vain has the pen of the scribe made books!"[12]

Chapter III

I will give thee two simple illustrations in support of my injunction that thou must be diligent in fulfilling all the practical precepts.

The first example is this: Concerning the wearing of fringes the reason is given, "that ye may look upon it, and remember all the commandments of the Lord."[13] How, you may ask in bewilderment, can the sight of fringes on a garment call to mind all the Lord's commandments, among them the four named above? The reply is, Certainly this is so. Let me explain briefly, and in terms suited to thy youthful capacity. Man is not an angel that his reason should always be working perfectly. Nor is he a mule, that his reason should never be active at all. He may be termed hermaphrodite, metaphorically speaking, half angel, half mule. Hence neither angel nor mule was bidden to wear fringes! As our honored Rabbis said, God asked the angels, What have ye to do with the Torah?[14] Man, however, received this and similar commandments, because he occupies an intermediate position, with his mind sometimes active, sometimes quiescent. The investiture of the fringed garment does recall all the precepts, until ultimately he remembers that God, blessed be He,

[12] Jer. 8.8.

[13] Num. 15.39.

[14] T. B. Shabb. 88, Ber. 28b.

תדע כי לא לשקר עשה עט סופר[24] ספרים:

פרק ג

אתן לך שני משלים קלים בחוזק מה שצויתיך להיות זהיר בכל המצות המעשיות:

המשל הראשון. כתוב בתורה במצות ציצית שהטעם הוא וראיתם אתו וזכרתם את כל מצות ה'. אולי תגע עדיך ותבהל איך בראיית הציצית נזכור כל מצות ה' שבכללם הארבע שקדם זכרם? התשובה כן הענין בלי ספק. ובאור זה בקצרה וכפי כחך היום. כי האדם אינו מלאך שיהיה שכלו[25] גמור בפעל תמיד. ואינו פרד[26] שלא יהיה שכלו[27] בכח[28] כלל. אבל הוא כמו אנדרוגינוס חציו מלאך וחציו פרד על צד הקרוב. ולכן לא נצטוה בציצית לא המלאך ולא הפרד. ואמרו רבותינו המכובדים כי השי"ת אמר למלאכים תורה מה תהא לכם? אבל נצטוה בזה וכדומה[29] לזה האדם. להיותו[30] ממוצע כמו שאמרנו. והוא פעם שכל ופעם אינו שכל בפעל. וההתעטפות בציצית יזכירהו כל המצות. עד שיזכור באחרית כי השם

[24] Jer. 8. 8; The quotation is not exact. So H. reads עט שקר סופרים. [25] H שכל. [26] L פרא throughout. [27] H שכל. [28] A, L נכח. [29] H ובדו מר. [30] H adds כמו.

is the First Cause. For the section relating to the fringes ends with the words: "I am the Lord thy God"—a truth thus made clear! This precept has other advantages, but above all is the statement of Scripture sure: "And ye shall look upon it, and remember all the commandments of the Lord," the text ending with the result: "that ye go not about after your own heart and your own eyes." It was by neglect of such warnings that Solomon, of blessed memory, erred, for he said: "I will multiply horses and yet I will not turn aside from God."[15] Take warning from this example.

My second example shall be a "light precept", to use our Sages' term[16]. I refer to the command to dwell in booths. The Torah assigns both the motive and the end: "that your generations may know that I made the children of Israel to dwell in booths, when I brought them out of the Land of Egypt."[17] Observe how truth is a testimony to itself! The text does not say, because the children of Israel *dwelt* in booths, nor does it say when they *came* out. But it does say, "because *I made them dwell*" and "when *I brought* them out." Thus there is a reference back to God, the First Cause; as though to indicate that this precept was not merely intended to recall the facts of the departure from Egypt and dwelling in tents but to recall Him who brought out, Him who made to dwell! In other words the intention was that they should practically realize this truth, just as the four primary precepts enforce it in theory.

[15] Deut. 17.16. Cf. T. B. Sanh. 21b.

ית' הוא[31] הסבה הראשונה כמו שכתוב אנכי ה' אלהיך הוא אמת וברור: ולזאת המצוה תועלות אחרות. אבל על כל פנים אמת מה שכתוב בתורה וראיתם אותו וזכרתם את כל מצות ה'. וסיים ולא תתורו אחרי לבבכם ואחרי עיניכם: ובזה טעה שלמה ע"ה שאמר אני ארבה ולא אסור. והקש על זה:

והמשל השני במצוה קלה כמו שאמרו רבותינו. והיא מצות סוכה. ונתנה התורה טעמה ותועלתה ג"כ. ואמר[32] למען ידעו דורותיכם כי בסוכות הושבתי את בני ישראל בהוציאי אותם מארץ מצרים. וראה איך האמת עד לעצמה כמו שפירשנו. כי לא אמר בסוכות ישבו בני ישראל ולא אמר ג"כ בצאתם. אבל אמר הושבתי וכן בהוציאי. שהוא כינוי להשי"ת שהוא הפועל הראשון. כלומר אין הטעם בזה כדי שנזכר היציאה והישיבה לבד. רק שנזכור[33] המוציא והמושיב:[34] והטעם כדי שידעו זה בפועל. וזה ענין ארבע מצות שזכרנו:

31 H שהוא. 32 L, A omit.
33 B, A שנזכיר. 34 So H. Others והמשיב.

---

16 T. B. 'Abodah Zarah 3a. 17 Levit. 23.43.

So, in general, all the practical precepts, positive and negative, are helpful in many ways; but one of their most comprehensive services is that they bring to their doer's consciousness the four basic precepts summed up in the idea of Knowing God; sometimes keeping this knowledge with him, at others restoring it if he momentarily lose it. For these two operations both fall within the scope of the physician's art; to maintain health if it be present, to restore it if it be absent. And it is a familiar truth that sickness of the soul and its cure are analogous to the disease and healing of the body.[18]

Chapter IV

The thought may occur to thee: "I will perform all the practical commandments, and I will also uphold the four inner, rational principles, knowing them by way of tradition on the authority of Scripture." Well, one who so acts is righteous and sincere, and belongs to the category of the good man. But there is a better than he. For the idea of the Good is susceptible of the less and the more, as in the proposition: "Gold is better than silver." Pure gold, in the case before us, is he who performs all the practical laws, and who maintains the inner, rational principles in the manner befitting them, that is to say, he knows them by way of demonstration. Although the

[18] Cf. Maim. *Eight Chapters*, 3; *De'ot* 2.

ובכלל כל המצות המעשיות הן עשה הן לא תעשה כולם מועילות תועלות רבות. ואחת מתועלותיהם הכוללות[35] היא כדי שנדע בפועל הד׳ מצות היסודיות שהסוג לכולם ידיעת ה׳. וזה אם לשמרו עמנו תמיד אם להשיבו אלינו[36] אם נשמט ונשכח כרגע מה. כי אלו השתי פעולות הן בגדר הרפואה. רצוני שמירת הבריאות העומדת וההשבה אם סרה. וידוע כי חלי הנפש ורפואתה הולך על דרך חלי הגוף ורפואתו:

פרק ד

כי תאמר בלבבך אקיים[37] כל המצות המעשיות וגם אקיים[38] אלו הארבע מצות הלביות והעיוניות כי אדעם דרך קבלה כמו שכתוב בתורה. דע כי עושה אלה הוא צדיק תם[39] וישר ובכלל איש טוב הוא. אבל יש יותר טוב ממנו: כי הטוב מקבל פחות ויותר. ואין זה אלא כמו שנאמר שהזהב טוב מן הכסף. והנה הזהב הטהור הוא המקיים כל מצות המעשיות והמקיים הלביות והעיוניות כראוי להם. רצוני שידעם במופת. וכבר מנה המורה כי

[35] H הכוללת. [36] So B, H. L להשיב אליו. A להושיבו אליו. [37] L נקיים. [38] A, L omit.
[39] A omits.

total number of the precepts is 613, Maimonides estimated that only sixty are of regular and general application[19]. This may be indicated symbolically by the verse: "Threescore are the queens."[20] Nay, if thou wilt probe the matter more deeply, thou wilt discover that the number of obligatory commandments is even less than sixty. Examine the *Book of the Commandments*, and thou wilt understand what I mean.

While he who fulfils all the precepts in the manner befitting them is perfectly good, he who does less than this attains by so much a lesser degree of good. Our Sages accordingly declared that "Every Israelite has a portion in the world to come."[21] But the portions are unequal, else were God unjust.

CHAPTER V.

Hear, my son! the instruction of thy father—and hold firm to my injunction to perform the practical precepts, doing so in the manner befitting them—i. e. by practice. These laws thou must derive from the Bible, from the encyclopedic Code of Maimonides, and also from the Compendium of Alfasi. "Give a portion unto seven"[22] and fix times for the study of the Talmud, as I shall further explain.

[19] Maim. *Book of the Commandments*, end of section on "Affirmative Precepts".

[20] Song of Songs 6.8.

[21] Mishnah, Sanh. 10.1.

[22] Eccles. 11.2. The expression in the text refers no doubt to the seven liberal arts.

אעפ"י שהמספר הכולל הוא תרי"ג אין[40] מהם תמיד וכולל רק ששים. וסימן להם ששים המה מלכות. והנה כאשר תדקדק[41] תמצא ההכרחיות יותר מעט מזה. תעיין בס' המצות ותבין זה:

ובכלל כל[42] המקיים המצות כלם כראוי להם הוא הטוב השלם. והפוחת מזה תהיה פחיתות מעלתו כפי פחיתות פעולתו. ולכן ארז"ל כל ישראל יש להם חלק לעה"ב. אבל אין החלקים שוים. כי אם אינו כן לא יהיו כל דרכיו משפט[43]:

פרק ה

שמע בני מוסר אביך. החזק במוסר לקיים המעשיות[44] כאשר צויתיך. ואלה תקיימם כראוי. והוא המעשה. ותעמוד על אלה ממה שכתוב בתורה. ופירשם רבינו משה בס' הכולל משנה תורה וגם מה שחבר רב אלפסי. ותן חלק לשבעה[45] וקבע עתים לגמרא כמו שאודיעך עוד בע"ה[46]:

40 So B, H. A. L איזה.
41 H adds יותר.
42 H כי.
43 L omits from אבל to end of paragraph.
44 A המצות.
45 B, H omit.
46 B, H omit.

But "if there arise a matter too hard for thee in judgment," as regards any of these practical laws, follow the ordinance of Scripture[23], "Arise and get thee up into the place which the Lord thy God shall choose." Note the selection of terms. "Thou shalt come unto the priests the Levites and unto the judge," "and thou shalt *do* according to the tenor of the sentence which they shall declare unto thee." It is written, "thou shalt *do*", and not, "thou shalt *know*". The Scripture had previously defined the kind of law to which this rule -(of seeking expert advice) was to apply. It starts with a very wide category, "between blood and blood", and further adds "between plea and plea", another general category, and then qualifies by the phrase "even matters of controversy within thy gates." The implication is that we are not all bound to know every detail of the law of the "four bailees"[24], of "claimant and respondent", of "loan and deposit". Acquaintance with such matters is commendable, yet is it enough for us if there be available in our age a judge or judges familiar with the law, who "shall judge the people at all times."[25] That is to say, if I am able to pass my whole life without litigation, then ignorance of the law as to disputes is no defect in my soul. And if, God forbid, contention should arise between me and another and I go before one of the Rabbis expert in these affairs, again it is no defect at all

[23] Deut. 17.8.

[24] Mishnah Baba Mezi'a 7.8, etc.

[25] Exod. 18.22.

וכי יפלא דבר ממך מאלה המעשיות עשה כמו שאמרה תורה. וקמת ועלית וגו׳ ובאת אל הכהנים הלוים ואל השופט אשר יהיה בימים ההם וגו׳ ועשית על פי הדבר אשר יגידו לך וגו׳: ראה הפלגת זה הלשון. כי אמר ועשית ולא אמר וידעת. וכן פרט תחלה על איזה מצוה יתנהג כן. ואמר סוג כולל מאד והוא בין דם לדם ואמר עוד בין דין לדין שהוא כלל אחר ואמר דברי ריבות בשעריך: והמשל בזה כי אינו הכרח שנדע כולנו על כל פנים דין ארבעה שומרים. או כל הלכות טוען ונטען שאלה ופקדון. ואם הידיעה הזאת טובה. רק[47] די לנו אם יש לנו בימינו שופט או שופטים ידעו זה ושפטו את העם בכל עת: וזה כי אם אוכל לשבת כל ימי ודבר אין לי עם אדם מענין ריב ומדון לא יהיה חסרון בנפשי כי לא ידעתי אלה הדינים. ואם ח״ו יארע לי ריב עם זולתי אלכה לי אל אחד מהרבנים היודעים דינים אלו. אין זה חסרון בנפשי

[47] A omits רק, L omits that and following 3 words.

in my soul. As the Sage Ibn Ezra remarks: "If all men were righteous, there would be no need for the tractate concerning Torts." Yet it would certainly be a defect in my soul if, when occasion arose for applying the law, I transgressed it.

On the other hand, as God liveth, the case is quite different with regard to the inner, speculative precepts. For their whole substance and being consists in the knowledge of them personally, by every individual, and this knowledge must be a continuous, rational apprehension. Nor does this of itself constitute perfection of fulfilment. This rational apprehension must be fortified by irrefutable proofs. For the knowledge of God, of His existence and His unity, means proven knowledge. Otherwise the term used ought to be "thought," "opinion," or "think," and not in the true sense unqualified "knowledge." Thus Maimonides avoids the terms "believe," "opine" and uses the term "know," after the Scriptural analogy: "Know therefore that the Lord thy God, He is God."[26]

Chapter VI

[When elsewhere Maimonides does use the term *faith*, the sense in which he employs it is clear]. In his *Guide for the Perplexed* Part I, ch. 50, he writes: "When reading my present treatise, bear in mind that by *faith* we do not understand that which is merely uttered with the lips, but that which is apprehended by the soul, the

[26] Deut. 4.39. Compare and contrast Mendelssohn's view in his *Jerusalem*. Cf. also Schechter, *Studies in Judaism*.

כלל. ואמר החכם אבן עזרא. אלו היינו כלנו צדיקים. לא נצטרך למסכת נזיקין. אבל יהיה חסרון בנפשי אם אעבור על זה[48] הדין:

ואמנם במצות הלביות והעיוניות לא כן חי ה'! כי כל עצמם ומהותם[49] הידיעה הנפשיית אשר[50] לאיש ואיש וזה בפועל תמיד ציור שלם ודבוק שכלי. וגם זה אינו שלימות גמור אלא אם כן תדע זה במופתים והקשים הכרחיים. ולכן אמרה התורה וידעת את ה' אלהיך. ואמר המורה לדעת שיש שם מצוי ראשון ולדעת שהוא אחד: וגדר שם הידיעה הוא הידיעה המופתית. כי זולת זה יקרא מחשבה או סברא לא ידיעה בסתם על דרך האמת: והנה המורה לא אמר להאמין או לסבור או לחשוב רק לדעת כלשון התורה וידעת:[51]

פרק ו

אמר המורה בפרק נ' מראשון. דע אתה המעיין במאמרי זה כי ההאמנה אינה הענין הנאמר בפה[52] אבל הענין המצוייר בנפש כשיאמינו בו שהוא כן

48 B, A, H omit על זה. 49 A, L ומתוכם.
50 H. omits. 51 L בידיעת התורה וכונתה.
52 B, H omit.

conviction that the object of belief is exactly as it is apprehended." To which he adds: "If in addition to this we are convinced that the thing cannot be different in any way from that which we believe it to be, and that no reasonable argument can be found for the negation of the belief or for the admission of any deviation from it, then the belief is true." When, again, in ch. 55, Maimonides discusses the kinds of attributes which are inapplicable to God, seeing that their application implies imperfection, he uses these expressions: "He who knows these things, but without their proofs, does not know the particulars which logically result from these general propositions; he will not be able to prove that God exists." Further Maimonides remarks in ch. 60: "But you must be careful in what you negative, to negative by proof, not by mere words, for each time you ascertain by proof that a certain thing, imagined to exist in the Creator, must be negatived, you have undoubtedly come one step nearer to the knowledge of God." In fine, Maimonides here and in many other pasages, and in agreement with all authoritative philosophers, asserts that perfect knowledge is only attainable when the mind's apprehensions are *demonstrated*.

כמו שיצוייר: ועוד אמר ואם יגיע[53] עם זאת האמונה שאי אפשר חלוף זאת האמונה בשום פנים ולא ימצא בשכל מקום דחיה לאמונה ההיא ולא לשער אפשרות חלופה תהיה אמיתית: עוד פרק נ"ה על ידיעת הדברים שראוי שירוחקו מהאל להיותם מונעים השלימות מאתו ית' אמר דבר זה לשונו. ואם ידע אלו הדברים ולא ידעם במופתיהם לא[54] ידע הפרטים המתחייבים מאלו ההקדמות הכלליות חיוב הכרחי. ולזה[55] לא יהיה אצלו מופת במציאת האלוה: עוד אמר בפרק פ' והשמר מאד שתוסיף שלילת מה שתשלול במופת לא שתשלול[56] בדבור בלבד. כי כל אשר תתבאר[57] לך במופת שלילת דבר שיחשב מציאותו לשם ממנו תקרב[58] אליו מדרגה בלא ספק. ובכלל הנה המורה בזה ובמקומות רבים וכל הפילוסופים השלמים הסכימו שלא יקרא ידיעה שלימה רק בידיעת אלו הציורים השכליים במופת:

53 L יהיה.
54 H has ולא.
55 H לזה.
56 H omits three words.
57 H כאשר התבאר.
58 B, H קרבת.

CHAPTER VII

When then we are bidden to know that there is a First Cause, how can this knowledge be obtained except by arguments and proofs which no sceptic can dispute? Our Sages ordained that the duty of studying the Torah is to be pursued to that very extent.[27] Again, how can I know that God is One, as is constantly proclaimed in our prayers, unless I know what constitutes unity, as it is expounded in the *Guide* and in the Metaphysics [of Aristotle]? Maimonides explains that the idea of unity does not attach to the sphere, nor to any of the separate Intelligences, nor even to the highest Intelligence which moves the diurnal sphere. Unity applies to God alone, who is above this highest Intelligence. Aristotle proved all this irrefutably; hence Maimonides burned with a mighty zeal when he saw that Aristotle had presumed to interpret our precious truths, attributing the exposition to himself, while he stole it all from the books written on the subject by King Solomon and others.[28] Maimonides was therefore impelled to compose his comprehensive treatise, the *Guide*, in which he includes these precepts

[27] Obviously Ibn Kaspi (with Maimonides) had before him the version of Mishnah Abot 2.14 (in which the imperative ודע is omitted, and which ran:—"Be diligent to learn Torah wherewith thou mayest make answer to Epicurus"). Cf. the Notes of the Tosafot Yomtob and C. Taylor to the passages.

[28] For this notion that Greek philosophy was derived from Hebrew sources, see above p. 129.

פרק ז

והנה צונו שנדע שיש שם מצוי ראשון. ואיך אדע[59] זה שהוא אמת אלא אם כן אדע זה בטענות וראיות שלא יוכל אפיקורוס לחלוק עלי[60]? כמו שצונו רבותינו ז"ל. שעד זה הגבול הוא חיוב למידתנו את התורה[61]: וכן איך אדע שהוא אחד שנאמר תמיד בקריאת שמע אלא אם כן אדע מהו האחד כמו שהתבאר בספר המורה וספר מה שאחר הטבע? כי שם התבאר שהגלגל אינו אחד. וכן אחד מן[62] השכלים הנפרדים[63] אינו אחד. ואף לא השכל העליון המניע הגלגל היומי. ואין שם אחד רק האל ית' לבדו שהוא למעלה[64] מזה השכל: וכל זה התבאר במופתים שאין בם ספק בספרי[65] האלהות לאריסטו: על כן קנא הרב השלם להשם[66] קנאה גדולה כאשר ראה שאריסטו התנשא לפרש המצות היקרות שלנו. וייחס פירושם לעצמו תחת אשר גנב כל זה מספרי שלמה וזולתו שחוברו בענין זה: ולכן חבר השלם ס' המורה שהוא כולל פי'

59 H, B נדע 60 A, L עליו 61 A, L לימודתנו בתורה.
62 A, L omit. 63 H omits. 64 L השלם.
65 B, H בדברי. In other contexts the readings vary between ספר and ספרי. 66 B, A omit. H לנו.

and their proofs, just as he had previously given in his Code a survey of all the other precepts.

Now how can any of us be said to appreciate the meaning of Unity as applied to God unless we have an inner understanding of the declaration so often on our lips that The Lord our God is One; unless we know, and know by demonstration, that this One is not the mover of the diurnal sphere but a power above it? So, too, with the precepts to love God and to fear Him. We are not to love God as a man loves his wife and children; not to fear Him as we fear a human being. But these emotions, as applied in our relation to God, need definition, of the kind supplied in the works of Maimonides. But to acquire the necessary knowledge a study of the natural sciences and metaphysics is indispensable.

Abraham, our first father, whom God termed His friend,[29] was the man who discovered for himself, by aid of his fine intelligence, this universal principle of ours: that above the celestial sphere there is a Unique Being. So, our Sages said, Abraham recognized His Creator when he was forty years of age.[30] This recognition, they would have us understand, was made by Abraham from actual demonstration; for it was not a tradition from his father, nor did he acquire it from his contemporaries. He originated the idea, while his contemporaries believed the physical sun to

[29] Isa. 41.8.

[30] The common reading in Genesis Rabbah, ch. xxx, is "forty-eight years of age", but Ibn Kaspi, like Maim., had the reading "forty". Cf. Theodor's note, p. 274.

אלו המצות ומופתיהם כמו שקדם לו ס׳ משנה תורה שהוא כולל פי׳ שאר המצות:

ואמנם מי מכולנו מבין ענין היחוד[67] באל ית׳ עד שנדע בלבנו מה כוונת אמרנו תמיד שמע ישראל ה׳ אלהינו ה׳ אחד. עד שנדע שזה האחד אינו הגלגל המניע היומי אבל הוא מה שהוא למעלה מזה כל שכן כשנדע זה במופת: וכן מצות לאהבה את ה׳. כי אין הטעם שנאהוב אותו כדרך אהבתינו אל נשינו ובנינו. וכן שנירא ממנו כמו שנירא מאחד מן האנשים. אבל כמו שפירש[68] המורה במדע ובמורה. ואין מי שידע[69] זה או יבין זה אלא היודעים ספרי הטבע ומה שאחר הטבע:

והנה אברהם אבינו הראשון שקראו השם אוהבו[70] הוא המציא מעצמו בדקות שכלו זאת האמונה שלנו הכוללית. שעל הגלגל יש מצוי שהוא אחד. ולכן אמרו בן ארבעים שנה הכיר אברהם את בוראו. והכוונה בפעל במופת. כי זאת ההכרה לא היתה לו בקבלה מאביו תרח או מזולתו מבני דורו. כי הוא היה המחדש[71] אותה. וכולם[72]

67 B האחד. 68 B, H שפירשם. 69 B, H ומי ידע.
70 A, L אוהבי. 71 H מחדש. 72 H כי כלם.

be divine. Abraham, in the rabbinical, story, appealed to argument and proof; he did not say to the others, I believe it, I have been told in a dream that I ought to think so and so true. "Look unto Abraham your father," cries Isaiah.[31] Assuredly it becomes us to imitate him. I am far from asserting that all men can reach the level of Abraham, but I do say that his level is the highest and most excellent though, as I have admitted above, those who stand below it are also good.

Chapter VIII

But I command thee, dear son of mine, to rise up, if thou canst, to this, the highest level. My son! be wise and make my heart glad![32]

Chapter IX

Yet, let not the fact that these works expound those four precious precepts, hurry thee to a premature study of the *Guide* or of Aristotle's *Metaphysics*. Not so my son! By gradual steps shalt thou rise to Truth. Not in a rush canst thou compass the whole ascent; slips and setbacks may impede thy progress. This is pointed out in the *Guide*, I 34, and in other places, as thou wilt hereafter see.

[31] Isa. 51.2.

[32] Prov. 27.11. The author intimates the importance he attaches to this counsel by devoting a whole chapter to it.

זולתו היו מאמינים שהגלגל שהוא גשם היה אלוה. ולכן טען כנגדם טענות מופתיות. לא שאמר להם אני מאמין כך וכך או חלום חלמתי שראוי להאמין כך וכך: לכן ראוי לנו שנתדמה אל אבינו הראשון. הביטו אל אברהם אביכם: ואין אני אומר שכל בני הזמן יוכלו להגיע אל זאת המדרגה. אבל אומר אני שזאת המדרגה היא היותר טובה והעליונה. ואשר למטה מזה טובים גם כן כמו שקדם לנו:

פרק ח

אבל אצוך בני היקר לי שתעלה אם תוכל אל המדרגה[73] היותר עליונה. חכם בני ושמח לבי!

פרק ט

לבך אל ימהר להתחיל[74] בלימוד ספר המורה וס׳ מה שאחר הטבע לאריסטו. בעבור שאלו הספרים מודיעים אלו הארבע מצות היקרות. לא כן בני! מעט מעט תעלה אל האמתיות. לא תוכל כלותם מהר פן תרבה עליך הטעיות והשבושים. וכבר באר זה המורה בספרו הנכבד פרק ל״ד מראשון. ובמקומות אחרים כמו שתראה עוד:

73 H המעלה.   74 H, B omit.

CHAPTER X

My son! Keep my words![33] To-day thou art twelve years of age. For another two years be a diligent student of the Scriptures and Talmud. When thou art fourteen, fix regular hours for continuing thy previous studies, and give also a good part of thy time to mathematics; first Ibn Ezra's Arithmetic, then Euclid, and the Astronomical treatise of Al-Fergani and [Abraham b. Ḥiyya][34]. Besides, appoint set times for reading moral books, which will introduce thee to all good qualities—viz. the Books of Proverbs and Ecclesiastes, the Mishnaic tractate *Fathers*, with the Commentary of Maimonides and his preface thereto, and the same author's Introductory chapters to the Code. Also read Aristotle's *Ethics*, of which I have made a digest. There is also available among us the Collection of the *Maxims of the Philosophers*.

This course should occupy thee for two years. Then, when thou art sixteen, appoint times for the Scriptures, for the writings of Alfasi, Moses of Coucy, and the Code of the perfect teacher (Maimonides). Also give much time to Logic. With the help of God I will make a compendium on this subject, sufficient for thy needs, as I did with the *Ethics*.

[33] Prov. 7.1.

[34] On the works named in the context see Steinschneider, *Hebr. Uebersetzungen*, §§ 343, 350, 502. On the Jewish educational schemes, cf. I. Abrahams, *Jewish Life in the Middle Ages*, chs. xix, xx.

פרק י

בני שמור אמרי! הנך היום בן שתים עשרה שנה. לכן שקוד בתורה במקרא ובגמרא עוד שתי שנים אחר כן.[75] ואתה בן י"ד שנה קבע עתים לכל מה שקדם. ותן חלק גדול לחכמות הלמודיות. וזה תחלה ס' המספר מאבן עזרא ואחריו ס' האקלידס ואחריו ס' אלפרגאני והשבון המהלכות. עם קבעך[76] עתים בספרים המוסריים[77] המישרים אורחותיך במדות[78]. והם ס' משלי וקהלת ומס' אבות עם פרוש המורה והקדמתו. וכן הלכות דעות מס' המדע וכן ס' המדות לארסטו אשר עשיתי ממנו קיצור. וכן ס' אחר נמצא אצלינו המקבץ מוסרי הפלוסופים:

הנה כל זה תבין בב' שנים. ואתה בן י"ו שנה תקבע עתים לתורה ולמקרא ולספרי הרב אלפאסי וס' רבינו משה מקוצי וס' משנה תורה מן הרב השלם: ותן חלק גדול למלאכת ההגיון. ובע"ה אעשה לך קיצור מזאת המלאכה יספוק לך[79] כמו שעשיתי קיצור מס' המדות:

[75] H puts stop at שנים and omits כן, begins new clause with אחר, and so in all similar contexts.

[76] A and L read וגם קבע. [77] B במוסריים. [78] A, L בכל המדות. [79] B, H omit.

In this way thou shouldst pass another two years, by which time thou wilt be eighteen years old. Then review all thy former work, and study natural science. By that date, being twenty years of age, "build thy house". Do not intermit the reading of moral books, but also take up theology, i. e., the *Metaphysics* of Aristotle and his disciples, as well as the *Guide* of Maimonides.

Marry a wife of good family, beautiful in form and in character. Pay no regard to money, for true wealth consists only of a sufficiency of bread to eat and raiment to wear. Why weary thyself to gain great riches, when neither thou nor any other could equal the vast store accumulated by the great mountain in our native city l'Argentière[35], even though that mountain is but a soul-less heap! Rather occupy thy mind continually with books of morals; I need not here repeat their lessons, but they will instruct thee as to the meaning of real wealth and as to other matters. Observe their injunctions faithfully. Above all things be chaste, just as thy father has been before thee. And use thy endeavors to live a virtuous life, and to order well thy home with thy wife and the children whom, God willing, thou shalt beget; in all things obeying the injunctions of the moralists. Never fail to read

[35] See above, p. 127.

ובזה תתמיד שני שנים אחרים. ואתה בן י״ח שנה תקבע עתים לכל מה שקדם. ושקוד בחכמת הטבע ובזה תתמיד שתי שנים אחר ובנית ביתך. ואתה בן עשרים שנים. אל תרף ידך מן העיון במוסרים[80] ותתחיל באלהיות.[81] הם ספרי[82] מה שלאחר הטבע לארסטו ותלמידיו וס׳ המורה:

אך קח לך אשה מבנות היחס. נאה בגופה ובמעשיה. ולא תתן עיניך בממון. כי העושר אינו רק ההסתפקות לחם לאכול ובגד ללבוש. ולמה תיגע בני להשיג כסף רב ולא תוכל אתה ולא זולתך להגיע אל הגבול שהשיג מזה ההר הגדול אשר בכספיא המקום עיר מולדתנו. עם היות ההר ההוא דומם שאינו בעל נפש כלל: על כן צויתיך להגות תמיד במוסרים. ואין רצוני להעתיקם בכאן. הלא הם יורוך על זה ועל כל הראוי. ועל כל פנים שמור כל הכתוב בהם: ועל הכל בני השמר לך מהסתכל בנשים כאשר נשמר אביך: אך בכלל תכלכל דבריך במשפט בסדור ביתך עם אשתך ובניך אשר תוליד אם ירצה הבורא על פי הדברים אשר יגידו לך הספרים[83] המוסרים. ועל כל פנים

[80] A, L בספרים. [81] B here and elsewhere spells באלוהיות. So H, though not so consistently. [82] A, L ספר.
[83] B, H omit.

a section of some ethical book daily after every meal, having first blessed the Lord. Above all set thy thought on that highest of attainments, the Knowledge of God, as expounded in the *Guide*, and in the *Vessels of Silver*, which, if God grant me life, I will make for thee.[36] "Then shalt thou understand the fear of the Lord, and find the knowledge of God."[37] In this course persist until the day of thy death. Ascending above the heavens, thou shalt then find entry into the company of the angelic spirits, into a delight which cannot be measured!

CHAPTER XI

There are, my son! two dispositions among contemporary Jews which must be firmly avoided by thee.

The first class consists of sciolists, whose studies have not gone far enough. They are destroyers and rebels; scoff at the words of the Rabbis of blessed memory, treat the practical precepts as of little account, and accept unseemly interpretations of biblical narratives. These men are false, through and through. They testify unmistakably against themselves that they are ill-acquainted with the philosophical writings of Aristotle and his disciples. This is obvious to those who are really familiar with those writings. I call heaven and earth to witness that I may

[36] Ibn Kaspi's *Ten Vessels of Silver* have been published by Isaac Last in 2 vols. (Pressburg, 1903).

[37] Prov. 2.5.

תקרא חלק מה מהם כל ימי חייך אחר גמר כל סעודה אחר וברכת את ה׳ אלהיך: ובכלל שקוד על טוב המדות. והם הדעות האלהיות כאשר תבין מספר המורה ומן הספרים כלי כסף אשר אעשה לך אם יחייני האל. אז תבין יראת ה׳ ודעת אלהים[84] תמצא: ובזה תתמיד עד יום מותך. ותעלה אז מעל לשמים. ותכנס בכת המלאכים הרוחניים בתענוג לא ישוער:

פרק יא

בני! שתים המה קוראותינו בתכונות בני הזמן מעמנו. בני אל תלך בדרך אתם. מנע רגלך מנתיבתם. המין האחד המתפלספים מבני עמנו. תלמידים אשר לא שמשו כל צרכם. הורסים בעיונם. ופורצים בלמודם. ומלעיגים על דברי חכמינו ז״ל. ומקילים במצות המעשיות ועושים ציורים לספורים בלתי ראויים. ואלו מזוייפים מתוכם ומעידים עדות נאמנה על נפשם שאינם יודעים ספרי החכמות שחבר ארסטו ותלמידיו כמו שמבואר זה למי שידעם: ואני מעיד עלי שמים

[84] So H. Others קדושים.

claim some not[38] inconsiderable scientific attainments. That being so, I swear by Him who lives eternally that Aristotle, his fellows, and his disciples, advocate all that is contained in the Torah and the Prophets, and particularly the performance of the practical precepts. For Plato said: "Slay him who is without Law[39];" and again, "Prayer is a halter to the lustful soul;" and yet again: "We cannot [by reason alone] reach the level of the prophets." Aristotle observes: "The end is not merely to know, but to know and do, receive and believe, all that is contained in the true Torah;" pry not too closely into possible causes and senses of the commands and prohibitions, nor dispute over them, for the Prophets, on whom be peace, knew all things from God, which is not the case with metaphysicians. This is the gist of their pronouncements; they said much more of the same kind.[40] Against these famous Saints of the Gentiles we have no possible complaint, and therefore our Sages asserted concerning them that they have a portion in the world to come.[41]

And note further how Aristotle, who at first derived his theory of the eternity of the world rationally, afterwards adopted the belief in Creation, expounded as it is in the Torah by those possessed of the prophetic soul, which is higher than the

[38] Some texts omit "not".

[39] Or: "religion."

[40] On these "quotations" from Plato and Aristotle see above, p. 129.

[41] Tosefta, Sanh. 13.2.

וארץ כי אין[85] אני מקטני חכמי הזמן. ואני נשבע בחיי העולם כי ארסטו וחביריו ותלמידיו כולם מזהירים לשמור כל מה שבתורה ובדברי הנביאים ובפרט להזהר במעשיות: ואמר אפלטון הרגו מי שאין לו דת. ואמר עוד התפלה[86] רסן הנפש המתאוה. ואמר עוד אנחנו לואים להבין מה שבא בתורה על ידי הנביאים: ואמר ארסטו אין הכונה[87] שתדע לבד אבל שתדע ותעשה ותקבל ותאמין כל מה שבא בתורה האמיתית. ולא תעמיק מאוד[88] לבקש טעמים וסבות למצותיה ואזהרותיה ולא תקשה לדבר שיונח בה. כי הנביאים ידעו הכל מאת אדון הכל. ולא כן אנחנו הפילוסופים חכמי העיון: זהו תורף דבריהם וזולת זה כהם וכהם. ולא נשאר[89] על אלה הנכבדים חסידי אומות העולם תרעומות אחרי כל זה. ולכן אמרו רבותינו ז"ל עליהם שיש להם חלק לעוה"ב:

והנה הקדמות הניח ארסטו מצד עיון הנפש. ואחר נכנע לאמונת החדוש כי בא בתורה מצד

[85] B, H omit.

[86] B התעלה.

[87] So H adds. [88] B תמיד.

[89] B, H omit ולא and read הנשאר.

rational faculty. The text says: "Whoso confesseth and forsaketh his transgressions shall obtain mercy."[42] But the sciolists who lightly esteem the precepts and the words of our Sages, will have to pay the penalty for their offence. They will be called to account, too, for the occasion they have given to the ignorant to scoff at philosophy, thereby profaning the name of heaven!

The second class referred to above includes those of our people who hold in contempt genuine philosophy as presented in the works of Aristotle and his like. They know not that they are speaking against their own soul! For these sciences were originally *ours*. Witness, how these sciences interpret and verify the precepts of our Torah; and further, how many of them are scattered in the haggadot of the Talmud, and the other rabbinic books, above all in the *Guide*, composed by Rabbi Moses, the father in Torah, the father in wisdom. And whom have we greater than Moses?[43] Now, my son! I do not blame this class because they devote all their time to the talmudic argumentation, for as Ibn Janaḥ said: "Every man deserves praise for his labor, eulogy for his effort." But I do blame them because they despise science and those engaged in its study.

[42] Prov. 28.13.

[43] Ibn Kaspi's whole-hearted esteem of Maimonides is noticeable throughout the Testament.

בעלי הנפש הנבואית.[90] שהיא למעלה מן העיונית. והכתוב אומר ומודה ועוזב ירוחם: ובכלל השחיתו התעיבו עלילה אלה התעלולים המקילים במצות ובדברי רבותינו ז״ל. ועתידים הם ליתן את הדין על זה ועל אשר נתנו יד להמון[91] לבזות החכמות וחללו שם שמים:

המין האחר הוא הנמצאים מעמנו שיבזו החכמות המיוסדות בספרי[92] ארסטו וחביריו. ולא ידעו כי בנפשם ידברו[93]. כי אלה החכמות היו שלנו מקדם והעד על זה כי הם פירוש ומופת למצות תורתינו. ועוד כי רובן מפוזרות בהגדות[94] בגמרא ובשאר ספריהם. וכל שכן בס׳ המורה שחבר רבינו משה אב בתורה אב בחכמה. ומי לנו גדול ממשה? והנה בני זה המין אין אני מגנה אותם בהיותם משימים כל ימיהם בשקלא וטריא מן הגמרא. וכל אחד כמו שאמר אבן גאנח מהולל על טרחו ומשובח על יגיעו. אבל אני מגנה אותם כי יבזו החכמות ולומדיהם:

[90] B, L הנביאית.
[91] B, H להאמין.
[92] L לספרו המיוחסות. A וספרי המיוחסות.
[93] L זדו. [94] B omits. H inserts before מפוזרות.

CHAPTER XII

My son! When thou meetest such men, address them thus: My masters! What sin did your fathers detect in the study of logic and philosophy? First as to logic. This art does not touch precepts or faith. As its name implies, it simply regulates and gives precision to the use of language. Is it a terrible crime to use words with accuracy? Do thistles grow on fig trees? 'Tis absurd to imagine that our Rabbis in their warning against logic[44], were thinking of this genuine discipline. For our Sages never laid an embargo on the good. Yet those who would fain evade the trouble of thinking "are glad when they can find the grave"[45] of sloth! And then, what say ye of the work of Aristotle and Maimonides? Have you examined the inside of their books? If ye know more than their covers, ye know of a surety that the books are an exposition and justification of our precious precepts. And if, God forbid, ye find something indigestible in these works, cast it out while eating the wholesome rest. So is it recorded of R. Meir: He ate the kernel, and threw away the husk.[46] This is the method pursued nowadays by Christian scholars. They highly esteem the

[44] T. B. Berakot 28b.

[45] Job 3.24. [46] Hagigah 9b.

פרק יב

בני כי תבא באנשים אמור להם. רבותי! מה מצאו אבותיכם עול במלאכת ההגיון ובמלאכת[95] העיונית? וזה תחלה בהגיון שאין בה[96] דבר נוגע למצוה ואמונה רק דקדוק הדבור והישרתו כמו שידוע מגדרה[97]. היש בהישרת הדבור עול ועוות? האם יש קוצים בתאנים? וחלילה כי מזאת החכמה האמתית אמרו[98] רז"ל מנעו בניכם מן ההגיון. כי הם לא מנעו הטוב[99] ממנו[100]. אמנם השמחים להקל מעליהם טורח הידיעה ישישו כי ימצאו קבר העצלה: ואחרי כן מה תאמרו מספר הטבע[101] ומה שאחר הטבע וספר המורה? ואין אחד מהם להם נראה[102] מבחוץ אף כי שוה מבפנים[102a]. ואלו ידעתם אותם תמצאו בם פירוש ומופת על מצותינו היקרות כמו שקדם: ואם ח"ו יש באחד מאלה דבר קשה אליכם השליכו אותו וקחו טוב השאר[103]. כי כן נאמר על רבי מאיר תוכו אכל קליפתו זרק. וכן יעשו חכמי הנוצרים.

[95] H omits these two words.

[96] A, L omit these 5 words and read כי אין בהם.

[97] H מגזרה. [98] L לא אמרו, A יאמרו. [99] H adds והאמת.

[100] A מעמנו. L ממנו מעמנו. [101] A, L השמע.

[102] A, L לפי הנראה. [102a] Read מה שבפנים, as the text seems corrupt [103] A ואכלו טוב. L ואכלו הטוב. H omits וקחו.

Guide, although it contains certain passages opposed to the Christian faith.[47]

Chapter XIII

Continue thy argument with them in these terms: I beg you to hear me, my masters! If ye are advanced in years, and have not yet read the words of the philosophers who demonstrate, clearly and indisputably, the four primary precepts, of which I have spoken, then open your eyes before the sun be darkened! Men asked the Sage whether it was becoming to an old man to learn; and he answered, "If ignorance is discreditable to him, learning is an ornament."[48] Should such a course involve any shame, our honored Rabbis have already given the admonition: Better be ashamed here than hereafter![49] Why, my masters, do ye regard the jibes of women, or of men who play the woman, when they cry: See this grey-beard gone again to school! What have ye in common with such people? Will they go with you, and take you on your way to the future world whose duration is eternal? Or shall a man redeem his brother? What concern have we with those children of this age who must die tomorrow, and who even now, in their lives, are called dead? How are we affected by the respect or scorn of the ignorant?

[47] On the vogue of Maimonides in Christian and Mohammedan circles see Yellin and Abrahams, *Maimonides*, ch. xii and the references in note 92.

[48] *Choice of Pearls*, ch. i (end).

[49] T. B. Ḳidd. 81a.

כל שכן שהם מנשאים ספר המורה ואם יש בו דברים סותרים לאמונת הנוצרים:

פרק יג

עוד תשוב ואמרת אליהם. שמעו[104] רבותי! אם באתם בימים ולא ראיתם עדיין דברי החכמים המודיעים במופתים וראיות ברורות ואמיתיות[105] אותן הארבע מצות הנכבדות. פקחו עיניכם בם[106] עד אשר לא תחשך השמש: ושאלו לחכם אם נאה לזקן שילמוד? והשיב אם הסכלות גנאי לו הלמוד נאה לו: ואם בשום פנים יש בושת מה בענין זה כבר יסרונו רבותינו המכובדים מוטב ליכסיף בהאי עלמא ולא ליכסיף בעלמא דאתא. ולמה רבותי תשימו[107] לב לדברי הנשים או האנשים אשר דרך נשים להם. כי יאמרו ראו זה הרב והרבן גם שב גם ישיש האדם הגדול חשבנוהו[108]. ועתה הוא לומד ועושה לו רב? מה לכם ולהם? האם ילכו אלה וילוו אתכם לעולם הבא שכולו ארוך? או אח פדה יפדה איש? ומה לנו ולדברי בני הזמן שמחר יהיו כולם מתים ומה גם עתה בחייהם קרויים מתים? ומה לנו

104 L, H בבעו.
105 B, H אמתת.
106 A, L omit.
107 B, H תשיתו.
108 A, L וחשבנוהו.

As our Rabbis of blessed memory have said: "Words neither kill nor quicken!"[50]

Chapter XIV

I will confess to thee, my son! that though in my youth I learned a great portion of the Talmud, I did not acquire (for my sins!) a knowledge of all the poseḳim.[51] Now that I am old and grey, I have often to consult rabbis younger than myself. Why should I be ashamed of this? Can one man be skilled in every craft? If, for instance, I want a gold cup, I go to the goldsmith, and I feel no shame; and so with other products, I turn, in case of need, to those whom God has gifted with the requisite skill.

Once I made a great feast at which all kinds of delicacies were served. I had the table prepared, I invited my friends to eat and drink with me, for it was a family party. Then the luckless handmaid put a milk spoon into the meat pot. I did not know the ritual law, how one ought to estimate the lawfully permissible proportion of intermixture.[52] Perturbed in mind, as well as famished in body, I went to one of the rabbis,

[50] This saying does not seem to occur in extant rabbinic books; Ibn Kaspi quotes the saying more than once in his works.

[51] Authorities on practical law.

[52] T. B. Ḥullin 97b. Literally: "The law was hid-

---

[113] L reads ולא אבוש כי לכל איש ואיש אומנותו יפה בעיניו.

[114] B טבחתי את טבחי ומרי ת'. H טבחתי את טבחי צאן ובקר ומרי תרנגולות.

[115] L משערין אם כמה תפוק מיניה.

לאנשים החסרים כי יכבדונו וכי יבזונו? ואמרו רבותינו ז"ל לא דברים ממיתים ולא דברים מחיים:

פרק יד

אודיעה דברי לך בני אמת כי[109] בבחרותי למדתי מן התלמוד חלק גדול. אבל בעונותי לא עלה בידי ידיעת הפוסקים כולם. והיום זקנתי ושבתי ואצטרך כמה פעמים לשאול הוראה[110] מהרבנים ואם הם צעירים ממני לימים. ולמה אבוש מזה? האוכל להיות בקי בכל המלאכות? הנה כשאצטרך אל כוס[111] זהב על דרך משל אלך אל צורפי זהב והאומנים ולא אבוש. וכן כל המצטרך אלכה לי לאיש ואיש[112] שהאל יפה לכל אחד אומנתו בפניו:[113]

ויהי היום זבחתי את זבחי. ותרנגולות[114] מפוטמות וברבורים אבוסים. אף ערכתי שולחני. קראתי למאהבי לאכול ולשתות עמי. כי זבח משפחה היה לי. והלכה השפחה הארורה והכניסה כף חולבת לתוך היורה. ונעלמה ממני הלכה. אם בכולה משערינן אם במאי דנפק מנה משערינן:[115] ואלך מר בחמת רוחי רעב וצמא לאחד מהרבנים

109 A, L אודיעך בני דבר אמת.

110 L omits. 111 L טס. 112 A omits.

held high in popular repute. He was (for my sins!) at table with his wife and family, eating, and drinking wine. I waited at his door until the shades of evening fell, and my soul was near to leave me. He then told me the law, and I returned home where my guests and the poor were awaiting me. I related all that had happened, for I was not ashamed to admit myself unskilled in that particular craft. In this I lack skill, but I have skill in another craft. Is not the faculty of expounding the existence and unity of God as important as familiarity with the rule concerning a small milk spoon?

Chapter XV

And thus further shalt thou speak unto them: My father solemnly impressed on me that neither timidity not diffidence is in place where truth is concerned. Why, then, should I deal insincerely with the Torah? My heritage of time I will share only with my Creator, the Giver of my soul; my heart shall seek its honor or find shame from Him alone! Hear me then,

den from me, whether we calculate the proportions by the actual amount of the admixture or by the quantity that has come out of it (has been absorbed by the dish)". See Jastrow, *Dictionary*, p. 1612.

הנכבדים שבעם[116]. והיה הוא בעונות[117] מסב על שולהנו עם אשתו ובניו ואוכלים ושותים יין. ואוחיל לו על פתח ביתו עד נטו צללי ערב. כמעט לא נותרה בי נשמה. ויורני ויאמר לי הדין כך וכך. ואשוב[118] אל ביתי והקרואים העניים[119] והאביונים וכולם שם[120] היו יושבים ומצפים לי. ואגידה אליהם כל המאורע לי[121] כי לא אבוש לומר אינני בקי בזאת[122] המלאכה. אבל אני בקי במלאכה אחרת. ולמה לא ישוה פסק או הוראה ממציאות הבורא או אחדותו[123] הגדולה ככף חולבת הקטנה?

פרק טו

בני! עוד דבר ואמרת אליהם. אבי השביעני לאמר. אין ראוי[124] לאמת שתהיה לא פחדנית ולא ביישנית. ולמה אשא פנים בתורה? ואין לי לחלוק נחלת זמני רק עם בוראי נותן נשמתי. חלילה לי משום לבי לכבוד או להפכו מכל בני הזמן זולת

116 B, H שבעירי. 117 A, L omit. 118 A, L ואשיב. 119 A, L והעניים. 120 A, L omit. 121 A, L omit. 122 A, L בהלכה זאת או בזאת. 123 A מידיעת הבורא אחדותו. L מידיעת הבורא או אחדותו. 124 A, L אין ראויה. B. omits אין.

my Masters, and God will hear you. I observe that those of you who are devoted to the Talmud, its glosses and commentaries, do so in order to probe the reasons of the practical precepts. You are not content to take the law from Maimonides' Code, though he asserted that no other book was necessary.

Take as an example the law formulated by Maimonides that a Sukkah (tabernacle) more than 20 cubits high is unfit for use on the festival. But ye regard this as ridiculously inadequate until ye ascertain the ground of the law, and satisfy yourselves whether it is because too high a roof is out of the line of vision, or because in such a case a man sits in the shade cast by the walls rather than by the roof, or because a Sukkah must be a slightly built structure, as the Talmud explains.[53] The keenest students are not content even with this, but feel impelled to exercise themselves in more penetrating questions, and to follow out the most detailed suggestions and inferences.

Of a verity, I admit that this is good. But why should a knowledge of the reasons for the practical precepts be obligatory, while the in-

[53] T. B. Sukkah 2a.

היחידי סגולה[125]. לכן רבותי שמעו אלי וישמע אליכם אלהים! רואה אני כי כונת המתעסקים מכם בגמרא וחדושים ושיטות היא[126] רק לדעת ראיות על המצות[127] המעשיות. כי לא יספיק לכם[128] הקבלה מספר משנה תורה שחבר רבינו משה ואעפ"י שאמר הוא ז"ל ואינו צריך לספר אחר ביניהם:

והמשל בזה. הרב המורה כתב בהלכותיו סוכה שהיא גבוהה[129] למעלה מכ' אמות פסולה. ותאמרו נואש! ולא ינוח לבכם עד שתדעו אם הוא משום דלא שלטא ביה עינא. או משום דאין אדם[130] יושב בצל סכך אלא בצל דפנות. או משום דסוכה דירת עראי בעינן. כמו שכתוב בגמרא: והמהדרין מן המהדרין לא יספיק להם גם זה. ולא ישבעו עד אשר יוסיפו על זה קושיות ושיטות ואם תמצא לומר ויש לומר וכאלה רבות:

ובאמת מודה אני שזה טוב הוא. אבל מדוע ידיעת הראיות במצות המעשיות חובה וידיעתם

125 B, H היחידים סגולות. L היחידים סגולת השם.
126 B ומשניות הן. H ושניות הן.
127 L omits. 128 L יסופק. 129 L omits.
130 B, H אתה.

vestigation of the grounds for the spiritual precepts is not even permitted but is absolutely barred? What is the sin of the four inner laws that ye treat them so differently, being content to take them on authority, without specification, without even an understanding of their terms? Woe unto us that we have sinned! Jews despise or neglect the *Guide* nowadays, though the purpose of that treatise is to demonstrate the existence and unity of God. The Christians [54] honor the work, study and translate it, while even greater attention is paid to it by the Mohammedans in Fez and other countries, where they have established Colleges for the study of the *Guide* under Jewish scholars![55]

CHAPTER XVI

But, my son, why should I attribute this good advice to my own initiative? Say to them: Seek from the *Guide* and particularly from ch. 51 of Part III. Then you will all know what course to follow. Maimonides was a qualified authority on whom to rely, it being recognized how he excelled all his contemporaries as accomplished rabbi and expert philosopher, especially as he adduced evidence for his view from our Sages. Far be it from you to neglect their

[54] Another reading "Egyptians". This variation between מצרי and נוצרי is not infrequent in medieval texts.

[55] See note 47 above.

במצות הלביות אינה רשות[131] או מקום פטור אבל[132] הוא אסור גמור: ומה חטאו אלו הארבע מצות הלביות שזכרתי שלא תעשו להם כמו זה הדרך אבל יספיק לכם הקבלה החלושה במעט דברים וגם עם העדר הבנת הענינים כמו שזכרתי. אוי נא לנו כי חטאנו[133] היהודים מואסים או עוזבים היום את ספר המורה שכל עצמו להביא מופתים על מציאות אלהינו ואחדותו וקדמותו[134]. והנוצרים[135] יכבדוהו וינשאוהו והעתיקוהו. וכל שכן הישמעאלים בפאס ובשאר ארצות אשר[136] קבעו שם מדרשות ללמוד ספר המורה מפי סופרים יהודים:

פרק טז

בני! למה איחס כל אלה דברים הטובים לעצמי? אמור אליהם! דרשו מעל ס' המורה וקראו ובפרט פרק[137] נ"א מחלק שלישי. אז תדעו כולכם מה תעשו. וכדאי הוא ז"ל לסמוך עליו עם היות מפורסם שהוא היה רב ורבן וחכם שלם מכל הנמצאים היום. כש"כ שהוא ז"ל מביא ראיות מדברי רז"ל. וחלילה

131 A, L וידיעת הראיות במצות הלביות רשות.
132 L או.
133 B, H אנו.
134 B omits.
135 A והמצרים.
136 L omits.
137 A, L בפרט.

words; but let your principle be to regard the speech not the speaker. "Take with you words"[56] —as the Sage enjoined: Take the truth from whoever uttereth it. This must be the guiding rule. Or to put the thought in fanciful terms: Receive my instruction and not Silver (the name of him who addresses you).[57]

Chapter XVII

I have shown thee, my son, the way to wisdom. Yet I will call to thy mind one matter, which must never be forgotten, seeing that, whilst still a boy, thou hast read the Talmud, and particularly the opening tractate. There are many haggadot the literal wording of which posits ideas inadmissible rationally, or attributes to God corporeality, change, or any other affection. Perchance thou mayest eat to satiety from these evil viands, these deadly poisons—I refer to the before-mentioned haggadot as literally interpreted, God deliver thee! Therefore my son, understand that most of the haggadot found in the Talmud and other rabbinic books, which on the surface seem to imply the ideas I have named, are figures of speech, with an inner meaning, which we can sometimes discern, sometimes not.

Ours it is to realize that he who is of the seed of Abraham our father,—who endangered his life to dissociate himself from all the people and the

[56] Hosea 14. 3. See Maimonides, Intro. to Mishnah Abot.

[57] Prov. 8.10. The author means by this play on

שתעברו על דברי חכמים ז"ל. וכלל[138] הדבר אל תביטו אל אומר הדברים. קחו עמכם דברים. כמו שצוה החכם. קבל האמת ממי שאמרו. ועל דרך מליצת השיר אומר אני קחו מוסרי ואל כסף!

פרק יז

בני! בדרך חכמה הוריתיך. אכן עוד אזכירך דבר[139] אחד פן תשכח בעבור היות לך גירסא דינקותא בגמרא. ובפרט במס' ברכות שהיא ההתחלה. ובאו בה כמה הגדות יורה פשוטם מציאת ענינים נמנעים[140] אצל השכל. או ענינים מיחסים גשמות או שינוי או הפעלות מה לשם. פן תאכל ושבעת מאלו המאכלים הרעים סמי המות. רצוני אותם הפשטים האלהים יצילך! לכן דע בני כי רוב ההגדות הנמצאות בגמרא וביתר ספריהם. אשר פשוטם יורה אלו הענינים אשר זכרתי. יש בהם תוך והסתר והם כולם משלים. הן שנבין אנחנו הנסתר הן שלא נבין:

ולנו יש לדעת כי מי שהוא מזרע אברהם אבינו. אשר השליך את נפשו לחלוק עם כל בני ארצו

138 A, L ובכלל.   139 So H. The other texts read דרך.
140 L שאינם נמצאים.

king of his country, believers in the corporeality of God—, we who are of Abraham's seed must share Abraham's principles! Whoever believes the contrary, who regards God as corporeal, testifies of himself that he is not of the seed of Abraham, but of the seed of Nimrod or the other Chaldean disputants with Abraham. Should any of thy rabbinic teachers desire to explain literally and not metaphorically any of the haggadot which are opposed to reason, or attribute corporeality or other inadmissible quality to God, as in the instance when "the children of Israel did impute things that were not right unto the Lord their God,"[58] do not assent to such a teacher, accept not the saying nor its utterer, for it is the opinion of a single unsupported authority. In fact, concerning the practical precepts there were just as various opinions, one prohibiting and another allowing, and the final decision necessarily adopted one view and rejected another, —so with the spiritual precepts, and particularly those which need intellectual assent, there were different points of view, as Maimonides often indicates.[59]

Chapter XVIII

But thou mayest be led on to think of similar difficulties in the case of the Scriptures where

words, take my instruction without any regard to me, Ibn Kaspi, who provide it. See above p. 127.

[58] See T. B. Mo'ed Katan 18b; Kimḥi on II Kings 17.9; Maim. *Guide*, III, ch. 19. Ibn Kaspi quoted the first words: "This pillar neither sees nor hears", not very aptly. Maim. uses it against the deniers of Providence.

[59] This principle that the *haggadot* were not neces-

ומלכם שהיו מאמינים גשמות באל יתברך. הוא מאמין באמונתו. ומי שמאמין חילוף זה בגשמות[141] הוא מעיד על עצמו שאינו מזרעו של אברהם אבינו. אכן הוא מזרע נמרד או מיתר בני כשדים בני מחלוקות של אברהם אבינו: ואם על כל פנים[142] ירצה אחד מרבותיך התלמודיים שקצת ההגדות אין להם תוך אבל הם כפשוטם. עם היותם אומרים דברים נמנעים או מיחסים גשמות או דבר מרוחק אצל הי"ת כמאמר האומר העמוד הזה אינו רואה ואינו שומע. לא תאבה לו ולא תשמע אל דברי[143] המאמר ההוא ולאומרו כי יחידאה הוא. והאמת כי כמו שהיה מחלוקת ביניהם במצות המעשיות זה אוסר וזה מתיר. זה מחייב וזה פוטר[144]. ונפסקה הלכה כאחד מהם בהכרח והאחר נדחה. כך הענין[145] במצות הלבבות. ובכלל בדעות העיוניות כמו שזכר הרב המורה רבים מזה המין:

פרק יח

כי תאמר בלבבך מה נעשה לכתובי התורה

[141] B, H omit.
[142] A omits these three words. [143] H omits.
[144] H מוכה. [145] B העיון.

the Law and the Prophets attribute corporeality to God. Such phrases as "in our image, after our likeness," may occur to thee; or the texts in which face and back, hands and feet are ascribed to God.[60] Understand that there is an explanation for all this, which must not be taken literally. But how canst thou realize it, while thou art a boy of twelve? For thou wilt find the explanation in the *Guide*,[61] and I have already directed thee not to study that work till thou art twenty. But in the freshness of thy childhood, and while the dew of thy young manhood is as the dew of light,[62] observe my commandments and live! Believe, as a tradition from me, that these matters can all be explained, that, in verity, unto God one cannot attribute body or bodily qualities or plurality of any kind, exalted as He is above all material and all angelic beings.

How all this is true, what is its significance, lo! as thou knewest not in the hour of thy entrance into the world, so thou wilt not know it until thou art twenty and over. Then wilt thou rise to this all-important knowledge, then wilt thou enter within the precincts of Pleasure and Delight, the Paradise of all dainty fruits, eating unto satisfaction of the Tree of Life, for as Solomon said of Wisdom: "She is a tree of life to them that lay hold of her, and happy is everyone that holdeth her fast."[63]

sarily unanimous or true expressions of Jewish opinion was strongly maintained by Naḥmanides in his famous Disputation. [60] Gen. 1. 25; Exod. 33.25, 34. 10; I Chron. 21.13. [61] See the opening chapters of Part I. [62] Isa. 26.19. [63] Prov. 3.18.

והנביאים שהם מיחסים לאל גשמות. באמרו בצלמנו כדמותנו. וכן יחסו לו פנים ואחור וידים ורגלים וכל הדומה לזה? דע כי לכל זה פירוש ואינו כפשוטו: אבל איך תוכל לדעת כל זה בהיותך בן שנים עשרה שנה:[146] כי פירוש כל זה תמצא בס' המורה. וכבר צויתיך שלא תעיין בו רק אחר שתהיה בן עשרים שנה: אמנם בטל ילדותך או בטל אורות טלך בימי בחורותיך שמור מצותי וחיה! האמן בקבלה ממני כי לכל זה פירוש. והאמת הוא שאין לאל גשמות או יחוס גשמות או רבוי בשום צד. והוא נעלה[147] מכל גשם ומלאך:

אמנם איך כל זה אמת ומה כונת זה. הנה כמו שלא ידעתו[148] ביום צאתך מבטן אמך. כן לא תדעהו עד היותך בן עשרים שנה ומעלה. אז תעלה לזאת הידיעה הנכבדת. ותכנס לפני ולפנים בגן העדון והעונג. פרדס[149] כל פרי מגדים. ואכלת ושבעת מפרי עץ החיים כמו שאמר שלמה על החכמה. עץ חיים היא למחזיקים בה ותמכיה מאשר:

146 B, H add או בן עשרים שנה.

147 A, L פנים, וכי הוא נכבד ונעלה. 148 A, L דעת.

149 A, L לפנים בגן עדן ותתענג בפרדס עם.

Chapter XIX

And as I have bidden thee, my son! to maintain from thy birth this supreme faith—the faith of Abraham thy first father,— refusing to attach to God the idea of body, so I command thee to hold through life to the trust that after thy death thou wilt be found worthy of the future life, where nothing bodily is. Thou wilt be as an angel of the Lord of Hosts, a brother and comrade of the other Angels there! What good or profit, what happiness or delight, is comparable to this? Yet mayest thou after thy death attain to this level of good, if thou hast in thy earthly life won for thy soul all that I have commanded. As our honored Sages in their figurative style said, "He who toils on Friday shall eat on Saturday,"[64] or again: "Hasten, thou wise, and eat; hasten and drink, for the world to come is like a marriage feast."[65]

Chapter XX

Dost thou ask how this is? Again my son, know that this is beyond thy capacity until thou art twenty, and canst turn thy mind to metaphysical investigations, among them the holy *Guide*. Then wilt thou see this in a light as clear as the sunshine. But till then trust and

[64] T. B. 'Abodah Zarah 3.

[65] T. B. 'Erubin 54a. This is not the usual reading. The ordinary text advocates making the most of the ephemeral present.

פרק יט

כאשר צויתיך בני להיות כל ימי חייך מלידה ומבטן ומהריון בזאת[150] האמונה הנכבדת. אמונת אברהם אביך הראשון. והוא העדר כל גשמות מהשם. כן אצוך להיות כל ימיך להאמין שאחרי מותך תזכה לחיי העולם הבא. ויהיה שם העדר כל גשמות. ותהיה[151] כמלאך ה' צבאות. אח וריע[152] עם יתר המלאכים אשר שם. ומה יש טובה והנאה ועדון ושמחה ועונג זולת זה? אך תזכה למעלה העליונה והגבוהה מזה הטוב אחרי מותך. אם זכית בחייך לקנות לנפשך כל אשר צויתיך. כמו שאמרו רבותינו המכובדים במשליהם. מי שטרח בערב שבת יאכל בשבת. ואמרו שיננא חטוף ואכול חטוף ושתה דהאי עלמא דאתי לבי[153] הלולא דמיא:

פרק כ

כי תאמר איך זה? דע בני כי לא תוכל לדעת גם את זה עד היותך בן עשרים שנה ותשים עיונך[154] באלהיות שמכללם ספר המורה הקדוש. ואז תדע זה ברור כשמש. ואולם בין האי ובין האי ראוי לך

150 A, L על זאת. 151 B, A, H אבל תהיה.
152 B, H omit. 153 B, H דבי. L כבי. 154 L עיניך.

lean on me. I am thy surety, my son, that if thou dost fulfil all my behests, thou wilt after thy death reach the highest degree of good appointed unto us for the world to come, and the expression "after death" will be only a figure of speech, and when thy house-hold think thee dead, then wilt thou be truly alive. As our Sages say: "The righteous in their death are called living."[66] Sufficient is it for thee to be inspired now with this glorious hope of the hereafter, when thou wilt be delivered from the diseases which befall thee in this world; there no bodily pains will wrack, nor faculties decay; there slumber will not be heavy on thine eyes, nor thy nostrils suffer from assail of noisome smoke; there, wilt thou behold thy sons and daughters, with all those near and dear unto thee, partaking of the banquet in joy. And what, my son, canst thou desire more than this?

Chapter XXI

"The end of the matter, all having been heard: fear God and keep His commandments."[67] This term, "His commandments", embraces those that concern conduct and those that concern thought; neither must be omitted, but each ful-

[66] T. B. Berakot 19.
[67] Eccles. 12.13.

שתאמין בי[155] ותבטח ותשען עלי: ובכלל אני ערב לך בני. כי אם תעשה כל מה שצויתיך תשיג אחרי מותך אל היותר טוב מן המדרגות היעודות לנו לעה"ב עד שאחרי מותך הוא על דרך העברה אבל כשתחשוב או כשיחשבו בני ביתך שתמות אז תחיה. וכן אמרו רבותינו המכובדים צדיקים במיתתם נקראים חיים: והנה רב לך היום שאתה[156] בזה התוחלת הנכבדה לעולם הבא. ואז תנצל מכל המכאובים המוצאים אותך בעולם הזה. כי אז בטנך לא תאכל ומעיך לא תמלא פרש רעי וזבל וקיא ומוגלא. או לחה מוראה ונגאלה ולא יכאבו לך עינים וברכים. ולא תצטרך לעביט של מימי רגלים. ולא תנום ולא תישן. ולא יעלה באפך ריח רע ועשן. ושם[157] תראה בניך ובנותיך אוכלים ושמחים ויתר הקרובים והאחים. ומה תבקש עוד בני?

פרק כא

סוף דבר הכל נשמע את האלהים ירא ואת מצותיו שמור! והנה בכלל מצותיו הן המצות המעשיות והמצות העיוניות. אחת מהנה לא נעדרה

[155] So H adds. [156] H שמחה. [157] H משם.

filled in the manner fit for each. This is the significance of the declaration of our fathers: "We will do and we will hear."[68] It is a deliberate, precise declaration, the reverse of hasty and confused as the heretic cited in the Talmud[69] pronounced it! For the two verbs "do" and "hear" are not illogically ordered, but refer to two different things. For when the word of Moses came before them, enjoining precepts of action and of mind, the people answered concerning all, "All that the Lord hath spoken we will do and hear." The term "do" applies to the practical precepts, and comes first; the term "hear" applies to the precepts involving the mind, and comes second. For practical precepts are incumbent at an earlier moment, while the others require for their understanding and fulfilment the examination of their proofs.

And this is obvious. For a child is first taught rules of conduct, among them the use of language. Thus our Sages say[70]: the father teaches his son: "Moses commanded a law", "Hear O Israel, the Lord our God, the Lord is One." That is, he initiates and teaches him to say this in Hebrew.[71] So, he teaches him to don the fringed garments and to pray; and similarly with the other practical precepts. But the acceptance by the heart, which is true knowledge, will come to thee, my son, after thy twentieth year, if God so will, though it may not come to others till they be past

[68] Exod. 24.7.

[69] T. B. Ketubot, 112a; T. B. Shabbat 88a.

[70] T. B. Sukkah 44.

[71] Some versions omit "in Hebrew".

כפי הראוי לכל אחת. וזה הלשון הוא מאמר אבותינו נעשה ונשמע! והוא מאמר מדוקדק. הפך שסבר ההוא מינאה עד שקראנו עמא פזיזא[158]. שחשב ששני אלו העניינים היו על נושא אחד. ואינו כן. אכן הוא על שני נושאים. וזה כי באשר קדם דבר[159] משה אליהם בצווי מצות מעשיות ועיוניות מאת ה׳. ענו הם על הכל. כל אשר דבר ה׳ נעשה ונשמע: והקדימו נעשה על המעשיות לנשמע[160] על העיוניות הלביות. כי המעשיות קודמות בזמן לעיוניות שידיעתם ושמועתם הוא בלימוד המופתים:

וזה מבואר. כי הנער יחונך תחלה במעשיות שבכללם הם הלשוניות. וכן אמרו חז״ל אביו מלמדו תורה צוה לנו. ושמע ישראל ה׳ אלהינו ה׳ אחד. כלומר יחנכהו וילמדהו שיאמר[161] זה בלשון הקודש[162]. וכן יתעטף בציצית ויתפלל. ובכלל המצות המעשיות: אבל שמיעת הלב שהוא הידיעה האמיתית[163] כמו שקדם לנו זה יהיה לך בני אחר עשרים שנה ברצון ה׳ ואולי לזולתך אחר

[158] L reads פחיזאה. B, H read הפך מה שסיפר ההוא אינש...פזיזא.
[159] B, H כבר. [160] ונשמע in B, H, A,L.
[161] H לומר for those 3 words. [162] B, H omit.
[163] H omits.

forty or fifty. In any case, this kind of knowledge, the acceptance and realization of truth by the intellect, belongs to those inner duties which can only be fulfilled by a man in his maturity. Therefore the declaration: "we will do and we will hear" included the two parts of perfection, our laws which are the perfection of the two parts of the soul—the practical and the rational. And thou, my son! wilt have rest, and wilt reach the place of thy destiny at the end of days. May God hold thee worthy of a life of felicity in this world and the next. Amen and amen!

[Ended is the Book of Admonition, called "A Guide to Knowledge". Thanks be to God, who stretcheth out the heavens as a curtain!][72]

[Ibn Kaspi thy father wrote this, in the month of Elul, in the year 92 of the sixth thousand (1332), in the city of Valencia].

[From thy yearning after thy silver comes thy wrath!
Never does this care leave thee, till it make an end of thee!
Yet, will it be thy comrade when thou goest to thy grave?
Or will it be a help unto thee in the distress that then befalls?][73]

[72] See notes to Hebrew text for the authorities which contain or omit this and the next two paragraphs.

[73] There are several puns in the Hebrew which could not be reproduced in an English version.

ארבעים שנה או חמשים שנה: ובכלל על כל פנים השמיעה בלב ובשכל כמו שהוא מונח בעברי בכמה מקומות על הציור השכל כראוי[164]. הנה יהיה זה במצות הלביות העיוניות אחר זמן רב כשיגדל האדם: ובכלל היה אמרם נעשה ונשמע כולל שני חלקי שלמות. המצות שלנו שהם שלמות שני חלקי הנפש. רצוני המעשי והעיוני. ואתה תנוח ותעמוד לגורלך לקץ הימין. והשם יזכך בני לחיים טובים בעולם הזה ובעולם הבא אמן ואמן:

נשלם ספר המוסר הנקרא יורה דעה.

תהלה לאל ית' נוטה שמים כיריעה:[165]

וכתב זה אבן כספי אביך. חדש אלול שנת תשעים ושתים לפרט האלף הששי למנין. בעיר ולנסיאה[166]

מִכָּסְפְּךָ אֶל־כַּסְפְּךָ הֵן קִצְפְּךָ!
בִּסְעִיפְּךָ לֹא יִרְפְּךָ עַד יֵאָסְפְּךָ!
הֲיִתְחַבְּרְךָ יוֹם עָבְרְךָ אֶל קִבְרְךָ?
אוֹ שֶׁבְּרְךָ אֶל שֶׁבְּרְךָ כִּי יְקָרְךָ?[167]

[164] A, L הראוי.
[165] B, H omit.
[166] In B, H only.
[167] B, H omit poem.

HEBREW ETHICAL WILLS

SELECTED AND EDITED

BY

ISRAEL ABRAHAMS

Reader in Talmudic in the University of Cambridge,
formerly Senior Tutor at Jews' College, London.

PART TWO

PHILADELPHIA
The Jewish Publication Society of America
1926

צואות גאוני ישראל

לקטו נערכו הוגהו ונעתקו

על ידי

ישראל בן ברוך בר אברהם

חלק ב

פילאדלפיא
החברה היהודית להוצאת ספרים אשר באמיריקא
תרפ"ז

צואה מחסיד אחד מוסר לבניו
(ר' יהודה בן אשר)

THE TESTAMENT OF JUDAH ASHERI

VIII

THE TESTAMENT OF JUDAH ASHERI

Asher ben Yeḥiel was born in Germany c. 1250, but migrated to Spain, where he died in 1327 or 1328. Judah, the author of this Testament, succeeded his father Asher ben Yeḥiel as Rabbi of Toledo, dying in 1349. Towards the end of his life he would seem to have recovered some of his financial property. A good account of Judah's life may be read in *J. E.*, vii, 340.

The text here printed is taken direct from the MS. (British Museum) from which S. Schechter published an edition in 1885. Some extracts have since been printed by L. Margoliouth in the third volume of his British Museum Catalogue, and some passages also appear in A. Neubauer's *Mediaeval Jewish Chronicles*, i, 103. The latter is collated in the notes as N. (S. refers to S. Schechter's readings and suggestions). One important change will be noted in the present edition. The reading 1285 adopted by Schechter for Judah's migration to Toledo must be emended to 1305 (the MS. clearly reads ס"ה and not מ"ה). Thus the received date 1305 is confirmed. It is not quite clear whether Judah implies that any long interval divided his two visits to Toledo. It seems scarcely possible that he was sent as an emissary at the early age of thirteen (See the passage p. 166 and n. 11, to the English translation below). All that is certain is that he went to Toledo in advance of his father and subsequently settled with him in the place.

ח

צואה מחסיד אחד מוסר לבניו

(ר׳ יהודה בן אשר)

אשר בן יחיאל נולד באשכנז בערך שנת י׳ לאלף הששי, אבל גלה לספרד ושם נפטר בשנת פ״ז או פ״ח. יהודה בנו, המחבר של הצואה הזאת, ירש את משרת הרבנות של אביו בעיר טולידה, והסתלק מן העולם בשנת ק״ט. כנראה, הושב לו מעט מהון כספו לקץ ימי חייו. תולדותיו וכל הקורות אותו אפשר למצוא באנציקלופדיה היהודית האנגלית, כרך שביעי, דף ש״מ.

הנוסח העברי הנדפס פה לקוח ישר מן הכ״י של המוזיאום הבריטי אשר ממנו הוציא שלמה שכטר את נוסחו בשנת תרמ״ה. מן העת ההיא נדפסו איזה לקוטים ממנו ע״י ל. מרגליות בכרך השלישי של רשימת המוזיאום הבריטי, ואיזה פסוקים מופיעים ג״כ ב„סדר החכמים וקורות הימים״ של א. נייבויער, כרך ראשון, דף ק״ג. בהערותי כניתי את האחרון N (S מורה על ההגהות של שכטר). שינוי חשוב אחד נמצא במהדורה הנוכחית. שכטר גרס שנת מ״ה לגלותו של יהודה לטולידה, אבל אין כל ספק שצריך לגרוס ס״ה (בכ״י כתוב ברור ס״ה ולא מ״ה), בהסכם עם המסורה שבאה לידינו מדור דור. לא נתברר עדיין אם כונתו של יהודה היא שימים רבים עברו בין סיורו הראשון והשני לטולידה. כמעט שאי אפשר הוא שנשלח בתור שליח בהיותו רק בן שלש עשרה (ראה להלן דף 166 והערה י״א אל ההעתקה האנגלית למטה). בודאות גמורה אפשר להחליט רק שהלך לטולידה קודם לאביו ואח״כ התישב עמו שם.

Apart from its ethical aspects, Judah's will has great historical value. The author's naïve delight in legendary lore, is characteristic of his age. But on the other hand his more famous brother Jacob (author of the Ṭurim) very pointedly disparages a belief in omens or dreams. More interesting is Judah's insistence on the ordinance of the *Tithe* (on which see *Jewish Life in the Middle Ages*, ch. xvii). More important still is the account of the personal relations between Rabbi and congregation. Judah writes at the transition period, when the Rabbi was passing out of the category of voluntary to salaried official. Judah throws a genial light on the new conditions. Unfortunately we do not know exactly what coin the author describes as the *zehub*, but the payments to him seem considerable on any estimate of the coin's value. Finally, Judah's remarks on family intermarriages have considerable importance for the social life of the Jews in the fourteenth century.

A Saint once indited a Testament in admonition of his sons, bidding them keep the way of God his Master. He thus exhorted them not because they were worse than their contemporaries, but because he desired to direct them into the paths of the ancients. They are called friends [of God] when they imitate the deeds of their fathers[1]. With this example in view, I said: "Better is open rebuke than love that is hidden."[2] Such rebuke entwines itself in the hearts of the hearers, and to the utterers it is pleasant, for they know that their words will be guarded as the apple of the eye. So it is said: "He that

[1] Sanh. 27b; Abot vi, beginning.

[2] Prov. 27.5.

מלבד ערכה המוסרי יש לה לצואת יהודה ערך היסטורי גדול. חבתו התמימה של המחבר לאגדות ולמעשיות היא מיוחדת לבני דורו. להפך, אחיו יעקב המפורסם ממנו (מחבר הטורים) מתנגד בכל כח אל האמונה באותות ובחלומות. חשובה היא ההטעמה שבה יהודה מטעים את מצות המעשר (עיין בספרי Jewish Life in the Middle Ages, פרק י"ז). חשיבות יותר גדולה יש לדבריו ע"ד היחס שבין הרבי והקהלה. יהודה כתב בתקופת המעבר, בשעה שהרבי אשר שרת את קהלתו שלא על מנת לקבל פרס התחיל לקבל פרס ידוע בעד משרתו, ודבריו משליכים אור על התנאים החדשים. לדאבוננו לא נדע בדיוק את ערך המטבע שהוא קורא „זהוב", אבל איזה ערך שיהיה לה הנה קבל משכורת הגונה. לאחרונה, דברי יהודה על ההתחתנות בין המשפחות יש להם ערך גדול בעד הכרת החיים החברותיים של היהודים במאה הארבע עשרה.

וצוה אותם לשמור דרך האל אדוניו. לא מפני שאינם טובים כבני זמנם. אלא כדי להנהיגם בדרכי הקדמונים. והם הנקראים רעים כשהם אוחזים מעשה אבותיהם בידיהם. ועל זה אמרתי טובה תוכחת מגולה מאהבה מסותרת. כי אז תהיה ללבבות נקשרת. ואז למוכיחים ינעם. ביודעים כי שמעם ינצרוהו כאישון עינם. כאמור מוכיח

rebuketh a man shall in the end find more favor than he that flattereth with the tongue."[3] So I will open with a voice of thanksgiving, I, Judah, to the Rock whose works are awe-inspiring, to whom appertain glory and greatness transcending man's capacity to express them; who, ere ever I was born, remembered me for good. My mother dreamed how she was told that she would bear a son, and was asked whether she wished him to be wise or wealthy? She chose wisdom. And though in reality dreams speak vain things, for I learned not wisdom, yet in a certain deceptive sense the dream was fulfilled. The world imagines that I am a scholar, one who giveth goodly words! Wealth, too, the Lord, blessed be He, hath bestowed on me beyond the ordinary, in that He hath provided me with the measure of mine allotted bread.[4] I rejoice in my portion.[5]

When I was an infant about three months old, my eyes were affected, and were never completely restored. A certain woman tried to cure me when I was about three years of age, but she added to my blindness, to the extent that I remained for a year confined to the house, being unable to see the road on which to walk. Then a Jewess, a skilled oculist, appeared on the scene; she treated me for about two months, and then died. Had she lived another month, I might

[3] *Ibid.* 28.23.

[4] I Kings 3.5 ff.; Gen. 49.21; Prov. 30.8.

[5] "Who is rich? He who rejoices in his portion" (Abot, 4.3).

אדם אחרי חן ימצא ממחליק לשון. ואפתח בקול תודה. וזאת ליהודה בתחילה. לצור נורא עלילה. אשר לו התפארת והגדולה. ומרומם על כל ברכה ותהלה. אשר בטרם הוציאני. לטובה זכרני. בהיות אמי מורתי הרה ממני אמרו לה בחלום שתלד בן. ואם היתה רוצה שיהיה חכם או עשיר? והשיבה שהיתה רוצה שיהיה חכם. ואם לפי האמת החלומות שוא ידברו. כי לא למדתי חכמה. לפי ההטעאה קצתו נתקיים שמדמים העולם שאני יודע ספר. ונותן אמרי שפר. גם עושר נתן לי האל ית' יותר מבן גילי. במה שמטריפני בית כור לחם חקי. שמח בחלקי:

ויהי בהיותי כבן שלשה חדשים בעיני חליתי. וממנו כבתחילה לא נתרפאתי. ואני כבן שלש שנים השתדלה אשה אחת לרפאני. והוסיפה על עורוני. עד אשר עמדתי שנה אחת כלוא בבית. לפי שלא ראיתי הדרך אשר הייתי הולך. עד שבאת יהודית אחת יודעת ברפואת העינים. והשתדלה כשני חדשים ומתה. ואלו חיתה עוד חדש אחד אפשר

have received my sight fully. As it was, but for the two months' attention from her, I might never have been able to see at all. Blessed be the Lord, who exercised marvelous loving-kindness towards me, and opened for me a lattice through which I might behold, with my own eye, the work of His hands.

Thenceforward I studied the tractates which my lord, my father,[6] taught in the College, as far as my capacity went, and without intricate discussion.[7] When I was about thirteen[8] he took me from the land of persecution, and "hurled me up and down with a man's throw."[9] I left the German method of study without entering on that of France.[10] For exile confuses the intellect, and I was able neither to write nor speak their language, nor understand their books. Moreover, I could not pore over my books day and night because of my weak eyesight. For this reason I could not write books nor compile treatises.

When I was twenty-eight[11] my lord, my father, of blessed memory, sent me to the city of Toledo,

[6] This form of reference to Rabbi Asher b. Yeḥiel (the Rosh) was usual with his sons: it is very frequent in the Ṭurim of Judah's brother, Jacob.

[7] Lit. without difficulty and answer.

[8] S. suggests the reading "thirteen": the MS. has 'ט.

[9] Isa. 22.17.

[10] On the method of studying in the thirteenth century see I. H. Weiss, *Dor dor vedoreshav*, vol. v, ch. 1 (1891)—, a chapter which first appeared in English (*J. Q. R.*, 1889, pp. 289–313). Perhaps in what follows the author does

שהייתי רואה כבתחילה. ואלמלא השני החדשים שהשתדלה עמי אולי לא הייתי רואה מאז מאורות מימי. ברוך השם שהפליא עמי חסדו ופתח לי מאורות לראות בעין מעשה ידיו:

ומאז למדתי המסכתות שהיה מגיד אאז"ל בישיבה. כפי השגתי בלבד לא בקושיא ותשובה. ואני כבן שלש עשרי[1] שנים מארץ גזירה הוציאני. וטלטלה[2] גבר טלטלני. ומשנות למוד אשכנז יצאתי. ולשנות צרפת לא באתי. כי הגלות מבלבל הדעת. וגם לא היה לי כתב ולא לשון ללמוד בכתב ספריהם. ולהבין לשון מליצותיהם. וגם לא יכולתי לטרוח ימים ולילות. מחולשת העינים כי הם אפלות. ולכן לא יכולתי לכתוב ספרים. ולא לחבר חבורים:

ובהיותי בן כ"ח[3] שנים שלחני א"א ז"ל לעיר

[1] So S corrects MS. which has 'ש. [2] MS. ולטליטלה. Cf. Introduction p. 163.
[3] So MS. S suggests correction to ל"ה.

not refer to his ignorance of the French language but of the methods of French scholarship.

[11] S suggests the reading 35. The incident is not clear. It possibly refers to the arrival of Asher, who was not allowed to leave Toledo to bring his family, a duty imposed on Judah, who was attacked on this journey.

to seek out a place there, and so I did. The Toledo community sent for him, insisted on securing him for their city, and they sent their delegates after I was gone. On my journey back, I was waylaid by bandits who sought my life. But all their purpose was frustrated. My father's God was with me, and His angels encamped round about me, so that I reached my father's house in peace. Twenty-three years later my father died. Though there were in the city men greater and wiser than I, the Lord, be His name blessed, inclined unto me grace and favor in the eyes of the inhabitants and they installed me in my father's seat. But I had no experience fitting me for such an honor, my scholarship was not enough for such an office. I was a foreigner of no account, with altogether insignificant attainments. I could find no quality in me.[12] I sat one day pondering in silence, my heart within me appalled.[13] In my hand was the book of Hagiographa, and I said: How will my lot ascend?[14] I will account it as a sign. I opened and there came up in my hand this verse:[15] "And Nathan said unto David, Do all that is in thine heart, for God is with thee." When this text providentially presented itself, I rejoiced, and said, Though one may not seek an omen, one may

Then the Toledo community sent a party to escort Judah back. Or, Judah returned home to report his success, and the Toledan delegates were sent later. What is clear is that once Asher came to Toledo he was never allowed to go away.

טוליטלה לתור שם מקום וכן עשיתי. ושלחו קהל
טוליטלה בשבילו ולא הניחוהו[4] לצאת מביניהם.
ושלחו אחרי שלוחיהם. ובחזרתי ארבו עלי גוים
עריצים לקחת נפשי קמו[5]. וננער מהם כל אשר
זממו. ואלהי אבי היה עמדי. ומלאכיו חנו סביבי.
ושבתי בשלום אל בית אבי: אחרי כן כ״ג שנים נפטר
א״א ז״ל: גם כי היו בעיר גדולים וחכמים ממני.
הטה אלי השם ית׳ חן וחסד בעיני אנשי העיר ועל
כסא א״א ז״ל הושיבוני. ואני ללכת באלה לא ניסיתי
גם לא עמדה לי חכמתי. ואני גר תושב. למאומה
נחשב. נמשל כבהמה. ולדעת חכמה לא הגיע שכלי.
ולא מצאתי און לי. ויהי היום ואני יושב ודומם.
ולבי בקרבי ישתומם.[6] ובידי ספר כתובים. ואומר
איך יעלה גורלי. ואחשבהו לסימן לי. ואפתח ועלה
בידי הפסוק הזה ויאמר נתן אל דוד כל אשר
בלבבך עשה כי האלהים עמך. וכאשר הפסוק הזה
נזדמן לי שמחתי. ואמרתי אעפ״י שאין נחש יש סימן.

[4] The MS. repeats ק״ט. [5] MS. זממו [6] MS. אשתומם.

---

[12] Hosea 12.9, where און means "strength" or "wealth". See Rashi on the text. [13] Ps. 143.4.

[14] For phrases cf. Oxford Gesenius, *s. v.* גורל.

[15] I Chron. 17.2.

read a sign.[16] By the gracious gift of the Merciful, the Faithful God, I have honorably fulfilled all my duties, and thus far the Lord hath helped me.

Likewise my desire for children was not due to my love for them nor expectation of pride in them; my desire was to obey the divine precept, and to raise up offspring to fill my father's place in study and righteousness. For this I often prayed at the graves of the perfect and upright. God in His mercy gave me five sons, and I considered myself through them as a live man[17] among my people and brethren. But for my sins there was taken the one, "the middle bar",[18] on which I thought my house founded; for there passed a smoking furnace and a flaming torch between my pieces[19]. But my courage revived and I call heaven and earth to witness that I deserve this and double from God, for I know that His judgments are right. Faithfully He afflicted me, He chastened me sore, but gave me not over unto death.[20] I found consolation in the knowledge that my son was not punished by heaven for any sin of his, for he spent his days, which were few, in the eternal Law. And when the turn of my time comes, I shall go and shall see him, in Beth-el (the house of God) I shall meet him.[21] I rely on the mercy of God that a substitute will be bestowed on me, and my

[16] Cf. Ḥullin 95b.

[17] Cf. Nedarim 64b. See below p. 193 note 125. Possibly in the variant of חי and חיל the author designed a play on the name of his father Yeḥiel.

ובזכות הרחמן האל הנאמן עברתי בטוב כל עניני. ועד הנה עזרני ה':

גם חפצי בבנים אינו מאהבתי להם. ולא להתכבד בהם. רק להתקיים המצוה שנצטוינו בה. ולהיות לי זרע ממלא מקום אבותי בתורה ובמצות. ועל זה היתה תפילתי רוב הימים על קברי הצדיקים התמימים. והשם ברחמיו נתן לי חמשה בנים. וחשבתי עצמי בהם בן איש חי. בתוך עמי ואחי. ובעונותי נלכד האחד הבריח התיכון. אשר חשבתי שהבית עליו נכון. ועבר תנור ועשן ולפיד אש בין בתרי ונתחי. והעמיד בקרבי איש חי. ומעיד אני עלי שמים וארץ שחייב אני לאל בזה וכפלים. וידעתי כי צדקו משפטיו. ואמונה עינני. ויסור יסרני. ולמות לא נתנני. וזאת נחמתי בידעי כי לא נענש בעונו בידי שמים. וימיו אשר מעטים עסק בדת קדומת יומים. ובהגיע תור זמני. אלכה ואראנו. בית אל אמצאנו. ובטוח אני ברחמי שמים שיתן לי

---

[18] Exod. 26.28. The author refers to the death of his third son, the middle of the five.

[19] Cf. Gen. 15.17. The last phrase is obscure.

[20] Ps. 118.18.

[21] Hosea 12.5. By Beth-el the author means Heaven.

heart's gladness renewed. Then shall both he and his substitute be holy![22]

Now because of the weakness of my eyesight, my father and mother left me to do whatever was right in my own eyes; they never punished or rebuked me. Wherefore I have never been wont to chide others, for they taught me not how; even my own sons I knew not how to reprove. If they reprove not themselves, they will receive no reproof from me. Nor have I the face to admonish them by word of mouth, lest I put them to the blush, even though evil unto me was the evil of their ways. No joy of mine on earth equals my happiness at their well-doing, no pain or distress can compare with my grief at their misconduct. I have hated life, when I have seen that they went not in the paths of the fathers, in their sitting-down, rising up and walking on the way.[23]

But now my heart has impelled me to write for them this Letter of Admonition, conveying a discipline. I command them to read it carefully once a month, that the Lord may renew a clean heart and a steadfast spirit within them[24]. Perhaps they will mend and listen to my voice, so that I may speedily bring salvation unto them.[25] Now stand ye still that I may plead with you.[26] Why walk ye not in your fathers' way, nor hold the fear of God ever before your eyes? In His Law ye meditate not continually day and night, nor do ye go morning and evening to your houses of prayer. All your study is

[22] Lev. 27.10. [23] Eccles. 2.17; Deut. 6.7.
[24] Ps. 51.12. [25] *Ibid.* 55.9. [26] I Sam. 12.7.

תמורתו. וששון לבי יחדש. והיה הוא ותמורתו יהיה קדש:

ובשביל חולשת עיני. עזבוני אבי ואמי לעשות כל הישר בעיני. ולא יסרוני. גם לא הוכיחוני. ועל כן להוכיח אחרים לא הרגלתי. כי לא למדוני. ואפי' לבני לא אדע להוכיח. ואם לא יוכיחו עצמם ממני אין להם מוכיח. גם אין לי פנים להוכיחם בפה פן אלבין פניהם. ואם רע עלי רוע מעשיהם. ואין לי שמחה בעולם כמו פעולתם הטובה. ולא יגון ואנחה כמו ברוע מעללם. ושנאתי את החיים כמו שראיתי שאינם הולכים בדרכי אבותם. בשבתם בקומם ובהליכתם:

ועתה מלאני לבי לכתוב להם זאת האגרת תוכחת. מוסר מגדת. ומצוה אני אליהם לקרואתה בכוונה פעם אחת בחדש. ולב טהור ורוח נכון בקרבם יחדש: כי תהיה להם למזכרת. ביני וביניהם למשמרת. אולי ישובו וישמעו בקולי. ואחישה מפלט להם: ועתה התיצבו ואשפטה אתכם. מדוע לא תלכו בדרך אבותיכם. ולא תהיה יראת השם תמיד לעיניכם. ובתורתו לא תהגו תמיד כל ימיכם ולילותיכם. ואינכם משכימים ומעריבים לבית

below the standard,[27] and when the law is discussed ye are as the dumb, and open not your lips. You associate with those who are unfit to be your companions, for it is unseemly that their ways should be yours. Again, ye honor not your mother and your father, your conduct is disrespectful in their presence. Know ye not that unto the honor of God is likened the honor of parents?[28] For three are partners in a man (God and his parents)[29]. What have I left undone for you that a father could do for his children? Regularly were your meals provided, and all your wants. You own many books, and my every thought was directed to you, to equip you and to leave behind me a blessing[30] for you. And if the Law was given to those who ate the manna,[31] surely ye are in similar case. Or if it were a question of marriage, ye are assuredly wed to wives of your own family, who make no extravagant demands on you, but on the contrary seek to encourage you in your study. What then will you do on the day of visitation, when you give account of all your conduct? And what will ye answer when reproved before Him who trieth your reins, on the day wherein He arraigneth you for all your works?[32] Nay, my

[27] Or merely for appearance' sake.

[28] Mekilta on Exod. 20.12 (p. 70a).

[29] Ḳiddushin 30b. [30] Bequest, provision.

[31] To those whose minds were free from worldly cares, Mekilta on Exod. 16.4 (p. 47b).

[32] Habakkuk 2.1; Ps. 7.10; Prov. 29.4. In several phrases the author has the liturgy (especially for the New Year) in mind.

תפילותיכם.[7] ולפנים הוא כל למודכם. ובמשא ובמתן בהלכה אתם כאלמים. לא תפתחו שפתותיכם: ואתם מתחברים עם מי שאינם הגונים לכם להתחבר עמהם. כי מן הראוי הוא שלא דרכיהם דרכיכם: גם אינכם מכבדים אמכם ואביכם. כי לא תבושו מעצמיכם. בעשותכם (זה) מטותיהם (וצי)[8] ושאר צרכיהם. הלא ידעתם כי לכבוד המקום הוקש כבודם. כי שלשה שותפים יש באדם. ומה יש (לאדם) לאב לעשות לבנים ולא עשיתי לכם? בכל עת וזמן מזומן מאכלכם ומשתכם. וכלי[9] צורכיכם. וספרים רבים יש לכם. וכל מחשבותי עליכם. לתקן עצמיכם. ולהשאיר אחרי ברכה לכם. ואם התורה לאוכלי המן נתנה הלא כמותם (בי) כמותכם. ואם בשביל נשים הלא אתם נשואים ממשפחתכם. אשר לא יבקשו גדולות מכם ואדרבה[10] להחזיק אתכם. בלימוד יחזיקו ידיכם: ומה תעשו ליום פקודה. בתתכם חשבון על כל מדה? ומה תשיבו על תוכחת לפני בוחן כליותיכם. יום למשפט יעמידכם על כל מעשיכם?

7 MS. תפילותכם.

8 So MS. S suggests deletion.

9 MS. ובכל. 10 MS. ואדברה.

children, act for the glory of God and the honor of your progenitors. Improve your ways and your doings, and listen unto Judah your father. Make the Torah your main object, remember your Creator in the days of your youth,[33] while ye are still in vigor, and take upon you the yoke of the Torah. Let not the Law depart from your mouth, act always with the motive to please God. And the good name which your fathers bequeathed, uphold it and leave it to your children as a heritage.

Now, therefore, ye children, hearken unto me, for happy are they that keep my ways.[34] Come, listen unto me, I will teach you the fear of the Lord.[35] Look unto the rock whence ye were hewn, and to the hole of the pit,whence ye were digged.[36] Why, forsooth, were ye brought into this world? Not to eat and drink and wear fine linen and embroideries, but for the service of the God who hangeth the earth over nothing.[37] And since His wisdom has ordained that the body cannot be sustained without food and raiment, He permitted man to eat, drink and clothe himself for the sustenance of the body, that body and soul might be associated to perform God's behests so long as their association continues. Food to a man is like oil to a lamp; if it have much it shines, if little it is quenched. Yet sooner is the lamp extinguished by redundancy than deficiency of oil. Therefore be diligently on your

[33] Eccles. 12.1. [34] Prov. 8.32.
[35] Ps. 34.12. [36] Isa. 40.1.
[37] Job 26.7.

אל בני! עשו למען כבוד השם יתברך ולמען כבוד אבותיכם והטיבו דרכיכם ומעלליכם. ושמעו אל יהודה אביכם. ועשו עיקר תורתכם. וזכרו בוראכם. בימי בחורותיכם. בעודכם בכחכם. וקבלו עול התורה עליכם. ולא תמוש מפיכם. ויהיו לשום שמים כל מעשיכם. ושם אשר הורישו לכם אבותיכם החזיקו בו והנחילו לבניכם:

ועתה בנים שמעו לי ואשרי דרכי ישמורו. לכו בנים שמעו[11] לי יראת ה' אלמדכם. הביטו אל צור חוצבתם ואל מקבת בור נוקרתם. ולמה לזה העולם הובאתם? לא לאכול ולשתות וללבוש שש ורקמה. רק לעבודת האל תולה ארץ על בלימה. ולפי שחייבה חכמתו שלא יקיים הגוף בלי אכילה ושתיה. ובבלתי כסות לכסות הגויה. נתן רשות לאדם לאכול ולשתות וללבוש לקיים הגוף. ולהיות חבור לנשמה לקיים מצות האל כל ימי חבורם. והאכילה לאדם כשמן לנר. אם ירבה יאיר ואם ימעיט יכבה. ויותר מהרה יכבה ברוב מבמעט. ועל כן יש לכם להשמר

11 MS. repeats ואשרי דרכי.

guard against over-feeding.[38] More heinous than homicide is suicide.[39] Gross eating is as dangerous to the body as a sword, besides that it bars one from occupation with the Law of God and the reverence due to Him.

Ever let the fear of God be before you, and accustom yourselves to recite with devotion, that it depart not from your mouths, the text: I have set the Lord always before me; surely He is at my right hand, I shall not be moved.[40] Keep your minds always alert on whatever may induce the fear of heaven; be not diverted by the jibes of others, nor by your own lusts.[41].

Make it your firm custom to study the Torah at fixed times, probe deeply into its contents, and endeavor to communicate daily a portion of the rabbinic law to others; for to accomplish this you will be compelled to make your own knowledge precise, moreover by the exposition orally it will be fixed in your memories. Always repeat, if possible going back to the beginning of the tractate. Our sages of blessed memory have said (with regard to perfect service): "He who repeats his chapter a hundred times cannot be compared to him who repeats it a hundred and one times."[42]

[38] Or "heavy meals".

[39] On suicide see Gen. Rabbah on Genesis 9.5 (ch. 34, with Theodor's notes, p. 324). There is an unidentified quotation from the Talmud Yerushalmi that the deliberate suicide has no portion in the world to come.

[40] Ps. 16.8.

[41] Cf. Jastrow, *Dictionary*, p. 278. The meaning here of the last clause may simply be: "nor by any other thing."

[42] Mal. 3.18; Ḥagigah 9b.

ולהזהר מאכילה גסה. ויותר עונש לאדם ההורג עצמו מהורג את אחרים. ואכילה גסה קשה לגוף כחרבות. מלבד שמונעתו לעסוק בתורת האל ויראתו:

תמיד יהיה יראת השם על פניכם. ופסוק זה הרגילו לומר תמיד בכונה ולא ימוש מפיכם. שויתי ה' לנגדי תמיד[12] כי מימיני בל אמוט. ותהיו ערומים לחשוב תמיד בכל דבר המביא לידי יראת שמים. ולא תניחוהו בשביל שום אדם המלעיג עליכם. ולא בשביל דבר אחר:

הוו זהירין לעסוק בתורה בקבע. ותשאו ותתנו בה. והשתדלו להגיד הלכה בכל יום לאחרים ובזה תצטרכו לדקדק בה. וגם בהוציאכם אותה בפה לאחרים תקבע בלבבכם. ותחזרו תמיד מלמעלה. ואם תוכלו מראש המסכתא. ורז"ל דרשו בין עובד[13] אלהים לאשר לא עבדו אינו דומה שונה פרקו מאה פעמים לשונה מאה ואחד. ועל כן כל הלכה תקראו מאה וא'[14] פעמים. וגם תקבעו שעות ללמוד הלכה

[12] The MS. repeats here the words כל דבר המביא ל' from the next clause.

[13] MS. reads אלים and in general confuses the text from Malachi.

[14] So S adds.

Read ye, therefore, every rule (halakah) 101 times, and appoint hours for studying halakah from the codifiers[43] every day, and also strive to read a tractate with Rashi's commentary. In fine, you must consider yourselves as laborers hired by the day to do the work of God, as it is said in the Talmud: "We are day laborers."[44] Much more is this the case with you, for all that you possess comes from the congregation and the trust fund.[45] This support is given to you for the purpose of your studies, so that ye are indeed daily hirelings. See to it that ye do your tasks faithfully, and faithful is your employer to pay your wage[46], nay your reward is already with you, for he has paid it in advance.

Think not in your heart that the Torah is an inheritance from your fathers, and needs no personal effort to win it. The matter is not so. If ye toil not therein, ye shall not acquire, and more than ordinary will be your punishment, in that ye forsake your family tradition. So we read in tractate Nedarim:[47] Why do not learned fathers invariably beget learned children? R. Joseph answered: So that people shall not say, Your Torah is inherited from your fathers. R. Sheshet said: Because they call men "asses". Rab said: To prevent them assuming an over-

[43] Famous among the Posekim were the author's father and brother.

[44] 'Erubin 65a.

[45] Cf. p. 181, below.

[46] Abot 2.14.

[47] fol. 81a.

מפוסקים בכל יום. וגם השתדלו ללמוד מסכתא עם פי' רש"י. סוף דבר יש לכם[15] לחשוב שאתם שכירי יום לעשות עבודת האל ית' כמו שאמרו בעירובין אנן אגירי דיומא אנן[16]. לא כל שכן אתם שכל מה שיש לכם הוא מהקהל ומן ההקדש. והוא נתון לכם בשביל למודכם. שאתם באמת שכירי יום. ויש לכם לעשות מלאכתכם באמונה. ונאמן הוא בעל מלאכתכם שישלם לכם פעולתכם. גם הנה שכרו אתכם. כי הקדימו לכם:

ואל תחשבו בלבבכם. כי התורה ירושה היא לכם מאבותיכם. ושאינכם צריכים לטרוח בה. כי אין הדבר כן. ואם לא תטרחו בה לא תזכו בה. ועונש שלכם גדול משל אחרים. כי תעזבו אומנות אבותיכם. וגרסינן במסכת נדרים מפני מה אין תלמידי חכמים מצואין לצאת מהם תלמידי חכמים? אמר רב יוסף[17] כדי שלא יאמרו ירושה היא לכם מאבותיכם. רב ששת אמר[18] משום דקרו לאינשי חמרי. רב אמר כדי שלא יתגברו על

15 MS. repeats יש לכם

16 The ordinary text of the Talmud reads אנן פועלי דיממי אנן.

17 MS. יוסיף.

18 MS. repeats כדי.

bearing attitude towards the congregation. Rabina said: Because they become careless with regard to the benediction before study.[48] For your part, avoid all these things.

Also appoint regular periods for studying the Bible with grammar and commentary. As in my childhood I did not so study it—for in Germany they had not the custom—I have not been able to teach it here. Read weekly the Pentateuchal lesson with Rashi and other commentaries. Also make yourselves familiar with homilies and midrashim; this will make you more effective in public preaching, and to bring men back from iniquity. Our Sages said: He who wishes to become saintly should fulfil the words of the Fathers.[49] So, I, after making my confession, accustomed myself to read a chapter of the tractate Abot every day. Do ye the same at table, before Grace after meals, read a chapter daily till you know the whole tractate by heart. This practice will habituate and attract you to saintliness.

Discourse of matters of Torah at your meals, then will ye be as those who eat at the table of the Omnipresent.[50] Read regularly in the *Duties of the Heart* and in the *Book of the Upright*,[51] and the *Epistle on Repentance* of Rabbenu Jonah,[52] and similar books. Set your hearts on

[48] The ordinary text of Ned. 81a presents variants to the author's readings.

[49] Baba Kamma 30a, in reference to the Mishnah Abot.

[50] Abot 3.4. [51] By Baḥya and Zeraḥyah ha-Yevani, respectively (Cf. *J. E.*, ii, 447, and xii, 661).

[52] On Jonah Gerondi, see *J. E.* v, 637.

הציבור. רבינא אמר מפני שאין מברכין על התורה תחילה. ואתם הזהרו מכל אלו הדברים:

גם תקבעו עתים ללמוד הפסוק בדקדוק ובפי'[19]. ולפי שבקטנותי לא למדתי אותו כי לא הורגלו ללומדו באשכנז לא יכולתי ללמדו[20] בכאן. גם על הפרשה תקראו בכל שבוע פירוש רש"י ופירושים אחרים. גם תרגילו עצמכם בדרשים ובמדרשים. ובזה יגדל שכרכם כאשר תדרשו ברבים ותשיבון מעון. ורז"ל אמרו האי מאן דבעי למיהוי חסידא יקיים מלי דאבות וכו'. ואני כשעשיתי הוידוי שלי הנהגתי[21] עצמי לקרוא ממנו פרק בכל יום. כן תעשו גם אתם על שלחנכם. קודם ברכת מזון תקראו ממנה פרק אחד בכל יום עד שתדעו המסכתא על פה. ודבר זה ירגילכם וימשככם להיות חסידים:

וגם תאמרו בכל יום דברי תורה על השלחן. וכאלו[22] תאכלו משלחנו של מקום. וגם תרגילו עצמיכם ללמוד בספר חובות הלבבות ובספר הישר ובאגרת תשובה לרבינו יונה ז"ל וכיוצא בהם.

19 So MS., prob. ובפירוש.

20 MS. ללומדו. This spelling is common with infinitives in later Heb. texts.

21 MS. והנהגתי. 22 MS. ובאלו.

that you read therein with devout intent to apply the lesson in your life. When you read, do so audibly.[53] And reason with yourselves *a fortiori* after this manner: If you had to speak before a king of flesh and blood, how carefully you would clear your hearts of all other thoughts. Your whole endeavor would be to word your speech acceptably, and you would think of nothing else. How much more should this be your method before the King of kings, blessed and sanctified be His Name! Pray with the congregation in the same place and in the same context.[54] See that you are among the first.[55] Discontinue your present habit of departing as soon as the lesson is over, thus failing to pray where the congregation is collected. Never speak from the passage "Blessed is He who spake" until you have ended the Eighteen Benedictions.[56] Be silent, too, while the Ḥazzan repeats the last-named prayer. For if there be not ten attentive to it, the repetition is not according to law.[57] Be ye always among these ten, and make it your rule to join in prayer so as to enable the many to do their duty.[58] Let the words be softly spoken, for thus is devotion aroused and prayer made acceptable.

See to it diligently that ye be not among the four classes who behold not the divine presence (Shekinah): liars, scoffers, hypocrites, and slanderers.[59]

[53] Berakot 13a. [54] Oraḥ Ḥayyim 90, 9, 10.
[55] *Op. cit.*, 14. [56] *Op. cit.*, 51,4. [57] *Op. cit.*, 124,14.
[58] By helping to constitute the necessary quorum (ten).
[59] Soṭah 42a.

ושימו לבבכם כאשר תקראו בהם שתהיה הקריאה על מנת לעשות. ותהיה בכוונת הלב. והשמיעו לאזניכם מה שאתם מוציאים מפיכם: ותקחו ק"ו בעצמיכם. אם היה לכם לדבר לפני מלך בשר ודם איך הייתם מפנים לבבכם מכל המחשבות. וכל כוונתכם לרעות דבריכם[23]. ולא תחשבו זולתי בדבר ההוא. ועל אחת כמה וכמה לפני מלך מלכי המלכים ית' וית' שמו: והתפללו עם הצבור במקום שהם מתפללים במקום שהצבור שם. והזהרו שתהיו מן הראשונים. ולא תעשו כמו שאתם עושים שאחר ההלכה אתם יוצאים מיד ואינכם מתפללים במקום שהצבור שם. והזהרו שלא תדברו מברוך שאמר עד שתסיימו התפלה. ולא בחזרת ש"צ התפלה. ואם אין עשרה ששומעים התפלה היא חזרה שלא כדין. והזהרו שתהיו לעולם מהם. והרגילו עצמיכם להתפלל להוציא הרבים. ותהיה התפלה בנחת. ובזה תתעורר הכונה ותהיה מקובלת:

הזהרו מאד שלא תהיו מד' כתות שאין רואות פני שכינה. והם כת שקרנים וכת לצים וכת חנפים וכת מספרי לשון הרע.

[23] S reads לדעת and omits next word.

(i) *The class of liars*: Let no falsehood or lying be found among you, but let truth and fidelity be a girdle round your loins.[60] There was a man of our family by name Eliakim, who was employed in the house of his prince. And all his property his master entrusted to him, being wont to laud him to his people because he never told a lie, whether for advantage or not. And they tell of a certain rogue who left no sin undone and who entreated a certain Sage to teach him an easy road to repentance. He answered, "Keep thyself from lying." The man went out gleefully and in high spirits, conceiving that his counsellor had permitted him to walk in the stubbornness of his heart as of aforetime. He planned a theft according to his wont, but then bethought himself: "If anyone inquires: whither goest thou? if I tell the truth I shall be caught, if I answer falsely I shall transgress the order of the Sage." Thus it was with all offences, and he became a completely reformed character.

(ii) *The class of scoffers*: "Now, therefore, be ye not scoffers, lest your bands be made strong and lest fire consume your spirit."[61] From all levity and frivolity guard yourselves, for man is forbidden to fill his mouth with laughter in this world.[62] Furthermore, play no game for money, for that, too, is a form of robbery.

[60] Cf. Isa. 11.5.

[61] Isa. 28.22. The author completes his quotation by a reminiscence of Isa. 33.11.

[62] Berakot 31a.

כת שקרנים. ולא ימצא בכם דבר שקר וכזב. אבל האמת והאמונה יהיו אזור חלציכם: איש היה במשפחתינו והר׳ אליקים שמו. והיה בבית השר שלו. וכל אשר היה לו היה בידו. והיה משתבח בו לעמו שלא יוציא שקר מפיו לעולם. לא לתועלת. ולא ללא תועלת: ואמרו שהיה איש אחד רשע שלא הניח עבירה שלא עבר. והילה פני[24] חכם אחד שיורהו דרך תשובה בדרך קל. אמר לו שמור עצמך מלשקר. יצא שמח וטוב לב. כמדומה לו שהתיר לו שילך בשרירות לבו כבתחילה. מלך בלבו לגנוב כמו שהורגל. אמר בלבו מי שישאלני אנה[25] אתה הולך. אם אומר לגנוב האמת אתפש.[26] ועם אשקר אעבור על צווי החכם. ועל זה הדרך כל העבירות. ושב בתשובה שלימה:

וכת לצים. ואתם אל תתלוצצו פן יחזקו מוסריכם. ופן תאכל אש רוחכם. ומכל התול ושחוק שמרו נפשכם. ואסור למלאת[27] אדם שחוק פיו בעולם הזה. גם שחוק למעות אל תשחקו. כי גם הוא עניין[28] של גזל:

[24] MS. עני. [25] MS. אנא. [26] MS. אתפוש
[27] MS. למאלאת. [28] MS. עניו.

(iii) *The class of hypocrites*: Never flatter any man, nor show partiality to any in judgment.

(iv) *The class of slanderers*: Avoid it to the utmost; for slander leads to many sins, and most men are liable to it. As our Rabbis of blessed memory said,[63] many are prone to theft, and a few to incontinence, but all to slander, explaining this last clause of those who are guilty of some shade[64] of the offence. Further they said,[65] Let no man praise another [too much], for it may result in disclosing something to his discredit; and in all such matters I have not found anything better for a person than silence.[66] Ever, then, let a man bethink himself before he speak; uttering his words if they be profitable, suppressing them if they would profit nothing. Silent above all must he be if speech would actually harm.

Avoid pride, for every one that is proud in heart is an abomination to the Lord.[67] Majesty, indeed, is the garment of God alone, and he that makes use of the crown shall perish.[68] As a certain Sage said: how can a man be proud, considering the way in which he was conceived and born?[69] But cleave to humility, that best of good qualities. For this virtue Moses our Master was praised, as it is said: Now the man Moses was very meek.[70] Be very lowly in spirit, say our Rabbis.[71] They said further that (the fear

[63] Baba Batra 165a.

[64] Lit., "dust".

[65] Arakin 16a. The passage exhorts men not to over praise lest others be provoked to contradict.

כת חנפים. הזהרו שלא תחניפו לשום אדם. ולא תשא פניו בדין:

כת מספרי לשון הרע. הזהרו ממנו מאד כי הוא מביא לכמה עבירות. רוב בני אדם נכשלים בו. ואמרו רז"ל במסכת בתרא רוב בגזל ומעוט בעריות והכל בלשון הרע. והעמידו אותו באבק לשון הרע. ואמרו רז"ל אל יספר אדם בטובתו של חבירו שמתוך כך בא לידי גנותו. וכל כיוצא בזה לא מצאתי לגוף טוב משתיקה. ולעולם יחשוב אדם עצמו קודם שידבר אם יהיה בו תועלת ידבר. ואם לא לא ידבר. כ"ש אם יהיה בו הפסד:

והוו זהירין מן הגאוה כי תועבת ה' כל גבה לב. והוא מלבושו של הקב"ה. ודישתמש בתגא חלף. ואמר חכם אחד איך יתגאה אדם והוא עבר דרך השתן ב' פעמים. והתדבקו בענוה שהיא המדה הטובה שבמדות. ובה נשתבח משה רבינו ע"ה שנ' והאיש משה עניו מאד. ורז"ל אמרו מאד

---

66 Abot 1.17.
67 Prov. 16.5.
68 Ps. 93.1; Abot 1.13.
69 Baḥya, *Duties of the Heart*, 6.5; cf. *Choice of Pearls* ch. 55. 70 Num. 12.3. 71 Abot 4.4.

of the Lord) which Wisdom makes a crown to her head, Humility makes the imprint of her foot.[72] Be punctilious in honoring all men, for therein shall you find your own honor, for God Himself has declared: "them that honour Me will I honour."[73] People remarked to a Sage: "We have observed that thou ever showest honor to every man;" and he replied: "I have never come across one in whom I failed to recognize superiority over myself; therefore have I shown him respect. Were he older, I said he has done more good than I; were he richer, I said he has been more charitable. Were he younger, I said I have sinned more; were he poorer, I said he has suffered heavier tribulations; were he wiser, I honored him for his wisdom; were he not wiser, I said his fault[74] is the lighter." Take this to heart and understand it.

Take heed to love and respect him that reproves you. For thus we read in Tractate 'Arakin:[75] R. Johanan said: I call heaven and earth to witness that many a time was 'Aḳiba punished through me, for I complained of him before Rabban Gamaliel; all the more did he augment his love for me, to fulfil what is written:[76] "Reprove a wise man and he will love thee." As the Sage said:[77] Love thy critic, and hate

[72] T. J. Shabbat 1.3; Tanḥuma Genesis (beginning). See Jastrow, *Dictionary*, p. 964. The idea is derived from a comparison of Ps. 3.10 with Prov. 22.4.

[73] I Sam. 2.30.

[74] Lit. punishment.

[75] Fol. 16b; the readings vary.

מאד הוי שפל רוח. ואמרו רז"ל מה שעשתה חכמה עטרה לראשה[29] עשתה ענוה עקב לרגלה.[30] והוו זהירין לכבד כל אדם ובזה תהיו מכובדים שנא' כי מכבדי אכבד. ושאלו לחכם ראינוך תמיד מכבד לכל אדם. והשיב לא ראיתי מי שלא[31] הכרתי לו מעלה עלי. ובשביל זה כבדתיו. אם היה זקן אמרתי זה עשה טובות יותר ממני. אם היה עשיר אמרתי זה עשה צדקות יותר ממני. אם היה בחור אמרתי חטאתי יותר ממנו. אם היה עני אמרתי זה סבל יסורין יותר ממני. אם היה חכם ממני כבדתיו בשביל חכמתו. אם לא היה חכם ממני אמרתי עונשו מועט משלי. שמעוהו ודעו לכם:

והוו זהירין לאהוב ולכבד המוכיח אתכם. והכי גרסינן בערכין[32] פרק יש בערכין אמר ר' יוחנן מעיד אני עלי שמים וארץ שהרבה פעמים לקה על ידי עקיבא ע"י שהייתי קובל עליו לפני רבן גמליאל וכ"ש שהוסיף אהבה. לקיים מה שנאמר הוכח לחכם ויאהבך. ואמר החכם אהוב את

[29] MS. לראשו. [30] MS. לראשו.
[31] MS. למה. [32] MS. בערבין.

---

[76] Prov. 9.18. [77] Simeon b. Eleazar, Abot de. R. Nathan 29 (ed. Schechter, p. מד).

thy eulogist, the former helps, the latter hurts thee. Consider also that man is but a sojourner on earth; his days are numbered, though he knows not their tale, nor when he will be summoned before the King of kings, to give judgment and account for all his works. Therefore let him do all that is in his power, nor think any good opportunity small, for there is no limit to the reward. In the world to come, when God, blessed be He, makes requital to the righteous, the recipient will ask: Why am I so rewarded? He will be told: On such and such a day thou didst do such and such a mizvah. Then, sighing, he will say: For so little do I receive so much? Alas for the days that I lost wherein I did no good! Therefore will a wise man be alert lest he waste an hour of his hours, but he will be energetic in well-doing, thinking ever of the fear of God and His service.

I will make mention of the mercies of the Lord according to all that He hath bestowed on me.[78] He has shepherded me from my birth even unto this day. In the way of truth He led me, taking me from my father's house, sending me before them to preserve life.[79] He directed me in a strange land, made me to find favor and love and mercy in the eyes of its people, and set me upon a throne of honor. This to the glory of His name, and not for my sake. For what is my life and what am I? Lo, the finger of the smallest among them is thicker than my loins, how much more their greatest excel me! I am to them as a grasshopper is in my

[78] Is. 63.7. [79] Gen. 45.5.

המוכיחך ושנא המשבחך כי המוכיחך יועילך והמשבחך יזיקך: ותחשבו כי האדם גר בארץ ימים ספורים. לא ידע מניינם. ומתי יהיה מזומן לפני מלך מלכי המלכים ליתן דין וחשבון מכל אשר עשה. וכל אשר ימצא בכחו יעשה. ולא תהיה בעיניו שום מצוה קטנה כי אין קץ למתן שכרה. ולעולם הבא כשהשם ית׳ משלם שכר לצדיקים. שואל הצדיק למה נותנין לי שכר כל כך? ואומרים לו על שעשית מצוה פלונית ביום פלוני. והוא נאנח ואומר על דבר קטון כזה נותנין לי כל כך שכר. אוי לימים שאבדתי שלא עסקתי במצוות. ועל כן החכם יזהר שלא יאבד שעה משעותיו. רק ישתדל במצוות ויחשב תמיד ביראת ה׳ ובעבודתו:

חסדי ה׳ אזכיר כעל כל אשר גמלני. האלהים הרועה אותי מעודי עד יומי. ואשר בדרך אמת הנחני. ומבית אבי לקחני. ולפניהם למחיה שלחני. בארץ נכריה להדריכני. ולחן לחסד ולרחמים בעיני אנשי הארץ נתנני. וכסא כבוד הנחילני. למען כבוד שמו לא למעני. כי מה חיי ומה אני. הלא הקטון שבהם אצבעו קטנה עבה ממתני. כ״ש גדול שבהם. ואני נגדם כחגב בעיני. ועלה על לבי מלאני.

eyes.[80] Fain, then, is my heart to record the wondrous things that the Lord performs continually on behalf of one so insignificant as I; He fed me with my allotted bread,[81] and I had no impulse to run after money; but He thought differently, and God caused it to come to my hand.[82]

I left Germany at the age of thirteen, and when fifteen I came to Toledo, in the new moon of Iyar in the year 65.[83] It is obvious that at my exodus when thirteen I possessed nothing; nor when I married first the daughter of R. Yeḥiel and later the daughter of R. Solomon, did I receive even enough to pay for the wedding garments and celebrations. From my lord, my father, of blessed memory, I inherited only a trifle as my share of his library. All that he owned at the time of his demise, together with all his household goods, did not suffice to carry out his testamentary bequests. Never in my life did I accept gifts from individuals, except 1400(?) gold pieces[84] which were given to me by three men, from whom I sought a loan but who insisted on making a gift. Because of their importance and position, I was unable to refuse their bounty. I used the money for my sister's marriage. I also lost money through those who transacted business for me, although

[80] Num. 13.33. [81] Prov. 30.8. [82] Exod. 21.13.

[83] =1305. On the two journeys of the author to Toledo see Introduction, p. 163.

[84] Heb. "gold pieces". On the Spanish coinage of the period, cf. S. Lane-Poole, *Coins and Medals*, 1894, p. 85. The standard gold pieces were the dinar and dirhem,

להזכיר מעשה נסים שעושה ה' תמיד עם הבל וריק כמוני. ועל לחם חקי שהטריפני. בלתי רודפי אחרי הממון. והוא לא כן עמדי. אבל האלהים אנה לידי:

יצאתי מאשכנז בן י"ג שנה. ואני כבן ט"ו שנה באתי לטוליטלה בראש חדש אייר שנת ס"ה.[33] דבר פשוט כי כשיצאתי בן[34] י"ג שנה לא היה לי כלום. וכשנשאתי שתי בנות הר' יחיאל והר' שלמה זצ"ל[35] לא נתנו לי עמהן כשיעור ההוצאה של הבגדים והחופות .ומאאז"ל לא ירשתי רק דבר מועט בחלקי מן הספרים. כי כל מה שהיה לו בעת פטירתו עם כלי ביתו לא היה בו כדי להשלים צוואתו. ולא לקחתי מימי מתנות מיחיד. רק אלף וארבע מאות זהובים שנתנו לי שלשה אנשים שבקשתי מהם להלוות לי מעות ולא רצו בהלוואה ונתנו לי[36] הסך הנזכר. ומפני גדולתם ומעלתם לא יכולתי להשיב פניהם מלקבלם. ונתתים לנשואי אחותי. והפסדתי ביד המשתדלים בעבורי. והממון לא היה שלי. כי

[33] So the MS. S prints מ"ה. [34] MS. בן ט' י"ג.

[35] MS. adds incorrectly לא ירשתי רק דבר מועט.

[36] MS. ונתלי. S corrects as in text. Perhaps the right reading is ונטרתי.

but it is questionable whether coins of such high value are intended. The text is hopelessly corrupt regarding the sums enumerated.

that money was not my own. For 7000 gold pieces of borrowed capital were in the hands of my brother Eliakim, 8500 were deposited with R. Mordecai the Frenchman, who only returned to me 2000, 3000 were entrusted to R. Nissim, and the rest in the hands of others whom it would weary me to mention. I could not have survived till now but for the mercy of God, who put it in the heart of men to lend me capital, from the profits of which I maintained myself. For from the time of the death of my lord, my father, of blessed memory, that is to say for twenty-seven years and three months—I have not taken from the Congregation (whom may God preserve!) under contract more than 1290 gold pieces. This I accepted for two years and four months, and I ceased to enter into any contract until the ten years mentioned[85] were completed. Thereafter I received up to August [1340][86] from them 1500 pieces annually for nine years and ten months, a total of 14,750. Thenceforth they contracted to increase the annual payment to 3000 pieces. They agreed that after my death an annual pension of 1000 pieces should be paid for ten consecutive years to my wife and children or to any of them

[85] As Schechter points out no such mention has been made.

[86] The date of the year is 5100=1340. From August, 1340 to November, 1348, are 7 years and 4 months, as stated in the text below. The reference to 27 years and 3 months after his father's death cannot, however, be accurate, for while the father died in 1328 the son died in 1349.

ז׳ אלף זהובים מהם ביד אחי ה״ר אליקים נר״ו. וח׳ אלפים ות״ק זהובים ביד ר׳ מרדכי צרפתי ו[לא השיב לי רק][37] אלפים זהובים. וביד ר׳ נסים שלשת אלפים זהובים. והאחרים ביד בני אדם הרבה. ונלאיתי לכותבם: ולא עברתי זמני עד ככה רק ברחמי שמים. אשר נתן בלב בני אדם להלוות לי מעות להשתדל בהם ולהתפרנס מן הריוח. כי מעת פטירת א״א ז״ל שיש לו כ״ז שנה ושלשה חדשים לא לקחתי מהקהל יצ״ו בתנאי מהם רק אלף ומאתים ותשעים זהובים. וזה מה שלקחתי בשתי שנים וד׳ חדשים ונסתלקתי מליקח מהם תנאי עד שנשלמו העשרה שנים הנזכרים. ומאז לקחתי מהם אלף ות״ק זהובים בשנה. עד אגושתו ה״א.[38] שהם ט׳ שנים וי׳ חדשים שלקחתי מהם י״ד אלף[39] ותש״נ זהובים. ומאז החזירו לי התנאי ג׳ אלפים זהובים בשנה. והתנו שישאר מהם אחרי לאשתי ולבני או למי שיהיה אז מהם בטוליטולה אף אלף זהובים בשנה עד י׳ שנים רצופים. ולכל מי מבני בחיי שיהיה לו מן התנאי

[37] S suggests the addition of the bracketed words.

[38] If we read הא as an abbreviation, there is no need to emend the text as in S.

[39] The word אלף is not in the MS. S supplies it.

then living in Toledo. During my lifetime each of my sons was guaranteed 300 pieces a year for ten years, so long as he should pursue his studies and dwell in Toledo. A similar sum was appointed, under similar conditions, to be paid after my death to each of my sons out of the total of 1000 pieces mentioned above. I received from them from the August named to the end of November in this year 1348,[87] for seven years and four months, 22,000 pieces. The total received by me from the congregation till the end of November has been 37,240 gold pieces. Of this sum, my son Solomon received, for two years and two months, 800 pieces in accordance with the arrangement already explained.

The contract which the Congregation granted was not entered into because I demanded of them, for I knew that I was unworthy of such consideration, but it was due to their abundant generosity and their affection for my lord, my father. But in the tenth year of my office, the Congregation heard that it was my intention to seek a resting-place elsewhere. They then fixed for me the payment of 1500 pieces annually. Had I been willing to accept more, they would have given it, as is expressly stated in their letter (which I still possess) of the year 1341.[88] When the aforesaid Mordecai absconded I lost in his hand more than 6000, and it became

[87] The text has 109 = 5109 = 1348.

[88] The text has 101 = 5101 = 1341.

שלו ס״ש[40] זהובים בשנה עד י׳ שנים. כל זמן שתהיה תורתו אומנותו (ולקחתי)[41] וידור בטוליטלה. ומי שישאר מבני אחרי תוך י׳ שנים הנזכרים שיהיה לו מן האלף זהובים הנזכרים ש׳ זהובים כל זמן שתהיה תורתו אומנותו. ולקחתי מהם מאגושתו הנזכר עד סוף נובײמרי זה בשנת ק״ט לפרט ז׳ שנים וד׳ הדשים כ״ב אלף זהובים: סך כל מה שלקחתי מהקהל יצ״ו עד סוף נובײמרי ל״ז אלף זהובים ומאתים וארבעים[42] זהובים. מאלו לקח בני שלמה בשתי שנים ושני חדשים ח׳ מאות זהובים על הדרך המפורש למעלה:

והתנאי שנתנו לי הקהל יצ״ו לא נתנו לי בשביל שבקשתי מהם שיתנו לי. כי ידעתי כי איני ראוי לכך. אך מרוב חסדם ואהבתם עם א״א הר׳[43] ז״ל. ובשנה העשירי שמעו הקהל שהיה רצוני לבקש מנוח במקום אחר. וקבעו לי אלף ות״ק זהובים בשנה. ואם היה רצוני ליקח מהם יותר שהיו[44] נותנים כמו שמפורש בכתבם אשר בידי משנת ק״א. כאשר ברח לי מרדכי הפסדתי בידו יותר מו׳ אלפים.

40 S reads מ״ט, but the MS. has ס״ש = סך ש׳. S. suggests the correction to מאה. 41 So the MS., but delete. 42 MS. ואחד. 43 i. e. הראש. 44 MS. שיהיו.

known to the heads of the congregation that I designed emigrating to Seville. They besought me to remain, and they increased the sum payable under the contract to 3000 gold pieces a year. I am aware that all this was not due to my own deserts. It was due to the bounty of the Merciful one, the faithful God, and to the merit of my fathers, the repairers of the breach, the holy ones who were in the earth.[89]

He who searcheth hearts knoweth that all my yearning desire for children in this world was solely dictated by my wish to raise up offspring which should fill my father's place in the study of the Law, in good works, and in the service of God. And in this sense I besought Him who is enthroned o'er the Cherubim, entreating God for myself, my children, and all our generations after us, that we may dwell in the house of the Lord all the days of our life, to behold the graciousness of the Lord[90] and to pass our time in the inner shrine of His Law from morn to eve and from eve to morn, in the precious presence of God. I prayed that He would keep us far from men of vanity and frivolity, that we might maintain the example of our fathers, who, as our tradition assures us, were for many generations before us men of learning, of right-doing, and God-fearers—men from whom the Torah went forth unto Israel. And this has been my constant prayer at the graves[91] of the righteous and perfect: "Lord of

[89] Isa. 58.12; Ps. 16.23.

[90] Ps. 27.4.

ונשמע לגדולי הקהל יצ"ו שהיה רצוני לילך למדינת אישביליא. בקשו לישאר והחזירו לי התנאי ג' אלפים זהובים בשנה: וידעתי כי אינו בזכותי רק בזכות הרחמן האל הנאמן ובזכות אבותי גודרי פרץ. קדושים אשר בארץ:

ובוחן לבות יודע כי כל חפצי ורצוני בבנים בעולם הזה אינו רק להיות לי זרע שימלא מקום אבותי בתורה ובמעשים טובים ובמצות. וזאת בקשתי מאת יושב הכרובים. אחת שאלתי מאת ה' אותה אבקש עלי ועל בני ועל כל דורותינו אחרינו. שבתינו בבית ה' כל ימי חיינו, לחזות בנועם ה' ולבקר בהיכל תורתו מבקר ועד ערב ומערב עד בקר לפני ה' לרצון. ולהרחיקנו ממתי שוא ולצון ולהחזיק במעשי אבותינו. אשר קבלה בידינו אשר מכמה דורות אשר לפנינו היו בעלי תורה ואנשי מעשה ויראי אלהים. ומהם יצאה תורה לישראל. וזאת תפלתי כל הימים על קברי הצדיקים והתמימים. רבון העולמים מלך יושב על כסא

---

[91] On such prayers see *Shulḥan 'Aruk, Oraḥ Ḥayyim* ch. 559 (end); ch. 581 (end) and commentaries.

the Universe, King that sittest on the throne of mercy! It is revealed and known before Thee that all my desire for children was not out of my love for them, nor to gain honor through them, but only to perform that duty of continuing the race which Thou hast ordained.[92] May it be Thy will to order us in all our affairs in good counsel before Thee. O may the fear of Thee be with us that we sin not, and may we live in Thy presence in reverence. Grant unto me sons who may grow into maturity, and may fill my fathers' place. And may God in His mercy raise up for us the merit of the righteous one buried in this grave. May my prayer be heard here, and may he too pray on our behalf, blessing us continually and at all hours."

One of the good methods which I desired for maintaining the family record was the marriage of my sons to members of my father's house. I had many reasons for this. First, it is a fair and fit thing to join fruit of vine to fruit of vine.[93] It is indeed an important duty, for as our Sages said:[94] He who loves his relatives, he who marries his sister's daughter, and he who lends to the poor in the hour of his distress—to him applies the text:[95] "Then shalt thou call, and the Lord will answer; thou shalt cry and He will say, Here I am." Furthermore, the women of our family have grown accustomed to the ways of students, and the love of the Torah has entered their hearts, so that they are a help to

[92] Gen. 1.28. [93] Pesaḥim 49a.
[94] Yebamot 62b. [95] Isa. 58.9.

רחמים. גלוי וידוע לפניך שכל חפצי בבנים לא בשביל אהבתי בהם ולא בשביל להתכבד בהם. רק לקיים מצוה שצויתנו בפריה ורביה. יהי רצון מלפניך שתתקננו בעצה טובה מלפניך בכל ענינינו. ותהיה יראתך על פנינו לבלתי נחטא. ונחיה לפניך ביראתך ויהיה לי זרע של קיימא זרע אנשים שימלא מקום אבותי. ויעמיד לנו השם ברחמיו זכות הצדיק הקבור בקבר הזה. ותשמע תפילתי במקום הזה. גם הוא יתפלל בעדינו תמיד כל היום יברכנו:

ואחת מן העצות הטובות שחשבתי בדבר הזה הוא שאשיא את בני במשפחת בית אבי. ויש לי בזה הרבה טעמים. האחד שהוא דבר נאה ומתקבל ענבי הגפן בענבי הגפן. וגם היא מצוה רבה כמו שאמרו רז"ל האוהב את קרוביו והנושא את בת אחותו והמלוה את העני בשעת דוחקו עליו הכתוב אומר אז תקרא וה' יענה תשוע ויאמר הנני. ועוד נשי[45] משפחתנו הורגלו עם לומדי תורה ונכנסה אהבתה[46] בלבן ויעזרו בעליהן לקיים תלמודיהם

[45] MS. reads אנשי. [46] MS. reads אהבת.

their husbands in their scholarly pursuits. Moreover, they are not used to extravagant expenditure; they do not demand luxuries, the provision of which disturbs a man from his study. Then again, children for the most part resemble the mother's family. Finally, if with changing times a man see fit to seek his livelihood in another city, there will be none to place obstacles in the way of the wife accompanying her husband.

The second plan is for me to write something of the history of my saintly progenitors, for the edification of those that come after us. Seeing that the Lord, blessed be He, "hurled us with a man's throw"[96] to Toledo, that great and renowned city, and that a little later the Jews were expelled from France, possibly some may think that we were among the exiles, or that we left our country in consequence of some whispered suspicion[97]. Therefore it seems desirable to me to disabuse everyone of such an imputation. And further, when our posterity regards the upright lives of our ancestors, they will be ashamed if they walk not in the same paths. Rather will they strive in all things to imitate their fathers, thus finding grace and good favor in the sight of God and man.[98] Otherwise,[98a] better were it for them never to be born,[99] like infants

[96] Cf. p. 166 above, n. 9.

[97] Job 26.14. The word *shemez* is used in this sense in rabbinic Hebrew. [98] Prov. 3.4.

[98a] The words ואם לאו seem to be missing.

[99] Cf. Lev. Rabbah, ch. 35.

בידיהם. ועוד שלא הורגלו בהוצאות יתירות ולא יבקשו מבעליהן מותרות. ובקשות המותרות הן המטרידות האדם מן הלימוד. ועוד שעל דרך הרב הבנים ידמו למשפחת האם. ועוד אם בשינוי הימים יראה לאיש לבקש מחייתו בעיר אחרת אין מי שיעכב ביד האשה ללכת אחרי אישה:

והעצה השנית היא שאכתוב קצת מתולדות אבותי הקדושים אשר בארץ לתועלת הבאים אחרינו. לפי שטלטלנו ה׳׳ית טלטלה גבר לטוליטולה[47] העיר הגדולה המהוללה. ומעט[48] זמן אחר כך נתגרשו[49] היהודים מצרפת. אולי[50] יעלה בלב[51] אדם שנתגורשנו[52] מארצנו[53] או משום שמץ דבר יצאנו משם. ועל כן יאות לי להוציא דבר זה מלב בני אדם. וגם כאשר[54] יראו זרענו יושר פעולת אבותינו יבושו מאד בנפשותם[55] אם לא ילכו בארחותם. וישתדלו בכל עניניהם להחזיק מעשה אבותיהם בידיהם. [ואם יעשו כן ימצאו חן ושכל טוב בעיני אלהים ואדם][56] [ואם לאו] נוח להם שנהפכה שלייתם על פניהם. כעוללים לא ראו אור

47 N לטוליטלה. 48 N ובמעט. 49 N יתגרשו.
50 N שמא. 51 N על לב. 52 N שנירשנו. 53 N omits.
54 N אשר. 55 S מנפשותם. 56 N omits bracketed passage.

who never see the light. As I left Germany when about thirteen years of age, I did not acquire exact information as to our fathers' righteous lives, except the little which I heard from my lord, my father of blessed memory, and from his sister and my grandmother, who related to me some of the family history. What little I heard of the doings of our first ancestors I set down here.

My grandfather, R. Yeḥiel b. Asher, was born in the year 1210.[100] When he was ten years old he had a firm friend in R. Solomon ha-Kohen. They entered into a pact that each should share the other's rewards, whether religious or secular. They held to this agreement all their days, and were unique in their generation for saintliness and benevolence. Now on the eve of the Day of Atonement in the year 1264,[101] early in the night, the candle of my grandfather went out in the synagogue. For it was customary in Germany to kindle a wax candle for every male in the synagogue, on the eve of the Fast, and the candle was of a size to burn the whole day and night.[102] Later (during the middle days of Tabernacles) my grandfather died and great honor was shown unto

[100] Text has 970=4970=1210.

[101] Text has 24=5024=1264.

[102] On this custom see *J.E.*, ii, 282.

---

69 N ריע אח. 70 N במעשהו. 71 S הן הן.
72 N במעשים. 73 N מעשים. 74 N omits. 75 N היום.
76 N omits bracketed words. 77 N נר המערבי.
78 N מנהג אשכנז שבעבור כל בן. 79 N להדליק.
80 S omits. 81 N omits.

בעיניהם:[57] [ו]לפי שיצאתי קטן כבן י"ג שנה מאשכנז לא השגתי לשמוע יושר מעשיהם[58] וצדקותיהם רק[59] מעט מצער[60] אשר שמעתי מא"א[61] ז"ל ומאחותו[62] ומזקנתי[63] ז"ל אשר ספרו לי מאבותיהם[64] ז"ל ואני[65] שמעתי קצת ממעשה אבותינו הראשונים כתבתיו[66] פה:

זקני הר' יחיאל [בר אשר][67] נולד בשנת תתק"ע. וכשהיה בן עשר[68] שנים היה לו חבר[69] נאמן ר' שלמה הכהן ז"ל. וכרתו ברית יחד שכל אחד יהיה לו חלק בכל מעשה[70] חבירו הן[71] במצות הן בעניינים[72] אחרים. ועמדו בברית כל ימיהם והיו חסידים ואנשי מעשה[73] יחידים[74] בדורם: ויהי בליל[75] יום הכפורים [בשנת כ"ד לפרט בתחלת הלילה][76] כבה הנר[77] של זקני ז"ל שהיה לו בבית הכנסת. כי כן [נהגו באשכנז שכל][78] זכר מדליקין בשבילו נר של שעוה בבית הכנסת בעיוה"כ שיש בו שיעור שידליק[79] יום ולילה. ובחול המועד [של סוכות][80] נפטר זקני ז"ל וכבוד גדול[81] עשו לו במותו. ובאו

[57] N omits. [58] N לשמוע מעשה אבותי. [59] N כי אם.
[60] N מזער. [61] N מאדוני. [62] N מאחותי.
[63] N omits. [64] S מאביהם. [65] S ואם.
[66] N לא כתביי. [67] MS. omits. [68] S אב כבן י"נ.

him at his death, people from neighboring places attending his funeral. Now it is the practice in Germany to set the coffin on a stone appointed for the purpose near the cemetery, and to open it to see whether the body has been dislocated by the jolting of the coffin. When they did this to him, R. Solomon ha-Kohen approached up to four cubits, and said in the presence of the assembly, "In your presence I call upon him to remember our covenant." • Within the coffin a look of joy lit his face, most of those present saw him smile, and I testify on the evidence of my father and grandmother that this happened.[103] A day came when R. Solomon ha-Kohen was studying in his college in the day-time, and lo! my grandfather of blessed memory was seated by his side. Amazed, R. Solomon asked how he fared, and he answered, exceeding well, and that a seat was ready at his side for his friend.[104] "I wonder", said R. Solomon, "that thou art permitted to be visible to mortals." He answered: "I have liberty to go to my house as of aforetime, but I am unwilling that they should say: How this saint prides it over other right-

[103] For a poetical version of a similar idea see my *Book of Delight*, p. 230.

[104] On the cathedras of the righteous in Paradise, cf. *J.E.* ix, 516.

ענייניו ואמרי. 94 N רבי שמואל הכהן עומד במדרשו ביום וראה.
95 N omits. 96 N והיה. 97 N תמיה.
98 והשיב לו שנותנין לו רשות לילך לביתו כבתחילה שלא היה.
99 N צדיק.

מן המקומות הסמוכות לקבורתו[82]. ומנהג [בני אשכנז][83] שסמוך לבית הקברות מניחין הארון על אבן אחת מיוחדת[84] לכך ופותחין אותו לראות אם נידלדלו[85] אבריו מחמת טילטול הארון. וכאשר עשו לו כן[86] קרב אליו[87] הר' שלמה[88] הכהן עד ד' אמות ואמר בקול רם לפני הקהל אני [אומר לפלוני][89] שיזכור הברית שכרת עמי. אז התחיל לשחוק בארון עד שראו אותו[90] רוב הקהל. [ומפי אדוני הרא"ש ז"ל וזקינתי ז"ל אני מעיד][91] שראו אותו [מצחק[92]. ויהי היום הר' שלמה הכהן ז"ל היה לומד בבית מדרשו ביום וירא והנה][93] זקני ז"ל יושב אצלו. ויתמה מאד וישאל לו על [עניינו. ויאמר][94] לו שהיה עומד[95] בטוב מאוד. ושהיה[96] לו כסא מוכן אצלו. ואמר לו הר' שלמה תמה[97] אני איך יש לך רשות להיראות לבני אדם. [ענה ואמר יש לי רשות לילך לביתי כבתחלה אלא שאיני][98] רוצה שיאמרו כמה מתגאה חסיד[99] זה יותר משאר

[82] N הסמוכים לקוברו.
[83] S באשכנז. [84] N גדולה מונחת. [85] S נתנדו.
[86] N omits. [87] N omits. [88] N רבי שמואל.
[89] S אני מזכיר לפניכם (?לפלוני) בפניכם.
[90] N omits אותו. [91] S וכן אמר א'א ז"ל וזקנתי מ"ב אני מעיד שאמרו. [92] N omits. [93] N והנה יום אחד הנה

eous men!"[104a] Six months after his death, at midnight on the Sabbath night, he appeared to his wife and said to her: "Haste and rise, take thy sons and daughters, and remove them hence, for tomorrow all the Jews of this place will be slain. So was it decreed against the whole neighborhood, but we prayed and our petition was successful except as regards this place."[105] She rose and obeyed, but returning to save her belongings, she was killed with the congregation. She had previously rescued my lord, my father, R. Asher of blessed memory, and his brother, R. Ḥayyim, fellow-disciple of R. Meir of Rothenburg, teacher of my father, who also was taught by his brother Ḥayyim. They had another brother, by name R. Eleazar, who died at the age of twenty-seven. He was reported to be as fine a scholar as his brother R. Ḥayyim. They had six sisters, the whole family saintly—all bearing deservedly high reputations among their contemporaries. The nine of them escaped on the day and under the circumstances narrated above. All of them had large families of sons and daughters, and I have heard that one

[104a] See Ketubot 103a, where a similar story is told of R. Judah ha-Nasi.

[105] On legends as to communication between dead and living, cf. *J. E.* iv, 484.

הצדיקים:[100] ויהי לששה[101] חדשים אחר פטירתו
בליל שבת בחצי הלילה נראה[102] לאשתו ואמר לה
מהרי וקומי[103] וקחי בניך ובנותיך והוציאם[104] מן
המקום הזה. כי מחר יהרגו היהודים אשר במקום
הזה[105] וכן נגזר על[106] כל הסביבות. והתפללנו[107]
ונתקבלה תפילתינו חוץ[108] מן המקום הזה. ותקם
ותעש כן וחזרה להציל את אשר לה ונהרגה בתוך[109]
הקהל אחר שהוציאה משם [ואת א"א הרא"ש ז"ל
ואת אחיו][110] הר' חיים חבירו של ר' מאיר
מרוטנבורק רבו של א"א[111] ז"ל. וגם לפני אחיו[112]
הר"ר חיים למד. והיה להם עוד אח ושמו הר'
אליעזר ונפטר בן כ"ז שנים. ואמרו עליו שהיה גדול
בתורה [כאחיו הר'][113] חיים ז"ל. והיו [114] להם שש[115]
אחיות כולן חסידות[116]. [והיו בעיני העולם חשובים
כפי ענינם. ותשעה מהם יצאו][117] מן המקום בליל
שבת הנזכר[118] על ידי המעשה הנזכר: וכלם הרבו
בבנים ובבנות לרוב. ושמעתי שאחד מבני דודי

100 N צדיקים. 101 S. בששת 102 N בא.
103 N omits. 104 S ומוציאם. 105 S ההוא. 106 N omits.
107 N ונתפללה. 108 S omits. 109 S עם.
110 S לא"א ז"ל ולאחיו. 111 N אדוני. 112 S לבני.
113 N כרב. 114 S והיה. 115 S ששה.
116 N צדקניות. 117 N ויצאו. 118 N omits.

of the sons of my uncle R. Ḥayyim, of blessed memory, married in Germany, and that there were at his wedding about five hundred men and women, all relatives, the relationship reaching to that of third cousins.

The cause of my father's departure from Germany was due to the imprisonment of R. Meir of Rothenburg,[106] of blessed memory. The Count, then head of the government,[107] arrested him, and the congregation of Germany ransomed him for a considerable sum.[108] The Governor refused to accept as guarantor any other person than my lord, my father, of blessed memory. He was compelled to become security for a large amount. But before the contributions were apportioned to the various congregations, R. Meir died in prison. The governor unjustly refused to admit my father's plea that as R. Meir died before his release, the guarantee had lapsed. Payment was still demanded from my father and the congregations, and my father escaped to another city; he left Germany altogether because of his fear of the authorities, and settled in the great city of Toledo. In the first year of his residence there, they sent him a written communication from the town-council[109] of the place where he formerly lived, inviting him to return home. They would despatch fifty officers to meet him on the German frontier, and would give him a

[106] Cf. *J. E.* viii, 437. He died in the fortress of Ensisheim, in 1293. The account of the ransom differs somewhat in the present narrative.

הר' חיים ז"ל נשא באשכנז והיו בחופתו כת"ק אנשים ונשים שהיו כולם קרובים. והרחוקים שבהם היו רביעי ברביעי:

וסבה[119] ליציאת א"א ז"ל היתה מפני תפישת הר' מאיר מרוטנבורק ז"ל שתפשו האדון המושל והקהילות של אשכנז פדאוהו בממון רב. והמושל לא רצה ליקח ערב רק לא"א ז"ל והוצרך ליכנס ערב בממון רב. וקודם שנחלק הממון על הקהלות נפטר הר' מאיר בתפישה. והמושל העליל א"א ז"ל באומרו כי מאחר שנפטר בתפישה קודם שפטרו מן המאסר שבאחריותו נפטר. והקהלות והוא שיהיו פורעין הממון. ונשמט מלפניו והלך לעיר אחרת. ומפני יראתו מן המלכות יצא מאשכנז. ובא לעיר הגדולה עיר טוליטלה: ובשנה הראשונה שבא שלחו לו כתב מהקונסיגו של העיר שהיה דר בה שיחזור אל ביתו. ושהם ישלחו חמישים שרים לקראתו עד תחלת אשכנז. ושיהיו נותנין לו כתב

119 MS. סבת.

---

107 Count Meinhard of Goiz (*op. cit.*, p. 438).
108 According to one account 30,000 marks.
109 Sp. consejo (?)

documentary safe-conduct from the Emperor. For they recognized his wisdom and excellence, and were wont to follow his advice in all matters. But in face of the frequent ill-treatment of the Jews there, he was unwilling to go back. This was the reason of the coming of my lord, my father, of blessed memory, to this country. "This was the Lord's doing,"[110] to the end that my father might raise up many disciples on Spanish soil. "He executed the righteousness of the Lord, and His ordinances with Israel."[111] For there were not in these lands any thorough commentaries.[112] He also wrote commentaries and decisions to the Talmud. Wherever his commentaries, responsa and decisions reached, they made known the statutes of the Lord and His laws. His sons walked in his ways, and maintained his opinions. "As for Asher, his bread was fat;" his Rock guarded him with every care, because he was faithful to his charge. "And of Asher he said: blessed be Asher because of his sons"[113]—all of them were interpreters of uprightness[114], who from the least to the greatest of them held fast to the law of God, the Lord of the Universe, and by what they wrought were a shield to their generation. I was by far the most insignificant of all of them; through His grace God raised me up in my father's place, a tendril of his stock, a shooting of his roots[115] and planting, to maintain his

[110] Ps. 118.23.

[111] Deut. 33.21.

[112] Comp. above, p. 166, n. 10

בטחון מן המלך. לפי שהיו מכירין חכמתו ומעלתו וכל ענייניהם היו עושין בעצתו. ומפני הגזירות המצויות ע״ם לא רצה לחזור. וזאת היתה סבת ביאת א״א ז״ל לזאת הארץ: ומאת ה׳ היתה זאת להעמיד תלמידים רבים בארצות ספרד. צדקת ה׳ עשה ומשפטיו עם ישראל. כי לא היו בארצות אלה פירושים מדוייקים. וגם עשה לתלמוד פירושים ופסקים. ובכל מקום אשר פירושיו[120] ותשובותיו ופסקיו יגיעו. חוקי האל ותורותיו יודיעו. ובניו הלכו בדרכיו. לא שנו טעמו. מאשר שמנה לחמו. וצורו נצרו בכל משמר. עקב אשר מצותיו שמר. לאשר אמר ברוך מבנים אשר. כולם מליצי יושר. החזיקו בדת האל אלהי עולם. מקטנם ועד גדולם. והגינו על בני דורם בפעולם: ואני קטונתי מאד מכולם. ובזכותו העמיד על כנו חוטר מגזעו. ונצר משרשיו ונטעו[121]. להעמיד ישיבתו על

[120] MS. פירושותיו. [121] MS. reads חוט and אונו.

---

[113] Gen. 49.20; Deut. 33.24 (with reference to the father's name Asher). In the latter text the meaning is "above sons", but our author seems to apply it in the sense given in the translation.

[114] Job 33.23. [115] Isa. 11.1.

School on its site, even better equipped than of yore. And also in what pertained to the affairs and organization of the community, we passed our time together in settlement of causes and judgments. Men of the government also agreed to abide by my decisions, not because of my wisdom or wit, for "I am brutish, unlike a man, and have not a man's understanding,"[116] but God filled them with a kindly disposition towards me, so that my words were acceptable to them, in that they deemed me in their thoughts an impartial judge.

As for me, my prayer is made before the Lord of the Universe, that He may requite with a good recompense this holy congregation for their labors, and for all the good which they as a body and as individuals have done unto me in granting all my requests and of their heart's generosity and not for any selfish motive. And so will it ever continue until I part from them in great love, "and my seed shall be established in their sight, and my offspring before their eyes."[117] And may it be their good will to prepare a way for my progeny to settle among them as they did with my father and me, kindness after kindness. For what has passed and for what is to come, unto the Rock tremendous in His doing, Judah shall lead the thanksgiving.[118] And may the bounty of God and the merit of our fathers cause that there never fail from us in Toledo—until the majestic and awful God establish Jerusalem and a Redeemer come unto Zion—one to fill the

[116] Prov. 33.2.

תילה. ובהוצאה גדולה יותר מבתחילה. גם עניין הקהל יצ"ו ותיקונו. ובדיניהם ובמשפטיהם עברו זמן עמי ואני עמהם. גם אנשי ממלכות הסכימו לסמוך עלי בדיניהם. לא מחכמתי ושכלי כי בער אנכי מאיש ולא בינת אדם לי. אבל נתנני השם לרחמים לפניהם. להיות דברי מקובלים להם. ומדמים ברעיוניהם שאיני נושא בדין פניהם:

ואני תפילתי לאלהי עולם לשלם לקהל הקדוש הזה שכר טוב בעמלם. ועל כל הטובה אשר עשו עמי כלליהם ופרטיהם. לתת כל שאילותי אשר שאלתי מהם מנדיבות לבם ולא לשום סבה. וכן יהיה תמיד עד שאפטור מהם באהבה רבה. וזרעי יהיה נכון לפניהם וצאצאי לעיניהם: ויהי רצון מלפניהם להכין להם דרך להתיישב עמהם כאשר עשו עם אבותיהם טובה אחרי טובה. ועל העבר ועל הבא לצור נורא עלילה. יהודה יהודה בתחלה. וזכות הרחמן וזכות אבותינו יעמוד לנו שלא יכרת ממנו בטוליטולה עד שיכוננה אל אדיר ונורא ובא לציון גואל. איש יושב על כסא א"א הר' אשר

[117] Job 21.8 –(with some variants).

[118] Ps. 66.5; Neh. 11.17.

seat of my lord, my father,[119] R. Asher of beloved memory; (may this be so) for all time until Shiloh cometh and people be gathered unto him, and there arise a priest with Urim and with Thummim.[120]

Ended and completed, praise to the God of the Universe!

My lord, my father of blessed memory, ordained in his city in Germany that every member of the congregation should pay a tithe of his whole income, and in the district of Toledo he likewise ordained that he and his children should follow the same course.[121] And after his death, I and all my brethren resolved to maintain the practice and to add to its terms. In Elul 1346,[122] I wrote out the ordinance which was signed by my elder sons. I append the form of the ordinance, so that with God's help (my younger children also) will sign it. Perchance another (not of my family) seeing it, may be prompted to assume the same obligation, of which these are the terms:

We, the undersigned, have stood by a certain ordinance, in the handwriting of our grandfather R. Asher of blessed memory, of which this is the text: "Hear my son the instruction of thy father and forsake not the teaching of thy mother."[123] Seeing that in the country whence we migrated, our fathers and our fathers' fathers were wont to set aside to God as charity for religious purposes, one part in ten of all business profits—as our Rabbis said in their com-

[119] Isa. 59.20; I Kings 2.4. [120] Gen. 49.10; Ezra 2.63.

ז״ל כל הימים. עד כי יבא שילה ולו יקהת עמים.
ויעמד כהן לאורים ולתומים:

תם ונשלם של״ע:

אדוני אבי ז״ל תיקן בעיר׳ז באשכנז שכל אחד מהקהל יהיה נותן מעשר מכל הבא בידו וכן תיקן במדינת טוליטולה שהוא ובניו יעשו כן. ואחר פטירתו ז״ל הסכמנו אני וכל אחי לקיימה ולהוסיף בה דברים. ובאלול שנת ק״ו תקנתי וחתמו בה בני הגדולים. וכתבתי בה נוסח התקנות בכאן בע״ה יחתמו בה[122]. וגם אולי יראה אדם אחר וידבנו לבו לקבלה עליו. וזו נוסחה:

אנו הבאים על החתום עמדנו על תקנה אחת מכתיבת יד זקיננו הר׳ אשר ז״ל וזה נוסחה: שמע בני מוסר אביך ואל תטוש תורת אמך. יען כי בארץ אשר יצאנו משם נהגו אבותינו ואבות אבותינו להפריש חלק אחד מהעשרה חלקים לגבוה לצדקה לצורך מצוה מכל מה שירויחו במשא ומתן כמו

[122] Add: בני הקטנים or similar words. Similarly MS. omits the name אשר at the end of the third line of the text above.

---

[121] On the tithe see *Jewish Life in the Middle Ages*, ch. xvii. [122] MS. has 106 = 5106 = 1346.

[123] Prov. 1.8.

ment on the text:[124] "Thou shalt surely tithe all the increase of thy seed," which text they applied to traders over-seas who devoted one tenth of their gains to those laboring in the Law —therefore we have continued in the footsteps of our fathers, and have taken on ourselves the obligation to set aside a tithe of all our profits in business, whether interest on investments or trade transactions. Three-fourths of that tithe we will deposit in a chest, controlled by two treasurers, by whose authorization all grants shall be made to the necessitous. And this undertaking we have assumed for ourselves and our offspring, to observe, to do and to maintain it. The reasurers whom we have selected are the brothers R. Jacob and R. Judah (whom may God preserve!). These obligations we have duly signed on the 9th day of the month Marḥeshvan, in the year 75 (in the abbreviated reckoning) anno mundi.

Asher b. Yeḥiel
Solomon b. Asher
Jacob b. Asher
Judah b. Asher[125]
Eliaḳim b. Asher

And close to these signatures is a document to the following effect:

We, the undersigned, have agreed that included in the terms of the ordinance written above shall be whatever is or shall be in the hand of any

[124] Deut. 14.22; see Pesiḳta de R. Kahana ch. 11, end (ed. Buber p. 99b).

[125] On the phrase following the name here see above, p. 168, note 17.

שאמרו רז"ל על המקרא ודרשו תעשר את כל תבואת זרעך מכאן למפרישי ימים שמפרישים חלק אחד מעשרה לעמלים בתורה. לכן יצאנו בעקבות[123] אבותינו וקבלנו על עצמינו להפריש חלק אחד מעשרה מכל מה שנרויח במשא ובמתן ברבית ובסחורה. ושלשה רביעים מאותו חלק עשירי נתן לתוך קופה ותהיה הקופה ביד שני גבאים ועל פי אותם הגבאים ינתן כל מה שיותן לכל מי שצריך ממנו: ודבר זה קבלנו על עצמינו ועל זרעינו לשמור ולעשות ולקיים. והגבאים שבירנו הם שני אחים שהם ר' יעקב ור' יהודה יצ"ו ומה שקבלנו עלינו חתמנו[124] בט' ימים לחדש מרחשון שנת ע"ה לפרט היצירה. אשר בן הר' יחיאל ז"ל. שלמה בן הר' אשר נר"י. יעקב בן הרא"ש יצ"ו. יהודה בן הר' אשר[125] איש חיל[126]. אליקים בן הר' אשר נר"ו: וסמוך לחתימות כתב שזה נוסחו: והסכמנו אנחנו חתומי מטה שיהיה בכלל תיקון זה הכתוב למעלה כל מה שבא ויבא ליד כל אחד ממנו. בין במעות

123 MS. בערבות. S corrects as in text.

124 Missing in MS. 125 MS. reads wrongly ז"ל.

126 S suggests the reading חי. But the Kere חיל and Ketib חי in II Sam 23. 20 explains the variation in the two passages of our text.

of us, whether it consist of money, legacies, gifts, marriage settlements, or any other property. Each of us shall be bound to set aside the proper amount and place it in the hands of the trustees within eight days of the same becoming due. So far the form of the second document. The signatories are:

Solomon b. Asher
Jacob b. Asher
Judah b. Asher
Simeon b. Asher

We, the undersigned, take upon ourselves all the ordinances, relating to the tithe, inscribed above, even as our lord, our father, did, and (we contract) that each of us shall pay the contributions[126] named, as is mentioned above. In attestation of this we have here signed our names on the New Moon of Elul, in the year 5106[127] anno mundi. So far the third document, which bears the signatures of

Solomon b. Judah
Yeḥiel b. Judah

Conscious as I am of the limitation of my capacity and the exiguity of my learning, and recognizing that I am unworthy to receive emoluments[128] even from a small congregation, and much less from the great and holy congregation of Toledo, which God preserve! it accordingly irks me greatly to be compelled to take a salary.

[126] The translation follows the reading החלקים. The MS. actually reads האלפים.

בין בירושה בין במתנה בין בנישואין בין באיזה צד שיהיה. ויהיה חייב כל אחד ממנו להפריש תחילה ממה שיש לו להפריש תוך שמנה ימים אחר שיתחייב להפרישו ולהשתדל ליד הגבאים. ע"כ נוסח הכתב השני: והחתומים עליו שלמה בן הרא"ש ז"ל. יעקב בן הרא"ש ז"ל. יהודה בן הרא"ש ז"ל. שמעון בן הרא"ש ז"ל. אנחנו הבאים על החתום מקבלים עלינו כל התקנות תקנות המעשר הכתובות למעלה כאשר הסכים א"א נר"ו[127]. ושיפרע כל אחד ממנו החלקים[128] הנזכרים כמו שנזכר למעלה. ועל אמתת דבר זה חתמנו שמותינו פה בר"ח אלול שנת חמשת אלפים וק"ו ליצירה. ע"כ נוסח הכתב השלישי: והחתומים שלמה בן הר' יהודה נר"ו. יחיאל בן הר' יהודה נר"ו:

ולפי שאני יודע ומכיר מעוט שכלי וקוצר ידיעתי ואיני[129] ראוי ליקח תנאי אפי' מקהל קטן כ"ש מקהל גדול וקדוש קהל טוליטולה יצ"ו. ועל כן קשה לי מאד להיות צריך לקחת תנאי, ואם הייתי יכול

[127] MS. wrongly ז"ל. [128] MS. האלפים.
[129] MS. repeats יודע.

---

[127] 1346.
[128] lit. to take a contract.

Had I been able to carry on without it, I would not have taken it. But what could I do, forced as I was to so much outlay? With my own funds I could not operate, while maintaining my studies, except by the hands of agents, thus risking the capital, while the gain was small. The agents deducted a commission first, and it was only under pressure that they gave me what they did. Hence I became, in my own eyes, as one dependent on other men's tables.[129] But if the Lord, blessed be He, prosper my undertakings, and I can pay my debts, I may be able to pass the rest of my life without salary—either wholly or in part—from the congregation. The surplus I will devote to students of the Torah, or to other religious purposes. Thus, in my humble opinion, I should fulfil my duty, for this seems to me a better course than to refund the money to the congregation (whom may God preserve!). I should be more careful than they in applying the fund to well-chosen objects. The credit will be theirs, for I and mine are theirs. The money, indeed, having been appropriated by them to what they thought a religious purpose, it would not be right that it should return to them for secular use. And as my aim in begetting children was to raise up a progeny engaged in the Torah and in the pursuit of virtue, my sons have not busied themselves in any other occupation, and so will it always be, with God's help. Our Sages said: A father is not bound to support his young children after their sixth year.[130] I say

[129] Cf. Bezah 32b; Shabb. 87a. The translation

לעבור זולתו לא הייתי לוקח אותו. אבל מה אעשה וההוצאה היא גדולה? ובממון שתחת ידי איני יכול עם למודי רק ע"י אחרים. והקרן בסכנה. והריוח מעט. והמשתדלים לוקחים חלק בראש. ובטורח גדול נותנין לי מה שנותנין. עד שאני בעיני כמצפה לשלחן אחרים. אבל אם יסכים האל ית' על ידי ואפרע החובות שעלי. אפשר שאעבור זמני בלא תנאי הקהל כולו או מקצתו. ואתן העודף ללומדי התורה או בשאר דברי המצוה. ובזה לפי מיעוט דעתי אצא ידי חובה. כי זה בעיני יותר טוב משאחזירו לקהל יצ"ו. כי יותר אדקדק אני לתיתן למקומות הגונים ממה שיעשו הם. והשכר הוא להם כי אני ושלי שלהם. ומאחרי שהקצו אותו למצוה בעיניהם אינו טוב שיחזור חול לידיהם. ואחרי אשר כל כוונתי בפריה ורביה כדי שיהיו לי בנים עוסקים בתורה ושבים לאל ית' עוד בני אינם עוסקים בדבר אחר. וכן יהיה תמיד בע"ה. ורז"ל אמרו שאין אדם חייב לזון בניו הקטנים רק עד שש שנים. אני אומר

"in my own eyes" is based on an emendation of the MS. בעוני into בעיני.

[130] Ketubot 49b. After that age a father's duty was the same for *all* his children.

that if I have money to spare from my salary to students who are not of my family, and of whose methods I am ignorant, it would be better to give it to my sons and expend it on them. In this way, the greater will be the reward[131] of those who give the money. I estimate that for food and clothing each would require one gold coin a day,[132] a sum which would be small enough for them while young, and quite inadequate when they grow older, and so I determined to reckon for them. Now up to the end of this November I received 37,240 gold pieces, as explained above. Of this sum I gave for religious purposes 3724 pieces, the tithe in accordance with the obligation of the tithe written above. On my sons, in the period named, I have spent a total of 18,090, which with the tithe amounts to 21,814 pieces. In order to reimburse these sums, I have resolved to dedicate my library (on the estimate made by three persons, as is explained in my account-book). These books are ready for the use of students. Great is the reward of those who provided the money, for as our Sages said, the text: "Wealth and riches are in his house, and his merit endureth forever"—applies to him who prepares books and lends them to others.[133] If the books realize an insufficient sum, I bequeath of my goods

[131] There would be no doubt as to the proper use of the fund.

[132] Clearly the coin intended would not be of high value. Cf. above, p. 180, n. 84.

[133] Ps. 112.3; cf. p. 82, above.

מה שיהיה לי ליתן מן התנאי שלי לאנשים נכריים שלומדים שאיני יודע עניינם שיותר טוב הוא ליתן אותו לבני ולהוציאו עליהם. ובזה יגדל שכר הנותנים. וחשבתי שצריך לכל אחד מהם למזון ולכסות א׳ זהוב לכל יום. ואם יחסר מהם בעודם קטנים בגדולתם צריך יותר ויותר. וכן הסכמתי לחשוב להם. ועד סוף נובײמרי זה קבלתי ל״ז[130] אלף זהובים ור״מ[131] זהובים כמו שמפורש למעלה ונתתי מהם בדבר מצוה ג׳ אלף ותשכ״ד[132] זהובים שהוא המעשר כפי חיוב התקנה הכתובה למעלה. והוצאתי על בני בזמן שנזכר לכל[133] אחד ואחד כפי הסך שנזכר למעלה שעולה י״ח אלף וצ׳ זהובים הסך עם המעשר שנתתי כ״א[134] אלף זהובים ותתי״ד. במקום אלו המעות הסכמתי שיהיו הקדש הספרים שלי על פי השומא ששמו אותם ג׳ אנשים כמו שמפורש בפנקס שלי. והם מזומנים ללמוד בהם. ושכר גדול יש לנותנים המעות כמו שאמרו רז״ל הון ועושר בביתו וצדקתו עומדת לעד זה העושה ספרים ומשאילם לאחרים. ואם לא ישוו זה הסכום

130 MS. reads לשבעה. 131 S corrects to ר״מ or ר׳. MS. reads רמ״א.

132 So S corrects the MS. which reads ותשב״א.

133 MS. שכל. 134 MS. כ״ח.

enough to equalize matters. I trust in God, blessed be He, who searcheth my reins and knoweth all my thoughts, that He will provide to me the means for refunding also the amounts which I have expended on my children in the manner named. And since it is my desire that my sons shall continuously engage themselves in study of the Torah and not in any other occupation, I have made up my mind not to bequeath from my estate to my sons by legal inheritance more than 100 gold pieces. The rest shall be set aside as a fund devoted to any of them who shall devote himself to the Torah. They shall not portion out the estate in equal shares, but each shall take according to his family and according to his needs,[134] at the decision of their mother, and after her of the treasurer or treasurers whom I shall appoint and in the manner which I shall indite in the trust. Any student of my own seed shall have first claim, next to them a student of my father's seed, and next to them whoever studies the Torah, and makes that study his main object in life.

The testament of our teacher R. Judah, of blessed memory, made in expectation of death: This is what I desire to be done with my property. They shall sell such of my books as will produce 3000 gold pieces. These shall be devoted for study, and shall be joined to the sum put in trust on lease,[135] both amounts being treated on the

[134] See Jastrow, *Dictionary*, p. 533b, s. v. טיפול.

[135] The text has *arrenda*, medieval Latin term from which the modern *rent* is derived. It is the annual return of investment on lease.

אני מניח מנכסי לתשלום הסכום הנזכר בע"ה ית'. ואני בוטח בשם ית' החוקר כליותי ומבין כל מחשבותי שיזמין לי ענין שאוכל להחזיר גם על מה שהוצאתי על בני על הדרך הנזכר. ולפי שכוונתי היא שיתעסקו בני תמיד בתורה ולא בדבר אחר. הסכמתי בלבי שלא אניח מנכסי לבני בתורת ירושה רק מאה זהובים והשאר יהיה הקדש מוקצה ומזומן לכל מי שיעסוק מהם בתורה. ולא יחלקו אותו ביניהם בשוה רק כל אחד ואחד מהם יקח כפי טיפולו ולפי צורכו. על פי אמם ואחריה ע"פ גזבר או גזברים שאמנה ועל הסדר שאכתוב בגזברות. ומי שילמוד מזרעי יהיה קודם. ואחריהם מי שילמוד מזרע אאז"ל. ואחריהם כל מי שילמוד ויהיה תורתו אומנותו:

צוואת מורנו הר' יהודה זצ"ל מחמת מיתה. זהו מה שאני מסכים לעשות מענייני. שימכרו מספרי עד ג' אלפים זהובים. ויהיו הקדש לתלמוד ויתחברו עם הקדש ארנדה ותטילו להיותם כדינם

same conditions. Two thousand full gold pieces shall be used in business, and the profit shall every year be added to the capital; no expenditure shall be made either of profit or of capital, but all shall be accumulated for the marriage of my daughter Dona, so that her marriage may be in accordance with her dignity. The surplus shall be joined with the residue of what I leave to be treated in the same manner. If it be possible to marry her in the family of my father's house, she shall not wed outside the family. I leave to each of my sons 100 gold pieces; the residue I and my wife dedicate from this date and after the death of the survivor of us two, on the conditions which I now detail. To every one of my sons, so long as the Torah is his main occupation, a sum according to his family. So long as there is profit these payments shall be made out of profits, but if the profit suffices not, they shall pay him the necessary sums for his maintenance out of the capital. If any of them possesses any means for his part support, they shall complete the amount from the trust fund. And if, God forbid, there be among them one who does not devote himself to Torah, and he be whole-hearted, upright, and one that fears God,[136] walking in a good way and endeavoring to supply the needs of his brothers so that they may engage in their studies, and in all other respects performing his religious duties,—such a one shall share in the trust as one of his studious brothers, seeing that he busies himself in their needs. "For (the Torah) is a tree of life to them that lay hold upon her,

[136] Job 1.1.

לכל דבריהם. להניח אלפים זהובים שלמים שתרויח בהם. ותעלה הריוח בכל שנה עם הקרן. ולא תוציא כלום לא מן הריוח ולא מן הקרן. אבל יהיה הכל שמור לצורך נשואי דונה בתי. ואז ישאנה לפי כבודה. והמותר יתחבר עם שאר מה שאניח מנכסי להיות כדינם[135]. ואם יתכן להשיאה במשפחת בית אבי לא ישאנה חוץ למשפחה. ואני מניח לכל אחד מבני ק׳ זהובים. והשאר אני ואשתי מקדישים אותם מהיום ולאחר מיתת האחרון ממנו על התנאים שאפרש. שיתנו מהם לכל אחד מבני כל זמן שתהיה תורתו אומנותו לפי טפולו. כל זמן שיהיה שם ריוח יתנו מן הריוח. ואם לא יספיק הריוח יתנו מן הקרן די מחסורו אשר יחסר לו ולטפולו. ואם יהיה לשום אחד משלו כדי העברה ישלימו לו אז מן ההקדש על שיהיה לו משלו. ואם ח״ו לא יהיה בהם מי שתורתו אומנותו אם יהיה תם וישר וירא אלהים וילך בדרך טובה וישתדל בצורכי אחיו כדי שיוכלו לעסוק בתורה ואם יתעסק בכל שאר המצות בכל יכולתו יהיה לו בהקדש כאחד מאחיו העוסקים בתורה. כיון שמתעסק בצורכיהם. כי עץ חיים

135 MS. בידינו.

and happy is every one that holdeth her fast,"[137] like Zebulun, brother of Issachar, and Simeon, the brother of Azariah.[138] A share from the annual profit shall be given to any necessitous member of my father's family. If I have a son-in-law who devotes himself to study, he shall have precedence in the endowment of the trust over all other persons in the manner mentioned. After them shall come any person engaged in the study of the Torah. And I appoint five treasurers for the said trust, viz.: Solomon and Yeḥiel, my sons, and R. Eleazar my brother, and R. Asher, the son of my brother Solomon, and R. Solomon Israel; so that whatever they or a majority do shall take effect provided one of my sons and R. Eleazar, my nearest relative, be in the majority. And so at every time. Should any of the trustees resign or leave the city or die, he shall previously appoint a successor with the approval of the remaining trustees or a majority of them, otherwise the remaining trustees shall appoint. In case of disagreement they shall employ as arbitrator the man with the highest repute for probity in the city at the time. And I and my wife absolutely bind ourselves under a penalty of a thousand double coins to the treasurers or their substitutes with regard to all the property which they shall declare mine

[137] Prov. 13.18.

[138] Zebulun, according to the Midrash (see Rashi on Gen. 49.13), engaged in commerce in order to support his brother Issachar in his studies. A similar relation is recorded with regard to Azariah and his brother Simeon (Levit. Rabbah 25).

היא למחזיקים בה ותומכיה מאושר כזבולון אחי יששכר וכשמעון אחי עזריה. והח׳ מן הריוח בכל שנה יותן למי שיצטרך לו ממשפחת א״א ז״ל. ואם יהיה לי חתן שיהיה תורתו אומנותו אז חתני יהיה קודם ליקח מן ההקדש הנזכר מכל אדם על דרך הנזכר. ואחריהם כל מי שתורתו אומנותו: ואני ממנה ה׳ גזברים על ההקדש הנזכר. והם שלמה ויחיאל בני. ור׳ אליעזר אחי. ור׳ אשר בן אחי ר׳ שלמה ז״ל. ור׳ שלמה ישראל. שכל מה שיעשו הם או רובם שיהיה עשוי. והוא אחד מבני ור׳ אליעזר שהוא הקרוב יותר. וכן בכל זמן וזמן. וכל אחד מהגזברים שיסתלק מן הגזברות או ילך אחד מן העיר או יפטר שימנה אחר במקומו קודם ובעצת הנשארים או רובם. ואם לא יעשה כן הנשארים ימנו. ואם לא יסכימו. יקחו מכריע הגדול והמפורסם במדות בעיר בזמן ההוא: והנה אני ואשתי מחייבים עצמינו בקנין שלם באלף כפולות לגזברים או למי שיהיה במקומם בכל הנכסים

at this juncture, as though on the testimony of two competent witnesses; reserving to ourselves the right with regard to this foundation of trust that we may both of us sell, pledge or mortgage at our will any of the property which we have acquired or shall acquire in due legal course. Moreover we agree to the full maintenance of this foundation of trust in a signed witnessed document, and in every form of legal obligation we confirm all that is written above regarding the upholding or the cancelling of the trust in all or in part. Nor shall anything therein become invalid because of a scribe's error or the omission of any point in the instrument of the trust which will be drawn up. And regarding all that is written above R. Judah gave his full and absolute assent in the presence of us the undersigned at the end of the month of Sivan in the year 5109[139] of the era of the Creation. The witnesses are: Moses son of R. Benjamin of Rome, Isaac son of R. Abraham Maimon[140].

[139] Text has 5109 = 1349. Schechter interprets, "towards the end of the author's life".

[140] The last named was a dayyan in Toledo (see ref., date 1358, in זכרון יהודה, 1846, p. 38).

אשר יאמרו שהיו לי עתה נאמנות גמורה כשני עדים כשרים מניחין רשות לעצמינו בעיקר ההקדש הזה שנוכל למכור ולמשכן ולשעבד שנינו בכל מה שנרצה מנכסינו שקנינו ושנקנה בשטר מקוים כהוגן. גם אנחנו מסכימים בעיקר ההקדש בשטר חתום מעדים שיהיה עשוי וקיים. ונטלנו קנין על הכתוב למעלה בכל חזוקים שיוכל בדין לעשות לקיים כל הכתוב למעלה בין לענין קיום ההקדש או בטולו כלו או מקצתו. ולא יפסד שום דבר ממנו בשביל טעות סופר או חסרון שום דבר שימצא בשטר ההקדש שיעשה בדבר: ועל כל מה שכתוב למעלה נטל בפנינו אנו חתומים מטה ר׳ יהודה נר״ו קנין שלם במנא דכשר למקניא ביה בשלה׳[136] סיון שנת חמשת אלפים ומאה ותשע לבריאת עולם. והחתומים עליה משה ב״ר בנימין נ״ע רומי יצחק ב״ר אברהם נ״ע מימון:

תם ונשלם של״ע

136 MS. בשלה; S corrects as in text.

לקוטים מתוכחת הרב רבינו יעקב בן הרא"ש ז"ל לבניו:

THE FRUIT OF PIETISM FROM THE TESTAMENT OF JACOB ASHERI

IX

THE FRUIT OF PIETISM

From the Testament of Jacob Asheri

Jacob was a son of Asher ben Yeḥiel (VI), and a brother of Judah (VIII). He was younger than the latter, but pre-deceased him. After a life of privation, he died in 1340 (*J. E.* vii, 27). He does not seem to have filled any rabbinical post (Graetz, *History*, E. T., iv, 88), but though not himself a Rabbi, he was a begetter of Rabbis. For his chief work, which won him a fame far transcending his brother's, was the Ṭurim, the basis and model of the still favorite Code (Ḳaro's Shulḥan 'Aruk).

There is no indication that any of Asheri's family regretted the migration to Spain. The assertion, quoted by Graetz, that Judah, in his Testament, recommended his children to return to Germany, is not borne out by the full text of the Testament which is printed above. Jacob was associated with his brothers in the Tithe ordinance, signing before Judah. Jacob's own Testament or rather Admonition is derived from the same MS. as Judah's (VIII). Jacob very pointedly speaks against believing in omens or dreams, doubtless with the knowledge that, as his brother Judah's Testament reveals, other members of the Asheri family had some inclination towards such beliefs. As one would have expected, Jacob Asheri's Testament (in the part preceding the selection here printed) shows a scrupulous regard for ceremonial minutiae, but it also offers pietism with spirituality. For

ט

לקוטים מתוכחת הרב רבינו יעקב בן הרא"ש ז"ל לבניו:

יעקב היה בנו של אשר בן יחיאל (ו׳) ואחיו של יהודה (ח׳). הוא היה צעיר מן האחרון, אבל נפטר לפניו. אחרי אשר חי חיים של מחסור ועוני גוע בשנת ק׳ לאלף הששי (ראה את האנציקלופדיה היהודית האנגלית, כרך שביעי, דף כ"ז). כפי הנראה לא שמש בכתר הרבנות (גרץ, דברי ימי ישראל, העתקה אנגלית, כרך רביעי, דף פ"ח), אבל אף כי לא היה רבי בעצמו הנה הורה והוליד רבנים רבים, כי חבורו הראשי אשר נתן לו שם הרבה יותר גדול מזה של אחיו היה „ספר הטורים", היסוד אשר עליו נוסד קובץ הדינים היותר אהוב וחביב על העם (שלחן ערוך של קארו).

אין כל זכר ורמז שאיש ממשפחת אשרי התחרט על הגלות לספרד. הסברא שמביא גרץ שבצוואתו צוה יהודה לבניו לשוב לאשכנז אין לה כל יסוד בנוסח השלם של הצואה הנדפס פה. יעקב השתתף עם אחיו במצות המעשר, וחתימת ידו היתה לפני זו של יהודה. הצואה או אגרת המוסר של יעקב שאולה מאותו הכ"י עצמו שבו נמצאת צואתו של יהודה (ח׳). יעקב מוחא מחאה נמרצה כנגד האמונה באותות ובחלומות, בלי ספק מפני שידע, כמו שאפשר לראות מן הצואה של יהודה, שלבני משפחתו האחרים היתה איזו נטיה לאמונות טפלות כאלה. כמו שאפשר היה לשער, הצואה של יעקב אשרי (בחלק ההולך לפני הלקוטים הנדפסים פה) מתיחסת באדיקות גמורה אל המנהגים היותר פעוטים, אבל יחד עם רוחניות היא דורשת גם

the same document which lays stress on dietary laws in all detail, is full also of counsels towards inner perfection, a combination which is so often illustrated in the present volume.

Love God, hallow His Name, and do Him reverence, with thy soul, thy body, and thy wealth, surrendering thyself, if need be, to the sword or the stake. Reckon the anguish of death as of no account in comparison with the delight thereafter, when thou wilt have "free access among those that stand by."[1] Give alms, exercise loving-kindness, show hospitality to wayfarers. But when thou givest alms, see to it that thy act be done for the glory of God; beware lest thou seek thine own honor or to win a reputation for generosity! Study the Law for its true end—for thyself, to know the right and to avoid the wrong; for others, to teach the men of thy generation, seeing that (for our sins!) the Law becomes ever more forgotten. Be a diligent student all thy days.

Ever turn thine eyes on thy superior in wisdom, and realize that the path to learning has no end. Nay, a man may even lose in a day or in an hour much that he has acquired, if he suffer himself to relax into worldly ambitions.[2] Probe long and

[1] Zech. 3.7. "Those that stand" is usually referred to the Angels. Ḳimḥi in his note on the text interprets it of the soul after its separation from the body.

[2] Güdemann renders: "jeder müssige Augenblick verursacht unersetzlichen Verlust."

דבקות דתית. האגרת הזאת המדגישה כל כך את מצוות האכילה לכל פרטיהן ודקדוקיהן היא מלאה ג"כ עצות ותחבולות להשתלמות פנימית, הרכבה אשר דוגמתה אפשר למצוא לפעמים קרובות בכרך שלפנינו.

והוי זהיר באהבת השם ית' ובקידוש השם ויראת השם בנפשך בגופך ובממונך עד שתתיר עצמך להריגה ולשריפה. ולא תחשוב בעצמך צער הכלה כלום כנגד העונג שאחר המיתה שיהיה לך מהלכים בין העומדים: והוי זהיר בצדקה ובגמילות חסדים ובהכנסת אורחים. וכשתעשה צדקה הזהר שלא תעשה אותה אלא לכבוד השם ולא לכבודך ולא לקנות לך שם: והוי זהיר בתלמוד תורה לשמה כדי שתדע המצות ותשמור עצמך מן העבירות. וכשתזכיר[1] בהם אנשי דורך. כי בעונותינו התורה משתכחת ממנו בכל יום. ולא תתעצל מללמוד כל ימיך:

ולעולם תן עיניך במי שהוא למעלה ממך במעלת החכמה. ודע כי למוד התורה וספרים אין קץ. והרבה אדם מפסיד ביום אחד ובשעה אחת ממה שלמד אם הוא מתבטל בהנאת העולם: והוי זהיר

[1] MS. reads וכשתזכור.

deep into the authorities to reach clear decisions of law in matters necessary to the world, but spend not overmuch time or thought in needless casuistry. The aim of most of those who so act is to win a reputation for skill in puzzling scholars. After reading a tractate of the Talmud, prepare a synopsis of all the results, and of intricate discussions write a general summary. The main heads will thus always be available, and easily found on a future occasion. Follow this plan, and thou wilt be able to express thyself with lucidity, and to retain what thou hast learnt. When studying the Talmud read it aloud, do not mumble it; for its words are "life to them that proclaim them, and health to all their flesh."[3] And when thou prayest, think only of thy prayer; be on thy guard lest thy mind wander to other matters, even though they be matters relating to religious duty.

Thy labor on the soil, ploughing and sowing, is directed to one end—to produce fruits. So, all a man's toil in the concerns of his body is to sustain his soul. And the fruit of one's activity during the day is—the time of prayer; the fruit of one's work throughout the week is—the Sabbath day!

[3] Prov. 4.22. This explanation of the text is derived from T. B. 'Erubin 54a.

להאריך ולהעמיק ולחפש אחר כל הספרים בדרך פסק ההלכה בדבר הצריך לעולם. ולא תאריך ולא תעמיק בדברי קושיות שלא לצורך. כי אינם עושים רוב בני אדם כי אם לקנות שם מערבב בעלי הגמרא: ובכל מסכתא שתלמוד תכתוב מעט בכל מן הפוסקים[2]. ומן ההלכות המעורבבות כתוב הכללים כדי שיהיו בידיך ואם תספק[3] באחד מהם[4] תמצאם בפעם האחרת ובזה יצאו דבריך לאור ותתקיים תורתך ותזכור שתקרא. ותוציא לשון הגמרא בפיך. ולא תגמגם בקריאתה כי חיים הם למוצאיהם ולכל בשרו מרפא למוציאיהם בפה: והזהר כשאתה מתפלל שלא תחשוב בשום[5] דבר ובשום ענין אפילו לדבר מצוה אלא לדבר תפלה לבד:

כל טורח שאתה טורח באדמה בחרישה ובזריעה הוא כדי להוציא ממנה פירות. כן כל מה שאדם טורח בעניני גופו הוא כדי לקיים הנשמה. ופרי מעשה כל היום עת בתפילה. ופרי מעשה כל השבוע יום השבת:

[2] So the MS. Read הפסקים. [3] MS. תספה.
[4] Some word must be supplied: perhaps פעם אחת.
[5] MS. repeats שום.

Give thy whole heart to God. Trust not in dreams or omens[4], inquire not of fortune-tellers. Never cast lots with dice or in any other manner. All such things are vanity; resort to them is due to lack of faith. Trust thou in God alone, and He will prove thy support! As our Sages said[5]: If one desire to become clean, heaven helps him to his wish.

[4] The author's brother Judah was more inclined to interest himself in dreams and portents. This is clearly shown in Judah Asheri's Testament (p. 164 above).

[5] T. B. Shabbat 104a.

הזהר שתהיה עם השם ית' תמים. ולא תבטח בדברי חלומות ולא בשום נחוש ולא תשאל לחוזים. ולא תשליך גורלות ולא בנקודות ולא בשום דבר כי הכל הבל ומחסרון הבטחון. בלתי אל ה' לבדו תבטח. והוא יעזרך כמו שאמרו ז"ל בא לטהר:

צואת אליעזר בן שמואל הלוי

THE IDEALS OF AN AVERAGE JEW

(Testament of Eleazar of Mayence)

X

THE IDEALS OF AN AVERAGE JEW[1]

(TESTAMENT OF ELEAZAR OF MAYENCE)

The author of this Testament died at Mayence on the first day of the Jewish New Year of 1357. He was buried on the second day of the festival. This we learn from the colophon of the Bodleian MS. Cat. Neubauer, No. 907 (fol. 166b). The colophon was written by the author's namesake and grandson.

Eleazar son of Samuel the Levite was not a Rabbi, he is merely described with the conventional honorary title of Ḥaber. In a fuller version of the colophon (*Hamazkir*, ix, 23) the author is called both a "saint" (איש חסיד) and "der gut Rabbi Zalman". His father was Samuel b. Yaḳar, surnamed Bonenfant, the Ḥazzan of Mayence. The genealogy is carried back to that rather mysterious figure, Asher the Levite, the presumed author of the Purim piyyut beginning אשר הניא. On him see Zunz, *Literaturgeschichte*, p. 4.

Just as Solomon b. Isaac (see p. 220) was described as an "average Jew" of the South, Eleazar of Mayence may be regarded as an average Jew of the North. Their main attitude towards life is the same, but there are nuances due to variations of social environment.

A text of the Testament is printed, from a Munich MS., in M. Güdemann's *Quellenschriften* (Berlin, 1891, pp. 295, seq.). A German translation had previously appeared in the *Jüdische Presse*, Berlin, 1870, p. 90. The present translation is made from a text prepared by collation of Güdemann's edition with the Oxford MS. referred to.

[1] For the choice of title see above p. 207. As to the MS. authority for the first two paragraphs, see Notes to Hebrew text.

צואת אליעזר בן שמואל הלוי

המחבר של הצואה הזאת מת בעיר מגנצא ביום הראשון של ראש שנת קי"ז לאלף הששי ויקבר שם ביום השני של החג. זה נודע לנו מן הקולופון של הכ"י הבודליאני (רשימת נייבויער, נומר 907, דף קסו:) שנכתב ע"י נושא שמו ובן בנו של המחבר.

אליעזר בן שמואל הלוי לא היה רב, והוא נכתר רק בשם הכבוד המקובל „חבר". בנוסח יותר מלא של הקולופון (המזכיר, כרך תשיעי, דף כ"ג) נקרא המחבר „איש חסיד" וגם „רבי זלמן הטוב". אביו היה שמואל בן יקר המכונה טוב עלם, החזן ממגנצא. שלשלת היוחסין שלו עולה עד לאותו איש המסתורין, אשר הלוי, אשר משערים עליו שחבר את הפיוט הידוע לפורים המתחיל „אשר הניא". בנוגע לו ראה צונץ, ליטעראטורגעשיכטע, דף ד'.

כמו שאומרים על שלמה בן יצחק (ראה דף 220) שהוא „יהודי בינוני" של הדרום כך אפשר לאמור על אליעזר בן שמואל ממגנצא שהוא „יהודי בינוני" של הצפון. יחוסם אל החיים בכלל הוא היינו הך, רק שיש שנוים קלים משום שינוים בסביבותיהם החברתיות.

נוסח עברי של הצואה הזאת נדפס מכ"י האצור במינכען בספרו של גידעמאן „קוועללענשריפטען" (ברלין תרנ"א, דף רצ"ה וכו'). העתקה אשכנזית הופיעה קודם לכן בעתון „אידישע פרעססע", ברלין תר"ל, דף צ'. ההעתקה הנוכחית נעשתה מנוסח עברי שהכשרתי ע"י השואת המהדורה של גידעמאן לכ"י אוקספורד הנזכר לעיל. בהערותי קראתי את המקור הראשון

In the notes these sources are cited as G. and O. respectively. There is another copy of the Testament of Eleazar b. Samuel in the National Library Paris (Heb. Cat. No. 837.16). It may be pointed out that one of the most significant features of this Testament is the author's concern for the studies and occupations of his daughters.

Among the directions for the author's funeral is a curious order which often meets us, in more elaborate guise, in subsequent wills. The Midrash (Gen. Rabbah § 65, cf. Midrash on Ps. 11, ed. Buber p. 104), tells us how the infliction of the "four deaths", or older methods of execution, was regarded as a penitential act of importance. Moreover, there is the more general idea that the death of a sinner atoned. Hence, as no man on earth is righteous who sinneth not, it was held desirable by many authors of these Wills, that the "four deaths" should be symbolically inflicted on the remains. We have no doubt there is something of the same idea in the inclusion of passages relating to guilt involving the penalties of the four deaths in the confession on the Day of Atonement (Singer, Auth. Daily Prayer Book, p. 262).

[My grandfather's Testament to his children; and as it is a rule good for every God-fearer, I write it here, that all men may follow it.]

[A worthy Testament, whose ways are ways of pleasantness; proven and seemly for publishing to all the people].

These are the things which my sons and daughters[2] shall do at my request. They shall go to the house of prayer morning and evening, and

[2] It is significant that the author throughout insistently includes his daughters in his admonition.

G ואת המקור השני O. יש עוד כ"י מצואת אליעזר בבית עקד הספרים הלאומי בפריז (רשימה עברית, נומר 16. 837). צריך להעיר שאחד הקוים היותר חשובים של הצואה הזאת היא דאגת המחבר ללמודי בנותיו ועסקיהן.

בין הפרטים הנוגעים לקבורת המחבר נמצא פרט אחד מוזר הפוגש אותנו לפעמים קרובות, בלבוש יותר מעובד, בצואות של תקופה מאוחרת. המדרש (בראשית רבה, פרק ס"ה; השוה מדרש תהלים, פרק י"א, הוצאת בובער, דף ק"ד) מלמדנו שהטלת העונש של ארבע מיתות בית דין, סקילה, שרפה, הרג וחנק, נחשבה למעשה תשובה גדול וחשוב. נוסף לזה הרעיון היותר כללי שמיתת החוטא מכפרת על עונותיו. ויען כי אין איש בעולם אשר יעשה טוב ולא יחטא, ע"כ חשבו מחברי צואות רבים לטוב ונכון ש„ד' המיתות" יוטלו על גויותיהם אחרי מותם בתור סמל. אין כל ספק בעינינו שמין רעיון כזה אחראי בעד הוספת כתובים המדברים בארבע מיתות בית דין לתפלת הודוי של יום הכפורים (ש. זינגער, סדר תפלות, דף רס"ב).

[צוואת זקיני לבניו. ומפני דהנהגה טובה היא לכל ירא שמים. אכתוב אותה כאן לנהוג כל אדם אחריו:][1]

[צוואה הגונה. דרכיה דרכי נעם. ראויה ובחונה. להודיע לכל העם:][2]

אלה הדברים אשר יעשו בניי ובנותיי בבקשתי. ישכימו ויעריבו לבית התפלה. ויזהרו מאד[3]

[1] G only. I have supplied the word אותה [2] O only.
[3] O omits.

shall pay special regard to the Tephillah and the Shema'. So soon as the service is over, they shall occupy themselves a little with the Torah, the Psalms, or with works of charity. Their business must be conducted honestly, in their dealings both with Jew and Gentile. They must be gentle in their manners, and prompt to accede to every honorable request. They must not talk more than is necessary, by this will they be saved from slander, falsehood, and frivolity. They shall give an exact tithe of all their possessions; they shall never turn away a poor man empty-handed, but must give him what they can, be it much or little. If he beg a lodging over night, and they know him not, let them provide him with the wherewithal to pay an inn-keeper.[3] Thus shall they satisfy the needs of the poor in every possible way.

My daughters must obey scrupulously the rules applying to women; modesty, sanctity, reverence, should mark their married lives. They should carefully watch for the signs of the beginning of their periods and keep separate from their husbands at such times. Marital intercourse must be modest and holy, with a spirit of restraint and delicacy, in reverence and silence. They shall be very punctilious and careful with their ritual bathing, taking with them women friends of worthy character. They shall cover their eyes until they reach their home, on return-

[3] The texts vary beteween *Heller* and *Mark* as the name of the coins to be presented.

בתפילה ובק"ש. ומיד[4] לאחר תפילה יתעסקו מעט בתורה או בתילים או בגמילות חסדים. ויהיו[5] משאם ומתנם באמונה וביושר עם הבריות ואפי'[6] עם הגוי[7]. ויהיו נוחים לבריות ורצויים לכל דבר הגון שיבקשום: ולא ירבו דברים כי אם הצורך. בזה ינצלו מכל לשון הרע וכזבי[8] ולצנות. ויתנו מעשר שלהם בדווקא. ולא ישיבו פני עני ריקם. אך יתנו לו הן רב הן מעט. ואם מבקש מלון ואין מכירין אותו יפייסוהו עם הלייי"ש[9] או שנים שיתן לאכסנאי[10]. על דרך זה כל בקשות העני יפייסו[11] אם יוכלו בכל צד:

הנשים יזהרו מאד מאוד[12] לבדוק עצמן בכל עת ולפרוש מבעליהם סמוך לווסתן ולשמש בהצנעה ובקדושה עם בעליהם בלא חציפות ובלא ליצנות. אך באימה ובשתיקה. מאד מאד ידקדקו בטבילותיהן לעשות במתון ולהוליך [נשים] הגונות עמהן שיפגעו בהן. ויכסו עיניהן עד שובן לביתן שלא

[4] O מיד.
[5] O ויהיה.
[6] G אפי'.
[7] G גוי. [8] O omits.
[9] O reads במרקיט for this and the preceding word.
[10] G לאכסניא. [11] G יפייסוהו. [12] O omits.

ing from the bath, in order not to behold anything of an unclean nature. They must respect their husbands, and must be invariably amiable to them. Husbands, on their part, must honor their wives more than themselves, and treat them with tender consideration.

If they can by any means contrive it, my sons and daughters should live in communities, and not isolated from other Jews, so that their sons and daughters may learn the ways of Judaism. Even if compelled to solicit from others the money to pay a teacher, they must not let the young, of both sexes, go without instruction in the Torah. Marry your children, O my sons and daughters, as soon as their age is ripe, to members of respectable families. Let no child of mine hunt after money by making a low match for that object; but if the family is undistinguished only on the mother's side, it does not matter, for all Israel counts descent from the father's side.

Every Friday morning, they shall put themselves in careful trim for honoring the Sabbath, kindling the lamps while the day is still great, and in winter lighting the furnace before dark, to avoid desecrating the Sabbath (by kindling fire thereon). For due welcome to the Sabbath, the women must prepare beautiful candles. As to games of chance, I entreat my children never to engage in such pastimes. During the leisure of the festival weeks they may play for trifling stakes in kind, and the women may amuse them-

יראו דבר טמא. מאד מאד יכבדו את בעליהן. ויהיו רצויין להם לילה ויום. וגם הגברים יכבדו נשותיהם יותר מגופם. ואל ישמשו עמהם מתוך כעס עד שירצו ויפייסו[13]:

בניי ובנותיי אם יוכלו בשום פנים[14] ידורו בקהילות למען ישמעו ולמען ילמדו בניהם ובנותיהם תורה ואפי' ח"ו[15] יצטרכו לחזור על הפתחים על ככה לא יניחום בטל. וישיאו בניהם ובנותיהם סמוך לפרקן למיוחסים. ולא ירדפו אחר ממון להתחתן במשפחה שפלה. רק אם ימצאו בנים המיוחסים מצד האב אין להקפיד אם אינם מיוחסים מצד האם. כי כל ישראל הם[16] מתיחסים אחר האב:

בכל ערב שבת יזהרו לזרז עצמם[17] לכבוד השבת בשחרית שיהיו מוכנים מבעוד יום להדליק נרות בעוד היום גדול. ולהדליק האש בתנור בית החורף בעוד היום גדול. שלא יחללו את השבת. והנשים יתקנו נרות יפים[18] לכבוד השבת:

אודות שחוק בקובייאות מאד בקשתי שלא לשחוק[19] בו כלל כי אם דמי אכילה ושתיה

13 G reads שיפייסום for this and the preceding word.
14 G צד. 15 G omits. 16 G omits. 17 G עצמן.
18 O יפות. 19 O ישחוק

selves similarly on New Moons, but never for money.[4] In their relation to women, my sons must behave continently, avoiding mixed bathing and mixed dancing and all frivolous conversation, while my daughters ought not to speak much with strangers, nor jest nor dance with them. They ought to be always at home, and not be gadding about. They should not stand at the door, watching whatever passes. I ask, I command, that the daughters of my house be never without work to do, for idleness leads first to boredom, then to sin. But let them spin, or cook, or sew.

I earnestly beg my children to be tolerant and humble to all, as I was throughout my life. Should cause for dissension present itself, be slow to accept the quarrel; seek peace and pursue it with all the vigor at your command. Even if you suffer loss thereby, forbear and forgive, for God has many ways of feeding and sustaining His creatures. To the slanderer do not retaliate with counter-attack; and though it be proper to rebut false accusations, yet is it most desirable

[4] The text is here defective, but this is apparently the meaning. It may denote that the author permits playing for stakes to be used by the men for providing festival meals and by the women for New Moon delicacies.

---

[24] O omits this and the preceding word.

[25] G מאמצת. [26] לזונים G, who corrects to לזונם. O ולזונם fully justifies the correction.

למועדים ולרגלים. והנשים בעד כלום[20] לראש חדש:

מאד מאד יהיו צנועים בניי שלא יהיה להם עסקי[21] עם נשים. לא במרחץ ולא במחול ולא בנגיעה ולא להתלוצץ עמהם: והבנות עם אנשים נכרים[22] לא ידברו ולא ישחקו. ולא ימחלו. ושום קלות ראש לא ינהגו עמהם רק עם בעליהן: תמיד יהיו בנותיי פנימיות ולא יוצאניות ולא יעמדו פתח הבית לראות כל דבר: בבקשה ובצואה שלא ישבו הנשים פנויות בלא מלאכה כי בטלה מביאה לידי שיעמום ולידי[23] זימה. או יטוו או יבשלו או יתפרו:

מאד מאד בקשתי לבניי להיות סבלנים ושפלי רוח בפני כל אדם. כן הייתי כל ימיי. וכל דבר ריב ומדון שיוולד להם לא יצאו לריב מהר. אך ירדפו שלום ויבקשו שלום[24] בכל מאמצי[25] כחם. אפילו אם יטלו היזק. ויסבלו וימחלו. הרבה שלוחים למקום ב"ה לזונם[26] ולפרנסם: חירופים וגידופים לא ילבינו ולא ישיבו. אך על שם רע ירבו להשיב

[20] So O, G reads ביצים.

[21] G להתעסק (he corrects as O).

[22] G נוכרום.

[23] G omits this and preceding word.

to set an example of reticence. You yourselves must avoid uttering any slander, for so will you win affection. In trade be true, never grasping at what belongs to another. For by avoiding these wrongs—scandal, falsehood, money-grubbing,—men will surely find tranquillity and affection. And against all evils, silence is the best safeguard.

Now, my sons and daughters, eat and drink only what is necessary, as our good parents did, refraining from heavy meals, and holding the gross liver in detestation. The regular adoption of such economy in food leads to economy in expenditure generally, with a consequent reluctance to pursue after wealth, but the acquisition of a contented spirit, simplicity in diet, and many good results. Concerning such a well-ordered life the text says: "The righteous eateth to the satisfaction of his desire."[5] Our teachers have said: "Method in expenditure is half a sufficiency."[6] Nevertheless, accustom yourselves and your wives, your sons and your daughters, to wear nice and clean clothes, that God and man may love and honor you. In this direction do not exercise too strict a parsimony. But on no account adopt foreign fashions in dress.

5 Prov. 12.25. See Maim. *De'ot* 8.1.

6 *Choice of Pearls*, ch. 1.

ולהתנצל ולשתק המוציאים.[27] ורק ירבו בשתיקה ולא ידברו לשון הרע. בזה יזהרו מאד מאד. ובזה יוסיפו עליהם אהבה: ויהיו ישרנים בכל דבר משא ומתן. ולא יהיו להוטים[28] אחר ממון חביריהם: במעוט לשון הרע וכזב ורכילות. ובשנאת ממון. יהיו בשלום ובאהבה. ושתיקה גדר וסייג לכולם:

בניי ובנותי[29] פחותו נא מאכילה ושתייה רק כדי צורך. ואל תבזבזו ממון לאכילה ולשתייה. כן היו אבותינו החסידים אוכלים כדי הצורך ולא אכילה גסה ולמלאות כריסן. להיות כל ימיהם כחוש. והרגל דבר זה מביא אדם לידי הספקות. ולא לרדוף אחר הממון ולהעשיר[30]. ולבש מדת שמח בחלקו. ומעוט סעודת הרשות וכמה דברים טובים. ועל זה אמר הכתוב צדיק אוכל לשובע נפשו. ואמרו רבותינו סדר ההוצאה חצי הסיפוק. אך הרגילו עצמיכם ונשותיכם ואת בניכם ובנותיכם ללכת בבגדים נאים ונקיים. בזה יהיו אהובים ומכובדים בעיני הש״י ובעיני הבריות. ועשו יותר מיכולתכם על דרך זה: אך כלל לא תתקנו

27 מוצאים G, who corrects as in O.
28 להושים G, who corrects as in O.
29 G omits. 30 G ולהעושר.

After the manner of your fathers order your attire, and let your cloaks be broad without buckles attached.

Be on your guard concerning vows, and cautious as to promises.[7] The breach of one's undertakings leads to many lapses. Do not get into the habit of exclaiming "Gott!", but speak always of the "Creator, blessed be He"; and in all that you propose to do, to day or tomorrow, add the proviso, "if the Lord wills, I shall do this thing." Thus remember God's part in your life.

Whatever happiness befall you, be it in monetary fortune or in the birth of children, be it some signal deliverances or any other of the many blessings which may come to you, be not stolidly unappreciative, like dumb cattle that utter no word of gratitude. But offer praises to the Rock who has befriended you, saying: "O give thanks unto the Lord, for He is good, for His mercy endureth for ever. Blessed art Thou, O Lord, who art good and dispensest good." Besides thanking God for His bounties at the moment they occur, also in your regular prayers let the memory of these personal favors prompt your hearts to special fervor during the utterance of the communal thanks. When words of gratitude are used in the liturgy, pause to reflect in silence on the goodness of God

[7] The author's words refer to the habit of saying "without vowing", "without swearing," in forming a resolve which may be incapable of fulfilment.

בלבוש נכרי.[31] אך דרך ומנהג אבותינו תקנו הבגדים ורחבים בלא קנופל"א לפנים:

הזהרו בנדרים. ולעולם הרגילו עצמיכם לומר בלא נדר ובלא שבועה. שעון נדרים גורם כמה תקלות. ואפילו אל תזכירו שם שמים לבטלה לומ' בל"א[32] גו"ט. אך הבורא יתברך. ומה שבדעתכם[33] לעשות היום או מחר תמיד אמרו אם ירצה השם אעשה דבר זה. כדי שיהא שם שמים שגור בפיכם[34] בכל עת:

כל דבר טוב שיבא לידיכם הן מפרנסתכם[35] הן מבנים שיוולדו לכם. הן מניסים והצלה שתינצלו הן כמה שאר ניסים ומאורעות טובים שיגיעו[36] לכם. אל תהיו כסוס כפרד[37] אין מבין להיות כפוי טובה. שלא להגיד בטובו. אך שבחו והודו לצור ית' על חסדיו הודו לה' כי טוב כל"ח בא"י הטוב והמטיב. ובתפילה בברכת מודים. ובברכת המזון בברכת נודך תזכרו באותם חסדים להודות בלב שלם על הניסים שנעשו לכם. כשתאמרו ניסיך שבכל יום עמנו[38] ועל נפלאותיך וטובותיך שבכל עת–

31 G נוכרי. 32 G omits.

33 O שבועתכם. 34 G בפיכם. 35 O and G read מפרנסכם. G corrects as in text. 36 O שינעו. 37 G ופרד.

38 G omits this and preceding two words.

to you that day. And when ye make the response: "May Thy great Name be blessed," call to mind your own personal experiences of the divine favor.

Be very particular to keep your houses clean and tidy. I was always scrupulous on this point, for every injurious condition, and sickness and poverty, are to be found in foul dwellings. Be careful over the benedictions; accept no divine gift without paying back the Giver's part; and His part is man's grateful acknowledgment.

Every one of these good qualities becomes habitual with him who studies the Torah; for that study indeed leads to the formation of a noble character. Therefore, happy is he who toils in the Law! For this gracious toil fix daily times, of long or short duration, for 'tis the best of all works that a man can do. Week by week read at least the set portion with the commentary of Rashi. And when your prayer is ended day by day, turn ever to the word of God, in fulfilment of the Psalmist's injunction, "passing from strength to strength."[8]

And O, my sons and daughters, keep yourselves far from the snare of frivolous conversation, which begins in tribulation and ends in destruction. Nor be ye found in the company of these light talkers. Judge ye rather every man charitably

[8] Ps. 84.8.

אז תפסקו מעט• ותחשבו בלבבכם כל הטובות שנעשו לכם ביום ההוא. וגם כשתאמרו יהא שמא רבא מברך חשבו בטובות:

הזהרו מאד לכבד ביתכם ולהחזיק בנקיות מאד[39] מאד. ובזה נזהרתי מאד כי כל מזיקים וחלאים ועניות[40] מצוי' בבתי' מטונפות: הזהרו מאד מאד בברכות שלא ליהנות מן העולם בלא ברכה. ותנו לבורא ית' חלקו מיד. זו היא הברכה וההודאה:

כל אלה המדות טובות. מי שעוסק בתורה מתרגל בהן. כי גדול תלמוד תורה שמביא לכל מעשים טובים. לכן אשרי מי שעומל בתורה: ובכל יום קבע עתים לתורה הן רב הן מעט. וכל הפחות בכל שבוע הפרשה בפי' רש"י. ותיכף בכל יום ללמוד כפי שתוכל. כי תלמוד תורה עדיף מכולם[41] ותיכף לאחר תפלה מאד טוב לקיים מחיל אל חיל וגו':

נא בניי ובנותיי אל תרגילו עצמכם[42] להתלוצץ, תחילתו ייסורין ואחריתו[43] כלייה. ואפי' לישב אצל ליצנים ולעמוד אצלם: ודונו[44] כל אדם לכף זכות.

[39] G omits. [40] G omits. [41] O omits from ותיכף to וכולם. [42] G omits. [43] G וסופו. [44] G נדונו.

and use your best efforts to detect an honorable explanation of conduct however suspicious. Try to persuade yourselves that it was your neighbor's zeal for some good end that led him to the conduct you deplore. This is the meaning of the exhortation: "In righteousness shalt thou judge thy neighbour"[9]. To sum up, the fewer one's idle words the less one's risk of slander, lying, flattery,—all of them, things held in utter detestation by God.

On holidays and festivals and Sabbaths seek to make happy the poor, the unfortunate, widows and orphans, who should always be guests at your tables; their joyous entertainment is a religious duty. Let me repeat my warning against gossip and scandal. And as ye speak no scandal, so listen to none, for if there were no receivers there would be no bearers of slanderous tales; therefore the reception and credit of slander is as serious an offence as the originating of it. The less you say, the less cause you give for animosity, while "in the multitude of words there wanteth not transgression."[10]

[9] Levit. 19.15. [10] Prov. 10.19.

אפילו אם תראו בבני אדם דבר כיעור צידדו כל מיני צדדין לדונו לכף זכות לומר כך הייתה[45] כוונתו לשם שמים הביאו לכך. ועל זה נאמר בצדק תשפוט את עמיתך. סוף דבר מיעוט דברים בטלים כי אם הצורך. זה הגדר ללשון הרע ולכזב ולחניפות שכולם שנואים מאוד בעיני המקום:

במועדים ורגלים[46] ובשבתות תשמחו[47] עניים ואומללים ואלמנות ויתומים עמכם על שולחניכם ויהא שמחות'[48] שמחת מצוה: ובניכם להתרחק מאד מאד מלשון הרע. שלא ידברו כזב דבה ולשון הרע. ולדון כל אדם לכף זכות. ולא יעמדו אצל מספרי לשון הרע. כי לולי המקבלים ומאמינים הלשון הרע לא יהיו[49] מספרים לשון הרע. לכן קשה הקבלה. והאמינה והעמידה[50] כמו הסיפור: ולא יתלוצצו ולא ישבו במושב לצים. ולא ירבו דברים בטלים ולא ידברו כי אם הצורך בכל עת ועת. וירבו בשתיקה וזה גדר גדול ללשון הרע ולכזב ולליצנות. ובשתיקה לא יפסידו דבר. וירחיקו מהם בשתיקה איבה ותחרות וקנאות מעצמם כי ברוב דברים

[45] O omits. [46] O omits.
[47] G השמיחו. [48] G omits. [49] O היו.
[50] G reads והאמינו for this and preceding word.

Always be of those who see and are not seen, who hear and are not heard. Accept no invitations to banquets, except to such as are held for religious reasons: at weddings and at meals prepared for mourners, at gatherings to celebrate entry into the covenant of Abraham, or at assemblies in honor of the wise. Games of chance for money stakes, such as dicing, must be avoided. And as I have again warned you on that head, again let me urge you to show forbearance and humility to all men, to ignore abuses levelled at you, but the indignant refutation of charges against your moral character is fully justifiable.

Be of the first ten in Synagogue, rising betimes for the purpose. Pray steadily with the congregation, giving due value to every letter and word, seeing that there are in the Shema' 248 words, corresponding to the 248 limbs in the human body[11]. Be careful too to let the prayer for redemption be followed immediately by the eighteen benedictions. Do not talk during service, but listen to the Precentor, and respond "Amen" at the proper time. After the morning prayer, read the Chapter about the Manna[12], the passages associated with it, and the eleven verses,[13] with due attention to clear enunciation. Then recite a Psalm in lieu of a reading in the

[11] This is an old idea, just as the following is an old liturgical rule.

[12] Exod. 16.

[13] Collections of Scripture passages consisting of eleven verses are to be found in several editions of the daily liturgy.

לא יחדל פשע. ותמיד יהיו הרואים ולא הנראים והשומעים ולא הנשמעים: ולא יסעדו סעודת הרשות כי אם סעודת מצוה. לשמח חתן ולהברות אבלים ולברית מילה ולכבד ת"ח: ולא ישחקו בשום מיני שחוק המאבד מעות. לא בקובייאות ולא בשאר דברים. ולא יהיה להם עסק עם נשים לא לחוף ראשם ולא לפלות ראשם: ושיהיו סבלנים ושפלי רוח בפני כל אדם. ואפי' אם יבזו בדבור או במעש לא יקפידו. אך יסבלו ולא יבזו אדם[51]. אך שם רע לא יסבלו. אך יתנצלו ויבטלו השם רע בכל יכולתם:

הזהרו להקדים להשכים לבית הכנסת להיות מן המניין הראשון. והתפללו עם הציבור במתון בכוונת ק"ש ולדקדק אותיותיו ותיבותיו. כי יש בו רמ"ח תיבות כמניין[52] איברים. ולסמוך גאולה לתפילה[53]. ולא לדבר בשעת תפילה אך ישמעו להזן לענות[54] אמן: ואחר התפילה יאמרו פרשת מן והשייך לו והי"א פסוקים בכיון אותיות. ויאמרו מזמור אחד מתילים לאחר כל תפילה להיות

[51] O omits from או to אדם.
[52] G כמה תיבות כמניין רמ"ח.
[53] G ולתפילה. [54] G ולענות.

Torah; though it were well not to omit the latter, passing, as I said above, from strength to strength, from prayer to the Bible, before turning to worldly pursuits. Or if ye can perform some act of loving-kindness, it is accounted as equal to the study of the Law.

I beg of you, my sons and daughters, my wife, and all the congregation, that no funeral oration be spoken in my honor. Do not carry my body on a bier but in a coach. Wash me clean, comb my hair, trim my nails, as I was wont to do in my life-time, so that I may go clean to my eternal rest, as I went clean to Synagogue every Sabbath day. If the ordinary officials dislike the duty, let adequate payment be made to some poor man who shall render this service carefully and not perfunctorily. At a distance of thirty cubits from the grave, they shall set my coffin on the ground, and drag me to the grave by a rope attached to the coffin. Every four cubits they shall stand and wait awhile, doing this in all seven times, so that I may find atonement for my sins.[14] Put me in the ground

[14] See introduction above, p. 208.

במקום תורה. אך אם יוכלו ללמוד מעט אחר בית הכנסת לקיים מחיל אל חיל בזה יזהרו מאד טרם יפנו לעסקים אחרים. או אם יוכלו לגמול חסדים זה חשוב כמ' תורה:

הנני מבקש בניי ובנותיי וזוגתי וכל[55] הקהל איש ואשה שלא יספידוני כלל[56] כלל. ובזה יניחוני על משכבי ולא ישאו אותי במטה חוצה[57] אך על קרון: בקשתי מאד מאד שיטהרוני מאד במתון ובטהרה[58] ובנקיות בין אצבעות ידים ורגלים ובין האחור. ויחופו ראשי וסרקוני במסרק כדרך החיים ויטלו צפורני ידיי ורגליי. כדי שאבא טהור ונקי למנוחה. כמו שהלכתי לבית הכנסת בכל שבת. בחפיפה ובנטילת ציפורניים ובסריקה ובבדיקת נקבים. כן יעשו לי גם למנוחת עולמים. ויתנו לעני שכר טוב שיעשה לי כל זה במתון בלא חפזון אם קשה למטהרים לעשותם: רחוק מקברים[59] שלשים אמות בריוח ישיבו ארוני[60] עמי על הארץ ויגררוני בארון עם חבל עד הקבר ובכל ד' אמות יעמדו וישהו מעט. ויעשו כך ז' פעמים עד הקבר להיות כופר

[55] O כל. [56] O omits. [57] G במטת חוצה.
[58] O ובהערה.
[59] מקבריי. [60] G אורני.

at the right hand of my father, and if the space be a little narrow, I am sure that he loves me well enough to make room for me by his side. If this be altogether impossible, put me on his left, or near my grandmother, Yuta. Should this also be impractical, let me be buried by the side of my daughter.

לעונותיי: אצל מורי אבי זצ"ל מצד ימינו יקברוני. ואפי' אם הוא מעט צר בטחתי באהבת אבי שיגנז עצמו להכניסני אליו. ואם לא יוכל להיות בשום פנים אצל אבי[61] בימינו יראו בשמאלו. או אצל זקנתי מ' יוטא ואם לאו[62] יקברוני אצל בתי[63]:

[61] O omits this and preceding word.
[62] O דאי לאו.
[63] For the colophon see p. 207 above.

הגדרים והצואה אשר גדר על עצמו וצוה את בניו שלמה בן יצחק

A REGIMEN OF SELF-TAXATION AND THE TESTAMENT OF SOLOMON SON OF ISAAC

XI

A REGIMEN OF SELF-TAXATION

AND THE TESTAMENT OF SOLOMON SON OF ISAAC.

Solomon, son of the "holy" R. Isaac son of Zadok, was a Provençal (or Spanish) Jew of the fourteenth or fifteenth century. He seems, however, to have lived in an Arabic-speaking country, possibly Egypt. Though his father is described as "Holy", it does not necessarily mean that he was a martyr. Steinschneider (Cat. Leyden, p. 264) conjectures that Solomon lived in the fifteenth century; Schechter suggests (*Studies in Judaism*, I, 166) the fourteenth century. Besides the Leyden MS. there is also one in Paris, in the Bibliothèque Nationale (No. 710). A fragment from an independent MS. also appeared in היקב 1894.

The document containing his Testament consists of two parts. The formal Testament occurs in the second part; the first part is much the more piquant. It contains the rules of self-taxation which the author also recommends his children to maintain. Solomon ben Isaac is characterized by Schechter (*J. Q. R.*, first series, v, 112) as an average Jew of the Middle Ages. Not a scholar by profession, he nevertheless devotes part of every day to study. Despite his self-inflicted fines for lapses into indulgence, he is no ascetic. "He rather likes his dinner and enjoys his glass of wine, but he exercises a strict control over his comforts."

In the second part (*J.Q.R.*, v, 114) he offers some fine moral counsels, which he desires his children to read once

יא

הגדרים והצואה אשר גדר על עצמו וצוה את בניו שלמה בן יצחק

שלמה בן ה„קדוש" ר' יצחק בן צדוק היה יהודי פרובינצלי (או ספרדי) של המאה הארבע עשרה או החמש עשרה; אבל כפי הנראה חי במדינה בעלת לשון ערבית, אפשר במצרים. אף כי אביו נקרא „קדוש" אין זאת אומרת שמת על קדוש השם. שטיינשניידר (רשימת ליידען, דף רס"ד) משער ששלמה חי במאה החמש עשרה; שכטר נוטה אל המאה הארבע עשרה (Studies in Judaism, כרך ראשון, דף קס"ו). מלבד כ"י ליידען יש כ"י גם בפריז בבית עקד הספרים הלאומי (נומר 710). גם קטע מכ"י מיוחד ועומד ברשות עצמו הופיע ב„היקב" בשנת תרנ"ד.

שטר הצואה של שלמה נחלק לשני חלקים: הצואה עצמה נמצאת בחלק השני, אבל החלק הראשון הוא הרבה יותר מענין, יען כי הוא מכיל את הגדרים אשר המחבר גדר לעצמו וצוה לבניו לשמור אותם. שכטר (ברבעון היהודי האנגלי, סדר ראשון, כרך חמישי, דף קי"ב) מתאר את שלמה בן יצחק בתור יהודי בינוני של ימי הבינים. אף כי לא היה תלמיד חכם החי על תלמודו בכ"ז הקדיש שעות אחדות בכל יום ויום ללמוד התורה. למרות היסורים אשר קבל על עצמו בעד תקלות חטא אי אפשר לאמר שהיה נזיר. „להפך, הוא אוהב את ארוחת הצהרים ומתענג על כוס יינו, אבל הוא שולט שלטון בלי מצרים בהנאות גופו".

בחלק השני (הרבעון היהודי האנגלי, במקום הנזכר לעיל) הוא נותן איזה עצות מוסריות טובות ומצוה לבניו שיקראו אותן

a week. They are to commend the same course to their own children in turn, and so throughout the generations. With his Testament they are also to read two letters of Naḥmanides, one of which in praise of humility, is printed above (p. 95) and the other, in praise of chastity, below (p. 229). The first letter was addressed to Naḥmanides' son Naḥman, the second (according to both Steinschneider and Schechter), to Naḥmanides' son Solomon. The writer of this Testament asks them always to have a volume of the Talmud or other rabbinic work spread on a stool, so that they can open it whenever occasion presents itself. At all events they should read four lines from any book they select before every meal. They must train all their children to study the Torah, but one of the family should devote his whole time to it. And it shall be the duty of his brothers to support this one, and to invest his money, and to provide that he and his family may live respectably, so that he be not distracted by worldly cares from his studies. Solomon is an advocate of the system of paying the tithe. Very interesting is the author's injunction that his children "shall apply all their powers to maintain the synagogues and schools which our ancestors have built, as well as continue the endowments established by my ancestors and myself." They must, he continues, endeavor to imitate their forbears, and "they must always remember that they come of a good family." A fine type this, and generous, of family pride.

The Hebrew text here printed is derived from Schechter's edition in the first series of the *Jewish Quarterly Review*, Vol. V. pp. 112–117. The English translation there given, has been freely used here, but not exactly copied. This edition is referred to in the Notes as S; the variants from the Paris MS. as P. A portion of the text is also printed (from an independent MS.) in the Hebrew periodical היקב 1894. This is collated as Y.

פעם אחת בשבוע ויצוו את בניהם ואת בני בניהם עד סוף כל הדורות לעשות כן. יחד עם צואתו צוה להם לקרוא גם שתי אגרות של הרמב"ן, אשר אחת מהן בתהלת הענוה נדפסה לעיל (דף 95) והשניה בתהלת הצניעות נדפסה למטה (דף 229). האגרת הראשונה נשלחה לנחמן, השניה (גם לדברי שטיינשניידר גם לדברי שכטר) לשלמה, בני הרמב"ן. כותב הצואה הזאת דורש מבניו שיהיה לכל אחד מהם תמיד בביתו על ספסל כרך מן התלמוד או אחד מחבורי הרבנים, באופן שיוכלו לפתוח אותו ולקרות בו בכל שעה שאפשר. בכל אופן יתחייבו לקרות ארבע שורות באיזה ספר שירצו לפני כל ארוחה. החובה עליהם להורות תורה לכל אחד מבניהם, אבל אחד מהם מחויב לעשות את התורה אומנותו כל ימי חייו, ואחיו „יתחייבו לסייעו בכל יכלתם ולהתעסק בממונו כדי שיוכל לעבור זמנו ולכלכל בניו ואנשי ביתו בכבוד", באופן שדאגות העולם הזה לא יטרדוהו מלמודיו. שלמה מאמין במצות מעשר. יש חשיבות בציוויו לבניו „שישתדל כל אחד מהם כל יכלתו לקיים הבתי כנסיות והבתי מדרשות וההקדשות שבנו והקדישו אבותינו ז"ל ואני ג"כ", והוא הולך ומוסיף שעליהם להשתדל לעשות כאבותיהם ו„שיראה כל אחד מהם שהוא מזרע כשר ומהמשפחה שהוא". הרי זו דוגמא יפה של גאות משפחה.

הנוסח העברי הנדפס פה הוא ממהדורת שכטר ברבעון היהודי האנגלי, סדר ראשון, כרך חמישי, דף קי"ב–קי"ז. השתמשתי הרבה בהעתקה האנגלית הנתנת שם, אבל לא העתקתיה מלה במלה. המהדורה הזאת נקראת S בהערותי; השינוים הנמצאים בכ"י פריז נתנים תחת P; קטע הכ"י שהופיע בקובץ העברי „היקב" בשנת תרנ"ד מכונה Y.

These are the regulations which I, Solomon, son of the holy[1] Rabbi Isaac, the son of Zadok, of blessed memory, have drawn up for myself:—

That so long as I enjoy good health, am free from constraint,[2] and think of it, I shall not eat on any day before I have studied one page of the Talmud or of one of its commentaries. Should I transgress this rule intentionally, I must not drink wine on that day, or I shall pay half a ducat[2a] to charity. Again, that I shall read every week the Pentateuchal Lesson twice in the Hebrew text, and once in the Aramaic version. Should I intentionally omit completing the Lesson as above, then I must pay two ducats to charity. Again, that I shall take three meals every Sabbath, consisting of bread or fruit. Should I intentionally omit to do so, I must give in charity half a ducat. Again, in order to subdue my appetites, and to restrain myself from enjoying in this world more than is necessary for the maintenance of my body, I must not eat at one meal more than one course of meat, or more than two courses altogether; nor must I drink more than two cups of wine at one meal, apart from the blessing cup,[3] except on Sabbath, Festivals, Ḥanukkah, New Moon, and

[1] Perhaps (but not necessarily) a martyr, a common sense of *Kadosh*. It also, however, means mystic.

[2] Schechter renders "accident".

[2a] On the denomination of the coins called here (and in Ibn Tibbon's Testament) simply *gold piece* (*Zehub*), see Zunz, *Zur Geschichte*. pp. 545, 552, 563, 564.

[3] The cup over which the grace after meals is said.

אלו הם הגדרים שאני שלמה בן הקדוש ר׳ יצחק בן צדוק זצוק״ל גודר על עצמי.

כל זמן שאהיה בריא ובלא אונס, שלא אוכל בכל יום עד שאלמוד דף אחת מהתלמוד או מאחד מחבוריו. כל זמן שאהיה זכור. ואם אעבור על זה מדעת שלא אשתה יין אותו היום, או שאפרע חצי זהוב לצדקה: ושאקרא בכל שבוע הפרשה, שנים מקרא ואחד תרגום. ואם אעבור על זה מדעת מלהשלים הפרשה כאמור למעלה, שאפרע שני זהובים לצדקה: ושאעשה שלש סעודות בכל שבת, בפת או בפירות. ואם אעבור מדעת, שאפרע חצי זהוב לצדקה: ועוד כדי להכניע יצרי, שלא ליהנות בזה העולם אלא כדי צורך קיום גופי שלא אוכל בסעודה אחת בשרי[1] כאחת, ולא יותר משני תבשילים. ולא אשתה יין יותר משני כוסות בסעודה אחת חוץ מכוס הברכה, לבד שבתות וימים טובים וחנוכה וראשי חדשים וסעודת מצוה: ועוד שלא

[1] Read שני מיני בשר or perhaps בשר ודגים.

at religious banquets.[4] Again, I must not have any regular meal on Fridays, nor on the day preceding a Festival if that day be not itself a Saturday, but shall be satisfied with a single course, so that I may enter upon the Sabbath or holiday with a keen appetite. Should I transgress this rule intentionally, I shall have to fast a day, or pay two ducats. Again, that I shall not eat the fish called *barbotte*[5] in French and *shuli* in Arabic, so long as I do not forget. Even on the above-mentioned days, I must not eat more than three courses at a meal, nor drink more than three cups of wine exclusive of the blessing cup, or a cup of which it is a duty to partake. And this on the conditions written above.

Again I must not swear by God, nor mention the name of Heaven without a purpose, nor curse any man in the name of God. Should I, God forbid, transgress this, I must not drink more than one cup of wine on that day, exclusive of the blessing-cup, provided that I remember. Should I, however, transgress this after dinner, I must abstain from wine the following day, if I do not forget. If, while remembering, I transgress this rule, I have to pay half a ducat to charity.

[4] Such as wedding dinners.

[5] On the *barbuta* (usually identified with the sturgeon) see L. Löw, *Gesammelte Schriften* II 260. The full Arabic name is *hut ash-shuli* and is identified with the sturgeon by the Latin translator (p. 41) of a text published by Dozy (*Le Calendrier de Cordoue* de l'année 961, Leiden, 1873). I have to thank Prof. A. Bevan for this information.

אעשה סעודת קבע בערב שבת. ולא בערב יום טוב שיהיה בחול. ושלא אוכל באותה סעודה יותר ממאכל אחד. וכל זה כדי שאכנס לשבת או ליום טוב תאב לאכילה: וזה הענין כל זמן שאהיה נזכר. ואם אעבור על זה מדעת, שאתענה ליום אחד. או שאפרע לצדקה ב׳ זהובים: וגם שלא אוכל הדגה קרוי בלשון לעז ברבוטה ובלשון ערבי שולי כל זמן שאהיה נזכר: ובאלו הימים הנזכרים שלא אוכל יותר מג׳ תבשילין ולא אשתה יותר משלשה כוסות של יין חוץ מכוס של ברכה זולתי אם יהיה כוס של מצוה. וזה על התנאים הכתובים לעיל:

ושלא אשבע בשם, ולא אזכור שם שמים לבטלה. ולא אקלל לשום אדם בשם. ואם ח״ו אעבור על דבר זה, שלא אשתה יין באותו יום, אלא כוס אחד חוץ מכוס של ברכה, אם אזכור לזה: ואם יהיה לאחר אכילה, שיהיה זה הקיום ליום אחר. וזה אם לא אשכח: ואם אזכור ואעבור על זה שאפרע חצי זהוב לצדקה:

Again, that I shall rise up every night to praise God, to supplicate for His mercy, and to confess. This shall be the rule on such nights on which confession is permissible. On other nights,[6] I shall say hymns and Psalms. Every night that I am at home, in good health, and free from constraint, and fail to perform the acts referred to, I must not drink more than one cup of wine the following day, exclusive of the cup of blessing, unless the morrow happens to be a Sabbath or Festival.

Moreover, I take upon myself to set aside for charitable objects the following taxes on my expenditure:—Of every garment which I have made for myself or for a member of my household, costing ten ducats or more, I must pay one peseta for every ten ducats. Again, if I should buy an animal or a servant, or a handmaid, or land, I must pay at the same rate. And if I buy clothes by way of trade, I must pay two pesetas for every garment which they call *fasa*. As often as I am bound to say the benediction ha-gomel,[7] I shall pay a ducat, except when I am travelling, in which case I shall have to pay the aforesaid ducat only when I reach my home, and two pesetas daily during the journey. Again for every bird bought for or by me, costing a ducat or more, I must pay a peseta. If the price be below a ducat but not less than half a ducat, I must pay half a peseta. If the price be between half a ducat and

[6] i. e. Sabbath and festivals.

[7] The benediction recited in synagogue by one who has undergone some dangerous experience, among which travelling was included.

ושאקום בכל לילה ולילה לשבח לבורא ולהתחנן ולהודות לפניו, בלילות שהן ראויין להודות, ובלילות האחרות לומר שירות ותושבחות: ובכל לילה שאהיה בביתי, ואהיה בריא בלא שום אונס, ולא אעשה[2] למה שנזכר למעלה, שלא אשתה אותו יום יין אלא כוס אחד חוץ מכוס של ברכה אם לא יהיה מהימים הנזכרים למעלה:

ועוד להפריש מהוצאתי מכל הדברים הנזכרים למטה. ואלו הן, מכל מלבוש שאעשה לאנשי ביתי ובני, מכל שיהיה מהסכום עשרה זהובים ולמעלה, שאתן פשוט לכל עשרה זהובים: ואם אקנה בהמה או עבד או שפחה או קרקע שאפרע מזה הסכום. ואם אקנה בגדים לסחורה, שאתן שנים פשוטים לכל בגד שקורין פאסה: וכל פעם שאהיה מחוייב לברך הגומל, שאתן זהוב, חוץ מהליכת הדרך, שלא אתחייב ליתן זה הזהוב, אלא היום שאגיע לביתי בלבד, ושאר הימים שני פשוטין ביום: ומכל עוף ועוף שיקנו לי או אקנה שיהיה מזהוב למעלה, שאתן פשוט. ומה שיהיה מזהוב ולמטה עד חצי זהוב, חצי פשוט. ומה שיהיה מחצי זהוב ולמטה עד פשוט,

[2] Supply אעשה which is missing in the MSS.

a peseta, I must pay a trifle. For every load of wood bought by or for me, I must pay a peseta; for every kid two pesetas, for every fish costing a ducat and upwards, a peseta for every ducat.

And if I shall be held worthy by God to marry my children, and to be present at their entrance under the canopy, I shall command them to give from the dowry brought to them by their wives, whether in money or in kind, at the rate of one per cent. So, if God bless me with sons, I shall give for every son according to my means at the time. And in addition to this, between New Year and the Day of Atonement in each year, I shall calculate my profit-balance, and give a tithe of it. Should I be unable to make an exact calculation, I will give approximately according to my impression of the proper sum. And I will include this tithe together with all the money accumulated as above, and the total shall be set aside for religious purposes, to dispose of as I deem best. I also retain the liberty to employ the money in any speculation which promises gain, in order to augment the fund for charitable purposes.

All the penalties which I have assumed on myself shall not fall due if my transgressions be the result of forgetfulness; but in order to guard against that, I shall read this through weekly if I remember to do so.

I also command my children (whom may God preserve and make worthy of performing His will) to take upon themselves as many of the

שאתן פרוטה אחת. ומכל משוי של עצים שאקנה או יקנו לי, שאתן פשוט. ומכל גדי שיקנו לי או אקנה, שני פשוטין. ומכל דג שאקנה או יקנו לי שיהיה מזהוב ולמעלה שאתן לכל זהוב פשוט:

ואם יזכני הבורא ית' להשיא בני, ולראות חופתם, שאצוה אותם שיתנו מכל מה שיקחו עם נשותיהם הן במעות הן בשוה, זהוב מכל מאה זהובים. וכן אם יזכני השי"ת לבנים זכרים,[3] שאתן לכל בן שיהיה לי, מה שיראה לפי מה שתשיג ידי באותו זמן: ויותר על זה, בכל שנה בין ראש השנה ויום הכפורים, שאעשה חשבון. ומה שיהיה לי יותר על שנה שעברה אחר ההוצאות, שאתן ממנו העשור. ואם לא אוכל לדקדק החשבון, שאתן אותו באומד לפי מה שנראה לי: ואכלול זה העשור עם כל מה שיעלה באלה הדברים הנזכרים, ויהיה הכל מונח ביחד לדבר מצוה לכל מה שיראה לי. ואם יראה לי ליתן אותו במקום שאפשר להרויח בו, כדי לעשות ממנו דבר מצוה, שיהיה הרשות בידי:

וכל מה שכתבתי עלי מאלו העניינים הנזכרים,

[3] S adds בשוה.

above regulations as may be in their power to observe. They shall in their turn ordain them on their children, and so throughout the generations for ever. And whoever puts pressure on himself to keep these rules, and to add others of his own formulation, on him may a blessing descend.

And this is the text of the Testament which I, the aforesaid Solomon, have drawn up for my children, may God preserve them! That each of them shall pray thrice daily, and strive to utter his prayers with devotion. Again, that prayers shall be said in the Bet Hamidrash[8] or in the Synagogue together with the congregation. Again, that each shall apply all his power to maintain the synagogues and houses of study and the endowments which our fathers, and I also, have built and established. Let each endeavor to imitate them to the end that good work shall never cease from among them.

Again, that each shall always have in his house a chair on which a volume or two of the Talmud, or any other talmudical work, shall rest; so that he can always open a book when he comes home. Let him read what he can, making it a duty to read in any book he likes at least four

[8] Used for study and for prayer.

לא אתחייב בהם אלא כל זמן שאהיה זכור מהם, וכדי להזכר מהם קבלתי עלי לקרות אותם[4] בשבוע, אם אזכור: ואני מצוה לבני ישמרם האל! ויזכם לתורתו ולמצותיו! שיקבלו עליהם מאלו הגדרים כל דבר שיכלו לעמוד בו. שיצוו בהן לבניהם, ובניהם לבניהם, עד סוף כל הדורות: וכל הדוחק עצמו להשתדל ולהרבות בגדרים אלו, תבא עליו ברכה!

וזה נוסח הצוואה שצויתי אני שלמה הנזכר לבני ישמרם האל! שיתפלל כל אחד מהם ג׳ פעמים בכל יום. ושישתדל שתהא תפלתו בכוונה. ושתהא בביה״מ או בבית הכנסת עם הצבור. ושישתדל כל אחד מהם כל יכלתו לקיים הבתי כנסיות והבתי מדרשות וההקדשות שבנו והקדישו אבותינו ז״ל ואני ג״כ. ושישתדל כל אחד לעשות[5] כמותם. בענין שלא יפסק מעשה הטוב מהם כלל:

ושיהיה לכל אחד מהם תמיד בביתו ספסל ועליו ספר[6] או שנים מתלמוד או מאחד מחבוריו.[7] בענין שיפתח ספר בבואו לביתו[8]. ויקרא מה שיוכל לקרות. ושיחייב עצמו לקרות באיזה ספר שירצה

[4] Some word must be supplied: perhaps פעם אחת.
[5] Y adds ג״כ. [6] S. סופר. [7] Y מחבריו. [8] Y לבית.

lines before taking his meal. Again that he shall not omit to read every week the Pentateuchal Lesson twice in the Hebrew text and once in the Aramaic version.[9] He shall partake, on every Sabbath, of three meals, consisting if possible of bread, and, if not, of fruits.

Again, that he shall be ever modest, merciful and charitable, for it is for these qualities that the seed of Israel is renowned.[10] Let, also, his aim and thought be directed day and night to the service of the Creator, and be as charitable and benevolent as possible, for this is all that remains to man of all his labor. He shall also endeavor, to the utmost of his ability, to regulate his diet according to the rules laid down by R. Moses[11] in the fourth chapter of the Introductory Section of his Code so as to fulfil the words of Scripture:[12] "The righteous man eateth to the satisfying of his soul."

He shall, moreover, be careful not to mention the name of God in vain, to be honest in all his business transactions, and to deal in just measure.[13]

Each of them shall have the obligation to train his children to the study of the Torah, and to strive that one shall devote his whole life to the study thereof. All his children and household shall be directed in the right way and in the service of the Creator. And it shall be the duty of his brothers to support the one who makes

[9] T. B. Berakot 8a. [10] T. B. Yebamot 79a.

[11] Maimonides. [12] Proverbs 13.28.

[13] Levit. 19.36. S. renders "let their yea be always yea."

מהם[9] ארבעה שורות לפחות קודם שיאכל. ושיהיה מחוייב לקרות בכל שבוע הפרשה שנים מקרא ואחד תרגום. ושישלים בכל שבת שלש סעודות אם יוכל בפת ואם לאו בפירות:

ושיהיה תמיד ביישן ורחמן וגומל חסד. כי באלו המדות נתפרסם[10] זרע ישראל: ושתהיה כוונתו ומחשבתו יומם ולילה לעבודת הבורא ית׳. ועשות מה שיוכל מצדקה וחסד. כי זה ישאר לאדם מכל עמלו. ושישתדל להנהיג עצמו במאכליו ומשתיותיו[11] כפי יכולתו במה שכתב רבינו משה ז״ל בפרק רביעי מהלכות דעות כדי שיתקיים בהם מקרא שכתוב, צדיק אוכל לשובע נפשו:

ושיזהר שלא להזכיר שם שמים לבטלה. ושיהיה משאו ומתנו באמונה. ושישתדל שיהיה הין שלו צדק:

ושיהיה מחוייב כל אחד מהם ללמד בניו תלמוד תורה כל יכלתו. ושישתדל שיהיה אחד מבניו תורתו אומנתו כל ימי חייו. ושידריך בניו ואנשי ביתו בדרך ישרה ועבודת הבורא. וכל שיהיה מהם תורתו אומנתו שיתחייבו שאר זרעו לסייעו בכל

9 S. omits. 10 Y נתפרנס. 11 Y ומשתיו.

the Torah his life work, to invest his moneys, making provision that he and his family may live respectably.[14]

Let the elder brother love the younger as his own child, and the younger respect the elder as a father. Thus may they bear in mind that they are of a God-fearing family. Let each of them love and honor scholars, so that they may have scholars for their sons and sons-in-law.[15]

Each of my children shall be bound to read this Will through once a week, and undertake to follow its directions. He shall also make it incumbent upon his children, and they upon their children, from generation to generation, to accept its teachings,[16] in order to fulfil the Scripture:[17] "For I have known him to the end that he may command his children and his household after him, that they may keep the way of the Lord, to do righteousness and justice." Then will be fulfilled in them that which is written in the text:[18] "And as for Me, this is My covenant with them, saith the Lord; My spirit which is upon thee, and My words which I have put in thy mouth, shall not depart out of thy mouth, nor out of thy seed, nor out of the mouth of thy

14 S. adds: "So that he be not distracted by worldly cares from his studies."

15 T. B. Shabbat 23b.

16 See S. Or "to perform its terms."

17 Gen. 18.19.

18 Isaiah 59.21.

יכלתם. ולהשתדל ולהתעסק בממונו כדי שיוכל לעבור זמנו ולכלכל בניו ואנשי ביתו בכבוד:

ושיאהב גדולם לקטנם כבנו[12]. ושיכבד קטנם לגדולם כאביו. בענין שיראה כל אחד מהם שהוא מזרע כשר ומהמשפחה שהוא[13]. ושיאהב ושיכבד לת"ח כדי שיזכה למה שאז"ל כל דרחים רבנן הוו ליה בנין רבנין. וכל דמוקיר רבנן הויין ליה חתני רבנן:

ושיהיה כל אחד מהם מחוייב[14] לקרות הצואה הזאת פעם אחת בשבוע. ושישלים אותה. ויקבל אותה עליו שיהא ג"כ מחוייב לצוות לבניו לקבל אותה עליהם. ושיצוו לבניהם לקבל אותה ג"כ עליהם. ובניהם לבניהם דור אחר דור עד סוף כל הדורות. כדי לקיים מקרא שכתוב כי ידעתיו[15] למען אשר יצוה את בניו ואת ביתו אחריו ושמרו דרך ה' לעשות צדקה ומשפט: ויתקיים בהם מקרא שכתוב, ואני זאת בריתי אותם אמר ה' רוחי אשר עליך ודברי אשר שמתי בפיך לא ימושו מפיך

12 S. בבניו.

13 Some words must be supplied, or שהוא must be emended.

14 This word, missing in S, must be supplied.

15 S. ידעתי.

seed's seed, saith the Lord, from henceforth and forever!"

And as often as they read this Testament, they shall also read the two letters, written below, which R. Moses b. Naḥman sent to his sons, in order that they may profit from the admonitions contained in them. They shall also read the regulations to which I myself submitted, so that they also may carry out such of them as they are able. For, from the reading of all these things they will derive great advantage, provided that they read them in the right spirit. Should, heaven forbid, they be by any sad accident prevented from fulfilling any of the foregoing injunctions, they must hold themselves bound to abstain from drinking wine on that or on the following day, or shall deprive themselves of something at table or shall give some coin to charity as a fine for their delinquency. The purpose of this is that each of them shall be constantly on guard in these matters, so as to receive on himself the yoke of the kingdom of Heaven. And let the fear of God be ever present that they sin not, for the fear of God is life-giving.

The Letter which R. Moses b. Naḥman, of blessed memory, sent from the Holy Land to Barcelona: "Hearken my son to the instruction of thy father," etc.[19]

And this is the Letter which the above-mentioned Rabbi sent while in the Land of Israel

[19] For text of this letter see above p. 95.

ומפי זרעך [ומפי זרע זרעך][16] אמר ה׳ מעתה ועד עולם!

ובכל פעם שיקראו זאת הצואה. שיקראו אלו שני אגרות הכתובים למטה ששיגר הר׳ משה בר נחמן ז״ל לבניו. כדי להועיל מכל אותם ענינים שצוה בהם לבניו: ויקראו גם כן אלו הגדרים שקבלתי אני על עצמי. כדי שיקיימו מהם[17] מה שיוכלו לעמוד בו: כי בקריאת כל אלו הדברים יהיה להם תועלת גדולה. וצריך להשתדל לשים לבו עליהם בענין שיועילו לו: ואם ח״ו יארע שום מאורע לשום אחד מהם שימנעו בשבילו לקיים דבר מכל הכתוב למעלה, שיהיה מחוייב באותו יום או למחרתו שלא ישתה יין. או שיחסר דבר ממאכלו. או יתן צדקה לעניים בקנס על אותו המאורע. בענין שישמור כל זה תמיד. כדי שיקבל עליו עול מלכות שמים. ותהיה יראת ה׳ על פניהם לבלתי יחטאו כי יראת ה׳[18] לחיים!

האגרת ששלח הר׳ רמב״ן ז״ל מארץ ישראל לברצילונה. שמע בני מוסר אביך וכו׳[19].

וזאת האגרת ששלח הרב הנזכר בהיותו בארץ

16 The word omitted in S. must be supplied.

17 MSS. read בהם.

18 S. omits.

19 For text see p. 95 above.

to Castile, where his son was standing before the King.[20]

"As a man chasteneth his son, so the Lord thy God chasteneth thee."[21] "The Lord bless thee and keep thee"[22]—keep thee from sin, keep thee from punishment.

Our lord the King David, of blessed memory, begot a son wise and prudent, like unto whom there was none before or after him. Nevertheless, David laid on him the injunction: "Keep the charge of the Lord thy God, to walk in His ways, to keep His statutes, and His commandments, and His ordinances, and His testimonies, according to that which is written in the Law of Moses, that thou mayest prosper in all that thou doest and whithersoever thou turnest thyself."[23] Moreover, he said: "And thou, Solomon my son, know the God of thy father, and serve Him with a whole heart and with a willing mind; for the Lord searcheth all hearts, and understandeth all the imaginations of the thoughts; if thou seek Him, He will be found of thee; but if thou forsake Him, He will cast thee off for ever."[24] Now, my son, measure thyself with Solomon and thou wilt find thyself a worm—not a man, merely a creeping thing on the earth; yet if thou wilt seek God He will aggrandize thee and raise thee from degree to degree, while if thou forsake Him, spurned and forsaken art thou!

[20] In the royal service.

[21] Deut. 8.5. [22] Num. 6.24.

[23] II Kings 2.3. [24] I Chron. 28.9.

ישראל לקאשטילייא בהיות בנו עומד לפני המלך.

כאשר ייסר איש את בנו ה׳ אלהיך מיסרך![20] יברכך ה׳ וישמרך! ישמרך[21] מן החטא. ישמרך מן העונש!

הנה אדונינו המלך דוד ע״ה[21a] הוליד בן חכם ונבון. אשר כמוהו לא היה[22] לפניו ואחריו לא קם כמוהו. והוא צוה לו לאמר, ושמרת את משמרת ה׳ אלהיך ללכת בדרכיו ולשמור חוקותיו ומצותיו ומשפטיו ועדותיו (כאשר צוה) ככתוב בתורת משה (עבדך)[23] למען תשכיל את כל אשר תעשה ואת כל אשר תפנה שם: ועוד אמר לו, ואתה שלמה בני דע את אלהי אביך ועבדהו בלב שלם ובנפש חפצה כי כל לבבות דורש ה׳ וכל יצר מחשבות מבין אם תדרשנו ימצא לך ואם[24] תעזבנו יזניחך לעד: ואתה בני! תמדוד עצמך כנגד שלמה ותמצא כי אתה תולעת ולא איש, רמש מרמשי[25] האדמה. ואעפ״כ אם תדרשנו יגדלך וממעלה[26] מעלה יעלך. ואם תעזבנו זנוח[27] ועזוב אתה:

20 Y מיסריך. 21 Y and S omit. 21a Y and S. omit.

22 Y נהיה. 23 So the MSS. add; but in MT the bracketed words do not occur. There are also other variants from the MT.

24 P. adds תניחנו (cancelled). 25 So Y. But S מרמש.

26 Y omits ו יגדלך. 27 So Y and P. S זרוק.

My son! Take care to recite the Shema' morning and evening and the Eighteen Benedictions three times every day. At thy meals, say the blessing before and after, in the proper form. Let nothing prevent thee from reading the Lesson from the Law every Sabbath. Acquire an accurate copy of the Pentateuch, and take it with thee wherever thou goest, that (the law) depart not out of thy presence, but thou shalt meditate therein day and night, for then thou shalt make thy ways prosperous and then thou shalt have good success.[25]

My son! "Cast thy burden upon the Lord![26]" for the thing which thou believest far from thee is often very near. Know again, that thou art not master over thy words, nor hast power over thy hand; but everything is in the hand of God to do (as He wills). Set thy heart ever to the thoughts:[27] "Except the Lord build the house, they labour in vain that build it," (while, if the Lord build it, they labor in vain that throw it down); "except the Lord keep the city, the watchman waketh but in vain" (while if the Lord keep the city, the watchman's toil is unnecessary).

Know that the olden sages likened the king with woman.[28] Take heed to stand in the courtyard in awe and rectitude; and beware of the women (of the court?) never to be drawn by their cords. Know that our God hates unchastity, and Balaam could in no other way injure Israel than

[25] After Joshua 1.8. [26] Ps 55.23.

[27] Ps. 127.1. [28] See note on Hebrew text.

בני! הוי זהיר בק"ש שחרית וערבית[28], ובתפלה שלשה פעמים ביום: בני! על אכילתך תברך לפניה ולאחריה כמשפט: בני! על כל פנים תקרא הפרשה[29] בכל שבת ושבת. ויהיה לך חומש מדוקדק. ויהיה עמך בכל אשר תלך. ולא ימוש מפניך[30]. והגית בו יומם ולילה. כי אז תצליח את דרכיך ואז תשכיל:

בני! השלך על ה' יהבך. והדבר המוכן והמזומן[31] לפניך תחשוב אותו רחוק[32] ממך מאוד: ודע כי אין פיך שלך ואין ידך בגבולך. אלא הכל ביד האלהים לעשות. תן לבך תמיד אם ה' לא יבנה בית שוא עמלו בוניו בו. ואם ה' יבננו שוא עמלו הורסיו בו. אם ה' לא ישמור עיר שוא שקד שומר. ואם ה' ישמור עיר חנם טרח שומר[33]:

ודע כי החכמים הראשונים השוו המלך והאשה[34]. השמר לעמוד בחצר באימה ובמוסר. ומן הבנות[35] הזהר מאוד לבלתי צאת[36] בעבותן[37] כלל: דע כי אלהינו שונא זמה הוא. ולא מצא בלעם הרשע מקום

28 Y .שחרים וערבים 29 P. .הסדר 30 S. .מפיך

31 S. .מוכן ומזומן 32 P. .מרחוק

33 P. wrongly adds וגומר.

34 In the Leyden MS. is the word והאשה, but partly cancelled. P. reads והאש.

35 Here the MSS. have הבנים. S. corrects to הבנות.

36 So S. corrects from the צא of the MSS.

37 MSS. בעבותם.

by inciting them with the daughters of Moab.[29] For he who commits this offence, profanes the Covenant of Abraham our father, since this is the purpose of circumcision. He excludes himself from the community of Israel, the people of the God of Abraham. Such a one is termed disloyal to God, as it is said:[30] "We have broken faith with our God, and have married foreign women of the peoples of the land." He is further termed a trespasser: "And Ezra the priest stood up and said unto them: Ye have broken faith and married foreign women to increase the trespass of Israel."[31] He is also termed a transgressor, as it is said:[32] "for we have greatly transgressed in this matter." And he is termed treacherous and abominable, a profaner of the sacred things of the Lord which He loveth, and he makes himself hateful to Heaven, for it is written:[33] "Judah hath dealt treacherously, and an abomination is committed in Israel and in Jerusalem; for Judah hath profaned the holiness of the Lord which He loveth, and hath married the daughter of a strange god. May the Lord cut off to the man that doeth this, him that calleth and him that answereth out of the tents of Jacob, and him that bringeth an offering unto the Lord of hosts." That is to say, He will cut off the seed of such a one, who

[29] Num. 25. A section which follows immediately on the parables of Balaam.

[30] Ezra 10.2. [31] Ezra 10.10. [32] *Ib.* verse 13.

[33] Malachi 2.10–12.

להריע[38] לישראל רק בבנות מואב. שכל הזונה עם בנות העמים מחלל בריתו של אברהם אבינו שזו היא כוונת המילה. ומוציא עצמו מכלל ישראל שהם עם אלהי אברהם. ונקרא מועל באלהים. שנאמר אנחנו מעלנו באלהינו ונשב נשים נכריות מעמי הארץ. ונקרא אשם. ויקם עזרא הכהן ויאמר אליהם אתם מעלתם ותושיבו נשים נכריות[39] להוסיף על אשמת ישראל. ונקרא פושע שנאמר, כי הרבינו לפשוע בדבר הזה. ונקרא בוגד ונתעב[40] ומחלל קדשי ה' אשר אהב. ומשניא[41] עצמו לשמים. שנאמר, בגדה יהודה ותועבה נעשתה בישראל ובירושלים כי חלל יהודה קדש ה' אשר אהב ובעל בת אל נכר. יכרת ה' לאיש אשר[42] יעשנה ער ועונה מאהלי יעקב ומגיש מנחה לה' צבאות: לומר שיכרית זרעו

38 P. להכניע.

39 MSS. add מעמי הארץ which is not here found in MT.

40 Corrected from MS. reading ותועבה.

41 S. ומשניא ומשניא.

42 So MT. MSS. read לאשר.

will have none to call or answer in the tents of Jacob, among those who bring offerings and serve that honored Name. Measure for measure! He bears children unto other gods, and the Lord of hosts cuts him off so that he has no seed to serve Him. They were transgressors in Israel in their body,[34] and the Lord will turn the wheel over them.[35]

My son! Remember me always, let the image of my countenance be ever before thee, never leaving thee. Love not that which thou knowest me to loathe. Thou wilt be ever with me. Keep my commandments and live. Have always on thy lips the Scripture:[36] "I am a sojourner in the earth; hide not Thy commandment from me." And God, who is good and the Dispenser of good, shall increase thy well-being, and prolong thy life in happiness, and promote thy honor and prosperity according to thy wish, and the wish of thy father who bore thee—Moses son of Naḥman.

34 Or themselves.

35 Prov. 20.26: a figure of retribution.

36 Ps. 119.19.

ולא יהיה לו ער ועונה באהלי יעקב[43]. אשר הם המגישים מנחה ועובדים את השם הנכבד. מדה כנגד מדה. מוליד[44] בנים לאלהים אחרים. וה׳ צבאות יכרת אותו מהיות לו זרע עובד ה׳. הם[45] היו פושעי ישראל בגופן והב״ה ישיב עליהם אופן:

בני! בכל עת תזכור אותי. ותהיה דמות דיוקני לנגד עיניך. לא[46] תסור מלפניך. וכל דבר אשר ידעת בי שאני מואס אותו. אל תאהב אתה[47] לעשותו. עמי תמיד תהיה. שמור[48] מצותי וחיה! יכון[49] תמיד על שפתיך מקרא שכתוב, גר אנכי בארץ אל תסתר ממני מצותיך. והאל הטוב והמטיב ירבה שלותיך.[50] ויאריך בנעימים שנותיך. ויגדל כבודך והודך כחפצך וכחפץ אביך זה ילדך משה בר נחמן ז״ל:

43 So P. But S omits previous 14 words.
44 S. הוליד 45 P. omits. 46 P ואל.
47 P אותה. 48 S שומר· 49 P. בכון.
50 P שלומך.

קינת ר' משה רימוס

PROTHANATÏON OF MOSES RIMOS

XII

PROTHANATÏON OF MOSES RIMOS

The interest in this poem is partly literary, partly circumstantial. Its inclusion in the present volume was suggested to the editor, and the suggestion accepted, because while it is not technically a Will, it was written in the immediate expectation of death (hence the title *Prothanatïon* invented for it here). Undeniably it is in itself an attractive composition. That one whose end was so imminent should indite so artificial a poem is not an altogether unique literary fact. Another, later, instance (of the year 1586) may be seen in Isaac D'Israeli's *Curiosities of Literature*, in which are cited the lines, full of quaint and intricate conceits, written by Chidiock Titchbourne, in the Tower of London, on the night preceding his execution on a charge of treason. It must be conceded, however, that the poem of Moses Rimos is immeasurably the more elaborate and recondite.

Moses Rimos was a physician born probably in Majorca and settled in Sicily. When only twenty-four years of age, he was arrested in Palermo, about 1430, on a charge of poisoning a patient. Such false accusations were not uncommon in the middle ages; they arose from popular prejudice as well as from professional jealousy. The reader may refer on this point to M. Güdemann, *Geschichte des Erziehungswesens und der Cultur der Juden in Italien*, p. 237.

Very little is known of the poet, beyond what his poem conveys. There is one further reference to him, written in a MS. which was a gift or inheritance from Rimos to Rieti. As Moses Rieti died c. 1460, the date of Moses

יב

קינתי ר' משה רימוס

הקינה הזאת היא חשובה מפני ערכה הספרותי וגם משום תכנה, ואף כי איננה צואה במלוא מובן המלה בכ"ז אספתיה לתוך הכרך הזה, יען כי נכתבה בשעה שמלאך המות כבר פרש את כנפיו על המחבר (וע"כ המצאתי לה את התואר „פרותנטיון"). אין כל ספק שכשהיא לעצמה הרי היא חבור יפה ונעים. אין זו הופעה ספרותית מיוחדת שאיש אשר קצו ממשמש ובא יחבר שיר מלאכותי כזה. דוגמא אחרת מזמן יותר מאוחר (1586) נמצאת בספרו של יצחק דיזראעלי, Curiosities of Literature, מקום מובאים הטורים המלאים רעיונות משונים ומסובכים שנכתבו ע"י טשידיאק טיטשבורן במגדל לונדון בלילה שלפני הריגתו על אשמת מרד. אבל עלינו להודות שקינתו של משה רימוס היא הרבה יותר מתוקנה ועמוקה.

משה רימוס היה רופא שנולד בלי ספק במיורקה ויתישב בסיציליה. בהיותו רק בן עשרים וארבע תפשוהו וחבשוהו בבית האסורים בפלרמו, בערך שנת ק"ץ, יען כי הלשינו עליו שנתן סם המות לחולה ערל. עלילות כאלה לא היו חזיוך בלתי־נפרץ בימי הבינים, הודות למשפטים קדומים ואמונות טפלות שנתפשטו בין המון העם וגם לרגלי הקנאה ששררה בין אנשים העובדים במקצוע אחד. בנוגע לענין זה עיין בספרו של מ. גידעמאן, געשיכטע דעס ערציעהונגסוועזענס אונד דער קולטור דער יודען אין איטאליען, דף רל"ז.

מעט מאוד נודע אודות הפיטן הזה, מלבד מה שאפשר למצות מקינתו. יש עוד רמז אחד אליו בכ"י שבא במתנה או בירושה מרימוס לריאטי. בהיות שמשה ריאטי נפטר בערך ר"ך

[1] S. קינה לרבי.

Rimos seems fixed for the early part of the fifteenth century. The same entry confirms the martyrdom of Rimos, "who died for the sanctification of the Name," and another entry in the same volume records that Moses Rimos "died for the sanctification of the Name, when bandits came from the West, and he is buried in Palermo, outside the city under the wall." This reference to "bandits" is not consistent with Rimos' own account, but he, too, asserts that he could have saved his life by an apostasy to which he indignantly refused his assent. His martyrdom was indeed an act of 'sanctification of the Name' of God.

Full discussions of the points involved regarding the life and period of Rimos, will be found in L. Dukes, *Zur rabbinischen Spruchkunde*, p. 85; Zunz, *Zur Literaturgeschichte der synagogalen Poesie*, p. 523, Anhang, p. 46; M. Steinschneider, *He-chaluz*, iv, 67; D. Kaufmann, *Steinschneider Festschrift* (1896), p. 227; N. Slousch in *Centenario della nascita di Michele Amari*, vol. ii, p. 186.

The poem was first printed in *He-chaluz* (loc. cit.); in the critical notes this edition (or rather the Berlin MS. on which it is based) is referred to as S. Another edition by A. Cahana (referred to as C.) is known to the present editor only from the useful edition by Slousch (referred to as Sl.). Slousch's edition (which is to be found in the *Centenario* as cited above) is based on an Oxford MS., Cat. Neubauer No. 2578 (here referred to as O.), which has been specially re-collated for the present edition. Slousch's French rendering and annotations have proved of considerable service. But the Hebrew text is in several passages corrupt, though the general sense is clear. Moses Rimos possibly had in mind the talmudic story of Eleazar son of Durdaya who, rendered desperate by his announced

הנה קרוב לאמת שמשה רימוס חי בחלק הראשון של המאה החמש עשרה. באותו מקום נמצא כתוב שרימוס „מת על קדוש השם", ובמקום אחר בכ"י הזה אנחנו קוראים שרימוס מת על קדוש השם בשעה ששודדים באו מן המערב ונקבר בפלרמו מחוץ לעיר תחת החומה. הרמז הזה ל„שודדים" אינו מתאים לספור המעשה של רימוס עצמו, אבל גם הוא מודיע שאפשר היה לו להציל את נפשו ע"י שמד, אולם לזה התנגד בכל כחו. עינויי מותו היו באמת מעשה של „קדוש השם".

משא ומתן מלא בנוגע לחייו ותקופתו של משה רימוס נמצא בספרו של יהודה ליב דוקעס, „צור ראבינישען שפרוכקונדע", דף פ"ה; צונץ, „צור ליטעראטורגעשיכטע דער סינאגאגאלען פאעזיע", דף תקכ"ג, נוספות, דף מ"ו; משה שטיינשניידר ב„החלוץ", כרך רביעי, דף ס"ז; דוד קויפמאן ב„פעסטשריפט לשטיינשניידר" (תרנ"ו), דף רכ"ז; נחום סלושץ בקובץ שיצא לאור לזכרון מאת שנים מיום לידתו של מיכל אמארי, כרך שני, דף קפ"ו.

הקינה נדפסה ראשונה ב„החלוץ" (במקום הנזכר לעיל). בהערותי קראתי את המהדורה הזאת (או כת"י ברלין אשר עליו נוסדה) S. הוצאה אחרת ע"י אברהם כהנא (המכונה C בהערותי) נודעת לי רק מן ההוצאה הטובה והמועילה של סלושץ (המכונה Sl בהערותי). המהדורה של סלושץ (הנמצאת בקובץ הנזכר לעיל) מיוסדת על כת"י אוקספורד, רשימת נייבויער, נומר 2578 (המסומן פה O), ועליו עברתי עוד הפעם בעד הוצאתי זו. ההעתקה הצרפתית של סלושץ והערותיו המאירות היו לי לעזר גדול. אכן הנוסח העברי הוא מעוות ומקולקל במקומות אחדים, אף כי הכונה בכלל היא בהירה וצרופה. אפשר שעלה במחשבתו של משה רימוס ספור התלמוד ע"ד אליעזר בן דורדיא, אשר נתמלא ספק ויאוש כשאמרו

exclusion from the possibility of repentance for his sins, invoked successively the hills and dales, heaven and earth, sun and moon, stars and planets, to appeal on his behalf for pardon. Though these failed Eleazar, his own contrition won its way to the throne of mercy (T. B. Abodah Zarah 17a). Moses Rimos regards the elements and many another force in nature and man as more sympathetic with his sorrow. The poet describes how the Universe of Nature and of Philosophy, the Oral and Written Law, Jewish and Greek learning, all masterpieces of science, grieve at the undeserved catastrophe that has befallen the author. The very Signs of the Zodiac are involved in the general lamentation. But his faith triumphs and he dies with a declaration of firm trust. The whole episode is at once fantastic and fascinating. The young scientist, proficient in "the three tongues" (he uses the technical medieval phrase), about to perish on a trumped-up indictment, spent his last evening on earth in composing an elaborate acrostic on his name. In it are close parallels to the poem of an earlier Moses Rimos (see especially lines 64–69 of the epistle published by Kaufmann). Yet amid all this artificiality is seen the natural, simple, immovable piety of the man. His "Prothanatïon" thus possesses a value which transcends its literary worth, though as literature its quality is by no means insignificant.

[I keened it on the last day,[1] whereon they told me that on the morrow they would execute me. Woe unto me!]. May it be the divine will that my death be an atonement for my

[1]Perhaps "on the last day (of his life)"; or on "the first day of the week"—Sunday: or "on a certain day".

עליו שלא יקבלו אותו בתשובה על דבר עברה חמורה ויקרא אל ההרים והגבעות, השמים והארץ, החמה והלבנה, הכוכבים והמזלות, לבקש רחמים עליו לפני כסא הכבוד. אף כי הללו לא נענו לבקשתו של אליעזר הנה תשובת עצמו פלסה לה נתיב לכסא הרחמים (תלמוד בבלי, עבודה זרה י"ז.). משה רימוס משער שארבעה היסודות וכחות טבעיים ואנושיים אחרים משתתפים בצערו. הפיטן מתאר את עולם הטבע והפילוסופיה, התורה שבכתב והתורה שבעל פה, החכמה היהודית והיונית, כל ספרי המדע הנבחרים, מצטערים על האסון הגדול שבא עליו לא באשמתו. גם גלגל המזלות כמו משתתף בקינה הכללית. אכן אמונתו מתגברת על כל המכשולים ונשמתו יוצאת בקריאת אמון ובטחון בה' על שפתיו. כל המאורע הזה הוא מהר ומרהיב יחד. איש־מדע צעיר, בקי ב„שלש הלשונות" (הוא משתמש במימרא האומנותית השגורה בימי הבינים), עוסק בערב האחרון לחייו עלי אדמות, קרוב להריגתו על אשמת שוא, בחבור אקרסטיכוס מעובד ומשוכלל על שמו! בשיר הזה יש קוים מקבילים ושרטוטים מתאימים מאוד אל השיר של משה רימוס אחר שחי לפני הרימוס שלנו (השוה ביחוד שורות ס"ד–ס"ט של האגרת שנדפסה ע"י קויפמאנן). ובכ"ז בתוך כל המלאכותיות הזאת מתגלית החסידות הטבעית, הפשוטה, העומדת ברשות עצמה, של הגבור הצעיר. וע"כ קינתו יש לה ערך יותר גדול מערכה הספרותי, אף כי גם בתור ספרות יש לה איזו חשיבות.

נקוננתי אותה יום א' כי אמרו לי כי היום הבא אחריו היו עתידים להרגני. אוי לי![2] יהי רצון שתהיה מיתתי כפרה לעונותי.[3] ובבכי[4] תמרורים

[2] S. omits. [3] S. על כל עונותי. [4] O. ובכיתי.

iniquities! In bitter weeping,[2] without thought or reflection, I [Moses Rimos] have taken up the pen, crying as I write. I adjure by the Lord, God of Israel, that whosoever may become possessed of this elegy shall transcribe it and read it, and send it to others, until it reach the hand of my desolated relatives. Indicated therein[3] is my name, Moses Rimos. Woe unto me! (It is a month of lamentation, for through our sins was the sanctuary laid waste).

Who had believed that, as a churl dieth,
  Would die a sage, a seeker after God?[4]
And that, as an ox is led to slaughter,[5]
  Moses, the man of God, would be borne along?
The Attribute of Justice accuses me, 'gainst me are incensed
  The Ze'er Appin and the Ba'al ha-ḥoṭem;[6]
The shining Face has withdrawn its brilliance,
  And the Ancient of Days has closed his ear.
The Absolute Being, One Incorporeal,
  Efficient, Formal and Final Cause, Eternal.
The Wise, the Potent, the Willing, Changeless and Formless.

[2]Jer. 31. 15.

[3]In acrostic.

[4]II Sam. 3. 35; Ps. 14. 2, 53. 3.

[5]Jer. 11. 19.

[6]Cabbalistic terms, indicating the divine anger and long-suffering. The succeeding terms are derived in part from the Cabbalistic doctrine of the Spheres.

בבלתי מחשבה והסתכלות [אני משה רימוס][5] לקחתי הקולמוס, והייתי צועק וכותב.[6] אשביע בה' אלהי ישראל שכל מי שתגיע לידו יעתיקנה ויקראנה[7] וישלחנה לאחרים[8] עד שתבא[9] ליד קרובי העלובים. ורשום בה שמי[10] משה רימוס. אוי לי! [והיא לנהי חדש. ובחטאינו חרב מקדש][11]:

מי האמין כי כמות נבל
ימות משכיל דורש אלהים
וכאלוף[12] לטבח יובל
הובל משה איש האלהים:
מקטרגת[13] מדת הדין בי נחרים
זעיר אפין[14] עם בעל החוטם
אספו נגהם פנים מאירים
ועתיק יומין אזנו אוטם:
מחויב[15] המציאות אחד בלי גשמות
פועל וצורה[16] תכלית קדמוני
חכם יכול רוצה בלי שנוי ודמות

5 S. omits. 6 S. ובוכה.
7 O. ויקוננה. 8 S. לאחדים. 9 O. שתגיע.
10 S. omits. 11 O. והיא לנהי אז בחטאינו. 12 O. ואלוף.
13 S. מקטרגני. 14 S. ועיר אפיו.
15 S. transposes the next two stanzas.
16 "Form", in the sense of formal cause.

My God, my God, why hast Thou forsaken
 me?[7]
Evil fate and corruption of choice,[8]
 With a hidden mystery were among my
 disturbers.
For verily the guerdon of transgression is
 wrath.
 For this my heart trembles and quakes.
Ye holy princes, fathers of eld, a Lament
 Raise ye, O Crown, Wisdom and Intelligence—
Love, Justice, with Mercy,
 Splendor, Victory, Foundation, World, the
 Shekinah!
Again have the depths of Nothingness gathered,
 The Shade passeth on the day my shade
 passes and I die;[9]
Were I impenitent to the Lord, I would requite
 Eye for eye—thus did I swiftly decide.
Abstract Intelligences, Chieftains on high,
 Angels of Peace bitterly weep;
They whose essence and high quality resides
 in Intelligence

[7]Ps. 22. 2.

[8] Abuse of the power to exercise free will on the part of his enemies has made it possible for these to wrong him.

[9] Sl. refers to the fancy that his shadow precedes a man when he dies.

אלי אלי[17] למה עזבתני!
מזל הרע עם קלקול בחירה
היו בעוכרי עם סוד נסתר
כי באמת שכר עבירה עברה[18]
לזאת יחרד לבי ויתר:
שרי[19] קדש אבות עולם קינה
שאו נא[20] כתר חכמה[21] ובינה
החסד והדין עם רחמנא
הוד נצח יסוד עולם[22] שכינה!
שבו נאספו עמקי האין
סר הצל יום סר צלי ומתי
לולי תשובה לה'[23] אשיבה[24] עין
תחת עין כן לגזור[25] רצתי[26]:
שכלים נבדלים שרי מעלה
מלאכי שלום מר יבכיון
עצמם ועלותם[27] בהשכלה

17 S. אוי אוי.

18 The MSS. read עבירה. In that case the reference would be to Ben Azzai's maxim in Abot iv. 2.

19 S. שדי. 20 So C. corrects, the MSS. read שאינה.

21 O. תורה. 22 Sl. הוד עולם יסוד נצח. 23 O. לה.

24 S. אשובה. 25 S. לנדוד. 26 S. C. רציתי.

27 So C.; MSS. read ועילתם or ועלתם.

Will vainly moan on the day they slay me.[10]
The Active Intellect will make mourning,
So my thoughts answer in my agitation[11]:
For none will be left, fit to receive
As I can, the flow of human thought.[12]
The heavens put on blackness, and sackcloth
The Spheres have donned as their garment;
At my death Araboth[13] ceaseth; nor yearns
After its wont to reach out to the sons of the mighty.
Astonished be the heavens[14] at the cruelty of my end—
The orbit of the stars deviates from its central line.[15]
As a Lamb, as a *Bull* they conduct me,
My hands and feet are en-*Twinned* below[16].
Lo, backwards as the *Crab* goeth,
My hands are tied, my neck broken;
While my executioner at my right is as Satan,
His figure as a *Lion* eager for prey.
Lo, with cry of the *Virgin* crieth he that appeals
For the *Scales* of justice, asking with none to answer,

[10] Ps. 39.7. The line may be rendered: On the day they who roar in vanity slay me.

[11]Job. 20. 2. [12]Or: there will remain no human intelligence capable as I to receive inspiration. [13]On Araboth (Psalm 68. 5), cf. T. B. Ḥagigah 12; cf. Maimonides, *Guide*, II. 4 on the angelic power of ideas to move the spheres. [14]Jer. 2. 12. [15]Or: the reference is to the equator. [16]In these and the following lines allusion is made to the signs of the Zodiac.

יום יהרגוני הבל[28] יהמיון:
שכל הפועל יעשה אבל
סעיפי ישיבוני בעבור חושי
כי לא ישאר מוכן לקבל
כמוני[29] שפעת[30] שכל אנושי:
שמים לבשו קדרות ושק
שמו כסותם הגלגלים
יום מותי ערבות נח לא חשק
כמשפטו להשיג בני אלים:
שומו שמים לאכזריות מותי
גלגל המזלות מרכז נטה[31]
ככבש כאלוף[32] יובילו אותי
ידי ורגלי תאומים[33] מלמטה:
הן אחורנית כהלוף[34] סרטן
ידי אסורות[35] וערפי יערוף
ומשופטי על ימיני כשטן
דמיונו כאריה יכסוף לטרוף:
הן צעקת בתולה צועק קובל
מאזני משפט שואל ואין עונה

[28] So C. (after Ps. 39.7); MSS. read הכל.
[29] O. כמו. [30] S. שפעו. [31] O. נוטה. [32] S. ואלוף.
[33] Sl. תואמים. [34] O. בהלוך. [35] S. אחורנית.

Chastized is he as by a *Scorpion*,[17] bound[18] by the cord
A bent *Bow* is directed against him.
Lo, as the *Goat* is rent they fain would rend me,
Woe to the eyes that behold such a thing!
I could drain in a *Bucket* the tears of my eye
Until the *Fishes* might swarm therein.
Moan and lamentations[19] the planets[20]
Will raise, confounded are the errant stars;
Saturn is idle, that dependeth on me,
For my wisdom is become a cast-off counsel.[21]
The just man perisheth, a soul noble and true,
Jupiter[22] sighs, that attends at his steps,[23]
Mars grows pale for a skilful healer
Condemned and slain, whom the prince of peace hath spurned.
Majestic in beauty, of the shining face,
Venus withdraws her light at the death of the innocent;
Mercury is anguished for a ready scribe,

[17] I Kings 12. 11.

[18] Or pained, wounded.

[19] Ezekiel 2. 10.

[20] In the next lines various constellations are named.

[21] Cf. T. B. Shabbat 156a.

[22] Note the many word-plays which are untranslatable.

[23] Isaiah 41. 2.

מיוסר[36] בעקרב נחבל בחבל
קשת דרוכה נכחו פונה:
הן כשסע הגדי ישסעוני[37]
אוי לעינים כן רואות הן
אדלה בדלי דמעות עיני
עד כי דגים ידגו בהן[38]:
הגא וקינים[39] כוכבי לכת
ישאו נבוכים כוכבי נבוכה
תשבות[40] שבתי בי[41] נסמכת[42]
כי תבונתי[43] עצה[44] נשלכה[45]:
הצדיק אבד[46] יקר רוח נאמן
צדק יקראהו לרגלו נאנח
מאדים יכהה[47] על רופא אומן[48]
דאין וקטיל שר שלום[49] זנח:
הוד יפה[50] עינים פרצוף בהיר
נוגה אסף נגהו בהרוג נקי
כוכב ידאג על סופר מהיר

36 Sl. מוסר; S. מיוסד. 37 S. שעסוני.
38 O. הם and בהם at ends of lines.
39 S. הנה זקנים. 40 O. ישבות. 41 O. כי.
42 S. נשכבת. 43 O. תבונתו. 44 S. עתה.
45 S. נשלחה. 46 O. ועד. 47 S. יבכה. 48 S. אמן.
49 O. שלי(?). 50 S. יפי.

In the three tongues[24] was he proficient.
Lo, even the *Moon* refuses to shine,
[25]The stars are eclipsed on the day I am smitten;
And o'er the *Sun*, tented among them,
Darkness shall spread when I am put to death.
The Origin of Being—Matter, Form
And Privation—will make moan as do crocodiles;
Nature and Motion, Extension and Depth,
The External Mould, the Form of Species.[26]
First of matters, the *Hylê*,[27] devoid of action,
Which does not receive the forms,
Potentiality resides therein always—
Over me they lift their voice in tears.
Trembling has seized the Four Elements,
The Principles of Action and Passivity;
Composition, Mixture, Fusion—qualities
Which are Emanations from on high.
The Four Compounds are shaken—

[24] Probably Hebrew, Arabic and Latin.

[25] Job 25. 5.

[26] Various metaphysical terms are cited in these and the following lines.

[27] The Greek ὕλη.

בשלש הלשונות[51] היה בקי:
הן עד ירח ולא יאהיל
לקו מאורות[52] יום לקיתי[53]
ולשמש שם בהם אהל
חשך משחור יום נהרגתי:
ראשית[54] הויה חומר וצורה
והעדר מספד[55] יעשו כתנים
טבע ותנועה רחוק נקורה[56]
התחלה חצונית צורת המינים:
ראשון לחמרים ההיולי נעדר
פועל הצורות אין מקבלם
כח האפשרות תמיד בו דר[57]
ועלי[58] יתנו בבכי קולם:
רעדה אחזתם ארבע יסודות
אבות[59] פועלים ומתפעלים
הרכבה ערוב מזג סגולות
אשר ממעל הם נאצלים:
רגשו המורכבים הארבע

51 O. בשלשה לשונות.
52 S. המאורות. 53 O. לקותי. 54 O. ראיית.
55 S. הספר. 56 S. רוחק נקודה.
57 S. ואפשרות המיר המתבודד. 58 O. ועליו.
59 O. אכיות; Sl. איכות.

Mineral, Vegetal, Animal, Rational;
Controlled by matter, Nature's servitors,
Inert with but faculty to combine.
The Vegetal Soul seeth (my calamity),
The Feeder, the Grower, the Engenderer, with their satellites,
Whose essential motion extends upwards,
Whose eye hath pity on their organs.[28]
The Sensitive Soul is troubled, Sight, Hearing
Smell, Taste, Touch—all external;
The Common Sense, the Imagination and the Judgment weep,
Also the Desiring and the Moving Sense, being internal.
The Practical Intellect with which men know good and evil shakes with anxiety.
Arts,[29] Ethics, and Politics also
Cry with a bitter lamentation.
The Theoretic Reason trembles
With the Material, the Acquired, the Active also.
Axiomatic principles with the derivative,

[28] כליהם means organs which the vegetal soul keeps alive. [29] Sl. renders: "L'Industrie."

דומם וצומח חי ומדבר
נצוחי[60] החומר עבדי הטבע
הדוממים אין בהם רקי[61] התחבר[62]:
ראתה[63] הנפש הצומחת
זן מגדל ומוליד[64] עם משרתיהם
תנועתה בעצם מעל רווחת[65]
ועינה תחוס[66] על כליהם:
רגשה המרגשת ראות שמע[67]
ריח טעם משוש החצונים
חוש משותף מדמה עם משער ידמע[68]
מתעורר[69] מניע אלה[70] בפנים:
רעש שכל מעשיי[71] מהדאגה
דעת טוב ורע בו מכירים[72]
מלאכות[73] ומדות עם הנהגה
מדינית יבכו בכי תמרורים:
רעש השכל העיוני
חמרי ונקנה ופועל אצלו
מושכל ראשון גם[74] הזמני

60 S. נצוחי. 61 C. כח.
62 S. ההתחבר. 63 S. רגזה. 64 S. ומגדל מוליד.
65 S. רוחות. 66 S. תהיס. 67 S. השמע.
68 S. omits last two words. 69 S. מתעודד.
70 O. מעני אלף. 71 S. מעשה. 72 מכירים is correct.
73 S. מלכות. 74 S. עם.

Treachery attached to my person they could
not conceive.[30]
Existence and Essence, Accident and Substance,
Genera and *differentiae*, individuals and species,
Properties and accidents, the abstract, the corporeal, and the power pervading body,
Over me utter lamentations.
Moan in dire pain, O thou Written Law,
And thou Oral Law for me raise a sigh;
Grammar and Masora, Rhyme and Script—
Weepeth Ibn Ezra, lamenteth Ḳimḥi.
Bitterly cries the "Guide of the Perplexed,"
The Secrets of Prophecy, the Homonymous names;
The Meanings of the Laws[31] weep over me,
The views of the Mutakallimun, the principles of the sciences.
The structure of the Chariot, the Act of the Beginning,[32]
These lift up a lament with the Secrets of the Torah;
The theoretical Cabbala and also the practical,

[30] They refused to believe in the poet's guilt.

[31] The 'Meanings of the Laws' occupy much space in Part III of Maimonides' *Guide*, Prophecy is treated in Part II, Homonymous names in Part I.

[32] Cf. Maimonides, *Guide*, iii. ch. 1 seq.

בוגד דבק לעצמי[75] לא השכילו:
ישות ומהות[76] מקרה ועצמי
סוגיו[77] והבדיליו אישים מינים
סגולתו ומקרו נבדל גשמי
כח בגוף עלי[78] יהגו בקינים[79]:
יללי וגוחי[80] תורה שבכתב
תורה שבעל פה עלי האנחי[81]
דקדוק ומסורת חרוז וכתב
יבכה אבן עזרא ידאג קמחי[82]:
יצעק במרה מורה הנבוכים
סודות נבואה שתוף שמות
טעמי מצות עלי בוכים
דעת מדברים שרשי חכמות:
מעשה מרכבה מעשה בראשית
ישאו בכי ונהי סתרי תורה
חכמת הקבלה עם המעשית[83]

75 So Sl. corrects. S. reads: מבוגדת דבק לעצמי, O. בו גדר דבק ועצמי.

76 O. ישותו מהות. 77 O. סיניו. 78 MSS. או (אז) לא.

79 S. omits כח בגוף and at end of line reads במינים.

80 C. and Sl. correct to יליל נצחי; O. reads ילילי; S. reads ונגחי for וגוחי.

81 C. מר תצרחי. 82 S. הקמחי.

83 O. המופית.

The Book of the Zohar, the Book of Yezirah.
The Midrash on Ruth[32a] with the Song of Songs,
The Book ha-Bahir, the Sefer ha-Razim;
The Seven Halls—all the volumes
Of Naḥmanides are set in agitation.
Woe is the day I am slain, a mother's pangs
—Alas for Philosophy—shall come upon her;
Human inquiry shall be utterly dismayed,
(Crying) "Must I be robbed of the walker in the middle-way?"[33]
Logic shall veil its lip[34]—
The art of Dialectic, what shall become of it?
Poetry's grace has passed, imagination
Shall be lost to it after the death of Moses.
Porpḥyry feareth and is disturbed,
The Categories and also the Interpretation[35];
Prior and Posterior Analytics,
Topics, Sophistics, Poetics and Rhetoric.
Mathematics, learn ye to sigh

[32a] A cabbalistic work still extant.

[33] Between mysticism and rationalism; or the reference may be to the Golden Mean.

[34] Levit. 13. 45.

[35] In what follows several works of Aristotle (and Averroes) are named as sharing in the universal grief.

ספר הזוהר ספר יצירה[84]:
מדרש רות עם שיר השירים
ספר הבהיר ספר הרזים
שבעה היכלות כל הספרים
של בן נחמני הם נרגזים:
ווי יום אהרג חבלי יולדה[85]
הפלוסופיא יבאו[86] לה
חקירה אנושית תחרד חרדה
שבגבול[87] האמצעי[88] אותו אשכילה[89]
ועל שפם יעטה ההגיון
חכמת הדיבור[90] מה תעשה?
נעים המליצה סר[91] הדמיון
לא ימצא בה אחרי מות משה:
ויחרד פורפיריוס[92] וילפת
המאמרות והמליצה
ספר ההיקש עם המופת
נצוח והטעאה שיר והלצה:
והלימודיות נהי[93] למדינה

84 O. היצירה. 85 S. יולידה. 86 S. יבא 87 O. שהגבול.
88 S. אמצעית. 89 S. ומשפילה. 90 S. הדבר.
91 O. הר; Sl. חד. 92 O. פורפיריאות.
93 S. שיר; C. תהי למדמנה.

—Geometry and the Science of Numbers;
Music and Astronomy.
How hath Natural Science become desolate!
Physics—how shall it be content?
The books of the Heaven and of Generation;
Meteorology and the treatise on the Soul,
The Sense and the Sensible, the book of Perception.
Straying they wept, the divine sciences,[36]
Abstracted they from aught material;
Causes far off and primordial,
The book *Lambda*[37] crieth in pain.
The tumult of death, dizziness hath seized me,
No more can I grieve, for they have sent the message:
"Tomorrow thou diest!" Alas, for me, poor man,
Dragged and cast out for the funeral of an ass![38]
My sadly sorrowing mother, what wilt thou miserable do
When the ill tidings shall reach thee?
"Delight of my eye, crown of my head!"
Thus wilt thou mourn over me from a fountain of tears.

[36] Theology, i. e. metaphysics.

[37] Book XII (Λ) of Aristotle's Metaphysics. Cf. באור תאמסטיוס על מאמר הנרשם באות הלמ״ד מספר מה שאחר הטבע לארסטו, ed. Landauer, Berlin, 1903. (Commentaria in Aristotelem Graeca, Vol. V, Part V).

[38] Jer. 22. 19.

והגימטריא והתשבורת
המוסיקא עם התכונה[94]
החכמה הטבעית איך נעדרת!
ספר השמע איך ינפש
ספר השמים ספר ההויה[95]
אותות[96] השמים ספר הנפש[97]
החוש והמוחש ספר חזיה[98]:
סבבו[99] ובכו האלהיות
אשר מופשטות מן החומר
סבות הרחוקות הראשיות
מאמר הלמ״ד הוי הוי אומר:
סערת המות השבץ אחזני[100]
לא אוכל לנוד עוד כי שלחו לאמר
מחר תמות! אוי לי עני
סחוב והשלך קבורת החמור:
סוערה עניה אמי מה תעשי
עת אשר תגיע לך השמועה
מחמד עיני עטרת ראשי
תספדי עלי במקור דמעה[101]:

94 O. התכומה.
95 S. החוזה; O. החייה. 96 S. אודות. 97 O. החפש.
98 S. has ההויה here. 99 S. ספדו.
100 S. שבץ אחזתני; C. נשני. 101 S. omits these two lines.

Thy tent has fallen, what wilt thou do my sire?
Passing evil will thine old age prove;
I pray thee forgive my sin and my debt
If I have not becomingly honored thee.
Lo the loud treading warrior, Satan accuses—
The creditor has found how to exact his due[39];
Yet know, O my friends, that I am not slain
For some dire offence that I have committed.
Deadly poison, they assert, I planned
To be put in the dregs of the cup of trembling[40]
For gentiles who died: I was not guilty.
They have crushed out my life on this false charge,
But the Secret of the Lord is with them that fear him—but for 'Akiba[41]
And his band my feet had well-nigh stumbled,
When I saw I must die without cause;
But the Lord is just in all that cometh unto me![42]

The Chief prosecutor offered to save my life,
Were I to change my Honour and serve his God;
I answered: Better death of body than of soul,

[39] Cf. Gen. Rabbah 85 § 2. The poet, protesting his innocence of the charge on which he was condemned, admits his sinfulness towards God on other counts.

[40] Isaiah 51. 17.

[41] 'Akiba was a striking example of fidelity even unto death.

[42] Nehemiah 9. 33.

סוכתך נפלה מה תעשה אבי
מה מאוד רעה תהי זקנתך
אחלי מחול[102] לי פשעי וחובי
אם לא כראוי כבדתיך:
סאון סואן ברעש שׂטן מקטרג
מצא בעל חוב לגבות חובו
דעו מיודעי כי לא אהרג
על עון גדול עויתי בו:
סם המות אומרים[103] כי יעצתי
להנתן קבעת כוס התרעלה
לערלים מתו, לא פשעתי
הצמיתו חיי בזאת העלילה:
סוד השם ליראיו לולי ר׳ עקיבא
וחביריו כמעט נטיו רגלי
בראותי מותי על לא סבה
אך ה׳ הצדיק על כל הבא עלי:
סח שר[104] הצורר להציל ראשי
אם כבודי אמיר לעבוד[105] אלו
עניתיו[106] טוב מות גופי ממות נפשי

[102] S. תמחול. [103] S. and C. אמרו.
[104] O. צר; S. שח שר צר הצורר. [105] S. לעבור.
[106] S. עניתי.

My portion is the living God, and the dead
shall be his.[43]
Set am I as ordure and refuse, trodden by every
foot,
For the cruelties of earth have destined me
for death.[44]
Who had believed this of Moses Rimos?
I am the man that hath seen affliction![45]
The bitterness of death hath passed,[46] yet alas
For my calamity—I that was in the flower of
my age;
Four and twenty years I have lived,
A man whole and with all his desires.
The end of the matter![47] The Justice of God I
acknowledge,[48]
I confess and declare: "Verily I have sinned!"[49]
I have done wickedly, but the Lord is righteous,
I entreat Thee, O Lord, forgive my trespass!
Sustain me, my Rock, and as an atonement
Be my death for my sin! And with the soul
of one confident
(I cry): "In the bundle of life let be bound
My soul with Thee unto the end of days![50]

[Here endeth the Elegy: it is a dirge which men shall chant, and it shall be for a lamentation!][51]

[43] Exod. 21. 33. [44] Or: for men threatened me with a cruel death. [45]Lam. 3. 1. [46]I Sam. 15. 32. [47]Eccles. 12. 13. [48]On the recognition of the zidduk had-din, see the editor's *Annotated Edition* of the Singer Prayer-Book, Notes to p. 317 sq. [49]The ancient formula of confession: T. B. Yoma 87*b*. [50]I Sam. 25. 29; Dan. 12. 13. [51]Ezekiel 19. 14, 32. 16.

חלקי הצור החי והמת יהיה לו:

סחי ומאוס הושם[107] כל רגלם[108] תרמוס

כי מות אכזריות ארץ זמוני[109]

מי האמין זאת על משה רימוס

אני הגבר ראה עני:

סר מר המות אמנם אוי לי

על שברי[110] הייתי במבחר חיי

ארבעה ועשרים שנה יש לי

גברא בכולא וכל מאויי:

סוף דבר הדין עלי אצדיק

אתודה ואומר אבל חטאתי

רשעתי כי ה׳ הצדיק

אנא אל[111] נא מחול לי אשמתי!

סעדני צורי ותהי[112] כפרה

מיתתי על עוני ובנפש מאמין[113]

בצרור החיים תהי צרורה

נפשי אתך קץ הימין!

[תמה הקינה וקינה היא וקוננוה ותהי לקינה][114]

107 Only O. adds this word.

108 Sl. רגלים. 109 So C. O. אז גזמוני.

110 S. omits these two words and reads כי הייתי, Sl. חייתי.

111 O. ה׳. 112 S. תהי.

113 S. suggests ובנפשי אאמין.

114 O. omits and ends with תם ונשלם וכו׳.

לקוטים מצוואות ר׳ אברהם ור׳ יעקב ור׳ שבתי הורוויץ

THE STUDY OF THE LAW
COUNSELS OF THREE GENERATIONS BY ABRAHAM, JACOB, AND SHABTHAI HURWITZ

XIII, XIV, XV.

THE STUDY OF THE LAW

COUNSELS OF THREE GENERATIONS.

BY ABRAHAM, JACOB, AND SHABTHAI HURWITZ

The Hurwitz family derived their surname (which is spelt in a variety of ways) from a city of Bohemia. (For a genealogical table see Güdemann, *Quellenschriften*, p. 104). Testaments by three generations of the family are represented by selections in the present volume. The most famous member of the family, Isaiah, is not among them, but his son Shabthai (Sheftel), who edited Isaiah's popular "Two Tables of the Covenant" (Sheloh), occurs third on the list. Thus we have the grandfather Abraham, his son Jacob, and his grandson Shabthai. The Testament of Jacob is sometimes wrongly attributed to his brother Isaiah (see e. g. *J.E.*, vi, 466).

The three generations cover a considerable part of the sixteenth and seventeenth centuries. They were first associated with Prague, which suffered disturbances. Isaiah Hurwitz is attracted to Safed, the home of the Luryan mysticism; indeed the Hurwitz family did much to spread its influence in Eastern Europe. Shabthai died in Vienna in 1660.

The Testament of Abraham Hurwitz is entitled יש נוחלין "Some inherit": a title taken from the Mishnah (Baba Batra, viii, 1). "Some inherit," says the author, "and bequeath wealth...I have nothing to offer but a rule of righteousness and guidance in the fear of God." The

יג, יד, טו

לקוטים מצואות ר' אברהם ור' יעקב ור' שבתי הורוויץ

משפחת הורוויץ לקחה את שמה (הנכתב באופנים שונים) מעיר אחת בבוהימיה (בספרו של גידעמאן, קוועללענשריפטען, דף ק"ד, נמצאת טבלה של שלשלת היוחסין שלה). בכרך שלפנינו נתנים לקוטים מצוואות שלשה דורות של המשפחה הזאת. ישעיה, בן המשפחה הזאת היותר מפורסם, לא נמצא ביניהם, אבל בנו שבתי (שעפטל) שהוציא לאור את ספרו הידוע של ישעיה „שני לוחות הברית" (של"ה) הוא השלישי בסדר. וכן אנחנו פוגשים פה את אברהם הסבא, בנו יעקב ובן בנו שבתי. יש אשר הצואה של יעקב היא מיוחסת על פי טעות לישעיה אחיו (עיין, למשל, באנציקלופדיה היהודית האנגלית, כרך ששי, דף תס"ו).

שלשה הדורות האלה חלים בחלק גדול ונכר של המאות השש עשרה והשבע עשרה. מקום מושבם בראשונה היתה העיר פראג, אשר פורעניות רבות עברו עליה. ישעיה הורוויץ בחר ללכת לצפת, ביתה של תורת המסתורים של לוריא; ובאמת עזרה משפחת הורוויץ הרבה להפיץ את התורה הזאת באירופא המזרחית. שבתי נפטר בוויען בשנת ת"ך.

הצואה של אברהם הורוויץ מכונה „יש נוחלין", שם שאול מן המשנה (בבא בתרא, ח' א'). בדברי המחבר „יש נוחלין ומנחילין בית והון... אומר אני כי אין טוב לאדם כי אם כשינחיל לבניו הנחלה האמתית והיא... יראת ה'". וכל הצואה היא

whole lives up to this noble exordium. Equally beautiful is the Testament of the son Jacob, which takes the form of Notes to his father's work. These Notes were completed early in 1616, and the first edition of the Testament of father and son appeared together soon afterwards in Prague. Shabthai's Testament appeared for the first time in 1690 in Frankfort-on-the-Oder. An interesting edition is that of Amsterdam, 1701. It contains all three Testaments.

Abraham's Testament consists of 18 Chapters written largely, as are Jacob's Notes, in rhymed prose. The whole forms a fine body of ritual and ethical teaching. In the Introduction to Abraham's Testament is the well-known Parable of the Three Friends (Money, Kinsmen, and Deeds), the last of which alone accompanies the dying man to the grave. (On the history of this Parable see *Revue des Etudes Juives*, xviii, 83). Abraham Hurwitz obviously derived it from Aboab's *Menorat ha-Maor* (§ 278), which took it from Abraham b. Ḥisdai's *Prince and Nazirite*, a Hebrew version of Barlaam and Josaphat. Jacob's Testament consists of 52 Notes to Abraham's work. That these Notes deserve to be called a Testament is clear from the fact that the author so describes his Notes several times. At the end of Note 40 he directs his children to read the Two Testaments annually in the penitential season (Elul-Tishri).

Shabthai's Testament consists of Introduction and 29 paragraphs. The whole Testament is a notable example of that combination of legalism with mysticism, which is found in Naḥmanides and other famous scholars of the Middle Ages.

Another important point in Shabthai Hurwitz' will is

בסגנון ההקדמה הנעלה הזאת. לא פחות יפה היא הצוואה של בנו יעקב הלובשת צורה של הגהות לחבורו של אביו. ההגהות האלה נגמרו בתחלת שנת שע"ו, וזמן קצר אח"כ הופיעה בפראג המהדורה הראשונה של צוואות האב ובנו יחד. הצוואה של שבתי הופיעה בפעם הראשונה בשנת ת"ן בפרנקפורט על נהר אדער. יותר חשובה היא מהדורת אמשטרדם תס"א המכילה את כל שלש הצוואות האלה יחד.

הצוואה של אברהם יש לה שמונה עשר פרקים, וכמו ההגהות של בנו רובם כתובים בפרוזה חרוזה. בכללה הרי היא קבוצה יפה על הוראות דתיות ומוסריות. בהקדמתה נמצא המשל הידוע ע"ד שלשת החברים: ממון, קרובים ומעשים טובים, אשר רק האחרון מהם מלוה את המת לבית עולמו (בנוגע לתולדות המשל הזה עיין ברבעון היהודי הצרפתי, כרך שמונה עשר, דף פ"ג). כנראה לקח אותו אברהם הורוויץ מ„מנורת המאור" לאבוהב (סעיף רע"ח), והאחרון, כידוע, קבל אותו מ„בן המלך והנזיר" (העתקה עברית של „ברלעם ויהושפט") של אברהם בן חסדאי. הצוואה של יעקב עשויה מחמשים ושתים הגהות לצואת אברהם אביו. ההגהות האלה ראויות הן לשם צואה, ובאמת מכנה אותן המחבר פעמים אחדות בשם זה. בסוף הגהת הארבעים הוא מצוה את בניו לקרוא את שתי הצוואות יחד בכל שנה ושנה לפני בוא יום הדין הגדול והנורא, דהיינו סמוך לראש השנה וכן בעשרת ימי תשובה (אלול-תשרי).

הצוואה של שבתי יש לה הקדמה ועשרים ותשעה סעיפים. כל הצוואה הזאת היא מופת חותך של חבור תורת ההלכה ותורת המסתורים הנמצא בספריהם של משה בן נחמן והחכמים מפורסמים אחרים של ימי הבינים.

דבר אחר יש לו חשיבות בצואת שבתי, והיא הטעמת

his profession of faith. Confession of *sin* by the dying is old (see the Baraita in T.B. Shabbat 32a). Naḥmanides did much to strengthen this custom. (Cf. his *Torat ha-Adam*, ch. iv). But with regard to the confession of *faith* the formal habit does not seem older than the sixteenth or seventeenth century. 'Aḳiba in the first part of the second century died with the declaration of the Unity on his lips, and a similar declaration was early made by the dying. Again, Jacob on his death-bed asks his sons whether they have any disposition to dispute the divine monotheism, and they reply, 'Hear O Israel' (our father), the Lord is One (Gen. Rabba 98 § 3 and parallels). But Shabthai Hurwiz gives a much more formal profession of faith. Starting with the cabbalist thought (quoted from his father) that in the hour of death a man's mind is liable to disturbance, and improper thoughts may find entrance, Shabthai proceeds to declare in advance that all such thoughts are null and void, and follows this up with a formal enunciation of his creed. In several of the later Wills the authors professed their faith also in the Thirteen Articles of Maimonides. David Friesenhausen (c. 1750-1828) writes in his Testament: "I believe with perfect faith that the whole human race, Jew or Gentile, wise or ignorant, righteous or wicked, will enjoy felicity at the end, after bearing the punishment due to each according to his acts. And I further believe that such punishment will be for his good, for without it he could not be fitted to receive the happiness which the Lord has appointed for him." Joseph Landau (d. 1837) asserts his faith not only in the Oral law, but in all true interpretations which may be made in the future.

אמונתו. וידוי הגוססים על עברות שעברו הוא עתיק (ראה את הברייתא בתלמוד בבלי, שבת ל"ב.). משה בן נחמן עזר הרבה לחזק את המנהג הזה (עיין ב„תורת האדם" שלו, פרק ד'). אבל המנהג להתוודות על עסקי דת ואמונה נראה שמוצאו הוא רק מן המאה השש עשרה או השבע עשרה. עקיבא יצתה נשמתו ב„אחד" בחלק הראשון של המאה השנית, וכדומה לזה קראו הגוססים במאות הקדומות. גם יעקב אבינו בשעה שהיה נפטר מן העולם קרא לבניו ויאמר להם: שמא יש בלבבכם מחלוקת על הקב"ה? והם אמרו לו: „שמע ישראל (אבינו) ה' אלהינו ה' אחד" (בראשית רבה, פרשה צ"ח, סעיף ד', ומקומות אחרים דומים לזה). אבל ה„אני מאמין" של שבתי הורוויץ הוא יותר מפורט ומדויק. הוא מתחיל ברעיון המקובלים (שאול מאביו) שבשעת מיתה השטן עומד לצד האדם ומפתהו לכפור באלהי ישראל, והרי הוא מוסר מודעה למפרע שאם חלילה יארע לו דבר כזה יהיה בטל ומבוטל, לא שרירא ולא קיימא, והוא מסיים בעקרי האמונה שהוא מקבל עליו מעכשיו ולעולמים. יש צואות מאוחרות שבהן הטעימו המחברים את אמונתם ע"י שלשה עשר העקרים של הרמב"ם. דוד פריעזענ־הויזן (חי בערך תק"י–תקפ"ח) כותב בצואתו: „אני מאמין באמונה שלמה שכל הגזע האנושי, יהודי או ערל, חכם או בער, צדיק או רשע, יחיו חיי אושר באחרית הימים, אחרי אשר כל אחד מהם ישא את העונש הראוי לו לפי מעשיו. ועוד אני מאמין שעונש כזה יהיה לטובתו, יען כי בלעדו לא היה יכול להיות מוכשר לקבל את האושר אשר הצפין לו אלהים". יוסף לנדוי (מת בשנת תקצ"ז) מדגיש את אמונתו לא רק בתורה שבעל פה כי גם בכל הפירושים והחידושים שתלמידי חכמים עתידים לחדש עד סוף כל הימים.

I

Now the proper times for the fixed study of the Torah, twice daily, are these: (a) In the morning, before breakfast, immediately after leaving Synagogue. Nothing must be allowed to interfere with this practice, so that you may fulfil the text: "They go from strength to strength,"[1] from house of prayer to house of learning. At all events never leave home, even on necessary business, before studying a passage, or even a single rule or sentence if the matter be very pressing. (b) At night, immediately after evening service in the synagogue, before the evening meal, and again before retiring to rest. It is good to study early in the evening, before supper, either the whole or the greater part of the set portion, for eating makes one drowsy, and in that condition one is unable to learn. Do not trust to your power to rise before dawn, and to read your appointed portion then. As likely as not your sleep will be too strong for you. Night, say our Sages often, was made for no other purpose than study. I have already spoken at length on this subject in the second part of my work *Emek Berakah*, and also in my smaller volume which I have named *Berit Abraham*[2],

[1] Ps. 84.8. See notes to Hebrew text for this and the next following quotation. It will be observed that this text is frequently quoted in these testaments.

[2] On these books see *J.E.*, vi, p. 466 f. and references there.

[2] Two sentences from T. B. 'Erubin 65a are combined here into one.

א

וזמן הראוי לקבוע עתים לתורה בכל יום פעמיים בבוקר ובערב: בבוקר קודם האכילה מיד אחר יציאת ב"ה. ולא תעסקו בשום דבר כ"א לעסוק בד"ת. כדי שתקיימו הפסוק ילכו מחיל גומר מבית הכנסת לבית המדרש וכו'[1]. ועכ"פ אל תלכו בבוקר חוץ לבית לשום עסק אפי' הוא צורך שעה עד שתלמדו מקודם הלכה אחת או דין אחד או אפילו פסוק אחד אם נחוץ הענין: ובלילה ג"כ תקבעו ללמוד מיד אחר יציאת ב"ה קודם האכילה ולאחר האכילה ג"כ קודם שכיבה. וטוב ללמוד בתחילת הלילה קודם האכילה שיעור הקביעות או רובו. כי האכילה מביאה לידי שינה. ואז אין יכולת ללמוד. ואל תסמכו שתעמדו קודם אור הבוקר ותלמדו שיעור הקביעות. כי שמא יתקף עליכם השינה. וכבר נזכר בהרבה מקומות דלא איברא ליליא אלא לגירסא[2]. וכבר הארכתי בזה בספרי עמק ברכה ח"ב ע"ש ובספרי הקטן אשר קראתיו ברית אברהם על

[1] T. B. Ber. 64b: אמר רבי לוי בר חייא היוצא מבית הכנסת לבית המדרש ועוסק בתורה זוכה ומקבל פני שכינה שנאמר ילכו מחיל וגו'.

in reference to the saying of the Rabbis, "Night is the objective of day." So I command you to study every night before going to bed. Even in the short summer nights read a little before retiring, to fulfil the injunction, "Thou shalt meditate therein day and night,"[3] and fall asleep straight from filling your mind with the Torah. [And, let your reading be audible, and with a chant]. King David said: "Thy statutes have been my song,"[4] i. e. he read the Torah as a melodious song. I have often had to blame you for your habit of reading silently.

II

I, on my part, order also that before the coming of the great and awful Day of Judgment, I mean the New Year—ye shall read through this Testament of my father and teacher, together with my Notes.[5] Do the same thing during the Ten Days of Return,[6] for all that we have written is inspired with the Fear of Heaven and is meant to be an incentive to the fulfilment of the Torah, the performance of acts of piety, sincere Repentance, and pure love of God. Our words should summon you to a God-fearing frame of mind, and they will have this effect if

[3] Joshua 1.1.

[4] Ps. 119.54.

[5] The author, Jacob, writes his Testament as a commentary on the Testament of his father Abraham Hurwitz. See p. 251.

[6] First ten days of Tishri, called the days of Teshubah, *i. e.*, lit. return (repentance).

מאמר רז"ל שאמרו תכלית הימים הלילות כו' ע"ש: והנה אנכי מצוה אתכם שתלמדו בכל הלילות קודם שכיבה ואפילו בלילות היותר קצרים בקיץ תלמדו מעט קודם שכיבה כדי לקיים והגית בו יומם ולילה וכדי לישן מתוך דברי תורה: ודוד המלך ע"ה אמר זמירות היו לי חקיך ר"ל שהיה לומד תורה בשירה וזימרה. וכבר היה לי עמכם תוכחת מגולה כמה פעמים ע"ז הדבר שאתם לומדים תורה בלחישה:

ב

הגהות. גם באתי לצוות אתכם שלפני בא יום הדין הגדול והנורא דהיינו סמוך לר"ה תקראו ותגמורו זו הצוואה של או"מ ז"ל עם כל מה שהוספתי בס"ד. וכן תעשו בעשרת ימי תשובה. כי כל דברינו הם כולם יראת שמים והתעוררות גדולה מאד לקיום התורה והמצוות ולתשובה על אמתתם ולשם שמים. ומזכירים את האדם להיות חרד ייךא לדבר

they be read in a serious spirit and not cursorily. And to this end, have always in your hand the well-known books[7] on Reverence and Repentance, which draw mankind to the service of our Maker, and humble the unruly heart. Therefore meditate on such books continually, and read a definite section in them every day.

III

My lord, my father, of blessed memory, wrote in his book, that on the approach of death, the Adversary [God forfend], stands by the dying man's side, tempting him to deny his faith in the God of Israel. At that time a man is weak in his mind,—may the Merciful save us! Therefore I stand from now onwards before God and His Shekinah, before the tribunal in heaven and the tribunal on earth, and I make protest that if, God forfend, I shall make any unseemly utterance near my death, the words so spoken shall be null and void, without binding reliance. But I proclaim that what I now say has lasting validity; in that I accept and testify that the Holy One, blessed be He, is Cause of all Causes, Creator of all things, Eternal, existing before the first and after the last, for: "Hear, O Israel, the Lord

[7] For quotations from some of these books see M. Güdemann, *Quellenschriften zur Geschichte des Unterrichts* (Berlin, 1891) sections III and IV.

ה' תמיד למי שעוסק בהם בישוב הדעת לא בדרך העברה. וכן תקראו ותתעסקו תמיד בכל ספרי היראה והתשובה הידועים. כי הם מושכים לבו של אדם מאד לעבודת יוצרנו ית'. ומכניעים את לב הערל למי שרגיל בהם. ע"כ לא ימושו ג"כ הספרים האלה מפיכם. והגיתם בהם דבר יום ביומו באחד מהם שיעור מה:

ג

כתב אדוני אבי ז"ל בספרו. אדם כשמגיע זמן למות עומד השטן בר מינן על צדו ומפתה אותו באמור לו כפור באלהי ישראל. ואדם אין לו דעת באותן הימים רחמנא ליצלן! על כן הנני עומד מעכשיו בפני השם יתברך שמו הגדול ב"ה ושכינתיה ובפני בית דין של מעלה ובב"ד של מטה. שהנני מוסר מודעה אם חלילה וחס שאדבר סמוך לאותו ענין איזה דיבור שלא כהוגן, יהיו אותן הדברים בטלים ומבוטלים לא שרירא ולא קיימין על עצמי. והדברים של עכשיו הם קיימין באשר אני מקבל על עצמי ומעיד אני שהקדוש ברוך הוא הוא מסבב כל הסיבות ומהוה כל הויות והוא נצחי ראשון לראשונים ואהרון לאחרונים. ושמע ישראל ה'

our God, the Lord is One," and "Blessed be the Name of His glorious Kingdom for ever and ever." These are the principles that I truly declare mine from now and to all eternity.

With regard to academic study, read what my father[8] has written at the end of his remarks on "The Oral Law". There he gives directions for reading Talmud and Tosafot, and how also to arrive at new thoughts. I should add that where the Tosafot raise objections to Rashi, it is a proper thing to reconcile the two, for this is the truly admirable type of ingenuity. For helping you to this desirable result, the works of Alfasi and R. Nissim and all the commentaries around the Alfasi are a fine specific and you will be able to do wonders with Rashi and Tosafot![9] Then, when you have filled yourselves brim-full of the Talmud and Codes, study, I bid you, the Cabbala, for without it the Fear of God is impossible. He who reverentially learns the Cabbala, will see his soul in the Realm of Emanation.[10] To gain this knowledge read through the *Dew-fall* and the *Garden*[11]. And ye, my daughters and daughters-in-law, if your husbands are angry, leave them, and after the time of wrath has passed, rebuke them for their conduct, and re-

[8] The author is grandson of Abraham Hurwitz, son of Isaiah, the author of the *Two Tables of the Covenant*, from the end of which he here quotes.

[9] Many of the comments of the Tosafot are criticisms of Rashi.

[10] On this mystical idea see *J. E.*, ii, 372 and iii, 475.

[11] By S. b. A. Hurwitz and M. Cordovero respectively.

אלהינו ה' אחד. וברוך שם כבוד מלכותו לעולם ועד. והן הן הדברים שאני מקבל עלי מעכשיו ולעולמים:

...על לימוד הישיבה עיין בסוף תורה שבע"פ של א"מ ז"ל. מה שהוא מדריך כיצד לקרוא הלכה ותוספות וכיצד יחדש. אני מוסיף להזהיר במקומות שתוספות מקשים על רש"י ז"ל ראוי ליישבו וזהו חידוד של אמת בחילוקים: וסגולה לזה עיין ברי"ף ובהר"ן וכל הפירושים סביב על האלפסי. ואז תוכל לעשות פלאות ברש"י ותוספות: וראו אחר שתמלאו כריסכם בתלמוד ובפוסקים הנני מצווכם שתלמדו חכמת הקבלה כי אין אדם ירא שמים מי שאינו לומד חכמה זו. ומי שלומד קבלה באימה וביראה יראה נשמתו בעולם האצילות. ואתם בני ספר שפע טל לברכה תלמדו מתחלה ועד סוף. ואח"כ יהיה לכם ספר הפרדס:... אתן בנותיי וכלותיי אם יתכעסו בעליכם תלכו חוצה. ולאחר שיכלה זמן הכעס תוכיחו לבעליכם על זה ותזכירו להם צואתי

mind them of this command of mine. Moreover, my daughters and daughters-in-law, for God's sake be careful not to let a child under two years of age sleep in the same bed with you. And habituate yourselves to read the Pentateuch in German, and also the book called *A Good Heart.*[12]

[12] A Judeo-German moral book by Isaac b. Eliakim of Posen.

מה שאני מצווה על זה: אתן בנותיי וכלותיי הזהרו למען הש"י שלא לשכוב תינוק במטה שלכם קודם שיהיה שתי שנים. ותהיו רגילין לקרות חומש בלשון אשכנז גם ספר לב טוב:

פטירת ר׳ נתנאל טרבוט וצואתו:

THE PASSING OF NATHANIEL TRABOTTI AS RECORDED BY HIS DISCIPLE SAMUEL BELGRADI

XVI

THE PASSING OF NATHANIEL TRABOTTI

As Recorded by his Disciple Samuel Belgradi[1]

Nathaniel, son of Benjamin, son of Azriel Trabotti (cf. Mortara, *Indice*, p. 65), was born in 1576, and died in Modena on the second day of the New Year festival (September 23) 1658. This date is given in one of the elegies in his honor (*Revue des Etudes Juives*, xxxv, 256). He was much beloved by his congregation, as is evidenced by the Testament itself, by the elegies referred to (five of them have been printed), and by the fact that the Society for the Study of the Torah founded by him on Nov. 23, 1638 still thrives at Modena and annually commemorates its Founder.

His wife Judith died long before him. She had a fine musical taste, and would accompany the sacred songs sung at home with the harp (*Monatsschrift*, xxxix, 356). Nathaniel Trabotti (or Trabot, Trabotto) himself was a musician, as is shown by his Responsum addressed to Samuel Norzi. His daughter had married Joseph d'Urbin and had left Modena. He had no son. But he was evidently much attached to his kinsman and successor Abraham Graziano (Cf. Mortara, *Indice*, p. 28).

According to Gross (*Gallia Judaica*, p. 219), the name Trabotti was borne by several French Jews who migrated to Italy. The name is probably derived from the place Trévoux (Latin Trevoltium), situated in Burgundy, in the department of l'Ain. Steinschneider's list

[1] See p. 260.

טז

פטירת ר' נתנאל טרבוט וצואתו:

נתנאל בן בנימין בן עזריאל טרבוט (ראה מורטארא, מזכרת חכמי איטליא, דף ס"ה) נולד בשנת של"ו ויגוע במודינה ביום השני של ראש השנה תי"ח (כ"ג לספטמבר 1658). הזמן הזה נמצא כתוב באחת הקינות שנתחברו לכבודו (הרבעון היהודי הצרפתי, כרך שלשים וחמשה, דף רנ"ו). הוא היה אהוב וחביב על קהלתו, כמו שאפשר לראות מן הצואה עצמה, מן הקינות הנזכרות לעיל (חמש מהן נדפסו), וגם מן העובדא שחברת התלמוד תורה שנוסדה על ידו ביום כ"ג לנובמבר 1638 היא עוד במציאות במודינה ובכל שנה ושנה היא מסדרת אזכרה לנשמת מיסדה.

אשתו יהודית הסתלקה מן העולם זמן רב לפניו. היא היתה בעלת טעם זמרתי יפה, ורגילה היתה ללוות בעוגב את שירי הקדש ששרו בביתה (מאנאטסשריפט, כרך שלשים ותשעה, דף שנ"ו). נתנאל טרבוט בעצמו היה מזמר, כפי שנראה מתשובתו השלוחה לרבי שמואל נורצי. בתו נשאה ליוסף ד'אורבין ותעזוב את מודינה. בן לא היה לו, אבל כנראה נקשר בחבלי אהבה וידידות לקרובו ויורשו אברהם גרציאנו (ראה מורטארא, מזכרת חכמי איטליא, דף כ"ח).

לפי דברי גראס (Gallia Judaica, דף רי"ט) השם טרבוט הוא מיוחד ליהודים צרפתים אחדים אשר גלו לאיטליא. אין כל ספק ששם זה נגזר מן העיר טרייבו (ברומית טרייבולט־יום) היושבת בבורגונדיה במחוז איין. רשימת שטיינשניידר של

of persons bearing the same name (in various spellings) was augmented by Berliner (op. cit. below). To these may be added the references in Schiller-Szinessy's Cambridge Catalogue, pp. 85, 96-8.

The text is here reprinted (with many verbal corrections) from the copy which appeared in the Berliner-Hoffmann *Magazin*, xiv, 1887 pp. 111–122 of the Hebrew section. The copy was communicated by Mortara. The writer of the narrative of Trabotti's death was his disciple Samuel Isaac Belgradi (Belgrado). His style is very diffuse. But the document presents an impressive picture of the passing of an esteemed Rabbi, and if it is too obviously reminiscent of talmudic scenes (especially T. B. Ketubot 103-104) and palpably strives after effect, it at all events in part attains its object, to describe the affectionate leave-taking of a beloved Rabbi.

One of the names referred to in the narrative is David Saba (צבע). This corresponds to the family dei Tintori (Mortara, *Indice*, 64). The fame of Jews as dyers was wide-spread (Cf. *Jewish Life in the Middle Ages*, ch. xi).

These are the words which he spoke, the counsels he offered, the ordinances he instituted—he, the man of sacred stock, valiant and great in achievement, a saint ruling in the fear of God,[2] the man of whom we said: "Under his shadow we shall live among the nations,"[3] the lofty tamarisk,[4] towering o'er the captivity of Ariel, a

[2] II Sam. 23.3.

[3] Lam. 4.20.

[4] I Sam. 22.6. Cf. Comm. of Rashi for the application of the tree to Samuel.

אנשים הנושאים את השם הזה (כתוב באותיות שונות) קבלה הוספות ע"י ברלינר (עיין בעתון הנזכר למטה). לאלה אפשר עוד להוסיף את החומר הנמצא ברשימת קיימבריניה של שיללער-שצינעסי, דף פ"ה, צ"ו–צ"ח.

הנוסח הנדפס פה הוא מן ההעתק של מורטארא שהופיע ב"אוצר טוב" של ברלינר והאפמאן, כרך ארבעה עשר, תרמ"ז, דף קי"א–קכ"ב, מלבד מה שתקנתי מלים רבות. כותב הספור ע"ד מות טרבוט היה תלמידו שמואל יצחק בלגרדי (בלגרדו), המצטיין בהרחבת הדבור ובפזור מלים. אבל הספור הזה נותן לנו תמונה מרהיבה מפטירת רבי מכובד, ואם אמנם נמצאים בו איזה קוים מן התלמוד (ביחוד תלמוד בבלי, כתובות, דף ק"ג–ק"ד) ומורגשת בו השאיפה להפתיע ולעשות רושם, בכ"ז הוא ממלא במקצת את תפקידו לתאר את הפרידה המעוררת של רבי חביב.

אחד השמות הנזכרים בספור זה הוא דוד צבע, והרי הוא מקביל אל שם המשפחה dei Tintori (ראה מורטארא, מזכרת חכמי איטליא, דף ס"ד). כידוע, היו היהודים מפורסמים בתור צבעים (עיין בספרי Jewish Life in The Middle Ages, פרק י"א).

אלה הדברים והתוכחות והתקנות אשר דבר והוכיח ותקן גזע קדושים. איש חיל רב פעלים. צדיק מושל יראת אלהים. אשר אמרנו בצלו נחיה בגוים. האשל הגדול ראש גולת אריאל. עונה לכל

guide to the doubtful[5], a judge at whom his generation marvelled, for he had no like on earth, his renowned Excellency Nathaniel Trabotti, Rabbi over all Israel in the holy congregation of Modena. It befell on the Sabbath when was read in the Lesson: "And the Lord thy God will keep with thee the covenant and the mercy which He swore unto your fathers,"[6] 1653, that he admonished his people to fear God and to love Him, to study His word regularly, and to shun every act of oppression against men. Yet were his words pleasant withal, sweeter than honey from the comb, words which were fitted not only to stir the heart, but also to extract tears from flints.

This scene was the more affecting seeing that for some ten days previously he had been stretched on a bed of sickness. Neither in mind nor in body was he at ease, he could neither sleep nor rest because of the fever which burned his frame and crushed his spirit. So little strength remained that he could not even raise his hand to his bosom after his wont. But he was indomitable in his devotion to the Law, for he continued his interest in it morn and eve as in the days when he enjoyed tranquillity of mind.

But when it pleased God to relieve his sickness and calm his thoughts, the holy spirit did shine upon him and a north wind blew in his ears, so that the bands of slumber fell o'er his eyes, and

[5] Lit. "answering every questioner." For a parallel to this rhyme, cf. the inscription on the Bodleian Bowl (*Transactions Jewish Historical Society of England*, vol. V, p. 187).

[6] Deut. 7.12; in weekly section 'Ekeb.

שואל. הדיין המופלא בדורו. אשר לא היה על עפר משלו. הגאון כמוהר״ר נתנאל טרבוט זצוק״ל על כל ישראל שבקק״י של מודינא: בש״ק ס׳ ושמר ה׳ אלהיך את הברית ואת החסד הת״ג הוכיחם על יראת ה׳ ית׳ לאהבה אותו. ולקבוע עתים לתורתו. ולבלתי יונו איש את עמיתו. ודבריו היו כל כך ערבים. ומתוקים מדבש ונופת צופים. שלא זולת היו כדאי לעורר לבבות האנשים. גם להוריד דמעות מחרבות צורים:

וזה לפי שהיה סביב לעשרה ימים מוטל על ערש דוי. ומכובד חליו היה מטורף מדעתו. וממנו נדדה שנתו. וגם במטתו לא היה מוצא מרגוע לגופו לפי שעצמותיו כמוקד ניחרו מחזזית שעלתה על רובו. עד שכמעט אפס כוחו ונס לחה ולא היה יכול להרים ידו אל חיקו כמשפטו. ואעפ״כ לא שליו ולא שקט מפלפולו תמיד יומו ולילו. כימים הראשונים שהיה מיושב בדעתו:

וכאשר אוה ה׳ אלהינו להקל חליו מעליו. ולהשקיט רעיוניו. מרוח קדשו הופיע עליו ורוח צפונית נשבה באזניו. עד כי חבלי שנה נפלו על

he slept from the Sabbath eve until sunrise on the next morning. As he awoke, the Lord sustained him, His spirit spake through him and His word was in his mouth, summoning the children of his people, making known unto them that though his body might still be ravaged, his mind had returned to its olden strength. He opened his mouth with wisdom, and the law of kindness was on his tongue; the Lord his God was with him, and the shouting for the king was in him![7]

He called to his disciples who stood round his bed, while he seemed to them as a prince on his divan[8]. He bade them summon the Rabbis, the lay officers, and the private members of distinction, for he desired to make confession to his God, to give commands to his household and set his affairs in order, that the children of Israel might know his wishes, and God rejoice in him, and they in their Maker. They hastened to obey, and those whom he had named were gathered there, the people of the God of Abraham, ready to see and to hear what he had to say. When he was told that all were present, he collected his strength and sat up in his bed, for God had blessed his effort. He bathed his face

[7] Prov. 31.26; Num. 23.21. The 'North Wind' alluded to a few lines earlier is a reminiscence of T.B. Baba Batra 147a, it was a wind that drove away the clouds. Cf. Job 37.22.

[8] A metaphor for heaven in Cant. R. on 1.12.

עיניו. ותנומה על עפעפיו. וישן מהערב ליל ש״ק הנ״ל עד אור בקר יזרח שמשו. ויהי בהקיצו משנתו ה׳ היה סומכו. רוח ה׳ דבר בו ומלתו על לשונו. לקרא לבני עמו ולהודיעם כי חכמתו ותבונתו חזרה לאיתנו. וירגיש מקו מצבו שלא היה מתום בבשרו מפני זעמו[1]. פיו פתח בחכמה ותורת חסד על לשונו. ה׳ אלהיו עמו ותרועת מלך בו:

ויקרא לתלמידיו שהיו סביב למטתו. והוא עליהם כמלך במסבו. ויצום לקרא למע׳ הרבנים ולמע׳ הממונים עם כל שאר יחידי סגולה ולהביאם לפניו. כי היה רוצה להתוודות לאלהיו. ולצוות על ביתו ולסדר עניניו. למען ידעו בני ישראל עלילותיו. וישמח ה׳ במעשיו. וישמח גם ישראל בעושיו: לקול דברו חשו ולא התמהמהו. מע׳ הרבנים ומע׳ הממונים ונדיבי עמים נאספו שם עם אלהי אברהם. ויעמדו מנגד לראות ולשמוע מה ידבר אליהם. ויגידו להגאון הנ״ל כי כל הקרואים עומדים סביב למטתו. גבורי כח עושי דבריו. לשמוע לקול דבריו: ויתחזק וישב על המטה. כי שם צוה ה׳ את הברכה. וירחץ פניו וידיו ויטהר

[1] Probably this sentence has been misplaced and belongs to the previous paragraph.

and hands, making his body clean as were his thoughts, and a feeling of awe came over the assembly. He asked for water to drink, the water of mercy to sweeten judgment and shatter "husks".[9] So he sanctified himself like an angel of the Lord of Hosts, and turning to the leaders of the Community, said:

"Hear me, ye saints of the Lord, my brothers, my friends, my seed and the holy seed whom God hath blessed, hear me this day! I am now 86 years of age, no more can I go and come in your midst as I have done from my early youth. Ye are aware how I have borne on my shoulders with none to help, the burden of your affairs.[10] I have wronged none, but have tried my best to maintain union among you all small and great, so as to prevent scandals in your midst. May God continue to be with you as He was with your fathers; may He make you a thousand times so many as you are, and bless you as He hath promised!"[11]

Then his voice took on a more pitiful note, as he proceeded: "Know ye, my noble friends, that for my many and grievous sins it hath pleased the Lord to crush me with disease[12]. For many days my strength has gone, and I can scarcely move. Full well do I realize that the owner of the deposit[13] seeketh it back from me. I know

[9] The "husks" (Kelifot) were in mystical literature a type of evil spirits. For the use of prophylactic of water, cf. L. Blau, *Das altjüdische Zauberwesen*, p. 158.

[10] Deut. 1.12. [11] Deut. 1.11. [12] Isa. 53.10.

[13] i. e. the soul. Cf. Dictionaries, s. v. פקדון.

גופו כרעיוניו. כי האלהים עשה שיראו מלפניו. וישאל מים לשתות מי החסד המתוקים למתק הדינין ולשבר הקליפות. ויקדש עצמו כמלאך ה׳ צבאות. ויפן אל ראשי הק״ק. ויאמר אליהם:

שמעו אלי קדושי ה׳. אחי ורעי זרעי זרע קדש ברך ה׳. את אשר אני דובר באזניכם היום! בן ששה ושמונים שנה אנכי היום. לא אוכל עוד לצאת ולבא בתוככם כאשר התהלכתי לפניכם מנעורי עד היום הזה: אתם ידעתם איכה נשאתי לבדי טרחכם ומשאכם וריבכם. ולא הרעותי לאחד מכם. והשתדלתי תמיד בכל עוז להעמיד השלום ביניכם למקטנכם ועד גדולכם. למען לא יראה ערות דבר במחניכם[2]. ויהי כן ה׳ עמכם כאשר היה עם אבותיכם. ויוסף ה׳ עליכם ככם אלף פעמים ויברך אתכם כאשר דבר לכם:

וירם קולו בבכי ויאמר. דעו נא אלופי! כי מפני שעונותי עברו ראשי כמשא כבד יכבדו ממני חפץ ה׳ לדכאני. ונחליתי היום כמה ימים עד שאפסו כל כחותי. וכמעט שכל תנועותי אבדו. ויודע אני שבעל הפקדון מבקש פקדונו שיש לו אצלי. ואיני

[2] Ed. reads במתנכם, but correct form Deut. 23.15.

not whether I can restore it in its pristine condition, nor do I know by which way I shall be taken. Be gracious to me, my friends, and let your prayers be made on behalf of my soul, that in the moment of passing my mind be not overwhelmed, and my tent be free from plague. And I, on my part, will never cease to pray for you. This very day will I indicate to you the good and straight path, I will cry unto God and He will answer you, and He will shower His mercies on you.

"Lo, here am I! Tell me frankly, have I injured any one, have I shown partiality?[14] If so I will make amends. If sometimes I have addressed you in harsh phrases, in the ten terms of appeal,[15] I beg of you, do not murmur in your tents, but over all my offences let your love and tender consideration draw a veil,[16] and give me the glad message of your forgiveness! For the Lord of the Universe knoweth that my intention was never to take advantage of my official position, but to guide you into the way of good and out of the path of Satan[17], wherein grow thorns and thistles.[18] And so with God's help

[14] Cf. the protests of Moses (Num. 16.14) and of Samuel (I Sam. 12).

[15] Lit. "prayer". See Deut. Rabbah, beg. of ch. 12.

[16] Prov. 10.12. [17] Lit. "the destroyer." [18] Gen. 3.11.

יודע אם אחזירנה לו כמו שנתנה לי ואיני יודע באיזה דרך מוליכין אותי. לכן למען ה׳ הענוני חנוני אתם אלופי וחלו נא פני אל שיחנני לרחם על נשמתי כאשר יקחנה ממני. ורעיוני אל יבהלוני וישמור צאתי בכל דרכי ונגע לא יקרב באהלי. וגם אני חלילה לי מחטא לה׳ מחדול להתפלל בעדכם. והורתי אתכם היום דרך הטובה והישרה. אקרא אל אלוה ויענכם ונתן לכם רחמים וייטיב לכם כאשר דבר לאבותיכם:

ועתה הנני! ענו בי נגד ה׳ את מי מכם עשקתי ורצותי ומיד מי לקחתי כופר ואעלים עיני בו ואשיב לכם. ואם לפעמים גערתי בכם. בעשר לשונות של תפלה. אל תרגנו באהליכם. ועל כל פשעים תכסה אהבתכם וענותנותכם כי רבה היא בתוככם. ויבא נא דברכם הטוב ותאמרו מחלנו מחלנו! ואלהי עולם הוא יודע כי לא עשיתי ח״ו להשתרר על ראשי קהל ה׳ כי לש״ש תמיד נתכוונתי למען תלכו בדרך מלך מלכי המלכים הקב״ה ולא בדרך המלי״ח[2a] אשר קוץ ודרדר תצמיח ח״ו. וכן יהיה רוכב שמים בעזרכם כאשר

[2a] מלי״ח = משחית להבל.

let us still hold each other in mutual remembrance. Let my name be mentioned among you, and I will raise my prayer that God may bring back your captivity as in former years, break the yoke from off you, and judge you leniently."

The bystanders were deeply affected, their emotions being almost beyond control. Added to their own distress was the sense that he was suffering so severely from his pain. Yet they took courage and said: "Our master! Thou right-hand pillar, thou strong hammer[19], thou shepherd of Israel! How can we justify ourselves before you? God has found out the iniquity of thy servants—for many are our sins and transgressions, [and the Lord hath made to light upon him the iniquity of us all.[20]] But we are his atonement, the expiation for his rest.[21] Because of us has this great evil come upon him. 'Twere becoming for us to prostrate ourselves at his footstool, entreating forgiveness for our neglect of his commands, stiffening our neck to walk in the stubbornness of our heart, all of us, young and old, in neglect of his exhorta-

[19] T. B. Ber. 28b; I Kings 7.21.

[20] Isa. 53.6. The bracketed passage must have been added by the narrator after Trabotti's death.

[21] T. B. Ḳidd. 31b.

לא ישכח זכרוני מכם. ובכל כוחי אשא תפלה לנורא עלילה ישיב את שְׁבותכם כימי עולם וכשנים קדמוניות. ישבור מוטות עולכם ויולך אתכם קוממיות וידין אתכם לכף זכות:

כשמוע הקק"י את דבריו ויתעצבו מאד ולא יכלו להתאפק. וישאו את קולם ויבכו בכי גדול ועצום. ולא יכלו לענות אותו כי נבהלו מפניו. ונוסף עליהם שנפרץ קולם מגודל הבכי בראותם כי גדל הכאב מאד ויחזקו לבם ויאמרו לו: אדוננו! עמוד הימני פטיש החזק[3] רועה ישראל. האזינה[4] מה נדבר ומה נצטדק לפני מעכ"ת. האלהים מצא את עון עבדיך כי חטאותינו ופשעינו רבים הם אתנו. וה' הפגיע בו את עון כלנו. הרי אנו כפרתו וכפרת משכבו. כי בשלנו הרע הגדול הזה עליו. ועלינו מוטל להתנפל לפני הדום רגליו. ולבקש סליחה וכפרה[5] מלפניו. על כי עברנו צוויו ומלוליו. והקשינו ערפנו ללכת אחרי[6] שרירות לבנו בנעורינו ובזקננו לבלתי הטות לבבנו אליו לשמור מצותיו.

[3] The adjectives are transposed in ed.

[4] This word should be deleted. [5] וכפריו.

[6] Ed. אחד ר. Several obviously necessary corrections have been made without note.

tions. But O, our master, thou man of God, remember not our former offences, but let thy condescension make us great. Pity us as a father pitieth his children. Blot out our transgressions as clouds and our sins as mists and cast them into the depths of the seas. O hasten thy benign message, lest we be turned away from before thy face in shame, with empty hands, and be found sinners to our Father in Heaven for all time."

When he heard this, his Excellency realized the sincerity of their plea, and in a burst of sympathy for them, all the work of his hands, cried: "Be strong and of good courage. Fear not and be not dismayed. Trust in the Lord, for He shall help you and fulfil your hopes. The Almighty will be your treasure, He will renew your youth like the eagle,[22] and will turn and heal you. Hearken unto me, eat ye that which is good, and let your soul delight itself in fatness.[23] If it be the Lord's pleasure, I will order my cause before you, and fill my mouth with admonitions.[24] Wash you, make you clean, put away the evil of your doings from before your eyes.[25] Purify your hearts from enmity and dissension. Remove the stony heart from your flesh, and as for the hidden one,[26] drive it far from you into a land barren and desolate, lest, which God forfend, it prove a stone of

[22] Ps. 103.5. [23] Isa. 55.2.

[24] Job 23.4. [25] Isa. 1.16.

[26] Joel 2.20. In the context, the locust is meant, but the "northern one" (translated "hidden one") was interpreted of the evil yezer (T. B. Suk. 52a).

ואתה אדוננו איש האלהים אל תזכור לנו עונות ראשונים. וענותך תרבנו על כל פנים. רחם עלינו כרחם אב על בנים. מחה פשעינו כעבים וחטאותינו כעננים. והשליכם במצולות ימים. עשה ואל תאחר כי עינינו אליך מיחלים. ולא נשוב מלפניך נכלמים בידים ריקנים. והיינו ח"ו חטאים לאבינו שבשמים כל הימים:

כשמוע מע' הגאון דבריהם אז ידע כי נכנעו מפניו. ועליהם נכמרו רחמיו. כי כלם מעשה ידיו ויאמר אליהם: חזקו ואמצו! אל תיראו ואל תערצו. ובה' בטחו כי הוא יהיה בעזרכם. וימלא משאלות לבבכם כחפצכם. והיה שדי בצריכם[7]. ויתחדש כנשר נעוריכם. ושב ורפא לכם. שמעו אלי ואכלו טוב ותתענג בדשן נפשכם. וברצות ה' צבאות. אערכה לפניכם משפט ופי אמלא תוכחות: רחצו הזכו הסירו רוע מעלליכם מנגדכם. וטהרו לבבכם מהשנאה ותחרות שביניכם. ולב האבן הסירו מבשרכם. והצפוני הדיחוהו אל ארץ ציה והרחיקוהו מעליכם. פן יהיה ח"ו לאבן נגף ולצור מכשול

[7] Ed. בצדיכם, but see Job 22.25.

stumbling and a rock of offence.[27] Support the teachers of the Torah in your midst, so that they may instruct your children, and the good result be associated with your name. Richly load the poor of your city with dainties, open wide for them your treasuries, and the God of heaven, who lays the beams of His upper chambers in the waters, will fill your storehouses. But above all, execute the judgment of truth and peace in your gates!"[28]

"'Tis a familiar fact," he continued, "how in past times this city was the perfection of beauty, great among the nations for its learning, a princess among the provinces[29] by reason of the Rabbis and Sages who illumined the earth and them that dwelt thereon, alike by their talents and their virtues.[30] But now, for our many sins, these have hurried to their rest, leaving us to lament, for fewer and fewer remain to take their place. No man makes it his concern to encourage scholars, but all turn to their own way, each to his gain,[31] one and all. As for the Torah, they cast it into a neglected corner, so that the prophecy of the Rabbis[32] is well-nigh fulfilled in us that 'the Torah will one day be forgotten by Israel'. Particularly is this appalling destitution

[27] Isa. 8.14.

[28] Zech. 8.16.

[29] Lam. 1.1.

[30] On the scholars of Modena see *J. E.*, viii, 638.

[31] Isa. 56.11.

[32] T. B. Shabb. 138b.

לכם: החזיקו ידי לומדי תורה בקרבכם. למען ילמדו את בניכם. והמצוה תהיה נקראת על שמכם. הענק תעניקו עניי עירכם. פתח תפתחו להם אוצרותיכם. ואלהי השמים. המקרה עליותיו במים. יתן ויחזור ויתן אליכם כפלי כפלים כחפצכם והברכה תהיה שורה באסמיכם. ורק אמת ומשפט שלום שפטו בשעריכם:

ויוסף מע' הגאון לקרוא למע' הרבנים ויאמר אליהם: מודעת זאת למעכ"ת! איך לשנים שעברו היתה העיר הזאת כלילת יופי רבתי בגוים ובדעות. שרתי במדינות מרבנים וחכמים. אשר היו מאירים לארץ[8] ולדרים. בגודל חכמתם ותבונתם ומעשיהם המופלאים. ועתה בעונותינו הרבים סעו המה למנוחות. ועזבו אותנו לאנחות. וגם עינינו רואות וכלות איך הנשארים הולכים ומתמעטים. ואין איש שם על לב להחזיק ידי לומדי תורה. אלא איש לדרכו פנו איש לבצעה מקצהו. והתורה מונחת בקרן זוית. וכמעט שנתקיים מאמר רז"ל עתידה תורה וכו'[9]. ובפרט עתה בעו"ה לפי שאזלת יד

[8] Ed. לארן.

[9] The quotation (T. B. Shabb. 138b) continues שתשתכח מישראל.

apparent at this moment, when but two or three students stand true to their charge, all the rest having chosen other careers. As for me, I am old and grey; for many years I have only been able to leave the house leaning on my staff, and also my eyesight has failed me. I have been powerless to spread the Torah as I should have wished. Therefore, my dear friends, make it your duty to restore the crown, whereby your seed will possess the land and for ever dwell therein. I lay my command on you that after my death ye shall restart the Yeshibah which existed aforetime in this place. Till now, indeed, because of your modesty and to save me from going to and fro, you have come here to my house. In future I insist that the meetings be in the Synagogue. Similarly I order all my pupils to attend those meetings, to sharpen each the other by study of the law after their olden custom, all for the glory of God, and not for the sake of disputing. No excuse shall avail to free them from this obligation, unless it be some unavoidable obstacle, such as illness, or absence from home on business. If any one disobey this rule, he shall give a ransom for his soul[33] unto the Lord."

[33] Apparently a fine is referred to; Cf. Exod. 30.12.

ואפס עצור ועזוב מהטפל בה. כי כלם דלו מאנוש נעו ונשאר בנו עוללות שנים ושלשה ת"ח עומדים על המשמרת. והנשארים בחרו להם דרך אחרת. ואני זקנתי ושבתי. ואתם ידעתם כי זה כמה שנים שהייתי הולך בחוץ על משענתי. ואור עיני גם אין אתי. ולא יכולתי להרביץ תורה כרצוני. על כן המצוה הזאת אלופי להחזיר העטרה. כי בזה זרעכם יירשו ארץ וישבו לעד עליה. והנני מצוה לכם שאחר פטירתי תחוייבו להתחיל הישיבה אשר היתה נהוגה להיעשות בעיר הזאת משנים קדמוניות. ואם עד עתה בגודל ענותנותכם כדי שלא להטריחני ללכת אנה ואנה באתם בביתי ובחומותי. מכאן ולהבא הנני מצוה שהישיבה הזאת תעשה בבית הכנסת. וכמו כן הנני מצוה וגוזר לכל תלמידי ללכת לישיבה הנ"ל. ולחדד זה את זה בהלכה כמנהגם הקדום. אך בזאת שתהיה כונתם לש"ש ולא לקנתר ח"ו. ולא יועיל להם שום התנצלות להסיר מעליהם העול הלז. זולתי בהיות להם אונס המונע כגון חולי ח"ו או שיוכרחו ללכת מעיר אל עיר בסחורתם ולא באופן אחר. ואם ח"ו יעברו ונתנו כופר נפשם לה'.

Then he turned to another topic, and specially addressed himself to the Rabbis. "You are aware how very important it is that, in the killing of animals for food, there should be no mistake as to the due preparations of the instrument used.[34] There are many who have not the skill, yet undertake the work. Let there be an end to this. Before my burial you (and I place this command also on the lay officers of the congregation) shall appoint two conscientious overseers, adept in the laws on the subject and practised in examining the knives, and they shall inquire into the qualifications of those who perform the work, separating the expert from the inexpert, so that no Israelite shall run the risk of partaking of unfit food. If any one refuses to submit to examination when called upon, he shall be denounced publicly by the shamash and his service rejected. The overseers shall keep under special observation the permanently appointed shoḥeṭ, who is established at the abattoir, for all the people rely on his service for their food. This officer may be implicitly trusted as a skilled and honorable man, but none the less shall he be required to present his knife for examination on demand, as a safeguard to the due fulfilment of his function."

[34] Cf. *J. E.*, xi, 253.

ויוסף עוד מע' הגאון לדבר אל מע' הרבנים ויאמר אליהם: כבר גלוי ומפורסם למע' כמה הררים[10] גדולים תלויים בשחיטה. ובפרט בבדיקת הסכין. ולעת כזאת הכל שוחטין ונקל בדיקת הסכין בעיניהם. ע"כ למען הרים מכשול מדרך עמנו. מעתה ומעכשיו הנני גוזר אליכם ואל מע' הממונים. שקדם שתקברוני תמנו שני יראי אלהים שיהיו בקיאים בדיני שחיטה ובפרט בבדיקת הסכין. למען יהיו עיניהם פקוחות ואזניהם פתוחות לראות ולשמוע מי שוחט ויבחינו בעין שכלם בין מי שהוא בקי בבדיקת הסכין למי שאינו בקי. למען לא[11] יאכילו נבלות לישראל ח"ו. ומי שיעיז פניו לבלתי שמוע אליהם להראות הסכינים לכל מראה עיניהם יכריזו תיכף ומיד על ידי שמש הקק"י שלא יאכלו משחיטתו. וכמו כן הנני מצוה שמע' הממונים יהיה להם השגחה פרטית על השוחט הקבוע היושב בבית המטבחיים. כי עיני כל ישראל עליו לאכול משחיטתו ובדיקתו הגם כי שחזקה שלא יוציא מתחת ידו דבר בלתי מתוקן. עכ"ז גם הוא יהיה כפוף להראות סכינו למע' הממונים הנ"ל לכל מראה עיניהם. ובזה יעשו סייג לתורה:

10 Per. הרהורים.   11 Ed. omits לא.

His Excellency's next counsel was addressed to the lay heads of the congregation. "Keep watch and ward," said he, "over the welfare of the community. Insist on proper deference being paid to your authority, not because you wish to display your personal power, but because you wish to enforce rules necessary for the public good. If you govern in this spirit, perfect will be your recompense; you will live long in your land, and your children will fill your places after you. Further I implore you to support the directors of the Yeshibah,[35] to pay them the annual salaries now fixed, and to add as a bonus the sum you were wont to give me, dividing that sum equally among the teachers. Let this bonus be associated with my name, that my memory may thus be kept alive, as though I too were yet living, and participating in the good work. Again, immediately after my passing, you shall appoint a Crier, whose duty it shall be to make his rounds every Friday afternoon, to announce to the citizens that the day declineth and the shadows of evening are stretched out,[36] so that men and women may add from the profane to the holy.[37] Then, when they hear the summons, the shopkeepers shall put up their shutters and close their doors. The women, too, shall show their worth by kindling the lights without delay, thus deserving God's

[35] The academy at which the Bible and Talmud were studied. See *Jewish Life in the Middle Ages*, 349, 368.

[36] Jer. 6.4. Cf. op. cit. p. 56.

[37] T. B. Shabbat 119, Oraḥ Ḥay. § 261.

ויקרא מע׳ הגאון אל מע׳ הממונים ראשי הקק״י ויצום ויאמר אליהם: בבקשה מכם! היו זהירין וזריזין לפקח בעין שכלכם הטוב על צרכי הקק״י. ומוראכם וחתכם יהיה עליהם לש״ש ולא להשתרר ח״ו כי אם להדריכם בדרך הישרה והנכונה. כי בזה תהיה משכורתכם שלמה. ותאריכו ימים על האדמה. ובניכם ימלאו מקומכם בקרב ישראל:

ועוד הנני מחלה פני מעלתכם שתחזיקו ידי מע׳ ראשי הישיבה ולא תגרעו מלתת להם שכרם הקצוב בכל שנה ושנה מפני למוד הישיבה הנ״ל ונוסף עוד הפרעון שהייתם נותנים לי. תחלקוהו ביניהם שוה בשוה. כי בזה זכותי לא תמוט וזכרוני לא יסוף מהישיבה כאילו התם קאימנא: ועוד הנני מצוה אל מע׳ שתכף אחרי פטירתי תמנו שמש שילך כל ערב שבת קודש להכריז בעיר ולהודיע כי פנה היום ונטו הצללים. למען יוסיפו האנשים והנשים מחול על הקודש. ובפרט על בעלי החנויות בשמעם קול הקריאה יתחילו לסלק התריסין ולהציב הדלתות. וכמו כן הנשים הכשרות תהיינה זריזות להדליק הנרות. כי בזה יקיים להן[12] הקב״ה

[12] Ed. לחן.

fulfilment in them of His promise."[38] He then turned to David Saba individually, commanding him to take in hand as a personal duty, the reparation of the Yeshibah which had been recently founded and to place it on a permanent basis, and to apply to the salaries of the two Rabbis the sum paid previously to himself out of his own generous contribution. Let not any regret fill his heart as to this outlay, for faithful is the Master to recompense the worker. A blessing would assuredly rest on Saba's benevolence, for he would be building his house firmly, raising a tent which would not be removed.[39]

The general body of members was next addressed. "Many a time and oft," he said to them, "as I went about I heard the idle talk of gossiping women, who stood in the cross-roads doing their work, and in all high hills were their pastures.[40] Nay more, they would croak like the frogs in Egypt while uttering the Name of God, and by the Lord,[41] these doings were like needles in my flesh. I desired to suppress the fashion, but for various reasons was unable to translate thought into act. But out of fear lest God will be wroth at such doings, I do now order that any instance be reported forthwith to the

[38] Cf. Baer, Prayer Book, p. 173. These ideas go back to the early rabbinic period, but were much developed in the sixteenth century, by the mystical school of Luria.

[39] Isa. 33.20. [40] Isa. 49.9.

[41] Lit. by the worship; a common rabbinic exclamation.

ההבטחה שהבטיחן: ואל המעולה כמ"ר דוד צבע חלה פניו ויצוהו שיחזק את בדק ישיבתו אשר כוננו ידיו זה שנים מועטים לבלתי יבטלנה עולמית. והשכר שהיה נותן לו צוהו שיחלקהו בין שני הרבנים למען יהיה לו חלק וזכות עמהם כנ"ל. ואל ידאג מן ההוצאה כי נאמן הוא בעל מלאכתו שישלם לו שכר פעולתו. וישרה ברכתו באסמיו. ויהיה משכיל בכל דרכיו. וכן יבנה לו ה' בית נאמן ואהל בל יצען:

ויאמר עוד מע' הגאון לכל בני הקק"י: גם זה אודיע לכם! כי פעמים רבות בלכתי בדרך הייתי שומע שיחות בטלות מאותן הנשים הפטפטניות. העומדות בפרשת דרכים לעשות מלאכתן. ובכל שפיים מרעיתן. ולא עוד אלא שהיו מקרקרות כקרקור הצפרדעים במצרים בהזכרת שם אלהים. והעבודה שנעשה בשרי חדודין חדודין. ועלה במחשבתי לגזור עליהן לבלתי תשבנה עוד במעמדן. ולסבות ידועות אצלי לא יכולתי להוציא מחשבתי מן הכח אל הפועל. ועתה כי יראתי פן יקצוף האלהים על קולן וחבל מעשה ידיהן ח"ו מעתה ומעכשיו הנני גוזר לכל מי ששמע מפיהן

Rabbi appointed in office at the time, and the latter shall prevent the continuance of the nuisance. One witness in this matter shall suffice; and let no one incur the iniquity of noticing the evil without reporting what he has seen.

"Similarly, I impose the same rule against male offenders, men who waste their time in gaming-houses, playing at dice and amusing themselves with cards,[42] which they always carry in their pockets. Let them desist from their habit of using the Name of God in vain. Woe to them, woe to their souls, woe to their latter end! They know not, neither do they understand, for their eyes are bedaubed that they cannot see,[43] and their hearts that they cannot understand that by their blasphemy the world is shaken to its foundations. Let them now and henceforward realize that of a surety bitter retribution will find them unless they mend their ways. I call heaven and earth to witness that they must perish under the dire wrath of God. But if they incline their ear to instruction so as to conduct their affairs honestly after the manner of worthy sons of Israel, having no slander upcn their tongue, speaking truth in their heart and showing due reverence to the Name of Heaven—then will their sins be neither remembered nor visited, and everlasting joy will be upon

[42] On medieval amusements and the rabbinic attitude to them, see *Jewish Life in the Middle Ages*, ch. xxii.

[43] Isa. 44.18.

הזכרת ש״ש שתקף ומיד יגלה אוזן מע׳ הרב אשר יהיה בימים ההם. והוא יגזור עליהן שלא תוכלנה לישב עוד שם כמנהגן הקדום. ועד אחד יהיה נאמן להעיד לפני מע׳ החכם כבי תרי. ואם ח״ו יהיה מי שיהיה ישמע ולא יגיד ונשא עונו:

וכמו כן אני גוזר ומצוה לאותם הבטלנים העומדים בבתי צחוקות לצחוק בקובייאות ולהשתעשע בקלפים אשר הורגלו תמיד לשאת בחיקם. שיהיו זריזים לבלתי שיזכירו ש״ש לבטלה כמנהגם. שאוי להם ואוי לנפשותם ואבוי לאחריתם. שלא ידעו ולא יבינו כי טח מראות עיניהם מהשכיל לבותם כי בדיבור הזה נזדעזע העולם. ואם לא יהיו נזהרים מכאן ולהבא ידעו נאמנה כי יעבור עליהם כוס התרעלה. העידותי בהם היום השמים והארץ כי אבוד יאבדון. ויחרה אף[13] ה׳ בהם וישמידם מהר מעל פני האדמה ח״ו. ואם יטו אזנם לשמוע בלימודים לישא וליתן באמונה כמשפט בני ישראל הכשרים. ושלא ירגלו על לשונם וידברו אמת בלבבם וש״ש לא יזכירו לבטלה כמנהגם. לא יזכרו ולא יפקדו חטאותם. ושמחת עולם תהיה

[13] Ed. אך.

their head. To divert their transgression and bring near their salvation, let them follow my advice and affix a tablet on the doors of the inner chambers of their homes. On the tablet let be written the text: Thou shalt not take the Name of the Lord thy God in vain. This device will serve as a reminder to them, to prevent the recurrence of the sin. Then will they prosper in the work of their hands.

"And this too", he went on, "let me impress upon you all. The penalty for leaving a promise undone[44] is greater than a man can bear! It is impossible to enter into all the details as to the nature of the offence and its consequences. The great teachers of Israel have dealt with the subject, and I do not desire to make your hair stand on end by going into the matter fully. But to keep your eyes from tears, your feet from stumbling, I strictly enjoin that whoever makes a promise or offering must fulfil his undertaking, lest he place himself outside the possibility of atonement. Especially those who shall buy, or who have bought, the annual right to certain ritual honors[45] shall pay the sum due to the treasurers of the congregation without procrastination. Should anyone stubbornly refuse to make payment after it has been twice demanded, the constituent members shall never again permit the debtor to acquire the honor. Nor shall this penalty release the defaulter from payment of what he already owes, for if so the

[44] T. B. Shabb. 232b.

[45] Cf. *Jewish Life in the Middle Ages*, p. 22.

על ראשם. ולהרחקת פשעם והקרבת ישעם ישמעו לעצתי וישימו פיתק על דלתי חדרי בתיהם. ועליו יהיה כתוב לא תשא את שם ה' אלהיך לשוא. כי בזה יהיה להם למזכרת ולא יארע תקלה על ידיהם ויצליחו במעשה ידיהם:

ויאמר: עוד הנני מודיע לכם! ולכל בני הקק"י כי חומר נדרים גדול עונו מנשוא. עצמו פרטיו מספר ועונשו מבואר כי חמור הוא. וכבר האריכו למעניתם ראשי אלפי ישראל. ואילו באתי להאריך גם אני בשום פרט מפרטיהם הייתי מעמיד שערות[14] ראשיכם. לכן למען הסיר עיניכם מדמעה ורגליכם מדחי. הנני גוזר ומצוה לכל מי שידור נדרים ונדבות שישמור מוצא שפתיו פן יקח משכבו מתחתיו או שיחבלו מעשי ידיו ח"ו. ובפרט לאותם שקונים המצות כל השנה ושכבר קנו יפרעם ליד גזבר בהכ"נ בלי איחור. ומי שיעיז פניו לתת כתף סוררת לבלתי נתון לכסף מוצא אחרי שישתדלו בהם מע' הגזברים פעם ושתים מעתה ומעכשו הנני גוזר לבעלי בתי כנסיות שלא יניחו להם שיקנו מצות מכאן ולהבא. ולא מפני זה יפטרו מפרעון מעתה

[14] Ed. שררות.

sinner would be the gainer. On the contrary, they shall use every process of the Jewish Court to enforce a settlement of the account. If he still continue recalcitrant, I hereby grant license to the Members to carry their cause before the public courts.[46] And while on this subject, I entreat the Committee of the Society for Fixing Times to use their best endeavors to collect the members' dues month by month, so that funds may be available to pay salaries and also the rent of the room punctually. The lessor will not then have to dun the Society for his rent as he has sometimes had to do. If, from any cause, when the rent falls due the official for that month has not collected all the subscriptions despite all his efforts, he shall meet the bill from his own purse, for the lessor is not a man of means, and depends on the payment. The performance of this service is a religious duty, which brings its sure recompense."

Manifold exhortations and words of persuasion to penitence did his Excellency speak to the heart of the people assembled. Repeatedly he bade them observe his mandates, derived as they were from the statutes of God. Then said he unto them: "Draw near and observe what I

[46] Throughout the middle ages it was considered in general reprehensible to carry disputes to any but the Jewish Court (Beth Din). As regards the society mentioned in the next sentence, see Note 15 to the Hebrew text.

ומעכשו. דאם כן מצינו חוטא נשכר. לא! אדרבא יכופו אותו בכל ב"ד ובכל משפט לפרוע פרעון כמשפט בני ישראל. ואם יאחרו מלעשות הפרעון הנני מרשה לבבה"כ לעבוט עבוטם בערכאות של גוים. וכמו כן הנני מחלה מע' הממונים על חק"ע[15] שישתדלו בכל עוז לגבות המסודרים מדי חודש בחדשו. כדי להריץ הפרעון ליד מע' הרבנים ובפרט לפרוע השכירות מחדר הישיבה מיד בבוא עתו ליד המשכיר. למען לא יצעוק כפעם בפעם ע"ד הפרעון. ואם לאיזה סבה בהגיע זמן פרעון השכירות מחדר הישיבה הממונה מאותו חדש לא גבה כל המסודרים הגם שעשה כל ההשתדלות האפשר יזיל הכסף מכיסו למצוה רבה כזו יען כי עני הוא ואליו הוא נושא נפשו. ובזה יהיה משכורתו שלם מעם ה' אלהיו:

ויוסף עוד מע' הגאון לדבר על לב הקק"י דברי כבושין ואזהרות רבות. ויצום וישביעם כמה פעמים לשמור מצותיו חוקי האלהים ותורותיו. ויאמר אליהם: גשו נא אלי! והטו אזניכם לאשר אני מצוה

[15] חברת קובעי עתים founded by Trabotti on Kislev 16, 5399, and still extant. On the anniversary of its foundation a eulogy of Trabotti is annually spoken.

am about to ask. Do not disobey me and give me ground for resentment. When it shall please the God of all flesh to take my soul from me, and lay me beside my father, then my pupils who have served me in my life-time and during my illness, shall also minister to me after my death. On them shall devolve the duty to lave my body that I may be clean outwardly as inwardly. Then when I am borne to sepulture, they shall drag my bier from the entrance of the cemetery to my grave.[47] I desire to chastize this stricken and worthless body of mine, which sinned so often from start to finish of my existence. And if for the honor of the Torah ye wish to have a memorial service in your holy encampment, be sparing, I adjure you, in your terms of eulogy. When you make mention of me, do so by my unadorned name,[48] for God knows and you know, never was my heart haughty, or mine eyes lofty, nor did I ever exercise myself in things too great, or in things too wonderful for me, nor did I ever turn unto the arrogant, nor unto such as fall away treacherously.[49] And if in my life-time I was not a fount of falsehood,[50] still less must I be so after my passing. For there is no rulership in the day of death[51] and it is unlawful to approach arrogantly the presence of the Cause of all causes. Obey me without fail in this, so that no occasion be given for an accuser to speak to my discredit. But I do ask you to set up a monument over my

[47] Cf. p. 208 above.

[48] i. e. without the usual titles of honor.

[49] Ps. 131.1.

[50] This seems the sense in which Jer. 15.18 is here used.

[51] Eccles. 8.8.

אתכם היום ואם תמרו את פי תלונותי עליכם. וכאשר ייטב לאלהי כל בשר ליקח נשמתי ממני ולהשכיבני עם אבותי. תלמידי ששמשוני בחיי ובמחלתי ישמשוני גם כן אחרי מותי. ועליהם תהיה המשרה לרחצני ולנקות גופי היטב. למען יהיה ברי כתוכי. וכמו כן הנני גוזר שתגררו מטתי מהקברים עד קברי. כי רצוני הוא ליסר הגוף הנגוף והבליעל הזה. כי ידעתי שפשעיו רבו למעלה מיום היותי על האדמה עד היום הזה. ואם מפני כבוד התורה תרצו להספיד עלי במחנכם הקדוש הנני גוזר ומצוה שלא תאריכו לספר בשבחי. וכשתזכירוני אותי בשמי לבד תקראו לי. כי אל אלהים ה׳ הוא יודע וישראל יודע כי מימי לא גבה לבי ולא רמו עיני ולא הלכתי בגדולות ובנפלאות ממני. ולא פניתי אל רהבים ושטי כזב ולא הייתי מקור אכזב וק״ו בנו של ק״ו אחרי פטירתי. כי אין שלטון ביום המות ואינו מן הדין ללכת בגדולות לפני עלת כל העלות וסבת כל הסבות. וזה יהיה לכם לדת ולחוק שלא תתנו פתחון פה לבעל דין לחלוק. ואם מצאתי חן בעיניכם הגדילו חסדכם עמדי לעשות זכרון וציון על קברי וידעתי שתעשו אותו לפי

grave, and I know that ye will do it in accord with your distinction not with mine. And since I have not been held worthy to leave behind me a son[52] for the sake of the Holy One of Israel, do not omit to pray for my soul at the time of its separation from my body, to save me from hard tribulations[53]. And I beg of you, my masters, to remain with me so long as the breath is in me, for while I converse with you, ye gladden my heart with exceeding happiness.

"Moreover I entreat you to offer up a memorial for my soul every Sabbath day and I from my grave will always be mindful of you praying to God on your behalf. May He prolong your days, and your years, and make you dwell in your land safely. May your name endure as long as the heavens. And God Almighty who put a limit to the bounds of earth will set no bounds to the blessings which He will shower upon you!"

Then answered the leaders of the congregation: "All that thou hast commanded we will do; none will refuse obedience. From of old have we been ready to regard thy merest hint as a precept rejoicing the heart.[54] But concerning this injunction to drag thy body to the grave our heart is faint, and our visage blacker than coal.[55] We know not what iniquity thou hast found in us to impose on us a duty like this. For when thine Excellency sleepeth with his holy and righteous fathers, we shall all be sinners for disobeying an

[52] Lit. "blessing."

[53] On prayer for the dead, see *Annotated* ed. of the Singer Prayer Book, p. ccxxxi. [54] Ps. 19.9. [55] Lam. 4.8.

כבודכם ולא לפי כבודי. ויען שבעו"ה לא זכיתי להניח אחרי ברכה למען קדוש ישראל הנאדרי בכח אל דמי לכם מלהתפלל בעד נשמתי כשתפרד מגופי שלא ידונו אותה ביסורים אכזריים ח"ו. ובבקשה מכם אלופי אל תעזבוני כל עוד נשמתי בי. כי מדי דברי בכם תשמחוני ותעלצוני:

עוד הנני מצוה ומחלה פני מעלתכם שתעלו זכרון נשמתי מדי שבת בשבתו לפני ה' לטובה. וגם אהיה לכם תמיד מקבר לעזור להתפלל אל אל בעדכם יאריך בשלוה ימיכם ושנותיכם וישבתם לבטח בארצכם. וכימי השמים כן יעמד שמכם. ואל שדי שאמר לעולמו די יריק עליכם ברכה עד בלי די. עד שיבלו שפתותיכם מלומר די:

ויענו ראשי הקק"י אל מע' הגאון: כל הדברות והציוים אשר דבר ותיקן מעכ"ת נעשה ונשמע! ואיש לא ימרה את פיך ח"ו. כי כן מושבעים אנו ועומדים מהר סיני לחשוב רמיזות וקריצות מעכ"ת כפקודים ישרים משמחי לב. אמנם על זה דוה לבנו וחשך משחור תארנו. כי לא ידענו מה מצאת בנו עול לצוות עלינו צווי כזה. שבשכב מעכ"ת עם אבותיו החסידים והצדיקים נהיה כלנו חטאים

affirmative precept,[56] to revere the learned, the more so when he is a man of God as thou art, the light of whose teaching is spread unto all the living, and whose wisdom is renowned in the isles. Put not this heavy burden upon us, but withdraw thy command, lest we become a disgrace and a laughing-stock in the eyes of our neighbors."

He answered: "Your generous response is very pleasant unto me; in it I recognize your amiable intent. In sooth, 'tis no new revelation; full well I knew you to be compassionate sons of compassionate sires, and the branch does not belie the root. As you desire to be excused, I will not insist, but will leave you to follow the dictates of your heart, in your treatment of me after I die. Not only do I declare my pardon, but I implore yours for having caused you distress. A thousand, thousand times I thank you. May God comfort you as you have comforted me! And now, with your consent, I will command my household and set my private affairs in order before you, and will convey my

[56] See Baba Kamma, 41b.

לעבור על מצות עשה. דכתיב את ה׳ אלהיך תירא לרבות ת״ח. ובפרט לאיש אלהים כמוך אשר אור תורתך פרוסה על כל החיים. וחכמתך יגידו באיים. ע״כ תיקר נא נפשנו בעיניך לבלתי הכניסנו בעובי הקורה. והסר מעלינו הצווי הזה. פן נהיה חרפה לשכנינו לעג וקלס לסביבותינו ח״ו:

ויען מע׳ הגאון ויאמר: תשובתכם הטובה מאד ערבה לי! כי ממנה הבנתי כוונתכם הרצויה. והעבודה כי לא היתה חידוש אצלי. כי ידעתי שאתם רחמנים בני רחמנים. וגודל ענותנותכם כי רבה היא ותהי לי משען ומשענה והענף לא יכזב השורש הטהור והנקי. ויען כי חפצכם כן הוא. לא אשיב את פניכם. כי אם שתעשו הטוב בעיניכם. ידעתי חכמתכם ובינתכם. כי לא רחוקה היא מכם. ועתה לא בלבד אענה ואומר סלחתי סלחתי כדברכם. כי אם במרי שיחי אשאל מאתכם סליחה ומחילה וכפרה על אשר צערתי אתכם. ואלף אלפים תשואות חן חן אשיב אליכם. וגם אני אקטיר ואגיש לשמכם ולזכרכם תודות ותשבחות. כן יואל אלוה וינחמכם כאשר נחמתוני בדבריכם. ואם ייטב בעיני מעלתכם אצו לביתי ואסדר לפניכם עניני.

inheritance to my heirs, after the rule appointed by our holy Law. I will make my last will with every legal circumstance, fastening its conditions as with nails so that it cannot be upset. Thus will I remove a stumbling-block from my heirs, and save them from utter neglect of my dispositions, which would not be executed unless I made them very precise. Otherwise I should appear as a trifler with the goods of this world and of the next, the sport of my juniors and the target of every other's pointed barbs. They would account me as a keeper of other men's vineyards who failed to keep his own!"[57]

Thereafter he summoned those distinguished men, Michael Modona and David Saba, and he said to them: "I have a request to make, do not refuse to grant it." And they rejoined: "Command us, and we will obey as we were wont to the utmost of our poor ability. For we will obey now as heretofore and will not turn aside from thy commands right or left." He then appointed the trustees of his estate, with the duty to execute all things set forth in the will he was about to make, and every particular of which he desired should be precisely observed. Then he gave the necessary directions as to his household affairs,

[57] Canticles 1.6.

ואשיב נחלתי ליורשי כדין תורתנו הקדושה. ואעשה צוואת ש"מ עם כל החזוקים האפשריים וההכרחיים. ואחזקנה במסמרים שלא ימיטו אותה. וזה למען הרים מכשול מדרך יורשי. כי בלתה ידעתי כי השחת ישחיתון אחרי מותי. ויסורו מהר מן הדרך אשר אצוה אותם. ואהיה נחשב ח"ו כמתעתע בעלמא הדין ובעלמא דאתי. וממני יצחקו צעירים ויורו בי המורים חצי גבור שנונים. עם גחלי רתמים. ויחשבוני לנוטר כרמים:

ויקרא אל האלוף כמוהר"ר מיכאל מודונא ואל הנעלה כמ"ר דוד צבע ויאמר אליהם: שאלה אחת אני שואל מאת מע' נא אל תשיבו פני ריקם! ויענו האלופים הנ"ל מעכ"ת יגזור אומר ויקם לו עד מקום שכוחותינו הצעירות מגיעות. כי לא נסור ממצותיו ימין ושמאל כאשר עשינו מאתמול: ויאמר אליהם: מעתה ומעכשו הנני מצוה אתכם אפוטרופסים על כל נכסי ותעשו כל אשר אבאר בשטר צוואתי אשר אעשה. ולא תפילו דבר ארצה בפרט שבפרטיה. יען כי כך עלה במחשבתי שיורשי ישמרו לעשות: ויצו לביתו ויסדר עניניו כחפצו. ויעש הכל יפה בעתו. וידעו כל בני הקק"י בודאי

doing all things in a manner which aroused admiration of the testator's character, and reverence for his wisdom and foresight.

Afterwards his Excellency turned to the wall and wept. Then he prayed to the Lord his God a short prayer in a still soft voice, saying: "Hear my voice, O Lord, when I address Thee, and let Thy word drop upon my tongue. Answer me when I call, O God of my righteousness; for into Thy hand I commit my spirit. Examine me, O Lord, and try me, test my reins and my heart[58]. O Lord, open Thou my lips, and my mouth shall declare Thy praise!"[59] Then he stretched his fingers toward heaven and began to confess after the fashion appointed by saintly men of yore.[60] And as his grief-stricken tones were heard, those who stood by wept in sympathy, and amid their tears besought the Lord not to snatch the crown from off their heads. But the gates of tears were closed against them,[61] for the decree had gone forth from before the King of the Universe, it was signed and sealed; and God is not a man that He should lie, nor the son of man that He should repent.[62]

When his Excellency had finished confessing, and had ended his deliverances of judgment and admonition fit to rouse the heart and to calm

[58] Ps. 26.2.

[59] Ps. 51.17.

[60] For various liturgical references, see Singer Prayer Book, Annotations p. ccxxv. Cf. T. B. Shabb. 32a.

[61] T. B. Ber. 32b.

[62] Num. 23.19.

כי מאת האלהים היתה זאת. למען ילמדו פושעים דרכיו וחטאים אליו ישובו. ודאי נפלאת היא בעיני ה׳ ובעיני השומעים:

ויסב מע׳ הגאון פניו אל הקיר ויבך בכי גדול. ויתפלל אל ה׳ אלהיו תפלה קצרה בקול דממה דקה ויאמר: שמע אלהים קולי בשיחי ומלתך תטוף על לשוני. בקראי ענני אלהי צדקי ובידך אפקיד רוחי. בחנני ה׳ ונסני צרפה כליותי ולבי. ה׳ שפתי תפתח ופי יגיד תהלתך: ויזקוף אצבעותיו כלפי מעלה ויחל להתוודות כמשפט חסידי וגאוני עולם. בבכי ותחנונים לפני אל עולם. לקול דבריו החלו מצוקים לבכות ולסלד וינהמו כולם כנהמת ים. ובעוד דמעתם על לחיים היו מתחננים אל אל לבלתי הסר המצנפת והסר העטרה מעל ראשם. וגם שערי דמעה ננעלו בעדם לפי שכבר יצא הדבר מפי מלכו של עולם. כי כן מלאו בפיו מע׳ הגאון לאמר שבפני נכתב ובפני נחתם. ולא איש אל ויכזב ובן אדם ויתנחם:

ויהי ככלות מע׳ הגאון להתוודות. ולדבר לאנשי הקק״י משפטים ותוכחות כדי לעורר הלבבות.

contention and remove the boughs of thick trees,[63] he said, "Know ye that I have here among you one dearly beloved,[64] whom I dandled and reared and whom I have set first among those called[65] this many a year agone. For such a time as this has he become a Sinai and a mover of mountains.[66] He is a man who makes appeal to the masses, and yet his decisions illumine the experts all the world over. I refer to my kinsman, my chosen disciple, in whom my heart delights, Abraham Graziano.[67] Let him go out and come in before you,[68] for I know that he will judge you in equity." Then he called him and blessed him. Graziano fell on his knees and wept mightily, whereupon the Rabbi said to him: "Equal to the sum of all my cares within me, is the pain of parting from *thee*."[69] He placed his two hands upon him and continued to give of his glory, so that a double portion of his spirit might be upon him.[70] He commanded him to let abundant waters spring forth from his well so that disciples after him might drink; he bade him always to be generous with his learning and on

[63] Used euphemistically for the evil yezer which was driven out by the "bough of thick trees", the myrtle (Levit. 33.20 is interpreted of the myrtle). For later mystical ideas, see *J. E.*, ix, 136.

[64] T. B. Baba Mezi'a 84b.

[65] I Sam. 9.22. Used of those called to recite the Law. See Jastrow, *Dictionary*, p. 1417.

[66] Two contrasted qualities, learning (Sinai) and dialectical skill (mover of mountains) are combined. They are kept distinct in T. B. Sanh. 24a.

ולהסיר מלבם דברי ריבות וענף עץ עבות. ויאמר אל כל בני הקק"י: דעו כי פרידה טובה יש לי ביניכם אשר טפחתי וריביתי והעליתיו בראש הקרואים זה כמה שנים. ולעת כזאת נעשה סיני ועוקר הרים. ומקהיל קהילות ברבים וכבר האירו פסקיו תבל. ה"ה קרובי בחירי רצתה נפשי כמוה"ר אברהם גראציאנו. אשר יצא ואשר יבא לפניכם. וידעתי כי בצדק ישפוט אתכם. ויקראהו ויעמידהו לפניו ויברכהו. ויפל על ברכיו ויבך בכי גדול. ויאמר אליו. ברוב שרעפי בקרבי פרידתי ממך קשתה עלי כנגד כלם. ויסמוך שתי ידיו ויוסף תת מהדרו עליו למען יהיה פי שנים ברוחו עליו. ויצוהו שיפוצו החוצה מעינותיו למען ישתו התלמידים הבאים אחריו. ושלא ימנע טוב מבעליו ושיהיה קרוב לכל קוראיו. כי אותו ראה חכם

---

67 He was Trabotti's cousin and died in 1865 (*J. E.*, vi, 84).

68 Used of Joshua, Num. 27.18.

69 Cf. Ps. 94.19.

70 Terms used of Joshua (Num. 27.20) and Elisha (II Kings 2. 9) are combined.

his part to be always ready to serve when called upon. And to the members of the Community he said: "Do this man all honor! I testify of him that he will attain fame, that his repute will be great among the scholars of this age, and I have confidence in his ability and tactfulness for representing you before kings."

This done, he said: "Where are my pupils? Let them approach that I may bless them." They came into his presence and said: "What wouldst thou say? Speak, that we may show our respect by obedience." He answered: "Ye know that from your boyhood I have reared you and that my love has never failed. As a nursing father carrieth the suckling child I have borne you.[71] I have shown you the road to wisdom, I have guided you in paths of righteousness. To the shore of the sea I led you,[72] and laid on your brows the crown of the Torah. I was found of you in all your hearts' desire; at the beginning of the watch I rose to instruct you, that ye might be able to carry a righteous message to your congregations. My table was prepared before you, and every fruit pleasant to the sight and good for food,[73] I did not withhold from you. Ye were the object of my unceasing thought, I ever watched your progress. But now

[71] Num. 11.12.

[72] Prob. an allusion to the expression "sea of the Talmud."

[73] Phrases from Ps. 23 and Genesis 2. Such biblical allusions abound in this Testament, and are not always indicated in the notes.

לפניו: ויאמר עוד אל בני הקק״י הזהרו בכבודו! כי מעיד אני עליו שיגדל בתורה ויעלה מעלה מעלה לשם ולתפארת ולתהלה מיתר החכמים הנמצאים בדורותיו. וידעתי שבגודל חכמתו ותבונתו לפני מלכים יתיצב:

ויאמר עוד: תלמידי היכן הם? יבואו נא לפני ואברכם. ויעמדו לפניו ויאמרו. מה ידבר מעכ״ת כי יבא דברך וכבדנוך. ויאמר אליהם: אתם ידעתם כי מנעוריכם גדלתי ורוממתי אתכם. אהבת עולם אהבתי אתכם. כאשר ישא האומן את היונק נשאתי אתכם. ארחות חכמה הוריתי[16] לכם. ומעגלי צדק הנחתי אתכם. לחוף הים הגשתי אתכם. ובכתר תורה הכתרתי אתכם. ונמצאתי לכם ככל אות נפשכם. ובראש אשמורות קמתי ללמד תורה אליכם. למען תבשרו צדק בקהלכם. שולחני ערכתי לפניכם. וכל פרי נחמד למראה וטוב למאכל לא מנעתי מכם. כל מעייני תמיד בכם. לראות ולשמוע מה בפיכם. ועתה הנני הולך בדרך

[16] Or הראיתי, ed. הוראתי.

I go the way of all the earth. Take heed to yourselves lest your heart be deceived, and ye turn aside[74] from the way which I showed you, and the Lord be wroth with me for your sakes.[75] But if ye diligently hearken unto my voice and keep my covenant, then the fear of the Lord will be your treasure-house and my lips will whisper in the grave[76] on your behalf in continual prayer that the Lord will satisfy your soul in drought,[77] and ye shall be as a fragrant garden, and like a spring whose waters fail not."

His disciples were deeply moved by this appeal, but despite their overwhelming grief found power to answer: "O master and our teacher, ever sure guide in our perplexities, thou man of God, we have heard thy exhortations and commands, pleasant they and upright. We will bind them on the tablet of our heart, tie them as garlands[78] on our head, throughout our lives. But grant us this solace in our affliction, that even as thou hast taught us, so do thou bless us." Then he lifted up his hand and blessed them, and said: "I lay my order upon you to attend the great Yeshibah which is to be opened on the New Moon of Ḥeshvan in the coming year 5414.[79] Lead your young flocks in the steps of the wise to feed in the gardens, to gather lilies.[80] By following this course ye may be confident that your learning will abide with you permanently. Let the fear of God be upon you. And He who loves the Gates of Zion will make to dwell among you

[74] Deut. 11.16. [75] Deut. 3.26.

[76] T. B. Yeb. 97a, in ref. to Cant. 7.10. [77] Isa. 58.11.

[78] Prov. 6.21. [79] i. e. 1653. [80] Canticles 6.2.

כל הארץ. השמרו לכם פן יפתה לבבכם וסרתם מן הדרך אשר הוריתי אתכם. ויתעבר ה׳ בי למענכם. ואם שמוע תשמעו בקולי ושמרתם את בריתי. דעו כי יראת ה׳ תהיה אוצרותיכם. ושפתי יהיו דובבות תמיד בקבר למענכם. ותפלתי תהיה ערוכה תמיד לפני ה׳ בעדכם ישביע בצחצחות נפשכם. ותהיו כגן רוה וכמוצא מים אשר לא יכזבו מימיו:

וישאו התלמידים קולם ויבכו בכי גדול ויעצבו מאוד ויענו אליו: אדוננו מעון השואלים מורנו ואלופנו. איש האלהים אב המון גוים. שמענו דברי תוכחותיך הנעימים ומצותיך הישרות. ונקשרם על לוח לבנו ונענדם עטרות לראשנו כל הימים. לבד זאת תהי נחמתנו בעניינו כי אחרי שלמדתנו ארחות חיים. תברכנו ותתפלל עלינו: וישא ידו עליהם ויברכם ויאמר אליהם: הנני גוזרני עליכם שתלכו לישיבה הגדולה אשר יתחילו אותה בר״ח חשון של שנת התי״ד הע״ל. ורעו את גדיותיכם אחרי החכמים לרעות בגנים וללקוט שושנים. ובזה תהיו בטוחים שתלמודכם תתקיים בידכם ויהא מורא שמים עליכם. ומי שאהב שערי ציון ישכין ביניכם

love and good fellowship, peace and exultation. Ye will be like the dew of Hermon that cometh upon the mountains of Zion. For there the Lord commanded the blessing, even life for all eternity."[81]

[81] Ps. 133.3.

אהבה אחוה שלום ורעות שמחה ועלצון. ותהיו כטל חרמון שיורד על הררי ציון. כי שם צוה ה' את הברכה וחיים עד עולם:

לקוטים מצואות

OCCASIONAL PRAYERS

XVII—XVIII

OCCASIONAL PRAYERS

(From the Opening of the Testament of Jonah Landsofer)

Jonah, son of Elijah Landsofer, was born in 1678 and died in Prague in 1712 (*J.E.*, vii, 616). His surname was due to his expert knowledge of the art of writing Scrolls of the Pentateuch. He was a man of many parts. Scribe, Cabbalist, he was also a mathematician, as his notes on Euclid show (these were written in 1710 and published after his death in 1737 by his grandson).

Moses Ḥasid, also of Prague, was Landsofer's contemporary and friend. Like Landsofer, Moses was a Cabbalist, whence his surname Ḥasid. The two were sent together to Vienna "to engage in a disputation with the Shabbathaians" (*J. E.* loc. cit.). They were sent by Abraham Broda, Rabbi of Prague from 1693 to 1708.

The Testaments of the two were first published together in Deutz' ס' דרך טובים (Frankfurt-a-M., 1717). There have been several editions; often the two Testaments appear in the same reprint.

Landsofer's Testament consists of 37 short paragraphs. Moses Ḥasid evidently wrote his Testament at various periods, for it consists of five distinct parts, containing 25, 16, 19, 8, and 3 paragraphs respectively. There is a curious difference with regard to improvised prayers. Landsofer advocates such innovations, while Moses Ḥasid strongly advocates restriction to the regular liturgy. Both commend the reading of German (Yiddish) litera-

יז-יח

לקוטים מצואת מהור"ר יונה

יונה בן אליהו לאנדסופר נולד בשנת תל"ח ויגוע בפראג בשנת תע"ב (עיין באנציקלופדיה היהודית האנגלית, כרך שביעי, דף תרט"ז), כנויו בא לו משום שהיה סופר סת"ם מנוסה ומומחה. הוא היה איש בעל צדדים רבים: סופר, מקובל, וגם בעל חשבון, כמו שאפשר לראות מהגהותיו לאוקלידוס (נכתבו בשנת ת"ע ונדפסו אחרי מותו בשנת תצ"ז ע"י בן בנו).

משה חסיד, ג"כ מפראג, היה בן דורו ורעו של לאנדסופר. כמו לאנדסופר היה משה מקובל, וע"כ כנוהו „הסיד". שניהם יחד נשלחו לוויען ע"י אברהם ברודא, רבי בפראג משנת תנ"ג עד תס"ח, לקחת חלק בוכוח עם השבתאים (עיין באנציקלופדיה היהודית האנגלית, במקום הנזכר לעיל).

צואות שניהם נדפסו בראשונה יחד ב„ס' דרך טובים" של דייטץ (פרנקפורט על נהר מאין תע"ז), ומאז עברו דרך מהדורות אחדות. לפעמים קרובות הן נדפסות יחד.

הצואה של לאנדסופר מכילה שלשים ושבעה סעיפים קצרים. משה חסיד, כנראה, כתב את צואתו בתקופות שונות, כי נמצאים בה חמשה חלקים מיוחדים, הראשון בן עשרים וחמשה, השני בן ששה עשר, השלישי בן תשעה עשר, הרביעי בן שמונה, והחמישי בן שלשה סעיפים. יש הבדל מפליא ביניהם ביחס אל תפלות חדשות שאינן מסודרות בסדורים: לאנדסופר מצדד בזכות תפלות כאלה, בעת אשר משה חסיד מתנגד אליהן נגוד גמור ובונה גדר סביב התפלות המסודרות. שניהם מצוים לבורים לקרוא ספרים בלשון אשכנז (אידיש), אבל בה בשעה

ture by the unlearned. But while Moses Hasid specially names Isaac b. Eliaḳim's *Leb Tob* and Moses Henoch's *Brant-Spiegel,* he also urges the study of Maimonides' *Sefer ha-Mizvot* (in the edition *Megillat Esther,* on which see Zedner 383, 582). So, too, Landsofer speaks with deep regard of Baḥya's "*Duties of the Heart.*" Both emphatically urge the close and regular study of the Scriptures and the Talmud. Both Testaments combine a strong mysticism with a sober regard for rational principles. The result is a curious glow of style even when ritual laws are being discussed.

Long ago I felt impelled to lay my commands upon you, to instruct you in the path and conduct which lead to the service of God. It is true that many books have been written for that purpose, by that link in a noble chain, Shabthai Hurwitz,[1] and by others after him. Nevertheless I know that the affinity between son and father, and their close attachment, must always give a father's words readier entrance than another's to the ear and heart of his child. It is as though they still stood face to face, bone of each other's bone, in the vividness of olden association.

In any such commands, first of all must be set the great principle that the purpose of man's creation is—the service of God. Of that service the root is fixed in man's innermost being, with the heart as watchman over it. Prayer, in its highest sense, is this heart-service, a complete

[1] See above, p. 250.

שמשה חסיד קורא ביחוד בשם „לב טוב״ של יצחק בן אליקים ו„בראנט שפיגעל״ של משה הענוך הוא מטעים ג״כ את „ספר המצוות״ של הרמב״ם (במהדורת „מגלת אסתר״, ראה רשימת צדנר, דף שפ״ג ותקפ״ב), כן גם לאנדסופר מדבר בהדרת כבוד ע״ד „חובות הלבבות״ של בחיי. שניהם מדגישים את ההתעסקות התמידית והמסודרת בספרי התנ״ך והתלמוד.

שתי הצואות האלה מחברות תורת מסתורים לתורת השכל, ומן החבור הזה יוצאת יפעת–סגנון מיוחדת גם כשהמשא ומתן סובב על מצוות ומנהגים.

אחרי שנתעוררתי לצוות אתכם, אשר עלתה במחשבתי לפני מאז מעולם, לצוות את בני יצ״ו הדרך אשר ילכו בה והמעשה אשר יעשון בעבודת ה׳ ברוך הוא וברוך שמו, ואף כי מלאים ספרים כאלה כהנה וכהנה מאותו השלשלת היוחסין של הגאון מוה״ר שבתי הלוי הורוויץ זצ״ל והבאים אחריו כהנה רבים, על כל זה ידעתי כי לעולם חקיקתי[1] הבן לאביו ודבוקו עמו יכנסו דבריו יותר באוזן וישימם בלבו, כאלו הוא עומד לפניו, בהיותו בפועל מחשבתו ועצם מעצמיו:

הראשון שבראשון הוא כלל גדול בתורה ובעבודה, וכוונת יצירת האדם לעבודת ה׳, ועיקר העבודה היא בפנימיות הנקודה ושמירה שבלב

[1] So in first two editions. Some later eds. read חשוקת. The word in the text is a common Zoharistic term.

absorption, which no preoccupation invades. This degree is not reached by one in a thousand of those who are weighed down by human cares. They may understand the meaning of the words which they utter, and yet fail to attain to the love which should accompany them. Therefore, on all happenings, write for yourselves some new prayer, keeping it, however, carefully within lawful lines. Let it be pieced together from verses of the Psalms; make particular use of the 119th.[2] He who is incapable of doing this, shall pray in German from the depth of his heart.

Similarly, none of you shall omit, after the morning prayer, to pray in German[3], with especial reference to those needs which are most regularly felt. Let each of you pray to God for a contrite and understanding heart, from which ill-will and envy shall be far. Let each pray for sustenance, that it may be won honestly without the crushing anxiety which drives out higher things. Above all, let each pray for loyalty and virtue in his offspring, for power to avoid sin. Let him pray that God may implant in his heart the love of Him, and in his home peace. And a petition shall be made that prayer itself be free from carnal and foul thoughts,

[2] Lit. "the eight-fold"; the 119th Psalm, with its eight lines to every letter of the Hebrew alphabet, is so called in T. B. Ber. 4b. As will be seen from the passage quoted in the Hebrew note, the author was a strong advocate of the study of Hebrew.

[3] By "German" the author means the Judeo-German dialect.

והיא התפלה, בלי מחשבה ופניה אחרת. ולזה לא ישיג אחד מאלף מאותן הטרודים בטרדת אנושית. אף כי ישיגו מחשבות פירוש המלות לא ישיגו אהבה עמו. ולכן על כל דבר אשר יקרה אתכם ח"ו במקרה תכתבו לכם איזה תפלה חדשה, ותראו בה שלא תהא נגד הדין, ותהא מקובצת מפסוקי תהלים ובפרטות מפסוקי תמניא אפי: ומי שאינו בר הכי יסדר תפלתו בלשון אשכנז מעומק הלב:

וכן כל אחד לא ימנע עצמו לאחר תפלתו שחרית להתפלל בלשון אשכנז[2] דוקא על הבקשות הצריכות לו תמיד, בכל יום ובכל עת ובכל שעה: שיתן לכם השם ב"ה לב מוכנע[3] ומושכל בלי קנאת החברים, ויסיר השם הקנאה הרעה מלבבכם. וכן על הפרנסה בהיתר ובלי טרדה גדולה שמבטלת מן התורה מכל וכל[4]. ושלא יצא מכם פורץ וחוטא ח"ו. וישמרכם מכל חטא ועון. ויטע בלבבכם אהבת ה' ושלום בית ומחשבת התפלה בלי מחשבת

[2] The author elsewhere in this same Testament commands, be it noted, מאוד הזהרו בני בבניכם ללמדם ספר ושידעו היטב לשון הקודש.

[3] So the first ed. The second reads מוכנת.

[4] Some eds. place the stop two words higher.

that good progress may be made in the study of the Torah. But each of you can choose the exact terms of his own supplication.

Every day a different form of words must be used, lest by familiarity the prayers lose their spontaneity. The real end of these prayers is not the petitions they contain, but the act of petition, the act of praying with genuine emotion. This is the true service, this the true recognition of the sovereignty of Him to whom prayer is addressed, and to whom belongs the power of answering. In other words, prayer is an aspiration for that purity of heart which shall inspire the service of God in love and reverence. Nor will God withhold this happiness from him who seeks it without intermission.

חמדת המשגל והרהורים רעים. ויתן לכם זכירה טובה בתורה. וכל אחד יכול לברך כהנה וכהנה:

והנה בכל יום יתפלל בסדר אחר, כדי שלא יהיה מורגל בסדר אחד, למען תבוא מעומק הלב שלא תהא עיקר המכוון על השאלות הדברים האלה, כי אם להתפלל מעומק הלב כי זאת היא העבודה גמורה ונתינת הממשלה אליו אשר לו התפלה ובעל היכולת למלאות הבקשות: ועיקר התפלה שיתן לו השם יתברך לב טהור לעבודתו בדחילא ורחימא. כי לא ימנע השם הטוב לכל הדורשים אותו תמיד:

COUNSELS OF A MYSTIC

FROM THE TESTAMENT OF MOSES ḤASID.

He that feareth, and trembleth at the word of the Lord, should take his chief meal not at night but at mid-day. At night, he should eat only a small quantity of bread and meat, or something else as a light repast. After partaking of this, he should proceed to read aloud some folios of the Talmud, satisfying himself with his toil in the Torah.

The abstinences imposed on the High Priest[1] on the eve of the Day of Atonement, lay thou upon thyself on the eve of every day throughout the year. More precious is this course than pearls. Be not like those who deny themselves flesh on week-days, but compound for their asceticism by eating cereal and other vegetable dishes so heavily that their sleep is coarsened, and they lose more than they gain. Assuredly, not for such persons did the Lion[2] advise abstention from animal food!

Read the Shema' on retiring to rest, making use of the directions of Luria.[3] 'Tis a ladder[4]

[1] Mishnah Yoma 1.4.

[2] Isaac Luria, sur-named the "lion" from the initials of the "Holy Rabbi Israel". Cf. Schechter, *Studies in Judaism*, ii, 251 ff.

[3] Directions as to devotion, ritual and spiritual. They are printed in many editions of the prayer-book.

[4] A common Zoharistic symbol for prayer, derived from Jacob's vision (Gen. 28.12).

לקוטים מצואת ר' משה החסיד

הירא וחרד לדבר ה' לא ישים עיקר אכילתו בלילה, רק באמצע היום. ובלילה יאכל מעט רק לחם כביצה אחת או שתים או מעט יותר עם בשר או שאר דבר קל. ואח"כ ילמוד איזה דפין גמרא בקול רם, כדי שיהיה שבע ויגע בדברי תורה:

וממה שכהן גדול היה נזהר בי"כ, אתה ג"כ תהא זהיר לעת ערב בכל השנה, כי יקרה היא מפנינים. ולא כאותן שאין אוכלים בשר בחול, ועל ידי זה אוכלים דברים מקמח ושאר תבשילין עד שבטנם נתמלא[1] ובאים לידי קרי. ויצא שכרם בהפסדם. בודאי לא על אלו אמר האר"י ז"ל להזהר מן הבשר:

תקרא ק"ש[2] על מטתך, ובפרט ק"ש של האר"י ז"ל. הוא סולם מוצב ארצה להעלות נשמתך

[1] Some eds. מלא. [2] D יקרא...מטתו. These variations between second and third persons are frequent in the versions of Testaments and are also common in one and the same version, as in this very paragraph in D, which begins in the third and ends in the second person.

set up on earth for thy soul's ascent on high, especially if the words are accompanied with copious tears. Tears are a strong deterrent against the soul's distraction mid the vanities of the world. Rather will it make its way upwards, returning to thee strong in the fear of the Lord, like a new creature.[5] "New every morning, great is Thy faithfulness."[6]

Ritual ablution is a most important discipline, and Luria, who has much to say on the subject, points out that for the comprehension of the divine mysteries nothing so avails as ablution and ritual cleanliness at all times.

As regards prayer, I counsel limitation to set forms as contained in the prayer-books. It is not desirable to recite many additional supplications.[7] They monopolize the time which should be devoted to the study of the Torah. Even at the midnight exercises,[8] I prefer to pray the less so as to read the more.

The study of the Torah must be regular. Over and over again repeat what you learn. It must be a table ever laid[9]; at this meal be not sparing; your teeth must be always ready to masticate the words of the Torah, as the millstone is ready to grind the grain. I need not

[5] Cf. p. 299 below.

[6] Lam. 3.23. Cf. Midrash, *ad loc.*

[7] This refers less to the extensive prayers advocated by Jonah Landsofer (above, p. 287), than to the many additions found in some rites.

[8] These were much developed under Lurian influence.

[9] Or render: That thy study may always be well-

למעלה. ובפרט אם תבכה הרבה, שזו סבה גדולה שלא תשוט נשמתך בהבלי עולם. רק תעלה למעלה, ותחזור אצלך חזקה ליראת ה׳ כבריה חדשה. וכמו שכתוב חדשים לבקרים וגו׳:

טבילה, הרי[3] היא דבר גדול מאוד ובשם האר״י ז״ל שמאריך בענין השגה אין דבר מועיל כמו הטבילה והטהרה בכל עת:...

בעניני התפלות, אומר אני להתפלל רק מה שמסודרים בסידורים. דהיינו מיהי רצון שני עד אחר עלינו... ולא להרבות בשארי תחנונים. כדי שלא תבטל מתורתך. ואפילו בתקון חצות אני מקצר מאוד עבור הלימוד:

בעניני התורה, עסוק תמיד בתורה. וחזור מאוד מאוד על למודך. כדי שיהיה למודך ערוך לפניך. מאד אני מזהירך בזה בכל עת ורגע לא תנוח ולא תשקוט מתורתך. ויהיו השינים שלך מוכנים תמיד לטחון דברי תורה. כמו שאבן הרחיים מוכן לטחון החיטים:...

[3] D adds טבילת קרי.

---

ordered before thee. Repetition was held to be a highly important aid to study.

admonish you to keep all your books well under cover. Yet, as I have seen some persons neglectful as to this precaution, I add this warning:[10]

Never allow anger to master thee. A father must guard himself against hasty temper in his treatment of his children and household. On the Sabbath, particularly, he must be very patient in his home, lest he destroy the Sabbath rest which should pervade his heart. It is a wise habit not to reprove a child immediately on the offence. Better wait till irritation has been replaced by serenity. Let melancholy and passion, born of spleen and bile,[11] be banished from all hearts on the Sabbath day. Happy the lot of those who succeed! For, while irreverence obstructs the reception of the Face of the Shekinah, anger is a yet greater obstructive.

Gloom, as Luria urged, is a reprehensible frame of mind; it is a barrier to the comprehension of the divine mysteries. So our Sages declared[12] it altogether unlawful to pray in a state of grief, for eager cheerfulness is the disposition in which a servant should minister to his master. The only part of the liturgy to which sorrow is appropriate is the confession of sins. Therefore habituate thyself to the casting out of melancholy from thy heart. Yet let not Fear of God be forgotten because of the strength of Love of Him. Love and Fear should be yoke-fellows.

[10] For this care of books, cf. p. 80f. above.

[11] *Tikkunim* 48.

[12] T. B. Ber. 31a.

איני צריך להזהירך לשים כל ספריך כלי בתוך כלי. אלא שראיתי מקצת בני אדם שמקילים בזה על כן הוי זהיר בזה:...

בענין הכעס, אני מזהירך שלא תכעוס כלל... וכן על בניו ועל בני ביתו ובשבת צריך להשים על לב לסבול יותר מבניו ובני ביתו שלא להשבית שמירת שבת בלבו. וטוב מאד שלא להוכיחם תיכף בעשייתם. אלא אחר זמן קצת[4] שכבר נתבטל ההקפדה מלבו ובנחת[5]. שלא יקרב אל הלב עציבו דטחול וכעס דמרה בשבת וזכאה חולקי' כמו שאמר הזהר... אפילו הליצנות שאינו מקבל פני השכינה אומר אני שהכעס גדול ממנו:...

העצבות, אמר האר"י ז"ל שמדת העצבות מגונה ובפרט להשגה... ואמרו[6] עוד שאסור להתפלל בעצבות כלל, אלא בשמחה גדולה, וכעבד המשרת לרבו בשמחה גדולה. זולת בהזכרת הוודוי או בהזכרת העון... ע"כ תרגיל עצמך לדחות העצבות מלבך... רק שלא תשכח היראה מכח האהבה,... ויהיו האהבה והיראה צמודים:...

[4] So D. Some eds. omit. [5] D ובנחת.

[6] D ואמר as though the sayings were Luria's.

I like to support an idea of mine on the text: "The word is very nigh unto thee, in thy mouth, and in thy heart, that thou mayest do it."[13] On this phraseology I base the thought that the precepts must be fulfilled in three several ways. *In thy mouth*—this refers to the study of the precepts.[14] *In thy heart*, that refers to the antecedent determination of the heart to perform the precepts when the time comes. *That thou mayest do them*, this obviously refers to the actual performance. These three aspects combine to make up a perfect fulfilment, and they correspond to the faculty which, also under three aspects, is termed breath, spirit, soul. The term *in thy heart* occupies the middle, applying backwards to study and forwards to performance. Of a verity, in all things the Merciful demands the heart![15]

I cannot refrain from reminding thee that in the prayers which thou utterest it is essential to associate thyself with all the sons of Israel. This is a rule oft formulated by the Rabbis.[16] It is in fact this merging of one's personality in the congregation that makes prayer unselfish. It shows that the worshipper is not speaking and begging for everything solely to his own advantage and happiness. In the *Tikkunim* the point is insisted on at great length.[17] "And he saw that

[13] Deut. 30.41.

[14] Cf. Josh. 1.8.

[15] T. B. Sanh. 106b.

[16] T. B. Ber. 6. Cf. *Book of the Pious*, 533, and cf. commentaries on O. H. § 116.

הנה נראה לי להסמיך על הפסוק בפיך ובלבבך לעשותו, שהמצות ראויות לנו לקיים בג' אופנים פרטיים. בפיך, שהוא לימוד המצות, ובלבבך, שיתן אל לבו לקיים המצוה גם קודם שתבא המצוה לידו... לעשותו, היא עשיית המצוה. בג' אופנים אלו האדם שלם. וכנגד ג' חלקים רוח נשמה ונפש שיש לנשמה:... ומלת ובלבבך באמצעי. לרמז שעולה לכאן ולכאן... ובכל דבר רחמנא לבא בעי:...

לא אמנע מלהזכירך שבתפלה שאתה מתפלל שתשתתף עצמך בתוך בני ישראל כנודע מדברי[7] חז"ל מכמה מקומות. וגם זה מורה על לשמה. שאינו[8] מדבר ומבקש הכל להנאת ולטובת עצמו בלבד. ובתקונים הפליג מאוד בענין זה, ויורא כי אין איש

[7] Eds. דברי. [8] D שאינה.

---

[17] The *Tikkunim* or *Tikkune ha-Zohar* (*J.E.*, xii, 691) are much beloved by Ḥasid. The passages here quoted are much abbreviated from the Tikkune ha-Zohar, §§ 21, 24, 25, and particularly the Zohar ha-Ḥadash § 11. The translation slightly deviates from the text in the direction of closer adhesion to the original in the *Tikkunim*.

there was no man...but everyone turneth to his own way."[18] Everyone, on the Day of Atonement, cries: "Give us life, give us sustenance, give us pardon and atonement! Inscribe us for life! O greedy pack of whining dogs. Not one cries for the spirit which brings God's Presence to the earth." And again, using the same comparison, the *Tikkunim* complains, "They cry like dogs: Give, give! they are unsatiated like Gehinnom, which cries: Give, give! as it is written, Destruction hath two daughters who cry, Give, give![19] Give us the wealth of this world, Give us the wealth of the world to come! misinterpreting the saying: Learn much Torah, and much reward will be given to you hereafter."[20] Whence we clearly see that one who acts to gain future reward is not of those who serve from pure motives. To return to our former point. 'Tis a serious matter. For, beyond a doubt, he who fails to sympathize with the sorrows of the Congregation of Israel, when praying: 'May the Lord bless His people Israel,' shows by this indifference that he has regard neither for the glory of God nor for the honor of Israel, the Lord's people, of whom it is said: Ye are children of the Lord your God, while it is said further: "Is Ephraim a darling child unto Me? My heart yearneth for him."[21] There is no profanation of the Name greater than this! A people unique in its acceptance of the God-

[18] Ps. 59.16; Is. 53.6.

[19] Cf. Abodah Zarah, 17a, commenting on Prov. 30.15.

[20] Mishnah Abot, 2 end.

[21] Deut. 14.1; Jer. 31.20.

אלא איש לדרכו פונה. וכולהון צוחין בצלותיהן ביומא דכפורא הב לן חייא! הב לן מזונא, סליחה, וכפרה! כתבנו לחיים! ואינון עזי נפש ככלבין דצווחין, ולית להו בושת אנפין, דלית מאן דקרא לתיוביתא ע"ש. ועוד בתקונים בִמקום אחר וז"ל. וצווחין ככלבין דאמרי הב הב! כגוונא דגיהנם דצווח הב הב! הה"ד לעלוקה שתי בנות הב הב! הב לן עותרא דעלמא דין והב לן עותרא דעלמא דאתי. כמה דאוקמי למוד תורה הרבה ויתנו לך שכר הרבה עכ"ל. משמע להדיא אפילו מי שעושה בשביל שכר עולם הבא לא מיקרי עובד לשמה... וזה שזכרנו הוא דבר גדול. שבלי ספק מי שאינו נותן אל לב צערן של כנסת ישראל, פי' צערן של ישראל בכלל ה' יברך את עמו ישראל, מורה שאינו חס על כבוד המקום ועם ה' שעליהם נאמר בנים אתם לה' ונאמר הבן יקיר לי אפרים. אין לך חילול השם גדול מזה. שאומה יחידה בקבלת אלהותו[9]

[9] So D; some eds. אלהות.

head and of the divine Law, is given over to the world's scorn, and lives in low estate. Assuredly, he who is not pained to the heart over this, who does not suffer in his every limb and sinew woe unto such a one! Yet he forsooth pours out plenteously his prayers for his own welfare, and has no shame, but puts out of sight all concern for the tribulations of Israel, of whom the Prophet said: "In all their afflictions He was afflicted." He refuses to sympathize with the sorrow of the King who is pained at his son's sufferings—such a man deserves to be classed with the greedy of soul!

And know, my beloved! that I oft ask myself: With what shall I come before the Lord, how lift up my face in the presence of my Maker? My iniquities rise over my head, as a heavy burden are they upon me. And we, of this age, are weaklings; too feeble to fast, too frail for penance, unable to endure frequent ablutions. But, I bethink myself, (how Luria has said) that the admonitions written by earlier and later moralists, with their ascetic rites severe as snow, were meant for those whose occupations did not permit them to apply themselves constantly to the Torah. But he who has the knowledge and fear of God, which are the true means of setting one's heart right, must not weaken his body nor interrupt his studies. Only one day in every week he may remove himself from the society of other men, and pass his hours alone in the near Presence of his Maker. His every thought will be bound up in Him, as though he stood before Him on the Day of Judgment. Then will he speak to the blessed God, as a child speaks to his father, and withal as a servant to his Master!

ותורתו, נתונה ללעג ולביזה ולשפלות. ובודאי מי שאין לו כאב על זה בלבו ברמ"ח איבריו ושס"ה גידיו חבל ליה. ועוד מרבה הכל בתפלה לטובת עצמו. ואין לו בושת פנים. ומעביר מלפניו צערן של ישראל שע"ז אמר הנביא בכל צרתם לו צר. והוא מעביר מלפניו צער המלך כי יעציב המלך על בנו והוא שאינו מצער בצער המלך ובניו בודאי מכת עזי נפש הוא:

ודע אהובי! שנתתי אל לבי במה אקדם לה' ובמה אשא פני לפני קוני על שעונותי עברו ראשי כמשא כבד. ואנחנו חלושי כח ואין אנו יכולין להתענות ולסגף עצמינו בסיגופים וטבילות... והנה כל מה שתמצא בדברי ראשונים והאחרונים תוכחות על עון וסיגופין ויסורים קשים כשלג לא נזכרו אלא למי שאין עמלו בתורה ואין תורתו אומנתו. אבל למי שיודע דעת ויראת ה' כי זאת היא תקנתם לא יחלוש גופו ולא יתבטל בלמודו. אך יום אחד בשבוע[10] יתרחק מן בני אדם ויתבודד בינו לבין קונו. ותתקשר מחשבתו בו כאלו עומד לפניו ביום הדין. וידבר לאל יתברך כבן אל אביו וכעבד אל רבו:

[10] D מן השבועה.

מספר צואות ריב"ש

IN DEFIANCE OF DESPONDENCY
FROM THE TESTAMENT OF
ISRAEL BAALSHEM

XIX

IN DEFIANCE OF DESPONDENCY

From the Testament of Israel Baalshem

The founder of the modern sect of Ḥasidim, Israel son of Eleazar, was born in 1700, and died in Miedzyboz on May 22, 1760 (*J. E.*, ii, 383). He is familiarly known as Besht, i. e. Baal Shem-tob. His career, with its mixture of fact and legend in the reports, is brilliantly told by S. Schechter in *Studies in Judaism* I, pp. 1–55.

An interesting romantic picture is drawn by I. Zangwill in the "Master of the Name" in his *Dreamers of the Ghetto*. The selection printed in this volume is characteristic of Besht's position. Besht did not attack the rabbinic scheme of righteousness under the Law, but he refused to regard Law as the end. The end, according to him, was union with God, the realization that life is a divine manifestation, and that every act, whether "material" or "religious," performed under that realization, is a sanctification of the soul.

The "Testament of Besht" is printed in ספר צוואות ריב"ש והנהגות ישרות, Zolkiew, 1820. See also E. Z. Zweifel's שלום על ישראל, 1868.

These Testamentary directions are taken from the literary remains of Isaiah of Janova, as having been derived from verbal communications by the Besht, with additions from the rules of Baer of Meseritz and of Isaac Luria. Mystical ideas on the soul's perfection are found here; also

יט

מספר צואות ריב״ש

מיסד כת החסידים החדשה, ישראל בן אליעזר, נולד בשנת ת״ס ונפטר במעזיבוז ביום ז׳ סיון תק״ך (עיין באנציקלו־פדיה היהודית האנגלית, כרך שני, דף שפ״ג). הוא נתפרסם תחת השם בעש״ט, זאת אומרת בעל שם טוב. תולדותיו, המעורבבות מעובדות ואגדות בפי השמועה, נכתבו בטוב טעם ודעת ע״י שלמה שכטר בספרו Studies in Judaism, כרך ראשון, דף א׳–נ״ה.

תמונה רומנטית מרהיבה ממנו צייר ישראל זאנגוויל בספורו „בעל השם״ בספרו „חולמי הגטו״. הלקוטים הנדפסים בכרך שלפנינו הם מפתח לנקודת ההשקפה של הבעש״ט. הבעש״ט לא לחם נגד רעיון הצדק והיושר של הרבנים כפי שהוא מוכח מן התורה, אבל הוא לא רצה להביט על התורה כמו תכלית בפני עצמה. לפי דבריו התכלית היא דבקות והזדווגות אל הבורא יתברך, ההוכחה שחיי האדם הם הופעה אלהית ושכל מעשה, חמרי או דתי, הנעשה תחת ההוכחה הזאת מטהר ומקדש את הנפש.

„צוואת בעש״ט״ נדפסה ב„ספר צוואות ריב״ש והנהגות ישרות״, זאלקיעוו תק״ף. עיין גם ב„שלום על ישראל״ של אליעזר צבי צווייפעל, זיטאמיר תרכ״ח.

דברי הצואה הזאת לקוחים מן העזבון הספרותי של ישעיה מיאנאווא, אשר קבל אותם מן הבעש״ט בשיחותיו עמו פה אל פה, ונוספו עליהם הוספות מן ההנהגות של בער ממעזעריטש ויצחק לוריה. יש פה רעיונות מיסתיים ע״ד

discussions of penances and solitude; fasting before prayer; in that prayer is a yielding up of the soul; bodily survival after prayer is an act of loving-kindness on the part of God; bodily health necessary for due worship; reverence of God essential as a safeguard to the familiarity of love. There is an urgent plea for the service of God at all times and in all conditions, and a strong protest against despair under a consciousness of sin.

Some of the wills take indeed a sombre view, and (as in Elijah of Wilna's) the text is the "Vanity of Vanities" of Ecclesiastes. Life, he says, is like a draught of salt water, its pleasures seem to quench, but they really inflame thirst. To-day's smile is to-morrow's tear. But this sombreness is not despair; it is merely the foil to the true happiness induced by a life of virtue.

I am indifferent to the world's call, and this is the meaning of the text Ps. 16.8.[1] If I possess the quality of equanimity I know that my one objective is God. Equanimity of this type is acquired by absorption in God, for the effort towards this end leaves no room for lower aspirations. So he who serves the Creator continuously has no leisure for vain pride . . . Similarly, if the vision of a beautiful woman come suddenly to a man's eyes, or if he perceive any other fair and lovely thing, he should unhesitatingly ask himself: Whence comes this beauty except from the divine force which permeates the world? Consequently the origin of this beauty is divine,

[1] The author plays upon the word שויתי, Ps. 16.8, to which he gives the sense of "liken", "make equal." Hence he derives the idea of 'equanimity.'

השתלמות הנפש, עיונים במיני תשובה והתבודדות, חקירות ע״ד צום לפני התפלה, כי תפלה הוא הכנעת הנפש, השארת הגוף אחר התפלה הוא מעשה חסד ורחמים מצד הבורא יתברך, בריאות הגוף נחוצה לעבודת הבורא, הערצת אלהים היא כתריס בפני קרבת אהבה. המחבר דורש עבודת הבורא בכל שעה ובכל מקרה ומוחא מחאה עזה כנגד יאוש הבא לרגלי הכרת עוון.

יש צוואות העומדות על נקודת־השקפה נוגה ועצובה, וכל דבריהן (כמו בצואת אליהו מווילנא) סובבים על „הבל הבלים״ של קהלת. „העולם הזה״, הוא אומר, „דומה לשותה מים מלוחים: ידמה לו שמרוה צמאונו והוא צמא יותר״. השחוק של היום הוא הדמעה של יום המחרת. אכן האספקלריה הכהה הזאת איננה יאוש; כמו בדבר והפכו היא באה רק להטעים ולהדגיש את האושר האמתי הבא לרגלי חיי צדק ויושר.

שויתי ה׳ לנגדי תמיד. שויתי לשון השתוות. ומכיון שיש לי מדה זו אצלי, אז יודע אני שה׳ נגדי תמיד: ודבר הגורם לזה הוא הדביקות, שמחמת טרדות הדביקות אין לו פנאי לחשוב בדברים תחתונים וכשעובד את הבורא תמיד אין לו פנאי להתגאות:..וכן כשתבוא ליד האדם בפתע פתאום הסתכלות בפני אשה יפה, או שארי דברים נאים ויפים שבעולם, יחשוב מיד מניין זה היופי אם לא מכח אלהי המתפשט בעולם? ונמצא ששורש

and why should I be attracted by the part? Better for me to be drawn after the All, the Source of every partial beauty! If a man taste something good and sweet, let the taster conceive that it is from the heavenly sweetness that the sweet quality is derived. Such perception of beauty then is an experience of the Eternal, blessed be He . . .Further if he hear some amusing story and he derives pleasure from it, let him bethink himself that this is an emanation from the realm of Love . .

Every man must devote all his capabilities to the service of God, for all things are intended to serve God. Under no circumstances of life must this service be intermitted. For instance, a man may be walking and talking with other men, and he cannot then be studying the Torah. None the less must he on those occasions cleave close to God, in full consciousness of His uniqueness. Or the man may be on a journey, and thus unable to pray in his usual fashion. At such times he must find a mode of service other than prayer. Let him not allow this to oppress his spirit, for God's will it is that service of Him takes now one form, now another. Accordingly, when starting on a journey, or entering on converse with his friends, he should hold himself ready to serve in relation to the opportunity. For a man, wherever he is or whatsoever he does, must concentrate his thoughts on the Shekinah, full of love for her, yearning for her love. And his recurrent thought must be: "When shall I be worthy of the indwelling in me of the Light of the Divine Presence?"

היופי הוא למעלה. ואם כן למה לי להיות נמשך אחרי החלק? טוב לי להמשך אחרי הכל, שהוא שורש ומקור כל היפויים החלקיים. וכן כשטועם טעם טוב ומתוק, יחשוב שמתיקת של מעלה הוא הוא הכח המחיה זה. והסתכלות כזו היא ההסתכלות באין סוף ב"ה:...וכן אם שומע איזה דבר שחוק, ועל ידי זה נולדה לו שמחה, יחשוב הלא זה חלק מעולם אהבה:

וכל האדם צריך לעבוד הש"ת בכל כחו שהכל הוא צורך גבוה.מפני שהש"ת רוצה שיעבדו אותו בכל האופנים. והכוונה כי לפעמים אדם הולך ומדבר עם בני אדם. ואז אינו יכול ללמוד. וצריך להיות דבוק בש"ת ולייחד ייחודים. וכן כשאדם הולך בדרך ואינו יכול להתפלל וללמוד כדרכו וצריך לעבוד אותו באופנים אחרים: ואל יצער את עצמו בזה כי הש"ת רוצה שיעבדוהו בכל האופנים. פעמים באופן זה ופעמים באופן זה. לכן הזדמן לפניו לילך לדרך או לדבר עם בני אדם בכדי לעבוד אותו באופן הב':... ויתבודד תמיד מחשבתו עם השכינה שלא יחשוב רק באהבתו אותה תמיד שהיא תדבק בו. ויאמר תמיד במחשבתו מתי אזכה שישכון עמי אור השכינה:...

Sometimes the evil yezer[2] betrays a man, persuading him that he has committed a deadly sin.[3] Possibly he has failed in some stringency of the law, possibly he had done no wrong at all. The yezer's purpose is to drive him into despondency over the supposed lapse, and by inducing a condition of gloom render him incapable of service. Let man beware of this dastardly trick! Let him retort on the yezer: "I perceive thy design to lure me from service. Thou speakest a lie! If indeed I have sinned a little, the more gratified will my Creator be if I refuse to let my offence interrupt the joyousness of my service. On the contrary, I will go on serving Him in a happy mood. For I serve not for my own ends but to give God pleasure. If I do not worry about this peccadillo, with which thou chargest me, God will not take it amiss. For I ignore it, that my service be not stayed for a single instant." This is the great rule of service: Bid melancholy, avaunt!

Weeping is an exceeding great evil,[4] for man must serve in joy. If, however, weeping comes through joy, then is it an exceeding great good.

Therefore let a man desist from anxiety as to his conduct, for such an attitude is produced by the yezer's plot to overawe him, to make him

[2] On the evil inclination or impulse, see *J.E.*, xii, 601.

[3] Cf. Schechter, *Studies in Judaism*, 1, 39.

[4] Other mystics took another view. Thus in his Testament Moses Hasid writes: "Weeping is good at all times," § 17.

לפעמים מטעה היצר הרע לאדם ואומר לו שעבר עבירה גדולה. אע"פ שאינו אלא חומרא בעלמא או שאינה עבירה כלל. וכוונתו שיהא האדם בעצבות מכח זה ויבוטל בהעצבותו מעבודת הבורא ית'. וצריך האדם להבין הרמאות הזה. ויאמר להיצר איני משגיח על החומרא שאתה אומר שכוונתך לבטלני מעבודתו ית' ושקר אתה דובר. וגם אם היא באמת קצת חטא יותר יהיה נחת רוח לבוראי שלא אשגיח על החומרא שאתה אומר לי לגרום לי עצבות בעבודתו. אדרבא אעבוד אותו בשמחה כי זהו כלל כי אין כוונתי בעבודה לצורך עצמי רק לעשות נחת רוח לפניו ית'. ואם כן אף שלא אשגיח על החומרא שאתה אומר לא יקפיד הבורא עלי. כי כל עיקר שאיני משגיח הוא מחמת שלא אבטל מעבודתו אפילו רגע א'. וזהו כלל גדול בעבודת הבורא שיזהר מעצבות כל מה שיוכל:

הבכיה היא רעה מאוד שהאדם צריך לעבוד בשמחה. רק אם הבכיה היא מחמת שמחה אז טובה היא מאוד:

ואל ירבה בדקדוקים יתרים בכל דבר שעושה שזה כוונת היצר לעשות לאדם מורא שמא אינו

despair of fully accomplishing his duty. A sure hindrance to service is this despair! Has a man really stumbled? Let him not yield overmuch to paralyzing grief. Let him indeed sigh for his sin, but then let him turn again in joy to the Creator, blessed be He!

יוצא בדבר זה. כדי להביא אותו לעצבות. ועצבות היא מניעה גדולה לעבודת הבורא ית'. ואפילו נכשל בעבירה לא ירבה בעצבות שיבטל העבודה. רק שיעצב על העבירה ויחזור לשמוח בהבורא ית':

דבר צוה ההוא סבא אליהו הלוי ס"ט בכמהר"ר רפאל שלמה סג"ל מעכשיו ולאחר מיתה

ELIJAH DE VEALI TO HIS CHILDREN FROM THE TESTAMENT OF ELIJAH SON OF RAPHAEL DE VEALI

XX

ELIJAH DE VEALI TO HIS CHILDREN

FROM THE TESTAMENT OF ELIJAH SON OF RAPHAEL DE VEALI.

Alessandria, in North Italy, was the site of a Jewish settlement after the expulsion of the Jews from Spain in 1492 (See *J. E.*, i, 340). The community rarely enjoyed tranquillity until it received equal and political rights in 1848. Yet, throughout the troubled history of the community, the Rabbis were not wanting in distinction.

Elijah the Levite, son of Raphael Solomon, surnamed Saba (according to *J. E.* the family assumed the name De Veali, beginning with Elijah), held the position of Rabbi in Alessandria between the years 1738 and 1792. Nepi tells us that he was associated in his studies with Lampronti; they certainly worked together under Rabbi Judah Briel of Mantua. Elijah had something of a reputation as a wonder-worker and visionary. But he also has more solid claims to fame. He was a poet, and many of his Marriage Odes have been published (See Zedner, p. 231). He was a Cabbalist, and an authority on rabbinic law; some of his Responsa are quoted.

His Testament is a very long, elaborate, and valuable treatise. He gives full directions for the funeral, and enters into many erudite disquisitions on subjects connected with death and repentance. He says much that is worthy of attention on the general principles of the moral life. His Testament has never been printed. The editor of the present volume possesses the author's original autograph

כ

דבר צוה ההוא סבא אליהו הלוי ס"ט בכמהר"ר רפאל שלמה סג"ל מעכשיו ולאחר מיתה

אלסנדריה באיטליה הצפונית היתה מקום מושב יהודים אחרי גלות ספרד בשנת רנ"ב (עיין באנציקלופדיה היהודית האנגלית, כרך ראשון, דף ש"ם). הקהלה הזאת היתה שקטה ושלוה רק לעתים רחוקות, עד אשר קבלה זכיות מדיניות שוות בשנת תר"ח. אבל למרות הפורעניות הרבות שעברו עליה מיום הוסדה הצטיינה ברבנים מצוינים ומפורסמים.

אליהו הלוי בן רפאל שלמה המכונה סבא (לפי האנציקלופדיה היהודית האנגלית בחרה המשפחה בשם De Veali מימיו של אליהו) שמש בכתר הרבנות באלסנדריה משנת תצ"ח עד שנת תקנ"ב. נעפי מודיענו שהיה חבר ללמפרונטי בלמודיו; בכל אופן ברור הוא שעבדו יחד תחת השגחת רבי יהודה בריעל ממנטובה. אליהו היה נודע בתור בעל נס והוזה הזיות. אבל גם במקצועות יותר מוחשים ומוצקים נתפרסם שמו. הוא היה פיטן, ורבים משירי הארוסין שלו יצאו לאור עולם (ראה רשימת צדנר, דף רל"א); גם היה מקובל ובר סמכא בהלכות הרבנים, ואחדות מתשובותיו מובאות בספרי שאלות ותשובות.

צואת אליהו היא חבור ארוך מאוד, מעובד ומפורט, ויש לה ערך רב. הוא מסדר את כל הפרטים של הלויה ומתעמק בחקירות חריפות ע"ד ענינים הקשורים במות ותשובה. גם על היסודות הכלליים של חיי המוסר הוא משמיע הרבה הראוי לתשומת לב. הצואה הזאת לא נדפסה עוד. יש לי כ"י ממנה

of the Testament; there is a clean copy, also apparently autograph, in the Bodleian (Cat. Neubauer, No. 2590). Neubauer (p. 1130) describes its contents as "ethical, casuistical, and kabbalistical." This is a fair characterization. A bundle of letters (chiefly in Italian) by members of the family, including Elijah, is also in the Bodleian collection (No. 2595).

In the course of his Testament, Elijah twice quotes the "Short Will" of Benjamin Cohen Vitali, who forbade any funeral oration in his own honor, and ordered that he was to be interred in a simple linen shroud. Elijah adopts both rules for his own obsequies. He appoints as one of his executors R. Solomon Michael Jonah, Rabbi of Torino (See Mortara, *Indice*, p. 30). Elijah directs that, during the whole week of mourning, prayers are to be held with minyan in his room, and that a short passage from his Testament is to be read by his son Moses Zakut. Though Elijah wrote Italian, he used the German term Jahrzeit. He requests that from funds left by him, and to be supplied by the community, books are to be purchased annually for the Talmud Torah school. The books are to include copies of the Bible, the Shulḥan Aruk and the Menorat ha-Maor.

So far I have given directions relating to myself. Now I will put forth my hand a second time and take the wisdom of the aged;[1] to give command unto my house. "Command" means rather encouragement[2] from now onwards to my offspring, to whom I would fain bequeath

[1] Is. 11.11; Job. 12.20. The author means he will follow the olden prescription to give testamentary exhortations to his children.

[2] Sifre Num. i; Num. Rabbah 7.

בעצם ידו של המחבר; ויש עוד כ"י כזה, כנראה ג"כ בעצם ידו של המחבר, בבית עקד הספרים הבודליאני (רשימת נייבויער, נומר 2590). נייבויער (דף א' ק"ל) מתאר יפה את תכנה כמו סך־הכל של מוסר, פלפול וקבלה. חבילת מכתבים (עפ"י רוב באיטלקית) שהריצו בני המשפחה הזאת, לרבות אליהו, זה לזה נמצאת ג"כ בבית עקד הספרים הבודליאני (נומר 2595).

במשך צואתו מזכיר אליהו פעמים את „הצואה הקצרה" של בנימין כהן וויטאלי אשר אסר איזה הספד שיהיה לכבודו ויצו שיקברוהו בתכריך בד פשוט. גם אליהו מצוה כזאת בנוגע לקבורתו, והוא ממנה בתור אחד מאפוטרופסיו רבי שלמה מיכאל יונה, אב"ד בטורין (ראה מורטארא, מזכרת חכמי איטליא, דף ל'). אליהו מצוה ג"כ שבמשך שבעה ימי האבלות יתפלל מנין בחדרו ובנו משה זכות יקריא מקרא קצר מצואתו. נחוץ להעיר שאף כי אליהו כתב באיטלקית בכ"ז השתמש במלה האשכנזית „יאהרצייט". הוא דורש שמן הכספים אשר השאיר אחריו ואשר תמציא הקהלה יקנו ספרים בכל שנה ושנה בעד בית התלמוד תורה, ושבין הספרים האלה יהיו ספרי תנ"ך, „שלחן ערוך" ו„מנורת המאור".

...הן אלה קצות דרכי אשר צויתי ואשר דברתי לי לעצמי. ועתה אוסיף שנית ידי וטעם זקנים אקח. לצוות אל ביתי. אין צו אלא לשון זירוז מיד ולדורות הבאים אחרי מיוצאי חלצי. להניח ברכה

a gift over which they must stand at guard. This legacy is my exhortation to them to learn the fear of God all their days. I will make them know my testimonies, I will adorn them with crowns. For if my children ask me: What servitude is this that I require of them?[3] this shall be my answer: I am offering unto you not servitude but a Kingdom, for the righteous rules by the fear of God. Many are the messengers of God and fathers are among them; they are His partners.[4] Father telleth unto son His truth—the truth of the Torah[5], the life-giving lot of His inheritance. If I shall have executed His mission, without wavering, therein shall be my rest forever!

Come listen unto me, my children, let not your minds despise my words! I would have you hold yourselves as men hired for the day's work, saying every morning: "To-day I will be a faithful servant to the All-Master." Keep yourselves the whole day from anger, falsehood, hatred, contention, envy and incontinence. Forgive every one who troubles you. For half an hour supplicate God's aid to bring you to Repentance; do this in synagogue, this day, and on the morrow also! At least appoint one day a week for such exercise. I do not ask you to torture yourselves with fasting, although nowadays the whole world ought to repent with

[3] There are throughout this paragraph many snatches of Scriptural texts.

[4] T. B. Kidd. 30b.

[5] Or this phrase may be joined to the next clause.

אחרי. ואלה יעמדו על הברכה. את הברכה אשר ישמעו בנים מוסר אב. וילמדו ליראה את ה׳ כל הימים. ועדותי זו אלמדם ועטרות להם אענדם: והיה כי יאמרו אלי בני, מה העבודה הזאת להם. זאת אשיב אל לבם. שררה אני נותן להם. כי צדיק מושל ביראת אלהים: הרבה שלוחים למקום והאבות הן הן שלוחיו הן הן שותפיו. ואב לבנים יודיע את אמיתו, אמיתה של תורה, חבל נחלתו מחיה חיים. עשיתי שליחותו ובה׳ בטחתי לא אמעד זאת מנוחתי עדי עד:

לכו בנים שמעו לי. הטו אזניכם אלי. ואל יבוז שכליכם מילי... ותעשו עצמכם כשכירי יום, בכל יום בבקר לאמר, היום הזה אהיה עבד נאמן לאדון הכל. ושמרו עצמכם בכל אותו היום מכעס ושקר ושנאה תחרות וקנאה ומלהסתכל בנשים. ותמחלו לכל מי שיצער אתכם. ותבקשו רחמים כמו חצי שעה בבה״כ לה׳ שיעזרכם על התשובה. וכן תעשו למחרתו. ולפחות תקבעו יום א׳ לשבוע לזה. ואיני מטריד לסגוף עצמיכם בתעניות. הגם דהשתא כל בני עלמא בעלי תשובה נינהו וצריכים סיגוף ותיקון.

the sharpest rites of betterment. But it would be a fine thing if at least on Mondays and Thursdays in every week, the days on which teḥinah[6] is recited, you would limit your morning meal to a morsel of bread and water by measure, for the good of your souls and the health of your bodies, to fit yourselves for the Divine Presence and to make atonement for what you have done amiss.

Now in the forefront of my petitions is this: Show all honor to your mother, in heart, in speech, in action. And this further I entreat. Live together in love and brotherliness and friendship, dwelling if possible together in one household[7], with peace within your walls, and prosperity within your palaces.[8] And as for you, O husbands, honor your wives; and the latter shall on their part do full honor to their husbands, being to them a garland of roses, sweet flowers whose scent is of Lebanon. Be faithful shepherds of your flocks, watching your offspring, regarding their doings, wisely leading them to bask in the garden of the Lord, in which they, your young ones, shall luxuriate and flourish. And as for you, be ye in your conduct a light to their paths.

[6] The special penitential prayers added to the morning service on those days.

[7] Lit. "bond," but apparently the author means in one residence, the common rule indeed in the great Italian homes.

[8] Ps. 122.7. The conceit that follows, based on Eccl. 4. 9, is scarcely reproducible in English.

ויהי מה טוב אלו לעצתי תשמעון לפחות ביום ב׳ וה׳ שבכל שבוע בימים שאומרים בהם תחנה מה טוב לנפשכם וגם יועיל לבריאות הגוף אם תנהיגו עצמכם לאכול לחם צר ומים במשורה בסעודת הבקר. ותכונו לתיקון שכינה ולכפרת נפשכם:

והן קדם אני מבקש מכם, ואומר לכם, הזהרו בכבוד אמכם בלב בדבור ובמעשה... ואם אב אני בן יכבד אב ואלי תשמעון לישב באהבה ואחוה וריעות. ומה טוב ומה נעים שבתכם גם יחד באגודה אחת. יהי שלום בחילכם ושלוה בארמנותיכם. כי טובים השנים מן האחד ר״ל כשבאים מן האחד: ואליכם אישים אקרא. אוקירו לנשייכו והנשים יתנו יקר לבעליהם כליל לאישים. כלילא דורדי מעשה שושן ריח לו כלבנון... שימו לבבכם לעדרים וצאצאיכם לעיניכם. עיניכם על כל דרכיהם. והתבוננו מאד וראו לרעות בגנים גן נטע ה׳ בניכם כנטיעים מגודלים בנעוריהם... ואתם במעשיכם תהיו אור לנתיבותיהם:...

If your wealth increase,[9] be not proud; unto the rich, more than others, is humility becoming. They that possess most should be the most lowly, gratefully recognizing that they have their all from God. Pride oft displays itself in men's dress; avoid this form of arrogance just as ye concern yourselves with your moral excellence. Be ye attired so that you and your garments harmonize. Let your dress be righteousness, wear modest stuffs, not embroideries or gold and silver. Grace is not shown by fine feathers, but is revealed by unobtrusive bearing.

Happy will ye be, my children, my disciples, and all who attend to my counsel, if ye keep strict account of your expenditure, avoiding all superfluities, acting parsimoniously to yourselves and generously to others! And what ye save from frivolous outlays, add bountifully to your charities, and to your loans to the poor in the hour of their need. So have I read[10] of the brother of Obadiah of Bertinoro, the expounder of the Mishnah, that he was extremely rich, but lived on bare necessaries in order to support his famous brother who was settled in Jerusalem. It has been a life-long sorrow to me to behold how, on the contrary, so many, of whatever station, spend extravagantly on themselves and their own pleasures, sparing nothing on their soul's desires, but acting the most miserly part

[9] Ps. 62.11.

[10] In Conforti's *Ḳore ha-dorot.*

וחיל כי ינוב אל תשימו לב להתגאות ח"ו כי יותר מוטל לעשירים לנהוג ענוה בעשרם מאחרים. ועשירים בשפל ישבו... שלא להיות כפויי טובה להב"ה ויש להם כל:... וגם זה מן הכלל הגסות הרוח של המלבושים. ובמטותא מינייכו תרחיקו ממנו. ותשגיחו שלא יהיה א' מכם ולא שום אחד מבני בתיכם יוצא מן המוסר והנהגה טובה. ותהיו נאים בלבושכם ולבושכם נאה לכם. וצדק לבשו וילבש אתכם בצניעות. לא בגדי רקמה זהב וכסף. כי החן אינו תלוי בזה אלא בשפלות וענוה:...

ואשריכם בני תלמידי כל הסרים למשמעתי! אם תשימו בבתיכם שימת עין ותניחו המותרות ותהיו מצמצמים לעצמיכם וותרנים לזולתכם. ומה שאתם גורעים מהוצאות לדברים שאין בהם ממש תוסיפו ותרחיבו יד בצדקות ובהלוואות במשכון לעני בשעת דוחקו. כמו שמצאתי כתוב מאחיו של רבי עובדיה ברטנורה מפרש המשניות שהיה עשיר גדול ומסתפק בהכרחי לבד כדי לזון ולפרנס הגאון אחיו שהיה דר בירושלים: וכל ימי נצטערתי בראותי להיפך בני אדם גם בני איש ותרנים לעצמם ולהנאת גופם. ואינם מחסרים לנפשם מכל אשר יתאוו. וימלאו

towards others, to whom they yield no services at all; not among such should be the portion of Jacob!

Beware of entering into obligations involving suretyship. I would not have you think that I myself avoided the mistake. I acted otherwise out of my willingness to help others. Often I paid. Often I became liable to serious troubles from which God delivered me. But miracles do not happen every day, and you must not rely on them.[11] Therefore flee from the act of becoming guarantor as from a sword. Never stand surety[12] whether in written or verbal promises. And, in general, in your business transactions, examine before you sign any document or obligation whatever it be. Do not rely on the skill of the official scribe, or of any other writer. I am grateful to the cheats who opened my eyes by their wiles. And in this connection, I warn you against making promises for fulfilment at a future time. Once I promised the Collectors for the Hebron Academy[13] seven Venetian lire annually for ten years in succession. Though I distinctly inscribed in the book that I made no absolute undertaking to pay the subscription, yet I felt bound to settle the whole ten years' account at once and I received the receipt for my advance payment. So reluctant was I to assume responsibilities which would not mature till a later date.

[11] T. B. Pes. 50b, 64b. [12] T. B. Yeb. 109a.

[13] The first modern Academy (Yeshibah) was founded in Hebron in the first part of the eighteenth century (cf *J.E.*, vi, p. 312).

תאותם והם קמצנים בתכלית הקמצנות עם אחרים ומודרים הנאה מהם. לא באלה חלק יעקב:...

אזהרה גדולה וחזקה לכם בני שתרחקו מערבונות... ואל תבטחו על שקר לאמר אבינו לא עשה כן... וכוונתי היתה רצויה להיטיב לאחרים ...והרבה פעמים פרעתי. וכמה רעות עברו עלי וגדול הרועה שהצילני. ולאו כל שעתא ושעתא מתרחיש ניסא. ואין סומכין על הנס. על כן תנוסו מהערבונות כמנוסת חרב ולא בכתב ולא בע"פ... וגם אני מזהיר אתכם... שאפילו בשביל עסקיכם... תעיינו היטב קודם שתחתמו שום שטר או חיוב איך שיהיה מה שאתם חותמים. ואל תסמכו על חכמת הסופר הערכי או סופר אחר... ואני מחזיק טובה לרמאים שהאירו עיני ברמאותם:... ועל מרכז זה אני מזהיר אתכם שלא תכנסו בחיוב שום נדר או נדבה למשך זמן... ונדרתי פעם א' לישיבת חברון ע"י מעלת השלוחים נר"י ז' ליטרין ויניציאה לשנה לעשר שנים רצופים ואע"פ שכתבתי בפנקס מפורש בלא שום נדר אעפ"כ חשבתי למשפט לתת לכסף מוצא ולפרוע במעות כל העשר שנים מוקדמים וקבלתי מהם שובר ולא רציתי על שכמי נדר של אריכות זמן בכל צד:...

Similarly, with any religious duty never postpone its performance. As our Sages said, duty must be done at the earliest eligible moment.[14] So, too, if you notice in your homes anything, whether insignificant or important, which is out of order, and which by neglect may in course of time prove seriously injurious to body, soul, or property, lose no time, but at once set the matter right, whether to destroy or to overturn, to build or to plant—for sometimes one must upset so as to straighten. Thus will ye eradicate the poisonous plant before it can take root and produce its noxious fruit.[15]

Keep careful accounts, and strike an annual balance. Apply the same rule to your moral conduct, and look to it that ye strengthen the house where necessary. Search with strong lights, make search on search—use light on light to pry into all the crevices of your soul[16], and make haste to ascend to your Father in Heaven with Prayer, Repentance, and Charity...

Love work, hate lordship[17], and the idleness which tires more than toil itself. No rest excels that derived from labor in the Torah and in affairs of real import. Be ye kings, not slaves to your passions, rulers over your own spirit. True is the epigram[18]: questioning is the half

[14] T. B. Pes. 3a.

[15] Deut. 29.17.

[16] Cf. Pesiḳta Rab. ch. 8, on Zeph. 12; see also Ps. 64.7.

[17] Abot, i.10.

[18] *Choice of Pearls*, ch. i (beginning).

וכן בכל דבר מצוה אל תאחרו כמשז״ל לעולם יקדים אדם לדבר מצוה... ואם תראו בבתיכם איזה דבר קטון או גדול בלא סדרים שיוכל ח״ו בהמשך הזמן להיות גרמא בנזיקין לגוף או לנפש או לממון מהרה חושו מעשיכם לתקן הענין להאביד ולהרוס לבנות ולנטוע. כלומר לקלקל על מנת לתקן. ותשחיתו השרש פורה ראש קודם שישתרש ויעשה פרי:

והזהרו אתם בני ידידי לעשות חשבוניכם... מדי שנה בשנה:.. וגם כן בכל שנה ושנה תראו מה מעשיכם ותביאו חשבון לבדוק ולחזק את הבית... ועל הכל חפשו בנרות חיפוש מחיפוש ונר מנר בבתי הנפש ומהרו ועלו אל אבינו שבשמים בתפילה תשובה וצדקה:..

אהבו את המלאכה ושנאו את הרבנות והבטלה שהיא מיגעת יותר מהיגיעה עצמה. ואין מנוחה יותר גדולה מהיגיעה בתורה ובדברים של ממש:... ואתם תהיו ממלכת ואל תהיו כעבדים כפופים ומשועבדים ליצר ותמשלו ברוחכם... באמת אמרו השאלה חצי

of wisdom. But questions may be inept, for inquisitiveness in itself is impudence. Judge ye therefore truly in your minds whether the question is a suitable one. But put not this restriction on yourselves with regard to matters connected with religion. There are no boundaries on high; never hesitate to ask where the acquisition of virtue is concerned, but ask without stint, bring your empty vessels not a few, seek ye righteousness, seek ye humility, and the Lord will not withhold good from you!

If ye render a kindness to any man, do not recurrently remind him of it. This is a despicable habit. It is comparable to the son who feeds his father on dainties, yet inherits Gehinnom.[19] So was Nehemiah punished—his Book not being named after him[20]—because of his boast: "Remember unto me, O God, for good, all that I have done for this people." But fix ye this maxim in your hearts: Do what you say, but say not what you do!

[19] T. J. Kidd. 1.7. The son fed his father on choice poultry, but did it with insults; hence his condemnation.

[20] Neh. 5.19. According to T. B. Sanh. 93b, the Book of Nehemiah was accounted as part of the Book of Ezra because of Nehemiah's pride in his virtue.

חכמה... אמנם יש שאלה שאינה הגונה. שהשאלה לבדה היא חוצפה... ושפטתם צדק בדעתכם אם השאלה ראויה... אך בזאת נאות לכם במילי דשמיא אין תחומין למעלה ולא תעזוב נפשכם לשאול מדה טובה מרובה. הרחיבו שאול כלים רקים אל תמעיטו. בקשו צדק בקשו ענוה כי ה' לא ימנע הטוב מכם:

אם תטיבו לאיזה אדם אל תשימוהו תחת עיניו כפעם בפעם. לאמר אנחנו עשינו עמך כך וכך שמדה מגונה היא זו... ודומה למאכיל אביו פטומות ויורש גיהנם... והרי נענש נחמיה שלא נקרא ספרו על שמו לפי שאמר זכרה לי אלהי לטובה כל אשר עשיתי על העם הזה... וזאת אל לבכם השיבו. הטיבו את אשר תדברו ואל תדברו את אשר תיטיבו:

אגרת הגר"א

LETTER OF ELIJAH (GAON) OF WILNA

XXI

LETTER OF ELIJAH (GAON) OF WILNA

Elijah b. Solomon, called the Wilna Gaon, was born in that town in 1720 and died there in 1797. A brilliant character sketch of this famous scholar may be read in S. Schechter's *Studies in Judaism*, first series, chapter III. There is also a good biographical article in *J. E.* v, p. 133. The Letter which is here printed was written when he was on a journey to Palestine. His plan was not fulfilled, and he did not proceed further than Germany. The Letter was written at Königsberg (*J. E.*, v, 134 b); he seems to have returned home soon afterwards.

Two of his sons, Aryeh Leb and Abraham, attained a reputation for learning and piety; one of his sons-in-law, R. Moses of Pinsk, is also known to fame. His wife, who was still living when the Letter was written, died in 1783 (Schechter, op. cit. p. 107). His mother, also, was still alive; the writer's references to both are among the most interesting features of the epistle.

For the discussion of the tone and contents of the Letter see Schechter (loc. cit.). Possibly his severity is there somewhat overrated, for the Letter (though ascetically inspired) is not lacking in the softer graces.

The text of the Letter differs considerably in the different Versions of it. The editions here collated are mainly those contained in the עלים לתרופה. This first appeared in Minsk in 1836 and in subsequent reprints;

כא

אגרת הגר"א

אליהו בן שלמה, הנקרא הגאון מווילנא, נולד בעיר ההיא בשנת ת"ף ונפטר שם בשנת תקנ"ז. ציור מצוין של טיב החכם המפורסם הזה נמצא בספרו של שכטר Studies in Judaism, סדר ראשון, פרק ג'. יש גם מאמר יפה על תולדותיו ודברי ימי חייו באנציקלופדיה היהודית האנגלית, כרך חמישי, דף קל"ג. האגרת הנדפסת פה נכתבה בשעה שהלך למסעו לארץ ישראל; אבל מחשבתו לא יצאה מן הכח אל הפועל, ומסעו זה נפסק בארץ אשכנז. האגרת נכתבה בעיר קייניגסבערג (עיין באנציקלופדיה היהודית האנגלית, במקום הנזכר לעיל), וכנראה שב הביתה כעבור זמן קצר.

שני בניו אריה ליב ואברהם היו נודעים ללמדנים וליראי אלהים, ואחד מחתניו, רבי משה מפינסק, היה ג"כ מפורסם. אשתו, אשר חיתה עוד בשעה שנכתבה האגרת, שבקה חיים לכל חי בשנת תקמ"ג (ראה שכטר בספרו הנזכר לעיל, דף ק"ז). גם אמו היתה חיה עדנה, ורמזי המחבר לשתיהן הם בין הקוים היותר חשובים של האגרת.

בנוגע לסגנון האגרת ותכנה ראה את מסקנותיו של שכטר בספרו הנזכר לעיל. אפשר שהוא מגזים מעט על חומרתו של המחבר, כי האגרת (אף כי רוח הסגוף נסוכה עליה) איננה חסרה רכות ועדינות במדה ידועה.

נוסח האגרת שונה הרבה במהדורותיה השונות. המהדורות אשר השויתי לתכלית הוצאתי הן עפ"י רוב אותן הנמצאות ב„עלים לתרופה". הספר הזה יצא לאור בפעם הראשונה

the Warsaw edition of 1856 has a Judeo-German paraphrase. It is also printed in the 1884 edition of M. H. Luzzatto's מסלת ישרים (p. 74). An important edition is to be found at the end of Ḥayyim b. Joseph Vital's ס' שערי הקדושה (Aleppo 1866). This is often preferable to the rest; it is referred to as A in the Notes to the Hebrew text; the other editions as V. Where the variants are too considerable for collation, the most important of them are given at some length in the Notes. The student should refer to the notes on the Hebrew text, for the variations often contain different meanings from those of the text here adopted.

Grieve not at all on my departure for the Land of Israel (may it be built and established!). You[1] gave me indeed a firm promise to that effect. And why should you be anxious? Many men travel years long, in search of money, leaving wives and children, themselves wanderers and strayers in want of all things.[2] But I, thanks be to God, am on my way to the Holy Land, which everyone is eager to behold; the desired of all Israel, the desired of God Himself, the land for which in heaven and on earth all beings yearn. And I journey in peace, blessed be the Lord, though thou knowest[3] that I have torn myself from my children, for whom my heart moans,

[1] V. "my mother gave, etc."

[2] Deut. 28. 48.

[3] This is a parenthetic remark to the author's wife.

במינסק בשנת תקצ"ו ונדפס פעמים רבות אח"כ. מהדורת ווארשא תרט"ז יש לה תרגום חפשי ליהודית-אשכנזית. מהדורה אחרת היא זו של תרמ"ד, יחד עם „מסלת ישרים" של משה חיים לוצאטו (דף ע"ד). מהדורה חשובה נמצאת בסוף „ס' שערי הקדושה" של חיים יוסף בן וויטאל (אחלב תרכ"ו). לפעמים קרובות יש לבכר את המהדורה הזאת על כל המהדורות האחרות. בהערותי לנוסח העברי קראתי את הראשונה A ואת האחרונות V. במקום שהשינוים הם רבים מאד הבאתי רק את היותר חשובים. מן ההכרח הוא שהתלמיד ישתמש בהערות של הנוסח העברי, יען כי לעתים קרובות השינוים המובאים שם יש להם הוראות שונות מאלה של הנוסח אשר בחרתי פה.

באתי לבקש מאתכם שלא תצערו בנסעי אל ארץ ישראל תבנה ותכונן[1] כלל. כמו שהבטחתם לי בדברים אמיתים[2]. וגם למה תדאגו? הנה הרבה אנשים נוסעים כמה שנים בשביל ממון. מניחים נשותיהם ובניהם. וגם הם נעים ונדים בחוסר כל. ואני תהלה לאל יתברך נוסע לארץ הקדושה שהכל מצפים לראותה. חמדת כל ישראל וחמדת השי"ת. וכל העליונים והתחתונים תשוקתם אליה. ואני נוסע לשלום[3] ברוך ה'. הגם שאת[4] יודעת שהנחתי ילדי[5]

[1] Some omit this and preceding four words.

[2] V. שהבטיחה לי אמי תחיה. [3] V. בשלום.

[4] Some eds. add נות ביתי קדושה=נוב"ק in reference to author's wife. [5] V. בני.

from all my precious books, and from the glorious splendor of my house,[4] and have become as a stranger in another country.

It is a familiar truth that this world is altogether vain, its delights ephemeral. Woe to them who pursue after vanity which profiteth nothing! Be not eager after wealth, for there are "riches kept by the owner thereof to his hurt."[5] As a man came forth from his mother's womb, naked shall he return[6]; as he entered, so shall he quit the world. What profiteth it him, that he laboreth for the wind and though he live a thousand years twice told, enjoy no good? Even if a man live many years, rejoicing in them all, yet must he remember the days of darkness, for they shall be many, all that cometh is vanity. As for mirth, what doth it accomplish?[7] What gives you pleasure to-day, will make you weep tomorrow. Neither be zealous after glory, which is likewise a vain thing. Time deceives, resembling a balance which raises the light and lowers the heavy.

Moreover, this world may be likened to one who drinks salt water; he seems to quench his thirst, but he grows thirstier from the draught. No man dies with half his desires attained, and what profit has he of all his toil?[8] Remember the former generations, whose love and ambition and joy have already vanished, and who are

[4] Esther 1. 4. The writer refers to his wife.

[5] Eccles. 5. 12. [6] Job. 1. 21.

[7] Eccles. 5. 15; 6. 6; 11. 8; 2. 2.

[8] Eccles. 1. 3. Cf. Midrash ad loc.

שלבי הומה עליהם וכל ספרי היקרים ואת יקר תפארת ביתי. והייתי כגר בארץ אחרת:

וידוע כי כל העולם הזה הכל הבל. וכל השעשועים הכל כלא היו. ואוי להרודפים אחר ההבל אין בו מועיל! ואל תקנא בעושר כי יש עושר שמור לבעליו לרעתו. כאשר יצא מבטן אמו ערום ישוב. כל עומת שבא כן ילך. ומה יתרון לו שיעמול לרוח? ואלו חיה אלף שנים פעמים וגו׳. כי אם שנים הרבה יחיה האדם בכלם ישמח ויזכור את ימי החשך כי הרבה יהיו. כל שבא הבל. ולשמחה מה זו עושה? כי מחר תבכה מאשר היום תשחק: ואל תקנא בכבוד המדומה להבל. כי הזמן בוגד. והוא כמאזנים יגביה הקל וישפיל הכבד:

והעולם הזה דומה לשותה מים מלוחים. ידמה לו שמרוה צמאונו[6] והוא צמא יותר. ואין אדם מת וחצי תאותו בידו. ומה יתרון לאדם בכל עמלו? זכור את הראשונים אשר היו לפנינו שכל אהבתם

[6] V. omit.

enduring their manifold penalties. Destined to the worms, what is man's enjoyment, when the grave transforms all enjoyments into bitterness? Death is near and inevitable,[9] it is no mere accident; life is a series of vexations and pains, and sleepless nights are the common lot. For every word judgment is exacted, no word (however light) is overlooked. Therefore I urge you to make solitude your habit, for the sin of the tongue weighs as much as all sins put together. So, after enumerating the sins, the punishment for which man eats in this world (while the stock remains for the world to come), our Sages add: "and slander equals them all."[10]

But why need I dilate on this most serious of sins? "All a man's labour is for his mouth," on which text our Sages remarked[11] that all a man's pious acts and studies fail to compensate for his frivolous speech. What should be man's chief objective in this world? To make himself as one dumb,[12] tightening his lips like the two mill-stones. The entire penalty of the "hollow of the sling" is due to man's idle words; for every vain utterance he must be slung from end to end of the world.[13] All this applies to words which are merely superfluous, but with regard to for-

[9] Lit. "is entwined round him," or "ever hastens after him."

[10] Tosefta Peah 1.2 (ed. Zuckermandel p. 18, though the reading there is somewhat different).

[11] Eccles. Rabbah on 6. 7.

[12] T. B. Ḥullin 89a.

[13] Shabb. 152b on basis of I Sam. 25. 29.

וחמד׳תם ושמחתם כבר אבדה. ומקבלים על זה דינים מרובים. ומה הנאה לאדם שסופו לפרוש לעפר רמה ותולעה. וכל ההנאות יתהפכו לו בקבר למרה. והמות כרוך באדם. ואיננו מקרה[7]. ובעולם הזה כל ימיו כעס ומכאובים. גם בלילה איננו מניח לו לישן. והכל יביא במשפט על כל דבור. ולא נאבד אפילו דבור קל. ולכן אני מזהירך שתרגיל עצמך לישב יחידי. כי חטא הלשון שקול ככל העונות כמאמר חז״ל אלו דברים שאדם אוכל עונשם כו׳ ולשון הרע כנגד כולם:

ומה לי להאריך בזה העון החמור מכל העבירות. כל עמל אדם לפיהו. ארז״ל שכל מצותיו ותורותיו של אדם אינו מספיק למה שמוציא מפיו. מה אומנותו של אדם בעה״ז ישים עצמו כאלם כו׳. וידביק שפתותיו כשתי רחיים כו׳. וכל כף הקלע הכל בהבל פיו[8] של דברים בטלים. ועל כל דבור הבל צריך להתקלע מסוף העולם ועד סופו: וכל זה בדברים יתרים. אבל בדברים האסורים כגון

7 A. adds these two words and omits below the clause והמות אינו מקרה which appears in several eds.

8 A. הכל בעון.

bidden speech—such as slander, scoffing, oaths, vows, dissensions, and curses, (particularly in Synagogue and on Sabbaths and festivals)—for all such must a man sink very deep into Sheol. 'Tis impossible, indeed, to estimate the chastisements and sorrows which a man bears because of a single utterance—every word of his is noted. Daily and inexorably angelic witnesses stand by and keep account, as it is said: "a bird of the air shall carry the voice, and that which hath wings shall tell the matter."[14] "Suffer not thy mouth to bring thy flesh into guilt, neither say thou before the messenger that it was an error, wherefore should God be angry?"[15] Therefore let a woman remember that "all glorious is the king's daughter *within* (the palace);"[16] whatever she needs, let her buy through a deputy; and even if she has to pay twice or thrice the price, is the Lord's hand waxed short?[17] God, blessed be He, feeds and sustains all creatures, from buffalo to mite, giving to each according to its need.[18] On Sabbaths and festivals speak not at all of matters which are not absolutely essential, and even in such cases be very brief. For the sanctity of the Sabbath is great indeed, and only with reluctance did the authorities allow even the exchange of greetings—so severe were they regarding even a single utterance.[19] Honor

[14] Eccles. 10. 20; applied to angels in the Midrash.

[15] Eccles. 5. 5. [16] Ps. 45. 14. [17] Num. 11.23.

[18] T. B. Abodah Zarah 3b.

[19] On the author's exceptional asceticism, cf. Schechter, *Studies in Judaism*, I p. 88. f.

לשון הרע וליצנות ושבועות ונדרים ומחלוקת וקללות ובפרט בבית הכנסת ובשבת וי"ט על אלו צריך לירד לשאול מטה הרבה מאד. ואי אפשר לשער גודל היסורין והצרות שסובל בשביל דבור א' ולא נאבד אפילו דבור א' שלא נכתב. בעלי גדפים הולכים תמיד אצל כל אדם ואדם ואין נפרדים ממנו וכותבים כל דבריו שנא' כי עוף השמים יוליך את הקול ובעל כנפים יגיד דבר: אל תתן את פיך לחטיא את בשרך, ואל תאמר לפני המלאך כי שגגה היא למה יקצוף האלהים: על כן כל כבודה בת מלך פנימה. וכל אשר צריך לה[9] תקח הכל ע"י שליח. ואף אם הוא פעמים ושלוש ביוקר. היד ה' תקצר? האל ית' זן ומפרנס מקרני ראמים ועד ביצי כנים ונותן לכל אחד ואחד די מחסורו: ובשבת ויו"ט אל תדברו כלל מדברים שאינם נצרכים מאד. וגם בדברים הנצרכים מאד תקצרו מאד. כי קדושת השבת גדולה מאד. ובקושי התירו לומר שלום בשבת. ראה בדבור אחד כמה

[9] A. לך.

then the Sabbath to the utmost, as was done when I was with you. Be in nowise niggardly, for though God determines how much a person shall have, this does not apply to Sabbaths and festivals.[20]

I also make an especial and emphatic request that you train your daughters to the avoidance of objurgations, oaths, lies or contention. Let their whole conversation be conducted in peace, love, affability and gentleness. I possess many moral books with German (versions); let them read these regularly; above all on the Sabbath—the holy of holies—they should occupy themselves with these ethical books exclusively. For a curse, an oath, or a lie, strike them; show no softness in the matter. For, (God forbid!) the mother and father are punished for the corruption of the children. Even if you do your best to train them morally and fail, woe to your shame here and hereafter,—"she profaneth her father." Therefore use your utmost rigor in their moral training, and may Heaven help you to success! So with other matters, such as the avoidance of slander and gossip; the regular recital of grace before and after meals, the reading of the Shema', all with true devotion. The fundamental rule, however, is that they gad not about in the streets, but incline their ear to your words and honor you and my mother and all their elders.[21] Urge

[20] T. B. Bezah 16a.

[21] V. Their mother. Throughout this translation the word "you" has been employed where it is difficult to decide whether the author is addressing his wife solely

החמירו! ותכבד את השבת מאד כאשר היה[10] לפני. אל תצמצם כלל כי כל מזונותיו של אדם קצובים חוץ מהוצאות שבתות וי"ט:

וגם באתי לבקש מאתך מאד מאד בבקשה גדולה ועצומה ושטוחה[11] שתדריך את בנותיך מאד שלא יצא מפיהם קללה ושבועה וכזב ומחלוקת. רק הכל בשלום באהבה ובחבה ובנחת: והנה יש לי כמה ספרי מוסר עם לשון אשכנז. יקראו תמיד וכ"ש בשבת קדש קדשים לא יתעסקו אלא בספרי מוסר: ועל קללה ושבועה וכזב תכה אותם[12] ולא תרחם עליהם כלל. כי ח"ו בקלקול הבנים יענשו אב ואם[13]. ואף אם תדריכם תמיד במוסר ולא יקבלו. אוי לאותה בושה והצער והבזיון בעה"ז ובעה"ב. את אביה היא מחללת! לכן בכל מאמצי כחך תדריכם במוסר. ומהשמים יסייעוך שיקבלו מוסרך ואל תתיאש: וכן שאר דברים לשון הרע ורכילות. ושלא יאכלו וישתו כי אם בברכה ראשונה ואחרונה וברכת המזון וקריאת שמע והכל בכוונה. ועקר הכל שלא יצאו ח"ו מפתח ביתם לחוץ. ויטו אזן לדבריך[14]. ויכבדו אותך ולאמי[15] ולכל הגדולים מהם בשנים.

10 A. הייתם. 11 A. omits. 12 A. adds במכות אכזריות.
13 A. reads יענש אב. 14 V. ושיצייתו. 15 A. ולאמם.

them to obey all that is written in the moral books.

Furthermore, bring up your sons in the right way and with gentleness. Their teacher must be constantly in your house, and you must pay him generously. All a man's expenditure is appointed from the New Year, but (as the Talmud adds) this does not apply to expenditure on education.[22] I have left the necessary books for tuition. Pay careful heed to the children's health and diet, so that they never lack anything. They should first study all the Pentateuch,[23] learning it practically by heart. Let not the teacher impose his yoke heavily on them, for instruction is only efficient when it is conveyed easily and agreeably. Give the children small presents of money and the like, to please them,—this helps their studies. To this apply your unfailing attention, all else is vanity. At his death a man carries away with him from all his toil naught but two changes of white garments.[24] "No man can by any means redeem his brother. Be not afraid when one waxeth rich...for when he dieth he shall carry nothing away."[25] Say not: I will bequeath to my children money and means for their support. Know that the sons of man are like the grasses of the field, some flourish and others wither, each being born under

or the whole family. In this passage it is clearly the wife who is intended.

[22] Economy in education is not a virtue: T. B. Bezah 16a. [23] V. Bible.

[24] Shroud and tallit. Cf. *Yoreh Deah*, ch. 351.

[25] Ps. 49. 8, etc.

וכל הכתוב בספרי מוסר תזרזם לקיימו[16].

גם לבניך הי"ו[17] תגדל אותם בדרך הישר ובנחת. ותשלם שכר למוד. ותתמיד[18] המלמד בביתך. ולא תצמצם בשכרו. כי כל מזונותיו של אדם קצובין לו מר"ה[19] חוץ מהוצאת בניו לתלמוד תורה. והנחתי להם ספרים שילמדו בהם[20]. ותשגיח על בריאותם ומזונותם תמיד שלא יחסר להם[21]. ושילמדו מקודם כל החומש[22] שיהיו רגילין כמעט בעל פה. ואל יכביד המלמד עולו[23] עליהם. כי הלמוד אינו נקבע בלב האדם[24] כי אם בישוב ובנחת. ותפזר[25] להם איזה פרוטות וכיוצא כדי לשמחם ויועיל ללמודם[26]: ועל זה תתן תמיד דעתך. והשאר הכל הבל. כי מאומה לא ישא האדם מעמלו במותו[27]. כי אם שני חליפות בגדים לבנים גם לא אח פדה וגו'. אל תירא כי יעשיר איש וגו' כי לא במותו וכו': ואל תאמר אניח לבני ממון ונכסים לחיותם. דע לך כי בני אדם דומים לעשבי השדה. הללו נוצצים והללו נובלים.

16 V. for these two words יתקיימו. 17 V. שיחיו.
18 V. ותחזיק. 19 Eds. מתשר"י.
20 V. ספרים ולמען השם תדריכם בטוב ובנחת וגם תשגיח.
21 V. לחם. 22 A. התנ"ך.
23 V. omit these two words. 24 V. באדם.
25 V. ונתון תתן. 26 V. omit these four words.
27 V. omit.

his star, and under the Providence of the Most High God. The heirs of a wealthy man rejoice at his death, to inherit his estate, while he descends to the grave and leaves his wealth to others. So it was said of R. Simeon ben Laḳish, who left behind him nothing more than a measure of saffron, that he applied to himself the text: "and leave their wealth to others."[26] Woe and alas for the sins of men who toil and moil to leave their children money and goods and full houses! All this is vanity, for the only profit in sons and daughters is their Torah and their virtue. Their sustenance, on the other hand, is appointed unto them by God. He who created them, creates also their means of support. A man's main concern should be to acquire the future world by the charitable and benevolent use of his money, honoring the Lord with his substance.[27]

Moreover, well known is the reward accruing to women for seeing that their sons attend school. I wish particularly to impress this on my wife. As our Sages say, no woman is regarded as worthy unless she performs her husband's will,[28] the more so when his words are the precepts of the living God. Though I am confident that she will carry out all my instructions, I nevertheless insist that there be no modification made, that this Letter be read every week—particularly on the Sabbath before the meal—and that it be

[26] Ps. 49. 11. T. B. Giṭṭin 47a.

[27] Prov. 3. 9. T. B. Berakot 17a.

[28] Tana debe Eliyahu, ch. 9.

כל אחד נולד במזלו ובהשגחת אל עליון ברוך הוא. והם שמחים במותו לרשת אותו והוא יורד לשאול ומניחו לאחרים. כמו שאמרו על ריש לקיש שהניח בתריה קבא דמוריקא קרי אנפשיה. ועזבו לאחרים חילם: אוי ואבוי על בני אדם שכולם[28] טורחים ויגעים להניח לבניהם אחריהם ממון ונכסים ובתים מלאים[29]. כל זה הבל. כי אין יתרון מבנים ובנות רק בתורתם ובמעשיהם הטובים. אבל מזונותם קצובים להם מהשי"ת. מי שבראם בורא פרנסתם. והעיקר שיקנה האדם עוה"ב בצדקות וג"ח שעושה מממונו וכבד ה' מהונך[30]:

גם כן ידוע אגרא דנשי באקרויי[31] בנייהו בבית הספר. ומאד אני מצוה אותה לנו"ב על ד"ז[32]. וארז"ל אין לך אשה כשרה בנשים אלא כשעושה רצון בעלה. כל שכן שאני כותב לה דברי אלהים חיים. ובטוח אני שתעשה ככל אשר כתבתי. אעפ"כ[33] באתי להזהירך באזהרה כפולה[34] שלא תשנה דבר מכל אשר כתבתי. ותקרא את האגרת הזאת בכל שבוע ובפרט בשבת[35] קודם האכילה. ותזהיר בני

28 A. אוי ואבוי על שכלם ודעתם של בני אדם שטורחים.

29 V. omit 5 words.

30 V. omit 16 words.

31 A. adds ובאתנויי.

32 V. omit 7 words.

33 V. גדולה.

34 V. omit 7 words.

35 V. פ"א בשבוע וביום השבת

impressed on your children during the meal to avoid conversing on frivolous or secular matters, and above all to be on guard against slander and the like.

When you lead your sons and daughters in the good way,[29] let your words be tender and caressing, in terms of discipline that win the heart's assent. Particularly, is this essential if we are to enjoy the privilege of settling in the Land of Israel, where it is necessary to walk firmly in the ways of the Lord. Therefore accustom them to a life of virtue and noble character, to which end much training is required. Habit dominates all things, and becomes nature; all beginnings are hard, continuations are easy. The wicked knows of himself that his way is evil and bitter, but it is difficult to tear himself from his folly. For this is the way of man. At the door sin coucheth,[30] and his yezer rules over him. Its spice[31] in the case of men is study of the Torah, and for women modesty. To his death-day must man chasten himself, not by fasts and penances, but by a bridle to his mouth and his lust. This bridle is Return[32] (to God). This is the whole fruit of the world to

29 T. B. Sanhedrin 76b. 30 Eccles. 12. 13; Gen. 4. 7.

31 i. e. remedy or preservative. Cf. T. B. Ḳiddushin, 30b.

32 Repentance would be an inadequate rendering.

---

46 This clause is added from A., which differs considerably in wording in the following passage.

47 A. קנין.

ביתך בתוך[36] הסעודה שלא ידברו דברים [בטלים] ודברי חול[37]. וכל שכן בלשון הרע וכיוצא:

כשתדריך בניך ובנותיך לדרך טובה, יהיו דבריך רכים וחנונים בדברי מוסר המתישבים על הלב[38]. ובפרט אם נזכה לדירת ארץ[39] ישראל. כי שם צריך לילך[40] מאד בדרכי ה'. ולכן תרגילם בדברי מוסר ומדות טובות שצריכים[41] הרגל רב. וההרגל על כל דבר שלטון ונעשה טבע[42]. וכל התחלות קשות ואח"כ יהיו נוחות[43]. כי הרשע[44] יודע בעצמו שרע ומר דרכו אך שקשה לו לפרוש מסכלותו[45]. כי זה כל האדם. לפתח חטאת רובץ ושליט עליו יצרו. ותבלין שלו לזכרים עסק התורה ולנקבות הצניעות[46]. ועד יום מותו צריך האדם להתיסר. ולא בתעניתים וסיגופים רק ברסן פיו ובתאוותו וזהו התשובה. וזה כל פרי[47] העולם הבא

36 V. omit 3 words and read ובתוך.

37 V. omit 2 words and read ח"ו.

38 V. differ in wording here, but the sense is the same.

39 V. לבא לארץ. 40 V. להתנהג.

41 V. omit 5 words and read כי הדבור והמדות צריך.

42 V. omit 2 words.

43 V. ואח"ך ואוזל לו אז יתהלל; A. adds ואם ח"ו קלקלו מעשיהם רע.

44 A. הכסיל.

45 V. omit clause.

come, as it is written: "For the commandment is a lamp and the Law is light," but "the reproofs of instruction are the way of life."[33] This transcends all conceivable fasts and penances; and he who succeeds in muzzling his mouth, will merit in measureless abundance of the Light treasured up in the future world.[34] And the Scripture saith:[35] "Who is the man that desireth life, and loveth days that he may see good therein? Keep thy tongue from evil, and thy lips from speaking guile." Thereby shall his iniquity find atonement, and he be saved from the depths of the netherworld. So is it said: "Whoso keepeth his mouth and his tongue keepeth his soul from troubles:" and again: "Death and life are in the power of the tongue."[36] Woe to him that slayeth himself by his speech! (If the serpent bite before it is charmed) what advantage hath the charmer? For slander once spoken there is no remedy. Therefore the rule must be: Speak of no man to his praise, still less to his dispraise. For what has a man to do with slander? "The mouth of slander is a deep pit, he that is abhorred of the Lord falleth therein."[37]

Against this offence the most effective hedge is solitude—to avoid ever leaving the house for the streets unless under pressure of extreme necessity or in order to perform an important

33 Prov. 6. 23. 34 T. B. Ḥagigah, 12 a.

35 Ps. 34. 13–14. 36 Prov. 21. 23, 18. 21.

37 Prov. 22. 14, applied to slander, blasphemy and evil speech in T. B. Shabbat 33a.

כמש"כ כי נר מצוה ותורה אור. אבל ודרך חיים תוכחת מוסר. וזהו יותר מכל התעניתים וסיגופים בעולם. ואדם הזוכה לחסום פיו זוכה לאור הגנוז בשפע בלתי שיעור[48]. ואמר הכתוב מי האיש החפץ חיים אוהב ימים לראות טוב? נצור לשונך מרע ושפתיך מדבר מרמה. ובזה יכופר לו כל עון ונצול משאול תחתית[49]. שנא' שומר פיו ולשונו שומר מצרות נפשו, וכתיב מות וחיים ביד לשון. אוי לממית עצמו בדבורו[50]. ומה יתרון לבעל הלשון ולכל יש רפואה חוץ וכו'. והעיקר שלא תדבר בשום אדם בשבחו[51] וכל שכן בגנותו. כי מה לו לאדם לדבר זרות. שנא' שוחה עמוקה פי זרות זעום ה' יפול שם:

והגדר העקרי הוא התבודדות[52]. שלא תצא[53] מפתח הבית חוצה. כי אם לצורך גדול מאד או

48 V. הגנוז שאין מלאך ובריה יכולים לשער.

49 V. מגיהנם. 50 V. add בשביל דבור אחד.

51 V. add שמתוך שבחו יבא לידי גנותו.

52 V. ועיקר הגדר בבדידות.

53 V. תצאו.

religious duty. The Scripture hints at this.[38] Even in Synagogue make but a very short stay and depart. It is better to pray at home, for in Synagogue it is impossible to escape envy and the hearing of idle talk. Men have to give account for it; as the Sages say,[39] he who merely listens and is silent is culpable. The more so on Sabbaths and festivals, when people assemble to talk, it would be better not to pray at all. It is also better for your daughter not to go to Synagogue,[40] for there she would see garments of embroidery and similar finery. She would grow envious and speak of it at home, and out of this would come scandal and other ills. Let her seek her glory in her home, cleaving ever to discipline, and showing no jealousy for worldly gauds, vain and delusive as they are,[41] coming up in a night and perishing in a night.[42] Thus is it written:[43] "Though his excellency mount up to the heavens," yet "riches are not for ever."

38 The author quotes Levit. 16. 4: "He shall put on the holy linen (tunic)." The Hebrew *bad* means "linen" and also "alone".

39 T. B. Pesaḥim 118a.

40 V. "to the women's synagogue."

41 Jer. 10. 15; 51. 8.

42 Jonah 4. 10.

43 Job 20. 6; Prov. 27. 24.

הקברות כי שם מתדבקים הקליפות באנשים וכל שכן בנשים. וצרות רבות באים מזה.

57 A. reads לבה"כ של נשים. 58 V. בגדים טובים.

59 V. omit clause. 60 A. אדם להבל דמה בן.

לעשות מצוה רבה ודרך רמז ב׳ד קד׳ש יל׳בש[54]. ואף בבית הכנסת[55] תקצר מאד ותצא. ויותר טוב להתפלל בבית. כי בבית הכנסת אי אפשר להנצל מקנאה ולשמוע דברים בטלים ונענשים על זה כמה שאמרו אף השומע ושותק נענש. וכל שכן בשבת ויום טוב שמתאספין לדבר יותר טוב שלא תתפלל כלל[56]. וגם בתך יותר טוב שלא תלך לבית הכנסת[57] כי שם רואה בגדי רקמה וכיוצא[58]. ומתקנאת ומספרת בבית ומתוך זה באין ללשון הרע ולדברים אחרים. אלא כל כבודה בת מלך פנימה[59]. ותתדבק במוסר תמיד. ואל תקנא בעולם הזה. הכל הבל מעשה תעתועים. שבן[60] לילה היה ובן לילה אבד. שנא׳ כי אם יעלה לשמים שיאו וגו׳ כי לא לעולם

54 V. omit clause from כי אם.

55 For what follows A. reads:
ואף בבית הכנסת תתבודד מהבריות לשבת יחידי. כי במקום אסיפת אנשים א״א להנצל מלשמוע דברים בטלים ולה״ר. ואף השומע ושותק נענש ע״ז כמשרז״ל וכל שכן בשבתות ויו״ט שמתאספים העם בבה״כ ולא יבצר שימצא מהם מדברים דברים בטלים ולה״ר השמרו לכם שתשבו במסבתם הרחק מן הכיעור ותשב בבה״כ בהתבודדות שהדבור בבה״כ הוא עון פלילי ועבירה גדולה בידו. עד שאמרו בזהר הקדוש מאן דמשתעי בבי כנישתא לית ליה חולקא באלהא דישראל. ובתי מדרשות דינם כבה״כ שאסור הדבור בהם.

56 V. add this (or similar clause) ואל תלך תמיד לבית

This world's pleasure, even in its hour, is vanity—condemned in the eyes of every intelligent being. Woe and alas that men go astray in this matter![44] Do you rather show zeal for the fear of the Lord all day, becoming worthy of the world hereafter. Say not: How shall I become thus worthy, what am I able to do? For it matters not whether one do much or little, so long as he directs his heart heavenwards.[45]

Among my books is the Book of Proverbs in German; for the Lord's sake let them read it every day, as it is chief of moral works. They should also read Ecclesiastes constantly, in your presence; for this book exposes the vanity of temporal concerns. But the end must not be a mere perusal of these books, for man does not thus gain incentive. Many a man reads moral words without rousing himself to moral works. Partly because they merely read, partly because they fail to understand—this renders the reading fruitless. This is shown in the Parable of one who sows[46] without ploughing the soil, so that the wind snatches the seed and satisfies the birds. Because he cannot restrain himself or make himself a fence, he is like one who sows without

44 Or "in this world".

45 Mishnah Menaḥot (end).

46 See *Prince and Nazirite* (by Ḥisdai) ch. 10. Cf. I. Abrahams, *Studies in Pharisaism*, First Series, p. 93.

---

the personal references.

66 V. לפרקים   67 The eds. read מבהיל

68 V. add ושאר ספרים.   69 V. בתוך הבריות.

חוסן וגו׳. ועונג העולם הזה[61] אף בשעתו הבל. ומאוס בעיני כל בעל שכל. אוי ואבוי ששוגה בזה! ותקנא ביראת ה׳ כל היום ותזכה לעה״ב[62]. ולא תאמר במה אזכה לעה״ב ומה יכולתי[63] לעשות? כי אחד המרבה וא׳ הממעיט ובלבד שיכוון לבו לשמים![64]

ובספרים שלי יש משלי בלשון אשכנז[65]. למען השם שיקראו בכל יום[66]. והוא ראש המוסרים. וגם ספר קהלת יקראו תמיד לפניך כי שם מהביל[67] עניני עוה״ז[68]. אבל ח״ו לא תהיה התכלית הקריאה לבד. כי בזה אין מתפעל האדם. גם כמה ב״א קורין בספרי מוסר ואינם מתפעלים והוא בשביל הנ״ל. ועוד בשביל יציאתם בלא הבנה[69] כי זה מאבד הכל. והמשל הזורע בלא חרישה שיחטוף הרוח וישביע עופות כו׳ והוא בשביל שאין יכול לחסום עצמו ולגדור והוא כזורע בלא גדר ואוכלין

[61] V. omit 3 words. [62] V. omit 4 words.

[63] V. איני יכולת. [64] Some texts add:

ולמען השם שתפרש את החומש כאשר צויתיך. ואל תפחות כאשר הזהרתיך. כי בפחות מזה עוברים כל רגע על כמה לאווין ועשין ושקול כאלו כפר בתורה הקדושה ח״ו. אבל העיקר לזכות העה״ב בשמירת פיו וזהו דבר יקר מאד. ואלו נקראו נשים שאננות כי הפה קודש קדשים:

[65] The ending differs here in the eds. A. omits the whole reference to the parable of the sower and some of

fence, and the pigs consume it and tread it down. Sometimes one sows on stone, the stony heart into which no seed enters at all, and it is necessary to strike the stone until it is split. Therefore I have bidden you to strike your children if they refuse to obey you. "Train up a child in the way he should go, and even when he is old he will not depart from it."[47] This is the great rule! I include in all this exhortation my son-in-law, who must follow the course of reading which I have prescribed. Let his study be from pure love of God, and for the Lord's sake let him train himself in this, disregarding the objection of those who hold it unnecessary for a young man. On the contrary, the shell of a green nut is easily opened. This is the root of all, for thereby man becomes worthy of all; as our Sages remarked: "R. Meir said, whoever is busied in Torah for its own sake (merits many things), and not only so (but he is worth the whole world)."[48] Accustom your children to the study of the Chapters of the Fathers, and in the Abot of R. Nathan and the tractate *Derek Erez*[49], for good manners (the subject of the last named) are precedent to the Torah. Show the utmost honor to your aged mother-in-law, and treat all men with mannerliness, with amiability and respect.

My dear mother! I realize that you need no instruction of mine, for I know your modest

47 Prov. 22. 6.

48 Abot vi., Chapter of R. Meir (beginning).

49 *J. E.* i. 81 ff., iv. 526.

החזירים וירמסון. ויש שזורע על האבן והוא לב האבן שאינו נכנס בו כלל וצריך להכות את האבן עד שיתפוצץ. לכן כתבתי לך שתכה את בניך אם לא ישמעו לך. וחנוך לנער על פי דרכו גם כי יזקין לא יסור ממנו. זהו כלל גדול[70]. וגם את חתני אני מזהיר בכל זה שיקרא לפניהם כנ"ל. ושיהא למודו לשם שמים. ולמען השם יחנך עצמו בזה. ואל ישגיח על האומרים כי הנער אין צריך לזה ח"ו. אדרבה! קליפת האגוז ירוקה נוחה כו'. ועיקר הכל הוא. כי בזה זוכה אל הכל. כמו שאחז"ל. רבי מאיר אומר כל העוסק בתורה לשמה כו' ולא עוד וכו': ותרגילם בלמוד מסכת אבות ואבות[71] דרבי נתן. ותלמדם[72] דרך ארץ. כי ד"א קדמה לתורה: ולחמותך הזקנה תכבד מאד. ועם כל אדם תתנהג בדרך ארץ ובנחת ובכבוד:

אהובתי אמי! ידעתי שאינך צריכה למוסר שלי. כי ידעתי כי צנועה את. אעפ"כ יקראו לפניך

[70] V. ועיקר בחינוך.
[71] V. ובפרט בפרקי אבות דרבי נתן.
[72] So A. adds.

disposition. Nevertheless, let them read in your presence this Letter, for it contains counsels derived from the words of the living God. And I earnestly implore you not to grieve for my sake, as you have promised. If, by God's grace, I have the privilege to be in Jerusalem, the Holy City, over against the Gates of Heaven, I will pray on your behalf in accordance with my undertaking. If we are so blessed we shall appear (in the City) together all of us, should the Master of Mercy so will it.

I also beg my wife to honor my mother in accordance with the prescript of the Law, es-epecially regarding a widow.[50] 'Tis an indictable offense to distress her, even in the smallest matter. My mother, too, I entreat to live harmoniously with my wife, each bringing happiness to the other by kindly intercourse, for this is a prime duty incumbent on all mankind. Each one is asked, in the hour of judgment: "Hast thou conducted thyself with friendliness towards thy fellow man?" The aim of the Torah, in large part, is to induce this desire of causing happiness. Let there be no dissension of any kind among all the household, men and women, but let love and brotherliness reign. In case of offense, forgive each other, and live for God's sake in amity. Of my mother I also ask that she shall lay her injunctions on my sons and daughters in tender terms so that she may win obedience; that she

50 See Ṭur, Yoreh Deah, ch. 40, on rights of widow in husband's house. See *J. E.* xxi, 515. Cf. also Micah 7. 6, quoted in T. B. Sanhedrin 97a, Soṭah 49b.

האגרת הזאת. כי הם דברי אלהים חיים. ומבקש אני מאד ממך בבקשה שטוחה שלא תצער בשבילי כאשר הבטחתני. ואי"ה אם אזכה להיות בירושלים עיר הקדש אצל שערי שמים, אבקש בעדך כאשר הבטחתי לך. ואם נזכה נראה יחדיו כולנו, אם ירצה בעל הרחמים:

גם באתי לבקש לאשתי שתכבד את אמי כמה שכתוב בתורה. ובפרט לאלמנה. שעון פלילי מאד לצערה אפילו בתנועה קלה. וגם לאמי בקשתי שיהא שלום בין שניהם. ואשה את רעותה תשמח בדברים טובים, כי זה מצוה גדולה לכל אדם. ושואלין לאדם[73] בשעת הדין כו' ההלכת את חבירך בנחת רוח? ובזה רוב התורה לשמח לאדם. ואל יהי שום מחלוקת בכל בני הבית באנשים ובנשים אלא אהבה ואחוה[74]. ואף אם יעשה אחד[75] מכם שלא כהוגן תמחלו זה לזה ותחיו למען ה' בשלום. וכן לאמי בקשתי שתדריך את בני ובנותי בדברים

[73] A. לנשמה.

[74] V. omit this clause.

[75] Eds. אם תעשה אחת מכם.

shall care for them and they shall honor her. Between them there shall be heard no strife or anger, but peace shall prevail. And may the Master of Peace grant unto you, unto my sons and daughters, my sons-in-law and brothers,[51] and unto all Israel, life and peace! These are the words of one who constantly prays for you—Elijah b. Solomon Zalman (be the memory of the righteous for a blessing!).

[51] These two words may be rendered as singulars.

רכים שיקבלום. ותשגיח עליהם. ולבני ולבנותי אני מצוה שיכבדו אותה. וגם ביניהם לא ישמע ריב וכעס כלל אלא הכל בשלום. ובעל השלום יתן לכם ולבני ולבנותי וחתני ואחי וכל ישראל חיים ושלום! כ"ד המעתיר בעדכם תמיד, אליהו במהור"ר שלמה זלמן זצ"ל[76]:

[76] V. מנאי אהובכם אליהו וכו'.

לקוטים מצואת מוהר׳ אלכסנדר זיסקינד

A TRUE MAN OF GIMZO
EXTRACTS FROM THE TESTAMENT OF ALEXANDER SUESSKIND

XXII

A TRUE MAN OF GIMZO

EXTRACTS FROM THE TESTAMENT OF ALEXANDER SUESSKIND

Alexander, son of Moses Suesskind, died at Grodno in 1794. He was author of a popular book on Prayer and Worship, the *Basis and Root of Service*, which appeared in Novidvor in 1782, and has often been reprinted. His Testament was published in Grodno in the year of his death. It, too, has been very often reprinted. The author's desire that it should be printed at the beginning of editions of the Prayer Book (see the first note to the Hebrew text) does not seem to have been fulfilled. The length of the work must have proved an obstacle, just as the same cause has compelled the editor of the present volume to limit himself to a few extracts.

In the Introduction to his Testament he refers to his treatise and explains that his design was to add points for which place could not be found in the former work. Then follow 46 paragraphs.

The popularity of the Testament is easily understood. Like Naḥum of old (T. B. Ta'anit 21a) he was a veritable "man of Gimzo", one who ever used as his motto the cheerful maxim "*Gam-zu le-tobah*" (*This, too, is for good*). With this optimism he combined much learning and still more naïveté. It is indeed his simplicity that gives his erudition its rare charm. To him religion was a personal experience, a conviction of the soul. No less than forty-seven prayers and benedictions of his own composition occur in the Testament. And as his own religion was

כב

לקוטים מצואת מוהר׳ אלכסנדר זיסקינד

אלכסנדר בן משה זיסקינד נפטר בגרודנה בשנת תקנ״ד. הוא היה המחבר של ספר ידוע על תפלה ועבודה, „יסוד ושורש העבודה״, אשר יצא לאור בנובידבור בשנת תקמ״ב ונדפס פעמים רבות אח״כ. צואתו נדפסה בגרודנה בשנת פטירתו, וגם היא עברה דרך מהדורות רבות. לפי הנראה, חפצו של המחבר שידפסוה בראש הסדורים (ראה את ההערה הראשונה אל הנוסח העברי) לא נתמלא. בלי ספק אריכותה היתה בעוכריה, ומטעם זה הוכרחתי גם אני להסתפק רק בלקוטים אחדים.

בהקדמה לצואתו מזכיר המחבר את ספרו על העבודה ומבאר שכונתו היתה להוסיף דברים בצואתו שלא היה אפשר להזכיר בחיבורו הנ״ל. אח״כ באים ארבעים וששה סעיפים.

נקל להבין מפני מה הצואה הזאת היתה כ״כ אהובה על הבריות. כמו נחום מימים עתיקים (תלמוד בבלי, תענית, כ״א.) היה זיסקינד „איש גמזו״ אמתי וישתמש תמיד בכלל הנחמד והנעים „גם זו לטובה״. אל שמחת-החיים הזאת נצטרפה למדנות גדולה ותמימות גדושה, ופשטותו הוסיפה לוית חן מיוחד לחכמתו. לו הדת היתה נסיון אישי, הוכחה נפשית. לא פחות מארבעים ושבע תפלות וברכות, אשר חבר הוא בעצמו, נמצאות בצואתו. ובהיות שדתו היתה חפשית ובלתי כפויה

so spontaneous, its appeal is also immediate. We seem to stand in the presence of a sensitive soul, which, fortunately, does not lack the saving grace of humor.

My beloved children! Though I have already compiled a treatise on subjects connected with the service of our Maker and Creator (be His name blessed and His memorial exalted for ever),[1] a treatise which I entitled *Foundation and Root of Worship*, and in which I designed to instruct not you only but the community also—for on every individual of the holy Israelite people rests the duty to fulfil all that is therein written in accordance with my exposition of the meaning and profound significance of every thought and practice to which allusion is made—nevertheless, I here address you personally and it is your heart, my dear children, that I know better than all the families of the holy Israelite people. Therefore, by virtue of the obligation imposed on you of showing honor to your father and with the authority of one dangerously ill,[2] I command you to undertake the performance of all that I shall expound in this Testament,—points which it is impossible to notice in my afore-mentioned treatise. I also hope in my Maker and Creator that other men, too, who cast their eyes on this Testament will incline their pure hearts to all its contents, and that there may reach our Creator

[1] This phrase, which appears repeatedly in the course of the testament, is often left untranslated.

[2] This double appeal—to the law of the decalogue and to the duty of obeying a dying man's orders—recurs many times, and is not always translated.

גם פעולתה היא ישרה ותכופה. כמדומה שאנחנו עומדים פה לפני איש אנין בעל מזג רך, אשר בכ"ז נחן במתנת הבדיחה וההלצה.

בניי אהוביי![1] הגם שכבר חברתי חיבור מעניני עבודת יוצרנו ובוראנו יתברך שמו ויתעלה זכרו לעד. שקראתיו שמו יסוד ושורש העבודה. ולא ללמד בשבילכם לבד יצאתי שם אלא על הכלל כולו. שעל כל איש מעם קדוש הישראלי חיוב לקיים כל מה שכתוב שם כפי שבארתי שם טעמו ונימוקו בכל כוונה והנהגה הנזכר' שם. אך אתכם בניי אהוביי! ידעתי לבבכם מכל משפחות עם קדוש הישראלי. לכן אני מצוה בגזירת כיבוד אב וצוואת שכיב מרע לקבל[2] עליכם להיות עושים כל מה שאבאר בצוואה זו. מה שלא היה באפשרי להזכיר בחיבורי הנ"ל. ואקווה ליוצרי ובוראי ית"ש ויתעלה זכרו לעד שגם שאר בני אדם שיעיינו בצוואה זו יתנו לבם הטהור בכל הכתוב בה. ויגיע

1 Preceding this paragraph are the lines:

צוואה סדורה וערוכה אשר הניח אחריו ברכה איש אלהי מהו' אלכסנדר זיסקינד במהו' משה זצוק'ל:

בעז"ה צוואה לבניי שיחיו וצוואה זו תבוא על הדפוס בהתחלת הסידורים:

2 Eds. לקיים.

gratification from their service of Him, blessed be His Name, and exalted His Memorial, for ever, Amen!

I command you, this day, my beloved children, to acknowledge the Godhead, the Kingdom, and the Lordship of our Maker and Creator, to keep His commandments, His statutes and laws, to perform them fitly and for their own sake, and not as a "commandment of men learned by rote"[3] (may the Merciful One deliver us!).[4] Your intention shall be that God may find satisfaction in your conduct.[5] Ye shall labor in His holy Law whenever you have leisure; even a single instant ye must not waste in the world's vanities. The intent of your study of His holy Law should be that the Name (be it exalted!) may obtain pleasure from your devotion. And ye shall fix firm in your minds the love and fear of Him, to do His will with a perfect heart. Ye shall glory in His holy Godhead ceaselessly; and shall at all times offer thanksgiving to Him, with lips and heart, for that He bestowed on you the boon of creating you in His holy portion, in the midst of the holy Israelite people (as it is written: "for the portion of the Lord is His people"),[6] and not among one of the peoples who worship idols, "which shall utterly pass away."[7]

[3] Isaiah, 29.13.

[4] This phrase, too, is very often repeated by our author, and will mostly be left untranslated.

[5] On this idea, that man's excellence gives pleasure and satisfaction to God, see my *Studies in Pharisaism*, ii, p. 179. [6] Deut., 32.9. [7] Isaiah, 2.18.

גם כן מעבודתם נחת רוח ליוצרנו ובוראנו ית"ש ויתעלה זכרו לעד. אמן!

אשר אנכי מצוה אתכם היום בניי אהוביי! בגזירת כיבוד אב ובצוואת שכיב מרע שתקבלו עליכם אלהותו ומלכותו ואדנותו של יוצרנו ובוראנו ית"ש ויתעלה זכרו לעד. לשמור מצותיו וחוקותיו ותורותיו לעשותם כראוי ולשמה ולא כמצות אנשים מלומדה רחמנא לצלן! וכוונתכם תהיה בכדי שיגיע ממעשיכם נחת רוח ליוצרנו ובוראנו ית"ש ויתעלה: ותהיו עמלים בתורתו הקדושה בכל עת שיהיה לכם פנאי. אף[3] רגע אחד לא תבלו[4] ח"ו בהבלי העולם. וכוונת לימודיכם בתורתו הקדושה תהיה גם כן בכדי שיגיע להשם יתעלה נחת רוח מהלימוד. ותקבעו בלבבכם אהבתו ויראתו לעשות רצונו בלבב שלם. ותתפארו באלהותו הקדושה בתמידות ותתנו לו ית"ש ויתעלה הודאה בכל עת בפיכם ובלבבכם על שזיכה אתכם וברא אתכם בחלקו הקדוש בתוך עם קדוש הישראלי כמ"ש כי חלק ה' עמו. ולא בתוך עם מן העמים עובדי אלילים כליל יחלוף:

3 Some Eds עַד.
4 Some Eds. תהבלו.

Besides the potential surrender of life in which every Israelite is bound to acquiesce when reciting certain parts of the liturgy, as I have indicated in my treatise in accordance with the views of the Zohar and Isaac Luria,—besides this, I command you, my beloved children, that if ye be called upon to suffer actual martyrdom (from which may God deliver you and all the holy people!), ye shall go to your death with whole-hearted joy. And the Creator will delight in you throughout the realms above. He will say: "See ye what manner of a man I made in My world; he spared not his body, but bore chastisements for My honor, and delivered himself up for the sanctification of My Name!" And my heart knows, that if I were myself required to make this supreme sacrifice, it would not be for the wondrous reward which eye hath not seen in the worlds on high, but solely for the great Name of God, that it might be magnified and sanctified in all worlds below and above, by my act of voluntary martyrdom.

Moreover, my beloved children, I command you to ordain on your children too all that I have commanded you—the acknowledgement of His Godhead, the study of His holy Law at all times, the performance of His holy precepts in all their particularities for their own sake, and in the actual surrender of life. Command also your children that they shall continue these in-

גם מלבד מסירת נפש בכח כפי שהזכרתי בחבורי שחיוב על כל איש ישראל מעם קדוש לקבל על עצמו במקומות הידועים בק"ש ובתפלה ע"פ זוהר הקדוש ובכתבי האר"י ז"ל. מלבד זה אני מצוה אתכם בניי אהוביי שאם יבוא ח"ו עליכם מסירת נפש בפועל. השם יצילכם וכל עם הקדוש. אזי תקבלו עליכם מסירת נפש בשמחה גדולה עד מאוד. והבורא ית"ש ויתעלה ישתעשע בכם בכל העולמות העליונים. ויאמר ראו מה בריה בראתי בעולמי שלא חס על גופו וסבל יסורים לכבודי ומסר עצמו על קדושת שמי:... ותדע לבבי שלא אמסור גופי למיתה בשביל גודל השכר הנפלא שעין לא ראתה בעולמות העליונים רק למען שמך הגדול והקדוש שיתגדל ויתקדש בכל העולמות עליונים ותחתונים במסירת גופי למיתה:

גם בניי אהוביי! אני מצוה אתכם בגזירת כיבוד אב ובצוואת שכיב מרע שכל זה שצויתי אתכם תצוו גם אתם את בניכם בקבלת אלהותו ית"ש ויתעלה זכרו לעד. ובלימוד תורתו הקדושה בכל עת. ובקיום מצותיו הקדוש' בכל דקדוקיהן לשמה. ובמסירת נפש בפועל: גם תצוו את בניכם שיצוו

junctions to their progeny, and so to the end of all the generations, whom God in His great mercy will grant me the boon of begetting. All of this I solemnly enjoin on you, and do ye pay full regard to my words.

If I perceived that I had committed any unintentional offense against the will of the Creator, whether in conduct, speech or thought, I made a broken-hearted confession without any delay before my Maker, and resolved in my mind to be extremely watchful against similar offenses thenceforth. It would be clearly impossible for me to lay before you all the details of conduct, speech, or thought; but I will select one illustration from each class, and you can infer the rest.

Concerning conduct: if I perceived that I had eaten more than was needful, thereby running the risk of neglecting devout study of the Torah and prayer, or if I thought that I might in consequence be compelled to spend excessive time in the hour of cleansing my body, I made immediate confession, and firmly resolved to be more abstemious in future. And so with all other actions.

Concerning speech: if I perceived that there went forth from my mouth utterances unnecessary for performance of duty or the fear of Heav-

גם את בניהם ובניהם לבניהם עד סוף כל הדורות. שיזכה אותי השם יתעלה ברחמיו הגדולים שיצאו מחלציי. וכל זה אני מזהיר אתכם בניי אהוביי! באזהרה הנ"ל ותזהרו מאוד בזה:...

אם הרגשתי בעצמי שעשיתי איזה שגגה נגד רצון הבורא ית"ש. הן במעשה הן בדיבור הן במחשבה. התוודיתי תיכף ומיד לפני יוצרי ובוראי בשברון לב מאוד. והסכמתי במחשבתי הסכמה וקבלה אמיתית שאזהר להלן מאוד בזה: ולהציג לפניכם בניי אהוביי! כל פרטי עשייה ודיבור ומחשבה בוודאי זה אי אפשר. אציג מכל ענין דבר אחד ומזה תקשו אל כל העניינים:

על מעשה. היינו אם הרגשתי בעצמי שאכלתי יותר מכדי צרכי שאוכל לבוא בשביל זה לידי ביטול תורה ותפלה בכוונה. או חשבתי אולי בשביל זה אהיה מוכרח לבלות זמן יותר בעת נקיית הגוף. הייתי מתוודה תיכף על זה ליוצרי ית"ש וקבלתי עלי קבלה אמיתית שאזהר בזה מכאן ולהבא. וכיוצא בכל עניני עשיית האדם:

על דיבור. היינו אם הרגשתי בעצמי שיצאו מפי דיבורים שלא לצורך מצוה ויראת שמים. אף שלא

en, even though there was not in these utterances any suspicion[8] of slander or tale-bearing (which God forbid!), the utterances being merely superfluous—I made confession forthwith and resolved as indicated above. Also if during prayer or grace after meals I spoke any word without due devotion of the heart, I contritely sought pardon from the Lord of all in my mind at the very moment,—taking care thenceforth not to repeat the offense. As soon as I had finished the prayer or benediction I made confession by word of mouth. My precaution was to pause a little between the phrases, even though they consisted of but two words, still more so after every three or four words, if there was any natural pause in the subject matter. Do you, my dear children, also be careful to apply this device, to which I have called attention also in my Treatise. And if, in the course of the prayer or the grace after meals or the other thanksgivings, at a point where it is unseemly to interrupt with a verbal confession, you observe that you utter any of the Sacred Names without due devotion of the heart, then you should immediately seek pardon in your minds, and when you reach the benediction: "He heareth prayer,"[9] you should make confession verbally. Needless to remark that in the confession after the eighteen benedictions[10] you

[8] For the force of the Hebrew word, see Jastrow, *Dictionary*, 879.

[9] The sixteenth of the "Eighteen [nineteen] Benedictions."

[10] Confession after the Eighteen Benedictions is al-

היו בדיבורים אלו שום נדנוד לשון הרע ורכילות ח"ו. רק שלא היו דיבורים הכרחים. הייתי מתוודה תיכף על זה וקבלתי על עצמי כנ"ל בענייני העשייה: גם אם יצאו מפי בתפלה או בברכת המזון ושאר ברכות איזה תיבה בלא כוונת הלב כראוי. בקשתי תיקף בלבי כפרה מלפני אדון כל בשברון לב מאוד. והייתי נזהר להלן מאוד בזה: ולאחר סיום התפלה או הברכה התוודיתי בפה מלא על זה: והזהירות היתה לי בזה היינו שהייתי נזהר להפסיק כמעט רגע בין ענין לענין אף אם היה הענין רק ב' תיבות ומכל שכן אחר ג' וד' תיבות אם היתה הפסקת ענין מה: ותזהרו גם אתם בניי אהוביי! מאוד בתחבולה זו והזכרתי תחבולה זו בחיבורי ג'כ: ואם תרגישו באמצע התפלה או בברכת המזון ושארי הודאות במקום שאין ראוי להפסיק בוידוי פה שיצא מפיכם איזה שם משמות הקדושים שאינם נמחקים בלא כוונת הלב ר"ל! אזי תבקשו תיכף בלבבכם כפרה מלפני אדון כל. ובברכת שומע תפלה תתוודו על זה בפה מלא. ומכ"ש בוידוי שאחר תפלת י"ח תתוודו עוד בזה הלשון. יוצרי

should again confess in these terms: "My Maker and Creator! I have sinned, I have done iniquity, etc., in that I uttered Thy Sacred Names without due thought, and was inattentive to Thy holy honor. Woe unto me, and woe unto my soul!" Similarly should you act at the close of the grace after meals and the other thanksgivings.

Concerning thought: If I noticed that I thought of any subject disconnected with duty and the fear of Heaven, I withdrew forthwith from such thought; made confession, with firm resolve to avoid the fault in future. Take the utmost care, my dear children, to make confession ever familiar in your mouth and heart, seeing to it in very sooth that you do not repeat the offenses concerning which you make confession —apart from which, confession of itself has a potency in the higher world, as is frequently pointed out in the Zohar, and let what precedes suffice on this subject.

While speaking of the Grace after Meals, I will write for you about one matter concerning the service of our Creator, a matter derived from our love and reverence of Him. This is that before saying Grace after eating in my small closed private room as is known to you—out of my excessive fear lest any person should come and knock at the door in the middle of my Grace, so that I must open it and thus interrupt my meditation, therefore before I began the Grace

luded to in the Talmud (T. B. Berakot, 17a), and became very usual under the cabbalist influence.

ובוראי! חטאתי עויתי כו׳ שהוצאתי מפי שמותיך הקדושים בלא כוונת הלב ולא חשתי לכבודך הקדוש אויה לי ואוי על נפשי! כו׳. וכן אחר ברכת המזון ושארי הודאות:

במחשבה. היינו שהרגשתי שחשבתי בענין מה שאין בה מצוה ויראת שמים. חזרתי תיכף לאחור ממחשבה זו. והייתי מתוודה בפה מלא על זה בקבלה אמיתית להבא כנ״ל: והזהרו בזה בניי אהוביי! מאוד ומאוד שיהיה הוידוי מרגלא בפיכם ובלבבכם בתמידות. ובוודאי תזהרו להלן בדבר שהתוודיתם לפני הבורא ית״ש מקודם עליה. לבד זה שהוידוי בעצמו עושה פעולה גדולה בעולם העליון. כנזכר בזוהר הקדוש במקומות רבים. ודי בהערה זו:...

עוד אני מדבר בענין ברכת המזון אכתוב לכם בניי אהוביי! ענין אחד בעבודת בוראנו ית״ש ויתעלה הבאה מגודל אהבתו ויראתו. וזו היא קודם ברכת המזון אחר אכילתי ביחידות בביתי הקטן מסוגר כפי שידעתם. הנה מרוב פחדתי פן יבא איזה אדם וינקש על הדלת באמצע ברכת המזון שאפתח לו ויבטל אותי מכוונתי. לכן קודם שהתחלתי ברכת

I prayed to God in these terms: "My Maker, my Creator! deliver me that no person come nigh me at the time when I recite the Grace after my meals, so that my good devotion be not annulled!" And after the Grace, if I had escaped interruption, I rendered for this a great thanksgiving to God with a mighty joy in these terms: "I give thanks unto Thee, my Maker, my Creator! in that Thou hast delivered me from the loss of devotion during this Grace." Also, when I restrained myself from superfluous eating, I spoke thus: "My Maker, my Creator! Thou knowest my thought that I restrained myself from superfluous eating so that I may avoid angering Thee (God forbid!) through the inability to study Torah or the loss of devotion in prayer, induced by overfeeding."

It was ever my wont to thank God for whatever happened unto me. If some misfortune, small or great, befell, of all that lips could tell or heart devise, I would acclaim with joy the justice of the decree. And I would put my happy thanks into words, as follows: "My Maker, my Creator! Thou art righteous in all that hath come upon me, for Thou hast dealt truly and I have done wickedly.[11] And now I offer my grateful acknowledgments for this, knowing of a surety that this occurrence is for my welfare." Similarly, on occasion of any good, small or great, I would offer thanks for the Lord's bountiful kindness.

[11] Neh. 9.33.

המזון התפללתי להשם יתעלה בזה הלשון. יוצרי ובוראי! הצילני שלא יבא שום אדם אצלי בעת ברכת מזוני שלא יבוטל כוונתי הטובה ע״כ. ואחר ברכת מזוני אם לא היה לי ביטול משום אדם נתתי הודאה גדולה להשם יתעלה בשמחה עצומה על זה בזה הלשון. מודה אני לפניך יוצרי ובוראי! שהצלתני מביטול הכוונה בברכת המזון זו ע״כ: גם בעת שמנעתי ממותרות האכילה אמרתי בזה הלשון. יוצרי ובוראי! אתה ידעת מחשבתי שמנעתי ממותרות האכילה בכדי שלא אכעיסך ח״ו בביטול תורה וכוונת התפלה מחמת ריבוי האכילה:...

הייתי נזהר מאוד ליתן הודאה ושבח להשם ית׳ על כל מה שהגיע עלי הן איזה רעה ר״ל קטנה או גדולה מכל מה שהפה יוכל לדבר והלב לחשוב הייתי מצדיק עלי את הדין בשמחה. ונתתי להשם ית׳ ג״כ הודאה על זה בשמחה עצומה בזה הלשון. יוצרי ובוראי אתה צדיק על כל הבא עלי כי אמת עשית ואני הרשעתי. ואני נותן לך שבח והודאה על זה יוצרי ובוראי כי בודאי לטובתי עשית לי סבה זו ע״כ: הן על איזה טובה קטנה או גדולה מכל מה שהפה יוכל כו׳ נתתי לו ית״ש הודאה ושבח

And He who knows my inmost secrets can testify of me that, over and above the obligation imposed in the sacred Mishnah[12]—a law from Moses delivered at Sinai—I have ever rendered this service of praise unto God out of the great love of Him which is fixed in my heart, which has made it thankful for evil as for good, seeing that both are His handiwork. I will, my dear children, give several instances, as they occur to my mind; from these examples you can infer my habit on similar occasions.

For His great goodness in providing me with a private apartment for His holy service, from the day I arrived at years of discretion, and this possession of a private chamber for meditation is the basis and root of a man's power to acquire perfection in this lower world[13],—for this boon I expressed my thanks...many times a day. Whenever I had to go past the tottering wall, on my way to Synagogue, I prayed before I reached the spot, and when I had walked the wall's length I offered thanks. Whenever I received a letter from you, my dear children, I thanked God in these terms: "My Maker, my Creator! I thank and praise Thee for that Thou hast sent to me good tidings of the health of my children and grandchildren." Similar thanks did I offer when I saw or understood that

[12] Mishnah Berakot 9.5.

[13] The mystical school frequently insist on the importance of solitude. The idea recurs in many of the Testaments. Cf. particularly p. 320 above.

על הטובה שגמלני:... והיודע תעלומות יעיד עלי בניי אהוביי שמלבד החיוב מהמשנה הקדושה שהיא הלכה למשה מסיני עבדתי עבודה זו בתמידות מגודל אהבת השם ית׳ שהיתה תקועה בלבי בתמידות נתתי לו ית״ש וית׳ הודאות ושבחים בתמידות הן על הרעות והן על הטובה שעשה עמי. ועתה אציג לכם בניי אהוביי כמה דברים מה שתעלה על דעתי ומהם תקשו אל הדומה:...

על גודל הטובה שעשה לי יוצרי ובוראי ית״ש וית׳ שנתן לי חדר מיוחד לעבודתו הקדושה מיום עמדי על דעתי כידוע לכם. ודבר זה הוא יסוד ושורש לאדם שרוצה לקנות שלימות בעה״ז השפל לכן נתתי לו הודאה על זה... אף כמה פעמים ביום: בכל עת שהלכתי מביתי לבהכ״נ... והייתי מוכרח לילך אצל החומה רעועה... הנה קודם שהגעתי אצל החומה התחלתי להתפלל... ואחר שעברתי משך החומה נתתי הודאה להשם ית׳:... בכל עת שהגיע אלי אגרת שלמים מאתכם בניי אהוביי... נתתי שבח בזה הלשון. יוצרי ובוראי אני נותן שבח והודאה לך ית״ש שבשרתני בשורה טובה מבריאות בניי ובני בניי. גם בעת שראיתי או הבנתי

ye were walking in the right way. On Fridays towards afternoon when I put on my Sabbath suit, I thanked God thus: "My Maker, my Creator! blessed be Thy Name! I render thanks that Thou hast provided for me decent clothes for the honor of Thy sacred Sabbath, a provision due not to my worth but to Thy mercy." Also I possessed for winter use a very warm garment made of lamb's wool, and whenever I put it on I thanked God for it.... Whenever I much needed any object, and I found it ready to hand, and had no cause to go seek it or borrow it from others, I joyously thanked God.

Similarly, with regard to the toothache (from which I suffered), when the pain ceased a little, I offered thanks with mighty joy in these words: "I give thanks unto Thee, my Maker and Creator whose Name be blessed in the mouth of every living being, in that Thou hast sent healing to my great pain." If the relaxation occurred in the course of the service, I offered thanks silently in mind and heart, in the same terms.

So, if I forgot anything, but soon remembered, and suffered no inconvenience by having to go back for it, I thanked God ... So when my snuff-box fell from my pocket, and nothing was spilt, as the lid did not come open; or if some glass vessel rolled over on the table and like to fall and

בשכלי שאתם הולכים בדרך הטוב: כשלבשתי בעש"ק סמוך למנחה בגדי שבת נתתי להשם הודאה... בזה הלשון. יוצרי ובוראי ית"ש אני נותן לך הודאה על שנתת לי בגדים חשובים לכבוד שבת קודש לא כפי מעשי הטובים רק ברחמיך הרבים וחסדיך הגדולים ע"כ:... גם היתה לי בימות החורף בגד מצמר כבשים חם מאוד ובכל עת שלבשתי אותו נתתי הודאה להשם... כל דבר שהייתי נצרך לזה מאוד והיה אותו דבר אצלי היינו שלא הוצרכתי לחפש אחר אותו דבר ולשאול מאחרים הייתי נותן הודאה בשמחה להשם ית':... גם בענין כאב השיניים. בעת ששקט ושעה מעלי הכאב מעט הייתי נותן להשם יתעלה שבח והודאה בשמחה עצומה בזה הלשון. מודה אני לך יוצרי ובוראי ית"ש בפי כל חי! ששלחת רפואה לכאבי הגדול. ובאמצע התפלה הייתי נותן הודאה זו בלשון הזה ממחשבתי ולבי:

וכן בענין השכחה אם נזכרתי בזמן מועט על הדבר ששכחתי ליטול היינו שלא היה לי טרחה כ"כ בחזרתי...וכן בעת שנפל מחיקי הכלי של השנו"ף טאב"ק אם לא הגיע אלי בזה הנפילה

break, but I was quick enough to save it; or if though it fell, yet it did not break; or if my spectacles dropped to the ground and I picked them up whole, I thanked God...In all these and similar cases, out of the immeasurable happiness and exaltation which burned in my heart, due to my never ceasing consciousness of His Godhead, it was my regular custom to make mention of Him, and to praise Him for whatever befell.

It is a common practice in all Jewish communities that when anyone dies overnight or in the early morning, the Shamash,[14] when summoning us to prayer, gives only two knocks at the door, as a token of the sad event. When I heard only two knocks I felt sorely distressed at the loss of one from the holy congregation. For it is self-evident that God, too, would have no satisfaction in the passing of one who must henceforth be void of the performance of the commandments. On the other hand when I heard the three knocks I rejoiced that the community retained its full complement.

My beloved children! There is another matter on which I add my very serious injunctions. When you were young, I forbade you to drink spirituous liquors,[15] and I command you to ob-

[14] On the Schulklopfer and Shamash, see *Jewish Life in the Middle Ages*, ch. iii.

[15] Lit.: "burnt wine," cf. the etymologically equivalent English word *brandy*, German *Brantwein.*

שום הפסד כלל שלא נפתח הכלי בנפילתה... אם נתגלגל צלוחית על השולחן וקרוב היה לפול לארץ ולהשבר והייתי ממהר להצילה שלא נפלה... ומכ"ש אם נפלה ולא נשברה. גם בתי עינים שלי שנפלו לארץ ולא נשברו וכיוצא:... מגודל ההתפארות והשמחה והחדוה שהיה בוער בלבי בתמידות באלהותו הי' מרגלא בפי להזכירו ולשבחו... על כל מה שאירע לי:...

הנה הנהוג בכל תפוצות ישראל כשמת איזה אדם בלילה או בבוקר כשהשמש קורא לבה"כ אינו מכה על השער רק שני הכאות. לסימן שיש בר מינן בעיר. ואני כששמעתי שהכה רק שני הכאות הייתי מכניס צער גדול בלבי על ההעדר אדם מעם קדוש הישראלי. כי מן הסתם נעדר גם הנחת רוח מבוראנו ית"ש מזה האדם כיון שמת נעשה חפשי מן המצות. ולהיפך ששמעתי שהכה ג' הכאות הכנסתי שמחה בלבי שלא נעדר אדם מעם קדוש בעיר הזאת:...

בניי אהוביי! גם זה אני מצווה אתכם באזהרה גדולה. וזה הוא כפי שנהגתי אני עמכם שגזרתי עליכם בהיותכם עדיין קטנים שלא תשתו יין שרף.

serve the same rule with the sons and daughters which God may graciously bestow on you. In their youth keep them from spirituous liquors as from absolutely forbidden things, and in their age they will observe the same abstinence. Do you enjoin on them, with all the force of parental authority, never to drink throughout their days, though they live to a hundred years. And if you are happy enough to marry wives to your sons, speak to the hearts of the mothers and fathers of your daughters-in-law, to induce them to order their daughters never to drink spirituous liquors from the time of their marriage, even though they had been accustomed to do so before that time. They will be bound to assent to this, for I lay this order on them with the solemnity of one on his death-bed, in that I command you to require this abstinence from your daughters-in-law. And though it is seemly for every Israelite, of the holy community, thus to exhort his children and all his household,—since I have seen (for our many iniquities!) many evil consequences accrue from the habit of drinking spirits among men and particularly (God save us!) among women,—yet, my dear children, I add my solemn injunction as a father and as one near his end, not only on you but on all the future progeny which God may graciously bestow on me throughout all generations. I mean that you shall command your children to command their children, and their children to transmit the com-

כן אני גוזר עליכם שתתנהגו ג"כ עם בניכם ובנותיכם
שיזכה אתכם הבורא ית"ש ויתעלה שמקטנותם
תרחיקו מהם שתיית היין שרף ממש כמו שתייה של
איסור. ואז גם כי יזקין לא יסור ממנה. גם תגזרו
עליהם על זה בגזירת כיבוד אב שלא ישתו כל
ימיהם עד מאה שנים: גם כי יזכה אתכם הבורא
ית"ש לישא נשים לבניכם תדברו על לב אביהם
ואמם שיגזרו גם הם על בנותיהם שלא ישתו יין שרף
מעת הנישואין כל ימי חייהם אף שהיו רגילין בזה
מקודם. ויהיו מוכרחים להסכים על זה כי כן צוואתי
בצוואת שכיב מרע עליהם שתתנהגו גם כלותיכם
בזה: ואף גם שראוי לכל איש הישראלי מעם הקדוש
להזהיר לבניו ולכל בני ביתו על זה כי בעוה"ר
ראיתי מכשולים רבים באים משתיית היי"ש למי[5]
שרגיל בזה אנשים ובפרט נשים ר"ל! אך עליכם
בניי אהוביי! אני גוזר על זה בגזירת כיבוד אב
ובצוואת שכיב מרע ולא עליכם[6] בלבד אלא על
כל יוצאי חלציי עד סוף כל הדורות שיזכה אותי
הבורא ית"ש ויתעלה זכרו לעד. היינו שאתם בניי
אהוביי! תצוו לבניכם שיצוו גם הם לבניהם ובניהם

[5] Eds. מי.   [6] Some Eds. על ידכם.

mand to the end of all the generations, following the example of Jonadab the son of Rechab, recorded in the thirty-fifth chapter of Jeremiah. Yet I do not go to the same lengths as he did, for I only require of you a promise of total abstention from spirituous liquors.[16] But, my dear children, as regards the drinking of wine, even *Kasher* wine,[17] I admonish you to drink no more than the cup used in the benediction of Kiddush and Habdalah,[18] and to avoid the practice of the multitude, even though the Lord bestow on you great wealth. Also, with regard to drinking[19] bees' honey, no God-fearing man would drink it on a week-day, but would reserve it for holy days—Such as Sabbaths and festivals and at "commandment-meals,"[20] and on these occasions would avoid excess. All this I enjoin on you, and it is clearly explained in the Zohar that a father after his death suffers shame from his sons' vices and achieves honor from their virtues,[21] so that though the father deserve some punishment, the Holy One takes pity on him and places him on his seat of honor. Therefore, my dear children, take due heed to all my efforts

[16] i. e., he permits the use of beer and wine.

[17] See J. E. ix, 227.

[18] On Sabbath and festivals and at the conclusion thereof. See *Authorised Daily Prayer Book*, pp. 124, 174, 230, 216, 231.

[19] In the Mishnah honey is treated as a beverage (Makshirin v. 9). The reference here is to a fermented syrup made from honey. Cf. the Arabic *dibs* made, however, from dates.

לבניהם עד סוף כל הדורות ממש כצוואת יונדב
בן רכב הנזכר בירמיה סימן ל"ה. אך לא הכבדתי
עליכם בניי אהוביי ויוצאי חלציי! הכבדה כבדה
כיונדב בן רכב ע"ה כנזכר שם רק בשתיית יין שרף
לבד. בניי אהוביי! בשתיית יין אף ביין כשר אני
מזהיר אתכם שלא תשתו רק כוס של ברכה של
קידוש והבדלה. ולא תרגילו ח"ו כמו המון עם אף
שירחיב ה' גבולכם בעושר רב. גם שתיית דבש
דבורים ראוי לכל מי שנגעה יראת אלהים בלבו
להרחיק שתייתו בחול רק ביום קדש כמו בשבת
קדש ויום טוב ובסעודת מצוה ואף גם זאת לא
שתייה מרובה ח"ו: כל זה אני מזהיר אתכם בניי
אהוביי! והרי מפורש בזוהר הקדוש איך יגיע לאב
חרפה גדולה ובזיונות גדולות אחר פטירתו בעולם
העליון על ידי מעשה בניו שאינם מתוקנים. ולהיפך
איך גורם לאביו בכשרון מעשיו כבוד גדול בעולם
העליון אף שראוי לאיזה עונש כמפורש במאמר
הקדוש הנ"ל. וקב"ה חייס עליה ואותיב ליה
בכורסיא דיקריה. לכן בניי אהוביי! תזהרו בכל

---

[20] See *Jewish Life in the Middle Ages*, 143, 318.

[21] See p. 316 above.

to direct you in the good path, and I will assuredly be your advocate and patron,[22] strong as an iron pillar, if ye fulfil my testamentary commands. Let this suffice on the subject.

And now with regard to the affirmative precept: "Thou shalt love thy neighbour as thyself,"[23] that great principle of the Torah, I have written at length in the first section of my book. Here I will add a few details, which occur in my mind, and may serve as illustrations of many similar rules. When I saw that the coat of a friend was slightly torn, I advised him to have it mended. But before offering this counsel, I said: "My Maker, my Creator! lo, here am I ready to fulfil the command of Thy holy Law, bidding man love his neighbor as himself." Thereupon I would address my friend, reminding him that a small hole grows into a big one...Once I obtained a well-tried remedy for bruises. When I saw in the bath any one troubled in that way, I bethought myself that it were rebellion and trespass against God if I refrained from offering my remedy...I could write much more on this subject, but the paper would be exhausted though the subject would not. Remember this com-

[22] *Patronus*, protector, used also in sense of pleader. With the rest of the phrase compare Plautus': "Patronus parieti" ("A patron in front of the wall").

[23] Lev. 19.19. See *Studies in Pharisaism* i. Ch. 2.

מה שהדרכתיכם בדרך הטוב. ובוודאי אהיה מליץ ופטרון בשבילכם כעמוד ברזל אם תקיימו צוואתי. ודי בהערה זו:

הנה ענין מ"ע של ואהבת לרעך כמוך שהוא כלל גדול בתורה כבר הזכרתי כמה ענינים ממצוה זו בחבורי בשער הראשון. ומה שעלתה על דעתי עוד להציג לפניכם בניי אהוביי דברים פרטיים בקיום מ"ע זו שמהם תקשו אל שאר דברים. וזה הוא כשראיתי ביודעי ומכירי קריעה קטנה בבגדו הזהרתי אותו שיתקן קריעה זו. ומקודם אמרתי בזה הלשון. יוצרי ובוראי ית"ש אני מוכן ומזומן לקיים מצוה של ואהבת לרעך כמוך שצויתנו בתורתך הקדושה ע"כ. אחר זה אמרתי לו בזה הלשון. אחי ורעי הלא ידעת קריעה קטנה נעשה קריעה גדולה...: גם קבלתי מאיש אחד רפואה בדוקה ומנוסה לפצעים... וכשראיתי במרחץ איזה איש במכות ופצעים ברגליו... חשבתי בדעתי בודאי הוא מֶרֶד ומעל נגד יוצרי ובוראי ית"ש אם לא אומר לו הרפואה זו... בניי אהוביי יש לי בעז"ה לכתוב לכם בקיום מ"ע זו עוד עניינים רבים אך יכלה הנייר והם לא יכלו... זכרו ואל תשכחו

mandment "when thou sittest in thy house and when thou walkest by the way, when thou liest down and when thou risest up." Verily if one pursue this course, he will never fall into sin, whether in matters between him and God, or in matters between him and his fellow-man.

It should be your constant desire to journey to the Holy Land; and of a surety, a man is guided (by heaven) in the way he wills to go. It is written in the books that unless an Israelite is thoroughly resolved in his heart to set his steps before he dies, towards the Holy Land, to die there, great is his punishment. How can a man be so resolved, unless the desire for it is constantly maintained? Therefore, my beloved children, keep your hearts clean in this matter, and salvation will come from the Lord!

מ"ע זו בשבתך בביתך ובלכתך בדרך ובשכבך ובקומך. ובודאי לא תבואו לשום עון בעולם הן בדברים שבין אדם למקום ב"ה הן בדברים שבין אדם לחבירו:

בניי אהוביי! תשוקתכם תהיה בתמידות ליסע לארץ הקדושה. ובוודאי בדרך שאדם רוצה לילך מוליכים אותו. והובא בספרים אם אין מוסכם בלב אדם הישראלי בתכלית ההסכמה שבוודאי קודם שימות יראה לשום פעמיו לנסוע לארץ הקדושה למות שם עונשו מרובה ר"ל! ובוודאי אם לא תהיה תשוקת האדם בתמידות לזה לא יהיה גם כן הסכמה בלבו בזה. לכן בניי אהוביי! ברו לבבכם בזה ולה' הישועה!

לקוטים מצואות ר׳ יואל בן אברהם שמריה

LOVE AND PEACE
EXTRACTS FROM THE TESTAMENT OF JOEL SON OF ABRAHAM SHEMARIAH

XXIII
LOVE AND PEACE
(Extracts from the Testament of Joel son of Abraham Shemariah)

Joel, son of Abraham Shemariah, died in the last year of the eighteenth century. His "Testaments" (the plural is used in the title) were published in 1799 or 1800, apparently at Wilna, where the author had lived.

He actually wrote his Will a quarter of a century earlier. He tells how on Iyar 21 of the year 1773 he was seized with faintness in his bath. After his escape he felt it incumbent on him to set his house in order, lest he be taken unawares by death.

The document was edited by his pupil Avigdor b. Meir ha-Cohen, who thus exhorts the public: "My friends, despise silver, despise gold, and buy this little book, small in quantity, great in quality." The Hebrew style is as poor as the matter is rich.

The Will constitutes a rule for conduct throughout the year, with some delightful exhortations, lucid and sound. There is not wanting passion amid the sobriety, when he commands the ordering of all things for God's sake. He shows at once profound trust in prayer and a manly belief in man's taking care for his own future. He gives full directions for his burial, "if possible in the old cemetery by my father; if not, in a place where there is room for eight graves near and around me." He adds that he would like to name the eight who should be interred near him, but refrains "because I do not wish to make invidious exceptions." There was to be no formal *hesped*, though

כג

לקוטים מצוואות ר׳ יואל בן אברהם שמריה

יואל בן אברהם שמריה נפטר בשנה האחרונה של המאה השמונה עשרה. צוואותיו (כך נקראה צואתו בלשון רבים) נדפסו בשנת תקנ״ט או תק״ס, כמדומה בווילנא, מקום מושבו של המחבר.

באמת כתב את צואתו עשרים וחמש שנים קודם לזה. הוא מספר שביום כ״א לאייר שנת תקל״ג תקפתהו חולשה בבית המרחץ, וכששב לאיתנו הרגיש חובה לצוות לביתו פן ישיגהו המות פתאום.

שטר הצואה יצא לאור ע״י תלמידו אביגדור בן מאיר הכהן המוכיח את העם בדברים האלה: „ידידי, הוו בזים לכסף, בזים לזהב, וקנו את הספר הקטן הזה מעט הכמות ורב האיכות״. הסגנון העברי הוא דל במדה שהתוכן הוא עשיר.

הצואה היא ספר מנהגים בעד כל השנה, יחד עם איזה הוכחות נחמדות, בהירות ותמימות. יש להכיר כעס ורוגז מהולים במתינות כשהוא מצוה לסדר את כל המעשים לשם שמים. יחד עם בטחון עמוק בכח התפלה הוא מאמין שכל איש צריך לדאוג לעתידו. במקום אחד הוא מצוה על אופן קבורתו, „אם אפשר בבית העולם העתיק קרוב לאבי, ואם לאו במקום שיש רוח בעד שמונה קברים קרוב וסביב לו״, והוא מוסיף שמאוד חפץ לקרוא בשם השמונה הצריכים להיות קבורים אצלו, אבל הוא מתאפק יען כי איננו חפץ לעורר קנאה בין אלה היוצאים מן הכלל. הוא אסר לעשות הספד

"men may study the Torah on my behalf during the first year after my death." There is the usual quaint combination of practical rules and general principles. God must be ever in man's mind, and "to keep your own mind free from strange imaginations stand on your two big toes," a counsel found also in the *Book of the Pious.* Abu Said, a tenth century Mohammedan, is reported to have exercised the same discipline. Joel says many good things about charity. "No man ever became poor by what he gave away." All that man has "is in trust, and the will of the Truster must be followed." He advocates the setting aside of an exact tithe. He thinks despicable those who are generous to others but neglect their own poor relations. He is very urgent on the duty of loving all men (see extracts below). Nor may seemingly unimportant duties be neglected. A villager finds a herb which heals far more than the physician's remedies. He gives many regulations for the Sabbath (see extracts). He bids his children take a siesta after lunch "for the honor of the Sabbath joy." "Between afternoon and evening service," he bids, "do not dance in the courtyard of the Synagogue." There are cabbalistic elements in the Will also. Thus he presents a mystic picture of heaven with its rivers of milk and of fire and snow, all this quite in the Apocalyptic manner.

To be at peace with all the world, with Jew and Gentile, must be your foremost aim in this terrestrial life. Contend with no man. In the first instance, your home must be the abode of quietude and happiness; no harsh word must

עליו, אף כי הוא מרשה לאנשים ללמוד תורה בעבורו במשך השנה הראשונה אחרי מותו. יש פה החבור הרגיל בין מנהגים מעשיים ועקרים כלליים. הבורא יתברך צריך להיות תמיד במחשבת איש, ובכדי שתהיה מחשבתו חפשית מדמיונות זרים עליו לעמוד על שתי בהונותיו הגדולות, עצה היעוצה גם ב„ספר חסידים". אומרים שאבו סעיד, מושלמי של המאה העשירית, הורה ג"כ את הכלל הזה. יואל משמיע דברים טובים ונכוחים ע"ד צדקה: „שום איש לא נתדלדל מעולם ע"י מה שחלק לעניים", וכל מה שיש לאיש הוא בפקדון וצריך לעשות את רצון המפקיד. הוא מאמין בהפרשת מעשר במדה נכונה, והוא חושב לנקלה ונבזה את האיש העושה חסד עם אחרים ועוזב את קרוביו העניים. הוא מטעים את החובה לאהוב כל איש (ראה את הלקוטים להלן). הוא מזהיר אזהרה לבלי לזלזל בחובות הנראות כבלתי חשובות. בן כפר מוצא עשב המרפא הרבה יותר מרפואות הרופא. גם בנוגע ליום השבת הוא מזהיר אזהרות רבות (ראה את הלקוטים להלן). הוא מצוה את בניו לישון אחר ארוחת הצהרים לכבוד שמחת השבת ולבלי לרקוד בחצר בית הכנסת בין מנחה למעריב. יש גם יסודות קבלה בצואה הזאת: הוא מצייר תמונה מיסתית מרקיע השמים עם נהרי נחלי חלב ואש ושלג, כל זה בנוסח הספרים האפוקליפטיים.

מאוד ומאוד תראו להיות שלום[1] עם כל אדם בעולם ממש. ואפילו עם גוי. ולא תריבו עם שום אדם בעולם: ופשיטא דפשיטא בביתכם יהי' שלום ושלוה. וחלילה חלילה וחס שלא יהא שום קללה

[1] So the ed. Perhaps read להיות בשלום.

be heard there, but over all must reign love, amity, modesty, and a spirit of gentleness and reverence. This spirit must not end with the home, however. In your dealings with the world you must allow neither money nor ambition to disturb you. Forego your rights, envy no man. For the main thing is peace, peace with the whole world. Show all men every possible respect, deal with them in the finest integrity and faithfulness. For Habakkuk summed up the whole Law in the one sentence: "The righteous shall live by his faith."[1]

The root of all the commandments consists of the 248 affirmative and the 365 negative precepts. But the branches, which include all virtuous and vicious habits, extend into countless thousands of thousands. To specify them is impossible, but the Scriptures[2] have in several places reduced them to general categories. One of these is: "In all thy ways acknowledge Him."[3] Another: "Keep thy feet in an even path."[4]

When, in the course of the prayers, you come to the "Sanctification," fulfil the text: "I will be hallowed among the children of Israel."[5] But you must at the same moment resolve to uphold the duty to love thy neighbor as thyself. For in the "Sanctification" (*Kedushah*) named

[1] Hab. 2.4.

[2] Possibly the author means that moralists and codifiers have cited certain texts as summing up the Scriptures. Cf. Abrahams, *Studies in Pharisaism*, ch. ii.

[3] Prov. 3.6.

[4] Prov. 4.26. Or "make plain the path of thy feet."

[5] Levit. 22.32.

רחמנא לצלן בביתכם כלל. רק אהבה וחבה וצניעות והכל בנחת וביראת שמים: אבל עם כל העולם ג"כ לראות להיות בשלום גדול. ולא תקפידו על שום דבר הן דבר שמגיע לממון. יותר טוב תותרו משלכם ופשיטא בעניני כבוד:... ופשיטא דפשיטא שלא לקנא חלילה לשום אדם:... אבל עיקר העיקר שתהיו מאוד בשלום עם כל העולם. הן באיזה חלוקת כבוד תכבדו מאוד את כל האדם. והן במשא ובמתן יהיה הכל באמת ובאמונה. כי בא חבקוק והעמידן על אחת. וצדיק באמונתו יחיה:

...שורש כל המצות הוא רמ"ח מצות עשה ושס"ה מצות לא תעשה אבל הענפים, והם המדות או טובות או רעות, הם אלפי אלפים עד אין קץ ומספר. ואי איפשר לפרטם רק הפסוקים[2] כללו אותם בכמה פסוקים בכללות. האחד, בכל דרכיך דעהו וכו'[3]. השני, פלס מעגל רגלך כו':...

וכשתגיע לקדושה, אז תקיים מ"ע ונקדשתי בתוך בני ישראל. ותכוין לזה. וגם מ"ע שניה לקיים ולקבל עליך ואהבת לרעך כמוך. כי אנו אומרים, כשם

[2] Perh. read הפוסקים.

[3] Read וגו'; so in next clause.

above,[6] we use the phrase: "We will sanctify Thy name in the world, *even as they sanctify it in the highest heavens.*" We must, indeed, strive to imitate the ministering angels, and as they are in a state of perfect love and unison,[7] such must also be our condition.

It was oft my way at assemblies to raise my eyes and regard those present from end to end, to see whether in sooth I loved everyone among them, whether my acceptance of the duty to love my fellow-men was genuine. With God's help I found that indeed I loved all present. Even if I noticed one who had treated me improperly, then, without a thought of hesitation, without a moment's delay, I pardoned him. Forthwith I resolved to love him. If my heart forced me to refuse my love, I addressed him with spoken words of friendship, until my heart became attuned to my words. So, whenever I met one to whom my heart did not incline, I forced myself to speak to him kindly, so as to make my heart feel affection for him. What if he were a sinner? Even then I would not quarrel with him, for I wonder whether there exists in this age one who is able to reprove another![8] On the other hand, if I conceived that he would listen to advice, I drew near to him, turning towards him a cheerful countenance. If, however, I fancied that he would resent my ad-

[6] On this prayer, see *J.E.*, vii, 463.

[7] Sifre Numbers § 42. *J.E.*, i, 586.

[8] T. B. 'Arakin 16b.

שמקדישים אותו בשמי מרום, דהיינו מלאכי השרת. וצריכים אנו להתדמות אליהם. מה הם באהבה ובאחדות גמור כך אנו צריכים להיות:...

דרכי היה כמה פעמים כשהיה קיבוץ עם, הייתי מגביה עיני לראות מקצה לקצה, אם באמת אני אוהב את כל אחד ואחד, ואם הקבלה[4] שלי באמת, ובעזרת השם כן מצאתי: ואף אם הייתי מוצא איזה שעשה לי איזה דבר שלא כהוגן, אז בתוך כדי דיבור מחלתי לו תיכף ומיד. וקבלתי לאהוב אותו: ואף אם היה לבי מכריחני שלא לאהוב אותו, אזי הייתי ממש מוציא מפי ברכות גדולות לאותו האיש עד שהוצאתי מלבי: וכן בכל פעם שפגשתי איזה אדם שלא היה לבי נוטה אליו, הייתי נותן לו הרבה ברכות בכדי להפוך לבי עליו לטוב ולאהבהו. אם לא חלילה מי שעשה עבירה. אבל גם כן לא רבתי עמו. כי תמה אני אם יש בדור הזה מי שיוכל להוכיח כו׳: רק אדרבה, אם הייתי משער שהוא ישמע תוכחתי אז הייתי מקרב אליו. ומראה

[4] i. e. קבלת המצוה ואהבת לרעך.

vances, I did not intrude on him. As there is a duty to speak, so is there a duty to be silent.[9]

Every Friday try your utmost to prepare the requirements of the Sabbath. It is good for you to do something with your own hand, though you have many servants[10]; such as to see that fish is provided for the Sabbath meal.[11] Everything must be done within the limits of possibility, everything with joy and for the glory of God. After completing these preparations, read the Pentateuchal Lesson in the proper manner, twice in Hebrew and once in the Aramaic version;[12] never interrupt the reading, not even with a word. 'Tis seemly to read wrapped in the fringed garment and with the phylacteries on, and if you are competent, use the Scroll.[13] Later in the afternoon of every Friday it was my habit to pray with a congregation (of ten persons), and then as an unbroken rule to cut my nails and proceed to the bath for the honor of the Sabbath. It is a fine thing to recite some devotions and to confess, while in the bath,[14] all one's doings during the past week. Then go (to Synagogue) to welcome the Sabbath, as one welcomes a great and renowned King, with

[9] T. B. Yeb. 65b; see note 5 to the Hebrew text.

[10] See *J.E.*, x, 594.

[11] See *Jewish Life in the Middle Ages*, p. 150.

[12] T. B. Ber. 8a.

[13] i. e. the written text, not a printed book.

[14] On the connection of bathing with penitence, see Abrahams, *Studies in Pharisaism*, ch. iv.

לו פנים צהובות: אבל אם שערתי שלא ישמע אלי, אז הנחתיו כשם שמצוה כו׳:...[5]

בכל ערב שבת תראו להשתדל להכין צרכי שבת. וטוב לעשות בעצמיכם איזה דבר לכבוד שבת, אף שיש לכם כמה משרתים. ולראות שיהי׳ לכם דגים בכל שבת. וכל דבר רק לפי יכולתו. והכל בשמחה ולשם שמים. ואחר כך לקרות שנים מקרא וא׳ תרגום כדינו. וחלילה וחס להפסיק אפי׳ בדיבור. ונכון לקרות בטלית ותפילין. ופשיטא אם תוכלו בספר תורה כידוע: ואחר חצי היום כמה שעות היה מנהגי להתפלל מנחה במנין. ואחר כך לחתוך הצפרנים בכל ערב שבת חוק ולא יעבור. ולילך למרחץ לכבוד שבת. חוק ולא יעבור: ומי שיזכה למעט כוונות ולהתוודות במקוה על כל מה שעשה בזה השבוע אזי מה טוב!... ואחר כך לקבל שבת באימה ובשמחה גדולה, כמקבל פני מלך גדול

[5] The full saying is: כשם שמצוה על אדם לומר דבר הנשמע כך מצוה שלא לומר דבר שאינו נשמע.

reverence and joy. Thence return home, to find the lamps lit, the chairs set, the table laid and a tranquil happiness in the heart of wife and family. See to it that this is so! For if I have exhorted you to a peaceful life on weekdays, on Sabbath let joy and love prevail to a yet higher degree. Say the Sanctification (over the wine) with devout gladness, eat the meal in joy and for the glory of God. And let words of Torah be spoken round thy board, or songs sung with joyous awe.[15] Ever let some respectable poor guest be with thee. End with the Grace recited with religious fervor and happy contentment.

[15] On the *Zemirot*, or table songs, see Singer Prayer Book, Annotated edition, p. cclix.

ונורא: ואחר כך לילך לבית ולמצוא נרות דולקות ומטה מוצעת ושלחן ערוך: ותזהר ביותר שיהא [שתהא] בשלוה ובשלום גדול ובשמחה גדולה עם אשתך וכל בני ביתך: כי אף בחול הזהרתיך על השלום למען השם אבל בשבת יהי' בשמחה ובחבה יתירה: ותקדש בכוונה ובשמחה. ותאכל בשמחה לשם שמים. ותראה שיהא דבר תורה על שולחנך או זמירות באימה ובשמחה. ומאוד מאוד נכון שתהדר שיהי' איזה עני הגון על שולחנך... ואחר זה ברכת המזון בכוונה עצומה ובנחת:

וקראתם דרור בארץ לכל יושביה

Proclaim liberty throughout the land unto all the inhabitants thereof Leviticus 25:10

Published in Philadelphia in the two-hundredth year of American Independence by The Jewish Publication Society of America